Creating the Secure Managed Desktop

Creating the Secure Managed Desktop

Using Group Policy, SoftGrid, Microsoft Deployment Toolkit, and Other Management Tools

Jeremy Moskowitz

Wiley Publishing, Inc.

Acquisitions and Developmental Editor: Allegro Editorial Services
Technical Editor: Jakob Heidelberg
Production Editor: Elizabeth Campbell
Copy Editor: Sally Engelfried
Production Manager: Tim Tate
Vice President and Executive Group Publisher: Richard Swadley
Vice President and Executive Publisher: Joseph B. Wikert
Vice President and Publisher: Neil Edde
Book Designer: Bill Gibson and Judy Fung
Compositor: Craig Woods, Happenstance Type-O-Rama
Proofreader: Scott Klemp, Word One
Indexer: Ted Laux
Cover Designer: Ryan Sneed
Cover Image: © Polka Dot Images/Jupiter Images
Library of Congress Cataloging-in-Publication Data
Moskowitz, Jeremy.
  Creating the secure managed desktop : using group policy, softgrid, Microsoft deployment, and other management tools / Jeremy Moskowitz.
       p. cm.
  ISBN 978-0-470-27764-5 (paper/website)
  1. Microsoft Windows (Computer file) 2. Windows (Computer programs) 3. Computer security. I. Title.
  QA76.76.W56M685 2008
  005.8--dc22
                                        2008011990

Dear Reader,

Thank you for choosing *Creating the Secure Managed Desktop*. This book is part of a family of premium quality Sybex books, all written by outstanding authors who combine practical experience with a gift for teaching.

Sybex was founded in 1976. More than thirty years later, we're still committed to producing consistently exceptional books. With each of our titles we're working hard to set a new standard for the industry. From the paper we print on, to the authors we work with, our goal is to bring you the best books available.

I hope you see all that reflected in these pages. I'd be very interested to hear your comments and get your feedback on how we're doing. Feel free to let me know what you think about this or any other Sybex book by sending me an email at nedde@wiley.com. Or, if you think you've found a technical error in this book, please visit http://sybex.custhelp.com. Customer feedback is critical to our efforts at Sybex.

Best regards,

Neil Edde
Vice President and Publisher
Sybex, an Imprint of Wiley

For Laura, who makes me feel as if I'm the most important person in the world.

—Jeremy

Acknowledgments

If you're holding this, it means you've found the companion book to *Group Policy Fundamentals, Troubleshooting, and Security*. That's great. I'm glad to have you aboard for this (extended) ride.

I want to thank my chapter authors for this book: Johan Arwidmark for stepping up to help with Chapter 1 ("Windows Deployment Services and Microsoft Deployment"); Greg Shields for doing a smashing job with Chapter 8, "WSUS 3.0 and MBSA"; and, Eric Johnson for hitting two big chapters out of the ballpark with his contributions to the SoftGrid community (Chapters 6 and 7). This book wouldn't be the same without you guys, so that you for your dedicated efforts.

Next, I want to thank Jakob Heidelberg for taking on the tough job as the book's Technical Editor (he helped with the other book too). Jakob was just the perfect guy for the job. If you ever get a chance to meet him, do so. He's awesome.

I want to thank Elizabeth Campbell for taking on this book as well (yes, if you're keeping score that's another person working on two books at the same time.) She's simply a rock star who just always comes through. Thank you.

Thank you to the Sybex and Wiley people who also worked on this book at the same time as the *Group Policy Fundamentals* book: Tom Cirtin, and Peter Gaughan. And behind the scenes, Jay Lessandrini, Dave Mayhew, Judy Flynn, and Neil Edde, who help me get the book on the shelves and in your hands. This is a great staff, and I'm really happy to be working with you guys.

A special thanks to Mark Gray from the Group Policy team at Microsoft. Mark is new to the Microsoft team but hacked and slashed through my tortuous questions one after another. A simple "Thanks!" simply isn't enough to convey my appreciation.

Thank you to the hordes of Microsoft folks who helped me get technical questions answered. From the Group Policy team, Judith Herman, Mark Gray and Kevin Sullivan. From other teams, Greg Lindsay, Jeff Sigman, Jason Popp, Ian Hammeroff, Emily Woo, Garrett Vargas, Reshma Nichani, Rob Elmer, Scott Dickens, and I'm sure lots of others who I just plum forgot to write down. Thank you for all you help.

Finally, I want to thank you for taking the time to bring a little piece of me into your lives. Writing a book takes, well, way too long, and sometimes it's not clear if the end will ever come. But when you tell me how this book has helped you out, it makes it all worth it. Come over to GPAnswers.com and let me know how this book helped you out and met your expectations.

About the Contributors

Jakob H. Heidelberg, the Technical Editor for the book, currently works as an IT Specialist for Interprise Consulting A/S, a Microsoft Gold Partner based in Denmark. He is also a writer for www.windowsecurity.com (see www.tinyurl.com/ypar82) and takes on freelance teaching and public speaking when possible.

Jakob is very engaged as a contributor at the largest online Microsoft community for Danish IT Pros, www.it-experts.dk, and spends a great deal of time in the www.GPanswers.com forum too. He also writes on his own blog, heidelbergit.blogspot.com (www.tinyurl.com/2mctjf), and likes to catch up on as much new stuff as possible within the Microsoft world. He currently specializes in Group Policy, scripting, and security.

Jakob dedicates his chapter to his wonderful wife—the better half who was and is always on his mind.

Eric Johnson, who wrote Chapters 6 and 7 about SoftGrid, started his career in IT over a decade ago and has run the gamut of IT jobs. Answering technical support calls, teaching technology classes, network administration, and Citrix administration were just some of his roles. His current role is as an infrastructure project manager at a nonprofit health system in Idaho. His current focus involves implementing a suite of Microsoft applications and tools including Windows Deployment Services (WDS), Systems Management Server (SMS), Group Policy, and SoftGrid / Microsoft Application Virtualization.

Greg Shields, who wrote Chapter 8 about WSUS and MBSA, is an independent author, speaker, and IT consultant based in Denver, Colorado. Having nearly 15 years of experience in IT systems administration and architecture, Greg is a contributing editor for *Redmond Magazine*, MCPMag.com, and *Virtualization Review Magazine*, as well as the resident editor for Realtime Publishers' Windows Server Community at www.realtime-windowsserver.com. He is also a highly sought-after instructor and speaker, regularly seen at IT conferences like TechMentor Events.

Greg dedicates his chapter to his three wonderful girls: Sharon, Lexus, and Shelby. Their never-ending optimism and support inspires him to do things he never thought possible.

Johan Arwidmark wrote Chapter 1 about Microsoft Deployment and contributed to the sections on Windows Deployment Services. He is a consultant and all-around ubergeek specializing in Enterprise Windows Deployment Solutions. He is currently employed by Truesec, an independent elite-team of security and infrastructure consultants. Johan speaks at several conferences each year, including IT-Forum, MMS, and TechEd. He has also been awarded Microsoft Most Valuable Professional (MVP) in Setup and Deployment.

Contents at a Glance

Contents

Introduction

If you already bought the first book, you already recognize the awesome power of Group Policy. And you realize that "more is more" with Group Policy. More power, more control, and an easier experience for your users.

But you can't do it all just with Group Policy.

And that's where this book comes in.

It's going to take a well-rounded approach to manage and secure your Desktops. And Group Policy *is* one of those integral pieces. But there are other pieces of the puzzle, too, and this book contains all of them. Like understanding how profiles work, and dealing with distributing software, and delivering printers, and dealing with patches, and the list goes on.

We also dive into some awesome new technology, Microsoft's SoftGrid, to keep our Desktops running smoother (and lighter) than ever.

Each chapter in this book is about "removing the friction" that you usually encounter with Desktop management. If you eliminate the friction, you can get back to why you loved IT in the first place.

I'm confident you'll have a happier end-user Desktop experience after reading this book.

Getting Ready to Use This Book

If you have the companion book, *Group Policy Fundamentals, Troubleshooting, and Security*, and you've worked through it, you've already seen this section. Here, I'll present my suggested test lab set up, with names of machines, procedures to kick off our test lab, and other items to ensure a successful work though with this book.

You'll need to have a management station (described in just a second) that has the latest GPMC 2.0 loaded. I'll show you how to do that, too, if you've never done it before.

So, this book is full of examples. And, to work through these examples, here's my suggested sample test lab for you to create. It's pretty simple really, but in its simplicity we'll be able to work though dozens of real-world examples to see how things work. Here are the computers you need to set up and what I suggest you name them (if you want to work through the examples with me in the book):

DC01.corp.com   This is your Active Directory Domain Controller. It can be a Windows 2000 Server, Windows Server 2003, or Windows Server 2008 Domain Controller. For this book, I'll assume you've loaded Windows Server 2008 on this computer, and that you'll create a domain called Corp.com.

It should be noted that some material, for instance the entire Chapter 9 on Network Access Protection, requires a Windows Server 2008 server, so, ideally, if you can get your hands on one for this book, that's your best bet.

In real life you would have multiple Domain Controllers in the domain. But here in the test lab, it'll be okay if you just have one.

I'll refer to this machine as DC01 in the book. We'll also use DC01 as a file server, software distribution server, and a lot of other roles we really shouldn't. That's so you can work though lots of examples without bringing up lots of servers.

In some examples DC01 has a D: drive to store data. You might want to consider a machine (or virtual machine) with an 8GB C: drive and another 8GB D: drive.

XPPRO1.corp.com   This is some user's Windows XP machine, and it's joined to the domain Corp.com. I'll assume you've loaded Windows XP's SP2 (though SP3 might be available by the time you read this). Sometimes it'll be a Sales computer, other times a Marketing computer, and other times a Nursing computer. To use this machine as such, just move the computer account around in Active Directory when the time comes. You'll see what I mean. I'll refer to this machine as XPPRO1 in the book.

Vista1.corp.com   This is some user's Windows Vista machine and it's joined to the domain Corp.com. I'll refer to this machine as VISTA1 in the book. Like XPPRO1, this machine will move around a lot to help us "play pretend" when the times arise. Windows XP works a little differently than Vista, so having both a Vista machine and a Windows XP machine in your environment will be good for testing. Having Windows Vista's SP1 is a good idea for this machine.

Vistamanagement.corp.com   This is your machine—the IT pro who runs the show. You could manage Active Directory from anywhere on your network, but you're going to do it from here. This is the machine that you'll run the tools you need to manage both Active Directory and Group Policy. I'll refer to this machine as VISTAMANAGEMENT. As the name implies, you'll run Windows Vista from this machine. Be sure to have Windows Vista's SP1 loaded before continuing here.

Figure I.1 shows a diagram of what our test network should look like if you want to follow along.

 You can build your test lab with real machines or with virtual hardware. I use VMware Workstation (for-a-fee tool) and VMware Server (free tool) for my testing. However, Microsoft's tools, like Virtual Server 2005 and Virtual PC 2007 (both free) are great choices, as well. That way, if you don't have a bunch of extra servers and desktops around, you can follow along with all the examples.

 Because Group Policy can be so all-encompassing, it is highly recommended that you try these examples in a test lab environment first before making these changes for real in your production environment.

Note that in the book, from time to time I might refer to some machine that isn't here in the suggested test lab, just to illustrate a point. However, this is the minimum configuration you'll need to get the most out the book.

Implementing the GPMC on Your Management Station

The GPMC isn't part of the standard Windows 2003 or Windows XP package out of the box. And it's already installed into Windows Vista and Windows Server 2008.

That's right—at first there's nothing to download, nothing to install, and nothing to worry about. That is, until Windows Vista + SP1 is installed, at which time the GPMC is uninstalled.

FIGURE I.1   Here's the configuration you'll need for the test lab in this book. Note the Domain Controller can be 2000 or above, but 2008 is preferred to allow you to work through all the examples in this book.

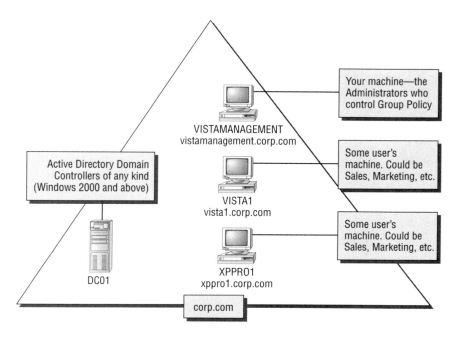

Don't panic. It's a quick hop, skip, and a jump to get the latest GPMC from Microsoft's website. I'll show you how to do this in a minute.

Remember earlier we stated that you could manage your Active Directory from anywhere. And this is true. You could walk up to a Domain Controller, you could install the GPMC on a Windows XP or Windows Server 2003 server, or you could use Terminal Services to remotely connect to a Domain Controller.

But in this book, you won't be doing that. Your ideal management station is a Windows Vista + SP1 + RSAT machine, or a Windows Server 2008 machine (which is ready to go, no downloads needed).

If you must use something else (Windows XP, Windows Server 2003, or Windows Vista RTM), I provide some advice for those. But you'll really want to use one of my two recommended configurations to get the most out of this book.

Using a Windows Vista or Windows Server 2008 Management Station

In this book, and in real life, I'm going to recommend that you use what's known as a Windows Vista management station. And, ideally, that Windows Vista management station would have SP1 with the updated (downloadable) GPMC installed on it.

You could also use a Windows Server 2008 machine as your management station, but it's not likely you're going to install that puppy on your laptop or desktop.

So, just to be clear, the following two ways to create and manage GPOs are equal:

- Windows Vista + SP1 + newly downloadable GPMC (contained within the RSAT tools)
- Windows Server 2008 with built-in GPMC

I'll usually just refer to a Windows Vista management station; and when I say that, I mean the first configuration I just mentioned. Just remember that you can use a Windows Server 2008 machine as your management station, too.

I delve into this in serious detail in Chapter 7, but here's the CliffsNotes, er, "Jeremy's Notes" version:

- Always use Windows Vista (or Windows Server 2008) as your management station, and you'll always be able to control all operating systems' settings: Windows Vista, Windows Server 2008, and all earlier editions.
- If you have even one Windows Vista client machine (say, in Sales, Marketing, etc.), you're going to need to manage it using a Windows Vista or Windows Server 2008 management station.
- If you create a GPO using Windows Vista or Windows Server 2008, but then edit it using an older operating system, you might not be able to "see" all the settings. And, what's worse, some might actually be set (but you wouldn't see them!).

 What if you're not "allowed" to load Windows Vista on your management station? Well, you've got another option. Perhaps you can create a Windows Vista or Windows Server 2008 machine and have it act as your management station, say, in the server room. Then set up Terminal Services or Remote Desktop to utilize the GPMC remotely.

Again, in our examples we'll call our machine VISTAMANAGEMENT, but you can use either a Windows Server 2008 or Windows Vista + SP1 + RSAT for your best management station experience.

Using a Windows Server 2008 Machine as Your Management Station

The latest GPMC is available in Windows Server 2008. Except by default, it's not immediately usable. You need to install it or you won't be able to use it. There are two ways to install the GPMC: using Server Manager and by the command line.

To install the GPMC using Server Manager:

1. Click Start, then point to Administrative Tools and select Server Manager.
2. In the Server Manager's console tree, click Features then select Add Features.
3. In the Add Feature Wizard dialog box, select Group Policy Management Console from the list of features.
4. Click Install.

Close Server Manager once you're done.

You can also install the GPMC using the command line:

1. Open a command prompt as an Administrator.

2. In the command prompt, type **ServerManagerCmd -install gpmc**.

3. Close the command prompt when the installation has been completed.

Using a Windows Vista + SP1 + RSAT Machine as Your Management Station

The first step on your Windows Vista management-station-to-be is to install Windows Vista SP1. Next, you'll need to install RSAT. RSAT installs like a hotfix, and you may or may not need to reboot after installation. Download RSAT for Vista + SP1 (x86 version) here: `http://tinyurl`
`.com/3xs2o6`. Download RSAT for Vista + SP1 (x64 version) here: `http://tinyurl.com/`
`337gfj`.

Then, on Windows Vista, go to Control Panel and select Programs. Select "Turn Windows features on or off." Locate the Feature Administration Tools and Role Administration Tools nodes. Select Group Policy Management Tools and Active Directory Domain Controller Tools as seen in Figure I.2.

Once you're done, close the Windows Features and, if prompted, reboot your Windows Vista machine. The next time you boot, you'll have Active Directory Users and Computers, the GPMC, and other tools available for use in the rest of the book.

FIGURE I.2   The RSAT tools install like a hotfix but then must be individually selected using Control Panel ➢ Programs ➢ Turn Windows features on or off.

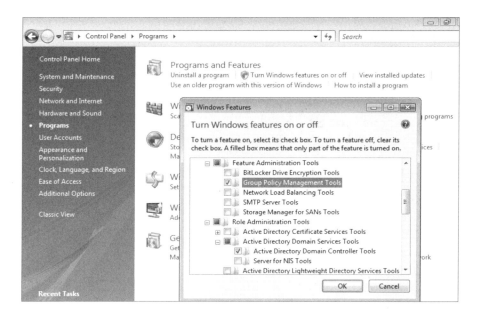

Other Management Station Options

If you positively cannot use a Windows Vista + SP1 + RSAT machine to be your management station, and you must limp along with Windows Vista RTM, Windows XP, or a Windows Server 2003 machine, you can.

But know that you won't get the full experience, and your screen might look different than my screenshots. And some features, like Folder Redirection, simply won't work the same or look the same.

If You Must Use a Windows Vista RTM Machine   On your Windows Vista machine, click Start and in the Start Search prompt type **gpmc.msc**. With Windows Vista RTM, the GPMC will just fire right up. I strongly encourage you to get to a Windows Vista + SP1 + RSAT machine as soon as possible. However, you can also perform the steps in the section titled "Adminpak on a Windows Vista Management Station" in *Group Policy Fundamentals, Security, and Trouble-shooting* in the introduction to make the most of your situation.

If You Must Use Windows XP or Windows Server 2003 Management Station   Now, what if you really, really cannot use a Windows Vista or Windows Server 2008 management station? Well, then, sounds like you're stuck with Windows XP or Windows Server 2003. With that in mind, you can check out the sidebar titled "If You Must Use a Windows XP or Windows Server 2003 Management Station."

If You Must Use a Windows XP or Windows Server 2003 Management Station

Again, I recommend against using the GPMC on Windows XP or Windows 2003 if you have even one Windows Vista machine to use. Read Chapter 7 in the companion book for the full rundown about why.

However, if you feel you must continue to use Windows XP or Windows Server 2003 as your management station, you can download the older GPMC for free from www.microsoft.com/grouppolicy. To be honest, I don't know how much longer they'll maintain the original GPMC. I wouldn't be surprised if, sometime soon, the only GPMC available is the updated edition (contained within RSAT), which runs on Windows Vista (and built into Windows Server 2008).

Click the link for the Group Policy Management Console to locate the download. Once it's downloaded, the GPMC is called GPMC.MSI. You can install this on either Windows 2003 or Windows XP with at least SP1, but nothing else. That is, you cannot load the GPMC on Windows 2000 servers or workstations; but, as I noted before, the GPMC can manage Windows 2000 domains with Windows 2000 and Windows XP clients as well as Windows 2003 domains with Windows 2000 or Windows XP clients.

Installing the GPMC does require certain prerequisites that must be loaded in the order listed here.

Loading the GPMC on Windows XP

If you intend to load the GPMC on a Windows XP machine to manage Group Policy in your domain, follow these steps:

1. At least Windows XP Service Pack 1 is required. If you are unsure whether SP1 (or later) is installed, run the WINVER command, which will tell you whether a service pack is installed. So, if your Windows XP system doesn't have at least SP1 installed, you should install the latest service pack.

2. The GPMC requires the .NET Framework 1.1 to run properly. Note that if you only have the newer .NET Framework (2 or higher), it won't work. It simply must be .NET Framework 1.1. If it's not installed, you'll need to download and install it. At last check, the .NET Framework download was at a URL I've shortened to http://tinyurl.com/7vshz. If it's not there, Google ".NET Framework 1.1."

   After downloading .NET Framework 1.1, double-click the install to get it going on your target Windows XP/SP1 (or greater) machine. It isn't a very exciting or noteworthy installation.

3. To install the GPMC, double-click the GPMC.MSI file you downloaded. If you're running Windows XP with SP1, the GPMC installation routine will report that a hotfix (also known as a QFE) is required and then proceed to automatically install the hotfix on the fly. This hotfix (Q326469) is incorporated into Windows XP's SP2. So, if installing on a Windows XP/SP2 machine, you won't be bothered to install it.

Technically, the GPMC runs fine on .NET 2.0 only, but the MSI installer chokes when checking .NET versions. If you have the skills to get around that, you're theoretically good to go with just .NET 2.0.

Loading the GPMC on a Windows 2003 Domain Controller

If you intend to load the GPMC on a Windows 2003 Domain Controller or a member server, there are just a couple of things to do:

1. Although there aren't any Windows 2003 prerequisites, it's a good idea to install the .NET Framework 1.1. If the GPMC installation doesn't complain, you're good to go. Otherwise, load it up.

2. To install the GPMC, double-click the GPMC.MSI file you downloaded.

The Results of Loading the GPMC on Windows XP

After the GPMC is loaded on the machine from which you will manage Group Policy (the management workstation), you'll see that the way you view things has changed. If you take a look in Active Directory Users and Computers (or Active Directory Sites and Services) and try to manage a GPO, you'll see a curious link on the existing Group Policy tab (as seen here).

Additionally, you'll see a Group Policy Management icon in the Administrative Tools folder in the Start Menu folder.

Creating a One-Stop Shop MMC

As you'll see, the GPMC is a fairly comprehensive Group Policy management tool. But the problem is that right now the GPMC and the Active Directory Users and Computers snap-ins are, well, separate tools which each do a specific job. They're not integrated to allow you to work on both Users and Group Policy at the same time.

Often, you'll want to change a Group Policy on an OU and then move computers to that OU. Unfortunately, you can't do so from the GPMC; you must to return to Active Directory Users and Computers to finish the task. This can get frustrating quickly. The GPMC does allow you to right-click at the domain level to choose to launch the Active Directory Users and Computers console when you want, but I prefer a one-stop-shop view of my Active Directory management. It's a matter of taste.

As a result, my preference is to create a custom MMC which shows both the Active Directory Users and Computers and GPMC in a one-stop-shop view. You can see what I mean in Figure I.3.

You might be wondering at this point, "So, Jeremy, what do I need to do in order to create this unified MMC console you've so neatly described and shown in Figure I.3?"

FIGURE I.3   Use the MMC to create a unified console.

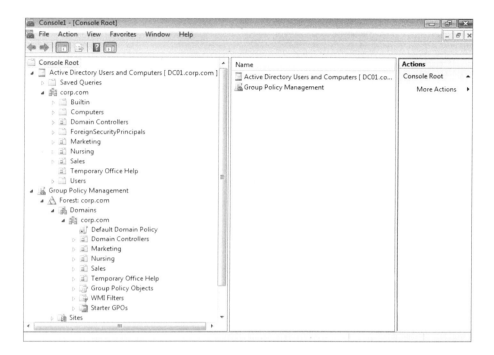

 By the time you read this, Microsoft will have hopefully released the RSAT tools, which are the Windows Vista equivalents to the Windows XP Administration Pack tools. By using these tools, you can have a management station with both Active Directory Users and Computers and the GPMC (both included in the RSAT tools).

Just click Start and type **MMC** at the Search prompt. Then add in both the Active Directory Users and Computers and Group Policy Management snap-ins, as shown in Figure I.4.

Once you have added both snap-ins into your console, you'll really have a near-unified view of most everything you need at your fingertips. Both Active Directory Users and Computers and the GPMC can create and delete OUs. Both tools also allow administrators to delegate permissions to others to manage Group Policy, but that's where the two tools' functionality overlap ends.

The GPMC won't show you the actual users and computer objects inside the OU; so deleting an OU from within the GPMC is dicey at best, because you can't be sure of what's inside!

You can choose to add other snaps-ins too, of course, including Active Directory Sites and Services or anything else you think is useful. The illustrations in the rest of this book will show both snap-ins loaded in this configuration.

FIGURE I.4 Add Active Directory Users and Computers and Group Policy Management into your custom view.

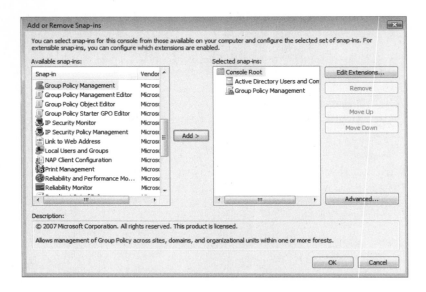

You can launch the GPMC from either the new link in Active Directory Users and Computers (or Active Directory Sites and Services) or directly from the new icon in the Start Menu. However, clicking Open in the existing tools has a slight advantage of telling the GPMC to "snap to" the location in Active Directory on which you are currently focused.

Deploying the Group Policy Preference Extensions Client to Your Machines

For this book, we're going to assume you have the Group Policy Preference Extensions client component installed on all your Windows XP, Windows Vista, and Windows Server 2003 machines.

It's free, and we cover the ins and outs in the companion book.

However, for reference, you would get the Group Policy Preference Extensions clients here: `http://tinyurl.com/2za5zz`.

As of this writing, the Group Policy Preference Extensions ship as "patch files" and not MSI files, which means it's not super easy to deploy them unless you're using a "big management tool" like SCCM 2007 or a patch management system like WSUS (which we talk about in Chapter 8).

However, if you want to mass-deploy the GPPEs today, you can create start-up scripts which would deploy the GPPEs to certain types of machines. Jakob Heidelberg, the Technical Editor of this book and the companion book, *Group Policy Fundamentals, Security, and Troubleshooting*, created a killer startup script that will do the dirty work.

Check out www.gpanswers.com/faq/55 for the complete script.

Note that Windows Server 2008 machines have the client components already installed (even though it's a server). In our world, we're going to assume you have a GPO linked to the domain, and the GPO is enforced on so every client computer will get a copy.

Understanding the Flow of This Book

A Desktop has a lifecycle.

It's born, gets configured, then starts grow strong and healthy.

It grows strong and healthy by feeding it applications, and also keeping the operating system updated and patched.

This book is all about the lifecycle. You'll see it's roughly grouped by five broad concepts:

Operating System Deployment   We have one chapter on deployment, but it could be all you need. That's Chapter 1, where we talk about Windows Deployment Services and Microsoft Deployment: two technologies that work in hand in hand to get your machines out the door, using free tools that Microsoft already provides.

Managed Desktop Part I: The User Environment   We have two chapters on creating a dynamic, managed Desktop. The idea is that whenever a user roams around, their basics "follow them." Their documents, their icons—their "life." We see how this works in Chapter 2 when we talk about Profiles and Chapter 3 when we talk about Redirected Folders and Offline Files and the Synchronization Manager.

Managed Desktop Part II: Deploying Software to Your Client Systems   Under this conceptual umbrella, we tackle the sticky issue of getting software to your client machines. And we want to do so in a very efficient manner. We have four chapters here. One chapter (Chapter 4) deals with the straight Group Policy solution. The rest of the chapters in this topic area, Chapters 5, 6, and 7, deal with SoftGrid, a new Microsoft technology used to deploy software—without actually installing it. (And, with a killer tip in Chapter 5, we show you how to use Group Policy to deploy your SoftGrid-based applications.)

Implementing Real-Life Security   Powerful security tools are the focus of two chapters. Chapter 8 deals with Microsoft's free patch management tool, WSUS 3.0, and their free security posture analyzer called MBSA. Using these tools together, you can learn where your trouble spots are, then patch any holes. Additionally, Chapter 9 helps you close the door on potentially unhealthy machines using Windows Server 2008's new Network Access Protection mechanism. That way if you have a machine that isn't "healthy enough" for your network, it won't be able to potentially infect others (but still allows it to make contact to machines that can help it get cleaned up).

Finishing Touches and Lockdown   In these last two chapters, you'll learn some additional techniques for crafting the perfect Desktop. It might seem odd that Chapter 11, "Lockdown with Windows SteadyState," falls under this concept rather than the security area. This makes sense because I believe that full lockdown isn't for every machine. It's a true "finishing touch" that you need under specific circumstances and not others. So, don't get all gung-ho and deploy this technology to all your machines; that's not what this is meant for. Be sure to read the chapter first.

And among *finishing touches*, we have a chapter on, well, finishing touches (Chapter 10). Here you'll learn how to control hardware, deploy printers, and save your client's bacon if they delete files they shouldn't.

Don't Go at It Alone

As always, at GPanswers.com I have lots of resources and updates to keep you going. Be sure to sign up for the GPanswers.com Newsletter (and confirm your subscription) at `www.GPanswers.com/newsletter`, and utilize our community forums and training classes to take your game to the next level.

Please e-mail me and let me know how this book helped you or anything else you'd like to tell me. See you at `www.GPanswers.com`.

Deploying Windows with Style: Windows Deployment Services (WDS), and Microsoft Deployment Toolkit 2008

This chapter is about getting Windows Operating Systems deployed with the least amount of pain and the best possible results. It is filled with tips and tricks, best practices, guidance, and notes from the field on how you can take advantage of the latest deployment tools and technologies.

Chances are that you are already working with image-based deployment. You might even be working with a third-party imaging solution and may be fine with that.

If you've already got it down to a science, then why should you read this chapter? Well, first of all, it's the first chapter—but beyond that, we think you should understand that the fundamental way to set up Windows has changed.

That means that new deployment tools and techniques have been made available. Some of those are free tools. Indeed, Windows now ships with its own imaging utility called ImageX (which we'll start exploring in the "Imaging Software Isn't About Speed" section). And the best part is, you can leverage these new tools to deploy Windows Vista and Windows XP if you want.

Let's start by busting a common myth:

"Ghost (or your current image tool) is faster than the new stuff Microsoft came out with." Really? Is it?

To prove it to you, I decided to put on my "Mythbusters" hat and put some science to the test.

This chapter was written by Johan Arwidmark with Jeremy Moskowitz

---

Check out the MythBusters TV show at http://dsc.discovery.com/fansites/mythbusters/mythbusters.html. Maybe they'll invite us on the show to prove our facts to you!

It's All About Imaging

I spent a good few days in my Lab Center, measuring speed and efficiency when deploying different Windows operating systems (and deploying to a large number of machines) using different imaging tools.

The results may surprise you.

 Real World Scenario

Quick Tips Before I Begin

Before giving you the details, let me give you some real-world tips about Windows deployment.

Tip #1: You'll Want to Use Image-Based Deployment

Trust me on this: image-based deployment is the way to go, whether you're deploying Windows XP, Windows Vista, Windows Server 2003, or Windows Server 2008.

With Windows XP and Windows Server 2003 you had an option; you could do a scripted setup and also work with images. With Windows Vista and Windows Server 2008 you *don't* have a choice; everything is now image based and for a reason: working with images has been proven to be the easiest, fastest, and most cost-effective way to deploy Windows.

Tip #2: Don't Fret About Your Imaging Tool

Which imaging tool you use (whether it's Ghost, Acronis, or ImageX, which we'll examine in this chapter) doesn't really matter that much. This is because the process of applying an image to disk is just one of many steps during deployment of a Windows operating system. Other steps might be driver injection, changes to the Windows setup, or adding post-install applications.

High-Level Imaging Process

In this section, I'll give you a high-level overview of Windows deployment processes and review the different terms and definitions involved.

First up are Windows deployment terms, where tools and technologies like Windows PE, Sysprep, and PXE will be explained. Then you'll learn about how the Windows setup process works, and last, we'll pull all the information together and match it to the deployment process.

Windows Deployment Terms

With Windows Vista, Windows deployment tools and processes have changed a lot. The new deployment tools can be used to deploy not only Windows Vista, but also Windows XP, Windows Server 2003, and Windows Server 2008. We can now have common processes no matter what operating system we are deploying.

Let's get some definitions out of the way first. That way, we can share a common vocabulary as we work through the issues with imaging.

Windows PE   Windows PE is a cut-down version of the Windows operating system that is used to start the deployment process, either by starting a tool for applying an image, or by starting the Windows setup engine. This operating system is also called a boot image.

Sysprep   You use Sysprep to prepare the machine for disk cloning and restoration via a disk image when working with operating system images. Sysprep will, for example, remove unique identifiers for a PC, clean the driver cache, and clear the event logs. The Sysprep processes can be automated by creating a text-based answer file called `sysprep.inf`.

PXE   PXE, or Preboot Execution Environment allows you to boot images over the network, for example, a Windows PE boot image.

Mini Setup   After deploying an image, Windows setup will reboot and enter the mini setup phase. This is when, for example, drivers are installed and the machine is joined to the domain. The `sysprep.inf` answer file is used to automate this process. In Windows Vista the mini setup phase, or pass, is called Specialize.

Unicast   Unicast is a protocol specification that delivers a set of packages to a single computer (destination).

Multicast   Multicast sends the same package to multiple computers (destinations) without affecting network bandwidth.

Windows System Image Manager (WSIM)   WSIM is an authoring tool for editing `unattend.xml` files. This is the replacement for Setup Manager, which was used with Windows XP or Windows Server 2003; this tool works only with Windows Vista and Windows Server 2008.

Windows Imaging (WIM)   WIM is a format for the new Windows Vista and Windows Server 2008 standard images. You can also create WIM images of Windows XP or Windows Server 2003. WIM images have a high compression rate (3:1), which leads to smaller images. Within each WIM image you have single instancing, which means you can combine multiple images to the same WIM image with only that difference between the two images being added to the wim image.

ImageX   ImageX is an imaging utility that is part of the Windows AIK (Windows Automated Installation Kit). It can be used to create (capture), deploy (apply), and edit WIM images.

Windows Desktop and Server Setup Overview

We'll start with exploring the setup of Windows XP and Windows Server 2003. They can be deployed in numerous ways:

Manually   If you choose to manually deploy Windows, you will boot the computer from the CD/DVD and answer all setup questions manually.

Unattended   If you want to install from CD/DVD media, but don't want to answer all setup questions manually, you can create a text-based answer file called `unattend.txt` with all the setup answers, name it `winnt.sif`, store it on a floppy or CD media, and then the setup will use it. Using an answer file like this is called a scripted setup.

Network-based Scripted Setup   If you like the idea about answering all setup questions using an answer file, but don't want to deploy from CD/DVD you can copy all setup and answer files to a server share, start a boot media like Windows PE, connect to the server share, and start the setup.

Network Image-based Setup   After installing the operating system using any of the preceding methods, you can run Sysprep and then capture the operating system to a network share using an imaging utility. This image can then be deployed unattended.

The setup of Windows Vista or Windows Server 2008 may look similar to the setup of Windows XP or Windows Server 2008, but under the hood, the setup is very much different. You can still automate the setup, but the setup is now exclusively image based. In fact, if you look in the \sources folder of a Windows Vista DVD, you will see a file called install.wim. This is a Windows Vista image that Microsoft prepared in their build lab.

The following are the setup options for Windows Vista and Windows Server 2008:

Manually   If you choose to manually deploy Windows, you will boot the computer from the CD/DVD and answer all setup questions manually. The difference, compared with the setup of Windows XP and Windows Server 2003, is that you actually deploy a sysprepped image.

Unattended   If you want to install from CD/DVD media, but don't want to answer all setup questions manually, you can create a text-based answer file called unattend.xml with all the setup answers, name it autounattend.xml, store it on a floppy, USB or CD media, and then the setup will use it.

Network Image-based Setup   If you like the idea about answering all setup questions using an answer file, but don't want to deploy from CD/DVD you can copy all setup and answer files to a server share, start a boot media like Windows PE, connect to the server share, and start the setup. This method is similar to the Network Image-based setup of Windows XP and Windows Server 2003.

Deployment Process

Here is a high-level overview of deploying Windows using a standard deployment process.

1. The deployment process begins when starting a boot image (Windows PE), either from a CD or over the network (PXE boot).
2. After booting the Windows PE boot image, it will connect to a server share containing the image(s) and other files such as drivers and applications.
3. An application or script will prompt for, or query a central configuration file or database for setup information such as what image to deploy, what computer name to use, and so on. This step will be explained in the "Microsoft Deployment Toolkit 2008" section.
4. Apply the image to disk.
5. Detect what hardware you are deploying to and copy the right drivers to disk.
6. Reboot into mini setup (or Specialize pass if deploying Vista).
7. Run post-install actions like installing applications or restoring user data and settings.

Imaging Software Isn't about Speed

As you can see, the imaging utility is only used in step 4, so it's not that important what imaging utility you are using. But since this step is what most people associate with Windows deployment, let's dive into that step for a while. I did promise you some test results, didn't I?

The two major imaging utilities today are ImageX from Microsoft and Ghost from Symantec. The end result is the same—they both apply an image to disk—but they work a bit differently.

Ghost is sector based, which means you can apply a Ghost image without having to partition the drive first. It's also fast both when capturing and deploying an image, and it supports offline editing of NTFS images (this feature is available in Ghost Solution Suite version 2.0 and later). However Ghost is not freeware.

ImageX is file based, which means you need to partition and format the drive first, then apply the image. It works like a very, very large file copy after the disk is partitioned. The bad news about ImageX is that it is very slow when capturing an image. However, it's pretty fast when *deploying* the image (see my results in Table 1.1). And ImageX is freeware. Like Ghost, it also supports offline editing of the image (which we'll explore in the "Servicing a WDS WIM Image" section a little later).

Table 1.1 shows my test results when capturing and deploying a 32-bit Windows XP image (fully patched and with some applications) and a 64-bit Windows Vista Enterprise (fully patched, no applications) with both Ghost and ImageX.

TABLE 1.1 Ghost vs. ImageX

	Ghost		ImageX	
	Time to Capture in	**Resulting Size**	**Time to Capture in**	**Resulting Size**
Creating (Capturing the 32-bit Windows XP Image), Initial Size: 4.4GB				
	7 min	2GB	18 min	1.3GB
Deploying Windows XP-32 bit image (plus some apps, fully patched), Initial Size: 4.4GB				
One computer	4 min		4 min	
Five computers (unicast)	4 min		4 min	
Ten computers (unicast)	6 min		5 min	

TABLE 1.1 Ghost vs. ImageX *(continued)*

	Ghost		ImageX	
	Time to Capture in	**Resulting Size**	**Time to Capture in**	**Resulting Size**
Creating (capturing the 64-bit Windows Vista Image), Initial Size: 10.3GB				
	13 min	4.5GB	30 min	2.5GB
Deploying the 64-bit Windows Vista image (plus some apps and fully patched), Initial Size: 10.3GB				
One computer	7 min		5 min	
Five computers (unicast)	9 min		8 min	
Ten computers (unicast)	12 min		10 min	

Our Mythbusters test shows that ImageX is slower when creating the image, but as fast or faster than Ghost when deploying the image.

It's okay to consider using something other than Ghost. If you're happy with what you're using, that's good. But I think you might be happier with the Microsoft way of things. I'll emphasize that way of things here because it's about as fast (if not faster) and will make your deployments easier to manage overall.

Windows Deployment Services (WDS)

Do you remember the high-level deployment overview earlier in the chapter? The first step was starting a boot image, followed by selecting an image. Windows Deployment Services (WDS) can help you with that. It's a core player and is frequently used in modern network-based deployment solutions. Later in the chapter, in the "Microsoft Deployment Toolkit 2008" section, we will dive deep into the Microsoft Deployment Toolkit 2008 (formerly known as Business Desktop Deployment, or BDD) and you will learn how these tools and pieces of infrastructure work better together and get some guidance on how to create and configure the deployment solution.

In a networked environment, and with a small investment of your time, WDS can help you better manage your Windows deployments. Its goal is to provide the administrator with the ability to roll out any number of Windows XP, Windows Vista, Windows 2003, and Windows Server 2008 configurations in a short amount of time. In a nutshell, you simply prepare your server for WDS, leverage the built-in hardware your client machine already has to connect to the network, answer a few questions (optional), and away the installation goes.

WDS is available in several forms. It is included in Windows Server 2003 SP2, as well as Windows Server 2008. Windows Server 2003 SP2 will upgrade your existing Windows Server 2003

so that it supports WDS. You can find it at www.microsoft.com/technet/windowsserver/
sp2.mspx. You can also get the update for Windows Server 2003 SP1 as part of the Windows
Automated Installation Kit (WAIK) here: http://tinyurl.com/37b42g. Both versions will be
covered in this chapter.

WDS is the descendant of RIS (Remote Installation Services). Under the hood, they've got
some similarities and, if you're still using RIS, that's okay: WDS on Windows Server 2003 will
upgrade your existing RIS server so it will keep on acting like an RIS server. However, we're
not going to go into RIS here. If you'd like information on RIS, you'll have to chase down an
older copy of this book (revision 3 and earlier).

Here, we'll assume you don't have RIS installed on your network and that you have
installed Windows Server 2008 to get the WDS functionality (remember, WDS is available
on Windows Server 2003, as well).

After you create your first WDS-based client machine, you can customize it with commercial
or homegrown apps and save that configuration to the server as well, making that machine
appear as another downloadable image.

Inside WDS

WDS is built on multiple components and also relies on some additional network components.

The Network Component Prerequisites

Before you can use WDS, you need to make sure several components are present on your network.

DHCP Server   The DHCP server is the first place the client machines look to get a temporary
TCP/IP address while the system is being installed.

DNS Server   DNS server is also required, mainly because it is a key ingredient in Active Directory.

Active Directory   You're not surprised, are you? Active Directory is also a requirement for
WDS. It doesn't mean you need to (or should) run WDS on a domain controller, but rather
that you need to run it on a member server in the domain. For test lab or educational purposes
you can, of course, run WDS on a domain controller.

> Unless you're a smaller company running Small Business Server as your only
> server, WDS should be running on a member server for performance and
> security reasons.

WDS Server   At least one server in your environment needs to be running WDS. We'll set up
this service later in the "Setting Up the WDS Server" section.

Although you can run all these services on just one server, in practice you probably
wouldn't want to due to the potential heavy processor and disk load the WDS server will have
to shoulder. Most real-world configurations run the DHCP and DNS servers on separate
boxes but configure one or more specific servers solely for the purpose of running WDS server
and dishing out WDS images.

For the sake of this example, however, you can use one server to run it all: DNS, DHCP,
and WDS. In this case, we'll use DC01.

What Does WDS Have That RIS Doesn't?

If you're wondering if you should make the switch from RIS to WDS, the answer is yes. But here's a quick rundown of what you'll get when you do:

- Native support for Windows PE as a boot operating system

- Native support for the Windows Imaging (.WIM) file format (which means support for Windows Vista and Windows Server 2008)

- An extensible and higher-performing PXE server component

- A new client menu for selecting boot operating systems

You'll get to see more details on these items as we progress during this chapter.

WDS Components

The following WDS components work together to enable you to deploy Windows operating system images:

Server Components   These consist of a shared folder (with the default name of RemoteInstall, shared as Reminst), which contains the images and files necessary for network boot, a Preboot Execution Environment (PXE) server, and a Trivial File Transfer Protocol (TFTP) server for network-booting clients.

Client Components   One client component is the WDS client; it's a GUI that runs in the Windows PE and allows for image selections (attended or unattended). Another client component is the PXE boot ROM. If your network card has the PXE boot ROM code embedded, you can boot directly to the network. You might need to turn this feature on in the network card's BIOS or in the PC's BIOS—or both.

Don't try to deploy all your laptops with one PXE-capable docking station. WDS machines are registered in Active Directory based on a GUID. The GUID is either hard-coded or based on the MAC address. If you deploy all your machines with a single docking station, you'll have multiple machines appearing to have the same GUID. Active Directory requires that machines have a GUID to function properly.

Setting Up the WDS Server

You can easily add the WDS to any Windows Server 2003 or Windows Server 2008 installation. (WDS is not available in Windows 2003 Server, Web edition.) In the following examples, you'll set up WDS on Windows Server 2008 and add a Windows Vista image for distribution.

Before you set it up, you'll need a decently sized NTFS partition for the WDS components and the WDS images. The size, of course, depends on how many images you want to support, but I consider 36GB to be a minimum. In the upcoming steps I'll use drive letter R: for my WDS server components and images, but you can use any drive letter. For most production environments you usually set it to D: or E:.

> Although you can use the boot partition or a second partition on the same hard disk, this results in poor performance of both WDS and the system as a whole. My recommendation is to install WDS on a separate physical disk from that on which Windows resides.

Loading WDS

The following steps apply only to Windows Server 2008. For Windows Server 2003, you add WDS using Add/Remove Windows Components in the Control Panel.

If you did not add the WDS role when you created the server, you can load it now. Follow these steps:

1. Choose Start ➢ Server Manager to open Server Manager.

2. Click Roles to open the Roles window.

3. Click Add Roles to start the Add Roles Wizard, as shown in Figure 1.1.

4. In the Roles list, click the Windows Deployment Services check box, click Next three times, click Install, and then click Close.

FIGURE 1.1 Adding the WDS role is easy via Server Manager on a Windows Server 2008 server.

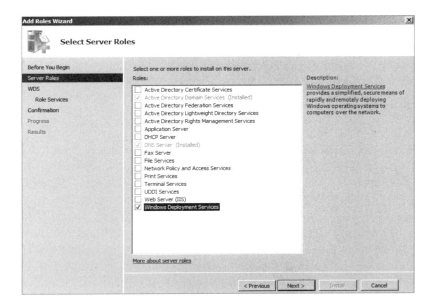

Setting Up the WDS Server

Once WDS is installed and the server is rebooted, you're ready to fire up WDS and get started with initial setup.

1. Choose Start ≻ All Programs ≻ Administrative Tools ≻ Windows Deployment Services.

2. In the WDS console, choose Expand Servers, right-click the DC01.corp.com server and select "Configure server." The first page of the WDS Configuration Wizard appears.

3. Walk through the wizard to answer the questions. Choose a folder on an NTFS volume that is not the system drive. In this example, I'm choosing R:\RemoteInstall. Click Next to open the "DHCP Option 60" screen. Note that you'll only see the "DHCP Option 60" screen if you have WDS and Microsoft DHCP on the same machine.

4. The WDS server needs to configure DHCP somewhat differently if the WDS machine is also a DHCP server. If it is, select "Do not listen on port 67" and "Configure DHCP option 60 to 'PXEClient'" when asked.

5. The WDS server must be configured to accept client connections. For our quick example, click the "Respond to all (known and unknown) client computers." For now, do not select the "For unknown clients, notify administrator and respond after approval."

 Clicking the "Do Not Respond to Unknown Client Computers Requesting Service" check box lets you lock down a computer's GUID to a specific WDS server. Make this connection when you're manually adding a computer to Active Directory Users and Computers by selecting "This Is a Managed Computer" and then entering the computer's 32-character-long GUID. You can find the computer's GUID in the computer's BIOS by using a WMI script (or you can use the MAC address of the network card instead) in the format of 20 zeros followed by the 12-character-long MAC address (hexadecimal); for example 00000000000000000000A309CDE24601.

Once your server is initially configured, you need to introduce it to the images you want to deploy. Let's first get a grip on the kinds of image files available to us, and then we'll install the image types we need.

Understanding WDS's Image Types

WDS has three types of images.

Boot Image   When your target machine performs a PXE boot to connect to the WDS server, this is what will be run on the client to "get it going." This is a cut-down version of Windows called WinPE which helps you (stay with me here) load the big version of Windows in the "Install Image" section (coming up next).

Install Image   This is the actual image you'll be downloading to your target machine. You might have one image for Sales, another for Marketing, and so on. However, a best practice is to have just one image which does it all. Note that images can be Windows XP, Windows Vista, Windows Server 2003, or Windows Server 2008.

Legacy Image   If you want to make your Windows Server 2003 WDS machine act like RIS, this is the place to do it. If you've upgraded an existing RIS server with RIS-style images, they will appear here. Ultimately, you'll want to convert these to the .WIM file format. The WDS help file, under the topic "Legacy Images" gives tips for how to do just that.

To use WDS successfully, you will leverage these images. If you're going to use WDS in native mode, you'll start out by booting a boot image then loading an install image. If you're going to use WDS in legacy mode, you'll leverage legacy images only.

Only WDS in Windows Server 2003 supports legacy mode. See the "New Features for Windows Server 2008" section for more information on Windows Server 2008 support for legacy images.

Adding the Boot Image

Let's start out by adding the boot image. Again, the boot image is a cut-down version of Windows to help you get started with your installation. Right-click the Boot Images node and select Install Image. The boot image you'll need is right on the Windows Server 2008 DVD in the \sources directory. Enter the path to the Windows Server 2008 DVD's \sources directory and specify boot.wim, as seen in Figure 1.2.

FIGURE 1.2   The boot.wim file gets your clients started with WDS.

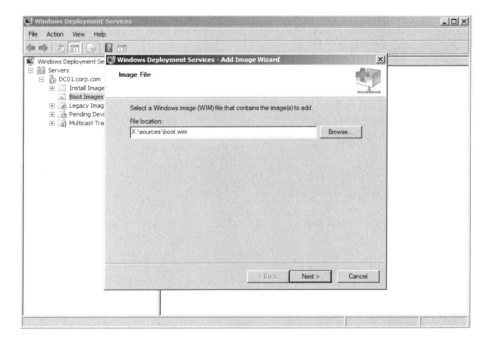

The boot image you are using must match, or be newer than, the operating system image (install image) you want to deploy. That's why we are using the `boot.wim` file from Windows Server 2008 and not from Windows Vista.

Once you click Next, you'll be able to enter in the image name. I'm not wild about the default name Microsoft Windows Longhorn Setup (x86), so I've changed it to Vista Boot WIM (x86) so it's much clearer. Another perfectly good name is Windows Server 2008 Boot WIM (x86), since we are using that media.

Adding the Install Image

Before we install the first image, you need to understand the concept of *image groups*. Image groups are like folders that contain similar images.

Here's the idea: within an image group, all the data is "single instance stored." That means if you have multiple images and they're very, very similar, you're only saving a copy of the differences. This is huge! Because the difference between the Sales and Marketing images might really be very small!

The other advantage of image groups is that you can specify who has access to different image groups. So, you can say that Server Installers have access to an image group for servers, but Desktop Installers have access just to an image group for desktops.

For our working examples, we're not going to have more than one image, so setting up multiple image groups isn't necessary. Follow these steps:

1. Right-click Install Images and select Add Install Image. You'll be prompted for your first image group. I'm naming mine VistaGroup, but you can call it anything you like.

2. In the Image File dialog, point WDS toward the file called `install.wim` in the `\sources` directory of the Windows Vista Enterprise DVD. When you do, you'll be presented with the "List of Available Images" screen, as seen in Figure 1.3.

FIGURE 1.3   You can select which versions of Windows Vista you want to put in the image group.

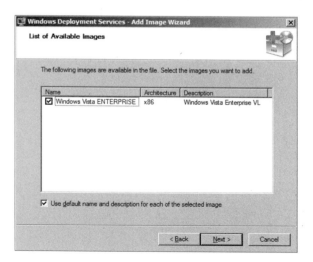

Because the images in the image group are single instance stored, you're not burning 1.7GB for each Vista image. It's 1.7GB plus a little more for each image you add.

3. Click Next until the image is added. This could take a while to complete.

Managing the WDS Server

Before you roll out your first client, you might want to tweak WDS. To do this, right-click the server name (dc01.corp.com) inside the WDS management tool and select Properties. Inside, you'll find various tabs.

There is nothing configurable on the General tab. It is informational only.

Directory Services   Space prevents us from diving into each option, but one you'll likely want to explore is Directory Services, as seen in Figure 1.4, where you can change the computer name of newly born computers as well as where to place newly born computers in Active Directory.

FIGURE 1.4   You can customize some WDS defaults, such as the client's computer name and where to drop it into Active Directory.

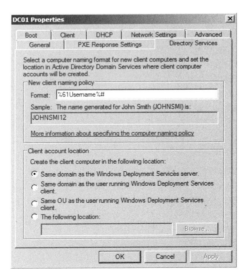

There are certainly lots of other options here, as well, including associating unattended installation files to your WDS client installations to make them hands off. This is done via the Windows System Image Manager (WSIM) tool to create the unattended files. Microsoft docs on the process can be found here: `http://tinyurl.com/y2sdbd`. The tool is found in the Windows Automated Installation Kit download (about 1200MB!) and can be found here: `http://tinyurl.com/37b42g`. You will find step-by-step guidance for associating unattended installation files in the "Beyond the Basics: Care and Feeding of WDS and Your Images" section later in this chapter.

In the past Windows Setup used multiple answer files, which are text files for different parts of the setup. Windows Setup used `unattend.txt` for scripted setups, `sysprep.inf` for automating Sysprep processes, `winbom.ini` in Windows PE and `cmdlines.txt` to perform operations during setup or Sysprep processes. All these text files have now been replaced by a single XML file (which is also a text file but a more structured one). And, to serve multiple purposes, it has been divided into different sections, or *configuration passes*. If you can't wait to learn more about this, you will find a section on how to create your own `unattend.xml` files in the section "Creating an Answer File Using WSIM."

PXE Response Settings   This tab instructs the server how to respond to known and unknown clients. A known computer is one that already has a record in Active Directory. When you create a new computer account in Active Directory, you can prestage it using the wizard when creating new computers. See Figure 1.5.

FIGURE 1.5   Set how a server should or should not respond to client requests.

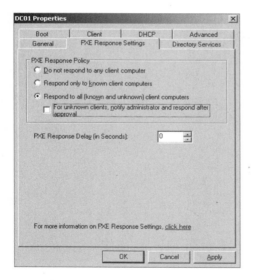

Boot   This tab is the PXE program that's downloaded right after you press F12 for a network boot. You can use this tab to automate the PXE boot or select the default boot image.

Client   Customizations in this area affect all clients when loading via WDS. You can basically customize the WDS Client installation here.

WDS Specifics for Windows Server 2008

Windows Server 2008 brings a new version of WDS. In this section you will learn the new features of WDS in Windows Server 2008 compared with the Windows Server 2003 version.

Before digging into the details about the new features, let's peek into the architectural changes. WDS in Windows Server 2008 still has the same network requirements as the Windows Server 2003 version (remember: DHCP, DNS, and Active Directory).

Server Components   The server components are pretty much the same as in the Windows Server 2003 version (a shared folder, a PXE server, and a TFTP server).

Client Components   A new multicast client has been added to the client components (WDS client and PXE boot ROM).

Management Components   The management components are same (WDS Console and WDSUTIL).

 Real World Scenario

Real-World Test Results

Here are some test results when deploying a 3.5GB Windows Vista image in a 100Mb connection (server connected using a gigabit connection):

- To 25 machines with multicast, 30 minutes

- To 25 machines with SMB (unicast), 30 minutes

- To 50 machines with multicast, 30 minutes

- To 50 machines with SMB (unicast), 43 minutes

Because we cannot multicast boot images and can only install images, this will be a limiting factor. Booting the Windows PE boot image takes about 50 seconds for 25 clients.

New Features for Windows Server 2008

Here is a detailed walkthrough of the new features:

Ability to Transmit Data and Images Using Multicast   WDS in Windows Server 2008 now has support for multicast, and not only that, but two different "versions" of multicast. We'll explore the multicast features in the section titled "Utilizing Multicast Deployment with WDS and Windows Server 2008."

Increased Efficiency   The WDS keyword here is efficiency, not speed. Multicast is not the fastest method for deploying, say, 25 clients on a 100Mb network—it actually takes about the same amount of time as with SMB (unicast). The difference is network utilization. Multicast will load the network about 5 percent, SMB about 95 percent.

This means that you may no longer be restricted to deploying your machines at nonpeak hours.

Standalone Server Support   When installing the WDS role in Windows Server 2008, you can choose to install only the transport server role service. This is for advanced scenarios; for example, when you don't have Active Directory Services present or a DNS or DHCP.

The cons to this are that Windows Server 2008 contains only the PXE listener, which is the server-side component. You will need to write a custom PXE provider and register it with WDS (see the Windows Server 2008 SDK for more information).

An Enhanced TFTP Server   WDS in Windows 2003 scales well up to 75 clients on a 1GB network; a slower network reduces scalability further. With multicast WDS in Windows Server 2008, WDS easily scales to 250 clients.

Network Boot x64-based Computers with EFI   EFI is the next generation BIOS, or rather a firmware layer between BIOS and the operating system.

Enhanced Diagnostics and Reporting   WDS now logs detailed information about its clients. The information is published to the event log. You will find the events under Application and Services Log ➤ Microsoft ➤ Windows ➤ Deployment-Services-Diagnostics.

These logs can be parsed for creating metric reports and can answer questions such as, "Which images are used most frequently?"

Logging for standard WDS client deployments is not enabled by default. See the "Troubleshooting WDS" section for information on how to enable this.

Ability to Deploy Windows Vista and Windows Server 2008   That says it all. You can now use the same processes and tools to deploy both servers and clients.

No Support for RISETUP Images or OSChooser Screens   Support for legacy image types and the OSC files is gone. This means that you need to convert any existing legacy images to native WIM images before upgrading. It also means you need to use Windows PE 2.0 for boot images, which requires 512MB RAM on all your client machines.

Installing and Managing Clients via WDS

You're almost ready to start rolling out your clients. Remember that your clients need network cards that are PXE-boot ROM–capable. To use the NICs that have the ROM code built right onto the card, watch for the PC to flash "Hit F12 for Network Boot" upon reboot. If your computer doesn't flash that message (or something similar), you'll need to check the network card's BIOS, the PC's BIOS, or both to see if the PXE feature is disabled.

Installing Your First Client

Once you're sitting down at your target machine, you're ready to install your first client.

 Running WDS on your workstations completely formats the first hard drive.

To use WDS to install a client, follow these steps:

1. Turn on the target system.

2. When prompted, immediately press F12 to see the boot menu, as seen in Figure 1.6.

FIGURE 1.6   Start WDS by pressing F12 and selecting which boot option you want.

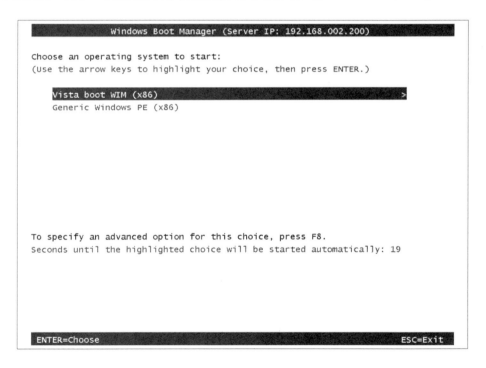

3. Select the boot WIM you want. (Maybe you have created the "Vista Boot WIM with Custom Network Drivers" using the information in the "Booting New Clients with VMware" Real World Scenario).

4. It will take some time to download the `boot.wim`. That's because the `boot.wim` is about 120MB, so be patient. When the first information screen appears, press Enter to open the Client Installation Wizard Logon screen.

5. The first WDS screen you'll see is called WDS and you simply select a Locale (like English/ United States) and a Keyboard Input Method (US). Click Next.

6. Enter a valid username, password, and domain. You'll have to enter it as ***DOMAIN\username*** or ***username@domain.com***.. Just about any username and password combination will work, like Frank Rizzo and our default password (if you chose to use it) of `P@ssw0rd`. In other words, users don't need to be (nor should they be) Domain Administrators to perform this function.

7. You can then select the Windows Vista image you want to install, as seen in Figure 1.7.

FIGURE 1.7   Select the Windows Vista image you want to deploy and select Next.

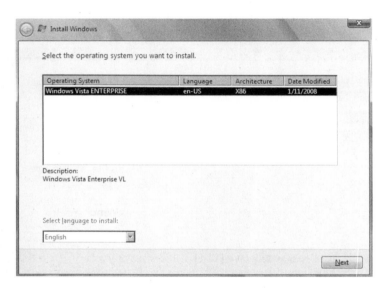

8. You'll then be able to partition the hard drive if you like; click Next, and you're off to the races.

If all goes well, the computer will be left at a logon prompt, waiting for the user to log on for the first time.

Converting Existing RIS Images to WDS Images

If you chose to upgrade your RIS server to a WDS server, you'll see your old RIS images in a folder called `Legacy Images`, as you saw in Figure 1.2 (though in that figure, we're not expressly showing the contents of the `Legacy Images` folder).

Real World Scenario

Booting New Clients with VMware

I do a lot of testing using VMware Workstation and Server. It's a great cheap way to emulate a lot of computers quickly. It's also great for when I need to take screenshots of the boot process. However, if you are not using the latest VMware Workstation release (version 6.0 as of this writing) when you try to spawn a new Windows Vista machine via WDS, it turns out that the network card that VMware emulates isn't part of the boot.wim (the file that's downloaded before you kick off WDS).

There are two options to getting older VMware Products to work with WDS: configure VMware to emulate an Intel 1000 MT adapter that is supported by default by Windows PE 2.0, or add the VMware Network Drivers to Windows PE 2.0 (boot.wim).

Implementing Option 1: Changing a VMware Client to Use Intel 1000 MT Adapters

Add the following information to your VMX file:

```
ethernet0.virtualDev = "e1000"
```

Remember that the latest release of VMware Workstation will automatically add this value if you select Windows Vista as your operating system when you're creating the virtual machine.

To add new or updated drivers you need the WAIK (Windows Automated Install Kit, found at http://tinyurl.com/37b42g), which can help you jam in the VMware network card driver. The tool you'll leverage is the imagex.exe utility, which can crack into an existing .WIM file, mount it in the file system, and allow you to put new drivers right into the file. Then, once the driver injection is completed, you can sew it up and use those drivers!

Implementing Option 2: Adding the VMware Network Drivers to Windows PE

1. Install the WAIK to the default location.

2. Create a new directory on your hard drive. This will be a temporary directory to "mount" the boot.wim file. For this example, I will use C:\6000 (the build number for Windows Vista). While you're here, create a subfolder under that called Mount (so the final path is C:\6000\Mount).

3. Copy the boot.wim file from the Windows Server 2008 DVD (in the \sources directory) to the C:\6000 folder.

4. The point is to jam in the network drivers you'll need that WDS doesn't natively support. In my case, I need the VMware drivers. To get them, leverage an ISO reading program (such as VCD, Daemon Tools, WinISO, and so on) to mount the C:\Program Files\VMWare\VMWare Workstation\Windows.iso file. You could also grab these files while telling VMware Work-station (or Server) that you want to "Install VMware Tools" from the VM menu. You'll then be able to see these files to copy (and you don't actually have to reinstall VMware tools if you already have them installed).

---

5. From that ISO, copy the following: `<root>\Program Files\VMware\VMware Tools\Drivers\vmxnet\win2k`. Copy all the files in that folder to a new directory: `C:\6000\vmxnet`.

6. Now it's time to use `imagex.exe` from the WAIK. Start the Windows PE tools command prompt (a standard Windows command prompt but with the path set to the different WAIK tools, like ImageX). Type: **`imagex /mountrw c:\6000\boot.wim 2 c:\6000\mount`**. Note the number 2 between `boot.wim` and `c:\6000\mount`. This designates the second index within the `boot.wim`.

7. In the command prompt, execute the next two lines, which will jam in the drivers and commit the drivers into the WIM:

```
peimg /inf=c:\6000\vmxnet\*.inf c:\6000\mount\windows
imagex /unmount /commit c:\6000\mount
```

8. Now your `boot.wim` will have the network drivers it needs inside the second image (the one Windows Vista uses when setup runs).

9. Now, use the WDS server manager to right-click the `Boot Images` folder and select Add Boot Image. Import your newly updated `boot.wim` (`c:\6000\boot.wim`) into your WDS server and give it a unique name, such as Vista Boot WIM with Custom Network Drivers (x86).

Before upgrading to the Windows Server 2008 version of WDS, you need to first upgrade your RIS Server to WDS (Windows Server 2003 version) and convert your existing legacy images. WDS needs to be in native mode in order to be upgraded to the Windows Server 2008 version.

Existing RIPREP images can be converted offline. RISETUP images need to be deployed and recaptured (which of course you can do with RIPREP images, as well). We will deal with how to do this in this section.

Converting Existing RIPREP Images to *.WIM* Offline

If you chose to upgrade your RIS server to a WDS server, you'll see your old RIS images in a folder called `Legacy Images`. Some of these could be RIPREP images, which are RIS images you made that already had the base applications inside the image. There's an alternate way to convert these to WIM format.

The command line `wdsutil.exe` (which is on your Windows Server 2003 WDS server) can convert an RIS image into a `.WIM` file. Your legacy RIS images are likely in a directory called:

`<driveletter>\RemoteInstall\Setup\English\Images\<imagename>\i386\templates\<something>.sif`

For example:

`R:\RemoteInstall\Setup\English\Images\WindowsXPSP2\\i386\templates\myriprepedimage.sif`

There will be additional SIF files for every RIS image with an answer file.

So, to convert the RIPREP image directly to WIM format, we'll leverage the `wdsutil` `/convert-riprepimage` command.

Now, a quick word about the `WDSutil.exe` command before we actually run the thing. It depends upon some libraries and DLLs in the WAIK tools, but those .DLLs aren't in the path in the standard Windows Command Prompt, so you need to start the conversion from the `C:\Program Files\Windows AIK\Tools\Servicing` folder. Once you started the Command Prompt, here are two example commands that should do the trick:

```
Cd /d "Program Files\Windows AIK\Tools\Servicing"
wdsutil /verbose /progress /convert-RIPREPImage /FilePath:"R:\remoteinstall\
setup\english\images\WinXPSP2ProImage\i386\Templates\riprep.sif" /
DestinationImage /FilePath:"R:\Windows XP SP2 Pro Eng X86.wim" /Name:"Windows
XP Pro SP2 Eng x86 Image" /Description:"Windows XP Pro SP2 Eng x86 Converted
RIPREP Image"
```

NOTE   The command lines beginning with `wdsutil` should be entered as one command, they have been wrapped for readability.

Again, this trick only works for RIPREP images, not flat (RISETUP) images where you just gave it the CD. For flat images, you need to deploy the image, run Sysprep, and then run the Capture Wizard.

Capturing Windows XP and Windows Vista Machines for WDS Deployment

You might have a Windows XP machine (or Windows Vista machine for that matter) that you want to deploy via WDS. But what about your applications? How you will get those onto the target systems?

You need to choose to do one of the following:

- Put your applications inside your WDS image. This is called a *thick image*.
- Have technologies like Group Policy Software Installation (GPSI) and/or assign application using tools from Microsoft Deployment Toolkit 2008. This is called a *thin image*.

Microsoft Deployment Toolkit 2008 (which is discussed in greater detail later in the "Microsoft Deployment Toolkit 2008" section in this chapter) allows you to assign applications per role, per hardware type, or per location (IP subnet).

You may also combine the two application deployment options; for example, you can have a few applications inside the image, like antivirus software and maybe some updates to the operating system like Windows Media Player 11 or Internet Explorer 7.0, and then deploy\ the other applications afterward.

On the one hand, it's certainly faster to load an application, such as Office 2003 or Office 2007, inside the WDS image and then deploy the image all at once rather than deploying a base WDS image and then using GPSI to shoot down Office 2007. The GPSI features have the added ability to upgrade packages and perform magic such as applying .MSP (Microsoft Patch) and .MST (Microsoft Transform) files into packages; these abilities are lost if the applications are embedded inside the WDS image.

Therefore, you'll need to analyze each application to determine if it's better to embed it inside the WDS image or deploy the package afterward. In my experience, in almost all cases it's better to deploy the applications after the image is installed. This makes it much easier to handle application upgrades and so on, or to remove applications from the deployment. If you do choose to embed applications in your WDS images, I'm presenting that information here. Again for the record, however, *I encourage you start working with thin images.*

After you install the applications on your target machine, you need to first run Sysprep on it, which prepares the machine for imaging. However, you won't be imaging it; you'll be capturing it, using the tools in the next steps.

We don't have room to go into all the Sysprep steps here, but you can see a screenshot of Windows Vista when it is being Sysprepped in Figure 1.8. However, if you want a quick Sysprep primer, check out the WAIK documentation.

FIGURE 1.8　　You need to have a Windows Vista machine (or Windows XP) Sysprepped in order to capture the installed machine to an image.

Creating Your Capture Boot Image

To get started, you need to first create a *capture image* and introduce that into your WDS boot images. The idea is that once you press F12, then boot from the capture image, you'll be able to push any machine up (Windows XP, Windows Server 2003, Windows Vista, or Windows Server 2008) that you want to deploy via WDS. Again, these machines can have no applications or a zillion applications preloaded (although, as I've said, I'm not a fan of preloading applications).

The capture boot is required so that the target machine can find a WDS server and push the existing machine up into an image. You'll leverage an existing boot image to create your capture boot image. Simply right-click one of your boot images and select Create Capture Boot Image as seen in Figure 1.9.

You'll be prompted for a name and location. Select any temporary location for now. Once the capture boot image is completely written, right-click Boot Images and suck it in from this temporary location. It's a bit convoluted, but it gets the job done.

When complete, you should see your new capture image as listed in Boot Images.

Leveraging Your Captured Boot Image

Let's assume you have a Windows XP machine you want to make as an available install image. Again, you have to have pre-Sysprep the machine in order to go on to the next steps. Without having Sysprepped your Windows Vista machine (or Windows XP, for that matter), the Capture Wizard (described next) won't be able to see the partition.

Once you Press F12 and select your new capture boot image, you'll be presented with the screen seen in Figure 1.10.

FIGURE 1.9   Right-click an existing boot image to create a capture boot image.

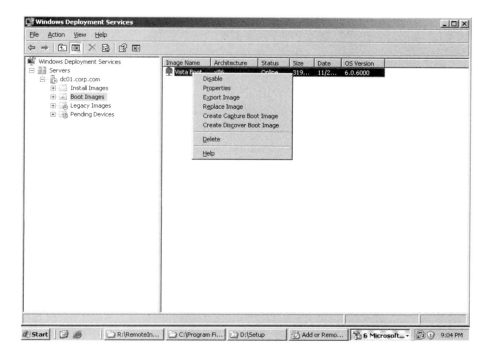

FIGURE 1.10   The WDS Capture Wizard can upload a Sysprepped Windows Vista machine.

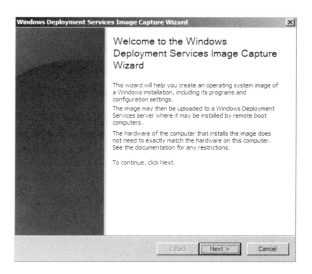

When you click Next, you'll be able to select a drive letter to capture, as well as name the image. I'll be calling my image Windows Vista Enterprise Master Image (x86), as seen in Figure 1.11.

FIGURE 1.11 You can name your image anything you like.

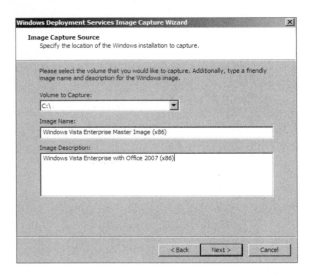

You'll then be able to specify the name of the server and the image group to plunk this in, and you're ready to go.

 The WDS capture utility (different from ImageX) creates the WIM image locally first and then copies it to the server. This is to address slow or high latency networks.

This image will then be available for deploying using WDS.

Utilizing Multicast Deployment with WDS and Windows Server 2008

The number one new feature for WDS in Windows Server 2008 has to be the multicast feature. And Microsoft didn't only give you multicast, they gave you two versions of multicast! (Don't worry, I cover both versions.)

Multicast should be used when you require many concurrent client installations and/or when you want to use the bandwidth efficiently. With multicast, you can limit the multicast deployments to a small fraction of your overall bandwidth.

Multicast does have some system requirements, and as I mentioned, the Microsoft implementation gives you two different multicast methods to choose from.

Requirements   Multicast is a very powerful ally. To use it on your network, your routers (if you have any) need to support multicasting. The needed feature is support for Internet Group Management Protocol (IGMP). Without this feature your routers might treat the multicast packages as broadcast packages and your network may become very busy or flooded.

You also need a boot image that is only available from Windows Server 2008. You cannot use the Windows Vista boot image for multicast.

Auto-cast   Auto-cast is the first of the multicast methods; it's like an ongoing stream of an image, present on the network as long as clients request it. A multicast client can join into this stream at any time. This is really neat when you see it in action.

Here's an example: You start the download for client 1, and, as suspected, it will start downloading data from the stream at the initial mark (0 percent). Then, later if you want to start client 2 downloading, but client 1 is now at 20 percent, client 2 just starts at 20 percent, finishes at 100 percent, and then goes back and gets the first 20 percent it missed! Wow!

Scheduled-cast   This is more like the multicast standard that has been around for years. You define how many clients you want to deploy and when the server "sees" that all clients have checked in the multicast deployment process starts.

Setting Up Auto-Cast Multicast Transmission

Creating an auto-cast multicast transmission is easy. You can choose between the management GUI, the WDS console, or the command-line management utility, WDSUTIL. In this example we will use the WDS console.

Adding the Boot Image

Remember, you'll need a Windows Server 2008 boot image for the multicast support. If you have not added a Windows Server boot image already, now is the perfect time to do it.

We already did something similar when we set up the WDS server earlier in this chapter, but this time, we'll use the boot image from Windows Server 2008. Since Windows Server 2008 and Windows Vista can use the same setup engine, this makes things easier. You will find the boot image in the same location on the DVD: \sources\boot.wim, as shown in Figure 1.12.

Creating the Transmission

In order to start deploying Windows using multicast, we need to create a transmission on the server that the client can connect to. Follow these steps:

1. Right-click the Multicast Transmissions node and select Create Multicast Transmission. This will start the Create Multicast Transmission Wizard.

2. On the Transmission Name page, enter a name (I entered Windows Vista Enterprise Eng x86) and click Next.

3. On the Multicast Type page, select the "Auto-Cast (multicasting starts automatically)" option and click Next. See Figure 1.13.

4. On the Task Complete page, click Finish.

FIGURE 1.12 Adding a Windows Server 2008 boot image

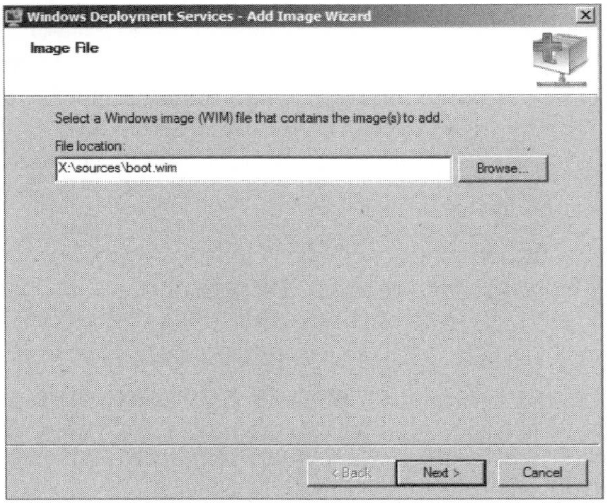

FIGURE 1.13 Selecting Multicast Type

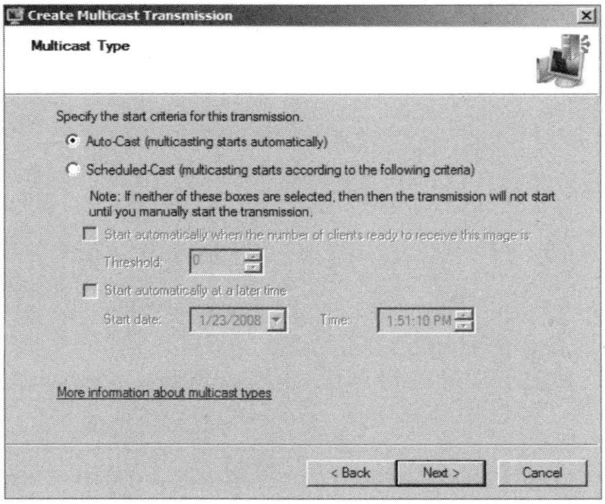

Installing Your First Client Using Multicast Transmission

Now it is time to start deploying our clients, as described in the following steps. The server transmission is set up and we only need to PXE-boot the client and it will download the boot image from the server. The boot image will then connect to our transmission and start down-loading our install image.

1. Turn on the target system.

2. When prompted, immediately press F12 to see the boot menu.

3. Select the boot WIM you want.

4. When the first information screen appears, press Enter to open the Client Installation Wizard Logon screen.

5. The first WDS screen you'll see is "Windows Deployment Services." Select a Locale (like English/United States) and a Keyboard Input Method (US). Click Next.

6. Enter a valid username, password, and domain. You'll have to enter it as *DOMAIN\username* or *username@domain.com*.

7. Select the Windows Vista image you want to install.

8. You'll then be able to partition the hard drive if you like. Click Next. When the client connects to the multicast stream, you will see the screen shown in Figure 1.14. After that, if all goes well, the computer will be left at a logon prompt, waiting for the user to log on for the first time.

FIGURE 1.14   Connecting to the multicast transmission

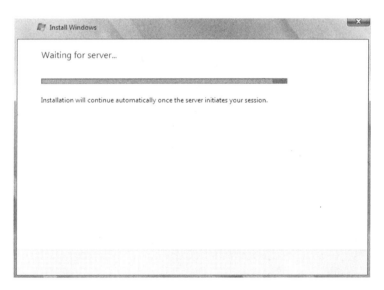

Monitoring Your Multicast Transmission from the Server

After the client connects to the multicast transmission, it will download the image locally and start the Windows Vista Setup, so using multicast actually requires a bit more disk space than unicast does. (Unicast expands the image directly from the server.)

You can see how your client progresses in the WDS console. You will see information like the MAC address, IP address, status (percentage complete), and transfer speed, as seen in Figure 1.15.

FIGURE 1.15   One multicast client

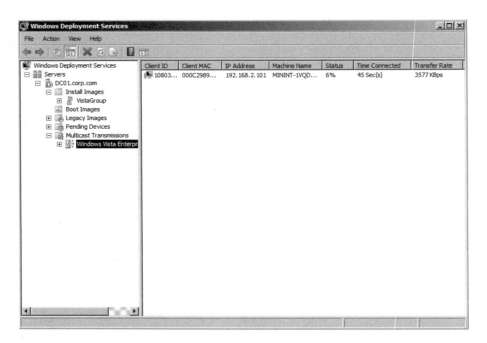

Installing More Clients Using the Existing Multicast Transmission

What if you want to install more than one client? That's easy! Just repeat the steps in the "Installing Your First Client Using Multicast Transmission" section. Then the second client will connect to stream at the current status. Figure 1.16 shows two clients downloading the image from the server using the same transfer speed. With multicast, it's the slowest client that determines the speed.

Managing Your Multicast Transmission from the Server

I just told you that the slowest client determines the speed of the download. So what if we have one super-slow client affecting the overall transmission to the other clients?

We can either disconnect the client that is slowing things down, or we can bypass the multicast transmission for that client. This is done by right-clicking the client's entry in the console and selecting "Bypass multicast," as seen in Figure 1.17.

This will not stop the download but will instead configure that client to download the image using unicast.

FIGURE 1.16   Two multicast clients using auto-cast mode

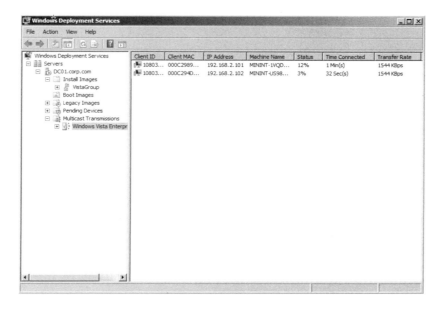

FIGURE 1.17   Bypassing a client

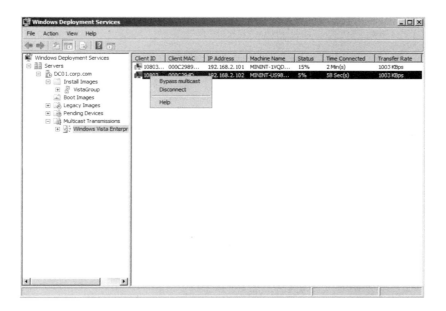

Configuring Multicast Transmission

Now that you have learned to create, monitor, and manage your transmissions on a per-client basis, it is time to configure the actual transmission.

Remember, clients join a transmission of a stream when they're installed during a multicast session. By using the transmission options, you can control all the connected clients at one time. Right-clicking the transmission gives you these options:

- Starting it. This option is only valid if the transmission hasn't started, such as when you are using the schedule-cast method. You can also enable clients to join in.

- Deleting it. This option will force all clients to continue the download using unicast.

- Deactivating it. This allows ongoing clients to complete their download using multicast but does not allow new connections.

- Viewing the properties. This option allows you to view the properties of the transmission, but you cannot edit the transmission after it has been created. To do that, you would need to delete it and re-create it.

Multicast Server Properties

In addition to managing the transmissions, we can configure other multicast settings such as bandwidth, IP address range, and so on. To configure those settings, right-click the server and select Properties, then go to the Network Settings tab, shown in Figure 1.18. In the Network Profile section, select the network speed. Each profile is tuned to match each specified network speed (such as window size, cache size, block size, and so on). You can create a custom profile or view the default profile settings in the Registry at HKLM\SYSTEM\CurrentControlSet\Services\ WDSServer\Providers\WDSMC\Profiles.

 If you have multiple WDS servers on your network running multicast transmissions, make sure to give them different IP address ranges. Don't forget to restart WDS after changing the IP address range.

Beyond the Basics: Care and Feeding of WDS and Your Images

By this point, you've got the WDS basics down. You can create your own new Windows Vista clients and you can zap your existing Windows XP machines up into .WIM files and into the WDS server—and you can zap them down, too. But there are several ways to go beyond the basics of WDS. That's what this section is about.

One of the key features of WDS and the WIM format (and the resulting .WIM files) is that you can maintain an image—even after it's captured. The result is that if you have a mere driver update or a hotfix to add, it's a piece of cake to add those to an existing image.

FIGURE 1.18   Multicast server properties

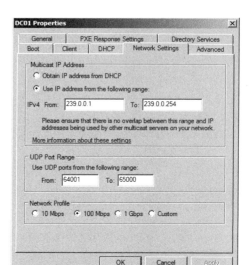

 The original idea with Offline Servicing was that you also should be able to apply service packs this way; however, that is not the case, at least not with Windows Vista SP1.

This idea of maintaining an image once it's captured is really only for Windows Vista and Windows Server 2008 WIMs, even though we've explored how to also capture Windows XP as a WIM. We'll spend most of our time here talking about how to perform these maintenance steps for Windows Vista WIMs.

Additionally, we'll cover how to associate an answer file with a WIM image, how to set up a larger WDS infrastructure, and finally, how to speed up WDS (under some specific circumstances).

Understanding Image Groups

As we've already discussed, WDS maintains WIM images in image groups. Image groups serve two functions: performing single instancing and maintaining security.

 The WIM file itself is a unit of single instancing. A single WIM file can contain multiple images. However, putting multiple images inside a WIM file isn't recommended if you use WDS, because WDS image groups already perform the function of performing single instancing. So, even though you can put multiple images inside a single WIM file, why bother? WDS's image groups go the extra mile and do the work for you.

Single Instance Storing

Windows Vista is about 1.7GB compressed on the DVD, so you might think that if you had seven versions of Windows Vista in an image group, that image group would be as large as 12GB! But it's not.

Again, that's because WDS will single-instance store all the images. Think about it: the differences between each Windows Vista version is ever-so-slight, and those differences are all that's captured between the various images.

If you dive into the actual image store via command line or Explorer, you'll see the images as various `.WIM` files with a big ol' `Res.RWM` file alongside them. Ninety-eight percent of all the images are contained inside that big file. The rest of the files are stored as the differences inside the remaining `.WIM` files.

> The Res.RWM file is really a WIM file, too. Technically, however, it's called a *resource WIM* and so is distinguished by a different filename.

You can see a list of my available images inside my VistaGroup image group and the corresponding underlying files in Figure 1.19.

FIGURE 1.19 WDS will perform single instancing inside an image group.

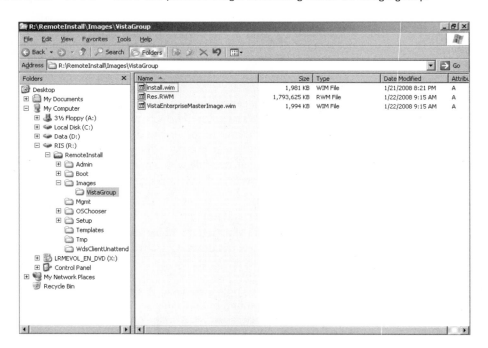

Setting Security for an Image Group

In addition to single instancing, the benefit of image groups is the ability to set security on them. By default, anyone who provides credentials when booting from a boot WIM can see the available images for download, format their machine, and get a fresh image.

I'll let that last sentence sink in for a while.

Go ahead and reread that if you need to.

The key word is *anyone*; specifically, Authenticated Users. This means that if you want to ensure that only the right people have access to WDS install images, you need to set permissions on an image group.

To do this, right-click the image group, say, VistaGroup, and select Security. Remove Authenticated Users' ability to "Read & execute," "List folder contents," and "Read." Add a group of people you trust, like DesktopAdmins or something similar, and give them those rights. You can see the default image group rights in Figure 1.20.

You'll need to get rid of Authenticated Users and add the group you want. However, Authenticated Users is being inherited at a higher level, so you'll also need to click the Advanced security button and uncheck the "Allow inheritable permissions from the parent to propagate to this object and all child objects" check box, as partially seen in Figure 1.21 (the Security pop-up that displays when you check this box is covering it). On the Security pop-up, choose Copy, which will copy the permissions from the parent, also seen in Figure 1.21.

FIGURE 1.20 By default, users can read and leverage the list of images inside an image group.

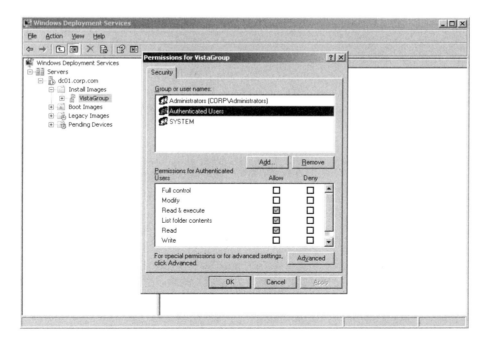

FIGURE 1.21   Remove the inheritable permissions and copy them from the parent.

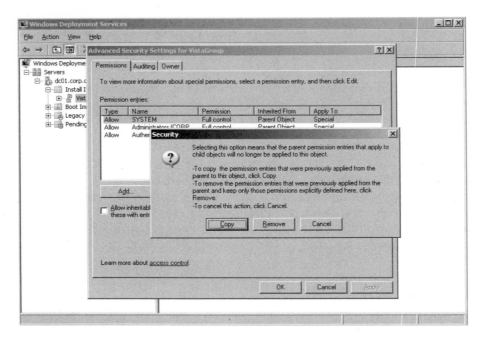

You'll be able to remove Authenticated Users and select just the users and groups you want. When a user log on using their credentials, and the WDS client will present only the images you've enabled them to see.

Servicing a WDS WIM Image

One really nice feature of Windows Vista is the ability to offline service drivers, language packs, and hotfixes. So when new hotfixes or security updates arrive, you'll want to just jam those hotfixes or that service pack into your existing image.

When you're done, you can either save the image out to another image (preserving the original one), or overwrite the original one. Here's the short version of how to do this:

1. Use the WDS MMC snap-in to mark the image as disabled (just right-click the image name and select Disabled).

2. Right-click the disabled image and select Export Image to export the image to a whole .WIM file. This can take a while.

3. Mount the image using the imagex.exe utility. Usually, the command will be imagex /mountrw <image.wim> 1 <mountpoint>, where <mountpoint> is a directory somewhere you can write to.

4. Service the image with the hotfix or driver. An example of how to add a driver can be found in the section, "Adding Drivers to an Existing Image."

5. Import the image back into the image group. If you want to completely replace the image, right-click the existing image and select Replace Image. If you want to add it as a new image while preserving the existing one, right-click the image group and select Add Install Image.

Adding Drivers to an Existing Image

With WDS you can easily add in new network, audio, video, and modem drivers by configuring the Vista setup to get the drivers from a folder during setup, or you can inject them offline into the image (offline servicing). Please note that only Windows Vista and Windows Server 2008 support offline servicing.

Option 1: Add Drivers Automatically During Windows Vista Setup

You can configure WDS to automatically inject drivers during setup. To do this, you create subdirectories with specific names within your image group's directory structure. In my examples, all the WDS stuff is being stored in R:\RemoteInstall in the \images directory. My first (and only) image group is named VistaGroup. To add drivers to your image, follow these steps.

Step 1: Prepare the Folder Structure and Add the Drivers   First, you create the folder structure needed for adding drivers to the Windows Vista Enterprise setup:

1. Create a subdirectory with the same name as the .WIM file, say, Install.

2. Then, create a OEM subdirectory and within that subdirectory create \$1, as seen here:

```
\Images
    \VistaGroup
        RES.RWM
        Install.WIM
        \Install
            \$OEM$
                \$1
                \Drivers
                  \NIC
                  \Audio
                  \SCSI
```

3. Copy the drivers to the corresponding folders.

 The OEM structure is also used for sysprep.inf when working with down-level operating systems like Windows XP or Windows Server 2003.

Step 2: Create the Answer File   Next, you use Windows System Image Manager to create an answer file containing information about which driver path the Windows Vista setup will

inject drivers from. Remember from the Windows deployment terms section that WSIM is an authoring tool for editing unattend.xml files, the replacement for Setup Manager used with legacy operating systems.

1. Using WSIM, in the Windows Image pane, right-click the "Select a Windows Image or catalog file" node and click Select Windows Image.

2. In the "File name" text box, type **C:\6000\CustomVistaEnterprise.wim** and click Open. In the Windows System Image Manager dialog box, click Yes to create a catalog for the image.

3. From the File menu, select New Answer File.

4. In the Windows Image pane, expand Windows Vista ENTERPRISE, expand Components, expand x86_Microsoft_Windows_PnpCustomizationsNonWinPE_6.0.6000.16386_ neutral, and expand DriverPaths.

5. Right-click PathAndCredentials and select "Add Settings to Pass 2 offlineServicing."

6. In the PathAndCredentials Properties pane, in the Key field, type **Drivers**, and in the Path field, type **C:\Drivers**.

7. From the Tools menu, select Validate Answer File.

8. From the File menu, select Save Answer File.

9. In the "File name" text box, type **R:\ImageDrivers.xml** and click Save.

Step 3: Associate the Answer File with the Image   Next, for Windows Vista setup to pick up and use your previously created answer file, you need to associate it with your Windows Vista Enterprise Image in the WDS Console:

1. Using the WDS Console, expand Install Images, and select the VistaGroup image group.

2. Right-click your Windows Vista Enterprise image and select Properties.

3. On the General tab, select the "Allow image to install in unattended mode" check box. Click Select File, browse to R:\ImageDrivers.xml, and click OK.

Once you add the answer file, it will be renamed ImageUnattend.xml and copied to the Unattend folder inside the image folder, for example, R:\RemoteInstall\Images\VistaGroup\Install\ Unattend.

When starting the deployment, the Drivers folder will be copied from the OEM\$1 folder on the server to C: on the client after the image is applied to disk but before the first reboot.

Option 2: Inject the Drivers into the Actual Image

Injecting drivers into the actual image involves exporting the WDS resource image to a standard WIM image, mounting it using ImageX, creating an answer file with WSIM, using PKGMGR to inject the driver, and then reimporting the WIM to WDS.

Follow these steps to inject the VMware NIC driver into the Windows Vista Enterprise install image. In this example, I have already created a C:\6000 folder to store the WIM image and a `C:\6000\Mount` subfolder that will be used to mount the WIM image. I have also copied the VMware NIC drivers to `C:\6000\vmxnet`.

Step 1: Export the WIM Image   Before you can mount the image, you need to export to a standard WIM image:

1. Using the WDS Console, expand `Install Images`, and select the `VistaGroup` image group.

2. Right-click the Windows Vista ENTERPRISE image and select Export. In the "File name" textbox, type **C:\6000\CustomVistaEnterprise.wim** and click Save.

Step 2: Create an Answer File for Package Manager   When injecting drivers into an install image, we need to create an answer file with the path to the driver(s). You will then use this answer file, together with Package Manager, to do the actual driver injection.

1. Using Windows System Image Manager, in the Windows Image pane, right-click the "Select a Windows Image or catalog file" node and click Select Windows Image.

2. In the "File name" text box, type **C:\6000\CustomVistaEnterprise.wim** and click Open. In the Windows System Image Manager dialog box, click Yes to create a catalog for the image.

3. From the File menu, select New Answer File.

4. In the Windows Image pane, expand `Windows Vista ENTERPRISE`, expand `Components`, expand `x86_Microsoft_Windows_PnpCustomizationsNonWinPE_6.0.6000.16386_ neutral`, and expand `DriverPaths`.

5. Right-click `PathAndCredentials` and select "Add Settings to Pass 2 offlineServicing."

6. In the PathAndCredentials Properties pane, in the Key field, type **vmxnet**, and in the Path field, type **C:\6000\vmxnet**, as shown in Figure 1.22.

7. From the File menu, select Save Answer File. In the "File name" textbox, type **C:\6000\Drivers.xml** and click Save.

Step 3: Using Pkgmgr to Inject the Driver(s)   Now you are ready for the heavy lifting; that is, mounting the image. You'll use Package Manager to inject the driver, and then unmount and save the changes.

1. Start a Windows PE tools command prompt. Type the following command to mount the image:

    ```
    ImageX /mountrw C:\6000\CustomVistaEnterprise.wim 1 C:\6000\Mount
    ```

2. Go the right location in the file system for driver injection (where the servicing stack is) by typing the following command:

    ```
    cd /d "C:\Program Files\Windows AIK\Tools\Servicing"
    ```

3. Inject the drivers using Package Manager by typing:

    ```
    Start /w pkgmgr /o:C:\6000\Mount\Windows /n:C:\6000\Drivers.xml /l:C:\
    6000\DriverInjection
    ```

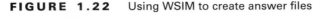

FIGURE 1.22   Using WSIM to create answer files

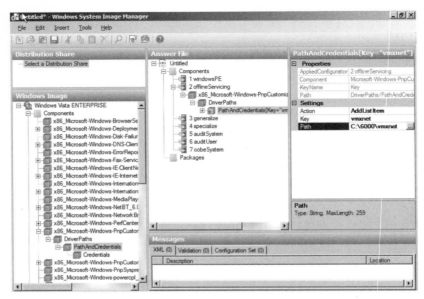

4. Verify the injection by opening the C:\6000\DriverInjection.txt log file in Notepad. A return code of 0x0 is considered a good thing.

5. Commit the changes by typing

    ImageX /Unmount /Commit C:\6000\Mount

Step 4: Add the Updated Image to WDS   Now, you need only to add the updated image back to WDS. You can choose between adding a new image or replacing the existing image. Remember, if you add the image as a new image to the same image group it will only use slightly more disk space due to the single instancing capabilities in WDS. This example, you will add a new image:

1. Using WDS Console, expand Install Images, right-click the VistaGroup image group and select Add Install Image. This will start the Windows Deployment Services—Add Image Wizard.

2. On the Image File page, in the "File name" text box, type **C:\6000\ CustomVistaEnterprise.wim** and click Next.

3. On the List of Available Images page, clear the "Use default name and description for each of the selected image" check box, and click Next.

4. On the Image Metadata page, in the Image Name text box, type **Custom Windows Vista Enterprise**, and click Next.

5. On the Summary page, click Next.

6. On the Task Progress page, click Finish.

The WAIK for Windows Vista and Windows Server 2008 has the rest of the story about customizing and servicing images. Be sure to read the documentation, specifically the section on DriverPaths and unattend settings to see how to best make use of this technique.

Creating an Answer File Using WSIM

As you know by now, we can configure the Vista setup by using an unattend.xml answer file. In fact, we can also configure the WDS client by using a second answer file. This means that when automating WDS deployments, we are using a two-stage approach with two different answer files.

First, the WDS client unattend file, WDSClientUnattend.xml, allows you to automate processes like image selection, logon credentials, and disk partitioning.

Second, the image unattend file, either ImageUnattend.xml or sysprep.inf, depending on the operating system, allows you to automate the remaining steps of the Windows setup.

The WDS console can assign unattend files only for Windows Vista and Windows Server 2008 images. For down-level images, you must use your existing sysprep.inf files and manually create an OEM directory structure. See the online documentation for more information: http://tinyurl.com/2kjlps.

The next sections will show you how to create those answer files and to associate them with the WDS server and a Windows Vista image. The end result will be a fully automated deployment solution.

Creating an Answer File for WDS Client

Here are the steps to create an answer file for the WDS Client. You will configure it to wipe the disk and create a 40GB partition, select UI language, log on automatically, and select an image automatically.

1. Using WSIM, in the Windows Image pane, right-click the "Select a Windows Image or catalog file" node and click Select Windows Image.
2. In the "File name" text box, type **C:\6000\CustomVistaEnterprise.wim** and click Open. In the Windows System Image Manager dialog box, click Yes to create a catalog for the image.
3. From the File menu, select New Answer File.
4. In the Windows Image pane, expand Windows Vista ENTERPRISE, expand Components, expand x86_Microsoft-Windows-Setup_6.0.6000.16386_neutral, and expand DiskConfiguration.
5. Right-click Disk and select "Add Setting to Pass 1 windowsPE."
6. In the Answer File pane, select Disk, then in the Disk Properties pane, set the following values:

    DiskID: 0

    WillWipeDisk: true

7. In the Answer File pane, expand `Disk(DiskID="0")`, and then right-click `CreatePartitions` and select Insert New CreatePartition.

8. In the CreatePartition Properties pane, set the following values:

    Order: 1

    Size: 40000

    Type: Primary

9. In the Answer File pane, right-click `ModifyPartitions` and select Insert New Modify-Partitions.

10. In the ModifyPartition Properties pane set the following values:

    Active: true

    Extend: false

    Format: NTFS

    Label: OSDisk

    Letter: C

    Order: 1

    PartitionID: 1

11. In the Windows Image pane, expand `WindowsDeploymentServices`, and expand `ImageSelection`.

12. Right-click `InstallImage` and select "Add Setting to Pass 1 windowsPE."

13. In the InstallImage Properties pane, set the following values:

    Filename: Install.wim

    ImageGroup: VistaGroup

    ImageName: Windows Vista ENTERPRISE

14. In the Windows Image pane, right-click `InstallTo` and select "Add Setting to Pass 1 windowsPE."

15. In the InstallTo Properties pane, set the following values:

    DiskID: 0

    PartitionID: 1

16. In the Windows Image pane, expand `Login`, right-click `Credentials`, and select "Add Setting to Pass 1 windowsPE."

17. In the Credentials Properties pane, set the following values:

    Domain: corp.com

    Password: <blank>

    Username: BuildAccount

For security reasons, you may not want to add all the credentials information, but to speed up the process for lab purposes, you can, of course, do it. If you add all the credentials, the process will be fully automated, and once a user presses F12, the old machine is gone.

18. In the Windows Image pane, right-click x86_Microsoft-Windows-International-Core-WinPE, and select "Add Setting to Pass 1 windowsPE."

19. In the Microsoft-Windows-International-Core-WinPE Properties pane, set the UILanguage value to en-US.

20. In the Answer File pane, expand x86_Microsoft-Windows-International-Core-WinPE and select SetupUILanguage.

21. In the SetupUILanguage Properties pane, set the UILanguage value to en-US.

22. From the Tools menu, select Validate Answer File.

23. From the File menu, select Save Answer File.

24. In the "File name" text box, type **R:\WDSClientUnattend.xml**, and click Save.

Answer File for the Vista Setup

Now the automation for the WDS Client is done. It is time to create the answer file for automating the Windows Vista Setup:

1. Using WSIM, in the Windows Image pane, right-click the "Select a Windows Image or catalog file" node and click Select Windows Image.

2. In the "File name" text box, type **C:\6000\CustomVistaEnterprise.wim** and click Open. In the Windows System Image Manager dialog box, click Yes to create a catalog for the image.

3. From the File menu, select New Answer File.

4. In the Windows Image pane, expand Components, expand x86_Microsoft-Windows-Setup_6.0.6000.16386_neutral, expand ImageInstall, and expand OSImage.

5. Right-click InstallTo and select "Add Setting to Pass 1 windowsPE."

6. In the InstallTo Properties pane, set the following values:

DiskID: 0

PartitionID: 1

7. In the Windows Image pane, right-click x86_Microsoft-Windows-International-Core-WinPE, and select "Add Setting to Pass 1 windowsPE."

8. In the Microsoft-Windows-International-Core-WinPE Properties pane, set the following values:

InputLocale: 0409:00000409

SystemLocale: en-US

UILanguage: en-US

UserLocale: en-US

9. In the Answer File pane, expand `x86_Microsoft-Windows-International-Core-WinPE` and select SetupUILanguage.

10. In the SetupUILanguage Properties pane, set the following values:

UILanguage: en-US

WillShowUI: OnError

11. In the Windows Image pane, expand `x86_Microsoft-Windows-Setup_6.0.6000.16386_neutral`, right-click `UserData` and select "Add Setting to Pass 1 windowsPE."

12. In the UserData Properties pane, set the following values:

AcceptEula: true

FullName: IT

Organization: Corp

13. In the Windows Image pane, right-click `x86_Microsoft-Windows-International-Core_6.0.6000.16386_neutral` and select "Add Setting to Pass 4 specialize."

14. In the Microsoft-Windows-International-Core Properties pane, set the following values:

InputLocale: 0409:00000409

SystemLocale: en-US

UILanguage: en-US

UserLocale: en-US

15. In the Windows Image pane, right-click `x86_Microsoft-Windows-International-Core_6.0.6000.16386_neutral` and select "Add Setting to Pass 7 oobeSystem."

16. In the Microsoft-Windows-International-Core Properties pane, set the following values:

InputLocale: 0409:00000409

SystemLocale: en-US

UILanguage: en-US

UserLocale: en-US

17. From the Tools menu, select Validate Answer File.

18. From the File menu, select Save Answer File.

19. In the "File name" text box, type **`R:\ImageUnattend.xml`** and click Save.

Associating Answer Files with a WDS

Associating answer files with WDS is easy. The hard part is creating the answer files first, as you just did.

Again, in WDS you have two types of answer files, one type for the WDS client that is associated on the Server, and one type for the images that is associated on the image. Let's start with the WDS Client answer file:

1. Copy the `R:\WDSClientUnattend.xml` to `R:\RemoteInstall\WdsClientUnattend`.

2. Using the WDS Console, right-click the WDS Server and select Properties.

3. On the Client tab, browse and select `WDSClientUnattend.xml` and click OK.

The process can be seen in Figure 1.23.

FIGURE 1.23   Associate an answer file for the WDS client directly with the server.

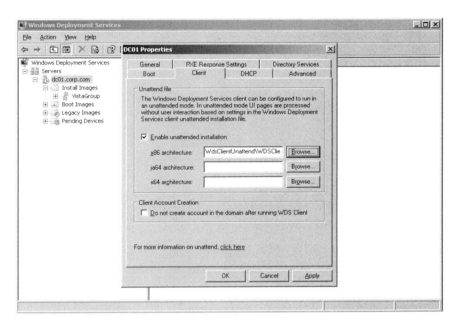

Next, associate the image answer file (I named mine `ImageUnattend.xml`).

1. Using the WDS Console, expand `Install Images`, and select the `VistaGroup` image group.

2. Right-click your Windows Vista Enterprise image and select Properties.

3. On the Client tab, browse to `R:\ImageUnattend.xml` and click OK.

The process can be seen in Figure 1.24.

Installing Your First Fully Automated Client

Once you're sitting down at your target machine, you're ready to install your first fully automated client.

Running WDS on your workstations completely formats the first hard drive on your system.

To use WDS to install a client, follow these steps:

1. Turn on the target system.

2. When prompted, immediately press F12.

FIGURE 1.24 Associate an answer file for the Windows Vista Setup directly with the image.

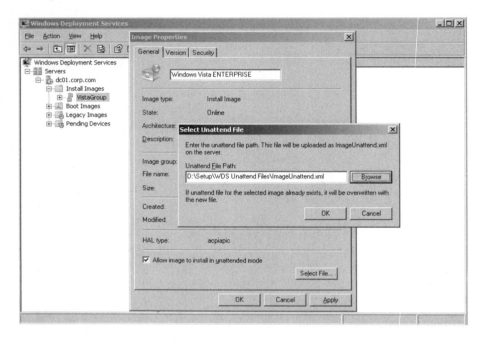

If you have done everything right, the setup process should prompt you for a password and then finish the process, fully unattended. Again, the password prompt can be automated too, but it may be a security risk since any user with access to the computer would then be able start the deployment.

Use at Your Own Risk: Speeding Up the Download Time of a *boot.wim* Image

For me, the only big drawback in WDS is the slow boot time of the boot.wim file. That's because it's about 126MB, which is, well, pretty big, even on most networks. Actually, the problem really isn't that the file itself is that big, it's the underlying protocol used to transfer the boot.wim from the server to your Windows Vista machine-to-be: TFTP (Trivial FTP) protocol, which really stinks. The major limitation is the TFTP block size used when downloading an image, which is around 1000 bytes; small enough to still fit in an Ethernet frame without causing packet fragmentation.

I need to stress this here: What I'm about to show you works only if your network cards and the switches and routers support it. If they do, you can bump up the frame size WDS uses when sending the boot.wim file via TFTP.

First, make sure you're network doesn't have too much network latency; TFTP transfers just hate that.

On gigabit connections you can increase the speed up to four times by increasing the frame size (measured on 50 and 75 clients), for example:

- Fifty boot images on gigabit connections typically take about 5 minutes to start with the default TFTP block size, about 3 minutes with a 4KB block size, and about 1.5 minutes with a 16KB block size.

- Seventy-five boot images on gigabit connection typically take about 8 minutes with the default TFTP block size, about 6 minutes with 4KB block size, and about 2 minutes with 16KB block size.

Now, let's say you have two kinds of network cards, three kinds of network switches, and four kinds of routers. All of the equipment (from the server's network card through the switch through the router to the target machine's network card) has to be able to support the increased block size trick I'm about to show you, which is how tell the WDS server to increase the frame size from 1000 to another number of bytes per block.

 Real World Scenario

WDS Best Practices

This sidebar could also be named "Common Issues" because one way of looking at best practices really could be about avoiding common issues.

Since WDS relies heavily on network configuration, most of the common issues relate to just that, but it doesn't stop there. Here are some tips to get the best environment for WDS possible.

- IPv6 is not supported by WDS, so if you are not using it for other services, unbind it from the network card.

- Always use the latest boot image version, which means use the one from Windows Server 2008 (required for multicast support).

- Don't use more than 13 boot images; the boot menu cannot list more than 13 boot images.

- When using Microsoft DHCP and WDS on the same server, configure WDS not to listen on port 67 and allow it to configure the 60 PXE option.

- When using a non-Microsoft DHCP and WDS on the same server, configure WDS not to listen on port 67 and use the non-Microsoft DHCP Server Configuration tool to configure the 60 PXE option.

- When using a DHCP server located in a different subnet, you will need to do one of the following:

  - Configure your IP helper tables (recommended).

  - Add DHCP options 66 and 67.

- If you have multiple domains, make sure they are in the right search order in your network card DNS settings.

The program you need to run, bcdedit.exe, is available only on a Windows Vista or Windows Server 2008 machine. So, to do this trick, you'll need to start on a Windows Vista machine and then map a drive to the REMINST\Boot\x86 on the server. You will then use the following command to edit the default Boot Configuration Data store, named default.bcd.

```
Bcdedit -store default.bcd -set
{68d9e51c-a129-4ee1-9725-2ab00a957daf} ramdisktftpblocksize
 <yourblock size here>
```

Just go up in even multiples: 4096, 8192, 16384. I wouldn't set it any higher than 16384. I've tried a lot of values. The two values that worked best were 4096 and 8192.

Finally, run this command when you're back on the server:

```
Sc control wdsserver 129
```

The next time you boot a client, it will use the new TFTP block size to download the Windows PE image.

Again, the maximum value isn't a function of your network bandwidth; it's a function of the maximum buffer size your PXE ROM allocates for UDP packets.

Troubleshooting WDS

When you need to troubleshoot the WDS, you will find that most of the time the log files and a good network sniffer are your very best friends.

PXE Client

One of the most common issues is that PXE client cannot locate the WDS server or can't find a network boot file to load, as shown in Figure 1.25.

FIGURE 1.25   PXE-boot failure due to wrongly configured DHCP or IP helpers

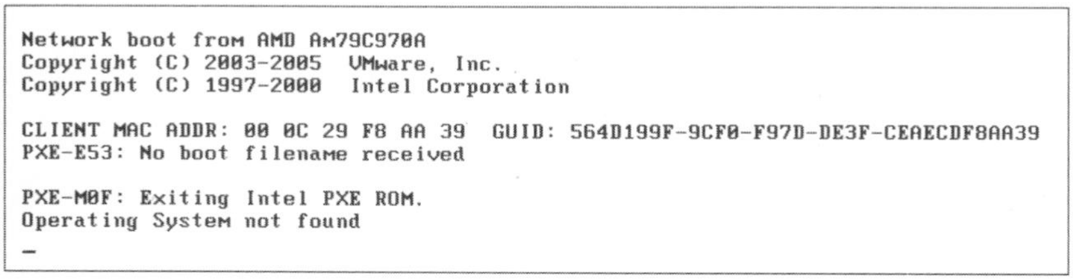

```
Network boot from AMD Am79C970A
Copyright (C) 2003-2005  VMware, Inc.
Copyright (C) 1997-2000  Intel Corporation

CLIENT MAC ADDR: 00 0C 29 F8 AA 39  GUID: 564D199F-9CF0-F97D-DE3F-CEAECDF8AA39
PXE-E53: No boot filename received

PXE-M0F: Exiting Intel PXE ROM.
Operating System not found
_
```

To troubleshoot this, first go back and verify your DHCP configuration according to the previous section. If that doesn't help, install a network sniffer and follow the traffic between the PXE client and DHCP/WDS server.

Setup

If you get any errors during setup, you can find additional information for the WDS setup for Windows Server 2008 in C:\Windows\logs\cbs\cbs.log. This CBS (component-based services) log, shown in Figure 1.26, is enabled by default and is used not only for WDS, but for all components (packages) in Windows Server 2008.

FIGURE 1.26   CBS log file entries when the WDS multicast components are installed

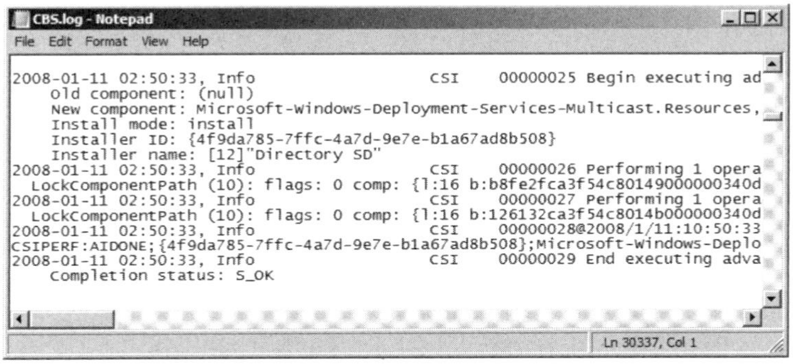

The component-based services will also raise events to the event log, but it is in the log file you will get all details. For example, an error like "cannot connect" in the UI might reveal itself as error code 5 in the log file, which is really an access denied error. Or, you may find that general "Setup failed" messages really mean something like a corrupt setup file is found, or that you have insufficient disk space to complete the operation.

Tracing and Logging

You can enable logging and tracing for all WDS components. This can be very useful when troubleshooting PXE client timeout issues due to high latency networks, or if the WDS server has problems contacting Active Directory.

Enabling Logging for the WDS Client   The WDS client supports four logging levels:

- NONE: No logging (default)
- ERRORS: Errors only
- WARNINGS: Warnings and errors
- INFO: Errors, warnings, and informational events

To configure WDS client logging, set the following Registry keys:

```
HKLM\System\CurrentControlSet\Services\WDSServer\Providers\WdsImgSrv\
ClientLogging\Enabled
```

- Type: REG_DWORD
- Value: not set or 0 means not enabled (default), and 1 means enabled

```
HKLM\System\CurrentControlSet\Services\WDSServer\Providers\WdsImgSrv\
ClientLogging\LogLevel
```

- Type: REG_DWORD
- Value: not set or 0 means OFF, 1 means ERRORS, 2 means WARNINGS, 3 means INFO

Enable Tracing for WDS Server Component   Set the following registry key to 1:

```
HKLM\Software\Microsoft\Tracing\WDSServer\EnableFileTracing
```

Log file: `C:\Windows\tracing\wdsserver.log`

Enable Tracing for Management Components   Set the following Registry key to 1:

```
HKLM\Software\Microsoft\Tracing\WDSMGMT\EnableFileTracing
```

Log files: `C:\Windows\tracing\wdsmgmt.log` and `C:\windows\tracing\wdsmmc.log`.

Enable Tracing for WinPE Client (WDS Capture) Components   After booting the image, when the capture wizard starts, press Shift+F10 to get a command prompt and set the following Registry key to 1:

```
HKLM\Software\Microsoft\Tracing\WDSCapture\EnableFileTracing
```

Log file: `X:\Windows\Tracing\WDSCapture.log`.

 Real World Scenario

Mere-Mortals Can Add Only Ten Workstations

In Windows NT, only administrators can add computer accounts to the domain. Under Active Directory, the Authenticated Users group can add computer accounts to the domain via the "Add Workstation to Domain" user right. But there's a catch. Each authenticated user can add only ten new computer accounts. On the eleventh try, the user is presented with the error message: "The machine account for this computer either does not exist or is unavailable." This is a little-known problem that has three little-known solutions:

Pre-creating Computer Accounts

Administrators can pre-create the computer accounts, as many accounts as they like. They are exempt from the "10 strikes and you're out" rule.

Granting Create Computer Objects and Delete Computer Objects Rights

You can grant the Create Computer Objects (and if desired) the Delete Computer Objects rights to the Computers folder in Active Directory. These rights are different from the "Add Workstation to Domain user" right that all Authenticated Users are given. To make this change, follow these steps:

1. Choose Start ➤ Programs ➤ Administrative Tools ➤ Active Directory Users and Computers.

2. Choose View ➤ Advanced to enable the Advanced view.

3. Right-click the Computers folder, and choose Properties from the shortcut menu to open the Properties dialog box.

4. Click the Security tab, and then click the Advanced button to open the "Advanced Settings for Computers" properties.

5. On the Permissions tab, click Authenticated Users, and then click the Edit button to open the Permissions Entry for Authenticated Users box.

6. Before proceeding, make sure the "This Object and All Child Objects" option is displayed in the Apply Onto box.

7. In the Permissions list, click the Allow check box for Create Computer Objects and, optionally, Delete Computer Objects, as seen here:

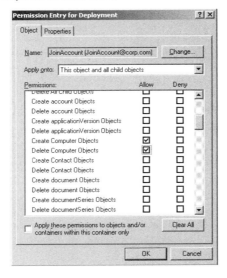

Use ADSI edit to manipulate the ms-DS-MachineAccountQuota to increase (or decrease) the value to the desired number of times a user can create a computer account. However, for security reasons, I prefer delegating the correct permissions rather than allowing any user to join computers to the domain.

Microsoft Deployment Toolkit 2008 (MDT), Formerly Known as BDD

Microsoft has a gift they want to give you: free Windows deployment tools and guidance. The best part: the guidance isn't just for Windows clients, but Windows servers, as well. The gift's name is Microsoft Deployment Toolkit 2008, or MDT for short, and it's the successor to BDD 2007, the Business Desktop Deployment Solution Accelerator.

If you are currently using BDD 2007, I strongly recommend that you look into Microsoft Deployment Toolkit 2008. You will find many goodies in this update, and the transition isn't terribly complicated. Microsoft Deployment Toolkit 2008 offers upgrade paths from existing BDD 2007 setups so you can take easily advantage of the new features.

The Microsoft Deployment Toolkit 2008 solution is called, in Microsoft-speak, a *solution accelerator*, but it's really tools and guidance wrapped up in a nice little gift pack. Microsoft Deployment Toolkit 2008 spans most aspects of a deployment project: planning, developing, piloting, executing, and more. In this section we will focus on the image engineering components.

By the time you're done with this section, you'll be able to do the following:

- Deploy Windows operating systems in a very rich and dynamic way
- Add drivers and applications to the deployment process
- Automate the Windows Desktop rollout experience

I know that you'll want to do even more, and that's great. To discover more about what Microsoft Deployment Toolkit 2008 can do, be sure to go to www.microsoft.com/deployment so you can find out about things like infrastructure remediation, application management, security, operation readiness, office deployments, deployment process, and testing processes.

Understanding Microsoft Deployment Toolkit 2008

Microsoft Deployment Toolkit 2008 has two core ways to be utilized. One is called *Lite Touch* and does not require much except a decent Windows server. In fact, it can even be run on a Windows workstation, but please don't go that route; you really want the power and performance of a real server.

The other way to use Microsoft Deployment Toolkit 2008 is *Zero Touch*, but it requires a lot more management infrastructure, like SMS 2003 or SCCM 2007. In this chapter we'll focus on the Lite Touch components so you can start working with it immediately.

You won't find it in Microsoft documentation, but we'll call Microsoft Deployment Toolkit 2008 Light Touch *MDLT* for short.

MDLT shouldn't to be confused with the McDonald's McDLT, a not so wonderful hamburger from the 1980s. If you want to walk down nostalgia lane, go to http://tinyurl.com/29yvh8 for a McDLT commercial.

The MDLT components have the following core features:

Wide Operating System Support   MDLT supports deploying Windows XP, Windows Vista, Windows Server 2003, and Windows Server 2008.

Deployment Workbench   This is an MMC 3.0 front-end for configuring most aspects of the deployment environment, as shown in Figure 1.27 (I'll show you how to get here in the next section).

FIGURE 1.27   The Deployment Workbench, viewing the driver repository

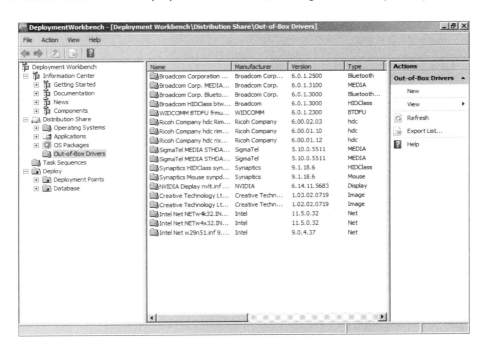

Task Sequencer   This uses technology from SCCM but does not require SCCM (or its high price). This is the heart and soul of Lite Touch. The task sequencer controls all steps of the deployment, as shown in Figure 1.28.

Driver Management   This is the central repository for drivers and tools for automatic driver injection during deployment. When deploying a client using Microsoft Deployment Toolkit 2008 the client will do a plug-and-play ID scan of the hardware and automatically download and install the needed driver from the driver store.

Patching   Microsoft Deployment Toolkit 2008 can add patches, language packages, and so on, both offline and online. There are also built-in functions for forcing Windows Update as part of the deployment process.

FIGURE 1.28 A sample task sequencer

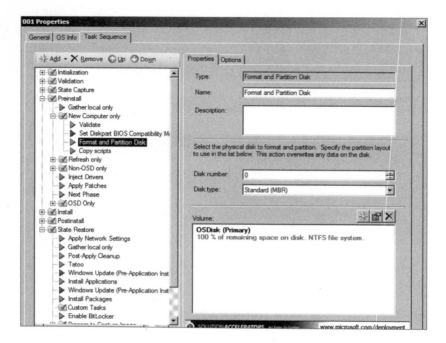

Advanced Disk and Network Configurations You can configure multiple disks, partitions, and multiple NICs (although these are mostly used for server deployments).

Server-side Rules Microsoft Deployment Toolkit 2008 uses central server-side rules to configure Windows deployment settings like regional settings, screen resolution, and so on.

User State Migration Support Microsoft Deployment Toolkit 2008 can back up and restore user state and data as part of the deployment process.

Backup Capability Microsoft Deployment Toolkit 2008 can take an optional full backup (image) of the old computer when deploying a new image.

Deployment Database Microsoft Deployment Toolkit 2008 also supports storing the configuration in a database. For example, you can create a role that will install five applications and then associate that role to a computer account (based on MAC address, serial number, asset tag, or UUID).If you start deploying that machine, it will query the database and install the five applications, as shown in Figure 1.29.

Server Roles You can select which server roles should be installed on an Windows Server 2008 operating system, as shown in Figure 1.30.

Configuration of some of the server roles is supported, as well, as shown in Figure 1.31.

FIGURE 1.29 The Applications pane of a role that can be assigned to a computer

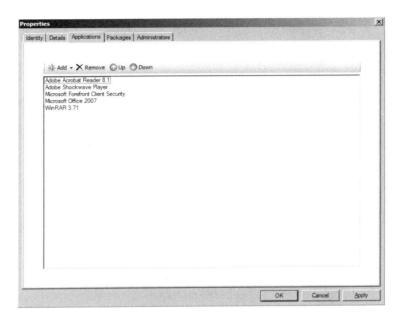

FIGURE 1.30 Install roles and features.

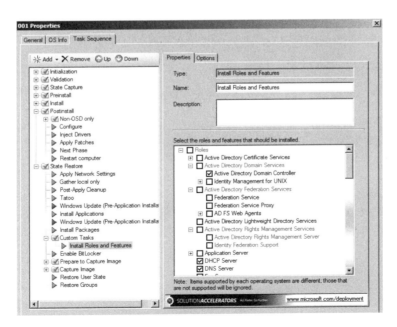

FIGURE 1.31   Configure Active Directory Domain Services.

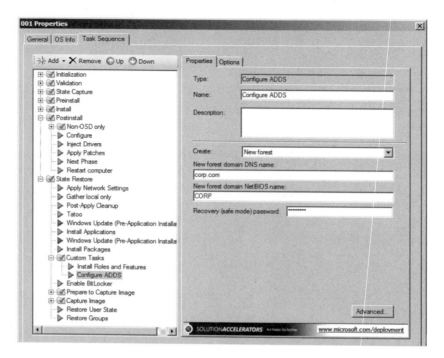

WDS vs. Microsoft Deployment Toolkit 2008 (Better Together?)

Before continuing, we need to clarify what roles WDS and Microsoft Deployment Toolkit 2008 play in your Windows deployment strategy. Will you use them together? Separately? What are the advantages of one versus the other?

Organizations tend to either just use WDS, or use WDS and Microsoft Deployment Toolkit 2008 together. The major difference between the two is that Microsoft Deployment Toolkit 2008 leverages a task sequencer. This task sequencer controls the deployment flow using static and dynamic server side rules and has many built in routines for things like driver injection, user state migration, monitoring, and so on.

If you want to configure more things than you can with a standard answer file, you should add the free MDLT components to your WDS solution. For example, with the built-in database support, you can assign role-based settings and applications to your deployments.

Let's review how WDS works, and I'll explain how the Microsoft Deployment Toolkit 2008 adds value.

Scenario 1: Image Engineering Using WDS   From an image-engineering point of view, WDS works like this:

1. A boot image (Windows PE) is downloaded over the network.

2. A client (the WDS client) connects to a server share containing the operating system(s).

3. Deployment settings (like regional settings and so on) are either prompted for or configured using answer files.

4. A Windows image is selected and applied to disk.

That's about it—a basic, straightforward deployment solution.

Scenario 2: Image Engineering Using WDS and Microsoft Deployment Toolkit 2008   From an image-engineering point of view, WDS and Microsoft Deployment Toolkit 2008 work like this:

1. A custom boot image (Windows PE, created by the Deployment Workbench) is downloaded over the network.

2. A client (an HTA-driven wizard) connects to a server share containing operating systems, updates, drivers, and applications and reads the deployment configuration.

3. Deployment settings (like regional settings, applications to install, and so on) are either prompted for or configured from the server-side rules.

4. The Task Sequencer starts and, as one of many steps, a Windows image is applied to disk.

As you can see, the scenarios are quite alike from a high-level overview. The major overt difference when leveraging Microsoft Deployment Toolkit 2008 is that you can take advantage of the Task Sequencer controlling the deployment.

However, underneath the surface there's quite a difference. Microsoft Deployment Toolkit 2008 starts where WDS functionality ends and will ease a lot of deployment pains for you. It will give you all the Microsoft Deployment Toolkit 2008 features like automatic driver injection and assigning applications to the deployment process. It will give you a whole rule-based driven central framework for doing all sorts of configurations to the operating system during deployment. And, since WDS can network boot the Microsoft Deployment Toolkit 2008 boot image, you are just an F12 keypress away from starting the deployment.

Inside Microsoft Deployment Toolkit 2008

Let's define a few terms first. That way, we'll share a common vocabulary as we work through the issues with imaging.

Deployment Workbench   This is the premium management tool, which also acts as a front-end for many of the WAIK tools and infrastructure support. Remember, the WAIK adds support to APIs like WIMGAPI, which allows you to manage WIM images; tools like PEIMG for driver injection; and OSCDIMG for creating ISO (CD/DVD) images. WAIK also contains Windows PE 2.0, our deployment platform. It is used as boot image for both WDS and Microsoft Deployment Toolkit 2008.

Task Sequencer   This controls all aspects of the setup, allowing you to select unique configurations and operating systems during deployment. This is the framework that drives the deployment process.

Distribution Share   This is a folder containing all setup files, updates, drivers, applications, deployment scripts, and so on. It is maintained by the Deployment Workbench.

Deployment Point   Here is where the deployment settings, the server side rules, are configured. This is also where you create the boot images used to start the deployment process. The boot image will connect to the deployment point and find out what deployment settings to use.

Boot Images   As WDS does, Microsoft Deployment Toolkit 2008 uses boot images to start the deployment process. Guess what service I recommend you use to boot these images over the network? Yep, the Windows Deployment Service!

Setting Up Microsoft Deployment Toolkit 2008

Implementing Microsoft Deployment Toolkit 2008 may seem hard, complicated, and unwieldy at first. But once you get into it, you'll see that it's not too bad. In this section, I'll take you from start to finish implementing MDLT components.

If you follow the steps, you will build a great deployment solution in just a few hours.

Microsoft Deployment Toolkit 2008 Prerequisites

Before installing Microsoft Deployment Toolkit 2008 there are some system requirements that need to be met:

- Microsoft Core Extensible Markup Language (MSXML) Services 6.0, found at `http://tinyurl.com/2h396u`.

- Microsoft .NET Framework 2.0. The Windows AIK 1.0 media includes the .NET Framework 2.0 installation file. Download WAIK (and .NET Framework 2.0) from `http://tinyurl.com/37b42g`.

- Microsoft .NET Framework 2.0 requires Microsoft Windows Installer 3.1, but you likely already have this. (If you are running SP2 on your Windows Server 2003 machine then you have it.) If not, check out `http://tinyurl.com/6camd`.

- Microsoft Management Console (MMC) 3.0 (part of Windows Server 2003 SP2) found at `http://tinyurl.com/2ytam3`.

- For database support (optional, but recommended) you need Microsoft SQL Server Express Edition SP2. Download it at `http://tinyurl.com/2ax2am`.

- Managing the database is a lot easier with Microsoft SQL Server Management Studio Express, which you can find at `http://tinyurl.com/mkvgw`.

 The first four components are dead easy to install and the default configuration works fine. The database components are another story, and that's why you'll find a step-by-step guide for configuring those components in the "Beyond the Microsoft Deployment Toolkit 2008 Basics" section later in this chapter.

Microsoft Deployment Toolkit 2008 Core Configuration

Setting up Microsoft Deployment Toolkit 2008 is a quite straightforward process. It involves the following steps, which are each covered in the next sections:

1. Installing the prerequisites software (listed in the previous section) and of course Microsoft Deployment Toolkit 2008 itself.

2. Creating a distribution share and importing setup files like operating system images, applications, updates, and drivers.

3. Creating one or more task sequences.

4. Creating a deployment point.

5. Adding database support (optional; this is covered in the section "Beyond the Microsoft Deployment Toolkit 2008 Basics").

    Let's explore each of these tasks right now.

Downloading and Installing Microsoft Deployment Toolkit 2008 Plus Some Updates

Installing Microsoft Deployment Toolkit 2008 is quite easy; The Microsoft Deployment Toolkit 2008 Setup files can be found at: `http://tinyurl.com/2xlp2y`.

Once you download these files, you are ready to install Microsoft Deployment Toolkit 2008. Run `MicrosoftDeploymentToolkit_x86.msi` and run through the Setup Wizard with the default settings.

After installing Microsoft Deployment Toolkit 2008 you will find the documentation in `C:\Program Files\Microsoft Deployment Toolkit\Documentation`. There is also a compiled help file of all the documents in the `C:\Program Files\Microsoft Deployment Toolkit\bin` folder. When working with the image engineering components, `Getting_Started_Guide.doc`, `Release Notes.chm`, and `Image_Engineering_Feature_Team_Guide.doc` are excellent reading materials to start with.

Creating the Server Structure

While you can use the administrator account for all credentials, this isn't recommended. Microsoft Deployment Toolkit 2008 is really designed for using role-based security. So let's create a few service accounts and an organizational unit and then assign the permissions as needed.

Creating an OU to Store Workstations   Using Active Directory Users and Computers, create an OU (for storing your computer accounts). I recommend naming it Workstations, and for our example, it can be right off the domain.

Creating Two User Accounts for Building and Joining Computers   Using Active Directory Users and Computers, create the following user accounts:

- BuildAccount, to be used to access the deployment server and start the deployment process when booting from our boot image.

- JoinAccount, to be used by Windows Setup to join the machine to the domain.

Using Active Directory Users and Computers, allow JoinAccount permissions to manage computer accounts in the Workstations OU by using the following lists of permissions. (The first set of permissions is for adding and removing computer accounts, and the second set is to update existing computer accounts). The end result should look something like Figure 1.32.

FIGURE 1.32   Active Directory permissions for JoinAccount

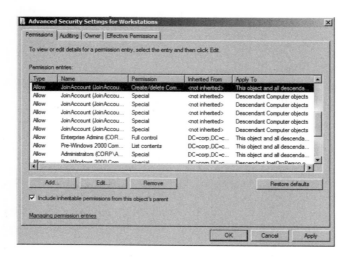

1. Start Active Directory Users and Computers. From the View menu, select Advanced Features. This will enable the Security tab on Active Directory objects.

2. Right-click the Workstations OU and select Properties.

3. On the Workstation Properties screen, in the Security tab, click the Advanced button.

    If you added the JoinAccount user directly on the first screen, the user would be given high permissions. For security reasons, assign only the minimum permissions needed.

4. On the Advanced Security Settings screen for Workstations, click Add.

5. In the "Select User, Computer, or Group" field, type **JoinAccount** and click OK.

6. On the Permission Entry for Workstations in the Permissions list, select Allow for the following permissions and then click OK:

    Create Computer Objects

    Delete Computer Objects

7. On the Advanced Security Settings for Workstations windows, click Add.

8. In the "Select User, Computer, or Group" screen, type **JoinAccount** and click OK.

9. On the Permission Entry for Workstations, in the "Apply to" drop-down list, select "Descendant Computer objects" (or "Computer objects" if doing this on a Windows Server 2003 server).

10. In the Permissions list, select Allow for the following permissions and then click OK.

   Read All Properties

   Write All Properties

   Read Permissions

   Modify Permissions

   Change Password

   Reset Password

   Validated write to DNS host name

   Validated write to service principal name

11. On the Advanced Security Settings for Workstations window, click OK.

12. On the Workstation Properties screen, click OK.

Next, create a folder, like D:\LOGS. Share it as Logs$ and configure the necessary permissions following these steps.

1. Using Windows Explorer, right-click the D:\Logs folder and select Properties.

2. In the Logs Properties window, on the Sharing tab, click Advanced Sharing. Select the "Share folder" check box, and in the "Share name" text box, type **Logs$**.

3. Still in the Advanced Sharing window, click Permissions. In the "Permissions for everyone" list, select Allow for Change permissions and click OK twice.

4. In the Logs Properties window, on the Security tab, click Edit.

5. In the "Permissions for Logs" window, click Add, type **BuildAccount,** and click OK.

6. In the "Permissions for Logs" window, select BuildAccount, and in the Permissions for BuildAccount, select Allow for Modify Permissions. Click OK and then click Close.

 In Windows Server 2008 the procedure has changed a bit for creating shares, but I'm sure you get the idea.

Creating the Distribution Share

The Distribution share will hold all your setup files, drivers, applications, scripts and so on, so let's go ahead and create it.

1. Using the Deployment Workbench, right-click the Distribution Share node and select "Create distribution share directory." The Create Distribution Share Wizard will start, as shown in Figure 1.33.

2. On the Specify Directory screen, in the "Path for new distribution share directory" field, type **D:\Distribution** and click Finish.

FIGURE 1.33   Creating Distribution Share Wizard

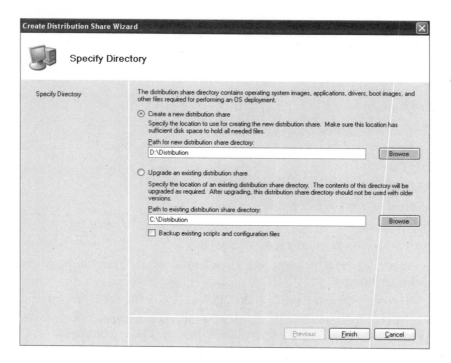

Adding Windows OS and Other Setup Files

To add Windows Vista Enterprise installation files to the Deployment Workbench follow these steps:

1.   Using the Deployment Workbench, expand the Distribution Share node, right-click the Operating Systems node, and select New. The New OS Wizard starts, as shown in Figure 1.34.

2.   On the OS Type page, select "Full set of source files" and click Next.

3.   On the Source page, in the "Source directory" text box, type the path to Windows Vista Enterprise media and click Next.

4.   On the Destination page, in the "Destination directory name" text box, type **Windows Vista Enterprise Eng x86** and click Finish.

Adding an Application to the Deployment Workbench

In this example you will be adding the Word Viewer 2003 application to the Deployment Workbench. You can download Word Viewer 2003 from this URL: `http://tinyurl.com/3q1b4`.

FIGURE 1.34 The New OS Wizard in Deployment Workbench

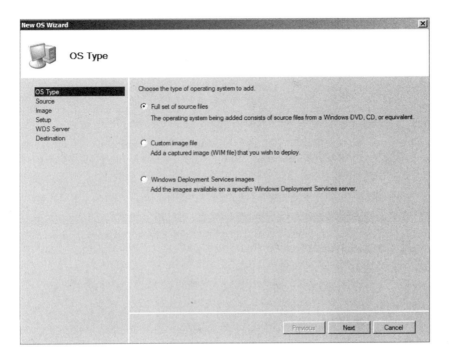

 When downloading files that you add to Deployment Workbench, make sure to unblock them first. (Right-click the file, select Properties, and click Unblock). If you don't, the deployment process will halt and ask you for permissions to execute the file, and this is not what you want during an automated deployment. The reason for this halt is that since Windows XP SP2 there is an Attachment Manager in Windows that will block certain file extensions from executing. For more information, see a description of how the Attachment Manager works in Windows XP Service Pack at http://support.microsoft.com/kb/883260.

For this example, I downloaded Word Viewer to a folder named D:\Setup\Word Viewer 2003 (and unblocked wdviewer.exe).

1. Using Deployment Workbench, expand the Distribution node, right-click the Applications node, and select New. The New Application Wizard starts.

2. On the Application Type page, select "Application with Source files" and click Next.

3. On the Details page, add the following information and click Next:

    Publisher: (Optional): Microsoft

    Application Name: Word Viewer

    Version: (Optional): 2003

4. On the Source page, in the Source Directory text box, type **D:\Setup\Word Viewer 2003** and click Next.

5. On the Destination page, in the "Specify the name of the directory that should be created" text box, type **Microsoft Word Viewer 2003** and click Next.

6. On the Command Details page, in the "Command line" text box, type **wdviewer.exe /q /c:"msiexec /i wordview.msi /qn"** as shown in Figure 1.35. Click Finish.

FIGURE 1.35   The New Application Wizard in Deployment Workbench

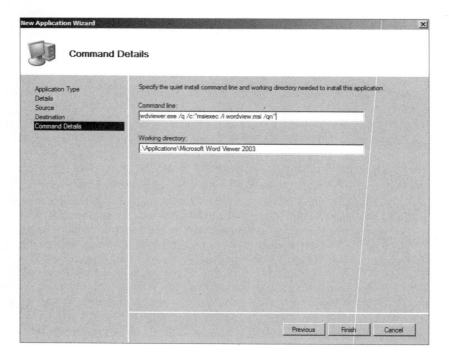

Adding an Out-of-Box Driver to the Deployment Workbench

In this example, you will be adding the VMware NIC drivers to the driver repository.

1. Using Deployment Workbench, expand the Distribution node, right-click the Out-of-Box Drivers node, and select New. The New Driver Wizard starts, as shown in Figure 1.36.

2. On the Specify Directory page, type the path to your drivers (in previous examples I stored mine in **C:\6000\vmxnet**) and click Finish.

FIGURE 1.36   The New Driver Wizard in Deployment Workbench

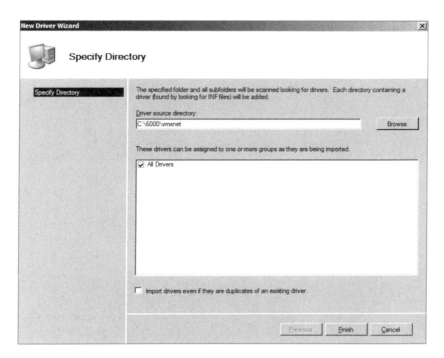

Creating a Task Sequence

Task sequences are core to the deployment process; it will control most aspects of the deployment. Here are the steps to create a task sequence.

1. Using the Deployment Workbench, right-click the Task Sequences node, and select New. The New Task Sequence Wizard starts.

2. On the General Settings page, add the following settings, as shown in Figure 1.37. Click Next.

    Task Sequencer ID: 001

    Task Sequence name: Windows Vista Enterprise Eng x86

    Task Sequence comment: Company Master Image

3. On the Select Template page, select the Standard Client Task Sequence and click Next.

4. On the Select OS page, select the Windows Vista Enterprise Eng x86 image and click Next. However, there's something important you need to know about. If the "Select OS" list box is empty it's either because you did not add an operating system or because of a well known bug in Microsoft Deployment Toolkit 2008. If you add an operating system without selecting (left-clicking) the operating system node at least once, the operatingsystems.xml file is not generated, and the Select OS list will be empty. The workaround is, of course, to cancel the guide, select the Operating System node once (so the operating systems list is generated), and start the guide again.

FIGURE 1.37 The New Task Sequence Wizard in Deployment Workbench

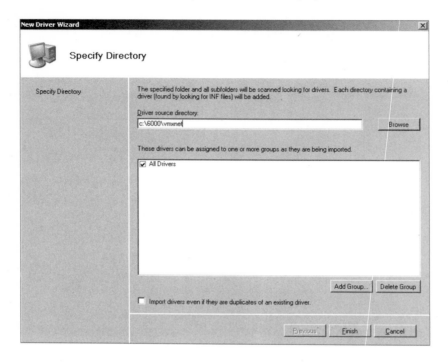

5. On the Specify Product Key page, select "Do not specify a product key at this time," as shown in Figure 1.38. Click Next. Since we are deploying Windows Vista Enterprise (Volume license) you should not specify the product key, it will be handled by the Key Management Service (KMS). In case you're doubting me, let me put it this way, if you do add the product key, you will break KMS activation.

6. On the OS Settings page, add the following settings:

   FullName: IT

   Organization: CORP

   Internet Explorer home page: `http://www.gpanswers.com`

   Click Next to continue.

7. On the Admin Password page, in the Administrator Password and Confirm Password text boxes, type the standard password we'll use for the rest of the book, **P@ssw0rd** (that's an "at sign" and a zero) and click Finish.

Creating and Configuring the Deployment Point

Creating a deployment point is basically sharing the `D:\Distribution` folder, configuring the rules, and then creating the boot image you will be using to start the deployment. Here are the steps for creating and configuring the Lite Touch deployment point.

FIGURE 1.38   The New Task Sequence Wizard Specify Product Key screen in Deployment Workbench

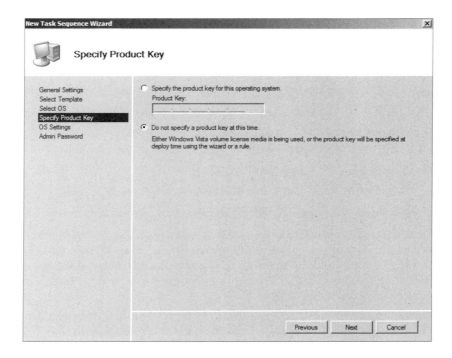

Creating the Deployment Point   Microsoft Deployment Toolkit 2008 supports several types of deployment points, but the one we will be creating here is called LAB and is the type we use for Lite Touch Deployments.

1. Using the Deployment Workbench, expand the Deploy node, right-click Deployment Points and select New. The New Deployment Point Wizard starts.

2. On the Choose Type page, select "Lab or single-server deployment" and click Next

3. On the Specify Deployment Point Name page, in the "Deployment point name" text box, type **LiteTouch** and click Next.

4. We're not making any changes here nor on the remaining screens in this wizard because we will override them when configuring the deployment point in the next section So, on the Application List page, just click Next.

5. On the Allow Image Capture page, click Next.

6. On the Allow Admin Password page, click Next.

7. On the "Allow Product key" page, click Next.

8. On the Network Share page, click Next.

9. On the Configure User State page, click Finish.

Configuring the Deployment Point Now that you've created the deployment point in Microsoft Deployment Toolkit 2008, you need to know a thing or two about it before going on to configure it.

When starting, the deployment client will connect back to the deployment point on the server and read its settings. These settings are called rules, and they will control the behavior of the Deployment Wizard (that is, what you see when you start the actual deployment) and configure Windows settings like keyboard, time zone, and so on. For example, the following rules will skip prompting for computer name during deployment and set the keyboard and time zone to Swedish for Windows Vista (I happen to be from Sweden, but you can set the time zone however you wish):

- SkipComputerName=YES
- KeyboardLocale=041d:0000041d
- TimeZoneName=W. Europe Standard Time

By adding more rules, you can fully automate the entire deployment if you like.

With that knowledge, you can go ahead and configure your deployment point:

1. Using the Deployment Workbench, right-click the Lite Touch Deployment Point and select Properties. If you are installing Microsoft Deployment Toolkit 2008 on a Windows Server 2008 with WDS installed, you can take advantage of the new multicast capabilities by checking the "Enable multicast for this deployment point (requires Windows Server 2008 WDS)" check box.

2. Remember all those rules I told you about? Well, now's the time to configure them. In the Rules tab, add the following rules for automating most of the Deployment Wizard screens:

NOTE For a great primer on Microsoft Deployment Toolkit 2008 rules, check out Ben Hunter's rule processing article on http://tinyurl.com/2zuw8t.

[Settings]
Priority=Default
[Default]
_SMSTSORGNAME=CORP
OSInstall=Y
DoCapture=NO
SkipCapture=YES
SkipAppsOnUpgrade=NO
SkipAdminPassword=YES
SkipProductKey=YES
SkipBDDWelcome=YES
SkipComputerName=YES

SkipDomainMembership=YES

SkipUserData=YES

SkipLocaleSelection=YES

SkipBuild=NO

SkipTimeZone=YES

SkipApplications=NO

SkipBitLocker=YES

SkipSummary=YES

SkipFinalSummary=NO

SkipBDDWelcome=YES

SLShare=\\DC01\Logs$

JoinDomain=CORP

DomainAdmin=CORP\JoinAccount

DomainAdminPassword=P@ssw0rd

MachineObjectOU=ou=workstations,dc=corp, dc=com

TimeZoneName= Pacific Standard Time

3. Click the `bootstrap.ini` and configure the following rules:

[Settings]
Priority=Default
[Default]
DeployRoot=\\DC01\Distribution$
userID=BuildAccount
UserDomain=CORP
UserPassword=
SkipBDDWelcome=YES

For security reasons, I don't recommend configuring the password in
`bootstrap.ini`, but if you want to speed up the process for lab purposes,
you can do it.

4. Save the file and click OK to close the Lite Touch Properties window.

5. Right-click the Lite Touch deployment point and select Update. The update process will
    take five to ten minutes.

Adding the Lite Touch Deploy Boot Image to WDS

Now it is time to add the Lite Touch boot image to WDS so you can boot it over the network.

1. In the WDS Console, right-click Boot Images and select Add Boot Image. The Windows
    Deployment Services—Add Image Wizard starts.

2. On the Image File page, in the File location text box, type **D:\Distribution\Boot\ LiteTouchPE_x86.wim** and click Next.

3. On the Image Metadata page, in the Image Name and Image Description text boxes, type **Lite Touch Windows PE (x86)** and click Next.

4. On the Summary page, click Next.

5. On the Task Progress page, click Finish.

Verifying Your Microsoft Deployment Toolkit 2008 Lite Touch Configuration

That's it! You have now configured all the components you need in Microsoft Deployment Toolkit 2008, in Lite Touch style, to start deploying Windows Vista to your client.

Before you start installing your first client using Lite Touch, however, let's review what you have done so far:

- You installed Microsoft Deployment Toolkit 2008 and its prerequisite software.

- Using Deployment Workbench, you created a distribution share (D:\Distribution).

- You added an operating system (Windows Vista Enterprise), some drivers (VMware NIC drivers), and an application (Word Viewer).

- You created a task sequence, which will drive the deployment process.

- You created the deployment point, and in that process you also configured the deployment rules and created the WinPE boot image that starts the deployment.

- You added the WinPE boot image to WDS so that you can easily start it by pressing F12 on the client.

This sounds easy enough, doesn't it? It *is* easy. Now it is time to put it to the test and install your first client.

Installing Your First Client Using Lite Touch

It's time to install your first client using MDLT. When booting the Lite Touch boot image, it will connect to the distribution share, read the rules, and start the deployment.

1. PXE-boot your computer, and select the Lite Touch boot image. After a while the Deployment Wizard starts.

2. On the "Specify credentials for connecting to network shares" page, enter the password and click OK.

3. On the "Select a task sequence to execute on this computer" page, select the "Windows Vista Enterprise Eng x86" image and click Next.

4. On the "Select one or more applications to install" page, select the Microsoft Word Viewer 2003 application, as shown in Figure 1.39. Click Next.

If you have done everything right, Windows Vista Enterprise will now install fully unattended with the settings you have configured. Figure 1.40 shows a screenshot of the process.

You should also end up with two log files from the setup in the D:\Logs folder on DC01.

FIGURE 1.39   Selecting application(s) during setup

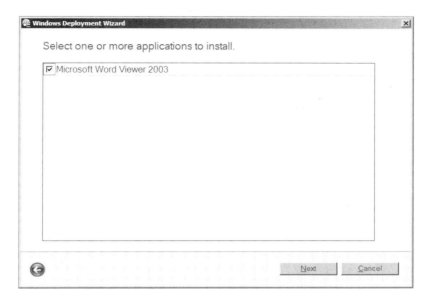

FIGURE 1.40   The Lite Touch setup running

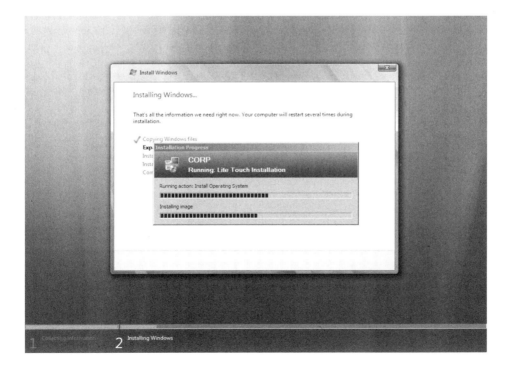

Beyond the Microsoft Deployment Toolkit 2008 Basics

In this section, we're going to go beyond the regular setup of Microsoft Deployment Toolkit 2008. Heck, there's a lot you can do with Microsoft Deployment Toolkit 2008, but here are two of my favorites.

First, I'll show you how to save user state as you upgrade from Windows XP to Windows Vista. That's right, you can preserve a lot of stuff from your users' Desktops and more using the User State Migration Tool.

I'll also show you how to add a deployment database (SQL database), which is nice if you have lots of systems and want to dig in and get more out of your data. This database is really useful even for smaller networks since it allows you to configure the client settings before you actually deploy the client. You can configure settings like the computer name, what applications it should have, what drivers it should install and so on.

Saving User State During an XP-to-Windows-Vista Upgrade

As I mentioned, Microsoft Deployment Toolkit 2008 supports migrating user settings and data when reinstalling a machine. This scenario is called Refresh and does not involve PXE booting or booting from a WinPE CD.

We will not go into great detail about this in here but you will find much more detail in the Microsoft Deployment Toolkit 2008 documentation. In fact, there is a whole document dedicated to user-state migration: User_State_Migration_Guide.doc. Reading up on the Refresh scenario in the Deployment_Feature_Team_Guide.doc is recommended, too.

Refresh Scenario

Say you want to upgrade a Windows XP machine to Windows Vista. You don't want to do an in-place upgrade, but you do want to keep the user data and settings. This is where the Lite Touch Refresh scenario comes in handy.

You can start the process by going to your XP Workstation, logging in as a local administrator and then running the LiteTouch.vbs script from the DC01 Server (for example, \\DC01\Distribution$\Scripts\LiteTouch.vbs).

The Windows Deployment Wizard will start and you will have to complete the wizard, but after that the process is fully automated. If you choose to do a refresh during this wizard, the following will happen:

- The User State Migration Tool (USMT) will back up your settings to the local MININT folder.

- Windows PE will be applied to the disk, the boot loader will be changed, and the computer will be rebooted.

- Windows PE will start and apply the Windows Vista Enterprise operating system to the disk.

- After Windows Vista is installed, the backed up user settings and data will be restored.

 The User State Migration Tool (USMT) version 3.0.1 is not included by default in Microsoft Deployment Toolkit 2008. You will have to download it and copy it to the Distribution\Tools\x86 folder. The URL is http://tinyurl.com/2jsb6h.

Adding Database Support

In order to get a more dynamic, database-driven deployment solution, you can configure Microsoft Deployment Toolkit 2008 to store some of its rules in a SQL Server Express Database (of course, a full-blown SQL Server 2005 will also work, but we'll use SQL Server Express because it's free).

 Adding a database may sound like a bit too much if you are a smaller organization, but trust me: it is really worth going that extra mile.

The benefits of using the database are that you get a central portal from where you can control all your client (and server) deployments in great detail. You even get a nice GUI to manage this information directly from the Deployment Workbench.

You can, for example, prestage all your computers into the database, complete with computer name, settings, applications and so on. So when you press F12 to deploy a client, it already knows how it should be configured.

Installing SQL Server Express Edition SP2

Install SQL Server Express Edition SP2 by following these steps:

1. Run the SQLSRV32.exe file. The Microsoft SQL Server 2005 Setup Wizard starts.
2. On the End User License Agreement page, accept the agreement and click Next.
3. On the Installing Prerequisites page, click Install, and then click Next.
4. On the "Welcome to the Microsoft SQL Server installation wizard" page, click Next.
5. On the System Configuration Check page, click Next.
6. On the Registration Information page, clear the "Hide advanced configuration options" check box and click Next.
7. On the Feature Selection page, expand Database Services and configure Data Files to be stored on D:\. Then click Next.
8. On the Windows Authentication Mode page, click Next.
9. On the Configuration Options page, clear the Enable User Instances check box, and click Next.
10. On the Error and Usage Report Settings page, click Next.
11. On the Ready to Install page, click Install.
12. On the Setup Progress page, click Next.
13. On the Completing Microsoft SQL Server 2005 Setup page, click Finish.

Installing SQL Server Express Edition Management Tools

The SQL Server Express Edition management tools are useful for configuring the database. Install SQL Server Express Edition management tools by following these steps:

1. Run the SQLServer2005_SSMSEE.msi file. The Microsoft SQL Server Management Studio Express Wizard starts.

2. On the Welcome to the Install Wizard for Microsoft SQL Server Management Studio Express page, click Next.

3. On the License Agreement page, accept the agreement and click Next.

4. On the Registration Information page, click Next.

5. On the Feature Selection page, click Next.

6. On the "Ready to Install the Program" page, click Install.

7. On the "Completing the Microsoft SQL Server Management Studio Express Setup" page, click Finish.

Configuring SQL Server Express Edition

To make SQL Server Express Edition work with Microsoft Deployment Toolkit 2008, you need to enable named pipes and start the SQL Server Browser service. Follow these steps:

1. Start SQL Server Configuration Manager and select the SQL Server 2005 Services node.

2. Right-click SQL Server Browser and select Properties. In the Service tab, change Start Mode to Automatic and click OK.

3. Right-click SQL Server Browser and select Start.

4. Expand the SQL Server 2005 Network Configuration node and select "Protocols for SQLEXPRESS."

5. Right-click Named Pipes and select Enable. In the Warning dialog box, click OK.

6. Select the SQL Server 2005 Services node, right-click SQL Server (SQLEXPRESS) and select Restart.

Creating the Deployment Database

Now you are ready to create the Microsoft Deployment Toolkit 2008 database. The database is created from the deployment database by following these steps:

1. Using Deployment Workbench, expand the Deploy node and select the Database node.

2. Right-click the Database node and select New. The New DB Wizard starts.

3. On the SQL Server Details page in the SQL Server name text box, enter **DC01**. In the Instance text box, enter **SQLEXPRESS**, and then click Next.

4. On the Database page in the "Create a new database—Database" text box, enter **MD** and click Next.

5. On the SQL Share page, in the SQL Share text box, enter **Logs$** and click Finish.

Configuring Microsoft Deployment Toolkit 2008 to Use the Deployment Database

In order for Microsoft Deployment Toolkit 2008 to use the database, we need to configure the rules on the deployment point. This process is a guide where you simply check the settings that you want to query the database for.

1. Using Deployment Workbench, expand the Deploy node and then expand the Database node.

2. Right-click Computers and select New. The Configure DB Wizard starts.

> As a general rule, start small. Checking every check box will cause a lot of database queries during deployment. This will increase the deployment time, especially if contacting the database over a WAN link.

3. On the Computer Options page, select the first two check boxes, clear the others, and click Next.

4. On the Location Options page, select the first two check boxes, clear the others, and click Next.

5. On the Make/Model Options page, select the first and the third option, clear the others, and click Next.

6. On the Role Options page, select the first two options, clear the others, and click Finish.

Adding Entries to the Database

Now you are ready to go ahead and create computer accounts, role-based settings, and so on.

1. Using Deployment Workbench, expand the Deploy node, and then expand the Database node.

2. Right-click Roles and select New. The Properties Windows is displayed.

3. On the Properties window in the Identity tab in the "Role name" text box, type **Standard PC**.

4. In the Details tab, in the "Full name" text box, type IT. In the Orgname text box, type **Corp**, and then click OK. You have created a role named Standard PC with some settings.

5. Right-click Computers and select New. The Properties window is displayed.

6. On the Properties window in the Identity tab, complete the Description and Identify fields for one of your target computer. I use the MAC address of one of my virtual machines in this example, as shown in Figure 1.41.

FIGURE 1.41 Adding a computer account

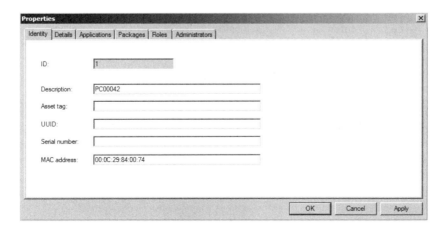

The database input fields in Microsoft Deployment Toolkit 2008 are a bit weird to edit in; you hardly ever see the cursor. I recommend editing in Notepad and then copying and pasting into the window.

7. In the Details tab, enter the computer name for the new computer. I use the name PC00042 in this example.

8. In the Roles tab, add the Standard PC role and click OK. Now you have associated the Standard PC role (and its settings) with PC00042, as shown in Figure 1.42.

FIGURE 1.42   Assign roles to a computer account.

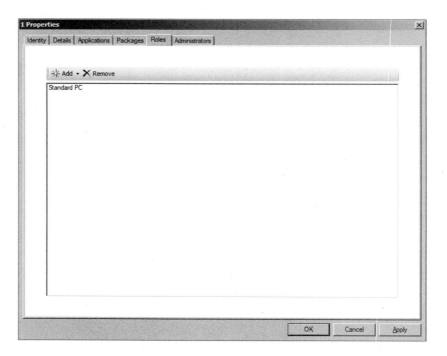

Troubleshooting Microsoft Deployment Toolkit 2008

When things go wrong (and things will go wrong), you need to find out why. Each Microsoft Deployment Toolkit 2008 script automatically creates a log file when it runs. Log files are stored in the C:\MININT\SMSOSD\OSDLOGS folder during the deployment process and are moved to C:\Windows\Temp when the deployment is completed.

Real World Scenario

Microsoft Deployment Toolkit 2008 Best Practices

You will quickly discover that Microsoft Deployment Toolkit 2008 is a very open platform, mostly driven by VBScripts, and you can tweak it to do most things with regards to deployment. With regard to tweaking, the first tip I want to give you is this: don't do that right away. Start small, get the basic built-in features working, and learn how the system works and how to troubleshoot it. Then take it from there.

Here, I summarize some tips and tricks that will help you steer clear of the most common pitfalls.

Get Rid of the Junk

The most common issue with Microsoft Deployment Toolkit 2008 is when leftover junk from a previous attempt of deploying an operating system prevents a new attempt. It could be a missing network driver; it could be a rule or setting you made on the deployment point that is causing it to fail in the first place.

If you try several deployments, make sure to either wipe the disk, or remove the MININT and _ SMSTaskSequence folders before trying again. (If you want to go real hardcore, check out my blog entry on how to configure the boot image to always remove the MININT and _SMSTaskSequence. You can find that at http://tinyurl.com/2x6ohq.)

Meet the System Requirements

Verify that the clients have at least 512MB RAM (and remember 512MB RAM is not always 512MB RAM, as sometimes shared video memory can be stealing "real" memory).

Group Boot Image Drivers

The boot image should have only Ethernet NIC and storage drivers. Adding wireless drivers to WinPE might even cause it to fail when loading other drivers. Group Ethernet NIC and storage drivers to a WinPE drivers group and configure the deployment point to use only that driver group.

Dealing with Two-Tier Drivers for WinPE

If you have two-tier network drivers, make sure to download the monolithic version and add it to the WinPE drivers group. The monolithic drivers are sometimes disguised under names like RIS, ADS, or WinPE driver.

Do a Final Reboot

Don't leave the system logged in as an admin; make sure it reboots after completing the setup.

See this URL for more information: http://tinyurl.com/yrhepn.

If You Don't Prestage, Then Generate Computer Names

Make sure you name the computers something useful, or else have the system generate a useful name. Here is information on how to configure a stored procedure for doing that: http://tinyurl.com/277bd3.

If Deploying XP or Windows Server 2003

Make sure to enable the Set Diskpart BIOS Compatibility Mode action in the Task Sequence. Address a disk partitioning bug in WinPE 2.0, also known as the WinPE 2.0 uberbug. See http://support.microsoft.com/?id=931760 and http://support.microsoft.com/?id=931761 for more information about the issue.

Make sure to add a storage driver to sysprep.inf before sealing the image (and install the necessary hotfixes). Install at least KB888111 and KB883667, which add support for HD audio and fix an issue with certain video cards freezing the Sysprep mini-setup.

Don't add every storage driver on the planet; add only those you do have. This helps solve issues with Sysprep and the magic CloneTag it adds to the Registry.

 The log files have been formatted to be read with Trace32 from SMS 2003 Toolkit 2, not with Notepad. You can download the Trace32 toolkit from http://tinyurl.com/2zy7no.

Creating a Test Environment

To speed up troubleshooting, you can configure a test environment where you simulate a deployment without actually performing a deployment. This is very valuable when testing new rules, scripts, database queries, and so on. Here are the steps:

1. On a client PC, create a folder named C:\ZTI.
2. Copy the Customsettings.ini file from \\DC01\Distribution$\Control to C:\ZTI.
3. Copy the following files from \\DC01\Distribution$\Scripts to C:\ZTI:

    ZTIGather.wsf

    ZTIGather.xml

    ZTIUtillity.vbs
4. Create a batch file (named LTITest.cmd in this example) with the following code:

    ```
    Cls
    if exist c:\minint\nul rd c:\minint /s /q
    cscript.exe ZTIGather.wsf /debug:true
    ```
5. Run the script from a command prompt, and review the output as well as the log files in C:\MININT\SMSOSD\OSDLOGS.

Interpreting the *ZTIGather.log* File

After running the script, examine the ZTIGather.log file. Remember, during deployment the WinPE boot image reads the settings from the deployment point. We are simulating that.

When you review the log file, you will find out how the client read the current deployment point rules (customsettings.ini). In the log file you will see, for example, the queries to the database and, if they succeeded, what result the client got back.

Following are some sample lines from a ZTIGather.log file and what they really mean. This entry means the MAC address is 00:0C:29:84:00:74:

```
MAC address = 00:0C:29:84:00:74
```

The next two entries show that the client has read the [Default] section in the rules and found out where to store the log files:

```
Processing the [DEFAULT] section
Property SLSHARE is now = \\DC01\Logs$
```

The next entries show that the client has connected to the deployment database, queried for settings related to its MAC address, and got one record back. In the record there was information on which role this PC had in the database, the Standard PC Role.

```
OPENING TRUSTED SQL CONNECTION to server DC01.
    Connecting to SQL Server using connect string: Provider=SQLOLEDB;OLE DB
    Services=0;Data Source=DC01\SQLEXPRESS;Initial Catalog=MD;Network
    Library=DBNMPNTW;Integrated Security=SSPI
Successfully opened connection to database.
    About to issue SQL statement: SELECT * FROM ComputerRoles WHERE UUID =
    '125B4D56-5CC1-2697-D688-A2755C840074' OR ASSETTAG = 'No Asset Tag' OR
    SERIALNUMBER = 'VMware-56 4d 5b 12 c1 5c 97 26-d6 88 a2 75 5c 84 00 74' OR
    MACADDRESS IN ('00:0C:29:84:00:74')
Successfully queried the database.
Records returned from SQL = 1
Property ROLE001 is now = Standard PC
```

The next entries show that the client has connected to the deployment database, queried for settings related to its role (Standard PC), and got five records back. These records had information about what five applications the client should install (retrieved from the role).

```
About to issue SQL statement: SELECT * FROM RoleApplications WHERE ROLE IN
('Standard PC') ORDER BY Sequence
Successfully queried the database.
Records returned from SQL = 5
The Above three lines
Property APPLICATIONS001 is now = {87099ba0-77df-4986-9eca-f0bc65c7b202}
Property APPLICATIONS002 is now = {53f4552a-6125-4b20-914e-5f9ffe5009cc}
Property APPLICATIONS003 is now = {8fece820-dc80-4cbe-a576-4841dd1a6e84}
Property APPLICATIONS004 is now = {0980e3d7-f9da-4006-a2e5-566429d28190}
Property APPLICATIONS005 is now = {26fb69a7-3f9b-4064-8f8a-efe739e6639f}
```

Final Thoughts

WDS and Microsoft Deployment Toolkit 2008 are big places. If I had to leave you with three things to remember as you work though the exercises in this chapter, they would be:

- When testing, remember that the client needs to have 512MB of RAM, even if you deploy down-level operating systems like Windows XP.
- To maintain a high-level overview, read through the exercises once before actually doing them.
- WDS and Microsoft Deployment Toolkit 2008 are best when used together. These components combined will form a very powerful deployment platform. Did I mention that they are free?

The following links will help you work with WDS and Microsoft Deployment Toolkit 2008:

- `http://www.truesec.com`: where I work as a deployment consultant, and where you can find training classes on WDS and Microsoft Deployment Toolkit 2008.
- `http://www.deployvista.com`: my blog.
- `http://blogs.technet.com/richardsmith`: a Microsoft Services Consultant from the U.K.
- `http://blogs.technet.com/benhunter`: a Microsoft Services Consultant from New Zealand.
- `http://blogs.technet.com/deploymentguys`: a team effort from some of your favorite deployment guys including Ben Hunter, Richard Smith, Adam Shepherd, Daniel Oxley, and more.
- `http://blogs.technet.com/mniehaus`: the Lead Developer for Microsoft Deployment Toolkit 2008.
- `http://blogs.technet.com/msdeployment`: the Deployment team blog.
- `http://www.myitforum.com/absolutevc/avc-view.aspx?v=735`: TechNet Webcast: Automated Windows Server 2008 Imaging and Deployment Using the Microsoft Deployment Accelerator (Level 300).

2

Profiles: Local, Roaming, and Mandatory

When a user logs onto a Windows machine, a profile is automatically generated. A *profile* is a collection of settings, specific to a user, that sticks with that user throughout the working experience. In this chapter, I'll talk about three types of profiles.

First is the *Local Profile*, which is created whenever a user logs on. Next is the *Roaming Profile*, which enables users to hop from machine to machine while maintaining the same configuration settings at each machine. Along our journey, I'll also discuss some configuration tweaks that you can set using specific policy settings—specifically for Roaming Profiles.

The third type of profile is the *Mandatory Profile*. Like Roaming Profiles, Mandatory Profiles allow the user to jump from machine to machine. But Mandatory Profiles force a user's Desktop and settings to remain exactly the same as they were when the administrator assigned the profile; the user cannot permanently change the settings.

Here's a little "cheat sheet" before we go much farther. That is, you need a guide to understand which operating system's profiles are compatible and which are not.

- Version 0: Windows NT
- Version 1: Windows 2000, Windows 2003, and Windows XP
- Version 2: Windows Vista and Windows Server 2008 (as clients)

We'll barely be talking at all about Version 0 profiles here. But we will be getting into Version 1 and Version 2 profiles. But, before we get too far down the line, let's just break the bad news: if you're interested in setting up Roaming Profiles for both your Version 1 type machines and Version 2 type machines, you'll be setting up "parallel worlds." That is, you'll set up two Roaming Profile infrastructures (one for Version 1 and one for Version 2) and the two shall never meet.

If the two shall never meet, how will you share data for a user if he roams from a Windows XP to a Windows Vista machine and back again? That's the next chapter, where we take on redirected folders. So, stay tuned for that after you've successfully set up Roaming Profiles for Windows XP and Windows Vista.

In general, your users will use desktop machines when roaming. However, users could, of course, roam to a server, like Windows Server 2003 or Windows Server 2008. Roaming Profiles will keep on working in those scenarios as well. Just remember that Windows Server 2003 is a Type 1 and Windows Server 2008 is a Type 2.

What Is a User Profile?

As I stated, as soon as a user logs onto a machine, a Local Profile is generated. This profile is two things: a personal slice of the Registry (contained in a file) and a set of folders stored on a hard drive. Together, these components form what we might call the *user experience*—that is, what the Desktop looks like, what style and shape the icons are, what the background wallpaper looks like, and so on.

The *NTUSER.DAT* File

The Registry stores user and computer settings in a file called NTUSER.DAT, which can be loaded and unloaded into the current computer's Registry—taking over the HKEY_CURRENT_USER portion of the Registry when the user logs on.

In Figure 2.1, you can see a portion of a Windows XP's HKEY_CURRENT_USER, specifically, the Control Panel ➢ Desktop ➢ Wallpaper setting, which shows c:\WINDOWS\web\wallpaper\ Bliss.bmp in the Data column.

This portion of the Registry directly maps to a file in the user's profile—the NTUSER.DAT file. You'll find that many of a user's individual settings are stored in this file. Here are detailed descriptions for some of the settings inside NTUSER.DAT:

Accessories   Look-and-feel settings for applications such as Calculator, Clock, HyperTerminal, Notepad, and Paint.

Application   Settings for things like toolbars for Office applications and most newer applications.

Control Panel   The bulk of the settings in NTUSER.DAT. Settings found here include those for screen savers, display, sounds, and mouse.

Explorer   Remembers how specific files and folders are to be displayed.

Printer   Network printer and local printer definitions are found here.

Drive Mappings   Stored, persistent drive mappings are stored here.

Taskbar   Designates the look and feel of the taskbar.

FIGURE 2.1   A simple Registry setting shows the entry for the wallpaper.

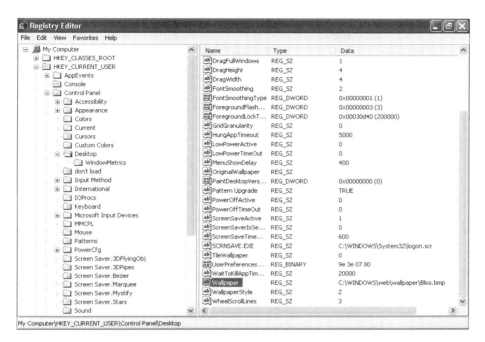

Profile Folders for Type 1 Computers (Windows 2000, Windows 2003, and Windows XP)

By default, Windows 2000, Windows 2003, and Windows XP profiles are stored in a folder underneath the C:\Documents and Settings folder.

Ultimately, what the user "sees" as their profile is an amalgam of two halves: their own personal profile and components from what is known as the "All Users" profile.

So, each user has a unique profile, and each user leverages a shared profile.

Understanding the Contents of a User's Profile (for Type 1 Computers)

Items in the profile folders can be stored in lots of nooks and crannies. As you can see in Figure 2.2, both visible and hidden folders store User Profile settings.

To show hidden files in an Explorer window, choose Tools ➤ Folder Options to open the Folder Options dialog box, and click the View tab. Click the "Show Hidden Files and Folders" radio button, and then click OK.

FIGURE 2.2 A look inside Frank Rizzo's profile reveals both visible and hidden folders.

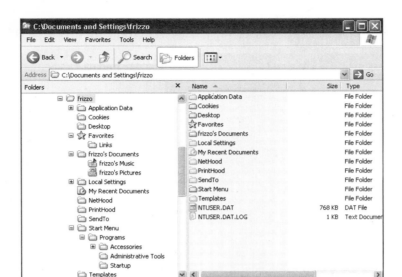

Here are the folders and a general description of what each contains.

Application Data Used by many applications to store specific settings, such as the Microsoft Office toolbar settings. Additionally, items such as Word's Custom Dictionary are stored here. MST files (Microsoft Transform Files) are stored here by default. MST files modify Windows Installer applications by providing customized application installation and runtime settings. (See Chapter 4 for more information on MST files.)

Cookies Houses Internet Explorer cookies so that pages on the Internet can remember specific user settings.

Favorites Houses Internet Explorer Favorites—the list of saved web page links.

Desktop Contains only files that users store directly on the Desktop. Special icons such as My Network Places, My Computer, and the Recycle Bin are not part of the Desktop profile.

Local Settings Contains application data specific to the user's machine, such as Internet Explorer History, temporary file storage, and other application data. This folder does not roam when Roaming Profiles are set up (see the "Roaming Profiles" section later in this chapter). Like the Application Data folder, this folder is to be used at an application vendor's discretion.

My Documents Now, users of all sophistication levels can leverage this centralized repository for their data files. The My Documents folder has the advantage that it's easily understood by end users, instead of them having to wonder about which file goes in which drive letter path. In fact, the default Office 2000, Office XP, and Office 2003 "Save as" path is to My Documents. This will come in handy, as you'll see in the next chapter. My Documents contains My Pictures, and Windows XP Profiles also contains My Music.

NetHood   Contains shortcuts to network drives. Even though the NT 4 Network Neighborhood was renamed to My Network Places, the NetHood folder is still around and still performs the same functions.

PrintHood   Contains shortcuts to network printers; similar to NetHood.

Recent   Contains a list of the most recently used application files and user data files like .TXT and .DOC files.

SendTo   Contains icons that applications can use to tie into Explorer to allow file routing between applications, such as Outlook, and folders.

Start Menu   Contains the shortcuts and information that users see when they choose Start ➤ All Programs. Each user's Start Menu folder is different. For example, if Joe installs DogFoodMaker 4 and Sally installs CatFoodMaker 8.1, neither will see the other's icons. To see each other's icons, the icons need to live in the All Users ➤ Start Menu folder (see next section). Note that if the application does a "per user" installation, then shortcuts will be present in the user's profile. If the application does a per machine installation then the shortcuts are in the All Users profile.

Templates   Contains the templates that some applications, such as Excel and Word, use to perform conversions. Like the Application Data folder, this folder is to be used at an application vendor's discretion.

The All Users profile (for Type 1 Computers), which is found at the variable location %ALLUSERSPROFILE%, typically maps to C:\Documents and Settings\All Users.

Applications often add icons to the %ALLUSERSPROFILE%\Start Menu to ensure that all users can run them.

Again, users end up seeing the combination of their own profile plus whatever is presented in the All Users profile.

Profile Folders for Type 2 Computers (Windows Vista and Windows 2008)

As I stated in the introduction to this chapter, the profiles for Windows XP and Windows Vista are basically incompatible. There might be some similarities between the two (and actually, Windows Vista goes the "extra mile" to try to help bridge the differences between the two). The items we'll be looking at here have moved from their original place in Windows XP to a new place in Windows Vista—the Users folder, which is typically found hanging off of C:\. The \Users folder in Vista is the equivalent of the Documents and Settings directory in Windows XP.

Additionally, all this information is valid for Windows Server 2008 machines too. Windows Vista and Windows Server 2008 share the same profile structure. However, we'll be concentrating on Windows Vista because it's what your users will mostly be logging onto.

Understanding the Contents of a User's Profile (for Type 2 Computers)

Inside the Windows Vista profile there are a lot of new folders and some that simply look familiar. Let's take a quick look at what's inside the Windows Vista profile.

Contacts   This is new for Windows Vista. This folder stores what are known as "Windows Contacts."

Desktop   Similar in function to Windows XP's Desktop (see earlier).

Documents   Was My Documents in Windows XP. Same basic function. Stores basic documents such as word documents and such.

Downloads   This is new for Windows Vista. It becomes a storage spot for users' downloads.

Favorites   Similar in function to Windows XP's Favorites (see earlier).

Links   This is where Explorer's Favorite Links are stored. You'll see these down the left pane of Explorer.

Music   Was My Music in Windows XP.

Videos   Was My Videos in Windows XP (though not officially part of the Windows XP profile).

Pictures   Was My Pictures in Windows XP.

Saved Games   This is a new folder to save users' saved games into. I'm sure network administrators everywhere are just *thrilled* about this.

Searches   This is new for Windows Vista and it will save stored searches for Explorer.

AppData   Was Application Data in Windows XP. Now in Windows Vista, AppData is bifurcated into two parts: Local (to the computer only) and Roaming (for the specific user). We'll be talking more about Roaming Profiles in a bit, but this part is important to understand for when we do tackle them.

The AppData\Roaming folder in Windows Vista performs the same function as the Documents and Settings*<username>*\Application Data folder in Windows XP.

The AppData\Local folder is now meant to hold machine-specific application data that isn't supposed to roam with the user. This folder is to be the equivalent for Local Settings\ Application Data in Windows XP.

The AppData\LocalLow folder is a special directory with "low integrity" rights. So files that get stored here will have a lower integrity level than in other areas of the operating system. See the sidebar entitled "The LocalLow Folder within AppData" for more information.

In the next section, I talk about how several Windows XP holdovers are mapped to directories within AppData.

The *LocalLow* Folder within *AppData*

Within a user's AppData folder, there are two obvious entries: Local and Roaming. These make sense and are used when that corresponding condition is true. However, also note the presence of a LocalLow folder.

Windows Vista has various ways applications can run. One way is Protected Mode, which guarantees a program will run with low rights. When running in this way, the application only has access to this portion of the User Profile. Windows Vista's Internet Explorer is one such application. Internet Explorer in Windows Vista runs in Protected Mode, so this prevents malware and other various nasties from infecting your computer, or possibly compromising user specific information.

Protected Mode uses the LocalLow profile folder.

Also note there are low integrity folders for Cookies, History, and Favorites.

For more on integrity levels, check out Mark Minasi's book entitled *Administering Vista Security: The Big Surprises* from Sybex (2006).

Adjusting for Windows XP Holdovers

Even though we're exploring the Windows Vista profile, something interesting should be noted. That is, Windows Vista profiles are set up to automatically handle older applications which are still looking for Windows XP locations. For instance, if an application wanted to expressly save something in My Documents, it would have a problem. My Documents doesn't exist anymore, right? Now, it's just Documents for Windows Vista. To that end, the Windows Vista profile has what are called Junction Points, so when an application visits My Documents it's really going to Windows Vista's Documents.

To see these pointers, we need to see the hidden files inside a Windows Vista profile. You can perform this by going to the user's profile and typing **dir /ah /og** (to show hidden files and to sort by directories first). You can see this in Figure 2.3.

Note that upon further inspection, the following folders appear at the top level of the profile, but really, they are placed into either AppData\Roaming or AppData\Local:

Windows XP Holdover	Linked to Windows Vista Folder	Directory path relative to c:\Users\{username}
My Documents	Documents	\Documents
Application Data	AppData	\AppData\Roaming
Cookies	AppData\Roaming	\AppData\Roaming\Microsoft\Windows\Cookies
Local Settings	AppData\Local	\AppData\Local

Windows XP Holdover	Linked to Windows Vista Folder	Directory path relative to c:\Users\{username}
NetHood	AppData\Roaming	\AppData\Roaming\Microsoft\Windows\Network Shortcuts
Start Menu	AppData\Roaming	\AppData\Roaming\Microsoft\Windows\Start Menu
Recent	AppData\Roaming	\AppData\Roaming\Microsoft\Windows\Recent
Templates	AppData\Roaming	\Appdata\Roaming\Microsoft\Windows\Templates
Printhood	AppData\Roaming	\AppData\Roaming\Microsoft\Windows\Printer Shortcuts
SendTo	AppData\Roaming	\AppData\Roaming\Microsoft\Windows\SendTo

Curious about what those `regtran-ms` files are? I was! According to my sources at Microsoft, these are the Kernel Transaction Manager (KTM) generated files. The Vista Registry uses KTM to avoid corruptions, so you should never see Registry corruption anymore. Let's hope anyway.

FIGURE 2.3   A view inside a Type 2 profile (dir /ah /og)

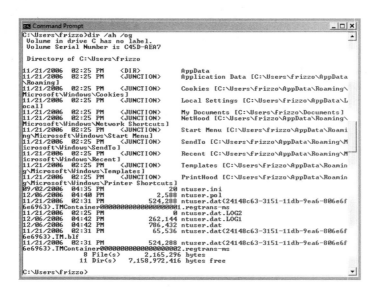

The Public Profile (for Type 2 Computers)

The Public profile in Windows Vista and Windows 2008 replaces the All Users concept in Windows XP and previous machines. However, it provides the same basic function. That is, the end user's experience becomes their own profile *plus* the contents of the Public profile. Again, categories like the Desktop and Start Menu become good candidates here, because the icons you place here affect everyone.

Virtualized Files and Registry for Programs

Some applications try to do bad, bad things. And Windows XP will (usually) let them. For instance, an application could try to write program data to `C:\program files\dogfoodmaker5\settings.ini`.

This DogFoodMaker application really has no business writing settings there. In reality, settings should be in the user's profile, specifically in the Application Data (AppData) section (either user or machine based).

To that end, Windows Vista will redirect writes like this to a location where the application should be writing. Microsoft calls this redirection *virtualization*. Specifically *file virtualization* and *Registry virtualization*. Specifically, `C:\users\`*<username>*`\AppData\Local\VirtualStore\Program Files\dogfoodmaker5`. And, because multiple users could be using the same machine, a separate copy of the virtualized file is created for each user that runs the application.

Indeed, if you wanted to see these redirected files right away, Windows Explorer has its own button to see these. If there is a virtualized version of a file related to the current directory, a Compatibility Files button appears that will take you to the virtual location to view that file. In this example, you can see that someone tried to put junk in the `\Windows` directory.

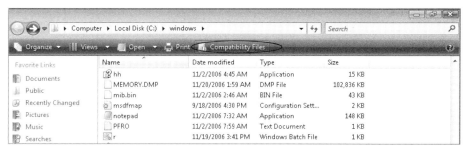

Writes to incorrect places to the Registry work the same way. Bad writes get redirected to `HKEY_CLASSES_ROOT\VirtualStore\MACHINE` or `USER\SOFTWARE`. This automatically takes effect if the application isn't UAC compliant. So, file virtualization doesn't affect applications that are run with a full administrative rights (when, say, someone elevates it to run as an admin).

This technology is, of course, a band-aid. It permits pre-Windows Vista applications to run in a predictable way. But, really, it should be considered a short-term fix rather than a long-term solution. The goal is to ensure that your application developers modify their applications such that they meet the guidelines of the Windows Vista Logo program instead of depending on file and Registry virtualization.

Note that file and Registry virtualization is disabled under some circumstances:

- File and Registry virtualization is simply not supported for Windows Vista 64-bit applications. These applications are expected to be UAC compliant and to write data to the correct locations.

- Virtualization is disabled for applications that include an application manifest with a desired execution level attribute. If you're a developer, you can learn more about application manifests here: http://tinyurl.com/ftvn5.

Additionally, note you can turn off virtual file and Registry abilities. That security policy is located in Computer Configuration ➢ Policies ➢ Windows Settings ➢ Security Settings ➢ Local Policies ➢ Security Options ➢ **User Account Control: Virtualize file and registry write failures to per-user locations**. You need to click "Define this policy setting," then select Disabled to turn it off.

The Default Local User Profile

The Default Local User Profile folder contains many of the same folders as any user's own Local Profile. Indeed, the Default User Profile is the template that generates all new local User Profiles when a new user logs on.

When a new user logs on, a copy of the Default Local User Profile is copied for that user to C:\users\%*username*%. As will often happen, the user changes and personalizes settings through the normal course of business. Then, once the user logs off, the settings are preserved in a personal local folder in the C:\Users\%*username*% folder.

This Default Local User Profile is different from the Default Domain User Profile described later.

As an administrator, you can create your own ready-made standard shortcuts or stuff the folders with your own files. You can also introduce your own NTUSER.DAT Registry settings, such as a standard Desktop for all users who log onto a specific machine. In the following example, you can set up a background picture in the Default Local User Profile. Then, whenever a new user logs on locally to this machine, the background picture is displayed.

For Type 1 computers (Windows XP, Windows 2003, Windows 2000) the Default User Profile is stored in C:\Documents and Settings\Default User.

For Type 2 computers (Windows Vista and Windows 2008) the Default User Profile is stored in C:\users\Default.

⊕ Real World Scenario

Changing the Profiles Folder for Windows XP Machines

Older applications sometimes balk at the new Local Profiles location, because they occasionally hard-coded information to the NT 4–style profile paths. This is probably why Microsoft chose to maintain the original profile location (C:\WINNT\PROFILES) when an NT 4 machine is upgraded to Windows 2000 or Windows XP.

If you come across any applications in your testing that prohibit you from using the new path, you can change the storage point for the Profiles folder. Although the storage point for the Profiles folder cannot be changed once a Windows 2000 (or Windows XP) machine is loaded, you can change it during an unattended setup. For instance, if you want to store the profiles under the old path of C:\WINNT\PROFILES or, say, under the Profiles folder on a large D: partition or hard drive, you can set up your answer file to contain the following:

```
[GUIUnattended]
Profilesdir="D:\PROFILES"
```

This technique works only for freshly installed systems, not for machines being upgraded from NT 4. Additionally, use this procedure when preparing servers for Terminal Services. This keeps users' profiles from choking the system partition with thousands of profile files and folders.

To set up your own Registry settings in NTUSER.DAT, follow these steps:

1. Choose Start ➢ Run to open the Run dialog box. In the Open box, type **regedt32.exe** and press Enter to open the Registry Editor.

2. Select HKEY_USERS, as shown in Figure 2.4.

3. Choose File ➢ Load Hive.

4. For Type 1 computers, browse to the C:\Documents and Settings\Default User folder, shown in Figure 2.4. For Type 2 computers, browse to c:\Users\Default. You might have to specifically type in the path, as the file requester may hide it from you if you are not displaying hidden files and folders.

5. Select NTUSER.DAT.

6. When prompted to enter a key name, anything will work, but for our example let's use **this is a dummy key name**, and click OK. Figure 2.5 shows an example. The key name is only temporary, so its name doesn't particularly matter.

7. Traverse to any Registry key and value. In this case, we'll change all future wallpaper to Coffee Bean.bmp. To do that, traverse to Dummy Key Name ➢ Control Panel ➢ Desktop and double-click Wallpaper. If you're using Windows XP, enter the value in this example, **C:\windows\coffee bean.jpg**, as shown in Figure 2.6. If you're using Windows Vista, enter **c:\windows\web\wallpaper\img35.jpg**. Note there might already be a default image set, but you're now changing it.

FIGURE 2.4 Load the NTUSER.DAT file into the Registry.

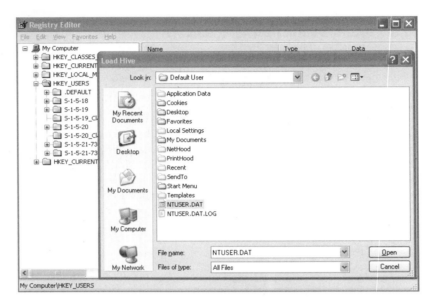

FIGURE 2.5 It doesn't matter what the temporary dummy key is called.

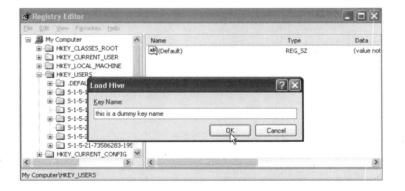

 If the wallpaper file does not reside on the local system, you must alter the path to point to a server share. If the wallpaper is not present in the folder specified, no wallpaper will show up.

8. After you complete your changes, select your dummy key name, unload it by choosing File ➢ Unload Hive, and click OK to save the changes. Again, you must highlight your dummy key name to unload the hive.

FIGURE 2.6   Enter the full path where the desired wallpaper is stored.

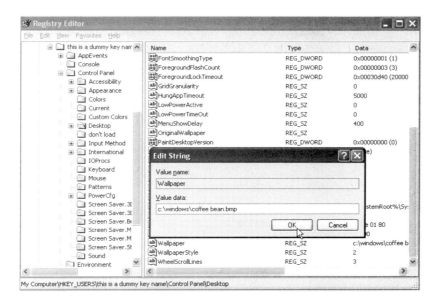

You can load the hive of any User Profile that is not currently logged on using the previously described method. This can be very useful in some situations, such as if you want to make a Registry hack as an admin on behalf of the user. Just remember to unload the hive or else you are blocking the profile.

Actually, you can also load hives from within a script (with REG.EXE). Jakob H. Heidelberg has a pretty cool article on this called "Efficient Registry Cleanup," which you can check out here: http://tinyurl.com/24dm5v.

Every time a new user generates a Local Profile, it pulls the settings from the Default Local Profile, which now has the coffee bean background picture. (Current users do not see the change because they already generated Local Profiles before the coffee bean picture was set in the default Local Profile.)

Test your changes by creating a new local user and logging on. Since this user has never logged on before, this should create a new User Profile from the default profile. See if the new user gets the coffee bean background for Windows XP and the water drop background for Windows Vista.

The Default Domain User Profile

The Default Domain User Profile is similar to the Default Local User Profile, except that it's centralized. Once a Default Domain User Profile is set up, new users logging onto workstations in the domain will automatically download the centralized Default Domain User Profile instead of using any individual Default Local User Profile. This can be a way to make default centralized settings, such as the background or Desktop shortcuts, available for anyone whenever they first log onto a machine.

> Don't create a Default Domain User Profile using Windows 2000, Windows XP, or Windows 2003 and expect your Windows NT clients to understand it. Remember: Windows NT is Type 0; Windows 2000, Windows XP, and Windows Server 2003 are Type 1; and Windows Vista and Windows Server 2008 are Type 2. Exchanging material between the types can be unpredictable.

For these examples, you'll need to create a new, mere-mortal user in the domain. In this example, we'll assume you created a user named Brett Wier.

Default Domain User Profiles for Type 1 Computers

It's easy to create a Default Domain User Profile for Type 1 computers. From any Type 1 computer, log on as Brett Wier and follow these steps:

1. Create a new, mere-mortal user in the domain. In this example, we'll create Brett Wier. From any workstation in your domain, log on as Brett.

2. Modify the Desktop as you wish. In this example, we'll use the Appearance tab in the Display Properties dialog box to change the color scheme to olive green. All you need to do is right-click the Desktop and select Properties. Then, select the Appearance tab. When you're done and back at the Desktop, create a text file, FILE1.txt.

3. Log off as Brett Wier.

4. Log back onto the workstation as the domain Administrator.

5. Click Start, and then right-click My Computer and choose Properties from the shortcut menu to open the System Properties dialog box.

6. Click the Advanced tab, and then click the Settings button in the User Profiles section to open the User Profiles dialog box.

7. Select bwier, as shown in Figure 2.7.

8. Click the Copy To button to open the Copy To dialog box, and in the "Copy profile to" field, enter the full path, plus the words **default user**, of the NETLOGON share of a Windows 2000 or Windows 2003 Domain Controller, as shown in Figure 2.8. In this example, it's \\dc01\netlogon\Default User. The Default User folder is automatically created.

9. Click the Change button in the Permitted to Use section, and change the default from the original user to Everyone, as shown in Figure 2.8. This lets everyone use the profile in the domain.

10. Click OK to actually copy the profile to the new folder and to close the Copy To dialog box.

11. Click OK to close the System Properties dialog box.

You can test your Default Domain Profile by creating a new user in the domain and logging onto any Windows XP or Windows 2000 machine. Verify that the Default Domain Profile is working by seeing if the olive green color scheme appears and that FILE1.TXT is present on the Desktop. Remember, you'll only see the magic for users who have no Local Profiles already on target machines.

FIGURE 2.7 Select Brett's entry in the User Profiles dialog box.

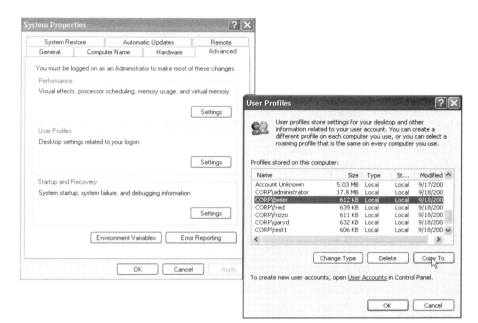

FIGURE 2.8 Copy the profile you just created to the NETLOGON share of a Domain Controller. Then, click Change to allow Everyone to use the profile.

Default Domain User Profiles for Type 2 Computers

For Windows Vista and Windows Server 2008, you can get the same control. But, here's the trick: remember how Windows XP (Type 1) and Windows Vista (Type 2) profiles are incompatible? Well, that's about to matter a whole lot, right here. To that end, we need to know a certain piece of Windows Vista magic. That is, Windows Vista will only read profile directories from the network if they end in a special moniker: .v2. That's right—the directory names must have a .v2 hanging off them for Windows Vista to read it. So, the steps we'll perform next will be almost like what we did for Windows XP earlier, except this time, we'll provide our name with the special `.v2` designation hanging off of it. Then, when users log onto Windows Vista machines for the first time, Windows Vista will recognize the special directory (Default User) with the extra-special `.v2` moniker and download the profile just for that operating system.

From any Type 2 computer, log on as Brett Wier and follow these steps:

1. Be sure you're logged into a Windows Vista machine as Brett.

2. Modify the Desktop as you wish. In this example, go ahead and simply plop a new text file on the Desktop: `vistafile1.txt` and put some fake data in it.

3. Log off as Brett Wier.

4. Log back onto the workstation as the domain Administrator.

5. Click Start, and then right-click Computer and choose Properties from the shortcut menu to open the System Properties dialog box.

6. Click the Advanced System Settings task, and then click the Settings button in the User Profiles section to open the User Profiles dialog box.

7. Select bwier, as shown previously in Figure 2.7. Note this figure shows Windows XP, but it should look similar in Windows Vista.

8. Click the Copy To button to open the Copy To dialog box, and in the "Copy profile to" field, enter the full path plus the default user of the `NETLOGON` share of a Windows 2000, Windows Server 2003, or Windows Server 2008 Domain Controller, as shown previously in Figure 2.8. In this example, it's `\\dc01\netlogon\Default User.v2`. Note that no quotes are needed, as seen in Figure 2.9. The `Default User.V2` folder is automatically created.

FIGURE 2.9   Be sure to put the .v2 extension in, because this is a Windows Vista (Type 2) profile.

9. Click the Change button in the Permitted to Use section, and change the default from the original user to Everyone, as shown previously in Figure 2.8.

    This lets everyone use the profile in the domain.

10. Click OK to actually copy the profile to the new folder and to close the Copy To dialog box.

11. Click OK to close the System Properties dialog box.

You can test your Default Domain Profile by creating a new user in the domain and logging onto any Windows Vista machine. Verify that the Windows Vista ".v2" Default Domain Profile is working by seeing if the VISTAFILE1.TXT is present on the Desktop.

Remember, you'll only see the magic for users who have no Local Profiles already on target Windows Vista machines. Also remember that Windows XP users will have their own Default User profiles, so this can get a little confusing.

Now that you're familiar with the files and folders that make up Local Profiles, you're ready to implement Roaming Profiles.

Roaming Profiles

Roaming Profiles are a logical extension to the Local Profiles concept. When users hop from machine to machine, the customized settings they created on one machine are automatically placed on and displayed at any machine they log onto.

For instance, you might have an organization in which 30 computers are at each site for general use by the sales team. If any member of the sales team comes into any office, they know they can log onto any machine and be confident that the settings from their last session are patiently waiting on the server.

Setting up Roaming Profiles for users in Active Directory is a straightforward process: share a folder to house the profiles, and then point each user's profile toward the single shared folder. By default, Roaming Profiles save a copy of the profile to the local hard drive. That way, if the network or server becomes unavailable, the user can use the last-used profile as a cached version. Additionally, if the user's Roaming Profile on the server is unavailable (and there is no locally cached copy of the Roaming Profile), the system downloads and uses a temporary Default User Profile as an emergency measure to get the user logged on with some profile.

As you'll see in the next chapter, another advantage associated with Roaming Profiles is that if a machine crashes, the most recent "set" of the user environment is on the server for quick restoration.

For those of you who threw up your hands and gave up using Roaming Profiles in Windows NT, I encourage you to try again with the newer operating systems.

From Windows 2000 onward, the Roaming Profile algorithm has been way improved since the NT 4 days. Specifically, there are three reasons why the improved algorithm is better than the old NT 4 counterpart:

Roaming Profiles Now Account for Multiple Logins   Most people had problems when a single user logged onto multiple machines at the same time. In NT 4, the profile was preserved only from the last computer the user logged off from—potentially losing important files in the profile. Modern Windows systems don't work that way. They do a file-by-file comparison of files *before* they get sent back to the server—sending only the latest time-stamped file to help quell this problem. So, give it another go if you despaired in the past.

However, one warning should be noted. All the user's settings are represented as one single file: NTUSER.DAT. Because the last writer wins, the NTUSER.DAT with the latest time stamp overwrites all others. If you make two independent changes to a setting on two different machines, you can lose one because only the NTUSER.DAT with the latest time stamp "wins."

Roaming Profiles Now Only Pull down and Push up Changed Files   NT 4 Roaming Profiles were on the slow side—especially over slow links. The good news about profiles from modern systems is that only new and changed files are specifically moved around the network. So, if someone logs onto the same machine over and over again, the user is not waiting for the whole gamut of profile files to be downloaded. Logging in is now faster than ever.

Better Terminal Services Support for Roaming Profiles   In Windows 2000, when the user logs off a session, the system tries 60 times—about once a second by default—to tidy up the NTUSER.DAT file and send it back to the server to be housed in the Roaming Profile. Usually, it only needs one try (and about one second) to do this task. This support has been increased since Windows 2000, so see the sidebar "A Brief History of the Unloading of NTUSER.DAT and UPHClean."

A Brief History of the Unloading of *NTUSER.DAT* and UPHClean

In Windows 2000, when a profile was ready to be unloaded, it simply waited for a little bit of time. If the handle was still not closed, Windows 2000 just gave up—nothing roamed and the hive was still (uh-oh) loaded. This caused profile corruption a-go-go. To that end, a policy setting named "Maximum Retries to Unload and Update User Profile" can tell Windows 2000 to increase the number of tries. Bad news: there's a bug in the policy setting description which makes it seem like this policy is meant to affect Windows Server 2003 and Windows XP machines. But it doesn't. It's just for Windows 2000 machines.

In Windows XP and Windows Server 2003, the same unloading process occurs but with a little work-around. The current Registry is saved into another file, and then at logoff, roams that file to the server's NTUSER.DAT. But the problem is that the real NTUSER.DAT file on the local machine is still loaded. If, after a while, the handle is closed, then the hive will be unloaded. But if the handle is *not* closed, and if user logs on again, the hive will continue to be used.

Uh-oh. Sounds like corruption city again, right?

In this case, Roaming Profiles will not be able to update this version of NTUSER.DAT even though the server's NTUSER.DAT might be newer. So, what's the solution?

Microsoft made a download available called "User Profile Hive Cleanup Service" (or UPH-Clean), to force the handle to be closed in just this situation. It solves this exact problem and is why it's suggested for Windows Server 2003 Terminal Services. You can locate the tool at http://tinyurl.com/5of5r.

In Vista (and Windows Server 2008), this "force unload" logic is already inside the profile service itself, so this simply won't be a problem anymore. Microsoft swears that it's a guarantee that the user hive will be unloaded and therefore roam it at logoff. It is doing the same thing as Windows XP and Windows Server 2003 UPHClean, but in a much better way.

Setting Up Roaming Profiles

The first thing we need to do on our server, DC01, is to create and share a folder in which to store our profiles. In this example, we'll choose a novel name: Profiles. Normally, you'd do this procedure on some file server somewhere, not on a Domain Controller. But we'll continue onward, because there's no harm here in our test lab. Again, I'll assume our server has two drives, C: and D:, and we'll perform these functions on our D: drive.

To create and share a folder in which to store Roaming Profiles, follow these steps:

1. Log onto DC01 as Administrator.

2. From the Desktop, click My Computer to open the My Computer folder.

3. Find a place to create a users folder. In this example, we'll use D:\PROFILES. After entering the D: drive, right-click and select New ➢ Folder. Name your new folder **Profiles**.

 You can substitute any name for Profiles. Additionally, you can hide the share name by placing a $ after the name, such as Profiles$.

4. Right-click the newly created Profiles folder, and choose "Share...", which opens the Properties of the folder, and is focused on the Sharing tab. Pull down the dropdown menu and select Everyone, and then click Add. Note that Windows Server 2003 and 2008 will default such that the share is Everyone:Read. Click "Share" and ensure that the share is set so that Everyone has Co-owner permissions, as seen in Figure 2.10. Keep the rest of the defaults, and click OK. (Note that Co-owner rights are almost the same as the "Full Control" rights of yore.)

Now you need to specify which network user accounts can use Roaming Profiles. In this example, you'll specify Brett Wier. Brett will now be able to hop from workstation to workstation. When he logs off one workstation, the changes in the profile will be preserved on the server. He can then log onto any other workstation in the domain and maintain the same user experience.

FIGURE 2.10   Share the Profiles folder such that Everyone has Co-owner permissions (in Server 2003). For Server 2003, utilize at least Change control.

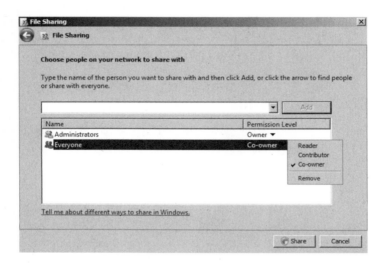

Caching and Roaming Profiles

Roaming Profiles are automatically cached with their own independent algorithm. In the second figure in this sidebar, you can see the Caching button, which controls caching on a share. We'll learn about offline files and caching in the next chapter. But, for now, we need to have a little side discussion about the Caching button.

Windows 2000 servers have caching turned off by default for all shares.

Windows 2003 severs have caching set up such that users can manually specify what files to keep offline.

A Windows XP machine tells you everything you need to know the first time you go to the event log when the default caching setting on a Windows Server 2003 is used in conjunction with a Roaming Profile share.

Windows XP explains that "…Offline Caching must be disabled on shares where roaming user profiles are stored." To do that, click the Caching button within the Profiles share and select "Files or programs from the share will not be available offline" as seen here for Windows Server 2008.

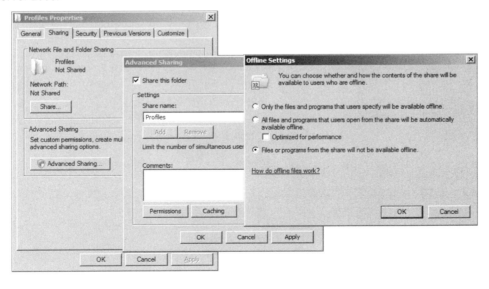

> When you do, you'll see Windows XP and Windows Vista stop complaining. (Windows XP and Windows Vista complain with the same Event ID.)
>
> For more information on this phenomenon, see the Knowledge Base article Q287566, "Offline File Caching Option Must Be Disabled on Roaming Profile." (For more on the Caching button, see Chapter 3.) Additionally, do not use the Encrypting File System (EFS) on shares containing Roaming Profiles. If you do so, roaming will not work.

To modify accounts to use Roaming Profiles, you'll leverage Active Directory Users and Computers as follows:

1. Choose Start ➤ All Programs ➤ Administrative Tools ➤ Active Directory Users and Computers.

2. Expand Corp.com in the tree pane, and double-click Brett Wier's account to open the Brett Wier Properties dialog box; click his Profile tab.

3. In the Profile Path field, specify the server, the share name, and folder you want to use, such as **\\Dc01\profiles**%*username*%. After you enter that, click OK. Then, just as a quick test, go back into the user account and look again at the Profile tab. When you do, you should see the username automatically filled in, as seen in Figure 2.11. For our purposes, you can leave all other fields blank.

> The syntax of *%username%* is the secret sauce that allows the system to automatically create a Roaming Profiles folder underneath the share. The *%username%* variable is evaluated at first use, and Windows springs into action and creates the profile. Windows is smart too—it sets up the permissions on the folder with only the required NTFS permissions, such that only the user has access to read and modify the contents of the profile. If you want administrators to have access along with the user, see the information in the "Add the Administrators Security Group to Roaming User Profiles" section later in this chapter.

4. Click OK.

FIGURE 2.11   Point the user's profile path settings at the server and share name.

Real World Scenario

Modifying Multiple Users' Profile Paths

After you set up Roaming Profiles and get comfortable with their use, you'll likely want the rest of your users to start using Roaming Profiles as well. The Windows Server 2003/2008 Active Directory Users and Computers tool allows you to modify the profile paths of multiple users simultaneously. To do so, follow these steps:

1. Select the users (hold down Ctrl to select discontiguous users).

2. Right-click the selection, and choose Properties from the shortcut menu to open the "Properties for Multiple Items" (previously called "Properties On Multiple Objects") dialog box:

3. Click the Profile tab, if necessary.

4. Click the Profile path check box, and enter the path.

5. Click OK to give all the selected users the same path, making sure you use the *%username%* convention in the path you specify.

If you're running Windows 2000 (or just want to put on your coding hat), you can use the following sample VBScript code to run though all the users in the domain Corp.com in the Phoenix OU and change their profile path so that they have access only to their own profile folder. Upon first use by the user, the folder is automatically created, and the user is granted exclusive access to that folder.

```
Set UserContainer = getobject("LDAP://ou=Phoenix,dc=Corp,dc=com")
UserContainer.filter = array("User")
```

```
for each User in UserContainer
    Username = User.SamAccountName
    Userprofilepath = "\\Profile_server\Profiles\" & Username

    Wscript.Echo User.ProfilePath

    If User.ProfilePath = "" Then
        User.Put "ProfilePath" , UserProfilePath
        User.Setinfo
        Wscript.Echo "Profile for user " & Username & " has been set to " &
UserProfilePath & "."
    Else
        Wscript.Echo "Profile for user " & Username & " was already set to " &
UserProfilePath & "."
    End if

next
```

Testing Roaming Profiles

You can easily test Roaming Profiles if you have multiple workstation machines. I suggest you log on as Brett from both a Windows XP machine (Type 1) and a Windows Vista machine (Type 2). Make sure these workstations are members in your domain.

Roaming from Windows XP to Windows XP

Log on first to the Windows XP machine. Then, make two simple changes to the profile for testing:

1. In the My Documents folder, create XPFILE1.TXT and save some dummy data inside.
2. Change the color scheme to something different—like silver.
3. Log off as Brett Wier.
4. Log onto another workstation as Brett Wier and make sure that FILE1.TXT was properly sent to the second machine and that the background has changed.

Right-click the XPFILE1.TXT and choose Properties from the shortcut menu to see the file's properties. Take note of the path where the file is actually residing. You can compare that file's location now (the local hard drive) with the file's location after the next chapter is completed. Hopefully, by the time the next chapter is completed, the file will be magically transported to the server, and the display will demonstrate this.

Roaming from Windows Vista to Windows Vista

Now, log on as Brett to a Windows Vista machine. Then, make two simple changes to the profile for testing:

1. In the My Documents folder, create VISTAFILE1.TXT and save some dummy data inside.

2. Change the color scheme to something different—like "Windows Classic."

3. Log off as Brett Wier.

4. Log onto another Windows Vista workstation as Brett Wier and make sure that VISTAFILE1.TXT was properly sent to the second machine and that the background has changed.

Right-click the VISTAFILE1.TXT and choose Properties from the shortcut menu to see the file's properties. Take note of the path where the file is actually residing. You can compare that file's location now (the local hard drive) with the file's location after the next chapter is completed. Hopefully, by the time you perform all the exercises in the next chapter, the file will be magically transported to the server and the display will demonstrate this.

Additionally, notice how XPFILE1.txt, the file created on the Windows XP machine is not present. Again, this is because Windows Vista (Type 2 profiles) and Windows XP (Type 1 profiles) don't intermingle.

Back on the Server

If you check out what's transpired on the server, two unique directories are created for Brett, one for each type of computer he logs onto (Type 1 and Type 2), as seen in Figure 2.12.

Additionally, note that even if you're an administrator, you cannot dive into Brett's profile folders. An example of this failure can be seen in Figure 2.13. This is a safety mechanism that gives Brett exclusive permissions over his personal sensitive stuff. If you want administrators to have access along with the user, see the information in the "Add the Administrators Security Group to Roaming User Profiles" later in this chapter.

FIGURE 2.12 On the server, a folder for each computer type has been generated.

FIGURE 2.13 Administrators cannot poke around User Profiles (by default).

Upshot of Roaming Profiles in a Mixed Windows Vista and Windows XP World

It's bad news for mixed environments. Logging onto Windows XP and then to Windows Vista (or vice versa) does not "share" information in any way.

As we saw, XPFILE1.txt was created (and available) only in the Windows XP profile. And VISTAFILE1.TXT was created (and available) only in the Windows Vista profile. So, Windows XP and Windows Vista profile data can never be shared.

What a bummer (on the surface at least). But don't worry; we'll overcome it.

To that end, if we want a "one stop shop" place for our documents, Start Menu icons, and more, we'll have to leverage the Folder Redirection mechanism in the next chapter. Not to get too far ahead of ourselves, but Folder Redirection's goal is to make various items (like the Documents of Windows Vista and the My Documents of Windows XP) point to the *same place* on a network share. That way, regardless of the kind of machine you log in with (Windows XP or Windows Vista), your data will *always* be available.

So, stay tuned for that in the next chapter.

The Impact of Users Latching onto *Documents/My Documents*

Because Documents (for Vista) and My Documents (pre-Vista) is part of the profile, there is the extra burden of lugging all the files in My Documents back and forth across the network each time a user logs on. This can have serious ramifications. Once users start using the My Documents folder, they generally don't want to stop. They place 50MB worth of PowerPoint files, 50MB of Word documents, and 50MB of Visio files in My Documents and then roam to another workstation, and they've just moved 150MB of data across the network at logon time! Ouch!

In any case, this pain can fortunately be mitigated in two ways. Windows 2000 and newer clients handle Roaming Profiles differently than their Windows NT cousin does.

Let's imagine that we have two users: one on Windows NT and another on Windows 2000, Windows XP, Windows Vista, or Windows Server 2003/2008. Each user puts 300MB of files into the Roaming Profile. When a user on Windows NT does this, all files in the profile are copied up to the server—lock, stock, and barrel—up to the server and then back over to the target workstation every time a user logs on or off. Can you say "painful"?

Windows 2000 and newer clients transfer *only* changed files up and back between the client and server. Thus, if a user transfers 60MB of data and then changes one file, only that file is sent back to be saved in the Roaming Profile. This feature is great news if a user uses the same machine day in and day out; only the changes are pushed up and back. But the usefulness of this feature breaks down any time a user roams to a computer they have never used before. In this case, the entire contents of the Roaming Profile (including Documents/My Documents) is brought down from the server.

That's why the real power comes with a key feature, Redirected Folders, which we'll explore in the next chapter.

Migrating Local Profiles to Roaming Profiles

In some situations, you might already have lots of machines with Local Profiles. That is, you didn't start off your network using Roaming Profiles, and now you have either many machines with Local Profiles or just pockets of machines with a combination of Roaming Profiles and Local Profiles. You can, if you want, maintain the user's Local Profile settings and transfer them to the spot on the server you set up earlier. You can convert a Local Profile to a Roaming Profile in two ways. Whichever option you choose, you first need to set up a share on a server.

Automatic Upload of Existing Local Profiles

In general, this step couldn't be easier. As we did earlier, on each user's Profile tab, point the profile path to \\servername\share\%*username*%, as seen earlier in Figure 2.11. The next time the user logs onto a machine with a Local Profile (and then logs off), the Local Profile is automatically uploaded to the server to become their future Roaming Profile. For most users, this is the way to go.

And, remember, profiles are zapped up to their source on the server independently. If a user has used both a Windows XP and Windows Vista machine in the past, and then travels back to these Desktops, then each computer's profile is zapped up into their own directory. Those directories can be seen in Figure 2.12, shown earlier.

But, what if the same filename exists, say, on the Desktop on three machines the user has logged onto in the past? The system will automatically figure out which is the last-written file based on the file date. And that file will end up being the only copy placed in the directory. In other words, you won't see three files with the same name in the profile directory—even if it exists on three local machines.

Manual Upload of Existing Local Profiles

If the user has logged onto multiple workstations and therefore has multiple Local Profiles, you might want to guarantee that one specific Local Profile becomes the Roaming Profile for that user. The procedure is nearly identical to the one you used to create the Default Domain User Profile. To preserve a specific Local Profile and convert it to a Roaming Profile, follow these steps:

1. Log on as the Administrator to the workstation where the desired Local Profile resides.

2. Choose Start, right-click My Computer (for Windows XP) or Computer (for Windows Vista), and choose Properties from the shortcut menu to open the System Properties dialog box.

3. For Windows XP, click the Advanced tab, or for Windows Vista, click "Advanced system settings."

4. Then in the User Profiles section, click Settings to open the User Profiles dialog box.

5. Select the Local Profile you want to convert to a Roaming Profile, and then click the Copy To button to open the Copy To dialog box, as shown in Figure 2.14.

6. Enter the server name, shared folder name, and folder name of the profile storage path. In Figure 2.14, this is the path for a Type 1 computer (like Windows XP). If this were a Windows Vista machine, you would have to type **.v2** at the end, like \\dc01\profiles\jkissel.v2, as shown in Figure 2.15.

7. Also, be sure to change the profile so that at least the user has access. It's generally okay to modify the profile permissions to Everyone.

8. Click OK.

When you do, the user's folder is automatically created in the shared folder.

FIGURE 2.14   In Windows XP, to move a specific profile to the server, use the Copy To dialog box.

FIGURE 2.15   If you want to push up a Windows Vista profile, you need to add a ".v2" at the end, as seen here.

Changing the Profile Type from Roaming to Local

Mere-mortal users (those without administrative privileges) can go to the User Profiles dialog (as seen earlier in Figure 2.7), choose their own profile, then change the profile type with the Change Type button. This will change their profile from Roaming to Local or back again and thus specify which copy of the profile (Local or Roaming) is to be used when they log on.

If a user selects Local Profile, a Roaming Profile reverts to a Local Profile. The Roaming Profile on the server stays there, but the user doesn't use it when working at this local machine. The next time the user works at this specific workstation, the changes are only saved to the Local Profile.

If the user selects Roaming Profile, and the Roaming Profile is on the server, the system determines which copy is newer. If the local copy is newer, the user is asked whether to keep or ditch the profile on the server.

Also, don't forget that for each specific user Local Profile you manually convert to a Roaming Profile, you'll need to modify the profile path (similar to that seen in Figure 2.11 earlier). Once you've done this, this user, Jimmy Kissel can now logon to any Windows 2000 or Windows XP machine as jkissel, and this specific profile (that you just pushed up) will follow him as a Roaming Profile.

Roaming and Nonroaming Folders

Oftentimes, you'll want to get a handle on specifically what, inside the Roaming Profile, is roaming and what isn't roaming. Things are different for Windows Vista and Windows Server 2008 (Type 2 computers) and Windows 2000, XP, and Windows Server 2003 (Type 1 computers). Let's check out those differences here.

Roaming and Nonroaming Folders for Type 1 Computers

Now that you have a grip on which folders constitute the profile and how to set up a Roaming Profile, it might be helpful to know a bit about what's going on behind the scenes. Remember that several folders make up our profile.

Type 1 Profile Directories That Do Not Roam

Local settings, including local machine-specific application folders and information, do not roam when Roaming Profiles are enabled. This is true for the local computer's `Application Data`. Some applications write information specific to the local computer here. The Application Data folder is located in `\Documents and Settings\`*`<Username>`*`\Local Settings`. Any subfolder below this folder also does not roam, including:

- `History`
- `Temp`
- `Temporary Internet Files`

Type 1 Profile Directories That Do Roam

All other folders do roam with the user.

There's an `Application Data` directory that does roam with the user. This `Application Data` folder is located in `Documents and Settings\`*`<Username>`*. This is typically a per-user store for application data, such as `Office 2000/Windows XP/2003 Custom Dictionary`. These are the kinds of things you would want to roam with the user.

- `Cookies`
- `Desktop`
- `Favorites`
- `My Documents`
- `My Pictures`
- `NetHood`
- `PrintHood`

- Recent
- Send To
- Start Menu
- Templates

Indeed, My Documents, My Pictures, Desktop, Start Menu, and Application Data have an additional property; they can each be redirected to a specific point on the server, as you'll see in the next chapter.

Roaming and Nonroaming Folders for Type 2 Computers

If we crack open a Windows Vista Roaming Profile, we can see some things are similar and some things are different compared to a Type 1 profile.

Figure 2.16 shows what the profiles look like when viewed from a pre-Vista machine. Note how the "My" prefix magically appears when viewed here, even though under the hood there is no "My" prefix. You can see this in Figure 2.17 when viewed directly from a Windows Vista machine.

 In order to see the contents in Figure 2.16, you need to be logged in as Brett Wier, or take ownership of the directory as the Administrator.

Let's get a grip on which directories roam and which don't roam.

FIGURE 2.16 Some of the contents of a Type 2 computer are similar to a Type 1 computer. Note that when viewed on a pre-Vista machine, Type 2 profiles have the "My" prefix due to viewing them within a pre-Vista machine's Explorer.

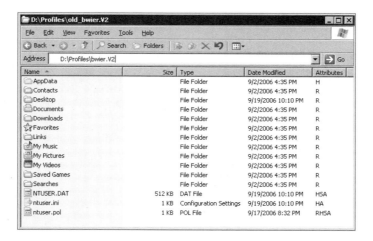

FIGURE 2.17 The same folder, when viewed directly from the command line. Note the absence of the "My" prefix for Music, Pictures, and Videos.

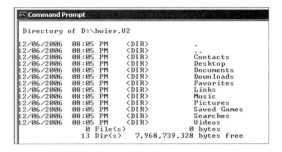

Type 2 Profile Directories That Do Not Roam

Local settings, including local machine-specific application folders and information, do not roam, even when Roaming Profiles are enabled. The nonroaming directories will stay on each local computer in the \Users\<Username>\AppData\ directory. Inside \AppData are two directories which contain this nonroaming data: Local and LocalLow.

Any subfolders within Local or LocalLow do not roam, including:

- History
- Temp
- Temporary Internet Files

 See the sidebar entitled "The *LocalLow* Folder within *AppData*" for more information about LocalLow.

Type 2 Profile Directories that Roam

All other folders do roam with the user. When a Roaming Profile is enabled, these directories are shot up to the server and stored within a user's own private directory with their <username>.v2:

- Contacts (new for Windows Vista)
- Desktop
- Favorites
- Documents (was My Documents in Windows XP)
- Pictures (in Windows XP this was under My Documents and now, in Windows Vista, it's at the root of the profile).
- Music (in Windows XP this was under My Documents and now, in Windows Vista, it's at the root of the profile).
- Videos (new for Windows Vista)

- Under \Appdata\Roaming\Microsoft you will find:

  - Credentials

  - Crypto

  - Internet Explorer

  - Protect

  - SystemCertificates

Of course, your users will need their day-to-day goodies as they roam from machine to machine. This is known as Per-User Application Data. This stuff is stored within the Roaming Profile's \Appdata\Roaming\Microsoft\Windows directory. Here, you'll see lots of stuff you know and love, including the following Desktop attributes, as seen in Figure 2.18:

- Network Shortcuts

- Printer Shortcuts

- Recent

- SendTo

- Start Menu

- Templates

- Themes

- Cookies (hidden for some reason)

FIGURE 2.18 The AppData\Roaming directory in the Type 2 computer contains the only directories that will roam with the user.

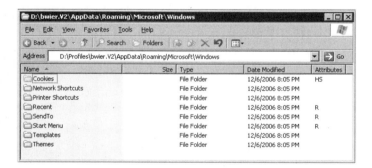

Managing Roaming Profiles

We've just been through how to set up and use Roaming Profiles. But don't leave home without these parting words about managing them day to day.

Additional System Profiles for Windows XP, Windows 2003, Windows Vista, and Windows Server 2008 (but Not Windows 2000)

Windows XP, Windows 2003, Windows Vista, and Windows Server 2008 contain two profiles that are meant to be used by newly installed services: Local Service and Network Service.

Local Service   Meant to be used by services that are local to the computer but do not need intricate local privileges or network access. This is in contrast to the System account, which pretty much has total authority over the system. If a service runs as Local Service, it appears to be a member in the local users group. When a service runs as Local Service across the network, the service appears as an anonymous user.

Network Service   Similar to Local Service but has elevated network access rights—similar to the System account. When a process runs under Network Service rights, it does so as the SID (Security ID) assigned to the computer (which in an Active Directory environment is a member of Domain Computers, and therefore also a member of Authenticated Users).

Windows XP, Windows 2003, Windows Vista, and Windows Server 2008 automatically create these profiles, which are basically normal but still a little special. For instance, you will not see the Local Service or Network Service in the listing of Profiles in the System Properties dialog box. You can see them in the Documents and Settings folder; however, they're "super-hidden" so that mere-mortals cannot see them by default. You can see them in the top window here:

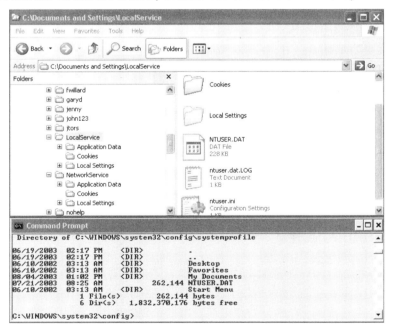

On Windows Vista and Windows Server 2008, the Local Service and Network Service profiles have moved to the %windir%\ServiceProfiles directory. Windows can also load software, services, and its own profile when the computer starts up. Indeed, you see this profile in the "Log on to Windows" dialog box, in which you are prompted to press Ctrl+Alt+Del. Basically, this is the profile for when no one is logged on.

When this happens, Windows loads what is called the .DEFAULT (pronounced "dot default") profile. In Windows 2000, the .DEFAULT profile was in c:\winnt\%computername%, in which %computername% is the name of the computer. But applications sometimes flipped out if services tried to load portions of this part of the profile's Registry. To adjust for this, Windows XP, Windows 2003, Windows Vista, and Windows Server 2008 plunked the .DEFAULT profile in c:\windows\system32\config\SystemProfile. Applications that leverage the .DEFAULT profile always use this Registry part, and troublesome application problems related to .DEFAULT should be quelled.

You can see the System Profile in the command prompt window in the lower half of the preceding graphic.

Merging Local Profile and Roaming Profile

Once a Roaming Profile is established, users can hop from machine to machine confident that they'll get the same settings. However, if a user with a Roaming Profile hops to a Windows XP machine on which they once had a Local Profile, something special happens: the previous Local Profile and the existing Roaming Profile are merged (except for the NTUSER.DAT settings). This data is then saved to the Roaming Profile folder on the server at logoff time.

This is helpful should a user have just the one copy of a critical document stored in the My Documents folder of XPPRO2. The next time he logs onto XPPRO2, that missing document will appear in his My Documents in his Roaming Profile. Oh, and you don't have to worry about overwriting existing files in the profile either; the latest time-stamped file is preserved.

Ditto for a Windows Vista machine and its profile. Just remember that these profiles are considered separate (because they are).

You can prevent this behavior on Windows XP and Windows Vista machines. For information on how to do this, see the "Prevent Roaming Profile Changes from Propagating to the Server" section later in this chapter.

Guest Account Profile

Who uses the Guest account anymore? Apparently someone, because Microsoft has slightly changed the behavior of the Guest account in Windows XP and onward. That is, the profile of a guest user is deleted at logoff—but only when the computer is joined to a domain. If the Windows XP or Windows 2003 machine is in a workgroup, no guest profiles (of users in the Guests group) are deleted at logoff.

If the Windows XP (and onward) computer is in a domain, and a user is a member of both the Guests and the Local Administrators group, the profile is not deleted—quite an unlikely scenario.

Cross-Forest Trusts

Roaming Profiles, like GPOs, are affected by Cross-Forest Trusts. Whether a user gets a Roaming Profile depends on the client operating system they're logged onto. (This operating-specific variance is documented in Chapter 3.) When clients log onto computers that enforce the rule, you'll get the message shown in Figure 2.19.

You can use a policy setting to prevent this from affecting your client computers. To do this, locate the **Allow Cross-Forest User Policy and Roaming User Profiles** policy setting by drilling down in Computer Configuration ➢ Policies ➢ Administrative Templates ➢ System ➢ Group Policy.

FIGURE 2.19   Users roaming within Cross-Forest scenarios receive this message.

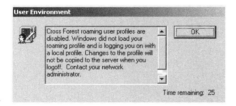

Manipulating Roaming Profiles with Computer Group Policy Settings

Roaming Profiles are simple to set up and maintain, but sometimes you'll want to use certain policy settings to affect their behavior. The policies you'll be setting appear in the Computer Configuration section of Group Policy. Drill down into Policies ➢ Administrative Templates ➢ System ➢ User Profiles, as shown in Figure 2.20. In Windows 2000, these User Profiles policies were not located under their own branch but in Administrative Templates ➢ System ➢ Logon.

Recall that computers must be in the OU that the GPO affects (or in a child OU that inherits the setting). Or the GPO could be linked to the root of the domain and scoped to a security group that the computer is a member of.

If a user is moved to a new OU then the user needs to log off and back on. If a machine is moved to a new OU then the machine needs to reboot.

Before implementing any policy setting that affects Roaming Profiles, read through this section and determine if it adds value to your environment. Then, create a test OU and ensure that the behavior is as expected.

FIGURE 2.20   There are many policy settings that affect profiles.

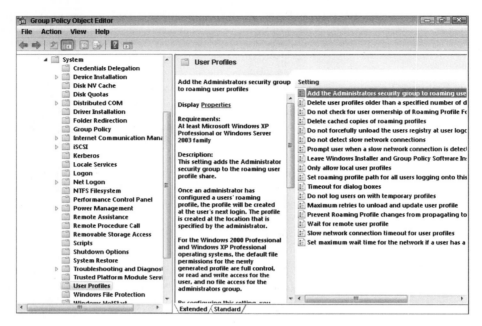

Do Not Check for User Ownership of Roaming Profile Folders

This policy setting applies only to Windows 2003 computers, Windows XP (SP1 and later) computers, Windows 2000/SP4 computers, Windows Vista computers, and Windows Server 2008 computers. Windows XP without a service pack and Windows 2000 with SP3 and earlier may have a potential security hole. If someone, such as a person in the Server Operators group, creates the user's target profile subfolder on the server, that creator is also the owner of the subfolder. When the user then pushes up their profile to the subfolder, the user isn't the only one with access to the profile; the creator/owner also has access. This could mean that the creator/owner can peer inside and get stuff they really shouldn't have.

If a client logs onto a Windows 2003, Windows XP (SP1 and later), Windows 2000/SP4 computer, Windows Vista, or Windows Server 2008, the machine is smart enough to first check to see if the user is the only one with permissions on the folder (as seen earlier in Figure 2.13) before moving sensitive profile data up. If you enable this policy setting, you're telling newer machines to act like older machines and allow sensitive profile information to move up to the server, even if the user doesn't have exclusive access and ownership to the subfolder. Personally, I would leave this unconfigured. (You can read more about this in the Knowledge Base article 327259.)

Delete Cached Copies of Roaming Profiles

This is a space-saving and security mechanism that automatically deletes the user's locally cached profile when the user logs off. The default behavior is to allow files to be downloaded and pile up on each and every hard drive to which the user roams. You can enable this policy setting to (as the forest rangers say) "Leave only footprints and take away only memories at your campsite." Heck, you won't even be leaving any footprints.

This policy setting has two downsides, however; let's walk through two scenarios to examine these potential problems. And, we'll look at one really good use for this setting.

Problem Scenario 1: Server Down at Login Time   This policy setting is set to delete cached copies of Roaming Profiles. The user logs on, makes some changes, and logs off. The profile is automatically sent back to the server, and the footprints are washed away on the local machine.

Now, let's say that the server that houses the Roaming Profiles goes down. By default, if the user tries to log on and the server is unavailable to deliver the Roaming Profile, the locally cached copy of the profile is summoned to take its place. Once you enable this policy setting, you're severing a potential lifeline to the user if the server that houses the Roaming Profile becomes unavailable. Enabling this policy setting sweeps up after the user on the local machine at logoff. If the server goes down, the user will not get their locally cached version of the Roaming Profile because there is no locally cached version of the profile. Rather, the only profile the user will get is a temporary Local Profile that is not saved anywhere when the user logs off.

Problem Scenario 2: Up and Back and Up and Back   Again, by setting this policy setting, you're deleting all cached files. So, when the user logs back onto the same machine, all the Roaming Profile files need to get redownloaded from the Roaming Profile on the server, which means you're killing the caching inherent in the Roaming Profile system. In essence, you're making your machine act like NT 4, where the whole profile gets redownloaded at login. Note, however, that at logoff time, things should still be faster than NT 4 because you're pushing up only changes (where NT 4 would have pushed up *all* the files).

Using This Setting in a High-Security Environment   This policy setting is useful in high-security environments where you need to make sure that no trace of potentially sensitive data in the profile is left behind. Be careful when using it with laptops, however, because users frequently need to use their copy of the locally cached version of the profile to get their work done. Additionally, enabling this policy setting does not prevent third-party tools from "resurrecting" deleted files inside the profile. It deletes the files but doesn't obliterate them to prevent industrious hackers from any possible recovery.

Once this policy setting is Enabled, the profile is erased only on logoff. And then it erases only profiles from machines on which users don't already have an existing cached copy! If you need to maintain a high-security environment, be sure to enable this policy setting early so that users don't have time to roam from machine to machine sprinkling copies of their profiles around (which won't get erased later by use of this policy setting).

To use this policy setting, you'll need to disable (or not configure) the **Do not detect slow network connection** policy setting, as described shortly. If a network connection is determined to be slow, it automatically tries to grab the locally cached copy of the profile, which doesn't exist if you've enabled this **Delete cached copies of roaming profiles** policy setting.

Delete User Profiles Older Than a Specified Number of Days

This policy setting applies only to Windows Vista computers (and Windows 2008 Servers). What happens when Sally User logs onto a Vista machine on the 4th floor—one time? All her profile junk gets downloaded on that machine and sits there—forever. Just eating up disk space, never to be reclaimed again. Until now.

If you set this policy setting and specify a certain number of days, the Roaming (and Local) Profiles on that Vista machine will be wiped clean—automatically. The user doesn't have to do anything. The system will automatically flush them down the, er, wherever it flushes them.

Here's a huge warning: Be careful with this setting. Any data that is, say, only in a Local Profile (like the `Documents` folder) will be gone once the profile is wiped clean. Note that the data stored in the server-side copy of a Roaming Profile, and also any data redirected using redirected folders, is not touched. See Figures 2.21 and 2.22 to see a before and after picture of how drastic profile cleanup really is!

FIGURE 2.21   A typical Vista computer after multiple users have logged onto it over time.

Slow Network Connection Timeout for User Profiles

Enabling this entry performs a quick ping test to the profiles server. If the speed is greater than the minimum value, the Roaming Profile is downloaded. If, however, the speed is not fast enough, the locally cached profile is used unless you've enabled the previous entry (**Delete cached copy of local profiles**). In that case, the user ends up with a temporary profile as described earlier.

 Setting the **Do not detect slow network connection** policy setting, as described in the next section, forces anything set in this policy setting to be ignored.

FIGURE 2.22   The same Vista computer after this policy kicks in within 24 hours. Note even local User Profiles are gone.

This policy setting has two modes, which it uses automatically: IP and non-IP. If the computer housing the profiles is connected to a network using IP, the speed is measured in kilobits (Kb) per second. If the computer housing the profiles is not connected using IP, the speed is measured in milliseconds (ms).

This policy setting is a bit strange: even if it's not configured, it has a default. That default speed threshold for IP mode is 500KB; that is, if the ping test determines that the bandwidth to the machine that houses the profiles is greater than 500KB, the profile is downloaded. If the ping returns a bandwidth of less than 500KB, the Roaming Profile is skipped, and the locally cached profile is used.

That default speed threshold for non-IP mode is 120ms; that is, if a machine that houses the profiles responds in less than 120ms, the profile is downloaded. If the machine that houses the profiles does not respond to the test in 120ms, the profile is skipped, and the locally cached profile is used.

You might want to enable this policy setting and decrease the value thresholds if you want to increase the chances of a dial-up connection receiving the Roaming Profile instead of the locally cached profile. If you enable this policy setting, you'll need to manually specify both an IP ping time test and a non-IP ping millisecond test.

Unrelated speed tests can verify the ability to apply GPOs for both the user and computer. They are in the Group Policy Editor under Computer or User Configuration ➢ Administrative Templates ➢ Policies ➢ System ➢ Group Policy ➢ **Group Policy Slow Link Detection**.

Do Not Detect Slow Network Connections

Like the previous policy setting, this one is a little strange. If it's not configured, it still has a default; that is, the users affected by this policy setting check the **Slow network connection timeout for user profiles** setting to see what a "slow network" actually means. If you enable this policy setting, you're disabling slow network detection, and the values you place in the **Slow network connection timeout for user profiles** policy setting don't mean diddly, nor do the default values of 500KB or 120ms.

Wait for Remote User Profile

Again, even if this policy setting is not defined or disabled, there is still a default; if the speed is too slow, it will load the locally cached profile. If you enable this policy setting, the system waits until the Roaming Profile is downloaded—no matter how long it takes. You might turn this on if your users hop around a lot and the connection to the computer housing the Roaming Profiles is slow but not intolerable. That way, you'll still use the Roaming Profile stored on the server as opposed to the locally cached profile.

Prompt User When a Slow Network Connection Is Detected (Was Named "Prompt User When Slow Link Is Detected")

When the ping test determines that the link speed is too slow, the user can be asked if they want to use the locally cached profile or grab the one from the server. If this policy setting is not configured or it's disabled, the user isn't even asked the question. If the **Wait for remote user profile** policy setting is enabled, the profile is downloaded from the server—however slowly.

For pre-Vista machines, if this policy setting is enabled, the user can determine whether they want to accept the profile from the server or utilize the locally cached profile.

For Windows Vista machines, if this policy setting is enabled, the user must determine before logon time (by using a check box at logon time) to use the local or remote profile, as seen in Figure 2.23.

If this setting is not configured or disabled, the system always uses the Local Profile instead of the Remote Profile when the link is slow.

If you've enabled the **Delete cached copies of roaming profiles** policy setting, there won't be a local copy of the Roaming Profile, so the user will be forced to accept the Default User Profile. If the **Do not detect slow network connection properties** policy setting is enabled, this GPO is ignored.

FIGURE 2.23   You can specify to allow users to download their profile over a slow network connection before they actually log on using Windows Vista.

Timeout for Dialog Boxes

This setting only applies to Windows 2000, Windows XP, and Windows Server 2003 clients (not Windows Vista or Windows Server 2008). If the **Prompt user when slow link is detected** policy setting is enabled, the user has a 30-second countdown to respond to whether they want to download their Roaming Profile anyway. Once this policy setting is enabled, the default value of 30 seconds can be changed. This dialog box timeout is also presented when the server that houses the Roaming Profile is unavailable, when the user logs off, or when the locally cached profile is newer than the Roaming Profile stored on the server. In all cases, the user can be prompted to determine what to do. The value you specify here is how many seconds to wait for an answer before the other policy settings make the decision for the user.

Do Not Log Users on with Temporary Profiles (Was Named "Log Users Off When Roaming Profile Fails")

This is the harshest sentence you can offer the user if things go wrong. By default, if the server is down (or the profile is corrupted), the user first tries to load a locally cached profile. If there is no locally cached profile, the system creates a TEMP profile from the Default User Profile.

However, if you choose to enable the setting, the behavior changes. If no Roaming Profile or locally cached profile is available (presumably because you've enabled the **Delete cached copies of roaming profile** policy setting), the user is not permitted to log on.

Maximum Retries to Unload and Update User Profile

As previously discussed, this policy setting is meant to assist Windows 2000 Terminal Services when trying to log users off and release their Roaming Profiles. Increase this value to increase the number of attempts made at unloading the pertinent Registry information, and update the profile when users start to complain that things aren't the same as when the last logged off (especially on Terminal Services). The current Explain text states that this policy is valid for Windows 2000, Windows XP, and Windows 2003 machines only. But it's not. Repeat after me: It does nothing for Windows XP or Windows Server 2003. Or Windows Vista or Windows Server 2008 machines for that matter. It's a Windows 2000–only policy setting.

Add the Administrators Security Group to Roaming User Profiles

As you saw in Figure 2.13 earlier in this chapter, only the user can dive in and poke around their personal User Profile. However, you can specify that the administrator and the user have joint access to the folder.

Oddly, this policy setting is found under the computer side of the house—not the user. Therefore, it's somewhat difficult to implement this policy setting on a small scale, because it's sometimes a mystery as to which client machine users will log onto. If you want to use this policy setting, I recommend creating a GPO with this policy setting at the domain level to guarantee that any client computers that users log onto will be affected. Setting this policy setting such that it affects the file server housing the profiles doesn't do anything for you. It's the target client computers that need to get this policy setting.

This policy setting *only* takes effect when new users first log onto affected client computers. Once they're on, they'll make some changes that affect the profile, and then log off. When they log off, a signal is sent back to the directory housing the profile, which then finalizes the security on the directory so that both the user and the administrator can both plunk around in there.

To be especially clear, as I implied, this policy setting works only for new users—that is, those users who don't already have a Roaming Profile. Users who *already* have established Roaming Profiles are essentially left in the dark with regard to using this; but there is a ray of light. If you want the same effect, you can take ownership of a profile and manually establish administrative access for the administrator and the user, as described in the upcoming section "Mandatory Profiles from an Established Roaming Profile."

This policy setting works with Windows 2000's Service Pack 2 and later, although the policy setting's Explain text states that it's applicable to Windows XP and Windows 2003 and higher. Additionally, the policy is supported on Vista and Windows Server 2008.

Prevent Roaming Profile Changes from Propagating to the Server

As previously discussed, when a user jumps from machine to machine and lands on one with an existing Local Profile, the system merges the Local Profile as a favor to the user. The idea is that if this Local Profile has a data file, say, RESUME.DOC, that's missing in the user's Roaming Profile, this is a perfect time to scoop it up and keep it in the Roaming Profile. You can dictate specific machines for which you don't want this to happen.

In general, you set this policy setting only on computers that you are sure you don't want the merge between Local Profiles and Roaming Profiles—perhaps because the Local Profiles contain many unneeded files. With the policy enabled, changes made to the profile are lost because the Roaming Profile is downloaded from the server logoff and not merged with the Local Profile.

In case you missed it, this policy setting makes the profile work like a Mandatory Profile, so don't save anything valuable in the profile, because it is going to be lost!

This policy setting affects Windows XP, Windows 2003, Windows Vista, and Windows Server 2008 machines (even though Windows Vista isn't listed in the requirements). Windows 2000 machines cannot be affected by this policy setting (and hence, will always merge, regardless if this policy setting is Enabled or not).

Only Allow Local User Profiles

This policy setting is useful when you have set up specialty machines, such as lab machines, library machines, kiosk machines, and so on. By setting this policy setting on the machines, you can ensure that a user's Roaming Profile doesn't "get in the mix" for what you designed this machine to be.

 If trying to figure out all the ins and outs of Roaming Profile policies is giving you a headache, use the handy flowchart in Figure 2.24 to help you figure out what each policy setting does and how it will affect your users.

Leave Windows Installer and Group Policy Software Installation Data

Earlier, we explored the **Delete cached copies of roaming profiles** policy setting. The idea was to "clean up" behind a user when he or she logged off. This is a great idea in theory but had an unintended consequence.

That is, if you opt to delete Roaming Profiles at logoff time, the information regarding applications deployed via Group Policy Software Installation (explored in Chapter 4) is also lost (by default). There is a new policy that affects users on Windows XP/SP2 (or Windows 2003/SP1) or newer (such as Windows Vista) called **Leave Windows Installer and Group Policy Software Installation Data.** Once enabled, the Group Policy Software Installation data remains on the hard drive, so subsequent logins for users are much faster.

So, if you're choosing to enable the **Delete cached copies of roaming profiles** setting, also enabling this one is likely a good idea. This policy was created to deal with the scenario where applications are deployed via Group Policy Software Installation as a full install of the application at logon time while the **Delete cached copies of roaming profiles** policy is enabled. More information at `http://support.microsoft.com/kb/828452`.

Do Not Forcefully Unload the Users Registry at User Logoff

In versions of Windows previous to Vista, the logging off process sometimes just "hung" there. In Windows' defense it was usually a service or something which kept the user's profile open. To that end, UPHClean (described earlier) was developed to help correct that problem on Windows Server 2003 Terminal Services. (See the sidebar "A Brief History of the Unloading of `NTUSER.DAT` and UPHClean.")

Now, Windows Vista goes the extra mile and will automatically do this.

So, the only time to enable this policy is if you think something is getting broken by this automatic process. For instance, you log on a second or third time and notice your application didn't save settings which would normally be stored in the user's Registry hives.

In other words, only enable this policy setting if you suspect some issue with the behavior of forcefully unloading the user's Registry at logoff.

This policy setting works with Windows Vista and Windows Server 2008.

FIGURE 2.24 Roaming Profile policy settings flowchart

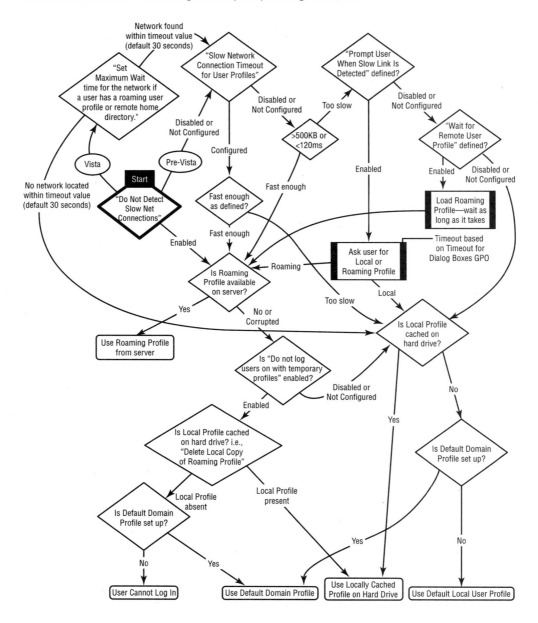

Set Roaming Profile Path for All Users Logging onto This Computer

The policy setting enables you to establish a shared User Profile path for a specific computer. Think of it as "Everyone who logs on to this computer gets the same profile."

But just because you enable this policy setting, doesn't mean it's 100 percent guaranteed to be embraced. That's because other values might have precedence before this one takes effect.

Windows reads profile configurations in the following order and uses the first configured setting.

1. The Roaming Profile path specified in the Terminal Services policy setting found at Computer Configuration ➤ Policies ➤ Administrative Templates ➤ Windows Components ➤ Terminal Services ➤ Terminal Server ➤ Profiles ➤ **Set path for TS Roaming Profiles**

2. The Roaming Profile path specific in the Terminal Server user object in Active Directory Users and Computers

3. The per-computer Roaming Profile path specified (using this policy setting)

4. The per-user Roaming Profile path specified in the user object in Active Directory Users and Computers

   This policy setting works with Windows Vista and Windows Server 2008.

Set Maximum Wait Time for the Network if a User Has a Roaming User Profile or Remote Home Directory

This is a wordy policy setting, for sure, but what it does is simple. You can increase the network timeout if you know the computer may not find the network right away after a user chooses to log on. This can happen a lot in the cases where a wireless card is searching, searching, searching for the wireless access point, but, meanwhile, the user has already pressed Ctrl+Alt+Del to log on!

Ouch!

By setting this policy, the computer waits a bit first to see if the network suddenly becomes present.

If the network still isn't available (based upon this value, or 30 seconds by default) then the cached profile is used and the user won't have access to the network home drive.

This policy setting works with Windows Vista and Windows Server 2008.

One More Policy Setting That You Might Like

This policy setting isn't specifically profile related, but it does relate to the logon experience.

Check out **Report when logon server was not available during user logon** found in Computer Configuration (and User Configuration) ➤ Policies ➤ Windows Components ➤ Windows Logon Options. They both work the same way.

Once Enabled, this gives an informative dialog telling the user if, more or less, he's working online or offline. This can be a great first step in knowing what's going on and if there's really a problem or not.

Manipulating Roaming Profiles with User Group Policy Settings

As you have just seen, most policy settings regarding Roaming Profiles are associated with the computer itself. Two policy settings, however, affect Roaming Profiles but are located on the user side of the fence: **Limit profile size** and **Excluding directories in roaming profile**. These policy settings are found under User Settings ➢ Policies ➢ Administrative Templates ➢ System ➢ User Profiles, as shown in Figure 2.25.

FIGURE 2.25   Some entries for profiles are found under the User Node in Group Policy.

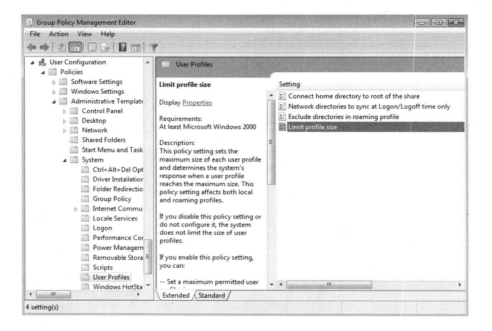

Limit Profile Size

This setting limits how big the profile can grow. Remember, now the My Documents folder is part of the profile. If you limit the profile size, the profile can hit that limit awfully quickly.

WARNING   It is recommended that you avoid using this setting unless you use the techniques described in the next chapter for redirecting folders for the My Documents folder. When that technique is applied, the redirected My Documents folder is no longer part of the profile, and the size can come back down to earth.

Once enabled, there are three other options:

"Show registry files in the file list"   If selected, the user will see the NTUSER.DAT as part of the total calculations on space. I suggest you leave this unchecked because most users won't know what the NTUSER.DAT file is. And, by leaving it unchecked, the NTUSER.DAT file doesn't count toward the space used.

"Notify user when profile storage space is exceeded"   This notifies the user about size infractions.

"Remind user every X minutes"   Use this setting so that it annoys the user every so often. This setting is only valid if the "Notify user when profile storage space is exceeded" box is checked, as shown in Figure 2.26.

Once this policy setting is configured, the affected users on Windows XP or Windows 2000 cannot log off until the files that compose their profile take up less than the limit. They are presented with a list of files in their profile, as shown in Figure 2.27, from which they must choose some to delete.

For Windows Vista machines, users get an extra notification in the notification area, as seen in Figure 2.28. To see the list of files, they have to double-click the X. (You might want to mention this in your custom message.)

Additionally, for Windows Vista, users can log off, but their changes aren't synchronized back to the server. At logoff, they get greeted with the message seen in Figure 2.29. It stays on the screen for a few seconds then goes away, allowing the next user to logon.

FIGURE 2.26   You can limit the Roaming Profile size, if desired.

FIGURE 2.27   Once the Roaming Profile size is set, users can't log off until they delete some files.

FIGURE 2.28   Windows Vista allows for a custom message in the notification area.

FIGURE 2.29   Users are notified their profile isn't completely synchronized.

Your roaming user profile was not completely synchronized. See the event log for details or contact administrator.

In general, this is a blunt instrument. The original use of this entry was for situations in which users stuffed lots of documents into their Windows NT Roaming Profile—onto the Desktop, for instance. Recall that Windows NT pushes the entire profile up and back, causing major bandwidth headaches. Indeed, because users rely heavily on the My Documents folder (which is part of the profile), there's even more reason to be concerned.

WARNING   Don't try to place disk quota restrictions on Roaming Profiles. Because applications sometimes put their own data inside the profile, users have a hard time tracking down files to delete if the quota prevented them from writing. Instead, use disk quotas on redirected folders, such as the My Documents folder.

But instead of being forced to use this policy setting as your only weapon to fight disk space usage, you have an ace in the hole; in the next chapter, you'll learn how to use Folder Redirection to redirect My Documents. You can then place a disk quota on the redirected My Documents folder.

In Windows Vista this policy setting will automatically exclude \Appdata\Local and Appdata\LocalLow directories (and all their subdirectories).

Excluding Directories in Roaming Profile

As previously stated, several folders in the profile will not roam.

For pre-Vista machines, these folders are Documents and Settings*Username*\Local Settings\Application Data (and everything below it, including Local Settings, History, Temp, and Temporary Internet Files).

For Vista machines, these folders are \Appdata\Local and Appdata\LocalLow and all their subfolders (like \Temporary Internet Files).

You can add additional folders to the list of those that do not roam, if desired. You might do this if you want to fix a specific file to a Desktop (if you maintain locally cached profiles). For instance, you can exclude Desktop\LargeZipDownloads if you want to make sure those types of files do not roam with the profile.

In Windows 2000, some, but not all, of the automatically excluded folders are presented in the Group Policy Editor. As far as I can tell, they're only there for show; deleting them produces no appreciable gain. (For example, you can't make the Temp, History, or other folders magically start roaming in the profile.) You can only add your own entries in addition to or in lieu of the presented entries. You will not see any of these folders listed when not using a Windows 2000 machine as your management station.

Enter additional entries relative to the root of the profiles. For instance, if you want to add the Desktop, simply add **Desktop** (not **c:\Documents and Settings\Desktop** or anything similar), because the Desktop folder is found directly off the root of each profile.

Connect Home Directory to Root of the Share

I'm pretty sure that by the time you get to the end of this book, you won't want to use old-style "Home Drives" anymore. That's because the changes in Roaming Profile behavior and redirected folders (see next chapter) present a better way for users to store their files. However, if you do end up using Home Drives for each user (located in the Account tab of each user's account's Properties), you can specify a location for users to store their stuff. Specific environment variables typically used when setting up home directories are defined differently in NT 4 and Windows 2000 (and later).

Those two environment variables, *%HOMEDRIVE%* and *%HOMEPATH%*, are automatically set when you set up, share, and assign a home directory for a user. NT 4 client computers aren't as smart as Windows 2000 computers, and they understand the meaning of the *%HOMEDRIVE%* and *%HOMEPATH%* shares a bit differently. To make a long story short, the fully qualified name path to the share isn't represented when those variables are evaluated on NT 4 clients; but it is for Windows 2000 and later clients. You can "dumb down" Windows 2000 and newer clients by applying this policy setting and making new clients act like old NT 4 clients.

This policy is not supported on Windows Vista or Windows Server 2008. Those operating systems *always* set *%HOMEDRIVE%* and *%HOMEPATH%* in the new way.

Mandatory Profiles

Mandatory Profiles enable the administrator to assign a single user or multiple users the same, unchanging user experience regardless of where they log on and no matter what they do. In non–mumbo-jumbo terms, Mandatory Profiles ensure that users can't screw things up. When you use Mandatory Profiles to lock down your users, you guarantee that the Desktop, the files in the profile, and the Registry continue to look exactly as they did when they were set up.

Mandatory Profiles are great when you have a pesky user who keeps messing with the Desktop or when you have general populations of users—such as call centers, nurse's stations, or library kiosks—on whom you want to maintain security.

Once the Mandatory Profile is set for these people, you know you won't be running out there every 11 minutes trying to fix someone's machine when they've put the black text on the black background and clicked Apply. Actually, they can still put the black text on the black background and click Apply, and it does take effect. But when they log off or reboot (if they can figure out how to do that in the dark), the values aren't preserved. So, voilá! Back to work!

You can create a Mandatory Profile in two ways—either from a Local Profile (or locally cached profile) or from an existing Roaming Profile. I recommend creating your Mandatory Profile from a local (or locally cached) profile. By default, if you try to dive into an existing Roaming Profile folder on the server, you are denied access, as shown in Figure 2.13 earlier in this chapter. The system utilizes the *%username%* variable and automatically sets up permissions such that only the user specified can access that folder. To dive in, you have to take ownership of the entire subfolder structure first and then give yourself permission to access the folder.

In the next sections, you'll find the steps for both methods.

If you previously set up the **Add the Administrators security group to roaming user profiles** policy setting, you won't need to worry about not being able to dive into the profile. However, the policy setting must be placed before the Roaming Profile is placed.

Establishing Mandatory Profiles from a Local Profile

The first thing to do when trying to establish the Mandatory Profile is to log on locally to any Windows 2000 or Windows XP machine as a mere-mortal user (without an existing Roaming Profile), make the modifications you want, and log off as that user.

Now that you have a local (or locally cached) profile that you want to use as your Mandatory Profile, follow these steps:

1. Log on as Administrator to the machine that houses the local (or locally cached) profile.

    For Windows XP and Windows 2000:

2. Click Start, and then right-click My Computer and choose Properties from the shortcut menu to open the System Properties dialog box.

    For Windows Vista:

    Click Start, right-click Computer, and select Properties from the shortcut menu.

3. Select "Advanced system settings" in the left pane.

    For both:

4. Click the Advanced tab, and then click the Settings button in the User Profiles section to open the User Profiles dialog box (as seen previously in Figure 2.7).

5. Click the Copy To button to open the Copy To dialog box, and then enter the full path plus a folder for the common users, as shown in Figure 2.30. This example has \\Dc01\profiles\allnurses. The allnurses folder is automatically created under the Profiles share.

FIGURE 2.30 For Windows XP (shown at left), use the Copy To dialog box to copy one profile for many users. If you want this profile to be used for Windows Vista (shown at right) computers, you need to specify a .v2 extension as seen here.

6. Click the Change button in the "Permitted to Use" section to open the "Select User or Group" dialog box and change the default from the original user to Authenticated Users. This lets everyone use the profile in the domain.

7. Click OK to actually copy the profile and to close the Copy To dialog box.

8. Click OK to close the System Properties dialog box.

Next, use Explorer to locate the share we created earlier, named Profiles. Inside the Profiles directory, you should now see the `allnurses` (or `allnurses.v2` for Windows Vista) folder. Locate the `NTUSER.DAT` and rename it to `NTUSER.MAN`, as shown in Figure 2.31.

FIGURE 2.31 Change a Roaming Profile to a Mandatory Profile by renaming NTUSER.DAT to NTUSER.MAN.

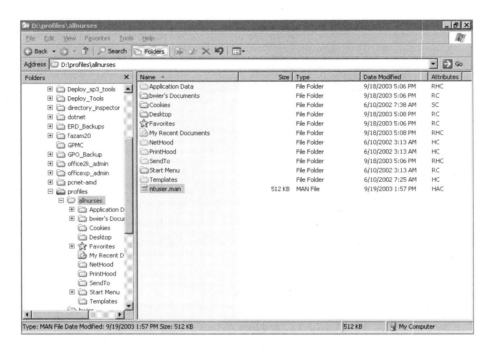

 Because `NTUSER.DAT` is hidden by default, you might have to change the default view options. In Explorer, choose Tools ➢ Folder Options to open the Folder Options dialog box. Click the View tab, click the "Show Hidden Files and Folders" button, clear the "Hide File Extensions for Known File Types" check box, and click OK.

Finally, in the Properties dialog box, change the profile path of all the users who are to use the profile to \\Dc01\profiles\allnurses, as shown in Figure 2.32. Note that you do not need to specify the `.v2` directory specifically for Vista users in the "Profile path" line. That is, just enter in \\Dc01\profiles\allnurses and Windows XP will use the non-`.v2` directory and Windows Vista will automatically find and use the `.v2` directory.

Since you copied the profile to the server with permissions for Authenticated User to use, you'll also want to modify the NTFS permissions of the `allnurses` folder under the Profiles share to make sure it's protected. You might choose to protect the `allnurses` folder by setting the Permissions as shown in Figure 2.33.

FIGURE 2.32   Point all similar users to the new Mandatory Profile.

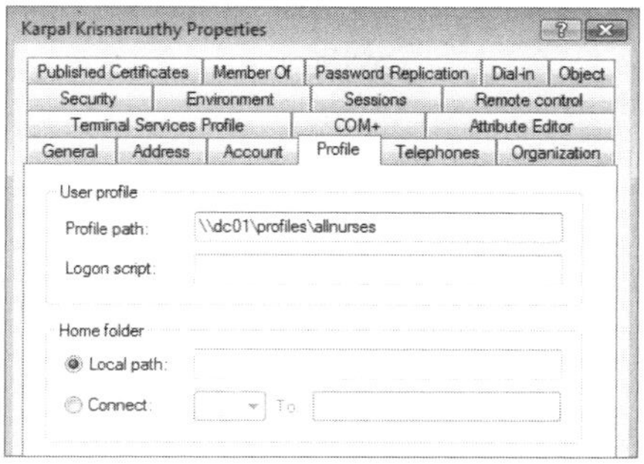

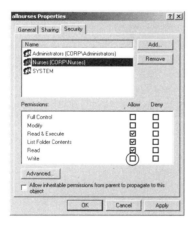

FIGURE 2.33   You can prevent people from inadvertently modifying the newly established profile.

Mandatory Profiles from an Established Roaming Profile

You might not be able to use a local (or locally cached) profile to generate the Mandatory Profile. This might be because you enabled the **Delete cached copies of roaming profiles** policy setting, and there are no locally cached profiles for you to use. In this case, you'll need to log in as Administrator on the server that houses the Roaming Profile, locate the profile folder, and take ownership of it. You can then copy the profile to another folder and have the user take back ownership of the folder. In this case, we'll take ownership of a profile for a user named garyd. To take ownership of a user's Roaming Profile, follow these steps:

1.   Log on at the server as Administrator.

2.   Locate the user's profile folder, right-click it, and choose Properties from the shortcut menu to open the User Properties dialog box.

3. Click the Security tab. You should get a message stating that the user is the only one with access to their personal folder.

4. Click the Advanced button on the Security tab to get the Advanced Security Settings dialog box. Next, click the Owner tab.

5. Select Administrator (or Administrators) from the list, click the "Replace owner on sub-containers and objects" check box (as shown in Figure 2.34), and then click OK. With Windows Server 2008, you'll have to hit the Edit button before modifying the ownership.

6. You will be prompted to confirm that you want to take ownership. Select Yes, and wait until you have ownership.

FIGURE 2.34   Take ownership of the folder.

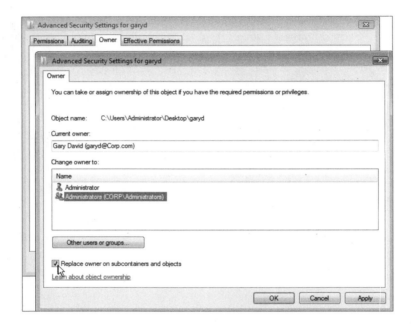

You can now rename the folder to a sensible name and then rename the NTUSER.DAT file to NTUSER.MAN. Last, specifically point each user account to use this new profile, as shown in Figure 2.32 earlier in this chapter.

Since everyone now has Full Control (inherited from the parent), you might want to restrict access to the profile, similarly to that seen in Figure 2.33 earlier.

You might need to add the Administrator account or the Administrators group to the ACL of the folder and let the permissions flow downward in order to be able to see the contents. In some extreme cases, you might also need to log off and back on as Administrator to get another access token.

Forced Mandatory Profiles (Super-Mandatory)

Mandatory Profiles might not always be so—if the server is down or a user unplugs their network cable, the Mandatory Profile does not load. Indeed, the user will get the Local Default User Profile. This could be a potential security problem and possibly a violation of your corporate policy.

In instances like this, you need to determine if it's more important that a user logs on (and gets the Default Local User Profile) or that, if they don't get the Mandatory Profile, they don't get to log on at all. Microsoft calls this type of profile "Super-Mandatory." In Figure 2.31 earlier in this chapter, we used a folder named `allnurses` as our Mandatory Profile folder. We can take this to the next step and ensure that no users using the `allnurses` folder can log on unless they can connect to the share on the server.

Don't forget: profiles are different for Type 1 (pre-Vista) and Type 2 (Windows Vista and Windows Server 2008) computers. To that end, you'll need to set up Mandatory Profiles that fit for each type.

To force users who log onto Windows Vista to use a Mandatory Profile or lose logon capability, you need to first rename the `allnurses.v2` folder such that it has `.man.v2` instead. So, the final folder name will be `allnurses.man.v2`.

To force users to use the Mandatory Profile, or lose logon capability, simply follow these steps:

1. Create a Mandatory Profile as described earlier, including renaming the `NTUSER.DAT` to `NTUSER.MAN`.

2. For Windows XP machines, rename the entire folder from `allnurses` to `allnurses.man`. For Windows Vista machines, rename the entire folder from `allnurses.v2` to `allnurses.man.v2`

3. Change the affected users' Profile tabs to point to the new location, such as `\\Dc01\profiles\allnurses.man`, as shown in Figure 2.35.

Once the forced Mandatory Profile is introduced onto a system, the system always checks to see if the Profile is available. If the forced Mandatory Profile is unavailable, the user is not permitted to log on.

 Technically, you can couple a Mandatory Profile with the **Log users off when roaming profile fails** policy setting to create the same effect. However, the method detailed here is preferred.

Final Thoughts

In this chapter, you learned about the three profile types: Local, Roaming, and Mandatory.

Local Profiles alone are great—for only the smallest of environments. However, remember that there's a lot you can do to get a similar look and feel for when new users show up on the job. You can craft a Default Local User Profile, or, even better, a Default Domain User Profile.

FIGURE 2.35   You can force a Mandatory Profile if absolutely necessary.

Step up to Roaming Profiles when you have even a handful of users and you want to allow them to bounce from machine to machine and keep their look and feel. Roaming Profiles have really grown up since the days of Windows NT. The algorithm to move the profiles up and back is much improved, and you should really give it another try if you once gave up in frustration.

Roaming Profiles are especially useful if you want to bring users' desktops and laptops back from the dead, as we'll explore in the next two chapters. Indeed, you can use Roaming Profiles as a handy way to upgrade users' machines while preserving their Desktops.

Remember that the Active Directory Users and Computers tool allows you to select multiple users at once and set their Roaming Profile path to a server. And, as stated earlier, there's no need to create the folder underneath the shared directory first—the system will automatically do that once the *%username%* variable is encountered.

Even though we set up Roaming Profiles for our Type 1 computers (pre-Vista) and our Type 2 computers (Windows Vista and Windows Server 2008), we still have a problem. That is, we have no way to exchange data between the two. If someone logs onto Windows Vista and drops some music files in their profile, then they log onto a Windows XP machine, they simply won't see those music files. In the next chapter, we'll discuss Redirected Folders. The idea is that instead of saving critical data in our profile, we save it on a point on our server. That way, if we're on Windows Vista or Windows XP, we'll be able to just reach out and touch the data that lives on the server. We'll get there right around the corner.

As stated earlier, there are a lot of policy settings you can utilize to hone how profiles work. You can set up your environment to be moderately secure when using the **Delete cached copies of roaming profiles** policy setting. And you can allow joint ownership of the user's Roaming Profile directory on the server by utilizing the **Add the Administrators security group to roaming user profiles** policy setting.

Use Mandatory Profiles sparingly. With Group Policy settings available to tie down all sorts of settings, Mandatory Profiles are really only a last resort. And Forced Mandatory Profiles are a really, really last resort (if there's such a thing).

3

Implementing a Managed Desktop, Part 1: Redirected Folders, Offline Files, and the Synchronization Manager

You get Active Directory, you get Group Policy. That's the good news. The better news is how you can put your knowledge of Group Policy to use to keep your users happy. Here's the idea: easily create a consistent environment for your users no matter where they roam.

In the previous chapter, you used Roaming Profiles to kick off your journey to a consistent environment. But that only got you so far—especially if you had both Windows XP and Windows Vista machines. That's because when you roamed from Windows XP to Windows Vista (or vice versa) you didn't maintain the goodies, like the stuff you put in My Documents (for XP) and Documents (for Windows Vista). Each computer type became its own island.

Now, let's explore how to create a *managed desktop*. A managed desktop is one where you can create a predictable environment for your users to log into and enjoy. It's not put together with wacky applications and icons all over the place. You know what to expect when your users log on, and so do they.

In this chapter, I'll give you an overview of what a managed desktop is and is not and show you how to implement a slew of its features: Redirected Folders, Offline Files, and the Synchronization Manager.

 Previously the idea of a managed desktop was called IntelliMirror. But you have to look far and wide to find Microsoft using that term nowadays. I wasn't even sure Microsoft was using the term IntelliMirror anymore. But after a little poking around I found this URL: http://tinyurl.com/y9tesn, which is a Vista page that clearly has the word IntelliMirror on it. But we decided not to include it in this book's title because the term just isn't in regular use anymore. So, instead, we'll just refer to IntelliMirror as a "Managed Desktop."

In the next chapter, I'll continue creating a managed desktop with a discussion of software deployment via Group Policy. We'll extend that even more when we explore SoftGrid (a new way to deploy software). Finally, in Chapter 10, you'll see how the "circle of life" for a computer, so to speak, comes together with more Group Policy Preference Extensions tricks, Shadow Copies, and more.

Overview of Change and Configuration Management

Believe it or not, you're expensive. Your salary, the percentage of rent your office takes up, the software you use that helps the business run—it all costs money. Making those costs tangible is a difficult proposition. Some costs are hard to put into concrete numbers. How do you quantify the cost of sending a technician to a user's desktop when they've inadvertently set the background color, the foreground color, and the font color to black and hit the Apply button?

Accounting for these costs is a constant challenge, and bringing these costs under control is even more difficult. The Gartner Group, in the early 1990s, generated a new strategy to help with this predicament and proposed a new *TCO (Total Cost of Ownership)* model. This philosophical model essentially attempted to take the voodoo out of accounting for computing services. Simply account for every nickel and dime spent around computing, and voilà! Instant accounting!

 You can find more info on Gartner Group's TCO model at www.gartnerweb.com/ 4_decision_tools/measurement/decision_tools/tco/tco.html (shortened to http://tinyurl.com/57f16).

Microsoft's first foray into aligning with the TCO philosophy was back in the NT 4 timeframe with their Zero Administration for Windows (ZAW) initiative. The first major technology set based on ZAW was called the Zero Administration for Windows Kit (ZAK).

Most organizations have two types of users: those who work on one application and one application only, and those who use a few apps (but seem to never stop playing with their Desktops). With those two types of users in mind, ZAK could be run in two modes: Taskstation, in which users were locked down to one (and only one) application, and Appstation, in which users could move between several strategically selected applications. ZAK's goal was noble: reduce the user's exposure to the Desktop and the operating system. Once that was reduced, less administration would be required to control the environment.

Although ZAK was a respectable first attempt, only a few organizations really used ZAK in the way it was intended. The adoption of ZAK never quite caught on due to the intricacy of implementation and lack of flexibility. Finally, in 2007, Microsoft took ZAK for NT 4 down as a free download.

With Active Directory as the backdrop to a new stage, a new paradigm of how administrators managed users and their Desktops could be created. Enter the Active Directory version of Zero Administration for Windows—now known as Change and Configuration Management (CCM) and the (now defunct) Microsoft term *IntelliMirror*.

Again, recall that the Zero Administration for Windows program was an "initiative," not a specific technology. With Windows 2000, Microsoft renamed the ZAW initiative to Change and Configuration Management and introduced several new technologies in order to move closer to the TCO philosophy.

In accordance with the TCO philosophy, by creating a managed desktop, each step you implement tries to chip away at each of the sore points of administrating your network by implementing specific technologies. Figure 3.1 shows how Microsoft envisions the Change and Configuration Management initiative and the Windows features and technologies therein.

ZAK was kind of an all-or-nothing proposition. But today with CCM, it's not like that. You can pick and choose the steps to perform: from setting up Roaming Profiles (which you learned about in the previous chapter) to setting up Redirected Folders and Offline Files (which you'll learn about in this chapter) to deploying software (which you'll learn about in the next chapters).

In short, you're in control of the features and functionality you want to deploy and when you want to deploy them. Although some features that I'll describe in detail here (such as Offline Files) are available when using a Windows workstation by itself, most features (such as Redirected Folders) are actuated only when you have the marriage between Active Directory and a Windows client.

Again, you built a bit of a foundation for your journey toward a managed desktop in the last chapter when you implemented Roaming Profiles. This enabled the basics of the "my documents follow me" and the "my settings follow me" philosophies. In this chapter, we'll explore the implementation of some of the other features needed to create a managed desktop: Redirected Folders, Offline Files, the synchronization capabilities (in both Windows XP and Windows Vista).

FIGURE 3.1   This is Microsoft's picture of how to create a managed desktop (the concept formerly known as IntelliMirror).

Change and Configuration Management	Managed Desktop	Features	Benefits	Technologies
		User Data Management	Increased protection and availability of people's data "My documents follow me!"	Active Directory Group Policy Offline Folders Synchronization Manager Redirected Folders
		User Settings Management	Centrally defined environment "My settings follow me!"	Active Directory Group Policy Offline Folders Roaming Profiles
		Software Installation and Maintenance	Centrally managed software "My software follows me!"	Active Directory Group Policy Windows Installer Service
		Remote OS Installation	Fast system configuration "Get Windows working on this machine"	Active Directory DNS DHCP Windows Deployment Services

Sometimes, in normal use, some people call Offline Files something else—"Offline Folders" and also "CSC" for "Client-Side Caching." In regular use, they're all the same thing, but strictly, Microsoft documentation refers only to Offline Files and not Offline Folders. So, to be consistent, we'll also try to call the feature Offline Files.

Redirected Folders

Redirected Folders allow the administrator to provide a centralized repository for certain noteworthy folders from client systems and to have the data contained in them actually reside on shared folders on servers. It's a beautiful thing. The administrator gets centralized control; users get the same experience they always did. It's the best of both worlds.

Available Folders to Redirect

Windows XP and Windows Vista have different folders that are available for redirection. In Windows XP you can set Redirected Folders for the following:

- `My Documents`
- `My Pictures`
- `Start Menu`
- `Desktop`
- `Application Data`

In Windows Vista, you can Redirect the following folders:

- `Contacts` (not previously available in Windows XP)
- `Start Menu` (like Windows XP, but see the note following this list)
- `Desktop` (like Windows XP)
- `Documents` (was called `My Documents` in Windows XP)
- `Downloads` (not previously available in Windows XP)
- `Favorites` (not previously "redirectable" in Windows XP, but available in the Roaming Profile)
- `Music` (was called `My Music` in Windows XP)
- `Videos` (was called `My Videos` in Windows XP)
- `Pictures` (was called `My Pictures` in Windows XP)
- `Searches` (not previously available in Windows XP)
- `Links` (not previously available in Windows XP)
- `AppData` (Roaming) (was called simply `Application Data` in XP)
- And (Lord help us), `Saved Games` (not previously available in Windows XP)

The Start Menu redirection support in Windows Vista is actually better than XP, because in XP you didn't have the ability to redirect each user's Start Menu folder to a different location. You could only do it to a shared location. It wasn't as flexible as My Documents.

For each of these settings, there is a Basic and an Advanced configuration.

The idea is to set up a GPO that contains a policy setting to redirect one or more of these folders for clients and "stick them" on a server. Usually the GPO is set at the OU level, and all users inside the OU are affected; however, there might occasionally be a reason to link the GPO with the policy setting to the domain or site level.

In the *Basic* configuration, every user who is affected by the policy setting is redirected to the same shared folder. Then, inside the shared folder, the system can automatically create individual, secure folders for each user to store their stuff.

In the *Advanced* configuration, Active Directory security group membership determines which users' folders get redirected to which shared folder. For instance, you could say, "All members of the **Graphic_Artists** Global security group will get their desktops redirected to the ga_Desktops shared folder on Server6" or, "All members of the Sales Universal security group will get their Application Data redirected to the AppData share on Server Pineapple."

Note that any folders that lived under the My Documents folder (pre-Vista) now have an additional option as seen in Figure 3.2. That is, you can choose to let these documents just "Follow the Documents folder" which will maintain the legacy folder hierarchy of My Documents if need be. Again, this option is only for folders within Documents (Music, Videos, and Pictures.)

FIGURE 3.2   Music, Videos, and Pictures can all "Follow the Documents folder."

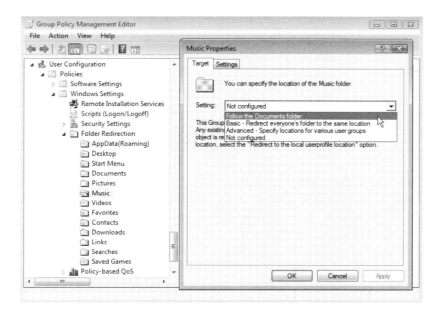

Redirected *Documents/My Documents*

For our journey through Redirected Folders, we'll work primarily inside the Documents folder. All the principles that work on the special Documents folder work equally well for the other special "redirectable" folders, unless otherwise noted. At the end of this section, I'll briefly discuss why you might want to redirect some other folders as well.

In the last chapter, we explored how to leverage Roaming Profiles to maintain a consistent state for users if they hop from machine to machine. Roaming Profiles are terrific, but one significant drawback is associated with using Roaming Profiles. Recall that My Documents (for Windows XP) and Documents (for Windows Vista) are now part of the profile. On the one hand, this frees you from the bondage of drive letters and home drives. No more, "Ursula, put it in your U: drive," or "Harry, save it to the H: drive."

On the other hand, once the user data is in Documents/My Documents, your network will be swamped with all the up-and-back movement of data within Documents/My Documents when users hop from machine to machine—20MB of Word docs here, 30MB of Excel docs there. Multiply this by the number of users, and it'll add up fast! Not to mention that (for XP at least) that data is synchronized at logon and logoff and hence, the user may have to wait until it's all completed. As we learned in the previous chapter, the Roaming Profiles algorithm does its best to mitigate that, but it's still got to move the changed files.

But with Redirected Folders, you can have the best of both worlds. Users can save their files to the place they know and love, My Documents (for Windows XP) and Documents (for Windows Vista), and anchor the data to a fixed location, so it *appears* as if the data is roaming with the users. But it really isn't; it's safe and secure on a file share of your choice. And, since the data is already on the server, there's no long wait time when logging on or logging off.

 There are two added bonuses to this scheme. Since all the Documents/My Documents files are being redirected to specific fixed-shared folders, you can easily back up all the user data in one fell swoop. Perhaps you can even make a separate backup job specifically for the user data that needs to be more closely monitored. Additionally, you can set up Shadow Copies for the disk volumes that house redirected Documents/My Documents files so users can restore their own files if necessary. The Shadow Copies function is explored in Chapter 9.

Basic Redirected Folders

Basic Redirected Folders works best in two situations:

- Smaller environments—such as a doctor's office or storefront—where all employees sit under one roof

- In an organization's OU structure that was designed such that similar people are not only in the same OU but are also in the same physical location

The reason these simple scenarios make a good fit with the basic option is that such situations let you redirect the users affected by the policy setting to a server that's close to them. That way, if they do roam within their location, the wait time is minimal to download and upload the data back and forth to the server and their workstation.

In the following example, I've created an OU called **LikeUsers** who are all using the same local server, DC01. Setting up a basic Redirected Folders for My Documents is a snap. It's a three-step process:

1. Create a shared folder to store the data.
2. Set the security on the shared folder.
3. Create a new GPO and edit it to contain a policy setting to redirect the Documents/My Documents folder.

To create and share a folder to store redirected Documents/My Documents data, follow these steps:

1. Log onto DC01 as Administrator.
2. From the Desktop, double-click My Computer to open the My Computer folder.
3. Find a place to create a users folder. In this example, we'll use D:\DATA. Once you're inside the D: drive, right-click D:\ and select the Folder command from the New menu, then type in **Data** for the name.

You can substitute any name for Data. Some use DOCS, MYDOCS, or REDIRDOCS. Some administrators like to use hidden shares, such as Data$, MYDOCS$, or MYDOCUMENTS$. This works well, too.

4. Right-click the newly created Data folder, and choose "Share..." which opens the Properties of the folder, focused on the Sharing tab. Pull down the drop-down menu and select Everyone, and then click Add. Note that Windows Server 2003 and 2008 will default such that the share is Everyone:Read. Click "Share" and ensure that the share is set so that Everyone has Co-owner permissions, as seen in Figure 3.3. Keep the rest of the defaults, and click OK. (Note that Co-owner rights are almost the same as the "Full Control" rights of yore.)

FIGURE 3.3 Share the Data folder such that Everyone has Co-owner permissions.

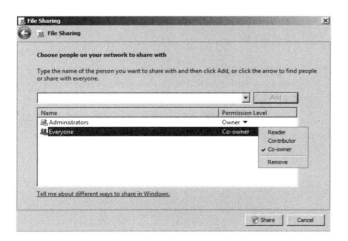

Be sure that the NTFS permissions allow write access for the users you want, as well. In other words, both the Share level and NTFS permissions must allow the user to write.

Now that the share is created, we're ready to create a new GPO to do the magic. Again, you'll want to do this on your Windows Vista management station, VISTAMANGEMENT. This machine should have Windows Vista + SP1 + the RSAT tools, which contain GPMC 2.0. For more information see the Introduction to this book for a lab setup guide.

To set up Redirected Folders for Documents/My Documents, follow these steps:

1. In the GPMC, right-click the OU on which you want to apply Folder Redirection (in my case, the **LikeUsers** OU), and choose "Create a GPO in this domain, and Link it here."

2. Name the GPO, say, "Documents Folder Redirection," as shown in Figure 3.4.

FIGURE 3.4 The LikeUsers OU has a GPO named "Documents Folder Redirection." After drilling down into the folder that you want to redirect, right-click and choose Properties.

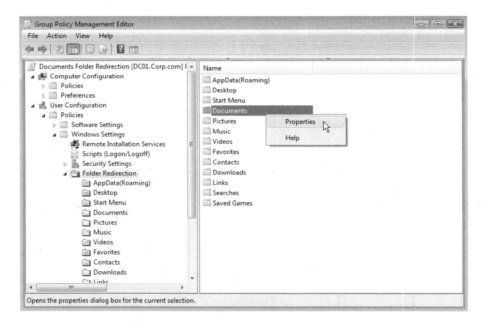

3. Right-click the new GPO, and choose Edit from the shortcut menu to open the Group Policy Management Editor.

4. Drill down to Folder Redirection by choosing User Configuration ➢ Policies ➢ Windows Settings ➢ Folder Redirection. Right-click the Documents entry in the Group Policy Management Editor, and choose Properties to open the Documents Properties dialog box, as shown in Figure 3.5.

5. In the Setting drop-down list box, select "Basic—Redirect everyone's folder to the same location."

FIGURE 3.5 The Basic settings redirect all users in the OU to the same location.

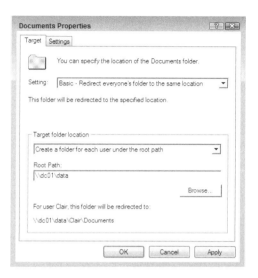

Don't click OK (or Apply) yet. There's more to do. If you do click OK or Apply, you're going to get a warning (which we'll talk about in the Real-World Scenario entitled "What Happens When You Edit a GPO from a Pre-Vista Management Station?").

 **Real World Scenario**

Share Permissions: Full Control (Co-owner) versus Change (Contributor)

In the last chapter, we set up a shared folder for our Roaming Profiles. We put Contributor/ Change control on the permissions, and this was enough. Interestingly, here, on the share that will house our Redirected Folders, we need Full Control permissions, or the Folder Redirection will fail.

So, is there a problem using Full Control, or Windows Server 2008's Co-owner rights? Is there a way to exploit an attack on a share with Full Control? Not really, unless the underlying NTFS permissions are open for an attack. Basically, as long as the root folder of the share is an NTFS folder with appropriate permissions, there is no reason to use anything other than Everyone:Full Control, or Windows Server 2008's Co-owner rights, on the share; though there's certainly nothing wrong with Authenticated Users:Full Control (or Windows Server 2008's Co-owner rights), either.

Some people used to insist on using share permissions, but it was often because they instituted the practice in the dark days of OS/2 and Microsoft LanManager and got used to it (and maybe they had the "insecure" FAT file system running). The share permission is simply a security descriptor stored in the Registry entry for the share in the LanManServer entries on the server. Giving Everyone:Full Control (or using Windows Server 2008's Co-owner rights) doesn't change the permissions on the Registry entry itself, so it cannot be used as an exploit for getting a toehold on the server.

The moral of the story: have the correct NTFS permissions underneath the folder that contains the share. Indeed, share permissions aren't sufficient if someone gets physical access, or near-physical access, to the box; for example, via Terminal Services access.

The Target Tab

The "Target folder location" drop-down list box has the following four options:

Redirect to the user's home directory.   Many companies use home drives for each user and have the users store all their stuff there. To set a home drive for each user, in Active Directory Users and Computers, click the Profile tab for the user and enter a path in the "Home folder" section. The idea behind this setting is that it's an easy way to help users continue to use a drive letter they already know and love, say, H: (for Home directory) in addition to the Documents/ My Documents redirection. If you choose this setting, both H: and Documents/My Documents point to the exact same place—the path you set in the Home folder section in Active Directory Users and Computers. In this book, we didn't set up home drives because Documents/My Documents redirection frees us from the need to do so. This setting is provided here only as a convenience for organizations that want to continue to use home folders. If you plan to eventually get rid of home drives in your company in lieu of just a redirected Documents/My Documents folder, my advice is not to use this setting; instead use the **Redirect to the following location** setting (explored shortly).

If the user has no home folder, this option is ignored, and the folder stays in its current location.

Create a folder for each user under the root path.   If you plan to redirect more than just the Documents/My Documents folder (say, the Application Data or Desktop), you might want to select this option. This creates secure subfolders underneath the point you specify. As you can see in Figure 3.5 earlier in this chapter, entering \\DC01\data in the Root Path box shows an example of how all users affected by this policy setting are redirected.

This choice might be good if you don't want to have to remember what the specific environment variables point to.

In the example, you can see that Documents for a user Clair will be redirected to her own folder in the Data share. Go ahead and perform this now.

In our example, we're using DC01, a Domain Controller. You usually wouldn't do this; rather, you'd use a regular run-of-the mill file server (as a member server, not a Domain Controller). We're doing that here simply for the sake of example.

Redirect to the following location.   This option makes sense if you plan to redirect only Documents/My Documents or just one other redirectable folder.

It also makes sense if you want to leverage the maximum flexibility. This selection allows you to specifically dictate where you want the folder placed. That's because you can use environment variables here.

For instance, to use this setting, type **\\DC01\data\%*username*%** in the Root Path text box. Then, a subfolder for the user is created directly under the Data shared folder. This is the selection to choose when none of the others are to your liking; that is, you have the most flexibility with this option.

In advanced configurations, you can use this setting to (get this) share a Documents/My Documents folder. But you need to ensure that you set the right ACLs on the folder as well as enable the policy named **Do not check for user ownership of Roaming Profiles,** which is located in Computer Configuration ➢ Policies ➢ Administrative Templates ➢ User Profiles.

Redirect to the local *userprofile* location.   With this option, you redirect the folder for the user back to their Local Profile. It's useful when you want to remove redirection for a particular folder without affecting the rest of the other Redirected Folders.

Don't click OK (or Apply) yet. There's more to do. If you do click OK or Apply, you're going to get a warning (which we'll talk about in the Real-World Scenario entitled "What Happens When You Edit a GPO from a Pre-Vista Management Station?").

The Settings Tab

When you click the Settings tab, you have access to additional options for Folder Redirection. The Settings tab is the hidden gem of Folder Redirection; it activates a bit of magic. Figure 3.6 shows the Settings tab for Documents.

By default, users have exclusive NTFS permissions to their directories, and the contents of their Documents/My Documents folders are automatically moved to the new directory. You can change this behavior, if desired, by making the appropriate choices on the Settings tab.

FIGURE 3.6   The Settings tab in Folder Redirection holds all sorts of magical powers!

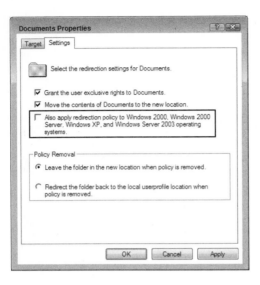

Because we're discussing My Documents (for Windows XP) and Documents (for Windows Vista) at this point, we'll dive into the Settings tab specifically for Documents for Windows Vista. However, each setting discussed here affects the other potentially Redirected Folders in exactly the same way. Let's take a look at some of the options available on this tab.

Grant the user exclusive rights to Documents.   By default, this check box is checked. You're instructing the system to create a secure directory underneath the redirection. This check box sets NTFS permissions on that directory such that only that user can enter the directory. This keeps prying eyes, even those of nosy administrators, out of people's personal business. If you want to change this setting, uncheck the box.

Unchecking the "Grant the user exclusive rights to Documents" check box sets no additional permissions, nor does it modify the target directory permissions in any way. When the folder gets created, it inherits its parent folder permissions instead of creating its own, exclusive, non-inherited permissions. The NTFS permissions are not modified. Because Windows Server uses NTFS inheritance, newly created folders receive the same permissions as the parent folder.

> If this box is checked and you do need to dig into someone's personal directory, you'll have to take ownership of the directory, as described in the previous chapter. Or, if you set it up in advance (using the information in the "How to Grant Administrators Access to *Documents/My Documents* (or Other Redirected Folders)" Real World Scenario, you'll be able to get in whenever you want! (Again, though, you need to set it up in advance.)

Move the contents of Documents to the new location. By default, this check box is checked. When you start out creating a managed desktop, Microsoft is betting that the first thing you do is to set up Roaming Profiles and then move on to setting up Redirected Folders. In between those two time periods, however, users have surely created their own documents and started putting them in their Documents folder in their Local or Roaming Profile. This check box magically moves (not copies) their documents from their profile (Roaming or Local) to the appointed place on the server the next time they log on.

 If users have bounced from machine to machine and sprinkled data in the local Documents folder, the files in Documents will move them to the redirected location the next time the user logs onto that machine. The only time to worry is when two files have the same name—the latest time-stamped file wins and stays on the server.

Also apply redirection policy to Windows 2000, Windows 2000 Server, Windows XP, and Windows Server 2003 operating systems. This setting gets the prize for most number of characters in a dialog box with just one check box. You'll only see this option when you create a GPO from a Vista management station. You can see this highlighted in Figure 3.6. Here's what happens:

This check box turns on or off what is called (unofficially) "downlevel compatible" Folder Redirection mode. This addition helps bridge the differences between the pre-Vista and Vista system profile hierarchies.

If you enable this box (downlevel compatible):

- The target folder name for Documents folder will automatically be set to My Documents; of course, you can change it to whatever you like.

- The Music and Videos folders will also automatically be redirected to the Follow the Documents folder, which means its target location will be <MyDocPath>\My Music and <MyDocPath>\My Videos. This is because pre-Vista Folder Redirection does not support individual redirection for these two folders.

- The Pictures folder, by default, will be set to follow the Documents folder. But there are some differences: since you can specify different locations in the pre-Vista system, you can do it on Vista as well. This means you can still change the Pictures folder to other places (including back to the Local Profile), as well.

If you disable this box (pure Vista mode):

- The target folder name will be Documents by default—you can still change it to other names.

- Pictures/Music/Videos will not automatically be placed within Documents as a parent. They remain where they are. You can configure them to redirect to any location you want, and the target folder name is also the new name without the "My" prefix.

The pure Vista mode gives the customer more flexibility; if you don't have pre-Vista systems in your environment, then it is better to use this mode.

Policy Removal   You must select one of the two settings under the Policy Removal heading. The point of having OUs is that you can move users easily in and out of them. If the user is moved out of an OU to which this policy applies, the following options help you determine what happens to their Redirected Folder contents.

Leave the folder in the new location when policy is removed.   If this option is selected, and the user is moved out of the OU to which this policy applies, the data stays in the shared folder and directory you specified. This is the default. The user will continue to access the contents of the Redirected Folder. However, there is one potential pitfall when using this option. To get a grip on it, read the Real-World Scenario "Folder Redirection Pitfalls."

Redirect the folder back to the local userprofile location when policy is removed.   If this check box is selected, and the user moves (or the policy no longer applies), a copy of the data is sent to the profile.

If Roaming Profiles is not set up, a copy of the data is sent to every workstation the user logs onto. If you've set up Roaming Profiles, the data gets pushed back up to the server and shared folder that houses the user's Roaming Profile when the user logs off.

This setting is useful if a user under your jurisdiction moves to another territory. Once this happens, you can eliminate their junk cluttering your servers (as long as you're not the administrator of the target OU). Use this option with care, though; since the user's data isn't anchored to a shared folder, the network traffic will increase when this data roams around the network.

It is recommended that you check with the target OU administrator to ensure that some Folder Redirection policy will apply to the user. This eliminates all the "up and back" problems associated with maintaining user data inside regular Roaming Profiles.

WARNING   Don't click OK (or Apply) yet. There's more to do. If you do click OK or Apply, you're going to get a warning (which we'll talk about in the Real-World Scenario entitled "What Happens When You Edit a GPO from a Pre-Vista Management Station?").

 Real World Scenario

Folder Redirection Pitfalls

Earlier, you learned about the "Leave the folder in the new location when policy is removed" setting when redirecting folders. However, let's work through a quick example—we'll assume that the check box is checked, and a user is being asked to use two machines.

Let's imagine the following scenario:

- There is a user Fred in the Sales OU.

- Fred uses ComputerA.

- There is a GPO linked to the Sales OU that contains a Folder Redirection policy. This policy redirects his Documents folder and has the "Leave the folder in the new location when policy is removed" setting enabled.

Fred logs onto ComputerA, and the Documents folder is redirected to \\server1\share1\Fred\ documents. As expected, Folder Redirection is working fine and dandy.

Now, let's assume Fred gets transferred to another job in Marketing, say, and his account is moved from the Sales OU to the Marketing OU. Let's assume Marketing does not have Folder Redirection policy for Documents in place.

What happens the next time Fred logs onto ComputerA?

Well, because the GPO doesn't apply to him, the policy for Folder Redirection will be removed. However, the Documents folder is still pointing to the server, and he can see all of his data on the server. Fred clicks his Documents folder and all is well. He sees the files on the server just fine. As far as the user is concerned, nothing "changes" because "Leave the folder in the new location when policy is removed" was selected.

A week later, ComputerA catches fire. Fred gets a brand new machine, ComputerB, which he has never logged onto before.

When Fred logs onto ComputerB his Documents folder will be pointing to C:\users\%*username*%\ Documents; not the server location like it was on ComputerA.

This makes sense: There isn't a Folder Redirection policy that affects Fred anymore. Remember— he's moved to Marketing, and they don't have a Folder Redirection policy. So, he never got the "signal" to use the server location he once did.

So, when Fred clicks Documents on ComputerB, he sees…nothing. However, Fred still has *rights* to get his files. So, if he wanted access to his files on ComputerB, he would have to navigate to \\server1\share1\%*username*%\documents via an Explorer window to be able to see his data.

 Real World Scenario

How to Grant Administrators Access to *Documents/My Documents* (or Other Redirected Folders)

As you learned in the last chapter, it's possible to grant administrators access to the folders where users store their Roaming Profiles. In that chapter, you set up a policy setting that affects the client computers; the first time the user jumps on the computer, the file permissions are set such that both the user and the administrator have joint access. However, that's not the case with Redirected Folders.

If you want both the user and the administrator to have joint access to a Redirected Folder such as Documents, you need to perform two major steps:

1. Clear the "Grant the user exclusive rights to Documents" setting (as seen in Figure 3.6).

2. Set security on the subfolder you are sharing that will contain the Redirected Folders.

In the Security Properties dialog box of the folder you shared, select Advanced. Uncheck the "Allow inheritable permissions from parent to propagate to this object" check box. Now, remove the permissions, and then add four groups, assign them permissions, and dictate where those permissions will flow. Here's the breakdown:

Administrators   Full Control, which applies to "This folder, subfolders, and files"

System   Full Control, which applies to "This folder, subfolders, and files"

Creator Owner   Full Control, which applies to "This folder, subfolders, and files"

Authenticated Users   Create Folders/Append Data, Read Permissions, Read Extended Attributes, which apply to "This folder only" (as seen here).

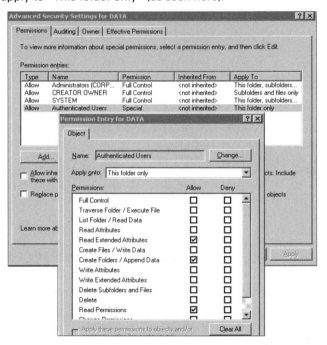

This information is valid for both Windows 2003 and Windows 2000 (and likely works for 2008 servers but I didn't specifically test). And you can find more details in the Knowledge Base article Q288991. Adding these groups and assigning these permissions appears to remove the automatic synchronization of Redirected Folders, as you'll see a bit later. However, you can restore this functionality with the **Administratively Assigned Offline Files** policy setting—again, explored later.

In some circumstances when redirecting to Windows 2000 servers, I needed to grant the Authenticated Users the List Folder/Read Data access for this process to work fully.

But we have a problem. What if you've already set up Redirected Folders and users already have their own protected subfolders? How do you go back in time and fix the ones that already were created? In our example, our Redirected Folders are in D:\data. Follow these steps:

1. Start cmd.exe, and type **AT nn:nn /interactive cmd.exe** (nn:nn is a couple of minutes in the future in 24-hour format) on the server where your share resides. This will get you access as the NT Authority\SYSTEM account which has the required permissions you'll need.

2. Wait until the new command window opens. This can take up to a minute. In this window, you are acting as the SYSTEM account.

3. Run **cacls "d:\data" /T /E /G DOMAIN\Administrator:F**.

This command edits the ACL (/E) rather than replacing it. It grants the user DOMAIN\Administrator Full Control (/G DOMAIN\Administrator:F) and sets the permissions on all subfolders (/T). This should allow you to set all previously created folders to nearly the same standard.

Advanced Redirected Folders

Anything beyond the basics as previously described isn't required. However, you can set up some advanced options using the Setting drop-down list box, as shown in Figure 3.5 earlier in this chapter. Advanced Redirected Folders works best in two situations, both larger environments:

- A campus with many buildings. You'll want to specify different Redirected Folders locations that are closest to the biggest groups of users.

- More likely, a specific department that is charged with purchasing its own server and storage. In this scenario, there's usually a battle over who can store what data on whose server. With this mechanism, everyone can have their own sandbox.

In either case, you can still have an OU that affects many similar users but breaks up where folders are redirected, depending on the users' respective security groups. For example, we have an OU called **Sales** that contains two global security sales groups: East_Sales and West_Sales. Each Sales group needs their folders redirected to the server closest to them, either East_Server or West_Server. First, you'll want to create the shares on both the East_Server and West_Server as directed earlier. For this example, they're each shared out as Data. To perform an Advanced Folder Redirection, follow these steps:

1. If you're not already logged onto DC01 as Administrator of the domain using your station VISTAMANAGEMENT, do so now.

2. Start the GPMC.

3. Right-click the OU on which we want to apply Folder Redirection, in this case the **Sales** OU, and select "Create a GPO in the domain, and link it here."

4. Enter a descriptive name, such as "Advanced Folder Redirection for the **Sales** OU," for the GPO. Select it, and click Edit to open the Group Policy Management Editor.

5. The GPO for the OU appears. Drill down to Folder Redirection by choosing User Configuration ➤ Policies ➤ Windows Settings ➤ Folder Redirection.

6. Right-click the `Documents` folder in the Group Policy Management Editor, and choose Properties from the shortcut menu to open the Documents Properties dialog box. In the Setting drop-down list box, select "Advanced—Specify locations for various user groups." The dialog box changes so that you can now use the Add button to add security settings, as shown in Figure 3.7. Click OK.

7. Click the Add button in the My Documents Properties dialog box to open up the Specify Group and Location dialog box. Click Browse under Security Group Membership, and locate the **East_Sales** global security group.

8. From the "Target folder location" drop-down, choose "Redirect to the following location" and enter the UNC path of the Redirected Folder. In this case, it's **\\east_server\data\ %username%**. Click OK to close the Specify Group and Location dialog box.

9. Repeat steps 7 and 8 for the **West_Sales** global security group.

FIGURE 3.7   Use the Advanced redirection function to choose different locations to move users' data.

Don't click OK (or Apply) yet. There's more to do. If you do click OK or Apply, you're going to get a warning (which we'll talk about in the Real-World Scenario entitled "What Happens When You Edit a GPO from a Pre-Vista Management Station?").

When you're finished, you should have both **East_Sales** and **West_Sales** listed.

The next time the user logs on, the settings specified in the Settings tab take effect; that is, by default, a new folder is generated specifically for each user, and the current documents in the user's `Documents` folder are transported to the newly Redirected Folder location.

Real World Scenario

What Happens When You Edit a GPO from a Pre-Vista Management Station?

If you took my advice in the companion book, *Group Policy Fundamentals, Security, and Trouble-shooting* (Sybex, 2008) and also in the lab setup guide in the introduction of this book, then you're using a Windows Vista computer as your management station. Why? Because you'll always have the full ability to edit whatever new goodies are in the Group Policy Object Editor.

And for Folder Redirection, this isn't any different. As you saw in Figure 3.4, Windows Vista has a lot more folders it can possibly redirect (like Links, Searches, and others listed previously) and some that are more familiar (like Start Menu and Documents).

So, whenever you click OK after editing any Folder Redirection policies on Windows Vista, you'll always get a warning like this one.

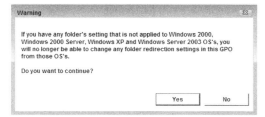

This warning is saying "You're editing this GPO on a Windows Vista management station. If you edit it on a pre-Vista management station, you're going to be in for a world of hurt."

Indeed, this is true. Take a look at the same GPO when viewed on a Windows Server 2003 management station if you had a policy for, say, the Links folder. The GPMC on that older machine doesn't know how to interpret the settings. This makes sense: Vista is newer; older management stations don't know what to do with this information. Sometimes, it displays only the information it can. For instance, older GPMCs can still sometimes figure out what's going on in the Documents folder when it's redirected. But not always, as attested by this screenshot.

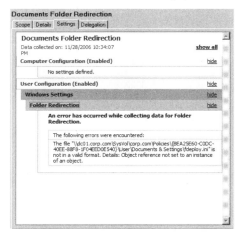

Then, if you decide to try and edit Folder Redirection policies of a GPO you created using Windows Vista by using a pre-Vista management station, again, it's a world of hurt. Take a look what happens when you try to make a change in, say, My Documents (if this was originally created on a Windows Vista management station). The system throws an "Access is denied" message. Which is pretty elegant considering the circumstances.

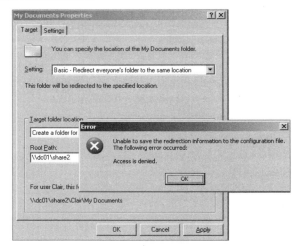

So, the message is clear: create and edit your GPOs using a Windows Vista management station. Don't create the GPOs using Windows Vista and then return to a pre-Vista management station.

In case you're interested, what's happening under the hood is this:

Vista Folder Redirection writes a new file into the GPT called fdeploy1.ini that doesn't overlap with the old one (called fdeploy.ini). However, it does populate fdeploy.ini when you select downward-compatible mode. But you see this message on a Windows XP management station because Vista sets the "old" fdeploy.ini file that it creates for downward compatibility as Read-only in the GPT, effectively preventing a downlevel GPEditor from writing to it.

It's a pretty low-tech solution; but it works.

Testing Folder Redirection of *Documents/My Documents*

In the last chapter, you used Brett Wier's account to verify that Roaming Profiles were working properly. You did this by creating a test file, FILE1.TXT, in the My Documents folder and noting that the file properly roamed with the user when he hopped from machine to machine. Additionally, you noted that the file location was on the local hard drive in his locally cached copy of his Roaming User Profile. To see whether My Documents is being redirected, move Brett's user account into an OU that has the My Documents folder redirected as specified in either the Basic or Advanced Folder Redirection settings.

You will need to log off and back on as Brett to see the changes take effect. Group Policy background refresh (as detailed in the companion book's Chapter 4) does not apply to Redirected Folders.

Let's first see what happens when we log onto a Windows 2000 machine as Brett Wier and open My Documents. Right-click FILE1.TXT and note its location, as shown in Figure 3.8.

FIGURE 3.8 Windows 2000 Folder Redirection in action.

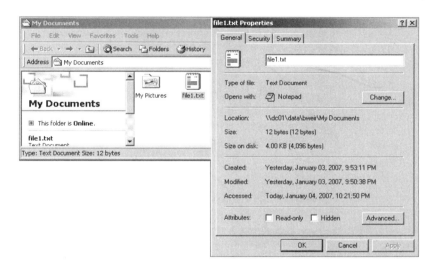

The file was automatically transported from the Roaming Profile and anchored to the fixed point on the server, in this case \\DC01\data\bwier\My Documents.

If you perform the same experiment on a Windows XP or Windows Vista machine, you'll see the same results, but notice the curious arrows on the files and folders (see Figure 3.9 for Windows XP and Figure 3.10 for Windows Vista).

The arrows signify that you're one step closer to having a managed desktop; a new feature is already working for you—Offline Files, which I'll talk about in the next major section. However, one point should be gleaned from these two figures. The behavior of Windows XP and Windows Vista is different from that of Windows 2000. That is, when a Windows Vista or Windows XP machine uses a Redirected Folder, the entire contents are automatically cached offline. Thus, when the network is offline, your users still have total access to the files they need.

Stay tuned for Offline Files, where we'll discuss how to actually put this knowledge to good use.

You will not see the arrows if you performed the procedure in the "How to Grant Administrators Access to Documents/My Documents (or Other Redirected Folders)" Real-World Scenario earlier in this chapter. However, you will see these arrows if you follow these instructions in the "Administratively Assigned Offline Files" section later in this chapter.

FIGURE 3.9 Windows XP Folder Redirection in action.

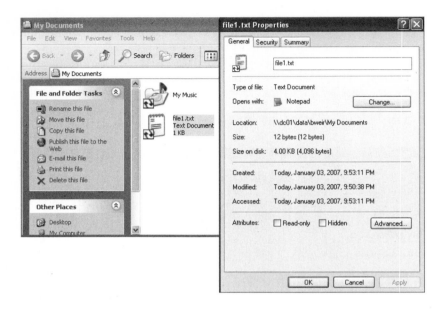

FIGURE 3.10 Windows Vista Folder Redirection in action.

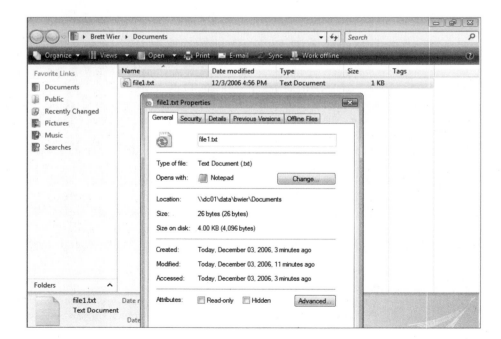

Redirecting the Start Menu and the Desktop

The Start Menu and Desktop might seem like weird items to redirect. However, there are some cases where you might want to.

One case is in a common computing environment—such as a nurse's station, library computer, or kiosk—where you want to make sure the same Start Menu and/or Desktop are always presented. Then, you can lock down the target location of the redirected items to ensure that they cannot be changed.

In cases like these, you specify a shared folder with Read-only access for the Security group who will use it and Full Control for just one person who can change the Start Menu or Desktop (such as a fake account that no one uses within that Security group). That way, no one in the affected group can normally change the common Start Menu or Desktop except for the administrative user of the bogus account you created, who has Full Control permissions over the share.

Instead of using the *%username%* variable, you fix the redirection to a specific shared folder and directory, as shown in Figure 3.11. Since all users are to use the same settings, there's no need to use *%username%*. Indeed, since you're locking the shared folder down as Read-only for the Security group, the username is moot.

FIGURE 3.11 Use one static path to ensure that all Desktops receive the same setting.

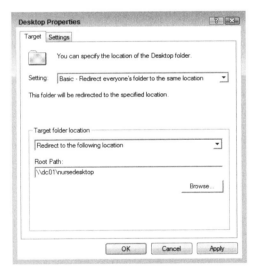

You could also argue that redirecting the Desktop is a good for those who have users who think the Desktop is a good dumping ground for big documents. If you redirect the Desktop, you're reducing the size of the Roaming User Profile. It's up to you if you want to explore this option.

You'll find additional Group Policy settings regarding the configuration of the Start Menu in User Configuration ➤ Policies ➤ Administrative Templates ➤ Start Menu & Taskbar.

Redirecting the Application Data

Because application designers can decide what to put in the Application Data folder in the profile, an administrator never knows what size this folder could grow to. By redirecting the Application Data, files—such as custom dictionaries or databases—can be firmly planted on the server instead of having to go up and back with each logon with the Roaming Profile.

In Windows 2000 and XP, there are some potential downsides to redirecting Application Data. One potential downside is that this folder contains the user's private PKI (Public Key Infrastructure) keys. If you use Windows 2000 or Windows XP and redirect this folder to a server, the keys are available to anyone with access to those files on the server. This isn't necessarily a security breach, because the keys are encrypted with a hash of the user's password and other elements, but take special precautions just in case.

The real danger in redirecting Application Data for Windows 2000 and XP shows up when users need to decrypt EFS (Encrypting File System) files. To do so, they need access to their private PKI keys. If you've redirected Application Data to the server, and the server goes down or the user's computer goes offline, how will users get their keys to decrypt their EFS files?

- Well, in Windows 2000, this is a big problem by default. Because, remember, Windows 2000 machines don't automatically make Redirected Folders always available offline. So, in the case of Windows 2000 the keys are cached in memory until they are cleared out by reboot.

- If the client is a Windows XP, the EFS files are cached offline automatically. The only issue would be if someone turned off offline caching of files. If offline caching is turned off and the Application Data is redirected and the computer is off the network, the user most likely wouldn't be able to access their encrypted files.

- In Windows Vista, things have changed even further. When you redirect the `Appdata\Roaming` folder, the following folders are not redirected to the server: `Appdata\Roaming\Microsoft\` with subdirectories `Credentials`, `Crypto`, `Protect`, and `System Certificates`. So, previous worries about where the keys are and who has access to them are reduced.

The final note here is that because Microsoft applications use this directory to store their settings data, this folder is heavily accessed (for example, by Outlook). Redirecting this, especially if it's not cached, can be painful from a performance perspective. (Note however, that Windows XP and Windows Vista should automatically cache this folder when redirected.)

Group Policy Setting for Folder Redirection

There are only a handful of settings that control Folder Redirection. They're located in Computer *and* User Configuration ➤ Policies ➤ Administrative Templates ➤ System ➤ Folder Redirection. If there's a conflict between the User and Computer side, the Computer side will win.

Do Not Automatically Make Redirected Folders Available Offline (User Side Only)

As you're about to discover, Windows XP and Windows Vista go the extra mile and automatically cache every scrap of data you have in, say, `Documents/My Documents` (or any other Redirected Folder). The idea is that if you're offline, you might need the data on the road. (Don't worry, we'll get to this in excruciating detail soon.)

This setting lets you disable that behavior. You might want to do this if you have laptops that travel to places with slowish links because all of the user's data will be downloaded over that slow link. See the section "Using Folder Redirection and Offline Files over Slow Links" a little later.

In versions prior to Vista this was an Offline Files policy. It is now a Folder Redirection policy. Why the change? There was no Offline Files API prior to Vista, so a feature like Folder Redirection had no way to pin a folder into the CSC cache. Now that Offline Files has an API, Microsoft chose to move this "decision" to pin files over to Folder Redirection. Now Folder Redirection decides whether or not it should pin the Redirected Folder. It becomes a much cleaner solution under the hood.

Because this policy is a user-side policy, it becomes very difficult to implement on a system-wide level.

Use Localized Subfolder Names When Redirecting *Start* and *My Documents* (Both User and Computer)

This setting is one that you might consider using in a multilingual corporate environment. However, it's very quirky.

The policy actually affects only legacy subfolders of Documents (My Music, My Pictures, and My Videos) and the Start Menu subfolders. This policy *does not* affect the root Documents or Start Menu folders.

It supports the legacy scenario where users may be sharing data between a multi-lingual Vista machine and a localized Windows XP or Windows 2000 machine. In that scenario, the legacy folder structure is preserved. The subfolders like My Music also map correctly to the localized name on the localized downlevel OS. The supported scenario is only when the user goes across the same languages, i.e., Vista French to XP Localized French (but *not* across languages).

This policy setting affects only Windows Vista.

Troubleshooting Redirected Folders

Occasionally, Folder Redirection doesn't work as it should. Or, maybe it does. We'll check out some cases in which it appears not to be working but really is.

Windows XP/Windows Vista Fast Boot and Folder Redirection

If you see the message in Figure 3.12, you might initially think that Folder Redirection isn't working as it should. This event tells us that the default is that Fast Boot is enabled in Windows Vista and Windows XP, and Folder Redirection will not take effect until the next logon.

FIGURE 3.12 Fast Boot in Windows XP (and Windows Vista) can delay Folder Redirection until multiple reboots.

With the default (that Fast Boot is enabled), Basic Folder Redirection needs two logons to take effect and Advanced Folder Redirection needs three logons to take effect (see Chapter 4 of the companion book, *Group Policy Fundamentals, Security, and Troubleshooting*, for more information).

Permissions Problems

Be sure that the user has access to the folder; specifically, make sure that the share you use for Folder Redirection is set for Authenticated Users:Full Control. Without it, you might encounter EventID: 101, as shown in Figure 3.13 (left) for Windows XP. Another common Windows XP event for security problems is Event 112: "The security descriptor structure is invalid." Again, the idea is that there are some permissions problems—usually share level permissions where Authenticated Users weren't set up properly for Full Control (or Co-owner).

You can see a similar error for Windows Vista, but with event ID 502, as seen in Figure 3.13 (right).

Use *GPResult* for Verification

First, make sure the user is actually being affected by the GPO you set up that contains your Folder Redirection policy. Use the GPResult tool we explored in Chapter 6 of the companion book. Figure 3.14 shows a snippet from the output of GPResult /v on Windows XP when Folder Redirection is working.

FIGURE 3.13   Be sure the user has permissions to write to the share you set up. The Windows Vista event ID is different, but the results are the same.

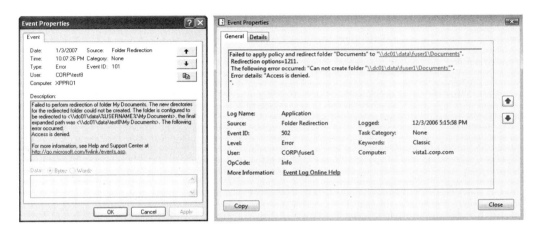

FIGURE 3.14   GPResult can help you determine if Folder Redirection is working.

```
Folder Redirection
----------------------
    GPO: My Docs Folder Redirection
        Setting:  InstallationType:  basic
        Grant Type:           Not Exclusive Rights
        Move Type:            Contents of Local Directory moved
        Policy Removal:       Leave folder in existing location
        Redirecting Group:    Everyone
        Redirected Path:      \\windc01\data\bwier\my documents\My Pictures

    GPO: My Docs Folder Redirection
        Setting:  InstallationType:  basic
        Grant Type:           Not Exclusive Rights
        Move Type:            Contents of Local Directory moved
        Policy Removal:       Leave folder in existing location
        Redirecting Group:    Everyone
        Redirected Path:      \\windc01\data\bwier\my documents
```

If no Folder Redirection policy displays in the output when you run GPResult /v, chances are the user is not being affected by the policy. Check to see if the user has permissions on the GPO for both Read and Apply Group Policy. If they are getting the GPO as indicated via GPResult /v, also make sure that the target server is still available, that the share is still shared, and that the users have rights to write to that share and folder. Last, make sure the user isn't hitting a disk quota on the volume on which the shared folder resides, as this can generate mixed results.

Enabling Advanced Folder Redirection Logging

Folder Redirection can provide a detailed log should the event log and GPResult not turn up what you're looking for. The procedure for this is different for pre-Vista and Windows Vista machines.

Turning on Advanced Folder Redirection Logging for Pre-Vista machines

For pre-Vista machines, you'll modify the Registry, which will create a log file for the Folder Redirection process. To do so, you need to modify the Registry as follows:

```
HKLM\Software\Microsoft\Windows NT\CurrentVersion\Diagnostics
```

If the `Diagnostics` key doesn't exist at the end of this Registry path, you'll need to create it. Then, add a new Reg_DWORD of `FdeployDebugLevel` and set it to `0f` in hex or 15 in decimal. Once you do this, you can find the log file at:

```
%windir%\debug\usermode\fdeploy.log
```

Only the administrator can read the log file, so you have two options. First, you can log out as the user and log back in as the local administrator to read the log file in action. Alternatively, you can use the `runas` command to view the log as an administrator while you're still logged in as the user.

Turning on Advanced Folder Redirection Logging for Vista Machines

You will essentially enable verbose logging the same way you did for pre-Vista machines, but you will have to do it with the elevated `CMD.exe` prompt. First, you'll need to click Start ➢ All Programs ➢ Accessories, right-click over the command prompt and select Run As Administrator. Then, in the new command prompt, run the following command:

```
reg add "HKLM\Software\Microsoft\Windows NT\CurrentVersion\Diagnostics"
/v FdeployDebugLevel /t REG_DWORD /d "0xF" /f
```

Log off and log on and check out the Application log in Event Viewer.

Offline Files and Synchronization

We've mitigated the amount of traffic our network will have to bear from Roaming Profiles by implementing Redirected Folders—especially for My Documents (for Windows XP) and Documents (for Windows Vista). But we still have another hurdle. Now that we're anchoring our users' data to the server, what's to happen if the server goes down? What happens if our network cable is unplugged? What if our top executive is flying at 30,000 feet? How will any of our users get to their data? The answer, in fact, comes from another feature—Offline Files.

Offline Files seeks to make files within shares that are normally accessed online available offline! You can be sitting under a tree, on an airplane, in a submarine—anywhere—and still have your files with you.

Here's a brief overview of the magic: Once you enable a particular share to support the function, the client's Offline Files cache maintains files as they're used on the network. When users are online and connected to the network, nothing really magical happens. Users continue to write files upon the server as normal. However, in addition to the file writes at the server, the file writes additionally get reflected in the local cache too, as a protection to maintain the files in cache. Moreover, reads are satisfied from the client, thus saving bandwidth.

You can use Offline Files for any share you like and practically guarantee that the data users need is with them. As we've noticed, Windows Vista and Windows XP already seem to do something special when you're using Redirected Folders. That is, when these operating systems notice that you've redirected a folder, they'll automatically make that data available offline for you.

However, it's certainly possible to use Offline Files for public "common" shares. For example, an administrator can set up shares for customer data, and a server can have a "general repository" from which multiple users can access files. We'll see how this works around the bend (especially when two people change the same file). Sounds bad, but it's not crazy-bad.

We'll also explore the differences between Windows XP and Windows Vista's Offline Files engine here.

So, for these examples, if you want to follow along, create a share called Sales on \\DC01. You wouldn't normally stick shares on your Domain Controller, but for our working example here, it'll be just fine. Additionally, stick 10 text files—salesfile1.txt through salesfile10.txt— in there, so you can watch the reaction as various flavors of Windows try to touch these files. Finally, map a network drive over to \\DC01\sales from your test machines (Windows 2000, Windows XP, and Windows Vista).

 There are three shares that you should not place Offline Files upon. Don't use Offline Files with the SYSVOL or the NETLOGON share. Nor should you use Offline Files with the Profiles share you created in the last chapter (more on this later).

Making Offline Files Available

When you set up any shared folder on your server, you'll notice an Offline Settings button, as highlighted in Figure 3.15 (seen as the Caching button on Windows 2000). The Offline Settings dialog box is slightly different in Windows 2000 and Windows 2003 (and a little harder to find in Windows Server 2008). Figure 3.15 shows the Windows 2003 and 2008 version, and the default in 2000 is "Manual Caching for Documents." The default setting named "Only the files and programs that users specify will be available online" may not really be the most efficient setting for this feature. The four settings are described in the following sections.

Only the Files and Programs that Users Specify Will Be Available Offline (or Windows 2000's "Manual Caching for Documents")

With this setting, users must specify which files they want to keep with them offline. They can do this in the Documents/My Documents folder by right-clicking a file (or more commonly, a folder) and choosing Make Available Offline in Windows XP and 2000 (see Figure 3.16) or "Always available offline" in Windows Vista (see Figure 3.16) from the shortcut menu. The unofficial term for this is *pinning* a file, but you won't see that term in any official Microsoft documentation. Users can pin as many files as they like; the number of files is limited only by the size of their hard drive (in Windows XP) or, in Windows Vista, this can be imposed by a hard "max space" limit via Group Policy (explored a little later).

FIGURE 3.15   Four offline settings for caching behaviors are available in Windows server.

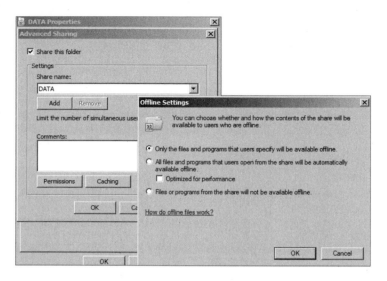

If a Windows 2000 or Windows XP user chooses to pin individual files manually, the Offline Files Wizard asks them some simple questions (see Figure 3.17). This wizard runs only the first time a user pins one or more files, and each user on a computer who pins files from that computer walks through the wizard once. As stated, in Windows Vista the command is slightly different, and there is no wizard. It just does it—short and sweet.

FIGURE 3.16   Users can pin files by right-clicking them and making them available offline for Windows 2000 and XP (top) and Windows Vista (bottom).

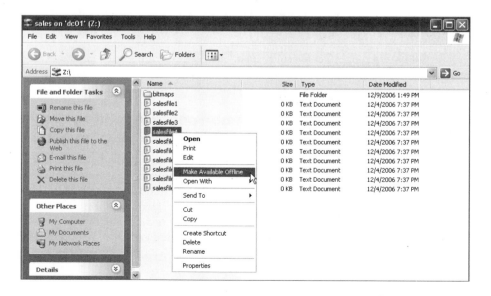

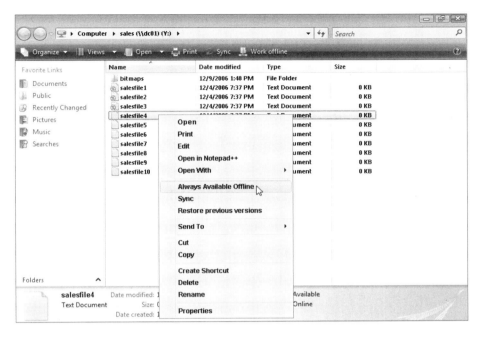

FIGURE 3.17   The Windows XP Offline Files Wizard asks if the user wants to synchronize upon logon and logoff (in Windows XP, usually a pretty good idea).

In pre-Vista systems, a balloon announces changes in Offline Files cache state, although a user who does not enable reminder balloons will still see the initial state change balloon tips. Once the wizard is finished, the pinned files are automatically brought down into the local cache. Users get a little graphical reminder attached to the pinned file's icon, as shown in Figure 3.18.

FIGURE 3.18 Pinned files can easily be recognized by their yin-yang (left) or "round-trip" (right) icon.

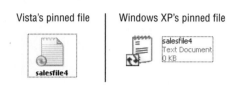

Vista's pinned file | Windows XP's pinned file

The reminder is an unobtrusive yin-yang icon symbolizing the harmony users will feel knowing their files are safe on the server and cached locally. Or maybe it's just two arrows showing the file can be "round-tripped." You can be the judge.

If you want, you can disconnect the network cable to your test client and still access any file that's now available offline.

As you saw in Figures 3.9 and 3.10 earlier in this chapter, users logging onto Windows Vista and Windows XP machines with the redirected My Documents folder already have these yin-yang icons on their files and folders. Windows XP and Windows Vista do a little extra magic and guarantee that all files in important Redirected Folders (such as the redirected Documents/My Documents) are available wherever the user roams.

All Files and Programs that Users Open from the Share Will Be Automatically Available Offline (or Automatic Caching for Documents for Windows 2000)

If you plan to use Offline Files for more than just the user's private data, you typically select this option. When users access any files in a share with this setting, the files are copied and stored in a local cache on the workstation, where, by default, 10 percent of the C: hard drive space is used to maintain files in a first in/first out fashion.

Before turning this on for any share or shares, be sure to read "It's Not Offline Files—It's Explorer!" a bit later in this chapter to understand how turning this on could be a potential headache.

For Windows Vista, that default is changed to 25 percent of free disk space when the drive cache is first created. This could mean that if you have only a little space left when the drive cache is created, it won't be 25 percent of the drive.

Later in this chapter, in the "Manually Tweaking the Offline Files Interface for Vista Machines" section, you can see this "25% of available disk space" formula in action. In Figure 3.36, you'll see that my offline cache size is only 15.2%. This number was calculated because it was 25 percent of free disk space at that time.

For example, let's say you're using Windows XP and have a 1GB C: partition. In this case, 100MB of data flows in and out of your cache. Let's also say that you have 11 files, each 10MB in size, named FILE1.DOC through FILE11.DOC. You consecutively click each of them to open them and bring each into the cache. FILE1.DOC through FILE10.DOC are maintained in the cache until such time as FILE11.DOC is read. At that time, since FILE1.DOC was first in the cache, it is also the first to be flushed from the cache to make way for FILE11.DOC.

 The files are ejected in a background thread called the CSC Agent. The agent periodically makes a pass over the cache removing auto-cached files as necessary. If a Write operation grows the cache size beyond the established limit, it doesn't immediately evict the least recently used auto-cached file. The CSC Agent is only periodically brought into memory for execution.

Additionally, files can be pinned, as they were in the "Only the files and programs that users specify will be available online" (or Windows 2000's "Manual Caching for Documents") option. Pinned files don't count toward the cache percentage in Windows 2000 or Windows XP but *do* count toward pinned cache size in Vista.

In all cases though, pinned files are exempt from being flushed from the cache and are protected, hence, "always available" to your users when working offline.

While it's tempting, do not use Automatic Caching for Documents for the share that houses the Roaming Profiles you set up in Chapter 2. See the next section, "Files or Programs from the Share Will Not Be Available Offline (or 'Disallow Caching for Files of Any Type' on Windows 2000)" for the reasons.

Files or Programs from the Share Will Not Be Available Offline (or Disallow Caching for Files of Any Type for Windows 2000)

If you choose this option, no files are cached for offline use, nor can they be pinned. This doesn't prevent users from copying the files to any other place they might have access to locally or to another network share they have access to that does have caching enabled.

Another Option: Optimized for Performance (or Automatic Caching for Programs for Windows 2000)

This option's name is highly misleading. The idea is to use this setting for Read-only files that you want available offline and in the cache, such as executables. According to Microsoft, this setting does a "version check" instead of creating a handle on the server if the access is Read-only. Since there is no server handle, the system tries to use the local version first to save bandwidth when it can use either the locally cached version or the network version.

Upon performing a network trace of the interaction of Optimized for Performance (for Windows 2003) and Automatic Caching for Programs (in Windows 2000), there seems to be no discernible difference between it and Windows 2003's "All files and programs that users open from the share will be automatically available offline" (or Automatic Caching for Documents for Windows 2000). Therefore, use "All files and programs that users open from the share will be automatically available offline" (or Automatic Caching for Documents) whenever possible.

Inside Windows XP Synchronization

Now, we want to spend a little time understanding what's going in synchronization land. Here, we'll explore Windows XP's synchronization engine. Then, we'll take some time and explore Windows Vista's synchronization engine.

Inside the Windows XP Offline Files and Synchronization Manager Interface

Most people would start out by exploring Tools ➢ Folder Options and selecting the Offline Files tab. You can see this in Figures 3.19 and 3.20.

FIGURE 3.19   The Folder Options item on the Tools menu is the first place to start your Offline Files configurations.

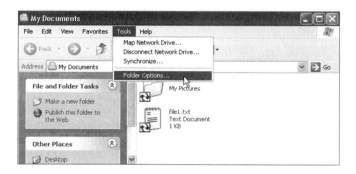

FIGURE 3.20   The default options for Offline Files on a Windows XP Professional machine. Only administrators can change all the options.

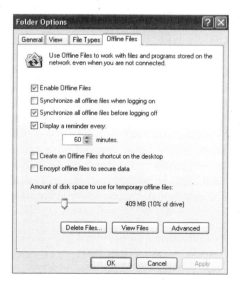

Indeed, this is where Offline Files live in Windows XP. But this is only half of where the synchronization magic in Windows XP *occurs*. That's because, in Windows XP, the Offline Files handler is used as a snap-in for a component called the Synchronization Manager. The Synchronization Manager is a framework for plug-ins such as Offline Files to use. The other half of the magic is in the Synchronization Manager itself.

You can open the Synchronization Manager (the Items to Synchronize dialog box, which is shown in Figure 3.21) in two ways:

- From the Desktop, choose Start ➤ All Programs ➤ Accessories ➤ Synchronize.

- In Explorer, choose Tools ➤ Synchronize.

FIGURE 3.21   Users can select specific shares on which to synchronize items.

Users can specifically choose which plug-ins they want to use, such as Offline Files or Offline Web Pages, as shown in Figure 3.21. For each plug-in, they can select which data (such as shares) they want the Synchronization Manager to handle. Additionally, the buttons in this dialog box perform the following functions:

Synchronize   Forces the Synchronization Manager to pop into the foreground and start the synchronization process.

Properties   Allows the user to open the Offline Files folder to view the files in the local cache. Same as the View Files button shown earlier in Figure 3.20.

Setup   Allows you to refine how synchronization is controlled. You can see the result in Figure 3.22.

Here a user can specify which Synchronization Manager snap-ins to use. In this case, the Offline Files snap-in is selected (with two entries), and the Offline Web Pages is also selected. The other entries on the Logon/Logoff tab that need specific attention are the "When I log on to my computer" and "When I log off my computer." These entries co-interact with the Offline Files "Synchronize all offline files when logging on" and "Synchronize all offline files before logging off" as in Figure 3.20 earlier in this chapter. Now, we'll take some time to explore that interaction.

FIGURE 3.22 The Synchronization Manager is a framework for snap-ins such as Offline Files and Offline Web Pages.

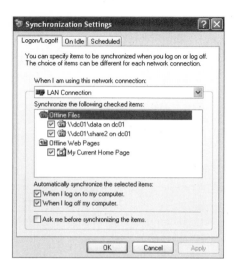

Understanding Offline Files and Synchronization Manager Interaction

Offline Files has two possible synchronization modes: Quick Sync and Full Sync. Here's how each works:

Quick Sync At logon, the files that were modified in the local client cache are pushed up to the server. At logoff, only the files that the user actually opened on the server are brought down into the local cache.

Full Sync At logon, *all* the files the user has in cache are synchronized with the copies on the server. Updated files on the server also come down into the cache. Also, if the user is caching an entire folder, those files come down into the cache. At logoff, the same occurs. That is, all the files the user has in cache and any new files on the server are synchronized in the cache.

For Full Sync, we're mainly concerned with the two options: "Synchronize all offline files when logging on" and "Synchronize all offline files before logging off." The key word to focus on in these options is *all*. You can see these settings in Figure 3.20 earlier in this chapter. Checking either of these options (or both) directs the Offline Files handler to utilize the Synchronization Manager to synchronize *all* content.

The Synchronization Manager settings (seen in Figure 3.22) control how the Synchronization Manager responds to the logon and logoff conditions on the computer. If these check boxes are *not* checked, *no* Synchronization Manager activity occurs at the corresponding time. These settings apply equally to all handlers registered with Synchronization Manager—not just the Offline Files handler.

So that's how they work together: the two dialog boxes' settings are interdependent for how Offline Files will synchronize. Indeed, if the corresponding Synchronization Manager setting is *not* enabled, the Offline Files setting has no effect.

Table 3.1 describes the behavior at logon. Table 3.2 describes the behavior at logoff.

TABLE 3.1 Logon Behavior with Synchronization Manager Settings and Offline Files Settings

Synchronization Manager Setting "When I log on to my computer"	Offline Files "Synchronize all offline files when logging on"	Resulting Behavior
Off	Off	No sync activity at logon
Off	On	No sync activity at logon
On	Off	Quick Sync at logon
On	On	Full Sync at logon

TABLE 3.2 Logoff Behavior with Synchronization Manager Settings and Offline Files Settings

Synchronization Manager Setting "When I log off my computer"	Offline Files "Synchronize all offline files before logging off"	Resulting Behavior
Off	Off	No sync activity at logoff
Off	On	No sync activity at logoff
On	Off	Quick Sync at logoff
On	On	Full Sync at logoff

Unfortunately, there is little coordination between the Synchronization Manager and Offline Files user interfaces. However, there is one small interaction: If you enable Offline Files' "Synchronize all offline files when logging on" or "Synchronize all offline files before logging off," Windows automatically enables the corresponding Synchronization Manager setting. The opposite is not true.

People often think there is more coordination between XP's Offline Files and Synchronization Manager than there really is. It's not uncommon for people to think that Synchronization Manager *is* Offline Files. Synchronization Manager is simply a place to host various synchronization plug-ins (such as Offline Files), a place where those plug-ins can display their items, and a place for users to select specific items for synchronization at specific times (and in response to specific events).

Inside Windows Vista File Synchronization

The Windows XP synchronization engine was good, but it could have been better. The Windows Vista File Synchronization was rewritten in several ways to try to address some of the shortcomings of the Windows XP version.

Better Handling of Downed Shares

If a user was using a Windows XP machine and was leveraging several offline-enabled shares and one network share went down, XP always thought the whole server went down. So, the upshot was that other shares (that you likely didn't set to be available offline) were then suddenly also not available. Again, that server itself really never went down, just one share on that server. While bad, it doesn't sound *that* bad on first blush. But, if you were using a domain-based DFS (Distributed File System) this could be a major problem. Especially if you put your redirected My Documents folder in a domain-based DFS. If even one share in the DFS went offline, XP would assume the whole caboodle wasn't available.

In Vista, things get smarter. If one share goes down, it doesn't assume (thankfully) that the whole server up and died. It just transitions that one share to offline and keeps trying the other shares. Same with domain-based DFS shares. If you can't access one, it doesn't assume the whole DFS up and died—it will make just the parts that appear offline to be available offline.

For more information on DFS, check out http://www.microsoft.com/ windowsserver2003/technologies/storage/dfs/default.mspx (shortened to http://tinyurl.com/9p7uh).

Better Handling of Synchronization

Synchronizing files gets much smarter in Vista. In Windows XP you had to close *all* your open files (handles, really) in order for synchronization to start. In Vista, it's supposed to be "absolutely seamless," to quote Microsoft. Now, in Vista, changes are just synchronized in the background, and the user doesn't really notice anything has happened. Of course, a file cannot be synchronized while it is held open for write. All files need to be closed, then they're automatically synchronized.

Also, modified files, or files currently in conflict, continue to stay offline while all other files and folders are transitioned online. The conflicting files are transitioned online after the conflict is resolved.

No More Logon/Logoff Syncing Files Dialog

On Windows XP, when you log off your machine, you'll see your files synchronizing (provided "sync at logoff" was turned on). This was often very confusing for a new user who had no training about what was going on. In Windows Vista, there are no more synchronization dialogs during logoff (or logon, for that matter). In fact, there's actually no more synchronization at logoff. I make note of this in case you have some reliance that absolutely guarantees that your files need to be synchronized at logoff in Windows Vista as they were in Windows XP.

Better Transfer Technology

In Windows XP, the following file types cannot be cached:

- .PST (Outlook personal folder)
- .SLM (Source Library Management file)
- .MDB (Access database)
- .LDB (Access security)
- .MDW (Access workgroup)
- .MDE (Access compiled module)
- .DB? (everything that has the extension .DB plus anything else in the third character, such as .DBF, is never included in the cache)

In Windows Vista, those limitations are out the window. Not only is there a brand new algorithm to help determine which files and directories are different, but also this same technology sends over *just the changed data* in a file. So, previous limitations on the types of files are gone. The new technology is called *Bitmap Differential Transfer* or *BDT* for short. BDT is so amazing, it keeps track of what *disk pages* of the files have changed. So, if you change 2 bytes in a 2GB file, only that block of data is sent to the server, instead of the whole 2GB.

And, did you catch that Outlook .PST files are no longer unsupported? That is you can use Offline Files with 2GB .PST files, and Microsoft will support you.

In my opinion, that's worth the price of Windows Vista right there.

The BDT technology only works (right now) when you change a file on the *client* and want to sync it back to the *server*. This is fine, as this is the usual case. However, should someone work directly on a file on the server (and hence, your file on Windows Vista is out of date), sadly, the entire file is pulled down to the Windows Vista client. BDT can't send just the changed bytes.

The other BDT limitation is that it isn't effective on *new* files. All of the new files are synchronized back to the server. And, this can be a pitfall, because some applications (like Microsoft Word) insist on creating new files sometimes—even though you're editing what *feels* like the same .DOC file.

Better User Interface Design and Experience

Vista doesn't show a pop-up and tell the client he's now offline. This is good. We don't need to scare the users any more than usual. Because the experience is now "seamless," there's nothing that needs to be said to the user. However, if you select an offline folder (such as the redirected Documents) you'll see a status in the bottom left as seen in Figure 3.23.

Additionally, a user can choose if they want to manually work offline (as also seen in Figure 3.23). A user might choose to do this if the connection to the server is slow or unreliable, or maybe it's an expensive connection or they just want to test the offline experience.

There's no pop-up window at logoff telling them anything about the offline synchronization—because there is no synchronization at logoff. Synchronization is just quietly happening in the background. The downside, as stated earlier, is that Windows Vista might not have all the files synchronized when a user logs off if synchronization hasn't recently occurred.

FIGURE 3.23 Windows Vista's Offline Files User Interface isn't as in your face as Windows XP.

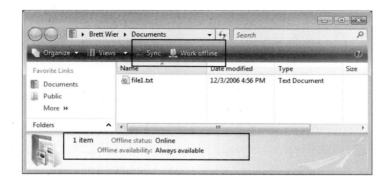

What's Really Happening in the Background on Windows Vista?

The Offline Files service automatically synchronizes files in several scenarios:

- If the user is working online, every five minutes the service "fills" in any sparsely cached files. This helps reduce the chance of transitioning offline and sparse files becoming unavailable to the user.

- Approximately one minute after user logon, the Offline Files service performs a full two-way synchronization of all content cached by that user. This is essentially the "logon sync" that was prominent in XP.

- Whenever a share transitions from offline to online, the Offline Files service performs a full two-way synchronization of that scope for each logged-on user.

Because of these background activities, the need to sync at logoff is reduced (since Windows XP). Since sync-at-logoff is not officially exposed in either the Offline Files or Sync Center UI, a user must manually sync using Sync Center prior to logging off if they wish to ensure that they have (in their local cache) all of the latest content from the server(s).

Windows Vista also has a new Sync Center (reborn as the next generation of the Sync Manager from Windows 2000/XP). It's a complete redesign/rewrite but it serves the same function. This Sync Center can be found from the Control Panel or by clicking the little green arrows in the toolbar. The idea of the Sync Center is that it's a common User Interface where all files and devices can get synchronized. So, expect things like handheld devices and other synchronizing things to make their way here. I don't know if this will end up being a nice unified experience or kind of a "catchall" place for anything in Windows Vista-land that synchronizes. You can see the Sync Center in Figure 3.24.

FIGURE 3.24   The new Windows Vista Sync Center

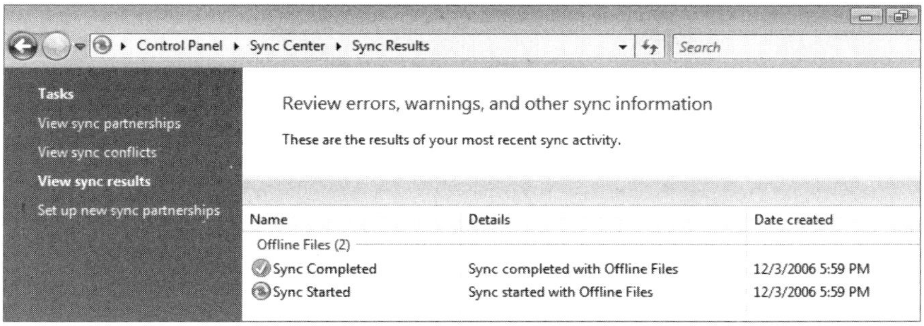

Better Offline Experience (Unified "Namespace" View)

Here's a common problem scenario with Windows XP: Let's assume Xavier chose to make three files out of ten available offline. When Xavier's computer went offline, the three files Xavier chose to keep offline were, of course, still there for Xavier to play with. However, the remaining seven files (which he didn't choose to Make Available Offline) simply—pop—disappeared. This was oftentimes confusing for users who weren't sure what the heck was going on. Windows Vista now introduces "ghosting" (which has nothing whatsoever to do with a product by Symantec).

Let's take the same scenario for Victoria on her Windows Vista machine. If she chooses to make those files Always Available Offline, as in Figure 3.25, then she gets a different experience. Windows Vista's Offline Files Ghosting will show the seven files "ghosted" as seen in Figure 3.26. Ghosts are namespace holders; they are visually different and are grayed out, plus they have an X icon overlay showing that they're not really accessible. The files are on the server, but because they're only on the server, Victoria can't access the files until she reconnects and makes them available offline.

FIGURE 3.25   Before Victoria goes offline, she pins salesfile1.txt, salesfile2.txt, and salesfile3.txt.

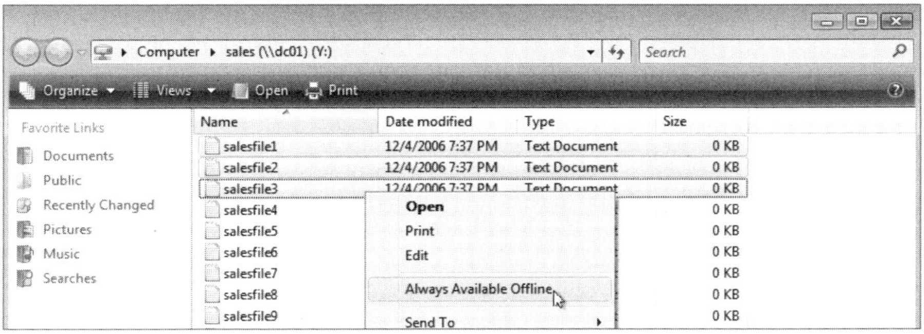

FIGURE 3.26 Files that are not available show a "ghosted" icon with a little "X."

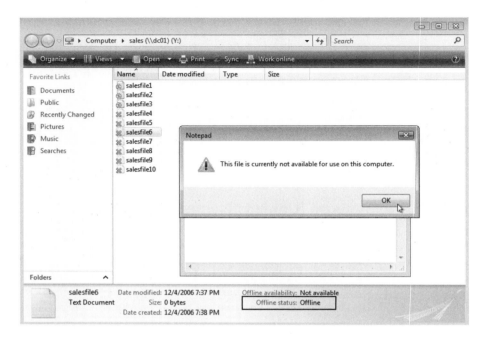

 The "Offline availability" status of "Not available" is an additional cue to the user that the file is not available for use. Note that these "Offline availability" and "Offline status" properties may be enabled as columns in the shell folder view. They're off by default because they take up valuable space, but some users may find them useful.

Better Cache Encryption

In Windows XP, offline files had the ability to be encrypted. This way if the laptop was stolen and the bad guy rooted around the file system, those offline files couldn't be seen in the clear. However, it wasn't long before it was realized that the encryption was based on the system account. Once you hijacked the system account, it was a trivial matter to see inside this encrypted cache. Just run a command prompt as the system account and, poof!, you're in!

In Windows Vista, offline files are now encrypted with the credentials of the first user who wants to encrypt a file. Using the user certificate is more secure (as hacking the system account is trivial), and this has a side benefit where multiple users of the same machine cannot see each other's encrypted cached files. However, this has a negative side detractor. What if Xavier and Victoria both have access to an encrypted file on a file server? Actually, this isn't a big deal if both Xavier and Victoria are online using different systems. Both XP and Vista have provisions for multiple certificates to be inside a file, allowing both users access to the file.

The problem comes in if Xavier or Victoria want to use that file while offline, and they both use the same Windows Vista laptop. Here's where it gets sticky. If you choose to enable Windows Vista's encrypted offline cache, you cannot share the same encrypted file with another user *on the same machine* (when that file transitions to offline). Only the user who initially encrypted the file can access that file when offline. The file is encrypted using only one certificate and that is the reason why multiple users cannot access them offline.

Again, this isn't a problem when Xavier or Victoria are online (and use the same Windows Vista laptop)—both users can continue to access the server version from the same client and get in using their certificate.

Other Random New Goodies

Here's a smattering of additional goodies you get with Windows Vista's Offline Files:

- One of the key problems with Windows XP's Offline Files feature was that it was never quite sure if you were using a slow link or not. That is, if you had connectivity, but it was slow, it would still use the file over the network rather than just use the copy it had cached locally. This would get really, really bad if you had lots of files over the network and even just looked at a thumbnail view (in Windows XP). The whole file would be downloaded. In Windows Vista, this can change. It's not changed by default, but see the section a little later entitled "Using Folder Redirection and Offline Files over Slow Links."

- Windows Vista's Offline Files is much smarter about detecting a slow-link condition (but only if you "explain" to Windows Vista what a slow link is; more on this later). And, during a slow link, it will simply transition to working offline. However, a user can, if desired, manually initiate a sync in the Sync Center. Finally, the user may force a transition to online mode if desired.

- You can, if you want, write your own scripts to manage the offline cache. Basically, all Offline Files functionality is scriptable and/or available via APIs. For instance, you could write a script to delete all files in cache, or initiate a sync, and other goodies as you wish. (See the section a little later entitled "Power Admins Rejoice: Scripting Offline Files.") See the note after the bullet points for some additional-geeky info about scripting.

- Windows XP had a 2GB maximum Offline Files limit. That limit is gone with Windows Vista.

- In case you missed it before, Windows Vista only sends the changed bits back to the server—not the whole file. This is via the Bitmap Differential Transfer (BDT) protocol. And, this new BDT magic works with (get this) any SMB server share back as far as Windows 2000. That's right. You don't need a Windows Server 2008 to take advantage of this. Your Windows Vista clients do all the magic on their own.

Not to get too geeky, but the script support is implemented as a WMI provider. Inline documentation is available in the CIM repository on a Vista system and may be viewed using a tool such as CIM Studio. This documentation doesn't show how to use the classes and methods, but it does provide descriptions. Look for classes that are prefixed with Win32_OfflineFiles.

Roaming Profile Shares and Offline Cache Settings

You should not use any caching with shares for Roaming Profiles. If any caching is enabled for profiles, Roaming Profiles can fail to act normally. Roaming Profiles has its own "internal" caching that is incompatible with Offline Files caching.

The correct choice for Roaming Profile shares is to select "Files or programs from the share will not be available offline" for shares on Windows 2003 or "Disallow Caching for Files of Any Type" for shares on Windows 2000.

The Windows 2003 caching default is to select "Only the files and programs that users specify will be available online," and the Windows 2000 default is to select "Manual Caching for Documents." These settings are not ideal, as there might be a way for a user to get into the contents of their profile and make portions available offline.

If you did set up a profile share in the last chapter, go back to that share and ensure that the share is set to disallow all caching.

Handling Conflicts

But a potential problem lies in these public "common" shares: what if someone on the road and someone in the office change the same document? In that event, the Windows XP Synchronization Manager or Windows Vista Sync Center handles conflict resolution on behalf of the Offline Files component.

When conflicts occur on a Windows XP machine, a user sees what's seen in Figure 3.27. As you can see, the user can inspect the contents of each version of the file, although that's usually not much help because there's no "compare changes" component to this resolution engine, and there's no way to "merge" the documents. But you can paw through the file yourself if you can remember where the last change was. It's not much, but it's a start.

In general, the Offline Files handler is fairly smart. If a file is renamed on either side (network or local cache), the engine wipes out the other instance of the file (because it thinks it's been deleted) and creates a copy of the new one. Hence, it appears a rename has occurred.

In Windows Vista, if a file changes both on the server and on the client, you'll get a message like what's seen in Figure 3.28 when you start to work online again. Then, a similar conflict resolution experience can be seen in Figure 3.29 where the user can press the Resolve button. Finally, the user can make a choice of how to deal with the conflict as seen in Figure 3.30.

FIGURE 3.27 The Windows 2000 and Windows XP conflict-resolution engine pops up when there's a conflict. It helps users decide which version of a file they want to keep.

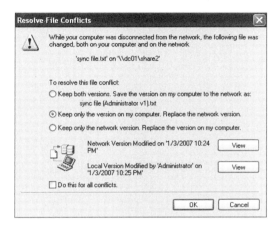

FIGURE 3.28 When Windows Vista connects up and recognizes a file has changed on both the server and the client, you'll get this message.

FIGURE 3.29 Use the Sync Center's Resolve button to handle conflicts.

FIGURE 3.30   Vista shows you your options to resolve a conflict.

Client Configuration of Offline Files

In the previous editions of my companion book, *Group Policy Fundamentals, Security, and Troubleshooting*, I suggested that you might just want to default your shares to "All files and programs that users open from the share will be automatically available offline"—also known as Autocache. And, we're about to explore what happens if you leverage Autocache. But, before we dive into it, be sure to read the Real-World Scenario "Autocache vs. Administratively Assigned Offline Files."

 Real World Scenario

Autocache vs. Administratively Assigned Offline Files

As mentioned, I have previously suggested that you simply enable "All files and programs that users open from the share will be automatically available offline" for every share. In retrospect, I think I could have given you better advice.

Here's why.

Because once that setting is enabled on a share, *everyone* who connects to this share will Autocache the files. So, for instance, if you set Autocache on the Sales share, an errant Human Resources person just poking around and opening up that share will start to stream those Sales files into the cache—even if they don't plan on using them. Sure, eventually, those files will be ejected after nonuse, but why get the user into a situation where he's merely looking at a share and then downloading all the junk in it? (Of course, it isn't junk to the Sales guys—but the Human Resources person certainly doesn't care about it much.)

A better approach is to specify that Sales guys need to Autocache the Sales share. And you can't do that directly in the share. To do that, you'll need a policy setting named **Administratively Assigned Offline Files**. Now, before I get too far ahead of myself, I will say that enabling this policy setting takes work. That is, every time you create a new share for the sales guys, you'll have to edit the GPO and specify the additional share. That way, only the sales guys will Autocache the Sales shares. Ditto for Human Resources and other folks around your Active Directory.

So, setting Autocache on all your shares (except the Profiles share) sounds like a good thing; but it's a better thing (if you can keep on top of it) if you hone in on the focus of *who* Autocaches *which* shares with **Administratively Assigned Offline Files,** explored a bit later in the text.

If you do decide to use Autocache, you can configure clients to use Offline Files with the aforementioned setting in three ways:

- Take the "do nothing" approach.
- Run around to each client and manually specify settings.
- Use Group Policy (insert fanfare music here).

This section explores the options a client can set on their own computer (or with your assistance). Then, in two later sections, "Using Group Policy to Configure Offline Files (User and Computer Node)" and "Using Group Policy to Configure Offline Files (Exclusive to the Computer Node)," we'll explore the broader scope of GPOs to see what sort of configuration we can do.

Another option is that you can script your changes via the Offline Files WMI provider described earlier. Of course, that only works for Windows Vista clients.

The "Do Nothing" Approach

If you do absolutely nothing at all, your clients will start to cache the files for offline use the first time they touch files in a share. This is called Autocaching. The underlying Offline Files behavior is the same for Windows 2000 and for Windows XP. However, Windows XP and Windows Vista have a trick up their sleeves, depending on what settings you're using for Explorer.

Windows Server 2003 and Windows Server 2008 acting as client computers are not enabled to cache files; this feature is specifically disabled in the operating system but can be turned on if really desired. See the sidebar entitled "Offline Files and Windows 2000 Server, Windows Server 2003 and Windows Server 2008."

This difference will be important and should be noted if you plan to enable caching for your shares to use Offline Files. In the examples in this section, we have a share called Sales, which contains some important files for our sales users. For this example, again, ensure that the "All files and programs that users open from the share will be automatically available offline" caching option is set on the share on our server.

Windows 2000 Reaction to Enabling Caching on Shares

Wanda is using her Windows 2000 laptop. She maps a drive to the Sales share (which maps as E:, as shown in Figure 3.31). When she uses Explorer to view the files on E:, she sees one she needs (`customer1.doc`) and double-clicks it to open it (as you can see in the bottom rightmost window in Figure 3.31). The file is now placed inside the Offline Files cache.

FIGURE 3.31 The files in the Offline Files folder cache are only those that Wanda (on her Windows 2000 laptop) has actually used.

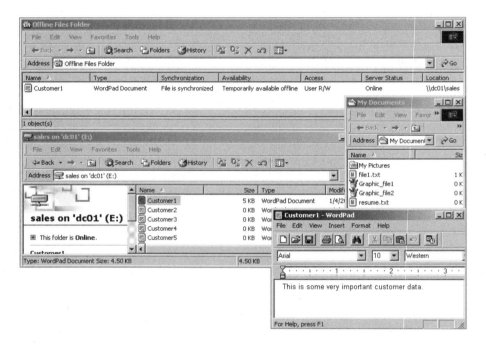

To see which files are within the file cache, Wanda chooses Tools ➢ Folder Options ➢ Offline Files ➢ View Files to open the topmost window in Figure 3.31. I'll discuss selecting View Files next, in the "Windows XP Reaction to Enabling Caching on Shares" section.

Wanda continues, using several documents in her redirected My Documents folder. Only the files she specifically opens will automatically be placed in the cache. She logs off and goes home.

Windows XP Reaction to Enabling Caching on Shares

Wanda's co-worker, Xena, is using a Windows XP laptop to do similar work. She maps a drive to the Sales share (which maps as Z:, as shown in Figure 3.32). When she uses Explorer to view the files on Z:, she sees one she needs (`hello1.doc`) and double-clicks it to open it (as shown in the bottom window in Figure 3.32). That file is immediately placed inside the Offline Files cache. It is now marked "Temporarily available offline."

FIGURE 3.32   An Offline Files folder in Windows XP shows much more activity than an Offline Files folder on a Windows 2000 machine.

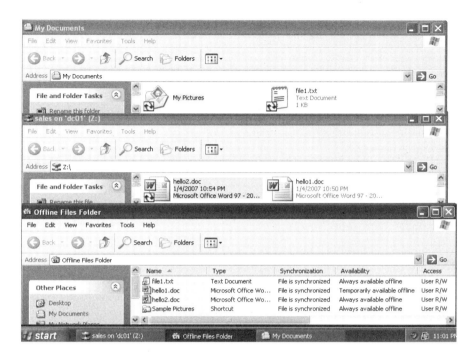

To see which files are in the file cache, Xena choose Tools ➢ Folder Options ➢ Offline Files ➢ View Files to open the topmost window (in Figure 3.32).

Additionally, as shown in Figures 3.9 and 3.10 earlier in this chapter, any files in redirected My Documents have the yin-yang round-trip icons. As I alluded to, this icon means that any file in a Redirected Folder is guaranteed to always be available offline (that is, pinned). What's interesting is that you can see the same icon demonstrating the file is round-tripped in two places: in a document in My Documents (file1.txt) and also in the Offline Files Folder window. The file will be listed as "Always available offline." The other files within the redirected My Documents are present within the Offline Files Folder window but are simply not displayed in Figure 3.32 due to space constraints.

When Xena then uses Explorer to open Z: to see the Sales files, she sets into motion a flurry of events that are particular to Windows XP. That is, as soon as Explorer touches the rest of the files in the Sales share, they begin to download and are *automatically placed in the offline cache*. Again, Xena didn't click each of the files in the Sales share; rather, she only opened an Explorer window. This behavior is specific to Windows XP (and not to Windows 2000). The Explorer in Windows XP is different from that in Windows 2000. Specifically, Windows XP Explorer performs an actual "file touch" to retrieve additional information, such as the file's Summary information or, for instance, when it tries to create a mini-view of a graphic. This "file touch" occurs only in Explorer's Thumbnails view in Windows XP, not in List or Details view.

The Offline Files window may occasionally display that a particular file's status is listed as "Local copy is incomplete." This signals that the files are currently being downloaded into the cache. Once the files are fully downloaded and the window refreshed, the field changes to "File is synchronized" as seen next to the file `hello1.doc` in Figure 3.32.

Additionally, note that Xena can pin any file from the Sales share that she wants to guarantee to be available offline. She's done this with `hello2.txt` which is now marked "Always available offline."

Windows Vista Reaction to Enabling Caching on Shares

Windows Vista is similar to Windows XP (perhaps even more aggressive in what it caches). That's because just about every View in Explorer will trigger a touch to the file and make it zoom down into the cache.

After connecting to the share and looking at the files via Explorer, you can see which files it cached.

It's more than a little cumbersome to see the list of offline files. But, if you click the Control Panel, select Classic View, and locate Offline Files you're almost there. Don't click Sync Center (which is something else entirely).

> Control Panel also has a search bar. You can type **offline** there and it will take you to the Offline Files Control Panel applet.

Then you can click through and hit the button "View your offline files." You'll see a screenshot of this a bit later in Figure 3.35.

Then, click through the Mapped Network Drives and find Sales. Tucked away in the far right is a column labeled Offline Availability (though you might have to move around the columns a bit). However, in Figure 3.33 you can see the Offline Availability column.

FIGURE 3.33   The Windows Vista Offline Availability column shows you the status of your files.

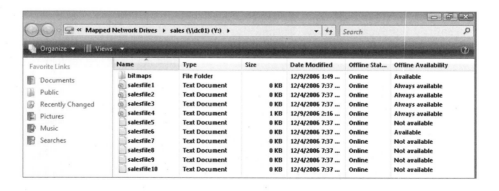

It's Not Offline Files—It's Explorer!

As you saw, Windows 2000 caches files differently than Windows XP, and Windows 2000 caches only files that are specifically pinned or files that are specifically used in shares that have caching enabled. Windows XP and Windows Vista cache files that are specifically pinned, files that are in Redirected Folders, and any file in a share that has caching enabled (once Windows Explorer is used to touch the file).

But it's not really the offline cache that changes at all—it's Windows Explorer! Because Explorer's Thumbnails view in Windows XP and Windows Vista is more rigorous than Windows 2000's counterpart, you're simply *more likely* to download stuff into the cache. Indeed, Explorer isn't the only possible program that works like this; any application that requires anything more than a basic touch to the file triggers a download of the file into the offline cache—regardless of whether the client is Windows 2000 or Windows XP! For instance, searching for files in network shares also plunks data into the cache. Basically, any time a file is opened for read, it's put in the cache.

On the surface, you might think this behavior of Windows XP's and Windows Vista's Explorer's Thumbnails view is a good thing. Sure, it's silently caching files! Indeed, how could this be a bad thing? Because if Wanda puts a 100MB file in the Sales share, Xena will be forced to download it. That's bad—especially if Xena comes in over a slow link. We'll explore at a detailed level what happens over a slow link in the "Using Folder Redirection and Offline Files over Slow Links" section coming right up.

But, for now, Table 3.3 has a sneak preview of what we're going to find. Table 3.3 shows specifically what happens with Windows 2000, Windows XP, and Windows Vista when Offline Files is used over fast and slow links.

TABLE 3.3   How Windows Explorer Reacts to Caching with Offline Files

Explorer View (Slow or Fast Link)	Action for Windows 2000 (Slow or Fast Link)	Action for Windows XP	Action for Windows Vista on Fast Link	Action for Windows Vista on Specified Servers and Shares Over Specifically Defined Slow Links
Thumbnails	Files are not downloaded into the cache when users open a window and are simply looking at the files. However, as soon as the file is clicked, it is downloaded into the cache.	As soon as you open a window in one of these views, all files begin downloading into the cache.	Not an option.	Not an option.

TABLE 3.3   How Windows Explorer Reacts to Caching with Offline Files *(continued)*

Explorer View (Slow or Fast Link)	Action for Windows 2000 (Slow or Fast Link)	Action for Windows XP	Action for Windows Vista on Fast Link	Action for Windows Vista on Specified Servers and Shares Over Specifically Defined Slow Links
Tiles	Not an option.	Files are not downloaded into the cache when a window is open and users are simply looking at the files. However, as soon as the file is clicked, the file is downloaded into the cache.	Not an option.	Not an option.
List	Files are not downloaded into the cache when a window is open and users are simply looking at the files. However, as soon as the file is clicked, the file is downloaded into the cache.	Files are not downloaded into the cache when a window is open and users are simply looking at the files. However, as soon as the file is clicked, the file is downloaded into the cache.	As soon as you open a window in one of these views, all files begin downloading into the cache.	Files are not downloaded into the cache unless specifically opened.
Details	Files are not downloaded into the cache when a window is open and users are simply looking at the files. However, as soon as the file is clicked, the file is downloaded into the cache.	Files are not downloaded into the cache when a window is open and users are simply looking at the files. However, as soon as the file is clicked, the file is downloaded into the cache.	As soon as you open a window in one of these views, all files begin downloading into the cache.	Files are not downloaded into the cache unless specifically opened.

TABLE 3.3   How Windows Explorer Reacts to Caching with Offline Files *(continued)*

Explorer View (Slow or Fast Link)	Action for Windows 2000 (Slow or Fast Link)	Action for Windows XP	Action for Windows Vista on Fast Link	Action for Windows Vista on Specified Servers and Shares Over Specifically Defined Slow Links
Large Icons (or Windows Vista Extra Large Icons, Large Icons, or Medium Icons)	Files are not downloaded into the cache when a window is open and users are simply looking at the files. However, as soon as the file is clicked, the file is downloaded into the cache.	Not an option.	As soon as you open a window in one of these views, all files begin downloading into the cache.	Files are not downloaded into the cache unless specifically opened.
Small Icons	Files are not downloaded into the cache when a window is open and users are simply looking at the files. However, as soon as the file is clicked, the file is downloaded into the cache.	Not an option.	As soon as you open a window in one of these views, all files begin downloading into the cache.	Files are not downloaded into the cache unless specifically opened.

Running Around to Each Client to Tweak Offline Files and the Synchronization Manager

If you wanted to, you could teach your users how to manage Offline Files themselves. (I'll wait a minute or two until the laughter stops.) Okay, maybe not, but if you ever needed to manage a computer that was using Offline Files but not using Group Policy, here's how you'd do it.

Manually Tweaking the Offline Files Interface for Pre-Vista Machines

As you saw, Windows 2000 and Windows XP have a baseline interaction with the synchronization of files. Optionally, you can manually configure your clients for some additional features of Offline Files and the Synchronization Manager. Earlier I described the synchronization mechanism of Offline Files as a "plug-in" for the Synchronization Manager. When you want to change the client-side behavior of how Offline Files works, you need to fundamentally understand this concept.

Since Offline Files is one entity and the Synchronization Manager another, they have two separate interfaces. Since they're independent entities, some pieces work independently; however, since Offline Files has a plug-in to the Synchronization Manager, they are also interdependent. To get a unified idea of how these two components work separately and together, you first need to locate their interfaces and see what goodies each has. You then need to know how they interact.

To manually tweak the Offline Files behavior, you'll need to get to the Offline Files interface. This is different for pre-Vista and Windows Vista machines.

To tweak the settings for, say, a Windows XP machine, open the My Documents folder, and choose Tools ➢ Folder Options to open the Folder Options dialog box as seen previously in Figure 3.19. In this case, we're using the My Documents folder, though any Explorer window returns the same results. As stated, 10 percent of the C: drive is configured to hold the cache as seen in Figure 3.20.

The defaults are different for Windows 2000 Professional and Windows XP versus Windows 2000 and Windows Server 2003. In Windows XP and Windows 2000 Professional, the "Enable Offline Files" check box is checked, but it is unchecked for Windows 2000 Server and Windows Server 2003. The key here is "server." Offline Files is predominantly a client feature and is therefore disabled by default on server installations.

On the Offline Files tab, click the Enable Offline Files check box to display the other options (as follows), which the user can configure.

Synchronize All Offline Files When Logging On   This setting is available only for Windows XP, and the user can change it. This entry co-interacts with the Synchronization Manager's similar entries entitled "When I log on to my computer" and "When I log off my computer." I talked more about this in the section "Understanding Offline Files and Synchronization Manager Interaction."

Synchronize All Offline Files Before Logging Off   The user can change this option. This entry co-interacts with the Synchronization Manager's similar entries entitled "When I log on to my computer" and "When I log off my computer." I talked more about this in the section "Understanding Offline Files and Synchronization Manager Interaction."

Display a Reminder Every (or Enable Reminders for Windows 2000)   When this box is selected (and a number is entered), users get a little pop-up balloon explaining that the connection to the machine where the files are stored has been severed. This is another win-lose area. On the one hand, if this option is selected, your users are well informed that the network has gone down. On the other hand, your users are well informed that the network has gone down, and they will probably call you, complaining. (This is because every new dialog box a user encounters automatically means that you need to be called, but I digress.) You can leave this option on or off here or use Group Policy to turn it off (as you'll see a bit later). Figure 3.34 shows a special case for balloon reminders that cannot be turned off. This occurs when the state changes.

FIGURE 3.34   Pop-up balloons inform your users that they have lost connectivity to the network.

Create an Offline Files Shortcut on the Desktop (or Place Shortcut to Offline Files Folder on the Desktop for Windows 2000)   Enabling this option displays a shortcut on the Desktop, the same as if you were to click the View Files button in the Folder Options dialog box. I'll discuss View Files in a moment.

Encrypt Offline Files to Secure Data   Only administrators of the machine can choose this setting. Administrators everywhere should be running to enable this setting. This is one of the major benefits for putting Windows XP on desktops and especially on laptops. That is, if the user uses EFS (Encrypting File System), the files stored in the offline cache are also encrypted. In Windows 2000, this was a major security hole. Specifically, if the laptop were stolen, the bad guy wouldn't be able to get to the encrypted data files on the hard drive, except for those still preserved in the Offline Files cache! With just a little know-how, this was a major exploit. Did I mention how major this is? Be sure to select this check box (or use a GPO to ensure the policy setting gets delivered to all your Windows XP and Windows 2003 machines). The bad news is that even with this nice plug, an attack is still possible on EFS. See two articles: `http://tinyurl.com/2vdfwm` and `http://tinyurl.com/2v668u`. (Note these articles may look a little funny because I've linked to their Internet archives, as the original articles are no longer available.)

Amount of Disk Space to Use for Temporary Offline Files   This slider goes from 0 percent to 100 percent of your C: drive. The default is 10 percent. Again, only files set up to use "All files and programs that users open from the share will be automatically available offline" (or Automatic Caching for Documents for Windows 2000) use this setting. Files that are manually pinned are not counted toward the percentage specified here; they are always available. You can change this percentage using Group Policy, as you'll see a bit later. Due to a limitation in the way Windows 2000 and Windows XP were written, a maximum of only 2GB of disk space can be used.

The following three additional option buttons are certain to scare away even the most fearless of end users. You just click each of the following three buttons, which gives you more stuff to play with:

Delete Files   This opens up the Confirm File Delete dialog box. Users run in terror when they see the word *Delete*. Because of this, there's a good chance that they won't go poking around here. Indeed, nothing actually gets deleted other than the files in the local cache. Files on the server stay on the server.

Note if you Ctrl+Shift when clicking Delete, it completely reinitializes the offline cache, which might help with any specific corruption issues on your Windows XP (or Windows Vista, for that matter) machine.

View Files This opens up the Offline Files Folder window. This button lets you peek into the local cache, as shown in Figures 3.31 and 3.32 earlier in this chapter. Files that are pinned are represented as Always Available Offline. Those that are just in the cache for now are listed as Temporarily Available Offline. This interface is similar to Explorer; it's really Explorer with rose-colored glasses on to make sure that the under-the-hood manipulations of the local cache are properly handled. The local cache is actually stored in the hidden directory C:\windows\CSC. Do not use Explorer or a command prompt to poke around there. The best way to manipulate locally cached files is through the View Files GUI.

This CSC directory is not created until Offline Files are enabled on your Windows XP machine, and Offline Files cannot be enabled without turning off Windows XP's Fast User Switching functionality. However, all of this happens automatically when you join a Windows XP Professional machine to the domain.

Also note that Offline Files are not available for Windows XP Home Edition.

Advanced This opens up the Offline Files—Advanced Settings dialog box. In this scary dialog box, you can specify what happens if a computer becomes unavailable. You can prevent the user of this workstation from accessing files in the local cache should the corresponding server go down. To be honest, I don't know why on earth you would ever do this, except for some wacky security concern. This is on a per-server, not per-share basis, so be especially careful if this user has many shares on one particular server.

 Real World Scenario

Offline Files and Windows 2000 Server, Windows Server 2003, and Windows Server 2008

By default, Offline Files is enabled only on the workstation versions of the operating system, such as Windows 2000, Windows XP, and Windows Vista.

On Windows 2000 servers and Windows 2003 servers, you specifically enable it (either via Group Policy or manually, as seen in the section "Manually Tweaking the Offline Files Interface for Pre-Vista Machines" and in Figure 3.20). The idea is that this function is largely used when mere mortals log on to their Desktop systems—not when administrators log onto servers. However, it can be manually enabled.

If you intend to use Offline Files when logged onto Windows 2003, you must (oddly) disable Remote Desktop. To do so, right-click My Computer and choose Properties from the shortcut menu to open the System Properties dialog box. In the Remote tab, ensure that "Allow users to connect remotely to this computer" is cleared. Of course, this will disable Remote Desktop connections, but, indeed, it will allow you to utilize Offline Files while logged onto Windows 2003 systems.

Note that this problem between Terminal Services and Offline Files no longer exists in Vista. All of the interlock UI between the two features has been removed.

Offline Files is also disabled on Windows Server 2008 by default but can be enabled via the Offline Files Control Panel applet. However, you'll also need the Desktop Experience Feature installed using Server Manager. Without the Desktop Experience feature, there is no access to the Sync Center UI.

Manually Tweaking the Offline Files Interface for Vista Machines

Again, if you needed to manually tweak Offline Files for Windows Vista, here's how you'd do it. There's an Offline Settings icon hiding in the Control Panel. There are two ways to find it:

- In "regular" view, click under Network and Internet, then select Offline Files.
- In Classic View you can see Offline Files just sitting there among the other icons.

Once you've made your selection, you'll note there are four tabs: General, Disk Usage, Encryption, and Network, as seen in Figure 3.35.

FIGURE 3.35   You can manually turn off Offline Files with local administrator credentials.

General Tab   On the General tab, you can select Disable Offline Files which, when presented with local administrator credentials will do just that.

You can also open the Sync Center (previously discussed) or view all the files from all shares which are available offline.

Disk Usage   The Disk Usage tab has two main items: changing the disk usage limits and flushing the cache with Delete Temporary Files. This only deletes any unpinned files from the cache. You can see this in Figure 3.36.

FIGURE 3.36   You can use the sliders to manage your hard disk usage.

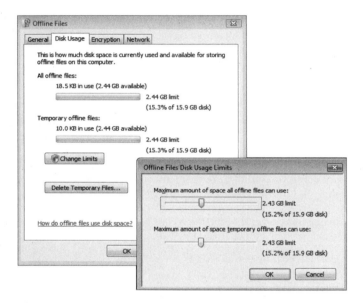

In Windows XP, the space used by pinned files was excluded from the cache-space-usage calculation. This meant a user could pin files until he was out of hard drive space. In Windows Vista, both pinned files and automatically cached files must fit neatly into a container size you specify. The first slider (shown in Figure 3.36) is the total space that all offline files will use on this machine (including pinned files). The lower slider is just for automatically cached files. You can use Group Policy to guarantee these numbers via the Windows Vista–only policy setting titled **Limit disk space used by offline files**.

Encryption   This tab literally only has two buttons on it: Encrypt and Unencrypt. Here, in the User Interface, a user can do this manually. You'll also see later that Offline Files supports a Group Policy setting (named **Encrypt the Offline Files cache**) that causes the cache to become encrypted.

When that policy setting is enabled, or the Encrypt button is clicked, the Offline Files service performs the encryption automatically on behalf of the first user who logs on, shortly after he logs on. But what if multiple users use the same Windows Vista machine, say, as a traveling laptop?

If it's desired to encrypt the redirected Documents folder, everything is hunky-dory for any user on a particular Windows Vista machine. However, if multiple users of a Windows Vista machine can access a given file (say, a share \\DC01\sales), the first user to log on and encrypt that file is the only user who can access that file while offline.

That's a subtle behavior, but it may be important if you share a specific laptop, encrypt the offline files which reside on a public share, and expect everyone to be able to read it when those users are offline.

Network   The Network tab allows you to choose how often to verify you're working on a fast or slow connection. But, here's the trick about slow connections: you have to be ridiculously specific to Windows Vista and explain to it (like to a two-year-old) exactly what servers and what shares and what speeds constitute a slow network connection.

So, even though Windows Vista automatically transitions to an offline state on a slow connection, you have to explain just what that slow connection is.

Not to put a fine point on it, but, as you're about to learn in the next big section, Windows Vista does not "believe" you're ever on a slow link by default. You'll have to teach it which servers and shares you consider slow. We'll see this a little later using Group Policy. The policy setting you'll use is entitled **Configure slow link mode** (which is a Windows Vista–only setting). I'm telling you this so you don't get confused with the unfortunately named **Configure Slow link speed** (which is a Windows XP–only setting).

Now, if you click the tab, you'll notice all the controls are grayed out.

So the check box in this tab is *only* available when the Windows Vista-specific policy setting **Configure slow link mode** is set. Once the check box is checked (by the policy being Enabled), the remainder of the controls will be enabled.

One more note here: this setting is a bit irregular. Once the policy setting is Enabled (which enables the controls), *any* user of the client is allowed to change that time value setting. And, that time value affects *all* users of the client computer. The rationale is that the setting must be per-machine to correspond with the per-machine cache, but any user of the client should be able to set it.

More to Tweak in Windows Vista: Offline Files Sync Schedule

Again, the Sync Center is where users can actually go to see what has synchronized or to manually kick off a synchronization. There are, however, some tweakable features.

I've already expressed how Windows Vista positively does not synchronize files at logoff (where Windows XP did). However, there are some options that can you can specify for the user in order to dictate when Offline Files actually performs its syncing.

In the Sync Center, click the Schedule button, as seen in Figure 3.37. When you do, you'll be presented with the "Which items do you want to sync on this schedule?" dialog, also seen in Figure 3.37. The check box called "Sync item name" is for selecting All or Nothing, but a minor bug seems to be involved, so clicking anywhere in the list field clears the list selections.

Yes, they just disappear—strange. Anyway, select the partnership and click next.

FIGURE 3.37   The Windows Vista Sync Center has options you can set for each item under Schedule.

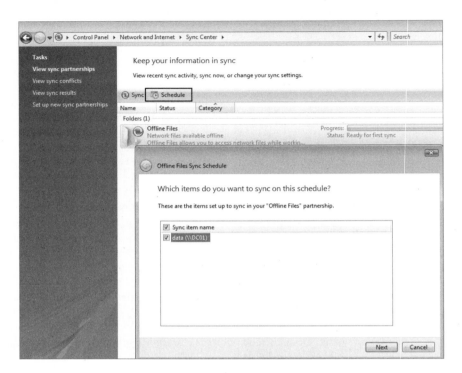

Next, you'll be asked "When do you want this sync to begin?" and you can choose "At a scheduled time" or "On an event or action." (This screen isn't shown here in the book.) You can see the options for "At a scheduled time" in Figure 3.38 (with its "More scheduling options" dialog box, also shown.) You can see the options for "On an event of action" in Figure 3.39 (with its "More scheduling options" dialog shown).

Again, these are optional settings for each Windows Vista machine. The bad news is that there is currently no direct way to dictate these settings using Group Policy.

Power Admins Rejoice: Scripting Offline Files

I've got good news and bad news for you admins out there. That is, if you want to do a lot of ultra-geeky command-line-only stuff with Offline Files (properly known as Client-Side Caching) there's a great tool.

Good news: the tool is free.

Bad news: the tool only works with Windows XP (not Windows Vista yet) and is only available if you call Microsoft PSS.

Did I mention the tool is free? If you call PSS and reference KB article 884739 they'll just mail it to you—no questions asked. Check out all the geeky fun at http://support.microsoft.com/kb/884739.

There likely won't be a Windows Vista version of the CSCCMD.EXE command line tool. And, even if there was, the scripting API provides much more flexibility (and capability) than CSCCMD. Microsoft's goal is to help you move toward using scripts. The Offline Files API can be found at http://msdn2.microsoft.com/en-us/library/bb530657.aspx.

FIGURE 3.38   The time-based schedule synchronization options.

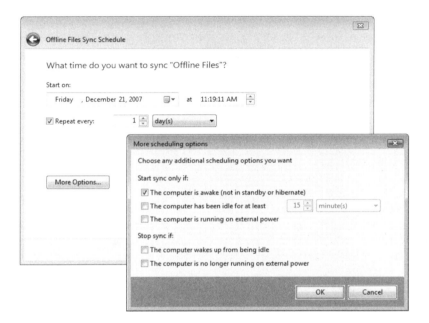

Using Folder Redirection and Offline Files over Slow Links

In Windows 2000 and Windows XP, Offline Files thinks a slow link is 64Kbps. Since no analog modem is going to achieve that speed, every normal dial-up user theoretically will be coming in over a slow link. When a user comes in over a slow link (less than 64Kbps), the system automatically uses their locally cached version of network files. Additionally, files will not sync when users log on.

FIGURE 3.39   The action-based schedule synchronization options

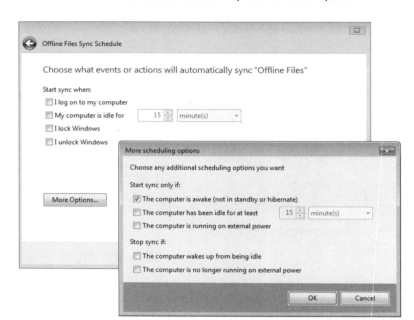

Windows Vista handles things differently. It assumes every connection to a share is a fast link until told otherwise. You'll see how to change this behavior right around the bend if you want to manage users' experiences.

When using Offline Files over a slow link, you need to consider the consequences of, say, a private folder like a redirected Documents/My Documents as well as a public folder, like our Sales share. Then, we'll see how Windows 2000, Windows XP, and Windows Vista react over slow links.

Synchronizing over Slow Links with Redirected *My Documents*

The first place you can run into trouble is if the user has never synchronized on a particular machine. For example, Charles is a member of the Marketing group. He's given a generic "workgroup" laptop to take to an emergency meeting in China. But Charles doesn't synchronize with the fast LAN network before he runs out the door to catch his plane. Of course, he won't have any files while he's on the long flight to China; but worse, when he gets to China and dials in, he won't see any files in his My Documents folder either, although we know they're still safe and sound on the redirected network share set up for him.

Why does this happen for Charles in China? Because the default behavior for Charles's computer is that it won't process Folder Redirection over slow links. If you're planning to make redirected My Documents a reality over slow links (for users who haven't ever synchronized with the

LAN), you'll need to set up a GPO that affects target computers; and, ideally, these target computers will receive this GPO before they leave for their trip. You'll need to set up a GPO that enables the policy under the Computer Configuration ➢ Policies ➢ Administrative Templates ➢ System ➢ Group Policy ➢ Folder Redirection policy processing policy setting and, inside, set it to "Allow processing across a slow network connection." Again, if you don't do this, users won't see their files in My Documents when they dial up unless they already performed a synchronization with the Synchronization Manager before they left for the trip.

Now, you have to consider what operating system Charles is using. If you give Charles a Windows 2000 laptop, the logon time won't be too long. However, if you give Charles a Windows XP laptop, the logon time might be tremendously long. Why? Remember that Windows XP in conjunction with any Redirected Folder, such as My Documents, attempts to Make Available Offline every file. If Charles has 300MB of files in his redirected My Documents folder, the system tries to automatically pin all 300MB of those files by copying the data from the server to the local system.

I hear you yelling at me now: "Jeremy, why on earth would I enable **Allow processing across a slow network connection** if I'm setting my Windows Vista and Windows XP users up for torture?" My answer? In the upcoming section entitled, "Using Group Policy to Configure Offline Files (User and Computer Node)" see the Windows XP policy setting titled **Do not automatically make redirected folders available offline,** which will return Windows XP to the behavior of Windows 2000 and not pin all redirected files. That way, the bandwidth your Windows XP users utilize when dialing up won't get crushed when using slow connections with Redirected Folders.

Remember though, that unless the user copies the files he needs locally or manually pins them, the files in My Documents will not be available offline. This philosophy is a yin-yang thing, just like the icon.

Synchronizing over Slow Links with Public Shares

Let's look at another example. Harold, Walter, Xavier, and Victoria are members of the Sales group.

- Harold stays put in the home office and works on a desktop machine.
- Walter has a Windows 2000 Professional laptop.
- Xavier has a Windows XP laptop.
- Victoria has a Windows Vista laptop.

Walter, Xavier, and Victoria are sometimes in the office and sometimes on the road. When in the home office, all employees plunk files into the share \\east_server\salesfigures, which is configured to use "All files and programs that users open from the share will be available offline." They all use the Frankfurt.doc file. Both Walter and Xavier normally synchronize their computers every time they log off, grabbing the latest version of Frankfurt.doc. And, because Victoria is using Windows Vista, her files are automatically synchronized in the background.

Walter, Xavier, and Victoria leave for Frankfurt, Germany to woo a prospective account. During the time that Walter, Xavier, and Victoria are on the plane, Harold (who's back in the office) modifies the Frankfurt.doc file with up-to-the-minute information on their prospective customer. Walter, Xavier, and Victoria all get drunk on the plane ride over and sleep the entire way. They don't even crack open their laptops to look at the `Frankfurt.doc` file on any of their laptops. In short, they don't modify their copies on the laptops; only Harold modifies a copy at the home office.

Walter, Xavier, and Victoria check in to the same hotel (different rooms) and dial the home office. They all want to ensure that the latest copy of `Frankfurt.doc` on the server is downloaded to their laptops to present to their client in the morning.

Windows 2000 Offline Files over Slow Links

When Walter connects, he's coming in over a slow link. Room service arrives just as he connects, and he forgets that he's logged on. An hour passes, and Walter remembers that he's dialed in! Frantically, Walter disconnects. Even with that hour-long connection, Walter does not receive any updated files via Quick Synchronization. Unfortunately, he will end up looking like a jerk in tomorrow's meeting.

Walter has four choices if he wants to get the latest copy of the file from the server:

- Manually copy the file from the share to a place on his local computer. (How quaint.)

- Right-click the file in the share and pin it with Make Available Offline. The file is now permanently available offline.

- Double-click the file to open it. Then, the synchronization field changes to "Temporarily available offline" (though it should be already), and the Modified field is updated to the current time stamp from the server. The file is then updated in the cache.

- Manually force a synchronization over the slow connection to synchronize any pinned file or file already in the cache, including `Frankfurt.doc`.

Windows XP Synchronization Manager over Slow Links

Xavier dials the office as well. Room service arrives just as he connects, and, like Walter, he forgets that he's logged on. If Explorer in Windows XP is set up to display files in Thumbnails mode, Explorer is actually opening the files. Because `Frankfurt.doc` is opened, it naturally makes its way into the cache. You can see this by peering into the Offline Files folder (shown in Figure 3.40); its status is changed to "Local copy is incomplete."

FIGURE 3.40   Compared to Windows 2000, Windows XP's Explorer is more vigorous in actually touching and opening files; hence, they are downloaded into the cache.

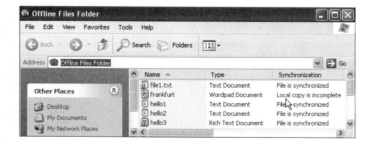

Some time later, the Synchronization column for Frankfurt.doc will change to "File is synchronized." Here's the upshot:

- Files aren't just automatically downloaded because it's Windows XP. They're downloaded because Explorer's Thumbnails view touches the files.

- All other files in the share that Xavier has used will try to update via Quick Synchronization (if Xavier hasn't updated the files himself on his laptop).

- As soon as Xavier uses Explorer to examine the files in the share with Windows XP's Thumbnails view, all the files in the share will try to be downloaded over the slow link. This could be painful.

Xavier's computer is connected over a slow, expensive connection. And now he's downloading the Frankfurt.doc file (small) and any other (potentially very, very large) file that is now on the share. This could be a major problem if Xavier just wants that one file fast. Poor Xavier is after just the Frankfurt.doc file that Harold modified. Xavier has some options while using the slow connection:

- Wait long enough, and Frankfurt.doc will automatically download in the background. Again, this happens because in Windows XP Explorer opens the file in Thumbnails view.

- Wait long enough, and all files on the share will synchronize automatically. Windows 2000 will not do this. Again, this happens because in Windows XP Explorer opens the file in Tiles or Thumbnails view. However, files Xavier might not care about are also being synchronized.

- Double-click the file to open it. The Synchronization column then immediately changes from "Local copy is incomplete" to "File is synchronized."

- Manually copy the file from the share to a place on his local computer.

- Right-click the file in the share and pin it with Make Available Offline.

- Manually synchronize Frankfurt.doc and all other files in the share. This spawns the Synchronization Manager to help ensure that Xavier has the latest file and also helps if any conflicts arise.

 Real World Scenario

Windows XP's Synchronization Manager State Transitions

Mobile users access their locally cached versions of files. They then return to the office and dock their systems—without a new logon or logoff. This is called a *state transition*. When a state transition occurs, the system evaluates several criteria to decide if it should keep working offline (using the files in the local cache) or start working online (using the files on the network).

A successful transition to an online state requires the following:

- All offline files in the local cache must be closed.

- The connection must be greater than 64Kbps (by default).

If either of these requirements is not met, the user will still be using the locally cached version of the file—even if the network share is theoretically usable across the network.

Again, if this user wants to use a fast connection instead of the locally cached files, they can choose Start ➢ All Programs ➢ Accessories ➢ Synchronize to kick-start the connection, or they can click the little computer icon in the notification area.

To get the latest files in the share, the user needs to synchronize again by choosing Start ➢ All Programs ➢ Accessories ➢ Synchronize. If the connection is determined to be a fast connection, changed files are automatically added to the cache for recurring synchronization.

Sometimes an automatic state transition does not function as it should. In this case, users are advised to log off before docking. Once they are docked and network connectivity is established, logging on causes a normal synchronization cycle. Sometimes automatic state transition functions as it should but a little slower than expected. Don't forget that Microsoft Office isn't the only application that can keep files open. Other day-to-day productivity applications you deploy for users can keep files open, and, hence, a state transition does not occur.

Moving the Client-Side Cache for Windows 2000, Windows XP, and Windows Vista

You might find a reason to change the original placement of the CSC folder. For instance, you might have some PCs with two (or more) physical hard drives. Perhaps you're running out of space on the C: drive, or maybe you just want to tune a machine's performance by splitting the duties over two hard drives.

You can use the Cachemov.exe utility in the Windows 2000 Server Resource Kit. Simply run Cachemov.exe on the workstation that has multiple hard drives. When you are done, you have a choice as to where to move the C:\%windir%\CSC, as shown here:

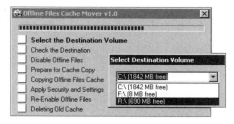

You can also use Cachemov.exe to execute batch-style in a logon script. If you want to affect multiple computers, you can run Cachemov.exe -unattend d:\, in which d is the drive to which the new CSC folder will move. Cchmvmsg.dll needs to be in the path when running cachemov.exe in unattended mode. This tool is not available in the Windows Server 2003 Resource Kit but seems to work fine with Windows XP. Use at your own risk.

Cachemov.exe won't work on Windows Vista. There is a procedure to move the cache for Windows Vista. As of this writing, it's not a KB article yet, but you can find the steps here http://tinyurl.com/yngfu3.

Windows Vista's Synchronization Engine over Slow Links

Victoria dials up just like Walter and Xavier. Will Frankfurt.doc automatically come down over the slow link (and the other potentially large files in the share)? By default, yes, if she looks at the share in any view which "touches the files." (See Table 3.3 earlier.)

But, here's the weird part about Windows Vista. It's much smarter about recognizing what a slow link is. Buuuut...by default Windows Vista will simply act like Windows XP and bring down every stinkin' file you even look at (even with a File List view in Explorer) over a slow link.

Ouch.

The good news is that you can control this. You simply have to tell Windows Vista which shares you want to throttle. The goal is to tell your Windows Vista clients which servers and shares should be cached over a slow link.

You tell the clients four things:

- The name of the server with the share(s)

- The name of the share(s)

- What constitutes a slow link (speed)

- What constitutes slow latency (wait time before the server responds)

Once your Windows Vista client "gets" this, it starts being *much* smarter about not downloading humongous files over slow links (like Windows XP would).

You do this with the **Configure slow-link mode** policy setting located in Computer Configuration ➤ Policies ➤ Administrative Templates ➤ Network ➤ Offline Files, as seen in Figure 3.41. Figure 3.42 shows an example of how to precisely set up one server's characteristics; you can see \\server1 and share1 being set to a slow link speed of 600Kbps and Latency of 50ms.

So, when should you use throughput or latency thresholds?

Well, this policy can be set to use *either* throughput *and*/or latency thresholds. So, you can decide to use throughput, latency, or both.

FIGURE 3.41 The Settings description doesn't express this, but you can specify a single lone * (asterisk) to turn on slow-link mode for all shares on all servers.

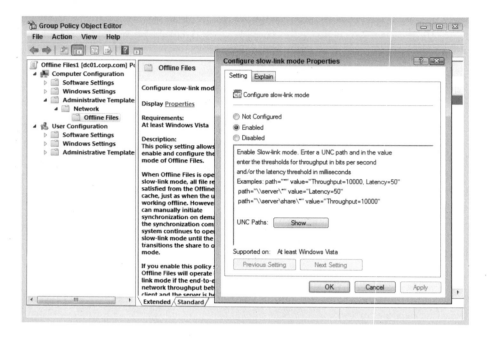

FIGURE 3.42 Specify Throughput = 600000 for 600Kbps and Latency=50 for 50ms, for instance, to define your slow link threshold. Note, all paths should have an ending slash (\) and asterisk (*) even if you're just specifying one server and one share.

About Throughput Estimates For Vista RTM, the throughput estimates are based on outbound traffic and can take some time to become available. That means, you may have to push some traffic to the server for the Windows Vista client to "wake up" and realize "Holy cow! This is slow!" The time taken to get throughput estimates depends on how long it takes for TCP/IP to "saturate" the outbound connection to the server. Offline Files checks this periodically and whenever it finds that the throughput is worse than the policy specified threshold, Offline Files transitions the connection to slow-link mode.

This behavior can be updated in one of two ways. There's a Windows Vista hotfix available at KB 934202. Or, when you load Windows Vista + SP1, the hotfix is built in. Once it's applied, Windows Vista will recognize both outbound *and* inbound traffic as potentially slow.

About Latency Estimates   Latency estimates, on the other hand are available more quickly. They do not have the outbound requirement either.

So, what should you use? Throughput, latency, or both? The short answer is, both. In our example, Victoria wasn't pushing anything up to the server. She merely viewed the share, and *blammo!* tons of stuff she wasn't really interested in came streaming down the slow link.

Again, Windows Vista RTM would cheerfully just stream all that junk down to her Windows Vista machine. But Windows Vista + SP1 is smarter and turns off the water before it becomes a flood.

So, can she at least get to the `Frankfurt.doc` file? I'm afraid to say the answer is maybe. During my testing, here's what I found (your mileage, as well as Victoria's mileage, may vary):

- If Victoria was really connected to a `\\server\share` (that is, a specific server and a share upon that server) and using a slow link (but still connected nonetheless), in my testing I found that she sometimes had access to the file, and sometimes she was blocked from getting the file. This is because the file was changed on the server. Since the share had transitioned to Offline, and I didn't have an up-to-date copy of the file, she couldn't access the changed file.

- If Victoria really wanted to get that file, she would have to choose to Work Online for that particular share. Of course, the bad news is that all the goo on the share she doesn't particularly care about will come streaming down (slowly) over that slow link. But at least Victoria could get access to the file.

- If, however, a user like Victoria was really 100 percent offline (i.e., Victoria never got a chance to dial-in back to the office), then she retains the last known copy of the file in cache (as might be expected).

So, the takeaway is that if a user like Victoria is connected, but slowly, she might not get access to the files she thinks she should have access to. That's going to be a tough one to explain to your users, I think. So, you may want to plan to show them how to transition shares to Online status if you choose to declare some shares eligible for slow link status. In Figure 3.43, you can see where the button is located that your users will need to learn to press. You can also see some files "ghosted" (with the little "X" indicator) because they aren't in the cache (and hence, not available for use) and those files which are available for use (not ghosted).

So, to use this policy setting, you add additional items for each server and share combination you needed to define individually. Or, you can also perform this operation en masse based on specific servers or, heck, have all Windows Vista clients react to all servers the same way.

Table 3.4 gives you some examples of some values you might want to specify using the **Configure slow-link mode** policy setting when entering in the "Enter the name of the item to be added" block and the "Enter the value of the item to be added" block and what the result would be if you used these suggestions.

FIGURE 3.43 When a slow connection transitions a share to Offline, only files already in the cache are accessible. To access files on the server over a slow link, select "Work online."

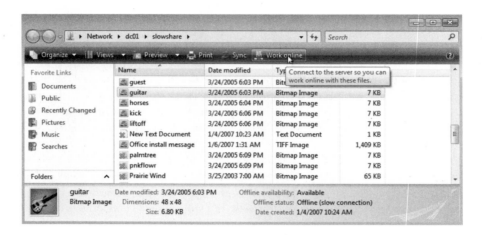

Once you're done, clients will only download files into cache when files are actually opened up. This will speed up their normal day-to-day connection because they're not downloading files into cache that they don't need.

 None of the **Configure slow-link mode** values require quotes, which can be confusing if you read the Explain text in the policy setting.

TABLE 3.4 Configure slow-link mode Policy Setting Examples

The "Enter the name of the item to be added" Block	The "Enter the value of the item to be added" Block	Result of these settings
\\server1\share1*	Throughput=600000,Latency=50	Only \\server1\share1 would react for Windows Vista clients affected by this policy setting. The share will automatically transition to offline if the speed is less than 600Kbps or the latency is less than 50ms.
\\server1*	Throughput=128000	All shares on \\server1 would react for Windows Vista clients affected by this policy setting. The share will automatically transition to offline if the speed is less than 128Kbps. Note that Windows Vista clients affected by this policy would not test for latency.

TABLE 3.4   Configure slow-link mode Policy Setting Examples *(continued)*

The "Enter the name of the item to be added" Block	The "Enter the value of the item to be added" Block	Result of these settings
**	Throughput=400000,Latency=20	All shares on all servers would react for Windows Vista clients affected by this policy setting. All shares would automatically transition to offline if the speed was less than 400Kbps or the latency was less than 20ms. Note the trailing star (*) at the end of the expression to signify all shares.
**	Latency=30	All shares on all servers would react for Windows Vista clients affected by this policy setting. All shares would automatically transition to offline if the latency was 30ms. Note the trailing star (*) at the end of the expression to signify all shares.

Using Group Policy to Configure Offline Files (User and Computer Node)

Asking users to configure their own Offline Files settings can be—to say the least—confusing. This isn't the fault of Microsoft—there are just a lot of options to play with. The good news is that most Offline Files settings can be delivered from up on high.

The policy settings for the Offline Files are found in two places in the Group Policy Management Editor. Some settings affect users specifically. To get to those settings, fire up the Group Policy Management Editor and traverse to Computer Configuration ➢ Policies ➢ Administrative Templates ➢ Network ➢ Offline Files, as shown in Figure 3.44.

Nearly all the same settings are also found in the User side of the house, at User Configuration ➢ Policies ➢ Administrative Templates ➢ Network ➢ Offline Files, as shown in Figure 3.45.

There are no policy settings for the Windows XP Synchronization Manager or the Windows Vista Sync Center.

This gives you flexibility in how to configure Offline Files. You can mix and match—within the same GPO or from multiple GPOs. The general rule is that if both computer and user settings are specified on the target, the computer wins.

In this section, I'll briefly detail what each Offline Files policy setting does. Since most of the policies overlap in both User and Computer configuration nodes, I'll discuss all the User and Computer configuration settings and then discuss those that apply only to the Computer configuration settings.

FIGURE 3.44   You'll find a slew of Offline Files options under the Computer node.

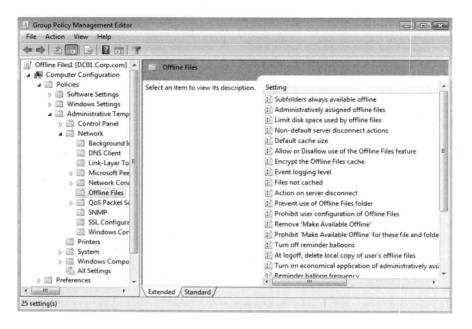

FIGURE 3.45   Many Offline Files options can also be found under the User node.

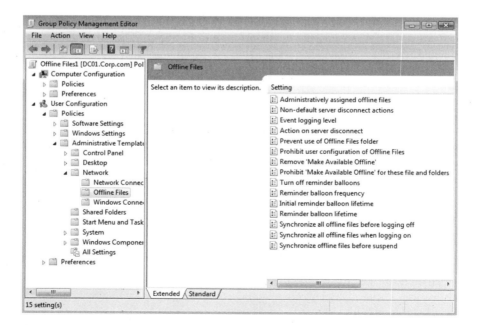

Prohibit User Configuration of Offline Files

If this policy setting is enabled, users on the target client computer embrace the default Offline Files settings and won't be able to change them. Indeed, this happens by the forceful removal of the Offline Files tab normally found in the Folder Options dialog box, as you saw in Figure 3.20 earlier in this chapter.

 This policy setting does not apply to Windows Vista machines.

Synchronize All Offline Files When Logging On

Enabling this setting grays out the "Synchronize all offline when logging on" check box in the Offline Files tab in the Folder Options dialog box (as seen in Figure 3.20) on the target machine, so the user can't change it. Be sure to read the section "Understanding Offline Files and Synchronization Manager Interaction" earlier in this chapter to understand how this setting works.

 This policy setting does not apply to Windows Vista machines.

Synchronize All Offline Files When Logging Off

Enabling this setting grays out the "Synchronize All Offline Files before Logging Off" check box in the Offline Files tab in the Folder Options dialog box (as seen in Figure 3.20) on the target machine, so the user can't change it. Be sure to read the section "Understanding Offline Files and Synchronization Manager Interaction" earlier in this chapter to understand how this setting works.

 This policy setting does not apply to Windows Vista machines.

Synchronize All Offline Files Before Suspend

Enabling this setting ensures that a full synchronization occurs before the user suspends or hibernates the machine (which usually means they will undock it or otherwise take it offline). The operating system must know about the change, and this will not work if you just close the lid on a laptop.

 This policy setting does not apply to Windows Vista machines.

Action on Server Disconnect

If this policy setting is enabled, you can select one of two options from the Action drop-down list box. This is analogous to the Advanced dialog box mentioned in the section, "Manually Tweaking the Offline Files Interface for Pre-Vista Machines." In a nutshell, you can allow normal operation of Offline Files or cease the use of Offline Files if the server goes offline. Again, avoid using this function, as it essentially defeats the whole purpose of Offline Files.

This policy setting does not apply to Windows Vista machines.

Non-default Server Disconnect Actions

This is similar to the previous policy setting. It corresponds to the Exception List, which is revealed after pressing the Advanced button—again, found in the Folder Options Offline Files tab. Whereas the previous policy setting specified the defaults for all servers, this policy setting specifies settings for specific servers.

Settings enabled here override those in the **Action on server disconnect** policy setting as well as any other policy settings set for the target systems. When this policy setting is enabled, the Exception list is removed to prevent users from making changes.

When you configure the Computer or User option of this policy setting, the box's radio buttons above the Exception list are gray, but the Exception list itself is not. You can add any computers you desire, but they will not take effect with the policy setting in place.

This policy setting is a bit wacky. That is, the policy setting will take effect on refresh, but the radio buttons don't show the actual setting until you reboot. My testing proved that a reboot was necessary for both Computer and User option settings to show in the interface. Also, when the User and Computer configurations conflict, the least restrictive setting takes precedence. If the Computer policy says you can't see the server when offline, but the User configuration says you can, you will be able to see the Offline Files when offline.

To configure this policy setting, choose Enable ➢ Show ➢ Add to open the Add Item dialog box. In the "Enter the name of the item to be added" field, type the name of the server that you want to have an explicit setting, such as **MysteryServer**. In the "Enter the value of the item to be added" field, enter either a 1 to keep the users offline or a 0 to keep them online, as shown in Figure 3.46. Click OK to add the server as an exception, click OK to close the Show Contents dialog box, and close the **Non-default server disconnect actions** policy setting.

This policy setting does not apply to Windows Vista machines.

Remove Make Available Offline

Enabling this policy setting prevents users from pinning files by right-clicking them and selecting Make Available Offline. Files are still cached normally as dictated through other policies or by the defaults. Additionally, enabling this policy setting will not unpin already pinned files.

Therefore, if you think you might not want users pinning files, you'll need to turn this setting on early in the game, or you'll be forced to run around from machine to machine to unpin users' pinned files.

FIGURE 3.46   Use this feature to prevent users from using a specific server's files when offline.

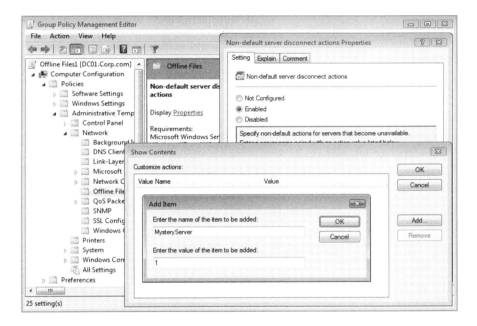

Enabling this setting does not interfere with either the Automatic Caching for Documents or the Automatic Caching for Programs setting on shared folders (as described earlier). Those files are not permanently cached (pinned).

Prevent Use of Offline Files Folder

This setting prevents users from clicking the View Files button inside the Folder Options dialog box. Once this option is set, users may not know which files are currently available in the cache or always available in the cache.

 This policy setting does not apply to Windows Vista machines.

Administratively Assigned Offline Files

This is arguably the most useful setting in the bunch. Recall that Windows XP and Windows Vista will automatically pin all files in Redirected Folders such as Documents (for Vista) or My Documents (for XP), which Windows 2000 will not do. However, with this policy setting, you can guarantee that your Windows 2000 users (especially laptop users) have all the files in their

My Documents folder both on the local hard drive and safely synchronized to the server—not just redirected there. This ensures that the copy is both synchronized at the server and pinned to the local hard drive.

Remember, though, that in Windows 2000 (and Windows XP) since these files are pinned, they are exempt from the percentage cache used (10 percent by default). That is, all files that are pinned are guaranteed to be available on the hard drive if the user transitions to offline.

A side benefit is that the modest 10 percent cache for temporarily available offline files can be used for other network files as your users use them. To make Windows 2000 files always available offline, follow these steps:

1. Enable the setting.

2. Click the Show button next to Files and Folders.

3. In the Show Contents dialog box, click Add to open the Add Item dialog box.

4. Enter the server and share name. If you want to guarantee the redirection of My Documents (only necessary for Windows 2000), enter the server, share and folder for the user, or leverage the *%username%* variable, as shown in Figure 3.47.

5. Leave the "Enter the value of the item to be added" field blank.

6. Click OK to render the share Assigned Offline.

7. Click OK to close the Show Contents dialog box and the **Administratively assigned offline files** policy setting.

The next time your users get this policy setting assigned, all the files affected will be pinned. Every newly created file will be pinned as well, as shown in Figure 3.48.

FIGURE 3.47   Use the Administratively assigned Offline Files policy setting to force specific files or folders to be pinned—like the My Documents folder!

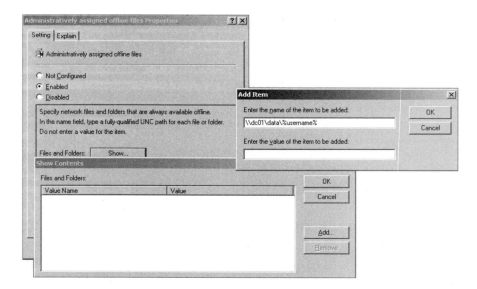

FIGURE 3.48   All files inside the My Documents folder on this Windows 2000 system are now pinned.

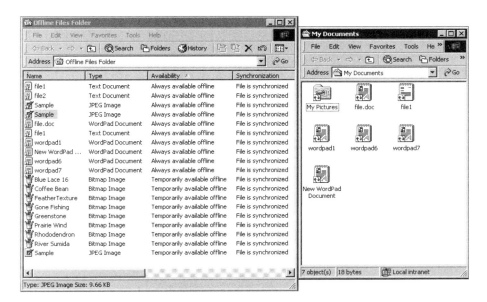

Additionally, by enabling this setting, you can force a file or folder to be pinned for a user in any other share you like. For instance, you can force the vice president of sales to always have their sales figures available. This might be useful if they're on an airplane without a 30,000-foot network cable plugged back into the network on the ground. You can forcefully command that they receive certain files—even if they didn't pin them.

If you're using Windows Vista machines, be sure to check out the computer-side policy setting named **Turn on economical application of administrative assigned Offline Files** (which, isn't named correctly, so definitely be sure to read about this a little later).

Turn off Reminder Balloons

This corresponds to Enable Reminders in the Folders Options dialog box. Again, you might want to disable the balloons, because they may only serve to spook the herd. See Figure 3.34 earlier in this chapter for an example of a reminder balloon (though that particular balloon cannot be removed). Enabling this policy setting disables the balloons. Disabling this policy setting prevents users from disabling the balloons.

This policy setting does not apply to Windows Vista machines.

Reminder Balloon Frequency

By default, balloons pop up every 60 minutes to remind the user that they are working offline. Enabling this policy setting and setting a time in the spin box sets that frequency and prevents the user from changing it. Disabling the policy setting keeps the default (60 minutes) and prevents users from changing the defaults.

 This policy setting does not apply to Windows Vista machines.

Initial Reminder Balloon Lifetime

The first balloon that pops up lasts 30 seconds. Use this setting to specify how long the first balloon stays up. Enabling this policy setting and entering a time in the spin box sets that duration and prevents the user from changing it. Disabling the policy setting keeps the default (30 seconds) and prevents users from changing the defaults.

 This policy setting does not apply to Windows Vista machines.

Reminder Balloon Lifetime

After the first balloon pops up, consecutive balloons pop up every 60 minutes by default (or for whatever value is configured in the **Reminder Balloon Frequency** policy setting) for a total of 15 seconds each, as defined by this policy setting. Enabling this policy setting and entering a time in the spin box sets that duration and prevents the user from changing it. Disabling the policy setting keeps the default (15 seconds) and prevents users from changing the defaults.

 This policy setting does not apply to Windows Vista machines.

Event Logging Level

This is a good debugging feature if users complain, er, report that their synchronizations are failing. Enable this policy setting, and enter a value of 0, 1, 2, or 3:

- Level 0 records an error to the Application log when the local cache is corrupted.
- Level 1 logs the same as level 0, plus an event when the server that houses the offline file disconnects or goes down.
- Level 2 logs the same as level 1, plus an event when the computer affected by this policy setting disconnects.
- Level 3 logs the same as level 2, plus an event when the corresponding server gets back online.

Figures 3.49 and 3.50 show examples of notifications when a server becomes available again. Remember, these logs appear in the log at the workstation, not at the server.

 This policy setting does not affect Windows Vista. For Windows Vista Sync Center troubleshooting, see the section "Troubleshooting Sync Center."

FIGURE 3.49   The workstation log shows that the server is available.

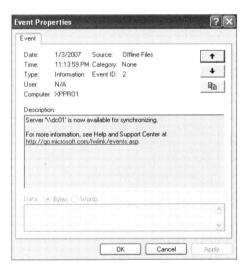

FIGURE 3.50   The workstation log shows state transitions in relation to the server.

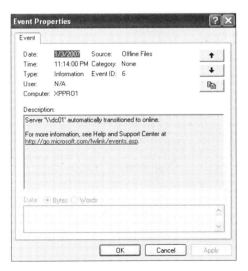

Prohibit Make Available Offline for These File and Folders

Okay, so there's a grammar problem in the name of this policy setting, but it's still useful. If you want to allow most users to pin files in a share but ensure that certain users can't pin files in a share, this is the policy setting for you. After you enable this setting, just add the full UNC (Universal Naming Convention) path to the share or share and file you want to block from being pinned. For instance, if you want to block \\DC01\sales from being pinned, enter it in this policy setting and then ensure that it applies to the appropriate users.

 This policy setting applies only when users are using Windows XP.

Do Not Automatically Make Redirected Folders Available Offline

I get several e-mails a month asking me how to prevent Windows XP from pinning all files in Redirected Folders such as Documents. Here it is. Ensure that it affects all the users you want. Of course, this trick should work for Windows Vista as well.

Actually, this policy isn't found (anymore) in Computer Configuration ➤ Administrative Templates ➤ Network ➤ Offline Files. In Windows Vista, it's been moved to User Configuration ➤ Policies ➤ Administrative Templates ➤ System ➤ Folder Redirection (and we discussed it earlier). But, I'm bringing it up again here because this policy does directly relate to Offline Files—even though it's been moved to the Folder Redirection section.

Because this policy is a user-side policy, it becomes very difficult to implement on a system-wide level. See the upcoming section "Turning off Folder Redirection for Desktops," which describes how to use the **Do not Automatically Make Redirected Folders Available Offline** policy setting by strapping on a set of fangs.

Using Group Policy to Configure Offline Files (Exclusive to the Computer Node)

As we just explored, most policy settings for Offline Files are duplicated in both the User and Computer halves of Group Policy. But several settings appear only on and apply only to the Computer half.

Allow or Disallow Use of the Offline Files Feature

This is the "master switch" for Offline Files. This policy can affect Windows XP and Windows Vista. Once a machine embraces this policy setting, a reboot is required. Disable (yes, disable) this policy setting and you effectively turn off Offline Files. Note that a restart is required.

In Windows XP, this policy setting is similar to the **Prohibit user configuration of Offline Files** setting discussed in the previous section. Once that policy setting is enabled, the Offline Files feature is active, and users cannot turn it off or change the settings. If *this* policy setting is enabled, Offline Files is enabled, but users can change the settings. If no additional GPOs are defined, the defaults are used. Once this policy setting is disabled, the target machine's Offline

Files tab in the Folder Options dialog box (seen in Figure 3.20) has grayed-out check boxes, and Offline Files is disabled.

Recall that Offline Files is enabled only for Windows 2000 Professional and Windows XP. It's disabled for servers by default. You can use the **Allow or Disallow use of the offline files feature** policy setting to your advantage to turn on Offline Files on all your Windows 2000 Servers or Windows Server 2003 computers easily—not that you would need to, as it's highly unlikely your servers will often be offline. Note that Windows Server 2003 requires that Remote Desktop Connections be *disabled* in order for Offline Files to function. See the Real-World Scenario titled "Offline Files and Windows 2000 Server and Windows Server 2003, and Windows Server 2008" earlier.

> If you enable this feature, it should kick in right away (when the background refresh interval hits). However, disabling this feature is another story. If one or more files are open in the cache when you try to disable the feature, that disable operation will fail; a reboot is required. You can experience the same behavior when trying to disable the feature through the user interface.

Default Cache Size

This corresponds to the "Amount of disk space to use for temporary online files" slider in the Offline Files tab in the Folder Options dialog box, as shown in Figure 3.20 earlier in this chapter. You can control what percentage of the C: partition is available for automatic caching.

If you enable this policy setting, you must enter a whole number that represents what percentage of the partition you will be using. If you want to use 31 percent, enter 3100. (The total range begins at 0 percent, then can be set to 100 or 1 percent, and ends at 10,000 or 100 percent.) This setting is then locked in, and users can't change it. If you disable this policy setting, the default of 10 percent is locked in, and users can't change it. Remember that this has a maximum size of only 2GB. Since this policy setting works with a percentage value, it can be difficult to know if that percentage exceeds 2GB on any target volume.

> This policy setting applies to Windows 2000, Windows XP, and Windows 2003 computers only.

> You might need to reboot the target machine for this policy setting to take effect. It does not always work when a background refresh is kicked off.

Files Not Cached

By default, for Windows XP and Windows 2000 several file extensions cannot be cached, due to their sensitive nature. Microsoft is concerned that especially large files will be shuttled up and back with just 1 byte changed. Therefore, the synchronization is hard-coded not to cache certain file extensions, most notably databases. That is, for extra protection, Microsoft prevents databases from being cached. The following file types cannot be cached:

- `.PST` (Outlook personal folder)

- `.SLM` (Source Library Management file)

- `.MDB` (Access database)

- `.LDB` (Access security)

- `.MDW` (Access workgroup)

- `.MDE` (Access compiled module)

- `.DB?` (everything that has the extension `.DB` plus anything else in the third character, such as `.DBF`, is never included in the cache)

If you enable this policy setting, you can add to this list. For instance, you can add your own file types in the form of `*.DOC`, `*.EXE`, and `*.JAM` to also eliminate the caching of only `.DOC`, `.EXE`, and `.JAM` files. In my testing, there appears to be no way to allow the caching of the hard-coded database files listed earlier. If users try to synchronize any of these file types, the Synchronization Manager balks with a "Files of This Type Cannot Be Made Available Offline" message. Windows XP/Service Pack 2 adds the capability to turn off the error every time users log synchronize. Although it is basically a manual endeavor, the hacks are described in KB 811660 in the section titled "Exclusion Error Suppression."

 This policy setting applies to Windows 2000, Windows XP, and Windows 2003 computers only. This policy setting isn't necessary for Windows Vista, because all file types are cached.

At Logoff, Delete Local Copy of User's Offline Files

This policy setting sort of defeats the purpose of using Offline Files in the first place. Its main purpose is for logon use at a kiosk-style machine. That is, a user logs on for a bit and then logs off. You'll want to ensure that their Offline Files are cleaned up behind them. Another reason I can see using this policy setting is to prevent files from being lifted off a user's hard drive. Theoretically, you can do this by digging around in the `C:\windows\CSC` folder. Even if the files are deleted at logoff, a good hacker could theoretically get the files back via an "undelete" program of some type.

Moreover, this policy setting doesn't guarantee a synchronization before it wipes the local cache clean upon logoff. Therefore, it is highly recommended that if you use this policy setting, you pair it with the "Synchronize all offline files before logging off" option (seen in Figure 3.21), which will save your users' bacon. Avoid using this option unless you have some workstation that needs extra security and is infrequently used, and you don't mind if the occasional file gets lost when using it.

If protection is what you're after, and you use EFS setup for your laptops users, a better option (for Windows XP machines only) is to use the **Encrypt the Offline Files cache** policy setting, discussed shortly.

This policy setting does not apply to Windows Vista machines.

Subfolders Always Available Offline

This policy setting is useful if you want to ensure that all subfolders are also available offline. Essentially, it prevents users from excluding the ability to cache subfolders and makes subfolders available offline whenever their parent folder is made available offline. Any new folder a user creates under cached subfolders is automatically cached and synchronized when the parent folder is scheduled for synchronization.

 This policy setting applies only to Windows XP.

Encrypt the Offline Files Cache

If you have EFS set up for your laptop users, enabling this policy setting is a good idea. By default, even files stored in an encrypted format on shares are not protected in the Windows 2000 file cache. With Windows XP, they can and should be.

 This policy setting applies only to Windows XP (regardless of all the notes in the policy setting's Explain text "Requirements").

Configure Slow Link Speed

Recall that the Synchronization Manager in Windows 2000 and XP thinks a slow link is 64Kbps. When a user comes in over a slow link (less than 64Kbps), the system automatically uses their locally cached version of network files. Additionally, the foreground Synchronization Manager does not run. You can change the definition of the speed of a slow link, but only for Windows XP and Windows 2003 clients.

 This policy setting applies only to Windows XP and Windows 2003 computers.

Configure Slow-Link Mode

We explored this earlier in the section entitled "Windows Vista's Synchronization Engine over Slow Links." Check out that section for detailed usage examples.

 This policy setting applies only to Windows Vista machines.

Real World Scenario

Synchronization Manager Limitations in Windows 2000 and Windows XP

You might see some weird behavior if a single computer is shared among multiple people. You can see this behavior in the following example:

Configure two GPOs that redirect My Documents to two different locations, \\WS03ServerA\UserDocs and \\WS03ServerB\UserDocs. Link the first GPO to OU-A and the second GPO to OU-B. OU-A contains Fred, and OU-B contains Robin.

Fred logs on and verifies that the My Documents redirection has taken effect by looking at the path in the Properties dialog box. If Fred opens the Synchronization Manager after creating or modifying a file in \\WS03ServerA\Data, he sees the \\WS03ServerA\UserDocs UNC in the synchronization list. When he logs off, he sees the synchronization happen for this UNC.

Now Robin logs onto the same Windows XP workstation and verifies that My Documents redirection has taken effect. When Robin opens Synchronization Manager, she sees the \\WS03ServerA\UserDocs UNC and the \\WS03ServerB\UserDocs UNC in the synchronization list. When she logs off, she sees both paths attempting to perform a synchronization.

You can take this to extremes, too. Try to configure five users in five different OUs with five different GPOs, each redirecting My Documents to one of five different servers. As each user logs on to a single Windows XP Desktop (or a Windows 2000 Desktop and chooses to manually cache the share), the UNC path for that user is added to the UNC paths for the other users in Synchronization Manager.

So what should you do? Allow only your laptop users to use offline caching. You can configure a GPO to prohibit offline caching for desktops and leave it enabled for laptops. Since laptop users don't tend to share their machines often, they don't build up many synchronization links. The workaround for those users is to open Synchronization Manager and uncheck all UNC paths except their own. But no user is going to do this.

After you have Windows XP/Service Pack 2 installed on the client, you have another option. You can leverage the tips in KB 811660, which explains how to perform several new feats of magic. One of the sections in the article describes how you can "Prevent admin pinning of files for non-primary users." Hence, when logging out, the main user of the machine will no longer resync the other user's settings. Here's the bad news, though: there are no Windows XP/Service Pack 2 policy settings to help you. This is basically a manual endeavor to enter in the hacks described in KB 811660. Or, you can come to GPanswers.com for a downloadable ADM template that can perform this action on multiple clients at once.

The caching of permissions on directory entries in the Offline Files cache has improved this situation significantly in Vista.

Turn On Economical Application of Administrative Assigned Offline Files

Read the name of the policy setting again. Then forget it.

It should have been called **Turn off economical application of administrative assigned Offline Files.** Yes, off.

Here's the history of this setting. Recall that you can use the **Administratively assigned offline files** policy setting to guarantee a share be offline for a user. This is great, except that with Windows XP, people found that their servers were experiencing very high file loads when users would log onto their clients (that is, at 9 a.m.). What was happening was that each client was trying to process their **Administratively assigned offline files** policy. Windows XP/SP2 had a Registry punch (found in KB 830407) to ease this problem. It was called "economical administrative pinning." Once it was enabled, any client with this behavior would perform the full pinning operation *only* if the top-level folder was not yet pinned in the Offline Files cache.

The result is that when the policy is processed once, subsequent logons to the server do not jam the server up.

This behavior was added and turned on, by default, in Vista. However, the policy title really should be **Turn off economical application of administratively assigned Offline Files.**" Once this policy setting is Disabled (yes, Disabled), the policy setting reverts back to pre-Windows XP/SP2 behavior.

 This policy setting applies only to Windows Vista.

Limit Disk Space Used by Offline Files

In Windows XP, files expressly pinned weren't counted toward Offline Files usage. In Windows Vista, with this policy setting, you can dictate how many megabytes you want to set aside for *all* Offline Files—those automatically cached and those pinned.

There are two settings here:

- One for total size of Offline Files (including those that are pinned) and
- One for the size of auto-cached files

The Group Policy interface allows you to set the second number higher than the first—but that setting isn't possible in real life. Indeed, if you go way back to Figure 3.36 you'll see the sliders for this setting in the interface. If you try it out, you'll notice you can't slide the second slider past the first. That's because you can't have a size bigger than the "Maximum amount of space all offline files can use." If you do that, the second number will automatically be set to the first number.

 This policy setting applies only to Windows Vista machines.

Troubleshooting Sync Center

The Windows Vista event log is a deep and rich place. To that end, there are two places in particular to go when troubleshooting Sync Center problems.

Enabling the Offline Files Log

The Offline Files log file is located in Event Viewer ➢ Applications and Servers Logs ➢ Microsoft ➢ Windows ➢ Offline Files. Once there, dive one level deeper into the Operational log. By default, this log doesn't grab any data. You need to turn it on. Right-click over the Operational log and select Enable Log as seen in Figure 3.51.

The events you'll find here are mostly the successful or unsuccessful startup/shutdown of the Offline Files feature as well as online/offline transitions.

FIGURE 3.51   To get data in the Offline Files ➢ Operational log, first enable it.

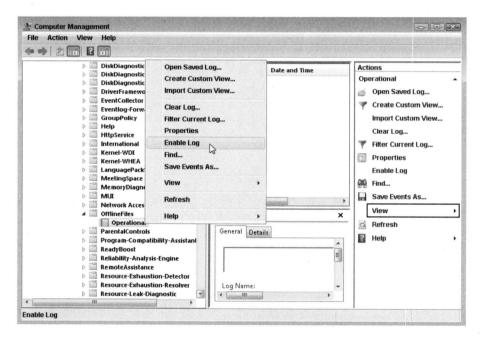

Enabling the Sync Log

There is also a Sync Log, but you need the super-secret entry key to know it's there. The thing to know how to do is called Show Analytic Channels, and here's how to do it.

As shown previously in Figure 3.51, in the rightmost pane of the Computer Management console's log view contains a View action. Click that View option and select Show Analytic and Debug Logs." You can see "View" highlighted in 3.51 for quick reference. Once you do, you'll then be able to find the Sync Log hiding under Microsoft ➤ Windows ➤ Offline Files. Right-click Sync Log and click the Enable item.

This is an analytic channel that reports sync activity *as it is happening* in the Offline Files service. It is not intended for use by end users but should prove useful to administrators (and could be asked of you by Microsoft PSS) to gather specific information about what's going on.

When that log is enabled, log entries appear for items that are being synchronized within the service. This means that any item synchronized by the service will be reported, not only items synchronized through Sync Center. You can see one of these events in Figure 3.52.

FIGURE 3.52   You can get blow-by-blow details of what is being synced via Offline Files.

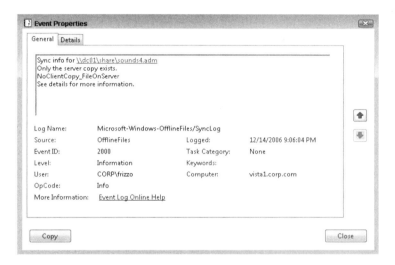

If you open one of these sync events to the Details tab in the event viewer, you can see the XML format containing the details; then, you can buy your favorite scripting pal some lunch to make some killer reports for you based on the XML data!

Turning off Folder Redirection for Desktops

I've never met a policy setting I didn't like. But I have met a few that missed their calling. The policy setting at User Configuration ➤ Policies ➤ System ➤ Folder Redirection ➤ **Do not Automatically Make Redirected Folders Available Offline** has missed its calling.

What on earth am I talking about?

Well, let's take a minute and analyze the normal function of Offline Files: its primary mission is to maintain files when you're not on the network so you can keep working. Super. So what kinds of computers are off the network a lot? Laptops, of course. And desktops generally *stay* on the network.

Assuming your laptops represent 10–30 percent of your workforce, do you need those files automatically cached on *every* machine in your enterprise like the remaining 70 percent of your desktops?

Why should you care about turning it off?

Because, depending on whom you ask, it could be a security risk. Do you want cached copies of your precious documents on every machine to which your users roam? Likely not. Isn't putting your user's documents on every desktop they roam to a security risk? In a way, yes!

Sure, you could encrypt the Offline Files using EFS or BitLocker, but, let's face it, most people simply don't use EFS today. And while BitLocker looks really promising, its deployment isn't very widespread. And, even then, if BitLocker is implemented it's most likely not on the desktop computers, but rather laptops (because it's usually only laptops that have the special TPM chip needed for BitLocker. But I digress.).

Finally, let's not forget that every time a user roams to a desktop, they're really just wasting space on the local hard drive. Remember, desktops are *normally* connected to the network just fine. Do they really need *another* copy of their documents clogging up the local disk?

So, in my analysis (and I'm just one guy with an opinion here), Offline Files doesn't make sense on a well-running network where your desktops and servers are on a fast LAN. Let me be clear: it won't hurt anything either. But with files flying around everywhere, being sprinkled from desktop to desktop, it can be a security risk, waste space, and promote unnecessary synchronization and bandwidth.

Let me be a zillion percent clear: I positively love this feature for my *laptops*. I'm just not that wild about it for my *desktops*. However, I likely would keep it on my desktops if I was connected to servers on a slow WAN like a branch office (especially if that WAN link was flaky).

So, my first thought when I read the name of this policy setting (**Do not Automatically Make Redirected Folders Available Offline**) was "Aha! They're thinking what I'm thinking! There's a policy setting that enables me to turn it off for desktops!"

Except that's not how this policy setting works. This policy setting is not on the computer side; it's on the user side. So, inherently, it cannot simply be put in a GPO and linked to, say, the Desktops OU to turn it off.

With this policy setting, you can only say, "The users in Sales don't automatically make their Redirected Folders available offline." But that's not the point, is it? You want the Sales guys to cache their documents on their laptops but *not* cache them on the various desktops they roam to (especially if they're public computers).

Now, cracking open the underlying ADMX file, I learned that the Registry key for this policy setting is really a value called HKEY_Current_User\Software\Policies\Microsoft\Windows\NetCache and it sets a REG_DWORD of DisableFRAdminPin to 1.

And then it came to me in a dream: If I could somehow only apply this policy setting (or the underlying Registry setting) to desktops, then, bam! I could turn off Offline Files for desktops (which would leave it on for laptops) and I would get the effect I wanted!

Let me jump to the end of the story and tell you what I found when I applied this policy setting (or the underlying Registry entry) on Windows XP and Windows Vista machines.

Turns out, that when I did this, Windows XP and Windows Vista didn't react the same way to it. Here's what I found, with Jakob, the technical editor of this edition to back me up (your mileage may vary):

When we applied the Registry value to Windows XP   Windows XP just eats the policy setting (or Registry value) and, bang! Offline Files goes out like a light. It's awesome. If you've never told Windows XP to try to use Offline Files, you'll be 100 percent successful immediately: Windows XP just won't try to use Offline Files with Redirected Folders.

However, there's a catch. If you have the Registry tweak set, and the desktop goes offline for some reason (e.g., network failure or the server is offline) for a period of time *and* the user creates or edits a document while offline, that document will be synchronized the next time the client is online (which is good). However, it will also stay in the local cache from that point.

That's not what we wanted. However, since we're talking about desktops (and they're usually online all the time) this shouldn't happen too much.

Now, with a little extra elbow grease and magic you might be able to flush the cache using CSCCMD (see the sidebar entitled "Power Admins Rejoice: Scripting Offline Files") but you're on your own for that.

When we applied the Registry value to Windows Vista   Windows Vista reacts kind of like Windows XP to the policy (or Registry addition), but it gets a little better actually.

If the client system goes offline, then files are created, Windows Vista will sync to the network share when it's available just once more (like XP).

But then it flushes those files from the local cache forever. So, with Vista you will be sure no Offline Files are stored locally once the policy setting (or Registry item) is set, then they perform one more sync.

Whew. Figuring all that out made both Jakob's and my head spin! Be sure to test our findings out thoroughly in your environment before you roll out one of our proposed plans in a widespread way. Now, once we know the predicted behavior, how do we get user-based policy setting (or underlying Registry entry) to *just* our desktops?

There are three ways to get this setting applied just on desktops (that is, turn it off just for desktops) but leave it on for laptops. Here are the three tricks I have up my sleeve:

- Create a custom WMI Filter to apply to a GPO (with the policy setting contained within it).

- Use Group Policy Preference Extensions to jam in the same Registry value that the policy setting would, but ensure that only users on desktops get the setting.

- Use the Loopback policy in Merge mode which makes the policy setting (which is really a user-based setting) affect the computers you want—in our case, desktops.

In Figure 3.53, you can see an example of what happens after a user logs onto a Windows Vista desktop after we make our setting. You can see that synchronization has been turned off, but Folder Redirected files are still stored on the server but not cached to the desktop (no little yin/yang symbols on the file icons).

Any of these will work, so, let's get started!

If you've figured out a more creative or alternate way to do this, let me know, and I'll include it in a GPanswers.com newsletter.

FIGURE 3.53 Documents are still redirected to the server, but for users on desktops, you can avoid the synchronization (copy) to the local computer.

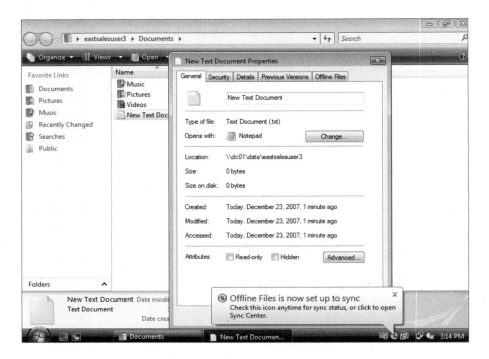

Using WMI Filters to Forcefully Apply This Setting Specifically to Desktops

This technique assumes you understand how to create WMI filters. If you need a refresher, please check out Chapter 5 in the companion book, *Group Policy Fundamentals, Troubleshooting, and Security* where we cover it in depth.

Here are the short steps you'll need to forcefully disable Redirected Folders from automatically making the contents offline upon desktops:

1. Create a new GPO that Enables the **Do not Automatically Make Redirected Folders Available Offline** policy. You don't need to configure any other settings in the GPO.

2. Link the GPO to OUs containing user accounts. Again, please, please read my warnings about how WMI filters can slow you down in Chapter 5 of the companion book.

3. Create a WMI filter that determines if a machine meets certain criteria. My suggestion is to check to see if it's a desktop (and not a laptop).

    ▪ If it's a desktop, then the users on those desktops will successfully embrace this GPO (and the adjusted synchronization behavior as described earlier will be performed).

    ▪ If it's not a desktop, then the standard behavior to sync Redirected Folders will continue (this is what we want).

All you need is a sample WMI query (once you've learned the basics). This query will work a lot of the time (perhaps not all of the time).

```
Select * From Win32_PhysicalMemory Where FormFactor != 12
```

This query returns True on computers that do not have SODIMM form factor memory and False on computers with SODIMM form factor memory. The assumption is that pretty much all laptops will have this style memory and desktops will not. We've tested this out and it really seems to work a lot of the time.

> More info on this class: http://msdn2.microsoft.com/en-us/library/
> aa394347(VS.85).aspx (shortened to http://tinyurl.com/2hq6e6).

How did we figure out this query? Hat's off to Jakob for launching a world-wide search for the answer. Check out the thread at http://heidelbergit.blogspot.com/2008/02/wmi-filter-contest-are-you-knight-in.html (Shortened to http://tinyurl.com/yvpshy).

Using Group Policy Preference Extensions to Force the Value (Just for Users on Desktops)

Because we can't just apply the policy setting to the user side, we need to get tricky. Again, the underlying Registry entry for the policy setting is User\Software\Policies\Microsoft\ Windows\NetCache, and it sets a REG_DWORD of DisableFRAdminPin to 1.

We need to get this to our desktops.

Now, the Registry entry itself can't figure out if the user's machine is a desktop or laptop. But with some of our Group Policy Preference Extensions super-powers we can set the same Registry value and ensure that it *only* affects machines that are desktops!

So, create a GPO and link it to your user population. Then, use the Registry Extension on the user side to specify the Registry value as seen in Figure 3.54.

However, at this point, you need to target the value so only users logged onto desktops get the preference setting containing the Registry entry. In Figure 3.55, you can see my suggested target. In short, I'm saying three things must be true for it to be a desktop:

- It is not a laptop (because the hardware profile says so).
- It has no battery.
- It has no PCMCIA slots.

Again, this might not be perfect in all situations, but it should suffice for most.

Alternatively, if all of your desktops had the word Desktop or some other distinguishing factor in the name, you could use a query like the one shown in Figure 3.56.

Using Group Policy Loopback in Merge Mode to Apply This Setting to Specific Computers

For a refresher on Group Policy Loopback modes, be sure to check out Chapter 5 of the companion book, *Group Policy Fundamentals, Security, and Troubleshooting*.

But, in short, Group Policy Loopback mode's job is to apply user settings to computers. The Loopback mode we're after is Merge mode, which will apply additional user side settings to specific computers as the user is logging on, as seen in Figure 3.57.

FIGURE 3.54 This is the same Registry entry that Do not Automatically Make Redirected Folders Available Offline would put in place.

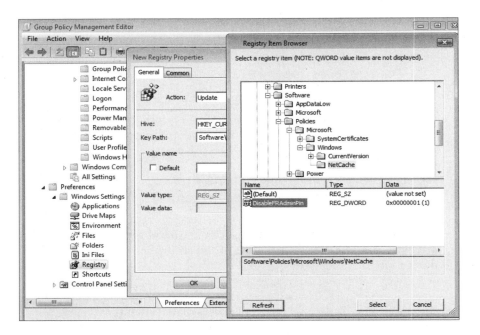

FIGURE 3.55 If you use this query, it will usually determine that your machine is a desktop and not a laptop.

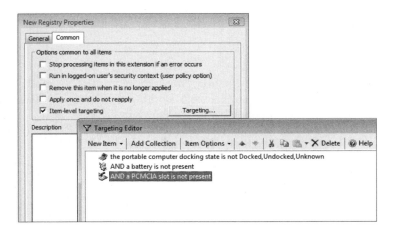

FIGURE 3.56 If you have a uniform naming convention for your desktops, this job is even easier.

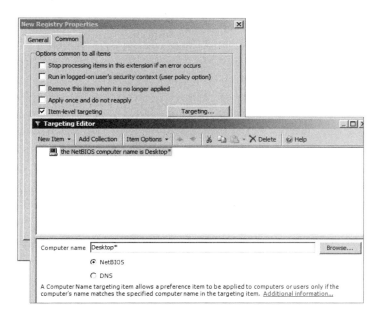

FIGURE 3.57 Use Group Policy Loopback in Merge mode to get user side settings to computers.

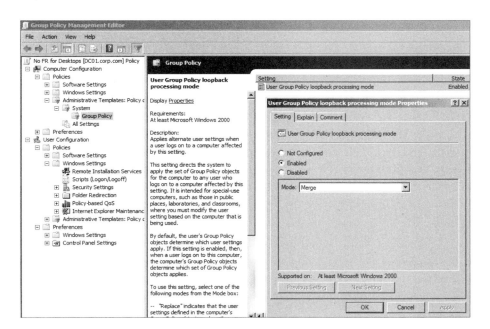

Here are the short steps you'll need to forcefully disable Redirected Folders from automatically making the contents offline on desktops:

1. Create a new GPO that enables the **Do not Automatically Make Redirected Folders Available Offline** policy.

2. Link the GPO to OUs containing desktop computer accounts.

3. In the same or another GPO, set the setting to enable Loopback in Merge mode, as seen in Figure 3.57. The setting is located within Computer Configuration ➢ Policies ➢ Administrative Templates ➢ System ➢ Group Policy ➢ **User Group Policy loopback processing mode**. Select Merge mode.

Now, reboot one of your machines in the OU containing desktops. That's because the Loopback policy doesn't kick in until after a reboot.

Now, when you log onto a desktop as any user who gets Folder Redirection, the **Do not Automatically Make Redirected Folders Available Offline** policy will kick in.

Note that Loopback policy can be a little hard to work with because you might inadvertently get even more settings than you bargained for. Again, for more information on Loopback policy processing, see Chapter 5 of the companion book.

Final Thoughts

In the last chapter, you set up Roaming Profiles. But there was a problem. If you had both Windows Vista and Windows XP machines, you wouldn't "see" files, say, in the Documents folder in Windows Vista show up in the My Documents folder on Windows XP. Here, you set up Redirected Folders, which anchored My Documents (for Windows XP) and Documents (for Windows Vista) to the same place.

This gave you several key features: a centralized backup place for critical files, the ability for users' Documents contents to be available on any workstation, and the ability to mitigate the generated traffic caused by Documents being located within the profile. By default, the Documents folder is located within the profile.

You also set up Offline Files so that files work offline as though they were online. You used Group Policy to specify how your users and computers would use this function. Recall that Documents/My Documents is already automatically pinned if you use Windows XP and Windows Vista. But Windows Vista thinks everything is "fast" until you expressly tell it what servers (and optionally shares) it should check to see if it's slow. Oh yeah, you have to tell it what "slow" means too.

If you're still using Windows XP/Service Pack 2, you should note that there are some additional hacks you can perform to squelch some noise generated by Offline Files (see KB 811660) during logoff.

If you just can't get enough information on Offline Files, be sure to check out the following resources:

- What's New In Offline Files for Windows Vista `http://tinyurl.com/2moatb`.

- Offline Files and Folder Redirection in Windows Vista webinar `http://tinyurl.com/27trbh`.

- Changes to Offline Files in Windows Vista article in *TechNet Magazine* (written by me): `http://tinyurl.com/2zkk8p`.

Creating a managed desktop isn't easy; there's a lot to configure. And you're well on your way to making your Windows life more livable. In the next chapter, we'll continue our desktop management story. We'll learn how to distribute software to our users and computers. So, turn the page and get started!

4

The Managed Desktop, Part 2: Software Deployment via Group Policy

Two chapters ago, I discussed and implemented the first big feature of getting your managed desktop story in gear: Roaming Profiles. Once Roaming Profiles are enabled, the user can roam from machine to machine, comfortable that their working environment will follow wherever they go.

In the last chapter, I discussed and implemented more features to get your managed desktop handled. First, we tackled Redirected Folders, which took Roaming Profiles one step further and anchored the user's Documents or My Documents folder to a share on a server. We then used the Group Policy settings on Offline Folders and the Synchronization Manager to ensure that certain files are always available in the cache if our connection to the server goes offline or if the server itself goes offline.

We're well on our way to implementing a fully managed desktop. That is, we want our users to roam freely across our entire environment and take all their stuff with them. But we're missing a fundamental piece of the equation: how can we guarantee that a specific application is ready and waiting for them on that machine? What good is having your user data follow you if an application needed to access the data isn't available? That's what we're going to handle in this chapter.

Group Policy Software Installation (GPSI) Overview

Without any third-party software distribution mechanism (such as SCCM 2007 (what was known as SMS) or Altiris, most environments require that you spend most of your time running from desktop to desktop. In a typical scenario, a user is hired and fills out the human resources paperwork, and a computer with the standard suite of software is dropped on their desk.

Usually this machine comes from some sort of "deployment farm" in the back office, where scads of machines are imaged (a la Symantec's Ghost) by the scores. Or, maybe the team is using Microsoft Deployment techniques as specified in Chapter 1.

The user then starts to surf the Internet—er, I mean—get to work. Soon enough, it's discovered that the user needs a specific or special application, and a desktop technician is dispatched to fulfill the user's request for new software. When the desktop technician arrives, they either load the user's special software via the CD drive or connect to a network share to pull down the software.

Group Policy Software Installation, or GPSI for short, is the next big feature we'll set up. It's with this feature that users can automatically pull applications through the network, without needing anyone to be dispatched. This feature further chips away at the total cost of ownership (TCO) regarding workstation maintenance.

There are essentially four steps to going from 0 to 60 in 4 seconds when it comes to deploying software with GPSI features:

- Acquire a software setup package with an .MSI extension.
- Share and secure a software distribution shared folder.
- Set up a GPO to deliver the software.
- Assign or Publish the software.

We will approach each of these steps in our software configuration journey in the next few pages.

The good news is that GPSI can solve many of your software deployment woes. The bad news is that, like all other Group Policy features, the magic only happens with the marriage between Active Directory on the back end and a Windows machine on the client.

Before we get too far along, I want to clear up a terminology misnomer. Specifically, many people incorrectly refer to the Group Policy Software Installation mechanism as the lone word IntelliMirror. As you might have noticed, we haven't included it in the book's title because the word IntelliMirror isn't being used very much; and I think this is why: IntelliMirror (the concept) was just one piece to the managed desktop story, where Group Policy Software Installation is only one of those pieces. Anyway, the term IntelliMirror has come and gone, but the idea of a *managed desktop* is here to stay.

Software installed this way—via Group Policy—is referred to in many Microsoft documents as *managed* software. Group Policy can perform what is generically known as an *advertisement* of software, and the Windows Installer Service picks it up and runs with it to perform the installation. Let's get started by understanding the Windows Installer Service.

Although it's true that Microsoft provides an "Active Directory Client" for Windows 9x and for Windows NT Workstation to be used with Active Directory, that "Active Directory Client" does not enable any Group Policy functionality. That client, by the way, is available on the Windows 2000 Server CD under the clients\win9x directory and provides additional features such as NTLMv2 authentication and some Active Directory searching. But it doesn't allow old clients to take advantage of Group Policy or GPSI.

The Windows Installer Service

A background service called the *Windows Installer Service* must be running on the client for the software deployment magic to happen. The Windows Installer Service can understand when Group Policy is being used to install or revoke an application and react accordingly. The Windows Installer Service has a secret superpower; it can run under "elevated" privileges. In other words, the user does not need to be a local administrator of the workstation to get software deployed via Group Policy.

So, the Windows Installer Service installs the software with administrative privileges. Once installed, however, the program is run under the user's context.

Windows Installer can install applications via *document invocation* or *auto-install*. That is, it is automatically started when you choose a specific extension or extensions. For instance, if you are e-mailed a file with a .PDF extension, and then double-click to open it (but don't yet have Acrobat Reader installed), the Windows Installer Service can be automatically invoked to bring down Adobe Acrobat Reader from one of your servers. This is described in more detail in the "Advanced Published or Assigned" section, later in this chapter. Additionally, Windows Installer can determine when an application is damaged and repair it automatically by downloading the required files from the source to fix the problem.

> You might have heard the phrase "Advertising a package" or, in short, an Advertisement. An Advertisement is a generic term which means that software is "offered" by Active Directory to the client machine. But, the client has three ways to accept that Advertisement. You'll see later that the shortcut can be selected, which will download the application (that's one way). Another way is to click a file extension that is registered for GPSI (we already mentioned this one), and finally, you can invoke an advertised COM object (which we really won't be going into here).

Do note, however, that there are several versions of the Windows Installer Service. For our purposes, they'll all pretty much act alike, but it's good to know about the history.

- Windows 2000 had Windows Installer 1.

- Since Windows 2000 was released, Windows Installer 2 was released. It is integrated into Windows 2000 Service Pack 3 and higher. For your Windows 2000 machines, if you don't yet have Windows 2000 Service Pack 3 (and I can't imagine why you wouldn't), you can install the Windows Installer 2 Redistributable, which, at last check, is located at go.microsoft.com/fwlink/?LinkId=7613.

- However, before you go forth and deploy that update, note that Windows Installer 3 is available. This is already included in Windows XP/SP2.

- And, finally, Windows Vista brings us Windows Installer 4.

We discuss the ins and outs of Windows Installer 3 (and higher) in the "Inside the MSIEXEC Tool" section coming up.

Understanding *.MSI* Packages

About 99 percent of the magic in software deployment with Group Policy is wrapped in a file format called .MSI. The .MSI file has two goals: increase the flexibility of software distribution, and reduce the effort required to make new packages. Files in the .MSI format are becoming more and more "standard issue" when a software application is rolled out the door (though sometimes they are not). For instance, every edition of Office since Office 2000 has shipped as an .MSI distribution.

On the surface, .MSI files appear to act as self-expanding distribution files, like familiar, self-executing .ZIP files. But really, under the surface, .MSI files contain a database of "what goes where" and can contain either pointers to additional source files or all the files rolled up inside the .MSI itself. Additionally, .MSI files can "tier" the installation; for instance, you can specify, "Don't bother loading the spell checker in Word, if I only want Excel." Sounds simple, but it's revolutionary.

Moreover, because .MSI files are themselves a database, an added feature is realized. The creator of the .MSI package (or sometimes the user) can designate which features are loaded to the hard drive upon initial installation, which features are loaded to the hard drive the first time they are used, which features are run from the CD or distribution point, and which features are never loaded. This lets administrators pare down installations to make efficient use of both disk space and network bandwidth.

With .MSI files, the bar is also raised when it comes to the overall management of applications. Indeed, two discreet .MSI operations really come in handy: Rollback and Uninstall. When .MSI files are being installed, the entire installation can be canceled and simply rolled back. Or, after an .MSI application is fully installed, it can be fully uninstalled. You are not guaranteed the exact same machine state from Uninstall as you are with Rollback, however. The GPSI features in Active Directory are designed mainly to integrate with the new .MSI file format. There is other legacy support, as you'll see later.

Utilizing an Existing *.MSI* Package

As stated, lots of applications come as .MSI files. Some are full-blown applications, such as Office 2000 and later. Others are smaller programs that you might use a lot, such as the GPMC (Group Policy Management Console) or the .NET Framework. All these aforementioned applications come as an .MSI. Be forewarned: just because an application comes as an .MSI doesn't necessarily mean it can always be deployed via GPSI; however, that's a pretty good indication. Yet even though versions of the Norton AntiVirus client shipped as an .MSI, it wasn't installable via GPSI until version 9. Ditto for Adobe Acrobat. Until Acrobat version 7, the Reader Program didn't ship as an .MSI, but the full version did. But even though earlier versions of Adobe Acrobat shipped as .MSI files, they simply weren't deployable via GPSI.

Additionally, some .MSI applications (such as Office 2000, Office XP, and Office 2003) can be deployed to *either* users or computers. However, some applications, such as the GPMC.MSI and the .NET Framework's .MSI can *only* be deployed successfully to computers.

You'll want to check with the manufacturer of the .MSI file to understand specifically how it needs to be installed. The .MSI files that can be deployed via GPSI usually come in three flavors:

- Some .MSI packages are just one solitary file, and they come ready to be deployed. The GPMC and the Windows Administration tools (Adminpak.msi) are examples in this category. (In Figure 4.1, you can see what happens if you try to deploy the GPMC to a user account.)

- Some .MSI packages have one file to "kick off" the installation. Then, there are a gaggle of other files behind it. The .NET Framework (netfx.msi) and service packs (update.msi) are examples in this category.

- Other .MSI files need to be "prepared" for installation. Usually, these applications are more complex. Office 2000, Office XP, Office 2003 (but not Office 2007), and Microsoft TechNet are examples in this category.

FIGURE 4.1   The GPMC 1 isn't meant to be deployed to users using GPSI. Indeed, when I hit OK, I just go into an endless loop!

Many people want to deploy big applications, such as the Office suite. I'm going to help you understand how to deploy both Office 2003 and Office 2007. Each one is somewhat different in how it's deployed and configured for setup (not to mention tweaking), so I'll show both.

So, for these examples, I'll assume you have a copy of Office 2003 or Office 2007. Note that only the Enterprise versions of these applications are guaranteed to work using GPSI. Other editions, like Home and School, may not work properly via GPSI.

Setting Up the Software Distribution Share

The first step is to set up the software distribution shared folder on a server. In this example, we'll use DC01 and create a shared folder with the name of **Apps**. We want all our users to be able to read the files inside this software distribution share because later we might choose to create multiple folders to house additional applications' sources. Later, we'll also create our first application subfolder and feed Office 2003 into its own subfolder.

To set up the software distribution shared folder, follow these steps:

1. Log onto DC01 as Administrator.

2. From the Desktop, click My Computer to open the My Computer folder.

3.   Find a place to create a Users folder. In this example, we'll use D:\APPS. Once you've opened the D: drive, right-click D: and select the Folder command from the New menu; then type in **Apps** as the name.

You can substitute any name for Apps.

4.   Share the Apps folder such that Everyone has Read access. The procedure for this is slightly different for Windows Server 2003 or Windows Server 2008. While you're in the Permissions for the Apps dialog, additionally ensure that the Administrators group has Full Control permissions upon the share.

You can use Share permissions, NTFS permissions, or both to restrict who can see which applications. The most restrictive permissions between Share level and NTFS level permissions are used. Here, at the Apps share, you want everyone to have access to the share. You'll then create subfolders to house each application and use NTFS permissions to specify, at each subfolder level, which groups or users can see which applications' subfolders.

Again, in this example, we're using a simple share on a simple server. Here, we'll be installing from a Domain Controller in our examples, which you wouldn't normally do in real life, but it's okay for our examples. Indeed, the best thing to do is to use Distributed File Systems (DFS) Namespaces to ensure that users can get to this share from another server, even if this server is down. DFS Namespaces is beyond the scope of this book, but do read the Real-World Scenario "Normal Shares versus DFS Namespaces."

It's a really good idea to exclusively use DFS Namespaces for package installation points. This is because if you move a package, you will likely cause a product reinstallation on your target machines. This happens whenever the original source location changes. By using DFS Namespaces, you can avoid this problem.

Setting Up an Administrative Installation (for *.MSI* Files that Need Them)

As stated, not all .MSI files are "ready to go"; some need to be prepared. To prepare Office 2000, Office XP, and Office 2003 you must perform an *Administrative Installation* of its .MSI file. In this procedure, the system will rebuild and copy the .MSI package from your CD-ROM source to a destination folder for use by your clients. While the package is being rebuilt, it injects the serial number for your users and other customized data. Again, to be clear, not all .MSI packages must be prepared in this manner. Be sure to check your documentation.

Office 2007 does not require this Administrative Installation step (see the section "Creating an Administrative Share for an MSI (for *.MSI* files that Don't Need an "Administrative Installation)" for Office 2007).

To perform an Administrative Installation of Office 2000, Office XP, or Office 2003, you'll use the msiexec command built into Windows 2000 and Windows 2003. The generic command is msiexec /a *whatever*.msi. For Office XP, the command is msiexec /a PROPLUS.MSI. For Office 2003, the command is msiexec /a PRO11N.MSI.

When you run this command, Office is not installed on your server (or wherever you're performing these commands). This can be confusing, as the Office Installation Wizard is kicked off, and it will write a bunch of data to your disk. Again, to be clear, an Administrative Installation simply *prepares* a source installation folder for future software deployment.

The Office Installation Wizard will show that it's getting ready for an Administrative Installation, as shown in Figure 4.2.

FIGURE 4.2   You need to perform an Administrative Installation to prepare a source installation folder for Office.

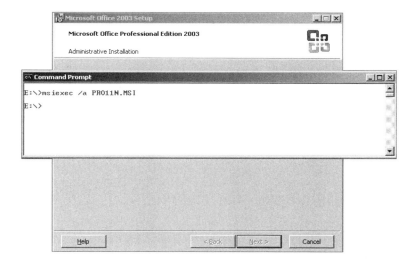

Your next steps in the Installation Wizard are to specify the organization and the installation location and to enter the product key. For the installation location, choose a folder in the share you already created, say, D:\apps\office2003distro. Be sure to enter a valid product key, or you cannot continue. The next screen asks you to confirm the End User License Agreement. Finally, the Administrative Installation is kicked off, and files are copied to the share and the folder (as shown in Figure 4.3).

Creating an Administrative Share for an MSI (for *.MSI* Files that Don't Need an Administrative Installation)

Office 2007 is different than its predecessors. It doesn't require any "preparation" from an Administrative Installation like Office 2003 or earlier. The only preparation you'll need to do is to create a subdirectory under APPS, perhaps Office2007Source, and copy the Office installation files to that directory.

FIGURE 4.3 The files are simply copied to the share; Office isn't being installed (despite the notification that it is).

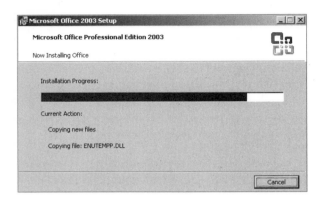

 Real World Scenario

About Underlying Share Permissions

When you set up shared folders, also lock them down with NTFS permissions to prevent unauthorized users from accessing the installations. Even though GPSI can *target* specific users, it makes no provisions for security. Rather, if your users discover the distribution shared folder, they'll have the keys to the candy store unless you put security upon the shared folder or, even better, utilize NTFS permissions as a deadbolt on the lock.

You can expose or hide your shared folders; to hide them, add a $ (dollar sign) to the end of the share name. You can have one shared folder for each package or one shared folder for all your software with subfolders underneath, each with the appropriate NTFS permissions.

It is not recommended (or really possible) to dump all the installations in one shared folder without using subfolders. Using subfolders lets you differentiate between two applications that have the same name (for example, Setup.msi) or two versions of the same application (Office 2000 and Office XP).

Assigning and Publishing Applications

Once you have an .MSI package on a share, you can offer it to your client systems via Group Policy. GPSI is located under both Computer and User Configuration directories and then Policies ➢ Software Settings ➢ Software Installation. Before we set up our first package, it's important to understand the options and the rules for deployment. You, the administrator, can offer applications to clients in two ways: *Assigning* or *Publishing*.

Assigning Applications

The icons of Assigned applications appear in the user's Start Menu. More specifically, they appear when the user selects Start ➢ All Programs. However, colloquially, we just say that they appear on the Start Menu. You can Assign applications to users or computers.

What Happens When You Assign Applications to Users

If you Assign an application to users, the application itself isn't downloaded and installed from the source until its initial use. When the user first clicks the application's icon, the Windows Installer (which runs as a background process on the client machine) kicks into high gear, looks at the database of the .MSI package, locates the installation point, and determines which components are required.

Assigning an application saves on initial disk space requirements since only an application's entry points are actually installed on the client. Those entry points are shortcuts, CLSIDs (Class Identifiers), file extensions, and sometimes other application attributes that are considered .MSI entry points.

Once the icons are displayed, the rest of the application is pulled down only when necessary. Indeed, many applications are coded so that only portions of the application are brought down in chunks when needed, such as a help file that is only grabbed from the source when it's required the first time.

When portions of an application are installed, the necessary disk space is claimed. The point is that if users roam from machine to machine, they might *not* choose to install the Assigned application, and, hence, it would not use any disk space. If users are Assigned an application but never get around to using it, they won't use any extra disk space. Once the files are grabbed from the source, the application is installed onto the machine, and the application starts. If additional subcomponents within the application are required later (such as the help files in Office XP's Word 2002, for example), those components are loaded on demand in a *just-in-time* fashion as the user attempts to use them.

What Happens When You Assign Applications to Computers

If the application is Assigned to computers, the application is *entirely* installed and available for all users who use the machine the next time the computer is rebooted. This won't save disk space but will save time because the users won't have to go back to the source for installation.

Publishing Applications

The icons of Published applications are placed in the Add or Remove Programs folder in Control Panel for Windows XP or "Install a program from the network" for Windows Vista. You can Publish to Users (but not computers). When you Publish applications to users, the application list is dynamically generated, depending on which applications are currently being Published. Users get no signals whatsoever that any applications are waiting for them in Control Panel.

Once the application is selected, all the components required to run that application are pulled from the distribution source and installed on the machine. The user can then close Control Panel and use the Start Menu to launch the newly installed application.

By default, the icons of Assigned applications are also placed in the Add or Remove Programs (or "Install a program from the network") folder for download. In other words, by default, all Assigned applications are also Published. The "Do Not Display this Package in the Add/Remove Programs Control Panel" option is unchecked by default; therefore, the application appears in both places by default upon Assignment. (I'll discuss this option in the "Advanced Published or Assigned" section.)

 Published apps are also advertised to be run automatically via document invocation (again, also known as auto-install).

Rules of Deployment

Some rules constrain our use of GPSI, regardless of whether applications are Assigned through the Computer or User node of Group Policy. As just stated, the icons of Assigned applications appear on the Start Menu, whereas the icons of Published applications appear in the Add or Remove Programs folder (or "Install a program from the network" for Windows Vista). With that in mind, here are the deployment rules.

Rule #1   Assigning to computers means that anyone who can log onto machines affected by the GPO sees the Assigned application on the Start Menu. This is useful for situations such as nurses' stations. You can also Assign applications to users in the GPO, which means that whenever users roam, their applications follow them—no matter which machine they reside at physically.

Rule #2   You can't Publish to computers; you can only Assign to computers within a GPO.

Why the funky rules? Although I have no specific confirmation from Microsoft, I'll make an observation that might help you remember these rules: most users can use the Start Menu to launch applications. Therefore, Assigning applications to users makes sense.

Additionally, since applications Assigned to computers apply to *every* user who logs onto a targeted machine, the users in question can also surely use the Start Menu to launch the Assigned applications. But using Published applications takes a little more computer savvy. Users first need to know that applications are Published at all and then check the Add or Remove Programs folder (or "Install a program from the network" for Windows Vista) to see if any applications are targeted for them. A specific user might know that applications are waiting for them, but it's unlikely that all users using a computer would know that. In any event, just remember the following rules:

- You can Assign to users.
- You can Assign to computers.
- You can Publish to users.
- You cannot Publish to computers.

Since this level of sophistication isn't really the norm, I bet Microsoft avoided providing Publishing capabilities for computers because there is no guaranteed level of sophistication for a specific user of a specific computer.

Package-Targeting Strategy

So far, we've set up our software distribution shared folder, prepared the package to the point of distribution, and (optionally) tied it down with NTFS permissions. Now we need to target a group of users or computers for the software package. Here are some possible options:

- Leverage an OU for the users you want to get the package, move the accounts into this OU, and then Assign or Publish the application to that OU. Whenever members of the OU log on, the application is available for download. Each user can connect to the distribution source and acquire a copy of the installation. This is best for when your users are mostly using desktops. Because desktops are connected to the network, the just-in-time fashion of the download really makes sense here.

- Leverage an OU for the computers that you want to get the package, and then Assign the application to the computers in that OU. When the computer is rebooted, then, whenever any user logs on to the targeted machines, the application is fully downloaded and ready to go. This isn't true for every application (like Office 2007, shown later). But it is true for just about everything else. This is best if you have a gaggle of laptop users. You'll want to ensure that the entire application is loaded before users go on the road with their machines. This strategy is ideal for this scenario.

- Assign or Publish the application at the domain or OU level, and then use GPO Filtering with Security Groups (see Chapter 2). This is a more advanced technique but can be very useful when you want to give someone only the ability to modify group memberships, and (by modifying the group membership) also deploy software to a group of users (or even computers).

- Assign or Publish the application at the domain or OU level, and then use WMI (Windows Management Instrumentation) Filtering based on specific information within machines. (See Chapter 5 of the companion book, *Group Policy Fundamentals, Troubleshooting, and Security*, in the "GPO Targeting with WMI Filters" section.) This is most useful if you want to strategically target machines based on very, very specific criteria. For instance, "Only deploy this software to users with 1GB RAM and hotfix Q24601."

 There's also the ability to permission individual packages within a GPO for more fine-grained targeting. Check out the "Security" tab for each package.

We could use any of these methods to target our users. The first two options are the most straightforward and most common practice. In our first example, we'll leverage an OU and Assign the application to our computers. We'll use the **Human Resources Computers** OU and Assign them Office 2007.

⊕ **Real World Scenario**

Normal Shares versus DFS Namespaces

The GPSI features are like the postal service; they're a delivery mechanism. Their duty is to deliver the package and walk away. But it's something of a production before that package is delivered into your hands, and that's what we'll tackle in the next section.

Before we get there, however, you need to prepare for software distribution by setting up a *distribution point* to store the software. You can choose to create a shared folder on any server—hopefully one that's close to the users who will be pulling the software. The closer to the user you can get the server, the faster the download of the software and the less saturated your network in the long run.

In a nutshell, GPSI delivers a message to the client about the shared folder from which the software is available. However, if you are concerned that your users will often roam your distributed enterprise, you can additionally set up DFS Namespaces.

DFS Namespaces is the *Distributed File System* technology that, when used in addition to Active Directory Site Topology definitions, can automatically direct users toward the share containing the software closest to them. The essence of DFS Namespaces is that it sets up a front end for shared folders and then acts as the traffic cop, directing users to the closest replica. To explore DFS technology, visit www.microsoft.com/dfs.

DFS Namespaces has an extra huge benefit over using normal shares. If a normal share on a normal server goes down (and the client application needs a repair), the client can just find another node on the network which contains the software. Or, if you want to repurpose that server for something else, you don't have to worry about the gruesome problem of removing the software from everywhere, putting the share on the new server, and redeploying the application. With DFS you just add a server with the share contents and change a few pointers around on the back-end.

But what if you're in one of these two traps already? Is there hope to move from a "one server" GPSI deployment to something more robust? Yep! And that, my friends, is what my Newsletter #19 is all about on GPanswers.com. It's called the File Server Migration Toolkit (or FSMT for short). The FSMT can move files from an existing server to another server. And, here's the magic: it can tell the new server to take on the additional name of the old server. So, your clients never know anything has changed under the hood. Really, really neat stuff (and it uses DFS technology to do the magic). Again, check it out in Newsletter #19.

Creating and Editing the GPO to Deploy Office

We are now ready to create our GPO and Assign our application to our users. In this example, we'll Assign Office 2007 to computers, but this procedure works to deploy Office 2003 as well.

Again, this performs the most basic of Office 2007 deployments. If you have a custom Office 2007 environment with bells and whistles and, like Burger King, want it "your way," there's a lot more that has to be done. Be sure to read the Real World Scenario entitled "Installing and Customizing Office 2007 via GPSI" a bit later.

Open the GPMC, and then follow these steps:

1. To create a GPO that deploys Office 2007 to the **Human Resources Computers** OU, right-click the OU and choose "Create a GPO in this domain, and Link it here" from the short-cut menu to open the New GPO dialog box. Enter a descriptive name, in the New GPO dialog box such as **Deploy Office 2007 (to computers)**. The GPO should now be linked to the **Human Resources Computers** OU.

2. Right-click the link to the GPO (or the GPO itself), and choose Edit from the shortcut menu to open the Group Policy Management Editor.

The software distribution settings are found in both Computer Configuration and User Configuration, as shown in Figure 4.4.

FIGURE 4.4 Right-click the GPSI settings to deploy a new package.

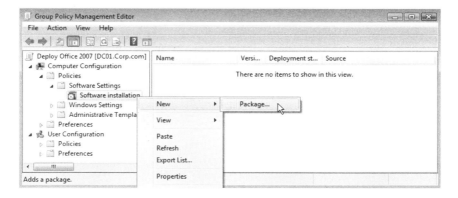

For this first package, we will Assign the application to the computers in the **Human Resources Computers** OU.

1. Choose Computer Configuration ➢ Policies ➢ Software Settings.

2. Right-click "Software installation" and choose New ➢ Package, as shown in Figure 4.4, to open the Open dialog box, which lets you specify the .MSI file.

You will need to specify the full UNC path on the shared folder for the application. Let me say that again: You'll need to specify the network path, not the "local" path, or else the installation will fail.

Earlier, we put our Office 2007 Administrative Installation inside the APPS share on the DC01 server inside the OFFICE2007SOURCE directory. If you take a look at the Office 2007 media, you'll note there are lots of .MSI files which might work. However, there really is only one which is meant for GPSI distribution. The precise name will vary depending on the version of Office 2007 you've got. In my case, I've got Office 2007 Pro Plus. The file which I'll need to deliver using GPSI is named `ProPlusrWW.msi`. Therefore, the full UNC path to the application is `\\DC01\apps\OFFICE2007SOURCE\ProPlusr.WW\ProPlusrWW.msi`, as shown in Figure 4.5.

FIGURE 4.5 Always use the full UNC and never the local path when this dialog box requests the file.

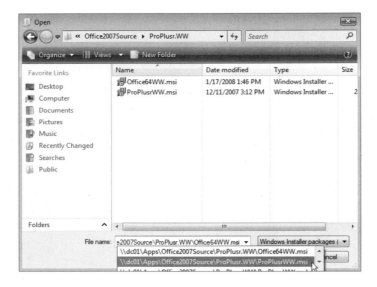

If you're deploying Office 2003, it is also based upon the version you have. For instance, the copy I have has an .MSI named `Pro11N.msi`.

Before You Ramp Up, Let's Talk about Licensing

A FAQ I get when I teach my Group Policy Intensive course is this: "If I use GPSI to deploy applications to my users, how does this affect my licensing agreements with Microsoft or other software vendors?" The next most frequently asked question about GPSI is this: "If I use GPSI to do mass rollouts, how can I keep track of licensing for reporting during audits?" Bad news on both fronts, friends.

Occasionally, the Microsoft technology doesn't work in lockstep with usable licensing agreements. Specifically, if you use GPSI as your mechanism to get software to the masses, you need to be especially careful with your Microsoft licensing agreements or any other licensing agreements. When you deploy any software via GPSI, you have the potential to load the software on a machine and make it available to any number of users who can log onto that machine. As I discussed, using GPSI to deploy to computers gives everyone who logs onto the machine (via the domain) access to the icons on the Start Menu. And, if you target users, whether the application is available only for that user depends on the application. For instance, a well-written .MSI, say Office XP, prevents users who aren't Assigned the application from using it; but other .MSI applications (especially those you create with third-party tools) may not. And when you use GPSI to deploy an application to, say, users in an OU, you won't know how many users accept the offer and how many users don't end up using the application.

With that in mind, GPSI is a wonderful mechanism for deploying software. But in terms of licensing and auditing, you're on your own. My advice is that if you're planning to use GPSI for your installations, check with each vendor to find out their licensing requirements when you Assign to Users and Assign to Computers.

Remember: you have a large potential for exposure by doing a GPSI to users and/or computers; protect yourself by checking with your vendor before you do a mass deployment of any application in this fashion. Additionally, it's important to remember that there is no facility for counting or metering the number of accepted offers of software for auditing purposes.

That's where Microsoft's SCCM 2007 is supposed to come into play to help you determine "who's using what." Also, as you'll learn in the next chapter, Microsoft's SoftGrid has the ability to meter usage as well.

Finally, if you're looking for an all-Group Policy solution to help mitigate these (and other) problems, check out Special Operations Software's Specops Deploy (www.specopssoft.com). But stay tuned—more on that later.

WARNING Do not—I repeat—do not use the Open dialog box's interface to click and browse for the file locally. Equally evil is specifying a local file path, such as D:\apps\office2003distro\pro11n.msi. Why is this? Because the location needs to be from a consistently available point, such as a UNC path. Entering a local file path prevents the Windows Installer at the client from finding the package on the server. Merely clicking the file doesn't guarantee that the package will be delivered to the client. Again—entering the full UNC path as shown in Figure 4.5 is the *only* guaranteed method to deliver the application to the client.

Once the full UNC path is entered, a dialog box will appear, asking which type of distribution method we'll be using: Assigned or Advanced. Published will be grayed out because you cannot Publish to computers.

For now, choose Assigned and click OK. When you do (and you wait a minute or two) you'll see the application listed as shown in Figure 4.6. Hang tight—it'll show up.

FIGURE 4.6   The applications you assign are listed under the node you chose to use (Computer ➢ Software installation or User ➢ Software installation).

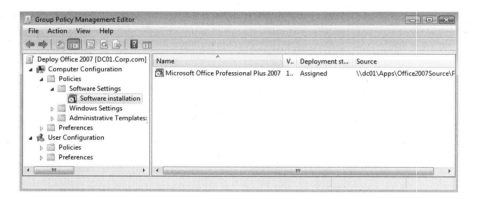

Understanding When Applications Will Be Installed

Once you've Assigned or Published an application, you'll need to test it to see if it's working properly. Here's how users and computers should react:

- Applications Published to users on any operating system should show up right away in Control Panel. No reboot or log out (and log back in) should be required, but you might have to refresh the Add or Remove Programs folder (or "Install a program from the network" for Windows Vista). An application isn't installed until a user specifically selects it or the application is launched via *document invocation* (also called *install-on-first-use* or *advertisement*). Recall that document invocation allows the application to be installed as soon as a file associated with the application is opened.

- Applications Assigned to users on Windows 2000 or Windows 2003 computers should show up on next logon on the Start Menu. Applications Assigned to Windows 2000 or Windows 2003 computers should install upon next reboot. All users logging onto those computers will see the icons on the Start Menu.

- If you're deploying to users on Windows XP or Windows Vista computers or directly to Windows XP or Windows Vista computers themselves, you need to know whether Fast Boot is turned on. Recall from Chapter 4 of the companion book, *Group Policy Fundamentals, Troubleshooting, and Security,* that Fast Boot is enabled by default for Windows XP and Windows Vista machines, and you will need to explicitly turn it off. To review:

  - If Windows XP or Windows Vista Fast Boot is enabled and you Assign applications to users, it will take two logoffs and logons for the icons to appear on the Start Menu.

- If Windows XP or Windows Vista Fast Boot is enabled and you Assign applications to computers, it will take two reboots before the Assignment is installed. Afterward, icons appear for all users on the Start Menu. If you want to turn off this behavior for Windows XP or Windows Vista, you can do so. Just check out Chapter 4 of the companion book to learn how.

- Note, however, that Windows XP and Windows Vista Fast Boot is always off if a Roaming Profile is used.

You'll need to adjust the deployment properties before certain applications will deploy properly to users. (More on this in the "Advanced Published or Assigned" section later in this chapter.)

Testing Assigned Applications

Before you go headlong and try to verify your deployment of Office 2007, first verify that a Windows 2000, Windows XP, or Windows Vista machine is in the **Human Resources Computers** OU, and then reboot the first test machine in the OU.

If you're Assigning an application to a Windows XP or Windows 2000 machine, you'll see this during startup as shown in Figure 4.7.

FIGURE 4.7 Applications Assigned to computers install completely upon reboot.

If you're Assigning an application to a Windows Vista machine, by default you won't see anything during startup except a "Please wait…" and a lot of disk activity. However, you can enable the policy setting called **Verbose vs normal status messages** located within Computer Configuration ➤ Policies ➤ Administrative Templates ➤ System, you'll see more information during startup, such as the application's title, as seen in Figure 4.8.

FIGURE 4.8 If you enable the Verbose vs Normal status messages policy setting to affect your Windows Vista machines, you'll see the name of the software installing instead of a lousy "Please wait…" message.

Installing managed software Microsoft Office Professional Edition 2003…

Go ahead and get a cup of coffee while this is installing. It takes a while. Really. Go ahead. I'll wait.

Once the application is fully installed, you can log on as any user in the domain (or the local computer) and see the application's icons on the Start Menu as seen later in Figure 4.11.

If you're deploying Office 2003 (or earlier), the icons will show up right away on the Start Menu for all users who log in.

However, if you've just Assigned Office 2007 to a Windows Vista computer—the first user who uses Office 2007 on that computer needs to w-a-i-t. When I deployed Office 2007 to Windows Vista computer and then immediately logged in as Frank Rizzo when the Ctrl+Alt+Del prompt was available, I got what's seen in Figure 4.9.

FIGURE 4.9   Users don't actually see all of Office 2007's icons until it has finished deploying itself in the background.

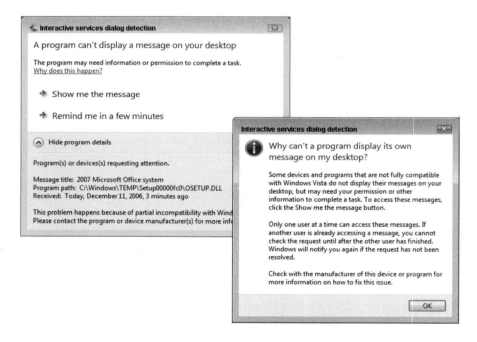

Strangely, the message basically states that Office 2007's setup isn't compatible with Windows Vista. How odd. If we can get past that, we can see what's happening behind the scenes is that Office 2007 is *still* setting up. If you click "Show me the message" (which would be better if it said "Show me the money" in one guy's opinion), you'll see what's going on "under the hood." You'll see this in Figure 4.10.

Eventually, this does finish. Or, if I chose not to immediately log in as Frank Rizzo, say, by getting a cup of coffee (maybe two) before logging in, Office 2007 would have completed on its own in the background. But, yes, you're reading this right; Office 2007 continues to install in the background even after you log in if you don't wait long enough.

So, when the installation is complete, you'll see your newly installed items on the Start ➢ All Programs menu. These are nicely highlighted for Windows XP and Windows Vista, as shown in Figure 4.11. If you try this experiment with a Windows 2000 client, you'll notice that the new icons and program titles are not highlighted.

FIGURE 4.10   You can watch Office 2007's display progress when installed via GPSI on a Windows Vista machine.

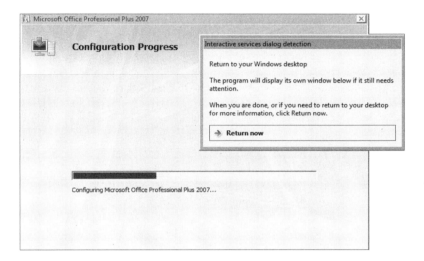

FIGURE 4.11   The Office icons and program names will appear on the Start Menu (more specifically on the Start ➢ All Programs menu).

This "extra setup time" after a user quickly logs on is new for Office 2007 and not very welcome, in my opinion. And, it seems that multiple users sometimes have to sit through at least some installation time to get Office 2007 configured the first time.

At this point, any user can select any Office application, and the application is briefly prepared and then displayed for the user.

Stay tuned for more information on Assigning and Publishing .MSI applications (particularly to users). For now, however, let's switch gears and look at another deployment option.

Understanding .ZAP Files

Using .MSI files is one way to distribute software to your computers and users, but one disadvantage is associated with this process: you must actually have an .MSI package that you deploy. Indeed, some applications don't come with .MSI packages, and repackaging them with a third-party tool doesn't always work as expected. If you already have your own Setup.exe (or similar program), you can leverage a different type of installation: .ZAP files, which invoke your currently working Setup.exe program.

Sounds great—but there is a downside: .ZAP files are not as robust as .MSI files. This "unrobustness" comes in several forms:

- They do not take advantage of the Windows Installer, and therefore they are not self-repairing should something go awry on the client.

- You can Publish but can't Assign .ZAP files. Their icons are available only in the Control Panel, and the application is installed all at once. And since .ZAP files are always Published, they can only be Published to users, not computers.

- The user is in full control of the install, unless you've magically scripted Setup.exe. This can create trouble for end users (and for you).

- The .ZAP files run with the user's privileges. They cannot run with elevated privileges. Again, only .MSI applications (not .ZAP files) automatically run elevated even for non-privileged users once deployed via GPSI.

Like .MSI files, .ZAP files (and their corresponding setup executables) can also be automatically invoked when a specific extension (or set of extensions) is chosen via *document invocation* (also called *auto-installer*). Auto-install is described in more detail in the "Advanced Published or Assigned" section, later in this chapter.

Creating Your Own .ZAP file

A .ZAP file resembles an .INI file. That is, it is a simple file created with a text editor such as Notepad, and it has headings and values. Instead of repackaging WinZip 8 with WinINSTALL (or any of the third-party applications), you can simply create a .ZAP file for a WinZip 8 setup executable, WinZip80.exe.

A sample WinZip 8 .ZAP file might look like this:

```
[Application]
FriendlyName = "Winzip 8.0 ZAP Package"
SetupCommand = "WINZIP80.exe"
```

```
DisplayVersion = 8.0
Publisher = WinZip Computing


[EXT]
.ZIP=
.ARC=
```

Let's briefly break down each entry. The [`Application`] heading is required, and the only other required elements are the `FriendlyName` and the `SetupCommand`, which are self-explanatory.

The entry pointed to the `SetupCommand` should be in the same folder as the `.ZAP` file itself. If it isn't, you can use UNC paths to specify, such as:

```
SetupCommand = "\\DC01\winzipsource\winzip8.exe"
```

Everything else is completely optional but might help you and your users sort things out. The [EXT] heading can list the file extensions that can fire off this particular `.ZAP` installation and the corresponding `WINZIP80.exe` setup executable. Listed in this sample file are `.ZIP` and `.ARC`, but you can also add file types such as `.TAR` and `.Z`. The [EXT] heading is not required and may not even be desired, depending on the application and its setup routine.

Publishing Your Own *.ZAP* File

If you want to Publish your own `.ZAP` file, you'll need to bring all the steps you've learned together:

1. Place the setup executable (in this case, `WINZIP80.exe`) in a subfolder (say, `WINZIPSOURCE`) underneath a shared folder (in this case `APPS`).
2. Lock down the `WINZIPSOURCE` subfolder with NTFS permissions.
3. Create the `WINZIP8.zap` file as directed earlier using Notepad.
4. Copy the `.ZAP` file to the distribution subfolder (`WINZIPSOURCE`).
5. Finally, distribute (Publish) the `.ZAP` package to your users.

Testing Your *.ZAP* File

Test your `.ZAP` file and distribution point by logging onto a workstation to which the GPSI policy applies. Open the Add or Remove Programs folder in Control Panel (or "Install a program from the network" for Windows Vista), and click Add New Programs in the column on the left, as shown in Figure 4.12. The application should appear in the list of programs available to add, named according to the entry in the `FriendlyName` field that you specified in the `.ZAP` file.

Once you've selected it and clicked Add, the WinZip setup program will launch and can be set up in any desired fashion.

 Alternatively, you can double-click either a `.ZIP` or an `.ARC` file to automatically launch the `.ZAP` file setup application via document invocation (also known as auto-install).

FIGURE 4.12 .ZAP files are always Published to Control Panel.

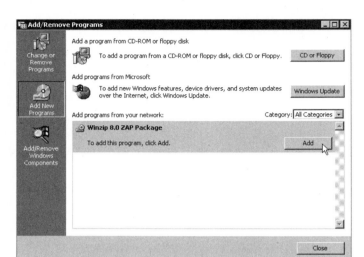

Testing Publishing Applications to Users

You can also test Publishing applications before continuing. Recall that the icons of Published applications appear in the Add or Remove Programs folder (or "Install a program from the network" for Windows Vista) in Control Panel. However, the usefulness of Published applications is minimal, which is why it's relegated to such a small section for discussion. Users must be specifically told there's something waiting for them, hunt it down themselves, and install it. And, applications can only be Published to users, not computers; so a user who is getting a Published application must be logged in.

To test this for yourself, simply select Publish when adding a new application, or right-click an existing package Assigned to users and choose Publish from the shortcut menu.

To see a Published application in action on a Windows XP or Windows 2000 machine, follow these steps from a client who is receiving a Published application:

1. Choose Start ➢ Control Panel ➢ Add or Remove Programs to open the Add or Remove Programs applet in Control Panel.

2. Click the Add New Programs button to display those applications that have been Published for the user as seen previously in Figure 4.12.

3. Ask the user to click the Add button next to the application, and it will be fully loaded on the machine.

The applications will then appear on the Start ➢ All Programs menu as seen previously in Figure 4.11, ready to be utilized.

To see a Published application in action on a Windows Vista machine, follow these steps:

1. Choose Start ➢ Control Panel ➢ Programs ➢ Get Programs ➢ Install a program from the network.

2. Select the application and select Install, as seen in Figure 4.13.

FIGURE 4.13   A Published application in Vista can be seen in Control Panel.

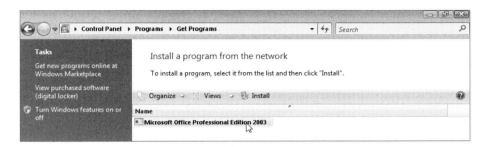

A Published application needn't be fully relegated to lying dormant until a user selects it. Indeed, the default is to specify that the application automatically launch via document invocation (also known as auto-install) as soon as an associated file type is opened. In this way, you can have the application available for use but just not have the application's icons appear on the Start Menu as you do when you Assign it. However, you can turn off document invocation by clearing the "Auto install this application by file extension activation" check box as specified in the section "The Deployment Options Section" a bit later.

WARNING

You'll need to adjust the deployment properties before certain applications will deploy properly to users. (More on this in the "Advanced Published or Assigned" section later in this chapter.)

 Real World Scenario

What Happens if You Try to Assign Office 2007 to Users?

In short: it doesn't work. Why not? The Office 2007 .MSI files are (apparently) written to be more "modular." And, in doing so, they couldn't guarantee that one .MSI would be able to call another .MSI when initiated as a user install. It works as a computer-side install; but not a user side.

This deployment to a user has worked since Office 2000 but is simply not available as an option to Assign Office 2007 to Users.

If you try it, the applications icons install on the Start Menu. However, when you try to run it, you get this (at least helpful) error message.

So, long story short—don't deploy Office 2007 to your users. It just won't work. It's an application that only works when Assigned to Computers as we did in our example.

Application Isolation

In many circumstances, applications are *isolated* for their intended use. Here are some examples:

- Users do not share Assigned or Published applications that an administrator has set up. For instance, User A is Assigned an application and installs it. User B can use User A's machine, but is not Assigned the application via Group Policy. Therefore, when User B logs on to that machine, they do not see the Assigned icons for User A.

- Users require their own "instance" of the application. If User A and User B are Assigned the same application, each user must contact the source and perform a one-time per-user customization that some applications require. In most circumstances, this will not double the used disk space, and the time for installation for the second user is not very long because portions of the application are already installed for User A.

- If two users are Assigned different applications that register the same file types, the correct application is always used. For instance, Joe and Dave share the same machine. Joe is Assigned Word 2000, and Dave is Assigned Office XP. When Joe opens a .DOC file, Office 2000's Word 2000 launches. When Dave opens a .DOC file, Office XP's Word 2002 launches. I even tried deploying Office 2007 to the computer and Office 2003 to a user, and the user side won. But, Office 2007's icons were available for selection, of course, via the Start Menu.

- Depending on the .MSI application, users might not be able to go "under the hood" and select the .exes of installed programs. For instance, if User A is Assigned an application, User B (who is not Assigned the application) cannot just use Explorer, locate the application on the hard drive, and double-click the application to install it. This is not a hard-and-fast rule and is based on how the .MSI application itself is coded. In Figure 4.14, you can see what happens when a user who is not specifically Assigned Office 2000 (yes, Office 2000) tries to run Winword.exe from Program Files. However, I tried this again with Office 2003, and, well, it let me run it just fine as another user.

- Users can uninstall applications that they have access to in the Add or Remove Programs folder (or "Uninstall or change a program" in Windows Vista parlance). This has a two-part implication. First, by default, all Assigned applications are also Published, and thus users can remove them using the Add or Remove Programs folder. The icons for the applications will still be on the Start ➢ All Programs menu the next time the user logs on. The first time the user attempts to run one of these applications by choosing Start ➢ All Programs ➢ *application*, the application reinstalls itself from the distribution point. The second implication deals with who, precisely, can remove Assigned (or Published) applications. First, users cannot delete applications that are directly Assigned to computers. Next, users cannot delete applications that aren't directly Assigned to their user account.

Office 2000 and later can prevent users from just clicking their installed .EXEs. These applications use .MSI APIs to verify the application state. For more information about how an application can become "installer-aware," see www.microsoft.com/msj/0998/windowsinstaller.aspx.

FIGURE 4.14 Some applications prevent users from just clicking the actual .EXE of the installed file. Again, this behavior is entirely application specific.

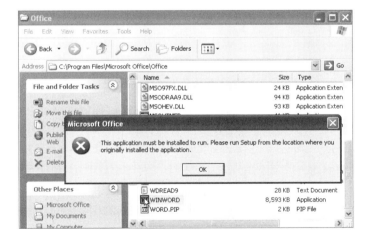

Advanced Published or Assigned

When you attempt to Publish or Assign an application to your users or computers, you are given an additional selection of Advanced. If you didn't choose Advanced when you initially deployed the application, that's not a problem. You can simply right-click the package and choose Properties from the shortcut menu to open the Properties dialog box. The only option that is not available in this "after the fact" method is the ability to add Microsoft Transform Files, which I'll describe in the "Modifications Tab" section later in this chapter.

🌐 Real World Scenario

Creating Your Own *.MSI* Package

It's great when applications such as Office 2003 come with their own .MSI packages, but not every vendor supplies .MSI packages. You can, however, create your own .MSI packages to wrap up and deploy the software you've already bought that doesn't come with an .MSI package.

Some of the popular ones are

- WinInstall from Attachmate: http://tinyurl.com/34f919

- Symantec/Altiris Wise Package Studio: http://tinyurl.com/2wexqw

- Macrovision Adminstudio: http://tinyurl.com/2q5hpu

The general steps for using a repackaging tool are as follows:

1. Take a snapshot of a clean source machine.

2. Run the current setup program of whatever you want to wrap up.

3. Fully install and configure the application as desired.

4. Reboot the machine to ensure that changes are settled in.

5. Take a snapshot again, and scour the hard drive for changes.

Once the changes are discovered, they're wrapped up into an .MSI file of your choice, which you can then Assign or Publish!

Due to page count, I can't go into the ins and outs of creating your own .MSI files. However, I have two options for you. First, you can take a look at my first book, *Windows 2000 Group Policy, Profiles, and IntelliMirror* (ISBN 0-7821-2881-5), which includes the step-by-step process. Or you can check out another resource that demonstrates this process with free and "pay" tools: *The Definitive Guide to Windows Installer Technology for System Administrators* (which is free and which I co-wrote) is available at http://desktopengineer.com/msiebook.

The third-party tools have some fairly robust features to assist you in your .MSI package creation. As I stated, the .MSI format lets you detect a damaged component within a running application. This feature is called *keying* files for proper operation. For example, if your Ruff.DLL gets deleted when you run DogFoodMaker 7, the Windows Installer springs into action and pulls the broken, but keyed, component back from the distribution point—all without user interaction.

Additionally, if you're looking for some heavy .MSI training, consider my pal Darwin Sanoy, who can be found at http://desktopengineer.com/windowsinstallertraining. (Let him know I sent you.)

The Properties dialog box has six tabs: General, Deployment, Upgrades, Categories, Modifications, and Security. In Figure 4.15, the Properties dialog box is focused on the Deployment tab, which is discussed in detail in this section.

FIGURE 4.15   These are the options on the Deployment tab when Assigning to computers. Note how just about everything is grayed out when Assigning to computers.

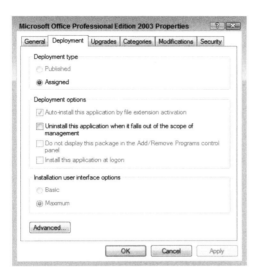

The General Tab

This tab contains the basic information about the package: the name that is to be displayed in the Add or Remove Programs folder (or "Install a program from the network" for Windows Vista), the publisher, and some language and support information. All this is extracted from the .MSI package.

If you're using the Windows 2003 administrative tools to deploy your package, you'll get another little goodie: you can specify the URL of a web page that contains support information for the application. For instance, if you have specific setup instructions for the user, you can place the instructions on a page on one of your intranet servers and include the URL with the package. The client's Add or Remove Programs folder displays a hyperlink to the URL next to the package. Although .ZAP files also display this information, you can't configure these files once they are Published.

The Deployment Tab

This tab, as shown in Figure 4.15, has three sections: "Deployment type," "Deployment options," and "Installation user interface options." There is also an Advanced button at the bottom of the tab. The options on the Deployment tab depend on how you want to deploy the application and whether you are Assigning to computer or Assigning or Publishing to users. In our first example, Figure 4.15 shows the options when Assigning to computers.

Figure 4.16 shows the options on the Deployment tab when Assigning an application to users. You'll notice that many more options are available than when Assigning to computers. The options in the "Installation user interface options" section are critical, and you will likely need to change them before applications are correctly Assigned or Published to users.

FIGURE 4.16   These are the options on the Deployment tab when Assigning or Publishing to users.

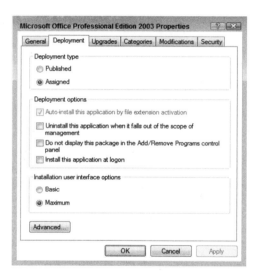

The Deployment Type Section

The options in this section let you instantly change the deployment type from Published to Assigned and vice versa, and it is available only when you are deploying applications to users. When you are deploying applications to computers, Assigning is the only option. If you're deploying to user accounts, you can also change the deployment type by right-clicking the package definition. You can see a package definition of an application in the Group Policy Management Editor dialog box in Figure 4.6. Then you can select the deployment type, Assign or Publish, from the shortcut menu.

The Deployment Options Section

This section has four check boxes:

Auto-install this application by file extension activation   When .MSI applications are Published or Assigned (or .ZAP packages are Published), each of their definitions contain a list of supported file types. Those file types are actually loaded inside Active Directory.

When a GPO applies to a user or a computer and this check box is selected, the application is automatically installed based on the extension. This is, essentially, application execution via document invocation. Note, this option is always automatically selected (and cannot be unselected) if you Assign the application. That is, document invocation is only optional when Publishing.

Document invocation is most handy when new readers and file types are released, such as Adobe Acrobat Reader and its corresponding .PDF file type. Simply Assign or Publish an application with this check box enabled, and Acrobat Reader will be automatically shot down to anyone who opens a .PDF file for the first time. This check box is selected by default when you are Assigning applications to users or computers.

Uninstall this application when it falls out of the scope of management   GPOs can be applied to sites, domains, or OUs. If a user is moved out of the scope to which this GPO applies, what happens to the currently deployed software? For instance, if a user or computer is moved from one OU to another, what do you want to happen with this specific software package? If you don't want the software to remain on the workstation, click this check box. Remember—the applications aren't removed immediately if a user or computer leaves the scope of the GPO. As you'll see shortly, computers receive a *signal* to remove the software. (This is described in the "Removing Applications" section later in this chapter.)

Do not display this package in the Add/Remove Programs control panel   As mentioned, icons and program names for Assigned applications appear in the Start ➢ All Programs menu, but, by default, they also appear as Published icons in the Add or Remove Programs applet in Control Panel. Thus, users may choose to install the application all at once or perform an en masse repair. However, the dark side of this check box is that users can remove any application they want. To prevent the application from appearing in the Add or Remove Programs folder or "Install a program from the network" for Windows Vista, check this check box. When the application is then earmarked for being Published, the application is available only for loading through document invocation.

Install this application at logon   This option is new and applies only to Windows XP, Windows Vista, and Windows Server 2003 clients. See the section "Assigning Applications to Users over Slow Links Using Windows XP, Windows Vista, and Windows 2003" later in this chapter for a detailed explanation.

The Installation User Interface Options Section

Believe it or not, the two little innocuous buttons in this section make a world of difference for many applications when Assigning or Publishing applications to users. Some .MSI packages can recognize when Basic or Maximum is set and change their installation behavior accordingly. Others can't. Consult your .MSI package documentation to see if the package uses this option and what it does.

Assigning applications like Office 2003 to users can be disastrous if you retain the default of Maximum. Instead of the application automatically and nearly silently loading from the source upon first use, the user is prompted to step through the Office 2003 Installation Wizard (the first screen of which is shown in Figure 4.17).

Simply choosing Basic remedies this problem. That is, Office 2003 is magically downloaded and installed for every user targeted in the OU. Why is Maximum the default? I wish I knew. It wasn't the default in Windows 2000. For now, if you're Assigning applications to users, be sure the Basic check box is checked. For information about how to change the defaults, see the "Default Group Policy Software Installation Properties" section later in this chapter.

The Advanced Button

Clicking the Advanced button opens the Advanced Deployment Options dialog box, as shown in Figure 4.18. This dialog box has two sections: "Advanced deployment options" and "Advanced diagnostic information."

FIGURE 4.17   The default of Maximum results in many applications (like Office 2003) no longer being a silent install.

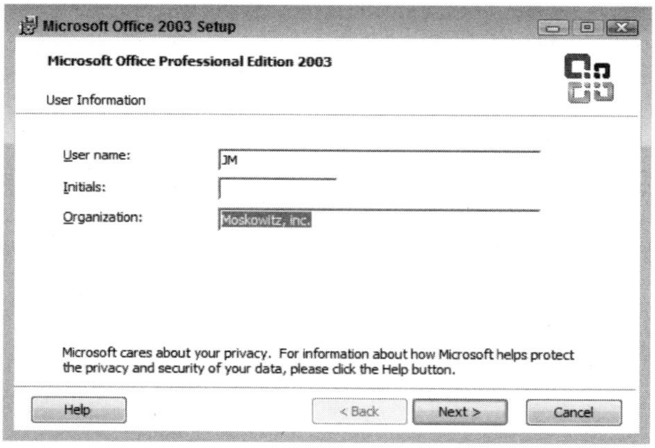

FIGURE 4.18   The options in the Advanced Deployment Options dialog box in Windows Server 2003

The Advanced Deployment Options Section

In Windows Server 2003, this section has three options, and in Windows 2000 Server, it has four options:

Ignore language when deploying this package If the .MSI package definition is coded to branch depending on the language, selecting this option can force one version of the language. Normally, if the language of the .MSI package doesn't match the language of the operating system, Windows will not install it. The exceptions are if the application is in English, if the application is language neutral, or if this check box is checked. If there are multiple versions of the application in different languages, the .MSI engine chooses the application with the best language match.

Remove Previous Installs of This Product for Users, If the Product Was Not Installed by Group Policy-Based Software Installation (older version of Windows 2000 only) If you use older Windows 2000 administrative tools to deploy your application, you'll see this option. However, in Figure 4.18, there is just an empty hole. For each .MSI application, a unique product code (which is shown in Figure 4.18) is embedded in the .MSI. If your users somehow get their own copy of the .MSI source and the product code matches the .MSI application, they can forcibly uninstall their copy before loading the copy you specified.

This can come in handy if the folks in your organization run out to BestBuy and buy a version of a program you weren't ready to deploy using Group Policy—say, Office 2003. If users acquire and install their own copy of Office 2003 before you're really ready to officially deploy it using Group Policy, you can forcibly remove the copy they install. Once you are ready to deploy Office 2003 using Group Policy, be sure to check this check box to remove all copies of Office 2003 that you did not deploy using Group Policy. The copy you're shooting down from on high will then be installed. In this way, you can ensure that all copies you deploy using Group Policy are consistent, even if your users try to sneak around the system.

This works because the unique product code you're sending via Group Policy matches the product code of the .MSI package the user loaded on the machine. The Office 2003 you deploy is essentially the same as the Office 2003 they deploy. The product codes match, and the application you deliver wins if you select this check box.

Why is this option absent from the later versions of the Windows 2000 tools or the Windows Server 2003 version of the Adminpak tools? Because this feature is built into the latest Windows 2000 Service Pack (SP4) and is standard issue for all other management stations. This procedure is performed automatically and is no longer required as an option.

WARNING Even if you repackage your own applications (such as WinZip, Adobe Acrobat Reader 6, and so on) using a third-party tool (such as WinINSTALL), a product code is automatically generated when the package is created, However, if you deploy those repackaged applications with Group Policy (in conjunction with this check box in Windows 2000), this procedure does not remove copies of applications that users installed with Setup.exe-style programs. It removes only applications on the target machine that have an .MSI product code.

Make this 32-bit X86 application available to Win64 machines   Software distribution with Windows Server 2003 gets a little more complex because of the support for 64-bit computers. The 64-bit version of Windows XP supports 32-bit applications by running them in a special Win32-on-Win64 emulator. This is similar to the way NT and Windows 2000 support 16-bit Windows applications. In general, 32-bit applications should run fine on x64 platforms, but you can encounter an ill-behaved application that does not function correctly in the emulator. Additionally, Service Pack 1 for Windows Server 2003 and Windows XP Service Pack 2 make 32-bit applications run even more stably on x64 computers.

Include OLE class and product information   This feature allows applications that contain COM services to be deployed such that COM clients can find their deployed applications. Basically, check with your application vendor to see if you need this switch; generally you don't. Enabling the switch increases the likelihood that the application will fail to deploy unless the application specifically requires this setting.

The Advanced Diagnostic Information Section

You can't modify anything in this section, but it does have some handy information.

Product code   As mentioned, if the unique product code of the application you are deploying matches an existing installed product, the application will be removed from the client.

Deployment count   A bit later in this chapter, you'll learn why you might need to redeploy an application to a population of users or computers. When you do, this count is increased. See the section "Using MSIEXEC to Patch a Distribution Point" a bit later in this chapter for more information.

Script name   Whenever an application is Published or Assigned, a pointer to the application, also known as an .AAS file, is placed in the SYSVOL in the Policies container within the GPT (Group Policy Template). The .AAS files are application advertisement script files and are critical to an application's ability to install-on-first-use. This entry shows the name of the .AAS file, which can be useful information if you're chasing down a GPO replication problem between Domain Controllers.

The Upgrades Tab

You can deploy a package that upgrades an existing package. For instance, if you want to upgrade from Office XP to Office 2003, you can prepare the Office 2003 installation (as we did earlier) and then specify that you want an upgrade, which can be either mandatory or optional.

   There is no Upgrades tab for .ZAP package definitions.

Moreover, you can "upgrade" to totally different programs. For instance, if your corporate application for .ZIP files is WinZip but changes to UltraZip, follow these steps to upgrade:

1. Create the UltraZip .MSI package, Assign or Publish the application, open the Properties dialog box, and click the Upgrades tab.

2. Click the Add button to open the Add Upgrade Package dialog box, as shown in Figure 4.19.

3. In the "Package to upgrade" section, select the package definition (in this case WINZIP 8). Note that WINZIP doesn't specifically appear in our example in Figure 4.19; it's just the dialog box.

> Although you can click the Browse button to open the Browse dialog box and select another GPO for this to apply to, it's easier to keep the original package and upgrade in the same GPO scope.

4. Use the options at the bottom of the Add Upgrade Package window to choose either to uninstall the application first or to plow on top of the current installation, and then click OK.

5. Back in the Upgrades tab, check the "Required upgrade for existing packages" check box and click OK to force the upgrade.

FIGURE 4.19 Use the Upgrades tab to migrate from one application to another.

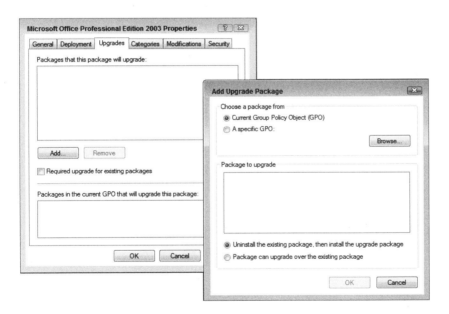

If the "Required upgrade for existing packages" check box is cleared, users can optionally add the program using the Add or Remove Programs applet in Control Panel. This can cause grief for some applications, such as Office 97 and Office 2000 if they're together on the same machine. Moreover, if the check box is not checked, the old application is started whenever an associated file extension (such as .DOC) is invoked.

> It is best if your package is specifically written to upgrade earlier (or different) products; sometimes, it may not actually remove the previous application.

When Assigning to computers, the "Required upgrade for existing package" check box is always checked and not available for selection.

The Categories Tab

The Categories tab allows administrators to give headings to groups of software, which are then displayed in the Add or Remove Programs applet in Control Panel. Users can select the category of software they want to display and then select a program within the category to install. (See earlier Figure 4.12 above the mouse cursor, which shows the Category drop-down box.)

For example, you might want to create the category Archive Programs for WinZip and UltraZip and the category Doc Readers for Adobe Acrobat Reader and GhostScript. If you want, you can list a package in multiple categories. You can also create categories. For information on how to do so, see the "Default Group Policy Software Installation Properties" section later in this chapter.

The Modifications Tab

The Modifications tab is used to support .MST files, or *Microsoft Transform* Files, or just Transform Files for short. Transform Files are applied upon current .MSI packages either to filter the number of options available to the end user or to specify certain answers to questions usually brought up during the .MSI package installation.

Each vendor's .MST transform-creation program is unique. Ask your application vendor if they have a transform-generation utility for your package. If not, you might have to step up to a third-party .MSI/.MST tool, such as Wise Package Studio or AdminStudio by InstallShield. Some applications, such as Office 2000, Office XP, and Office 2003 come with their own .MST generation tool.

Office 2007 does not ship with a .MST generation tool. See the Real-World Scenario "Installing and Customizing Office 2007 via GPSI" for more information on how to modify Office 2007 installations.

In Figure 4.20, you can see I've loaded an .MST file named NOMSACCESS.MST. This .MST will prohibit the use of Microsoft Access 2003 from Office 2003 but allow all other functions of Office 2003 to run.

The Modifications tab is available for use only when Advanced is selected when an application is to be initially Published or Assigned. If a package is already Published or Assigned, the Modifications tab is not usable. As you can see in Figure 4.20, all of the buttons on the Modifications tab are grayed out. Again, this is because the .MST file was loaded at package deployment time, and afterward there is no way to add or remove .MST files after deployment. We'll reiterate and reexamine this issue a bit later.

FIGURE 4.20 You can only add .MST files during the package definition.

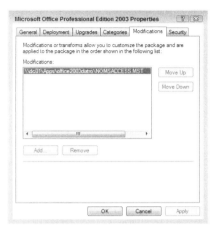

 There is no Modifications tab for .ZAP package definitions because Transform Files apply only to .MSI files.

You might be wondering how you can create your own .MST files for Office—and that's what the next section is about. After you're done, you'll have the chance to load your .MST file to test it out.

 Office 2007 doesn't seem to use Transform Files, and hence, you wouldn't use the Modifications tab. Office 2007 has its own wacky way of describing settings during installation time. See the Real-World Scenario "Installing and Customizing Office 2007 via GPSI."

Installing and Customizing Office 2007 via GPSI

Earlier, I mentioned the fact that Office 2007 isn't like its predecessors. It's made up of smaller .MSI files. Doesn't sound like much of a change, but in practice this really throws a monkey wrench into what was a really beautiful system.

Recall: To deploy earlier versions of Office, you'd usually Assign the .MSI to the user or computer. Then, you'd use the Office Custom Installation Wizard to create an .MST file and add that .MST file to the Modifications area when deploying the software.

Easy.

But not Office 2007. As we've already seen, you cannot deploy Office 2007 to Users. Nope. Only Computers. And we also saw that if you don't wait awhile before logging in, Office 2007 keeps installing—even after the user has logged on.

Bah.

Oh wait, this gets worse: there's no more Custom Installation Wizard tool that you download.

Customization and deployment happens in four steps.

Step 1: Create a *config.xml* File   This file is to be placed in the root directory of the installation location so certain parameters can be set when the computer gets the Assignment. There are two documents from Microsoft which have steps for producing a `config.xml`. This document, located at `http://tinyurl.com/utaf4`, shows all the available options normally available in a `config.xml` file. Buuuut, here's the trick. The document `http://tinyurl.com/327dnx` was removed from Microsoft's site, so I'm linking to a Google-cached version of it that tells the whole truth: The available configurable elements are pitiful for Group Policy installations—only four options can be set (Installation Location, Options and Features, Product Key, and Languages). Though one person on the `GPanswers.com` forum also suggested that Company might work, too. This affects every installation you use from this particular source. So, in our examples, we used the `Office2007Source` directory to perform our deployment to our client computers. If we deployed to Sales, Marketing, Human Resources, and Facilities, all these people would get these same four options because our `config.xml` file is rooted to this source. If you're only going to customize with `config.xml` files (to deploy to various categories of computers with different requirements), then you will need to maintain separate install locations per group of computers.

Step 2: Create a Custom MSP File   The `config.xml` file in Step 1 can only take us so far. In fact, not very far at all when it comes to customization. However, the tool to create more Office customizations is built in to the Office 2007 setup tool. Simply run `setup.exe /admin`, and—poof—instant customization tool. (Nice touch!) Note that trial and non-Enterprise versions will not show the customization tool.

So, take a big, deep breath, read the next two steps, then scream out the nearest window.

So, you might expect this new Office 2007 customization tool to produce `.MST` files like all the previous versions of Office before it.

Nope.

It produces `.MSP` files. A document at `http://tinyurl.com/39ru47` describes the way to produce `custom.msp` files.

`.MSP` files? Does that mean we can't use the Modifications tab to deploy our customization? That's exactly what it means.

Grrr.

Step 3: Deploy Your *.MSI* File Using GPSI   No big deal here. You're just using the information in this chapter to get Office 2007 installed. Remember, it only Assigns to the computer. At this point, it should pick up the `config.xml` configuration changes you made in Step 2.

Step 4: Patch Your Target Machines   Now that you've installed Office 2007 to your zillions of machines, here's the painful part. Use a logon script, batch file, or manually walk around to each machine to have it embrace your .MSP customization. Use the same information found in the section "Using MSIEXEC to Patch a Distribution Point." Except you don't update the distribution point. Instead, you patch the specific machines, individually.

Ow. Ow ow ow. That means you cannot use GPSI as a "unified" way of delivering Office 2007, and also customize it. This makes me spittin' mad, because Group Policy is *the way* to do oh so much goodness in the world.

What I've just described is likely your best option for deploying a custom installation of Office 2007, even if it isn't pretty. But there is another way.

The Office 2007 team suggests that you use a technology (any technology) which allows you to run the setup.exe program from Office 2007, because the setup.exe will call all the .MSI files it needs for the installation you desire.

Well, earlier, you learned about .ZAP files in the "Understanding .ZAP Files" section.

Recall that .ZAP files really just run the underlying setup.exe of an application. Well, Office 2007 has a setup.exe. And, if you put your .MSP files (that you created by running setup /admin) in the Updates directory on your distribution source and then deploy using a .ZAP file, you should be able to install a customized Office 2007 in one fell swoop.

But don't forget—.ZAP files make the application's installation icons appear only in the Add or Remove Programs applet in Control Panel (or "Install a program from the network" for Windows Vista). And, .ZAP applications aren't manageable. So, if you wanted to update Office 2007 later with more patches, you're basically asking the user to handle it on their own.

As you'll read later, in the "Removing Published .ZAP Applications" section, once you've deployed an application using a .ZAP file, you have no way to really upgrade it or revoke it. Once you've deployed it, consider it gone and basically "unmanaged" using Group Policy.

But wait! There's another (not-super-awesome) option: deploying Office 2007 via Group Policy and startup scripts. Microsoft has a document that can walk you through how to do this here: http://tinyurl.com/utaf4.

So, what's the *ideal* answer?

Well, if you read through the haze of Microsoft's Office 2007 deployment documentation, they seem to be really banking on everyone using Microsoft SCCM 2007. I've got some feelings about where SMS or SCCM might fit into your organization, and you can read about those a bit later. But for now, the idea of spending a lot of money just to deploy a package because it has a lot of .MSI files upsets me a little bit.

If you've found a creative way to work around these issues, I want to hear about it. Be sure to e-mail me at jeremym@moskowitz-inc.com and let me know your best techniques for deploying a customized Office 2007 using Group Policy.

Using the Office .*MST* Generation Tool (Pre-Office 2007)

You can deploy Office 2000, Office XP, and Office 2003, for instance, whole hog by using their included .MSI package. Indeed, you saw this earlier. All applications of Office were available when our users chose to use Office. But what if we didn't want, say, Access available to our users? Or what if we want to adjust an Office property at a global level?

Using the Custom Installation Wizards from the Office Resource Kit, you can create an .MST Transform File that can limit which options can be installed, as well as specify all sorts of custom options, including the default installation path, the organization name, the custom Outlook behavior, and more! The tool has the same name in all three versions of Office (but the application is unique to each). Table 4.1 shows you where to find the downloads.

TABLE 4.1   Location of Office Resource Kit Downloads

Office Version	Where to Find the Resource Kit
Office 2000	http://office.microsoft.com/en-us/ork2000/default.aspx
Office XP	http://office.microsoft.com/en-us/orkxp/default.aspx
Office 2003	http://office.microsoft.com/en-us/ork2003/default.aspx
Office 2007	http://tinyurl.com/vf9e3 (goes to Microsoft website). But remember, there is no tool to create .MST files for Office 2007. You create .MSP files (yes, .MSP files) with setup /admin. (See the Real-World Scenario entitled "Installing and Customizing Office 2007 via GPSI.")

The procedure to create an .MST is straightforward but quite long, and I simply don't have room available to dedicate to each and every step. In this example, I'll assume you're using the Office 2003 Custom Installation Wizard (CIW). Here is the basic overview:

1. Choose Start ➤ All Programs ➤ Microsoft Office Tools ➤ [*the version of the tool you loaded*] ➤ Custom Installation Wizard to start the CIW.

2. Tell the CIW where your administrative installation of that version of Office is. Remember, you created an administrative installation of Office 2003 in the section "Setting Up an Administrative Installation (for .*MSI* Files that Need Them)" earlier in this chapter.

3. Give your .MST file a creative name, for example, nomsaccess.mst.

4. Continue to follow the wizard's instruction, choosing your specific installation options. In this example, on screen 7 (of 24), as shown in Figure 4.21, we'll tell Office 2003 that we don't want Access available to users.

5. At the final screen, click Finish and save the .MST file to a handy location.

As the CIW presents the final wizard screen, it will give you information about how to run the .MSI file along with the .MST file manually. But you can ignore this because you're about to use the .MST file in a Group Policy Software Installation GPO.

FIGURE 4.21 Use the CIW to choose the options you want and create the .MST file.

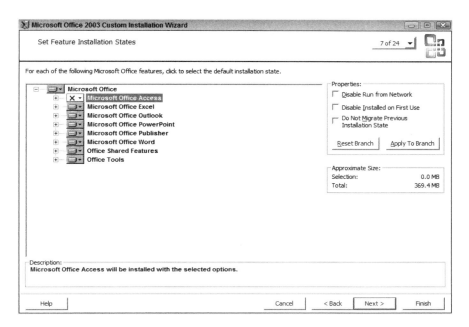

Applying Your *.MST* File to the Installation

As previously stated, you can add .MST files only when you're initially Assigning or Publishing a package. .MST files are valid, say, for Office 2003, but, it turns out, like I said, Office 2007 doesn't support them. See the Real-World Scenario "Installing and Customizing Office 2007 via GPSI" for the details.

You previously performed these steps in the "Creating and Editing the GPO to Deploy Office" section as shown in Figure 4.4. When you follow those steps, the "Select deployment method" dialog box will appear. Afterward, follow these steps:

1. In the "Select deployment method" dialog box, click Advanced to open the Properties dialog box.

2. Click the Modifications tab, and click Add to open the Open dialog box.

3. In the "File name" field, enter the full UNC path of the .MST file, for instance, **\\DC01\ apps\office2003distro\nomsaccess.mst**.

The .MST file needn't be in the same location as the .MSI distribution, as long as the path is available via the UNC name.

4. Click OK.

Your screenshot should be similar to what is seen in Figure 4.20 in the "Modifications Tab" section.

Once you click OK, the .MST file will be locked in and cannot be changed. You have only two options if you are unhappy with the .MST file:

- Remove the package and deploy it again.
- Create an upgrade package as described earlier.

Removing the entire Office suite and reinstalling it can be a pain for your users, so, if you want to deploy Office with (or without) .MST files, be sure to test in the lab before you really get started in your actual deployment.

What's with the Move Up and Move Down Buttons in the Modifications Tab?

If you wanted to, you could add multiple .MST files before clicking the OK button to lock in your selection. You can see this ability and the move up/move down buttons in Figure 4.20. But why would you do this?

Multiple, autonomous administrators can individually create .MST files and layer them such that each Transform File contains some of the configuration options. These files are then ordered so that the options are applied from the top down. If configured options overlap, the last-configured option wins.

However, in my travels I really haven't seen administrators choose to add multiple .MST files for the same .MSI. Typically, only one .MST file is used as we did in this previous example.

The Security Tab

Individual applications can be filtered based on computer, user, or Security group membership. For instance, if you Assign Office 2003 to all members of the **Human Resources Users** OU, you set it up normally, as described earlier.

 WARNING   If a user who happens to administer the application in the GPO is not given Read access, they will no longer be able to administer the application. Therefore, don't use filtering based on user or Security group membership on the administrators of the application.

If, however, you want to exclude a specific member, say, Frank Rizzo, you can deny Frank Rizzo's account permissions to Read the package. A better strategy is to create a Security group—say, DenyOffice2003—and put those people not allowed to receive the application inside that group. You can then set the permissions to Deny the entire Security group the ability to read the package as shown in Figure 4.22.

FIGURE 4.22   Use the Security tab to specify who can and cannot run applications.

Default Group Policy Software Installation Properties

Each GPSI node (one for users and one for computers) has some default installation properties that you can modify. In the Group Policy Management Editor, simply right-click the GPSI node and choose Properties from the shortcut menu, as shown in Figure 4.23, to open the "Software installation Properties" dialog box (also shown in Figure 4.23), which has four tabs: General, Advanced, File Extensions, and Categories.

The General Tab

Most settings on the General tab are self-explanatory. Do note that you can specify a default package location, such as `\\DC01\apps`, so that you can then use the GUI when adding packages. Avoid using direct paths such as `C:\apps\` since `C:\apps` probably won't exist on the client at runtime.

You can also specify the behavior for when you add in new packages; where Assign is the default action.

Last, you can establish the critical setting of Basic vs. Maximum here (when Assigning applications to users). The bummer is that these default setting changes are local only for this specific GPO. That is, the next GPO you create that uses GPSI will not adhere to the defaults you set in this GPO.

The Advanced Tab

The Advanced tab, as shown in Figure 4.24, allows you to set some default settings for all the packages you want to deploy in this GPO. You saw some of these settings with similar names before in the Advanced Deployment Options dialog box (Figure 4.18).

FIGURE 4.23   Use the GPSI Properties dialog box to set up general deployment settings.

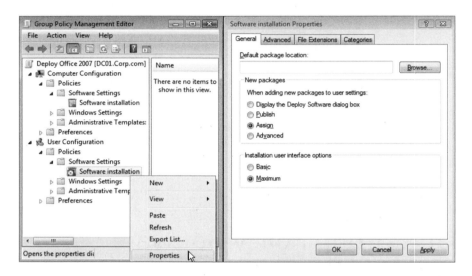

FIGURE 4.24   You can set up some default settings for new packages in this GPO.

Uninstall the applications when they fall out of the scope of management I'll discuss this setting in the "Removing Applications" section later in this chapter.

Include OLE information when deploying applications As stated earlier, this feature allows applications that contain COM services to be deployed such that COM clients can find their deployed applications. Again, check with your application vendor to see if you need this switch; generally you don't.

The "32-bit applications on 64-bit platforms" Section As stated, it's possible to run 32-bit applications on Windows XP/Vista 64-bit editions. You can set the defaults to block x64 machines from downloading 32-bit software packages. If you want to find out more about Windows Vista 64-bit Edition just check out `www.microsoft.com/windows/products/ windowsvista/editions/64bit.mspx`. If you're looking for info on Windows XP 64-bit Edition, try here `http://tinyurl.com/2ddp4h`.

The File Extensions Tab

As stated earlier, you can install and start applications by double-clicking or by invoking their document type. For instance, double-clicking a `.ZIP` file can automatically deploy a Published or Assigned WinZip application. The correspondence of a file type to a package is found in either the `.ZAP` file definition or the `.MSI` file database. Once the application is set to be deployed, the file types are automatically entered into Active Directory.

Occasionally, two Published or Assigned applications are called by the same file extension. This can occur if you're upgrading a package from, say, WinZip to UltraZip, and both are using the `.ZIP` extension, or if you're upgrading from Office 2003 to Office 2007 and both Word applications use the `.DOC` extension.

In those cases, you need to specify which extension fires off which application. To do so, follow these steps:

1. In the "Software installation Properties" dialog box, click the File Extensions tab, as shown in Figure 4.25.

2. Click the "Select file extension" drop-down list box, and select the extension to display all the applicable Assigned or Published applications in the Application Precedence list.

3. Select an application, and then click the Up or Down button to change the order.

The Categories Tab

Categories is a domain-wide property that puts Published or Assigned software into bite-sized chunks instead of one giant-sized alphabetized list in the Add or Remove Programs folder or "Install a program from the network" for Windows Vista. As noted earlier, you might want to group WinZip and UltraZip in the Archive Programs category or put Adobe Acrobat Reader and GhostScript in the Doc Readers category. On this tab, simply click the Add button to enter the names of the categories in the "Enter new category" dialog box.

FIGURE 4.25 Use the File Extensions tab to set the priority for conflicting file extensions.

This whole business of Categories is a bit strange, as it lets any OU administrator add categories into Active Directory. Oddly, there appears to be no way to centrally manage this property.

Therefore, if possible, select one administrator to control this property, set it up to be centrally managed, and then use the Properties dialog box to associate a package with a category or categories.

Removing Applications

You can remove applications from users or computers in several ways. First, under some circumstances, users can manually remove applications, but, as an administrator, you hold the reigns. Therefore, you can set applications to automatically or forcefully be removed.

Users Can Manually Change or Remove Applications

If an application is Assigned (and also Published) to a user, they can use Control Panel to change the installed options or remove the bits to save space. However, Microsoft's position is that it provides the best of both worlds: the user can remove the binaries, but if the application is Assigned, the icons and program names are forced to appear on the Start ➤ All Programs menu.

But, in practice, I've found that this is a bad thing. Users remove their applications and then go on the road with their laptops. Well, on the other hand, if they do this, they deserve what's coming to them. Note, however, that applications Assigned to the computer cannot be changed or uninstalled by anyone but local computer administrators. This is a good thing.

Automatically Removing Assigned or Published *.MSI* Applications

Applications can be automatically uninstalled when they no longer apply to the user. Earlier in the "Advanced Published or Assigned" section, you saw that in the Deployment tab of the "Software installation Properties" dialog box you can check the "Uninstall this application when it falls out of the scope of management" check box. This was back in Figure 4.16. You can specify that the application is to be uninstalled if any of the following occurs:

- The user or computer is moved out of the OU to which this software applies.
- The GPO containing the package definition is deleted.
- The user or computer no longer has rights to read the GPO.

The software is never actually forcibly removed while the user is logged onto the current session but is removed a bit later in the following manner:

- Applications Published to users are removed upon next logon.
- Applications Assigned to users are removed upon next logon.
- Applications Assigned to computers are removed upon next reboot.
- Applications Assigned to computers that are currently not attached to the network are removed the next time the computer is plugged into the network, rebooted, and the computer account "logs on" to Active Directory.
- Applications Assigned or Published to users on computers that are currently not attached to the network are removed the next time they log on and are validated to Active Directory.

In these cases, the software is automatically removed upon next logon (for users) or upon next reboot (for computers). For example, Figure 4.26 shows what happens when a computer is moved out of an OU and then rebooted. Moving users and computers in and out of OUs might not be such a hot idea if lots of applications are being Assigned.

These rules assume Fast Boot is not enabled. That is, you've specifically *disabled* Fast Boot. If Fast Boot is enabled (the default), these rules don't apply; expect two logons or two reboots for the change to take effect.

FIGURE 4.26   When applications fall out of the scope of management, they uninstall.

One final warning about the automatic removal of applications. GPSI cannot remove the icons and programs names for the application if the GPO has been deleted and the user has a Roaming Profile and has roamed to a machine after the application was uninstalled. In this case, there is not enough uninstall information on the machine, and, hence, the icons and program names will continue to exist, though they will be nonfunctional.

Forcefully Removing Assigned or Published .*MSI* Applications

You have seen how applications can be automatically removed from users or computers when the user or computer object moves out the scope of management. But what if you want to keep the user or computer in the scope of management and still remove an application? You can manually remove Published or Assigned applications. To do so, simply right-click the package definition, and choose All Tasks ➤ Remove, as seen in Figure 4.27. This will open the Remove Software dialog box. The options presented in this dialog box depend on whether you deployed .MSI or .ZAP applications.

FIGURE 4.27   You can revoke deployed applications by selecting Remove.

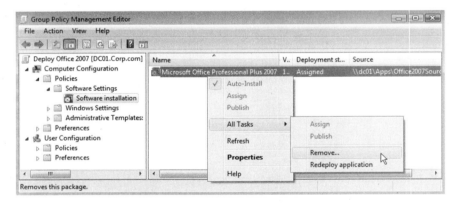

If you are removing an .MSI file, you have two options, as discussed in the next sections.

Immediately Uninstall the Software from Users and Computers

If you choose this option, all connected computers receive a signal to uninstall the software, and they follow the rules for uninstalling as in the previous section.

The signal to remove an application (such as Office XP) lives in the actual GPO definition. Therefore, if you're looking for success in the forceful removal of applications, don't delete the GPO right after selecting this option. If you do, the signal to remove the application won't be available to the workstations. Rather, remove the application, and leave the GPO definition around for a while to ensure that the computers get the signal to remove the software. If you remove the GPO before the target user receives the signal (upon next logon) or the computer receives the signal (upon next reboot), the application is orphaned on the Desktop and must be manually unloaded via Control Panel or by some other means (for instance, MSIEXEC, as described later in this chapter).

This is a second warning in case you overlooked the ominous message in the previous paragraph: if you remove the GPO definition before a target user or computer receives the signal, the application is orphaned on the Desktop. You can, however, likely get out of this trap if the application was specified with the "Uninstall this application when it falls out of the scope of management" check box. You can move the user or computer out of the scope of management to remove the application and then bring it back in when the application removal is completed. It's a bit rough, but it should work.

Allow Users to Continue to Use the Software, but Prevent New Installations

When you remove applications using this option, current installations of the software remain intact. Users to which this edict applies, however, will no longer be able to install new copies of the software. Therefore, those who do not have the software will not be able to install it. Those who do have it installed will be able to continue to use it.

The self-repair features of the Windows Installer will still function (for example, if Winword.exe gets deleted, it will come back from the dead), but the application cannot be fully reinstalled via Control Panel.

Once you use this option, you will no longer be able to manage the application and force it to uninstall from the machines on which it is installed.

Removing Published *.ZAP* Applications

You have only one option for removing .ZAP applications. When you right-click the package definition and select Remove (as seen in Figure 4.27), you'll have to answer but one question: "Remove the Package but Leave the Application Installed Everywhere It Is Already Installed?"

Remember that since the .ZAP file really calls only the original Setup.exe program, ultimately, Setup.exe is in charge of how the application is uninstalled. Therefore, once applications are deployed using .ZAP files, the power to forcibly uninstall them is out of your hands.

Troubleshooting the Removal of Applications

Sometimes, applications refuse to leave the target system gracefully. Usually, this is because an application has been Published or Assigned, and the user has "double-dipped" by throwing in the CD and installing a program on top of itself. Sometimes, the Windows Installer becomes confused. When you then try to remove the application from being Published or Assigned, the application doesn't know what to do.

If an application refuses to go away (or you're left with entries in the Add or Remove Programs applet in Control Panel), you have two tools at your disposal: The Windows Installer Clean Up Utility (also known as MSICUU) and MSIZAP. Both were originally in the Windows 2000 Support Tools located in the \SUPPORT folder of the Windows 2000 Server CD. Updates are now available at Microsoft's download site. Both do essentially the same thing: they manually hunt down all Registry settings for an application and delete them. This should remove all vestigial entries in the Add or Remove Programs applet in Control Panel.

Windows Installer Clean Up Utility (also known as MSICUU)   This tool has a GUI. Programs displayed in the Installed Products list, as shown in Figure 4.28, are the same as those in the Add or Remove Programs applet in Control Panel. At last check, the tool was available at `http://support.microsoft.com/kb/290301`.

MSIZAP   MSIZAP is a command-line tool with a similar function. You must specify an .MSI product code (GUID) to hunt down and destroy. At last check, additional reference and download for MSIZAP is at `http://tinyurl.com/2kobm3`. However, you'll have to download and install the monstrous Windows Installer SDK just to get it.

FIGURE 4.28   The MSICUU program in the Windows 2000 Support Tools can whack entire programs off your system.

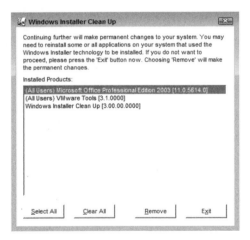

Using Group Policy Software Installation over Slow Links

First things first: applications Assigned to computers cannot ever be installed over a slow dial-up link or a VPN (virtual private network) connection. Why? Because the computer must see the network, log onto it, and then start to actually download the program. If you're using a dial-up or other slow connection, manual intervention to connect to the network must be involved. Hence, in general, no applications Assigned to computers will ever install unless the computer is connected to the LAN.

 I say "in general" in the previous sentence, because it does depend a bit on your VPN technology. For instance, you could have a hardware VPN, separate from the client, and a computer assignment could work over that should a slow-link not be detected.

However, when applications are Assigned or Published to users (not computers), it's a different story. When a user connects via a slow link, they will not see new Assignment offers. By default, only users connected at 500Kbps or greater will see new Assignments on the Start ➢ All Programs menu. This is a good thing too, as you wouldn't want someone dialing in over a 56Kbps modem to try to accept the offer of Office XP.

You can change this behavior by modifying the GPO at Computer Configuration ➢ Policies ➢ Administrative Templates ➢ System ➢ Group Policy ➢ **Software Installation Policy Processing**, as shown in Figure 4.29.

FIGURE 4.29   Use Group Policy to change the default slow-link behavior.

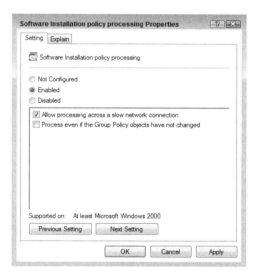

Checking the "Allow processing across a slow network connection" check box forces all clients, regardless of their connection speed, to adhere to the policy setting. If you want to be a bit less harsh, you can change the definition of a "slow link" and modify the **Group Policy Slow Link Detection** policy setting. After you enable the policy setting, set a value in the "Connection speed (Kbps)" spin box.

One word of warning with regard to slow links: users who are Assigned or Published applications can find other ways to install applications over slow links. First, they can trot out to the Add or Remove Programs applet and select the application. Sure, the offer isn't displayed on the Start ➤ All Programs menu, but it's still going to be available in the Add or Remove Programs applet in Control Panel. To prevent this, select the "Do not display this package in the Add/Remove Programs control panel" check box, which is found on the Deployment tab of the application's Properties (see Figure 4.16).

Last, check out this scenario. Imagine that while on a fast link, a user named Fred accepts the offer for Excel. Super-duper—Excel is now installed. Now, Fred is dialed up and receives a Word document in e-mail. And, Fred hasn't yet installed Word. Look out! Because .DOC is a registered file type for Microsoft Office, Word will attempt to install over a slow link (if Assigned to a User). This happens because Fred has accepted the "offer" for Office (he got Excel over a fast link) and now selects to get Word via document invocation. To prevent this, simply clear the "Auto-install this application by file extension activation" option in the Deployment tab in the Properties dialog box of the application (again, seen in Figure 4.16).

Assigning Applications to Users over Slow Links Using Windows 2000

If you are planning on utilizing GPSI with Windows 2000 laptops, there are two things to keep in mind. Here they are.

Dealing with Already-Assigned Applications

Here's a scenario that illustrates the problem with Assigning an application, such as Office, to users. While at headquarters in Washington, D.C., Wally, on his Windows 2000 Professional laptop, sees and accepts your offer for Office. Specifically, Wally clicks Word on the Start ➤ All Programs menu. Because Wally is connected over a fast link, the download is quick and painless. Wally is shipped off from Washington, D.C. to Walla Walla, WA.

 Oh, by the way, to learn more about the fine city of Walla Walla, WA, be sure to visit www.ci.walla-walla.wa.us/.

While on the airplane from Washington, D.C. to Walla Walla, WA, Wally decides to accept the offer for Excel and clicks that item on the Start ➤ All Programs menu. He gets the message shown in Figure 4.30.

This is a major problem for Wally because the source files are only available on the server from which he originally received the installation (or from DFS Namespaces, if that's available). Long story short, Wally is woeful. Wally calls the help desk, and the help desk calls you. Worst part of the story—there's not a whole lot you can do to help him now.

You can ask Wally to dial in, but that's likely going to be fruitless. Trying to install Excel over a dial-up connection won't be painless. Can Wally with his Windows 2000 laptop be helped? Not easily, now that he's on the road. He really needs to connect using a fast link to download the rest of Excel.

FIGURE 4.30   This is what happens when a user tries to use a program that isn't fully installed.

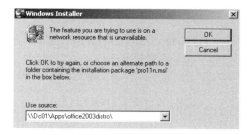

However, Wally could have been helped *before* he set out on the road in two ways:

- The application could have been Assigned to his computer (instead of to his user account), which would have ensured that the entire application was available and ready to go when he hit the road. You saw this earlier when we installed Office 2003. The entirety of Office 2003 was installed on the next reboot. Sure, it took a long time, but when it was done, it was done.

- Even though the application was Assigned to Wally's user account, the application could have been fully installed via a little scripting magic. We'll explore that option right now.

"Fully Installing" New Applications to Users on Windows 2000 When Using Assign

As I stated earlier, users dialed up over a slow link will not see *new* Assignment offers. The key word here is *new*.

However, this wasn't Wally's problem. He wasn't accepting a new offer over a slow link; rather, Wally had already accepted an offer before he left. Therefore, his problem could have been prevented if the application were already fully installed. But I already said that when you Assign applications to users, the .MSI file is downloaded in chunks—not all at once—which is precisely why Wally had problems when he tried to download Excel. He had the "chunk" for Word, but not for Excel. Hence, he needed to reach the original source for a download.

To that end, you can install a special logon script for users on Windows 2000 laptops. Here's the gist. When users connect at a high speed, the computer sees the new offer. This special logon script downloads and installs each chunk of the .MSI all at once to ensure that the application is fully installed. Hence, even though the application is Assigned to Wally's user account, the entirety of the application is available.

Sure, the application takes a while to download the first time the offer is available, and, of course, all the disk space the application will ever use is used right away. But it's a darn good idea to set up this logon script for your Windows 2000 laptop users. You don't want them to get the message seen in Figure 4.30.

Space doesn't permit me to print the script right here, but you can download it from my website, www.GPanswers.com. One warning about this script: if the user has already accepted any part of the offer (that is, already downloaded Word, but not Excel), this script won't work for them. You need to set up the script *before* you start Assigning applications to users—that is, before they start accepting your offers. If you've already deployed applications in this way, you'll need to remove them (see the section "Removing Applications" earlier in this chapter) and then Assign the applications again after the special logon script is in place.

Assigning Applications to Users over Slow Links Using Windows XP, Windows Vista, and Windows 2003

Microsoft has fixed the problem that plagued Wally. However, the solution is available only when the client system is greater than Windows 2000 (say, Windows XP, Windows Vista, or Windows 2003). However, it's doubtful you'll have many Windows 2003 systems for use "on the road."

When a modern machine sees an offer for a newly Assigned application for a user (which it will only see when connected over a fast link), the entirety of the application can be installed—instead of waiting for it to come down in chunks.

Ideally, you'll set this up for packages you want to Assign to users using Windows XP laptops. When you Assign this application to users, in the Deployment tab of the Properties dialog box, click the "Install this application at logon" check box (as seen in Figure 4.16). This setting is only valid for Windows XP or higher. When applications are Assigned to users. Windows 2000 machines simply ignore it.

WARNING   If the user opens the Add or Remove Programs folder or "Install a program from the network" for Windows Vista and manually uninstalls the application, neither the logon script nor the "Install this application at logon" setting will kick back into high gear and install the application. This might be a big deal if your users dink around trying to add or remove stuff. You might also want to select the "Do not display this package in the Add/Remove Programs control panel" check box, also located on the Deployment tab in the Properties dialog box.

Managing .*MSI* Packages and the Windows Installer

Users might occasionally want to install their own .MSI packages. Those packages can come on CDs from software vendors, like Microsoft (with an MSI packages such as Office 2003.) Or, perhaps you have MSI applications that you've created in house using a third-party "wrap-up" tool like WinInstall or Wise Installer.

To manually install an .MSI application on a workstation, you can either double-click the application or use a command-line tool called MSIEXEC to kick off (or repair) the installation.

This section explores the options when manually installing existing .MSI packages that you've deployed via Group Policy. As you've learned throughout the chapter, most of the things we need in order to deploy applications can be performed using the GPSI GUI. However, some functions are available only in the command-line tool.

Inside the *MSIEXEC* Tool

MSIEXEC is a command-line tool, which helps you get applications installed. There are three versions of MSIEXEC, but you're likely to encounter only two versions.

If your machine is Windows XP (pre-SP2), simply typing **MSIEXEC /?** on the command line is no help at all. In this case, to get the full syntax of MSIEXEC, you'll need to use the Windows help file and search for MSIEXEC.

However, if your machine is Windows XP/SP2, MSIEXEC has been upgraded to version 3. Now, if you type **MSIEXEC /?**, you'll get some useful feedback about how to use it.

For the purposes of this book, MSIEXEC for Windows XP/SP2 (that is, MSIEXEC version 3) and the non-Windows XP/SP2 versions of MSIEXEC (that is, MSIEXEC versions prior to 3) will act functionally equivalent. However, you might be interested in precisely what MSIEXEC 3 has to offer. And, if you like what you see, you'll be happy to know that MSIEXEC 3 is redistributable to your Windows XP (non-SP2) and Windows 2000 clients! Specifically, you can load Windows Installer 3 on Windows 2000 Service Pack 3, Windows 2000 Service Pack 4, Windows Server 2003, Windows XP, and Windows XP Service Pack 1. Note, however, you'll need to find some non–Group Policy way to deploy the update because you can't update the .MSI engine while in use (very clear chicken-and-egg problem). You should be able to update these systems with Microsoft WSUS.

You can find out about what MSIEXEC 3 is all about at MSKB 884016 with the plucky little title, "Windows Installer 3.0 is Available."

You can use MSIEXEC in several ways, but here we're going to look at how to use it to manage existing .MSI packages. Indeed, you can use MSIEXEC to script an installation of an .MSI package at a workstation, but why bother? You're already using the power of Group Policy. However, you might need to check out how an installation works by hand or enable additional logging for deeper troubleshooting. Or you could trigger a preemptive repair of an application at specific times. You can even use MSIEXEC to remove a specific application.

You can also use MSIEXEC as a maintenance tool for existing packages on distribution points. We'll explore a bit of both uses.

Instead of diving into every MSIEXEC command here, I'll simply highlight some of the most frequently used. Indeed, you may never find yourself using MSIEXEC unless specifically directed to do so by an application vendor's Install program.

Using *MSIEXEC* to Install an Application

The first function of MSIEXEC is to initiate an installation from a source point. This is essentially the same as double-clicking the .MSI file, using the /I switch (for Install). The syntax for your application might be as follows:

```
Msiexec /I \\DC01\apps\yourapp.msi
```

Using *MSIEXEC* to Repair an Application

You can script the repair of applications by using MSIEXEC with the /f switch and an additional helper-switch, as indicated in the Windows help file. For instance, you might want to ensure that Pro11n.msi (Office 2003) is not corrupted on the client. You can do so by forcing all files from inside the Office 2003 .MSI to be reinstalled on the client. Use the following command from the client (which overwrites older or equally versioned files):

```
Msiexec /fe \\DC01\apps\office2003distro\pro11n.msi
```

If you simply want to ensure that no older version is installed, you can execute the following command:

```
Msiexec /fo \\DC01\apps\office2003distro\pro11n.msi
```

Again, be sure to consult the Windows help file for the complete syntax of MSIEXEC in conjunction with adhering to your specific application vendor's directions.

Using *MSIEXEC* to Patch a Distribution Point

You can also use MSIEXEC to *patch*; that is to incorporate vendor-supplied bug fixes and the like to the code base of an existing package. The vendor supplies the patches by using an .MSP file, or *Microsoft Patch* file. Office XP's service packs, for instance, come with several .MSP files that update the original .MSI files.

Office 2003 has multiple service packs. You can download the latest one (SP3) from http://support.microsoft.com/kb/923618. It contains mainsp3.msp, owc11sp3.msp, and owc102003sp3.msp.

Microsoft seems to have changed their tune midway with this technology. In some instances, you needed to apply each successive service pack's .MSP files to be sufficiently protected. However, Office XP's Service Pack 3, for instance, expressly states that it contains all the fixes contained within all previous service packs. So, be sure to read your manufacturer's instructions on whether or not to install every .MSP file from every update, or if you can make due with just the most recent.

Throughout this chapter, we've leveraged our Office 2003 administration point. We'll continue with that trend. In the following example, the Office 2003 distribution, located at \\DC01\apps\office2003distro, is to be patched with the MAINSP3.msp patch that comes with Office 2003 Service Pack 3. The resulting log file will be called logfile.txt.

Because each vendor may have a different way of patching, be sure to check out the Readme file that comes with the patch files.

The following command line is written as directed from the Office 2003 SP3 whitepaper:

```
Msiexec.exe /a \\<path>\PRO11n.MSI /p \\<path>\MAINSP3.msp SHORTFILENAMES=True
/qb- /Lv* c:\Logfile.txt
```

Again, you'll have to run the command for each and every included patch file to update an Office 2003 distribution point to SP3. However, the good news is that included in the download are all updates that were previously contained in the previous service packs. So, at least you don't have to download and install Office 2003 to SP1, or SP2 for that matter. Just install all the patch files in SP3, and you're good to go.

This next step is a point of order that I left out of the second (and first) edition of my book *Group Policy Fundamentals, Troubleshooting, and Security*. That is, once the .MSI is patched, all your users (or computers) need to reinstall the application. The underlying application has changed, and the client system doesn't know about the change until you tell it. You can see how to redeploy an application in Figure 4.31. Again, this is only required after an .MSI source is patched.

FIGURE 4.31 Once you patch an .MSI source, be sure to select "Redeploy application."

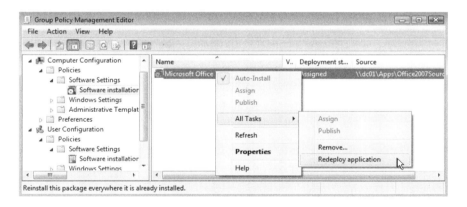

Users also need to do this because of what is termed the "client-source-out-of-sync" problem. Until the client reaches and reinstalls from the updated administrative image, it won't be able to use the administrative image for repairs or on-demand installations. This is because a source location is validated by the Windows Installer before use. The criteria for validation are the name of the package file and the package code (seen as a GUID) of the package. When you patch the administrative image, you change the underlying package code GUID. Thus, the client needs the recache and reinstall in order to pick up the updated package code information.

So, specifically, after you patch a distribution point (or otherwise change the underlying .MSI package in a distribution point), you need to right-click the offer and choose All Tasks ➢ Redeploy application, as shown in Figure 4.31.

Microsoft has some Office 2003 upgrade guidance at `http://office`
`.microsoft.com/en-us/ork2003/HA011402381033.aspx` (shortened to
`http://tinyurl.com/2qce97`).

Affecting Windows Installer with Group Policy

You can use several policy settings to tweak the behavior of the Windows Installer. Most tweaks do not involve how software is managed or deployed via GPSI because there's not much to it. You deploy the application, and users (or computers) do your bidding. Rather, these settings tweak the access the user has when software is not being Assigned or Published.

There are two collections of policy settings for the Windows Installer; one is under Computer Configuration, and the other is under User Configuration. As usual, to utilize these policy settings, just create a new GPO, Enable the policy settings you like, then ensure that the corresponding user or computer account is in the scope of management of the GPO.

Computer Side Policy Settings for Windows Installer

To display the settings in Computer Configuration, as shown in Figure 4.32, choose Computer Configuration ➤ Policies ➤ Administrative Templates ➤ Windows Components ➤ Windows Installer.

Note that Windows Installer 3 has four specific Computer-side policy settings. That is, for these four settings to work, your machine needs to be running Windows Installer 3. As stated, Windows XP/SP2 and Windows 2003/SP1 both have Windows Installer 3 already loaded. And, as also stated, the Windows Installer 3 redistributable is available for Windows XP (no Service Pack), Windows 2003, and Windows 2000 (SP3 and later). Again, check out MSKB 884016. Once your client has at least Windows Installer 3, it will respond to the newest settings. These are specifically called out and listed in the next sections.

Disable Windows Installer

Once enabled, this setting lets you specify one of four options:

Not Configured   Uses the settings at a higher level.

Enabled/Never   Always keeps the Windows Installer active.

Enabled/For Nonmanaged Apps Only   Turns off the Windows Installer when users try to manually install their own applications. This is useful if you want to guarantee no foreign `.MSI` packages are making it through the doors. This option permits users to install only those programs that a system administrator Assigns or Publishes.

Enabled/Always   Essentially turns off all methods (managed and unmanaged) for loading `.MSI` packages.

These settings specify only settings for `.MSI` packages—not other programs that users can install, such as those from `SETUP.EXEs` and the like.

FIGURE 4.32   Use Group Policy to affect the Windows Installer settings.

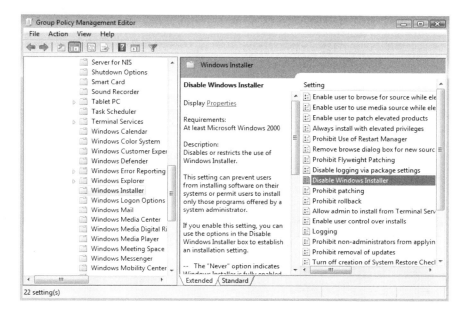

Always Install with Elevated Privileges

Deploying applications with GPSI is awesome: we do all the work with .MSI files, and we don't have to worry about users having administrative privileges. As we've already seen, we can deploy applications to users, and have the system take care of the installation in the system context (not the user context).

And, what's more, mere-mortals cannot just download an .MSI application and necessarily expect it to install correctly. Many .MSI applications will fail installation if attempted in the user context. You can, however, bypass the normal security mechanism so that users can install .MSI files by Enabling this policy setting. You'll need to do the same with the corresponding policy setting in the User Configuration, as discussed in the "User Side Policy Settings for Windows Installer" section.

If you are deploying .MSI applications with Group Policy, you need not use and enable this setting.

Prohibit Rollback

As stated, .MSI files can be "rolled back" during the actual installation of the application. For instance, a user can click Cancel during an installation, or the computer could suddenly be turned off.

If you enable this policy setting, you're effectively telling the system not to maintain "backup files" in the case of an on-the-fly rollback. Since a rollback can be initiated during the actual installation, a "fractured" and, hence, nonworking program could remain on the system.

Personally, I would never use this policy setting.

Remove Browse Dialog Box for New Source

Recall that, at any given point, only the components required to run an .MSI application are actually downloaded. For instance, the help files in Word are downloaded the first time it is used from the installation source (usually the server), not necessarily the first time Word runs. But what happens if you move the source?

When you move an application from one shared folder to another, the application can become confused, and users need to specify a different installation point to get to the source. By default, users can browse to any source.

If you Enable this setting, users are only allowed to use specific sources.

Prohibit Patching

If users can install some .MSI applications under their own security context, by default, they can also patch their own .MSI files with .MSP (Microsoft Patch) files by using the MSIEXEC command-line application. Enabling this setting prevents users from patching even their own installed .MSI applications.

Prohibit Flyweight Patching

This setting is new when a GPO is created from a Windows Vista management station. However, it is valid on machines that have Windows Installer 3. Windows Installer 4 is not required.

If you enable this setting, you're instructing the engine to be meticulous during its patching of applications. If you disable this setting (or leave it Not Configured), you are telling the system to utilize a faster algorithm when patching is needed.

Disable IE Security Prompt for Windows Installer Scripts

Recall that users can manually install .MSI applications from a CD or a shared folder or a web page. The default behavior before executing any downloaded application via Internet Explorer is to warn the user about potentially damaging content. Enabling this setting squelches this warning.

This scenario should be rare, because normally you Publish or Assign applications in order to install them to your users' Desktops. At times, however, some applications may be best suited for downloading via Internet Explorer, and, hence, a warning message could appear and frighten your users.

Enable User Control over Installs

When an administrator Publishes or Assigns applications, all the settings specified in the .MSI application are forced upon the user. Sometimes this behavior is undesirable. For example, you might want to let the user specify the destination folder or decide which features to download. If you enable this setting, you grant users the ability to change the default .MSI application settings.

This policy setting affects all applications installed on the client system. However, if you want to let the user set up a specific product in their own way, you can use a transform that sets special properties inside the .MSI. You can use the .MST tool to set the `EnableUserControl` property to 1 or add specific properties to the `SecureCustomProperties` list (using a customization transform). If your application doesn't have a way to create .MST files, you can create them with third-party .MSI creation tools.

Enable User to Browse for Source While Elevated

When an administrator Publishes or Assigns applications, all the settings specified in the .MSI application are forced upon the user from the installation point the administrator specifies. Sometimes this behavior is undesirable because the user knows of a closer source to the application in their branch office. In cases like this, you might want to let the user specify the source to locate a closer source point. If you enable this setting, you grant users the ability to change the default .MSI source location.

Once users are affected by this policy setting, they can basically browse anywhere they like, including the local system. If you have locked down the Desktop to prevent such behavior, enabling this setting could be a potential security hole during .MSI application install times.

Enable User to Use Media Source While Elevated

When users install .MSI packages under their own security context, they can choose whatever source they desire for the software. But when you, the administrator, Assign or Publish an application, you are essentially dictating the source of the .MSI file. If you enable this setting, you permit the user to choose a nonnetworked source, such as a CD or floppy drive, from which to install a program you specify. Enable this setting only if the **Enable the User to Browse for Source While Elevated** policy is enabled.

Enable User to Patch Elevated Products

By default, only the administrator who Assigns or Publishes the application can use an .MSP file (in conjunction with `MSIEXEC`) to patch a program. If you enable this setting, users can use `MSIEXEC` to patch their local versions of Published or Assigned applications.

Allow Admin to Install from Terminal Services Session

By default, administrators using the Terminal Services Remote Administration Mode on Windows 2000 or Windows Server 2003 are prevented from installing additional Published or Assigned applications.

If you want Administrators to be able to install .MSI applications while logged in via Terminal Services session, just Enable this setting so that servers and Domain Controllers download the setting and, hence, reverse this default.

Cache Transforms in Secure Location on Workstation

Recall that you can specifically customize an .MST file to hone an .MSI application. Transform Files are applied on .MSI packages either to filter the number of options available to the end user or to specify certain answers to questions, usually raised during the .MSI package installation.

Once a user starts using an .MSI application applied with an .MST file, that .MST file follows them in the Roaming Profile—specifically, in the Application Data folder, as described in Chapter 2. You can change this default behavior by enabling this setting, which takes the .MST file out of the Roaming Profile and puts it in a secure place on the workstation. On the one hand, this closes a small security hole that sophisticated users might use to hack into their own .MST files in their profiles. On the other hand, users are forced to return to the machine that has their .MST files in order to additionally modify their application.

Avoid using this setting unless specifically directed to do so by your application vendor, a security bulletin, or Microsoft.

Logging

Applications Assigned or Published using Windows Installer do not provide much information to the administrator about the success of their installation. By default, several key tidbits of information are logged about managed applications that fail. The log files are named .MSI*.LOG; the * represents additional characters that make the log file unique for each application downloaded.

Per-computer logs are in C:\windows\temp and per-user logs are in %temp%.

Thus, centralized logging and reporting is an arduous, if not impossible, task for anything more than a handful of users who are using Windows Installer. For additional logging and reporting, Microsoft recommends their Systems Management Server, as described in the section titled "Do You Need a 'Big' Management Tool for Your Environment?" later in the chapter.

To add logging entries, modify the Logging setting. Some settings that might come in handy are Out of Memory and Out of Disk—two common reasons for Windows Installer applications failing to load.

 You can also turn on Application Management debugging logs by manually editing the Registry of the client machine. Simply run regedit or regedt32 and edit the following key: HKEY_LOCAL_MACHINE\Software\Microsoft\ Windows NT\CurrentVersion. Create a key called Diagnostics, then add a Reg_DWORD value called AppMgmtDebugLevel and set it to 4b in hexadecimal. You'll then find a log in the local %windir%debug\usermode folder named appmgmt.log, which can also aid in finding out why applications fail to load.

Prohibit User Installs

On occasion an administrator might dictate that a user is Assigned Office 2003, and another administrator dictates that a computer gets Office 2003 (but perhaps without Access). What if the user who is Assigned Office 2003 sits down at a computer that is Assigned Office 2003 without Access? Which one wins? The application (and settings therein) Assigned to the user takes precedence.

This policy setting has three options (once enabled): Allow User Installs, Hide User Installs, or Prohibit User Installs. Computers that are affected by Hide User Installs display only the applications Assigned to the computer. However, the user can still install the applications Assigned to them using the Add or Remove Programs applet in Control Panel (hence, overriding the applications Assigned to the computer).

If you set Prohibit User Installs, the user won't get the applications Assigned to them on the machines to which this policy setting applies. And the user cannot load Assigned applications to their user account via the Add or Remove Programs folder or "Install a program from the network" for Windows Vista. If they do so, they'll get an error message. If this policy setting is set somewhere else, you can also return the default behavior by setting Allow User Installs.

This policy setting can be especially handy in Terminal Services sessions or kiosk settings (for example, lab machines) where you want all users of the machine to get the applications Assigned only to computers (not to users).

This setting is valid for Windows XP and Windows 2000 machines (with Windows Installer 2 or later loaded). See the section "The Windows Installer Service" earlier in this chapter.

Turn off Creation of System Restore Checkpoints

On a Windows XP machine, a System Restore Checkpoint is created when users load their own `.MSI` files unless there is no user interface. The `.MSI` system creates System Restore Checkpoints on first installation and uninstall. System Restore Checkpoints are not created when deploying (or repairing) applications via GPSI.

Enable this setting if you want to ensure that no System Restore Checkpoints are created when `.MSI` files are loaded.

This setting is only valid on Windows XP machines.

Prohibit Removal of Updates

Windows Installer 3 has new technology to help roll back patches once installed. If you enable this policy, no one can remove software updates and patches once installed—not even an administrator. You might want to do this if your environment has special security requirements. That is, if, by unloading a patch, you might be putting the system and your company in harm's way, you might want to enable this setting. This will ensure that no one can uninstall installed patches.

If this policy setting is disabled, a user can remove updates from the computer if the user has been granted privileges to remove the update. This all depends on how the patch was deployed. Read the Explain text on this policy setting for more information.

This setting is valid only on machines that have Windows Installer 3.

Enforce Upgrade of Component Rules

Windows Installer 3 can be stricter about how applications allow themselves to be updated, via .MSP files, for example. That is, some .MSP files can perform some no-no's that could inadvertently render an application to malfunction once updated.

The Explain text of this policy setting describes two of these no-no's: when an .MSP changes the GUID of a function and when a new component is added in the wrong place of the `.MSI` tree. These have to do with the way an `.MSI` file is represented internally to the system. If these things are changed, the application could fail to function.

To that end, Enabling this policy setting forces the .MSI engine to ensure that certain safeguards are in place and that the .MSP file doesn't actually perform these no-no's.

If you disable this policy setting, Windows Installer is allowed to perform these no-no's.

This setting is valid only on machines that have Windows Installer 3.

Prohibit Nonadministrators from Applying Vendor Signed Updates

When a patch comes out from an application vendor, how do you want to handle it? Application vendors can come out with patches that only the administrator can install—or conversely, they can also come out with patches that theoretically even the user should be able to install. And these patches are digitally signed, so you can be sure that they're not really coming from Evil-Software, Inc. You can then allow the user to just patch their own applications, but this is likely fraught with peril.

However, this policy setting controls just that. If you Enable it, you're forcing only administrators to install updates that have been digitally signed by the application vendor.

If you disable this policy setting, mere-mortal users can install these nonadministrator updates without needed administrative access.

This setting is valid only on machines that have Windows Installer 3.

Baseline File Cache Maximum Size

Don't you just hate it when you're asked for the original installation media when an update is available? In theory, this is silly: The application is already installed on my hard drive, why on earth do I need the original media?

Well, with Windows Installer 3, this policy setting tries to help fix that. It sets the percentage of disk space available to the Windows Installer "baseline file cache." The idea is that you can have these required files hanging around, ready for whenever an update is ready to go. Then, when the original source is needed, it goes to the baseline file cache and doesn't ask for the original installation source.

If you enable this policy setting, you can then modify the maximum size of the Windows Installer baseline file cache. Note that if the baseline cache size is set to 0, Windows Installer cannot store new files. Previously stored files will stay in place (until the application that uses it is uninstalled), but new applications (if loaded in the future) cannot store information here. Windows Installer will stop populating the baseline cache for new updates. The existing cached files will remain on disk and will be deleted when the product is removed.

Setting the baseline cache to 100 means "Use as much space as you need!"

By default, 10 percent of the hard drive is used for this purpose. Disabling this policy setting forces the value at 10 percent.

This setting is valid only on machines that have Windows Installer 3.

Prohibit Use of Restart Manager

The Restart Manager is a very, very cool new addition to Windows Installer 4. The idea is that applications can basically save their currently open files, get upgraded, and then present the saved document in the newly upgraded program. I saw a demo of this and it blew my socks off. This policy setting controls the Restart Manager. Why you would want to turn this neat thing off is a mystery to me; so leave it on unless instructed not to.

This setting is valid only on machines that have Windows Installer 4 (like Windows Vista and Windows Server 2008, which have it installed by default).

Disable Logging via Package Settings

This is another Windows Installer 4-only feature. .MSI packages can choose to log their own actions if the property is turned on within the package.

With this policy setting, you can let that behavior stand, or turn it off.

Again, this setting is valid only on machines that have Windows Installer 4 (like Windows Vista, which has it installed by default).

User Side Policy Settings for Windows Installer

To display the Group Policy settings that affect the Windows Installer, as shown in Figure 4.33, choose User Configuration ➢ Policies ➢ Administrative Templates ➢ Windows Components ➢ Windows Installer. These settings affect the behavior of the users in the scope.

FIGURE 4.33   The Windows Installer user settings

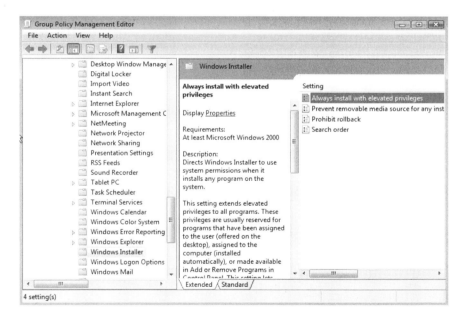

Always Install with Elevated Privileges

Enabling this policy setting allows users to manually install their own .MSI files and bypass their own insufficient and lowly user rights in order to correctly install applications. Some applications install correctly in the users' context, but many don't.

After you enable this setting, you'll also need to set the corresponding setting in the Computer half, as noted in the "Computer Side Policy Settings for Windows Installer" section.

Prevent Removable Media Source for Any Install

If you enable this setting, which works only for .MSI application, users cannot install applications under their own context from removable media. Rather, only administrators can install applications, or applications must be Published or Assigned for users to use them. This prevents users from running down to the computer store, obtaining the latest version of a program, and installing it via CD.

Prohibit Rollback

See the **Prohibit Rollback** policy setting in the "Computer Side Policy Settings for Windows Installer" section.

This setting is found in both User Configuration and Computer Configuration. Recall that computer settings have precedence over user settings.

Search Order

By default, applications that are Published or Assigned using the Windows Installer search their original location for updates or repairs. If that original location is not available, the application tries other locations.

This policy setting allows you to specify any or all of the following locations: Network, removable media, or URL (website).

 Real World Scenario

One for the Road—Leave Windows Installer and Group Policy Software Installation Data

Back in Chapter 2, we discussed a specific problem with regard to GPSI and roaming user profiles. That is, if you chose to enable the **Delete Cached Copies of Roaming Profiles** policy setting, the machine "cleans up" as a user logs off.

This has an unintended consequence with regard to GPSI.

Specifically, if the Roaming Profiles data is deleted at logoff time, the information regarding applications deployed via Group Policy Software Installation is also lost (by default). To that end, you should enable a new policy that affects users on Windows XP/SP2 (or Windows 2003/SP1) called **Leave Windows Installer and Group Policy Software Installation Data**, which addresses this. Once that policy is enabled, the Group Policy Software Installation data remains on the hard drive, so subsequent logins for users are much faster.

Again, enable this setting if you're also choosing to wipe the Roaming Profile away when the user logs out. Note that it is not a Windows Installer setting, per se, so it's located in a different area. Specifically, you'll find the policy you need at Administrative Templates ≻ System ≻ User Profiles ≻ **Leave Windows Installer and Group Policy Software Installation Data**.

If you're interested, this problem is specifically discussed in MSKB 828452 "An Assigned Package Is Reinstalled Every Time Clients Log on to the Domain."

Do You Need a "Big Management Tool" for Your Environment?

Microsoft's *SMS*, or *Systems Management Server*, is a big deal in corporations around the world. The newest iteration isn't called SMS 4, but rather, System Center Configuration Manager 2007, or SCCM 2007 for short. However, because I'm an old-school kind of guy, I'll just call it SMS in this brief discussion.

SMS costs an arm and a leg, has a thoroughly esoteric licensing scheme, and requires a client component on every Windows PC and server on your network. But, if you can get over these drawbacks, it houses a pretty amazing collection of core features:

- Software and Hardware Inventory
- Remote Control
- Software Metering
- Software Deployment
- Operating System Deployment
- Patch Management
- System Health Validation

Most of these features would be a welcome addition to any managed environment.

There are, of course, other management systems that don't ship from Microsoft. Companies like Altiris and LanDesk make their living selling similar tools. These all have one thing in common: more moving parts on your client and usually additional servers and components to move things around. They get the moniker of "Enterprise Management Systems" because they scale pretty well.

But what's also true about these tools is that they don't, fundamentally, use the Group Policy infrastructure that's already there. In other words, the "moving parts" to Group Policy are already installed on every client computer.

So, the question often comes up—do I need a "big" management tool if I'm already using Group Policy? To answer this question, we'll do a brief head-to-head comparison with, say, Microsoft SMS versus Stock Group Policy. However, when available, I'll also mention some third-party tools which hook right into Group Policy—leveraging the "moving parts" you already have deployed.

SMS vs. GPOs: A Comparison Rundown

Each feature of SMS is meant to chip away at that golden nugget of Total Cost of Ownership. I often get asked which has more power, SMS or Group Policy. Let's take a look at how SMS stacks up against the stuff we get in the box, that is, all the stuff we've looked at thus far.

Hardware and Software Inventory

Hardware inventory and software inventory are two critical elements that administrators need to keep in touch with what's currently out there in their environment. With this information in hand, they can rein in rogue installations of software and hardware.

Without SMS, once software is added via GPSI (or by hand or otherwise), there is no native way, using just Active Directory with GPSI, to really know who has installed what software. Although using GPSI to set up an OU, a package, and an Assignment is a pretty good yardstick for measuring what's out there, you're never certain until an actual inventory of the machine is performed.

No hardware or software inventory is built into Windows. You could build your own WMI scripts to pull out the hardware and software inventory data you want, but in doing so you'd go insane. So installing SMS would seem like a slam dunk.

It should be noted, though, that a nice pay tool is available that hooks into Group Policy to do this function. It's called Specops Inventory (`www.specopssoft.com`). So, if you wanted to do this function with Group Policy, it's now, basically, an even playing field. And, it can be argued that Hardware and Software Inventory is the most popular part of SMS, and it's not available a la carte: you have to buy the entirety of SMS to get this most requested feature. With a product like Specops Inventory, you're able to just buy the functionality you need.

Remote Control

The Remote Control feature is Microsoft's version of Symantec's pcAnywhere, but it is extremely lightweight and takes up almost no disk space. However, it could be argued that having a program such as SMS that specifically contains Remote Control is becoming less important. You can implement remote control on the cheap with various other options. In Windows 2000, you can use Netmeeting, which is workable, if not optimal. Or you can use the 100 percent–free multiplatform VNC from `www.realvnc.com`.

Additionally, Windows XP and Windows Vista have quite decent remote control built in via its Remote Assistance facilities. Oh, and Terminal Services has its own version of Remote Control called "shadowing."

So, although Remote Control is a great feature, it isn't as important as it used to be.

So, who wins in this category? SMS or "in the box"? It's a tie.

Software Metering

The Software Metering component has two methods of operation: Lock Out and Log Only.

Lock Out   This method (only available in SMS 2 and dropped from SMS 2003) is for strict license compliance. With this option, you can lock out users from applications if the number of licenses dries up across the environment. For example, if you purchased only 25 copies of DogFoodMaker 4.5, the 26th person cannot run it.

Log Only   This version doesn't lock users out of applications; rather, it simply logs the amount of copies in use. This is useful for gauging licensing compliance but not quite as intensive as the Lock Out method.

Without SMS, there is no way to gauge who's using what or to force users into compliance. Winner: SMS (if you really need this feature at all).

Operating System Deployment

Group Policy itself doesn't have operating system deployment as a feature. But, as we learned in Chapter 1, the Microsoft Deployment features handily perform that job.

And, while the process to kick-start an installation isn't 100 percent hands off, it's pretty close.

The SMS Operating System Deployment can hook into the Microsoft Deployment features to make the whole operation completely hands free. If this 100 percent hands-off capability is something you need, then the SMS (or SCCM) version is great.

But most people don't really need 100 percent hands-off deployment. They just need a way to make the process smooth. Is it smoother with or without 100 percent hands off?

That's debatable. But, if I had to pick a winner here, I'd say SMS because in the end analysis, if you needed 100 percent hands off, the only way to get it is via SMS.

That said, we also explored the Microsoft Deployment (formerly known as Business Desktop Deployment, or BDD) in Chapter 1. It might be just the free thing you need to ease the pain of deploying Windows clients and servers.

Software Deployment

The Software Deployment feature does overlap with the Active Directory feature of GPSI. As we explored in this chapter, Group Policy has a decent set of features when it comes to deploying software to clients.

In my first book, *Windows 2000 Group Policy, Profiles, and IntelliMirror*, I said that "SMS's Software Deployment features trounce the built-in features of Active Directory." I don't know if I would still agree with that. SMS does have quite a robust deployment mechanism, and one reason is that it can leverage the WMI query data to target to machines' CPU speeds, amount of RAM, BIOS revision, and so on. But we just did the same thing several pages ago with our Windows XP clients, so GPSI is certainly catching up!

Several facets of SMS software deployment are better than the GPSI. Specifically, SMS can do the following that GPSI cannot:

- Deploy software to users or computers any time of the day or night—not just on logon or reboot.

- Compress the application and send it to a distribution point close to the user. Even if we set up GPSI with DFS Namespaces, we cannot do this. However, the replication that DFS Namespaces uses, called *DFSR*, does have the superpower of only sending over the changed bytes if possible (and that's really sweet).

- Once a machine is targeted for a delivery and the package is received, the machine can send back detailed status messages describing success or failure of the transaction.

- Dribble the applications to clients over slow links without slowing down the connection. Only when the software is fully downloaded is the install initiated.

- Get detailed, central logs about which users or computers did or did not get the package.

And, SCCM loses an edge where it once had one. That is, SCCM 2007 can no longer target Windows 9*x* or Windows NT (but hopefully by now that's a small loss).

So, against Group Policy alone, SMS wins in this category. However, with a little elbow grease you can really get an amazing amount of mileage out of GPSI—even in really big environments. The big hit Group Policy takes in GPSI seems to be that the Office 2007 team really suggests that you don't use it for deploying their app. Again, for the gory details here, see the Real-World Scenario entitled "Installing and Customizing Office 2007 via GPSI."

However, those guys at Specops Software have another product which competes here, and, you guessed it—it hooks right into Group Policy. It's called Specops Deploy (www.specopssoft.com). And it overcomes some of the thorniest problems that Group Policy out of the box cannot solve. Specifically Specops Deploy can:

- Deploy .MSIs and .EXEs to client computers or users (where normal GPSI only targets .MSIs)
- Target based on time of day
- Deploy applications without requiring a reboot
- Use the "BITS" protocol to dribble applications to clients over slow links
- Give you detailed reports about which machines and users received the software and which ones don't

So, for SMS versus "naked" Group Policy, SMS wins.

But add a moderately priced third-party tool which hooks directly in to Group Policy, and it's a much closer horse race.

Health Management

SCCM 2007 comes with an enhanced way to work with NAP (Network Access Protection), which we talk about in Chapter 9.

You can read how it works here: http://tinyurl.com/ywv7nv.

I think it's a neat idea that there's some enhanced coverage to remediate unhealthy clients, but I'm not sure that there's sooo much extra value here that I'd want to use the SCCM 2007 + NAP solution over just NAP itself.

So, I'll give SMS the nod here, because, heck, sure, I like added protection too.

Patch Management

SMS also has decent patch management support, which is really just a customized extension of its Software Deployment feature. It's really, really good. You can target specific machines with specific patches. Once the patches are received, you can dictate how to react: wait for reboot, reboot now, and so on.

However, Microsoft has Windows Server Update Services (WSUS), found here: http://technet.microsoft.com/en-us/wsus/default.aspx. WSUS is pretty darned okay for most organizations, and it's in a very slick interface. WSUS is controlled by Group Policies on the client side—very neat indeed.

Winner? SMS, by some margin. But from WSUS 3.0 updating clients has never been easier: it has detailed feedback, a cool admin interface, computer groups, useful reports, and it's almost fun just sitting there controlling the patch level of your clients and servers. So, check it out in Chapter 8.

GPSI and SMS Coexistence

So, who wins?

If we're talking about SMS versus "naked" Group Policy, then, yes, I'm forced to admit it— SMS does have more raw power. However, I would argue that with a little finesse, you can squeeze quite a lot out of the desktop management tools you have come to learn about with Group Policy. And, add a third-party tool or two to Group Policy and you've got some serious competition—with a very lightweight back-end infrastructure.

Some organizations use either GPSI or a "big" management tool for software deployment. And some use both. Although no two organizations ever do anything exactly the same way, there does seem to be a general trend in those places where SMS and GPSI coexist.

In cases where using GPSI or SMS is a toss-up, GPSI is generally used to deploy smaller applications that need to be rapidly fired off due to document invocation. For example, if a user is sent an Adobe Acrobat .PDF file via e-mail but doesn't have the reader, double-clicking the document automatically installs the application on the machine.

SMS, on the other hand, is typically used to deploy larger applications, such as the Office suite, when you need definitive feedback about what went wrong (if anything). This philosophy provides a good balance between the "on demand" feel of GPSI and the "strategic targeted deployment" feel of SMS.

As you've seen, most of the features do not overlap, making a bigger management tool, like SMS, a solid addition to any medium or large environment. However, before you invest in a bigger management tool, be sure to check out the kinds of add-ons available that hook directly into Group Policy and can match the feature set. And, again, you can get those features a la carte instead of all-in-one as is only available in a bigger management tool.

Final Thoughts

In this chapter we inspected Software Installation using Group Policy, or just GPSI for short. GPSI works with Active Directory and Windows clients. Use Microsoft SMS (or another tool) for non–Windows 2000, Windows 2003, and Windows XP clients. Use WSUS for patch management because patches to Windows are not deployable using GPSI (more on this in Chapter 8).

In order to make the most of GPSI, you really need to leverage .MSI applications. You can either get .MSI applications from your software vendor, or wrap up your own with third-party tools (listed in this chapter and also in the companion book's Appendix and "Third-Party Group Policy Tools" on this book's website).

Share a folder on a server you want to send the package from. Plop the application in its own subfolder, and use both share and NTFS permissions to crank down who can read the executables and install files. Remember, though, that not all .MSI applications are ready to be deployed. Some are, indeed, ready-to-go (like the .NET Framework or Office 2007), others require an Administrative Installation (like Office 2003), and still others ship as .MSI files but cannot be deployed via GPSI (such as older versions of Adobe Acrobat Writer).

Once you have your package, you can Assign or Publish your applications.

Assign applications when you want application icons to appear on the Start ➤ All Programs menu; Publish applications when you want users to dive into the Add or Remove Programs folder or "Install a program from the network" for Windows Vista to get the application. You can leverage Microsoft Transform Files (.MST files) to hone an .MSI and customize it. (Though do note that Office 2007 doesn't use .MST files.) You can patch existing .MSI applications with Microsoft Patch Files (.MSP files), but afterward, you need to redeploy the application.

Try not to orphan applications by removing the GPO before the target computer gets the "signal" upon the next reboot (for computer) or logon (for user). If you think you might end up doing this, it's best to ensure that the "Uninstall this application when it falls out of the scope of management" check box is checked, as seen in Figure 4.16.

Use the material in Chapter 5 of the companion book (on creating WMI filters) to change the scope of management for when a GPO will apply. You can use WMI filters for any GPO you create—not just ones that leverage GPSI. However, the most common use for WMI filters is usually for GPOs that leverage GPSI. Don't forget that Windows 2000 clients don't honor WMI filters (the policy will just apply, no questions asked). Additionally, Windows XP, Windows 2003, Windows Vista, and Windows Server 2008 clients set to evaluate a WMI filter will take some extra processing time for each filter they need to work through. Be sure to test all your WMI filters in the test lab first.

Additionally, Darren Mar-Elia, on his GPOguy.com website, has a free tool called GPSIViewer that provides a nifty list view of all deployed applications in a domain and has some printout and .CSV reporting capability as well. Check it out at **www.gpoguy.com/gpsiviewer.htm**.

5

Application Virtualization and SoftGrid Essentials

Let me guess: Your users have been working, and things have been going great. Then, over time the machine starts to, oh...let's call it "deteriorate." You load more applications, and things get slower. You add a patch, and some applications start acting funny—things start crashing and users are rebooting more.

And you know why.

Because Windows doesn't do a really great job at isolating applications and keeping them from kicking each other in the shins. If you have DogFoodMaker 2.0 and CatFoodMaker 3.0 and they each use a DLL named FOOD.DLL, which application is going to use which file? And what if CatFoodMaker 3.0's DLL doesn't work quite right with DogFoodMaker 2.0?

Chaos and performance deterioration, that's what happens.

In this chapter, we're going to talk about something that I think is going to be really big, really soon: the realm of application virtualization. By now, almost everyone knows about Virtual PC, Virtual Server, and other VMware–style products. Their goal is to give you an entire "fake" PC inside your real PC. That way you can run additional computer instances (or "Guests" as some people call them). Application virtualization is awesome, and I use it all the time in the test lab and in my demonstrations.

But application virtualization is different. The goal is to give you your own *application sandbox* where your application runs, unbeknownst to the other applications on the system. So, even if Dog-FoodMaker 2.0 has its FOOD.DLL and CatFoodMaker 3.0 has its FOOD.DLL, there's never a conflict. They each cheerfully run in their own sandbox, unaware of each other.

But, before we get going, I need to start off with the bad news: In order to use the stuff we're going to talk about in this chapter, you have to pay Microsoft. That's right. Everything else in this book we'll be going over is free. That is, if you define *free* as the stuff that's in the box when you buy Windows and spin up an Active Directory, install your Windows clients, and pay for regular licensing, and so on. In this chapter we're going to talk about a Microsoft tool called SoftGrid—and it's a really cool tool. Which is why Microsoft is making you pay extra for it. But, before we go too far down the road, how do you get this tool?

Some readers might know that SoftGrid was recently renamed Microsoft Application Virtualization (MSAppVirt). Most people will continue to use SoftGrid for some time. MSAppVirt won't even be out of beta until Summer 2008. So we opted to talk about the current software, and we hope to have some updates available when MSAppVirt is a reality. In upcoming chapters, we express where we think things might change in the upcoming MSAppVirt 4.5.

First, you positively *must* be a Microsoft Software Assurance (SA) customer. This means you pay a little extra insurance money up front, hoping that Microsoft produces updates that you want to install. The misconception is that SA customers must be large companies. They don't have to be. You can be an SA customer with as few as 50 seats. You can learn more about becoming an SA customer here: www.microsoft.com/licensing/sa/.

Next, you must be willing to buy SoftGrid in a pack of five big products which are bundled as the Microsoft Desktop Optimization Pack (MDOP) for about 10 dollars per seat. People who pay *now* get the benefit of using these tools right away.

Perhaps some time in the future, Microsoft might remove one of these tools from MDOP, like SoftGrid, and make it available in some other manner. Maybe they'll make it available to all Microsoft customers, not just SA customers. In any case, if you want to learn more about the three other tools in the MDOP package, check them out here: www.microsoft.com/windows/products/windowsvista/enterprise/mdopoverview.mspx (shortened to http://tinyurl.com/2j38g2). You might also see Chapter 10 of my companion book, *Group Policy Fundamentals, Troubleshooting, and Security*, where one of the tools, Advanced Group Policy Management (AGPM), is described. And even then there are three more cool tools in that package.

But we're going to break apart one (big) piece of the MDOP in the next several chapters. That is, the idea of application virtualization. Sure, you already know what virtualization is; but we're gonna scramble your brain and show you what the next generation of virtualization looks like (from Microsoft no less!).

About Application Virtualization

In the introduction we talked about one problem—well, two problems really. We talked about the idea that Windows deteriorates over time, when multiple applications are loaded on the machine.

And, we also talked about how different applications could be trying to use .DLLs with the same name. These are big problems, but there are other big problems application virtualization can solve, as well.

Why Would We Need Application Virtualization?

So, without further ado, let's examine some of the additional problems that Application Virtualization solves:

App1 and App1A on the Same Machine   Similar to the DLL issue we've explored already, this is a case where a user needs to have both DogFoodMaker 2.0 and DogFoodMaker 2.2 on the same machine. Each application has a *slightly* different feature set, and the user needs both.

Except there are a few problems.

- The first problem might be that you can't load both instances of DogFoodMaker on the same machine. The installer for DogFoodMaker 2.2 wants to upgrade DogFoodMaker 2.0, and that's not what you want. You want to run them side by side. Except you can't, because the installer won't let you.

- The second problem might be that even if you can successfully install them side by side, one or both applications flip out because they share a common DLL. This situation is common for applications like Office 2000, 2003, 2007, as well as Java Runtime Environments. These applications don't really like different editions being loaded on the same box, even if there's a business case for it.

App1 and App1A on the Same Terminal Server   This issue is equally relevant for Terminal and Citrix servers. Historically, you've had to install different flavors of applications on different Terminal and Citrix servers for exactly the same reason I just described. Actually, the problems with Terminal Services and Citrix could even be worse because of things like shared .INI files, or locks on common files which might prevent one application from working properly. Additionally, some applications write to HKEY_LOCAL_MACHINE (which usually affects everyone on the machine) instead of the one user who needs to use that application. So, one user makes a small change to the application's settings, and that change can potentially affect everyone who uses that same application.

Installations of Software Affect Other Areas   This might sound like variations on a theme, but this problem is subtly different. Let's say you want to deploy a new application to a bunch of users. Except there's some mistake in that installation that deletes some key file or otherwise adversely affects the applications. Even if you remove that test application, the damage is done, and you've got to figure out how to keep that damaged box alive.

General Creeping Crud   What are some symptoms of the creeping crud? For no specific reason, Windows Explorer windows take longer to open. Or Internet Explorer hangs. Or an application that took 3 seconds to load takes 35 seconds to load. This happens because some application auto-updates itself with a file, or Windows gets populated with programs that affect what happens when you right-click items. Figure 5.1 shows my real machine—the one I do most of my work on—and when it runs slowly, I really have no one else to blame for that but me. And you can see why. I load tons of junk, er, applications which I think will help me do my job better. But we all know the fastest Windows system is the one that's freshly installed and has the fewest number of applications.

FIGURE 5.1   This is Jeremy's real machine. What a mess.

How Does Application Virtualization Solve the Aforementioned Problems?

Let's analyze that last sentence in the previous section:

> ...the fastest Windows system is the one that's freshly installed and has the fewest number of applications.

If only it were possible to run Windows and nothing else. If we could all just get by with Notepad to do our jobs, we wouldn't have to worry too much about Windows crashing, applications hanging, and drivers failing.

But we don't have that luxury. We *have* to install and run applications to really do anything with Windows. If only there were a way to have the freshly installed Windows system and *run* the applications without actually *installing* them.

That's what Application Virtualization does. Application Virtualization provides a sandbox for the application to run in. It's never really installed. I'll let that sink in for a second. The application that you're running on your Windows box isn't actually ever *installed* within Windows—even though it's *running* on Windows.

 Sandbox isn't a term all application virtualization solutions use when they talk about what they provide, though some, like Thinstall, do use the term sandbox specifically. I like the term sandbox and will continue to use it generally, even when talking about SoftGrid.

So, let's take another look at each problem, and see where Application Virtualization comes to the rescue.

App1 and App1A on the Same Machine   Instead of installing applications side by side on the same machine, the applications run in their own sandboxes, side by side on the same machine. That way, they never see either other's DLLs and there are no conflicts.

App1 and App1A on the Same Terminal Server   Since the applications are now running in their own sandbox, you see two huge improvements where Terminal Services/Citrix servers are involved:

- First, you can immediately reduce the number of Terminal Servers if you had to add more just to run conflicting applications.

- And second, since each application runs in its own sandbox, you don't have to worry about one user's preferences suddenly affecting all users on the machine. Again, each application runs in its own sandbox, isolating each application, but also isolating every user who uses that same application.

Installations of Software Affect Other Areas   Making a mistake during a deployment to dozens or hundreds of machines doesn't have consequences anymore. Since the application runs in a sandbox (and is never really installed on the machine), it's a cake walk to roll back that deployment. Then, just fix the application's issue (missing file, misconfiguration, etc.) then redeploy.

General Creeping Crud   Because applications aren't really installed on Windows, just running in the sandbox, the creeping crud problem goes away. Applications can share data (depending on the application virtualization solution), but that doesn't mean they actually interact with each other. If applications aren't really installed, they won't slow you down. It'll feel like a fresh install every day of the week.

How Does Application Virtualization Work?

Each vendor that provides application virtualization does so in a slightly different way, but generically, there are three parts to application virtualization:

Application Virtualization Agent or Client   Most application virtualization solutions require an agent or client. This is the sandbox I keep talking about. The applications you want to run in the sandbox will be called by the agent, but then the actual application really does run on Windows. You will see the launched application running in the Task Manager. It's running, but never installed.

Application Sequencing   This is the act of taking an existing application and putting it though a process which enables the agent or client to run it. You'll see how to sequence a simple package in this chapter.

Housing and Running the Application   Most application virtualization solutions have some sort of central storage or server-side component to serve up the application when the user wants to run it. Just click the icon on the Start Menu or Desktop and watch the application come down to the Desktop.

Good and Bad Applications to Virtualize

Not everything is an optimal application to virtualize. Indeed, ultimately, you'll have to make some decisions about which items you can and should virtualize and which things you'll still need to install directly within Windows.

Applications which are "normal" are good candidates. Common applications such as Office, WinZip, and Quicken are excellent candidates for application virtualization. (Though I do point to some documentation for how to best virtualize Office in the next chapter in the "Sequence Troubleshooting" section.") But here's a list of items which you'll likely not want to virtualize; in other words, installing them directly within Windows is a better option:

Drivers   Anything that needs direct access to the hardware. So, printer drivers are a poor choice, as well as anything that produces a "phony" printer driver. (There might be some workarounds in those instances, or that particular function may not be available when running with application virtualization.)

"Helper" Applications for Hardware   Some Print/Scan/Fax Multifunction devices have drivers, and they usually also have Helper applications (to send faxes, scan, etc.). Even though these aren't exactly drivers, they do touch the hardware, and might not be a great choice to wrap up as an application to virtualize.

Operating System Hotfixes   You'll want to load these directly within Windows. 'Nuff said.

Internet Explorer Versions   Some application virtualization solutions (like Thinstall) do a good job at wrapping up older Internet Explorer editions for use on the same machine. But some application virtualization solutions might have issues wrapping up IE. If you positively must repackage IE for some reason, ask your application virtualization vendor for guidance.

Antivirus Software or Other Filter Drivers Filter drivers are gateways between the operating system and the file system. Virtualizing them usually won't work.

Services Some application virtualization solutions can virtualize applications that run with services, but others cannot. Check your application virtualization solution to see if this is supported. (This is usually supported with SoftGrid.)

In SoftGrid, boot-time services are usually not virtualizable. Check out this blog post for some guidance on what kinds of applications can be virtualized: http://tinyurl.com/2pnm36.

Who Makes Application Virtualization Solutions?

Again, application virtualization is going to be hot, hot, hot because it solves so many interesting little problems. As a result, multiple vendors are creating their own application virtualization solutions. Here's a list of the players and a little about them.

Microsoft SoftGrid This is the one we'll be specifically exploring in this chapter. Again, you can only get it if you're an SA customer (www.Microsoft.com/SoftGrid) and pony up 10 dollars a seat for the whole MDOP package.

Altiris, oops, Symantec SVS (Software Virtualization Solution) Altiris has two solutions; one is paid and the other is a free solution for "personal, noncommercial use." So, if you're like me and have a laptop full of junk but want a free solution to keep it feeling spring-clean fresh, the Altiris SVS solution is a good deal. The free SVS download page is found here: www.altiris.com/Download/svsPersonal.aspx; the general product information can be found here: www.altiris.com/svs.

Citrix Applications Virtualization Citrix's implementation is mostly geared toward use on their own Citrix servers. The idea is to consolidate the number of Citrix servers you have, because you can eliminate application conflicts that occur when different applications are loaded on the same server. Learn more about it here: http://tinyurl.com/22detu.

Thinstall/VMware Thinstall, now owned by VMware, is the only solution where the agent is packaged along with the sequenced application. So, instead of deploying an agent first, then getting the sequenced application on the target machine second, you do it in one step. That way, you can just e-mail someone an .EXE file and they've got the whole virtualized application—ready to rock.

You might be wondering why I don't list VMware Workstation or Server, Microsoft, again, with their Virtual Server product). That's because those packages don't work the same way. Those are system virtualization solutions. When you press Start on one of those, they beep, count fake RAM, access a fake disk, and boot a whole operating system. That's not what the technology we're going to describe does.

If you haven't settled on Microsoft SoftGrid (the rest of what this chapter is going to focus on), then I would encourage you to check out all the options listed here. Each one has something a little different to offer, so checking them all out and making an informed decision is the way to go. One enterprising geek, Ruben Spruijt, put together a really amazing matrix of all the application virtualization solutions. You can check it out here: `http://tinyurl.com/2c5wyz`.

SoftGrid Architecture and Server-Side Installation

SoftGrid is a big application with lots of functionality. First we'll go over the components of Soft-Grid, then we'll cover the installation of the server components. But even then, all we've done is spin up a new server with a whole lot of nothing going on. It's going to take the next big section "Installing and Using the SoftGrid Client" to sling out our first application to our clients. Well, sling isn't a technical term. The proper term is *stream*.

So, settle in for a long haul, dear reader—it's going to be a while before we see the fruits of our labor.

SoftGrid Components and Requirements

One of the nice things about SoftGrid is that it isn't too terribly complex. While there are some moving parts that make the magic happen, it isn't too difficult to understand the parts and their interactions.

Right now, we're going to assume a simple SoftGrid deployment. There are lots and lots of advanced configurations possible with SoftGrid. My goal is to simply jumpstart your SoftGrid exposure and get you started with the tool. We'll talk a little later about getting advice and help with advanced SoftGrid configuration and deployment.

Active Directory   Active Directory is the backbone of SoftGrid. This is because Active Directory group membership is in charge of determining who is to receive which applications. Note that Group Policy is not involved at this stage. You don't use Group Policy to deploy SoftGrid applications natively. We'll see a little later how Group Policy is involved; but for now, keep in mind that normal Active Directory/NT–style group membership dictates who receives which applications.

SoftGrid Data Store   This is SQL Server. Indeed, this can be SQL Server Express to a fully clustered SQL Server enterprise server. Because this chapter is titled "SoftGrid Essentials," we're not going to be overly concerned with sizing of SQL Server.

However, in nice, round numbers, you only need to allocate about 1MB of space per 100 applications you want to deploy using SoftGrid and about 1KB of space per SoftGrid transaction (deploying, shutting down, and metering an application). So, in short, the SQL data store doesn't really need to be a rocket ship and, yes, it can certainly be housed along with other SQL databases without much fuss. Clustering your SQL server is a decent idea if you want to avoid single points of failure on your network.

SoftGrid SVAS Service   This is the actual service which regulates SoftGrid. Its proper name is Microsoft System Center Virtual Application service, but that's such a mouthful, that "the SoftGrid service" or "the SVAS service" is typically what it's called. This service interfaces with IIS, which, for speed's sake, should be loaded on the same box (at least in our sample environment).

If you want some guidance on planning for the size of the SVAC server, assume that a dual processor machine with 2GB of RAM can handle about 1,400 concurrent users or so (or 40 Terminal Servers, if you want to go that route), as long as the NIC is a gigabit Ethernet. In short, the SVAC isn't really a processor-intensive application. TechNet has a guide for server sizing about a third of the way down the following page: `http://technet.microsoft.com/en-us/library/bb608286.aspx` (shortened to `http://tinyurl.com/3aphtt`).

It's best to have the SVAC on a separate server than the SoftGrid Data Store (SQL) box because you likely already have a SQL box doing SQL things. But in our tests, we're going to make an all-in-one box.

SoftGrid Client   This is the piece that must be on every Windows XP or Windows Vista client you want to stream applications to. You can load each individual client by hand, or deploy them using (insert fanfare music here) Group Policy with Group Policy Software Installation. We'll perform this step later.

SoftGrid Files and Theory FAQ

Before we get too far along, let's be sure to take a moment to understand the "moving parts" of SoftGrid along with some of the theory about its workings. Here's a little FAQ about what's going on.

What Exactly Are We Running?

On a normal Windows environment, you install .MSI files (then run their contents); a SoftGrid Client runs something that feels similar to an .MSI file, called a *sequenced application*. Later in this chapter, we're going to create our own sequences with applications you already have, so stay tuned.

What Exactly Is Doing the Running?

Recall that SoftGrid applications aren't installed. Yet they actively *run* on the machine. How does this happen? This is the job of the SoftGrid Client. You'll learn how to load this a little later. This client (or agent) needs to be present on every machine that you want to participate in the SoftGrid system. This little application is loaded on Windows and calls the application that needs to be streamed from the SoftGrid server. This is really all that's genuinely "installed" on the client system.

What's Faster: Sequenced Apps or Installed MSIs?

A sequenced application is broken down into two *feature blocks* (or *chunks* as I like to call 'em). Here's the idea: If a user has never yet launched an application, the first chunk gets brought down. That first chunk is enough to get the application running. But what if a user wants to actually use the application, instead of just looking at it? No problem, additional chunks are brought down on demand.

But an MSI application deployed via Group Policy feels similar. Indeed, when you deploy (Assign) an application to users, the whole enchilada isn't brought down. Users need to request .MSI components and features as they need them. However, if you deploy an .MSI via Group Policy to computers, usually the whole thing is preinstalled.

So, in the end, I would say that .MSI applications installed to computers are the fastest (because they're 100 percent preinstalled for all users on the machine). But then it's about the same for both SoftGrid streamed applications or applications deployed to users via GPSI.

What, Exactly, Is Sequenced?

Just about everything. Here's a list of things that will be wrapped up into a sequence. (We'll be going over sequencing a little later in detail in the "SoftGrid Sequencing" section).

- Files (including System files)
- Registry
- Fonts
- .INI files
- COM/DCOM objects
- Services
- Namespaces
- Semaphores, Mutexes (programming constructs and details that admins don't much see)

Files are stored in what's known as the *Virtual File Store* or *VFS*. Registry data is stored in what's known as the *Virtual Registry*.

Where Is It Stored on the Client?

When any application is streamed down, the application's chunks are stored in a single file. Actually *all* streamed apps are stored in the same file, the sftfs.fsd file. That file is located in the All Users ➤ Shared Documents folder under SoftGrid Client. The more you stream, the bigger that file gets.

What if I'm Working Offline?

This isn't a problem. The client has a cache in it to maintain applications you already use. The default is 2GB, which might not be enough for you (though it's configurable).

What If I Need More Application Features on the Road?

So, if you're on the road and want to use more of an application, what happens if something isn't in the cache? Sounds like you might have found a hitch.

If you're on the road and want to use, say, the spell checker feature, but you have never used it before, you could have a little problem. Well, a big problem. In fact, depending on the application, you could receive a terse message telling you that you have two minutes to close your application or it will shut down. Ouch, harsh!

There are some ways to avoid this problem:

- You can ask your users to try to use all the functionality in the office before they go on the road.

- There is a command-line switch you can specify (we'll talk about it later) which will command the client to try to force a particular application (or all applications) into the cache before they take off for their trip. There's no reason why you couldn't use a Group Policy script (logoff, shutdown) to force this to occur under certain creative conditions. For instance, you could generate a shutdown script which asks users which applications they want to take on the road with them, but that's an exercise beyond the scope of this book, so I leave that to you, dear reader.

- There's a way to configure the SoftGrid Client (SoftGrid Client 4.2.1) to work in *Offline mode*. Then, you can specially deploy sequences using .MSI applications which can force 100 percent of the application into the cache. This is likely the best way, and we'll see how to do this in the section "Using an .*MSI* Package to Deliver SoftGrid Applications (via Group Policy and Other Methods)."

Can Multiple Users Customize the Same Application?

Let's say that in DogFoodMaker, Sally decides to change the spelling error color to green from the default of blue. When she restarts that application, she'll get the green color. How does that happen? Here's the geeky explanation.

On launch, a folder is created in Sally's *%appdata%*\SoftGrid Client directory. The folder is named after the specific application. So, you might see something that looks like dfmaker.v1-12345678-1234-1234.

The first time Sally launches this application, there isn't anything in the folder. When she changes her color preferences and then closes the application, a new file is written to this location. Here's what weird: The filename is *exactly* the same for every app: UsrVol_sftfs_pkg.v1.

That is the preference file for Sally for that application. When Sally launches the application again, her preference file should be read, and her color preferences should appear.

What if Fred uses the same machine with the same streamed application but wants to use the color teal? He gets his own UsrVol_sftfs_pkg.v1—but of course this lives in Fred's profile. So, there's never any conflict between the two.

Can SoftGrid Applications' Settings Be Managed Using Group Policy?

The short answer is maybe. It depends on if the application is "Group Policy aware." Recall that that there are "proper" Group Policy Policies keys (blue dot/scroll icon) and "improper/preference" keys.

If your application is coded to look at the proper Group Policy keys for setup information (like Microsoft Office is, for instance) a special exception is made to honor "real" Group Policy over the preferences inside the application. So, the Microsoft Office ADM and ADM templates will work against a sequenced SoftGrid Microsoft Office, because Microsoft Office knows how to properly use the Policies keys and the SoftGrid Client knows to look in those Policies keys for authoritative configuration information.

But if your application isn't coded to look in the proper Group Policy keys (for instance, Adobe Acrobat Reader will not), then even creating an ADM or ADMX template to modify the target application will not work, because the application is only looking within the virtual Registry, not the real Registry, which is being modified by a Group Policy ADM or ADMX file.

Is There an Alternative to Using an ADM or ADMX File?

So, if my sequenced application can't be controlled via Group Policy using an ADM or ADMX file, is there an alternative? Yes. PolicyPak software (`www.PolicyPak.com`) will "punch in" values to your existing sequenced application using its PolicyPak CSE. This feature is only available in PolicyPak Professional and not in the free version.

Full disclosure: The author, Jeremy Moskowitz, is a primary partner in PolicyPak.

What Are the Four "Golden File Types" in SoftGrid?

We're going to get to the heart of sequencing an application, then you'll learn more about these four golden file types in the "SoftGrid Sequencing" section.

One of the great things about SoftGrid is that it ships with a default sample application (to help us make sure it's working), and that sample application, as well as any other application we want to use with SoftGrid, has to be sequenced.

During sequencing four files are produced:

ICO file   This is the icon file which users click to kick off the application.

OSD file   OSD stands for Open Software Description. This file houses information about the "meat" of the file without being the meat itself. The OSD file describes, among other things, which operating systems this particular application can be used on, the path to the .SFT file, and lots more, so be sure to read the next chapter for more information.

SFT   This is the Softricity file (the name of the company which produced SoftGrid, which was bought out by Microsoft). This is the meat of the file. This contains both feature blocks. FB1 (Feature Block 1) is the first chunk that gets downloaded by the client system. This gets the application started. FB2 (Feature Block 2) is the rest of the application which is streamed on demand to the client in 32KB chunks, by default. This is the recommended setting, but there are other options. By default, only what's requested is sent. So, if you never use the spell checker in, say, Word 2007, you don't download that chunk.

SPRJ   SPRJ is the Sequencer Project file. Really it's short for *Softricity Project*, but since it's really only used for the Sequencer, I'll keep calling it the Sequencer Project file. We'll explore the SoftGrid Sequencer application, which takes our existing applications and turns them into sequenced applications. The SPRJ file is the result of the sequence. If you ever needed to tweak an existing application, the Sequencer application would need this SPRJ file to reopen the project.

What's With the Drive Letter Q, and Why Do I Need to Give My Sequences 8.3 Names?

When we create our SoftGrid sequencing station, you'll see that we specifically need two partitions on our hard drive (or two hard drives): our C: drive and our Q: drive. And when we create our sequenced applications, we'll need to give them unique old-school 8.3 filenames.

Sounds a little crazy, right? So, the short answers are that:

- Q: helps you "trap" more stuff when you're doing sequences.

- Using 8.3 names ensures that you don't have collisions in the name if you try to run multiple, similar packages.

You can get long answers here (both in one place): `http://tinyurl.com/2hbdlh`. Be warned, it's a geeky post by the SoftGrid team.

Another post, here, `http://tinyurl.com/yrzmpw`, explains how you can prevent the Q: drive from showing up on your users' Desktops. And, guess what? It's Group Policy to the rescue in order to do it.

WARNING The Q: drive letter should be free and not used as, say, the Homedir map or anything else. And if it is, you should either change the current use of the Q: drive on the network (so it's not used anymore) or change the SoftGrid drive letter.

SoftGrid Accounts and Shares

There are various user and group accounts you'll need to create and then configure to make a SoftGrid deployment possible. If you're working through the exercises with me, then go ahead and create these accounts in Active Directory now, so you'll have them ready to go when we spin up the SoftGrid server.

SoftGrid Browser Account   This can be any regular ol' user in Active Directory. I like to call mine sgBrowser (with the display name of SoftGrid Browser), but you could call him Joe if you want. It doesn't matter; it just has to be a simple User account. The idea is that you need at least one Active Directory user for the SoftGrid Client to leverage in order to browse Active Directory to see Group membership. I also suggest you configure this account such that the password never expires.

SoftGrid Managers   These are the people who have the rights to "do stuff" with SoftGrid. This should be a regular Active Directory group. You may or may not choose to put the Domain Administrator account in here (that's up to you). But the users you specify within this group will be able to make major decisions about the SoftGrid system. In my example, I've called it sgManagers. In my testing, I like to put the Domain Administrator account in here. This will enable us to start managing the SoftGrid system right away, using an account we already have.

SoftGrid Users   This is a group containing all users who will ever utilize any applications using the SoftGrid system. Heck, your environment might be such that you eventually want everyone to be able to access applications using SoftGrid. In that case, you can simply plunk Domain Users into your (newly created) SoftGrid Users account and never think about it again. Or, if you want more finely grained control, you can plunk in specific groups (like the Human Resources group), or just individual users. But, if your user isn't part of this group (or a member of a group that's a part of this group), SoftGrid will simply stop working for that user.

In my example, I've called it sgUsers. In my testing, I like to put the Domain Administrator account in here. Hey, the Administrator is a user too, and when we use our first SoftGrid Client, we'll already have a user in the sgUsers group, making our testing go smoothly.

Specific Group for a Specific SoftGrid Application   You'll want to set up a specific Active Directory group for each application you want to stream using SoftGrid. In our tests, we're going to (eventually) stream Adobe Acrobat Reader. So, at this point, let's go ahead and create a group so that when users are in this group, they'll be destined to get Adobe Acrobat Reader. In my tests, I've called this group sgAcroReaders and you can see it in Figure 5.2. As I mentioned, I also like to put the Domain Administrator account in here. This will enable at least one user to see the application—once it's ready to go.

FIGURE 5.2   SoftGrid requires groups for access, including specific groups for each application.

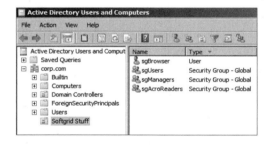

Shared Directory for SoftGrid Content   You'll need to share a directory on your server (or in alternate configurations, another server) which houses the applications you want to stream. You'll provide this directory during installation. For now, keep it on your SoftGrid server. In my examples, I'll create a directory on my server called C:\sgContent and share it with the same name (that is, a share named sgContent). The share should be available as Everyone:Read, but you can configure NTFS permissions so that, say, only Administrators can write to it.

Installing SoftGrid Server

We don't have unlimited page count (not even in the downloadable eChapter edition of this chapter). With that in mind, I'm going to make some assumptions before we continue. We've already discussed how there are several moving parts to SoftGrid: SQL server and IIS, and of course, the SoftGrid SVAS service. We're going to put all these moving parts on one box to make our world as simple as possible.

But, you're going to have to do some legwork (on your own) to prepare for our tests. To follow along from this point forward, you're going to need to install SoftGrid server somewhere.

You can choose to install it on your Domain Controller (if you're strapped for test machines), but you might also want to consider spinning up a new server and loading the components on there.

Installing SoftGrid on a Windows Server 2003 Machine

If the machine is a Windows Server 2003 machine, you'll first need to load the following components:

IIS 6.0   This is found within Add/Remove Programs in Windows Components.

ASP.Net server   This is a subcomponent of IIS 6.0. Be sure to load it at the same time as IIS 6.0.

MMC 3.0   You must download this update and install it on your server and anywhere else you want to manage SoftGrid from. That installation can be found here: `http://support.microsoft.com/kb/907265`.

.NET 2.0   Again, you must download this update and install it on your server and anywhere else you want to manage SoftGrid from. It can be found here: `http://tinyurl.com/758p8`.

If you don't install these extra components, you'll get prompted during the SoftGrid installation. Then, you'll have to stop the installation, load these components anyway, and restart the installation. So, just go ahead and do it now to save yourself some hassle.

Installing SoftGrid on a Windows Server 2008 Machine

If the machine is a Windows Server 2008 machine, my understanding is that you'll first need to load the following components. You do these steps within Windows Server 2008's new Server Manager tool.

IIS 7.0   This is found within the Select Server Roles Wizard.

.NET 3.0   You'll find this component within the Role Application Server.

At the time of this writing the SoftGrid server did not run on Windows Server 2008. A new upgrade or fix should be available soon.

Performing the SoftGrid Server Installation

The SoftGrid server installation (as well as the other components of MDOP) are located on the MDOP media Microsoft provided to you. To start, click SoftGrid Application Virtualization as seen in Figure 5.3.

Then, on the next screen, click Install the Microsoft System Center Virtual Application Server icon as seen in Figure 5.4.

FIGURE 5.3   This is the main screen for MDOP. Choose SoftGrid Application Virtualization.

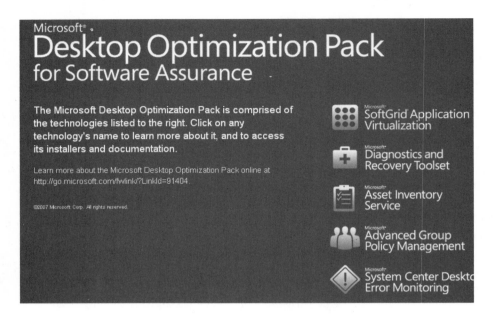

FIGURE 5.4   You can install SoftGrid components from this screen.

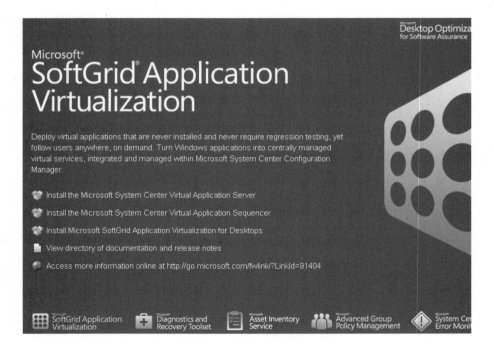

When you do, the server installation will be kicked off. There are a lot of screens to the Soft-Grid server installation, so we'll go over all of them, but we won't "screenshot you to death" with every page of the installation wizard.

1. In the Welcome Screen, click Next to get started.

2. In the License Agreement screen, click the "I accept" button, then Next when you're ready.

3. Enter a username (not specifically related to an Active Directory user account) and Organization name (not specifically related to an OU) in the Customer Information screen. Click Next when you're ready.

4. For set up type, you can click Typical or Custom. I suggest you select Custom and also install the component not installed by default—that would be the SoftGrid Client Management Console option. You can also change the default installation location for SoftGrid here, as well. Note that this isn't the location where you'll be storing the applications you'll be streaming to the clients. That selection is coming up.

5. In the Database Server screen, you are prompted to install the in-the-box MSDE, or connect to an available database. I'm going to choose to install MSDE, but in production, you'll likely want to use an existing SQL server.

6. If you selected MSDE, you'll have to provide an MSDE administrator and an initial SoftGrid user account password. In my tests, I use my favorite password "p@ssw0rd." (that's an at sign and a zero). You can see this screen in Figure 5.5.

7. In the Directory Server screen, seen in Figure 5.6, you'll enter the credentials for the sgBrowser account you created earlier. Again, this can be any user account in Active Directory.

8. The Administrator Group screen, seen in Figure 5.7, is asking for the sgManagers group you created earlier. Again, this can be any group you like, just know that these people will have the maximum authority within the SoftGrid system.

FIGURE 5.5   Here's where you can enter MSDE account information.

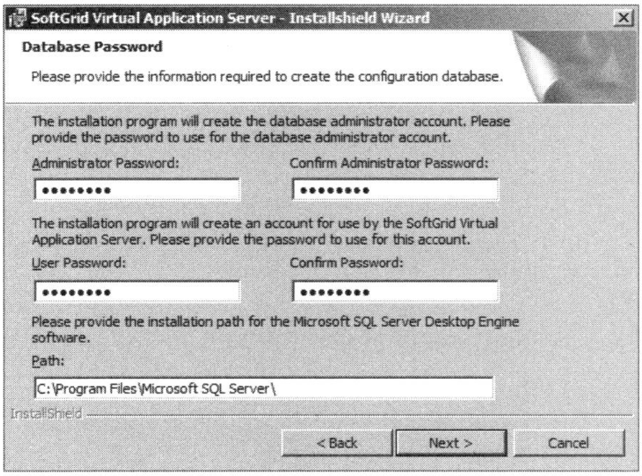

FIGURE 5.6 Enter in your directory information. The sgBrowser account is just a regular account to perform Active Directory lookups.

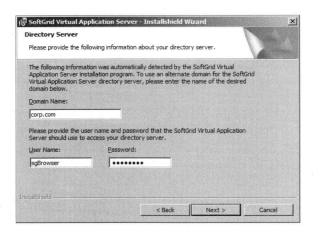

FIGURE 5.7 sgManagers is the group name I'm using to provide access to modify SoftGrid.

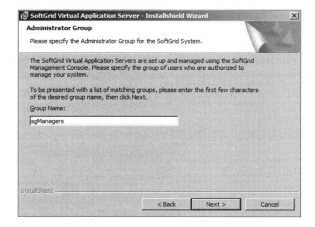

9. The Default Provider Group screen, seen in Figure 5.8, is asking for the sgUsers group you previously created. This group will be the people who are simply allowed to use the SoftGrid system. A little later, once SoftGrid is all set up, you'll specify who has access to each application.

10. SoftGrid can be set up into multiple groups for easy management of multiple servers. We're not going to leverage this feature now, so the default of Default Server Group will be just fine for our first server.

11. The Content Path screen, seen in Figure 5.9, is asking where you want to store the applications you'll be streaming to your clients. The suggested default is buried down in `C:\Program Files\Softricity\SoftGrid Server\content`.

I suggest you change it to something simple, like `C:\sgContent` (or a D: drive, etc.). The directory must exist before you continue past this screen, but you can just use Windows Explorer to create the directory, and then continue.

12. At this point, just click Install and sit back. Again, at the time of this writing the RTM edition of SoftGrid that ships in the box with MDOP cannot install directly on a Windows Server 2008 server. An update to the installation should be available soon.

Congrats. You've got a SoftGrid up and running. Now, let's take this baby for a spin.

FIGURE 5.8 sgUsers is the group that controls access to SoftGrid use.

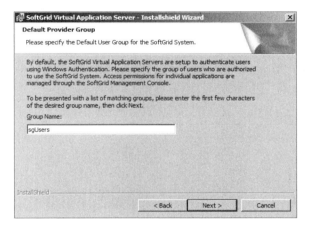

FIGURE 5.9 Change the content path to C:\sgContent (or another location where you want to share the applications).

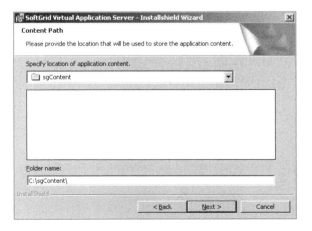

Launching the SoftGrid Console for the First Time

At this point, SoftGrid is installed, and you're ready to get started using it. The console icon is located in Start ≻ Programs ≻ Administrative Tools ≻ SoftGrid Management Console. When it's launched, you still need to tell it what server to connect to (even if you're currently using that machine).

To do that, perform the following steps:

1. Right-click over the SoftGrid Systems node, and select Connect to SoftGrid System as seen in Figure 5.10.

FIGURE 5.10 Connecting to the SoftGrid system via the console.

2. At this point, you can enter the actual name of the SoftGrid server, or the word localhost as seen in Figure 5.11, and click OK. If you get an error like the one shown in Figure 5.12, don't panic. One of two things is wrong: either you're not logged in as a member of the sgManagers group, or you are logged in as a member of the sgManagers group but the system doesn't know it yet.

FIGURE 5.11 Use localhost or the actual SoftGrid server name to access the console.

FIGURE 5.12 Don't panic if you are not immediately authorized for access.

3. Be sure you're logged in with an account that's a member of the sgManagers group, as seen in Figure 5.13.

FIGURE 5.13 Put the administrators you trust in the sgManagers group.

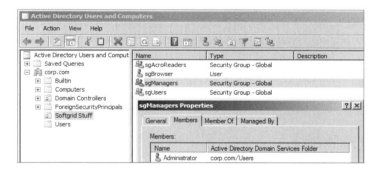

4. You may need to log out and log back in (to pick up the new group membership change). Or alternately, when presented with the Login screen (as seen in Figure 5.11), you can select the Specify Windows Account button and manually enter in a user's information, provided the user is contained within the sgManager group (like the Administrator account you just added).

At this point you should be able to see the SoftGrid console as seen in Figure 5.14.

FIGURE 5.14 The SoftGrid console once you're logged on.

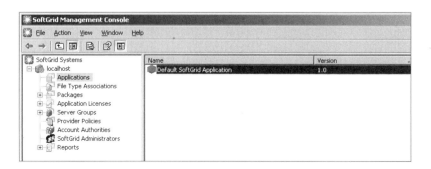

Configuring the Sample SoftGrid Application

SoftGrid ships with a dummy test application. It doesn't do anything; but you will know your client and server are talking correctly when the application launches. Except that even right out of the box, the sample application isn't correctly configured.

To correctly configure the application, we're going to perform the following items:

- Change the paths of the required files.
- Ensure we have the right shortcuts and icons.
- Adjust our file associations.
- Check out the required permissions to run the application.

Let's get started!

Changing the ICO and OSD path

Recall that earlier you set up a directory called sgContent and shared it. You also pointed the SoftGrid installation toward the sgContent directory at installation. During installation, Soft-Grid put four files in there as seen in Figure 5.15.

FIGURE 5.15   The DefaultApp is there to help you test your application.

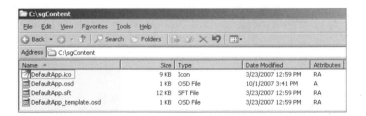

Also recall that we talked about the four golden SoftGrid file types. Three of those four file type are represented in the sample application. (See the earlier FAQ section for more information about the four file types.)

But even though the sample files are there, they're not quite ready to be used. To address this, we'll click SoftGrid Systems ➢ localhost ➢ Applications, and in the right pane, double-click Default SoftGrid Application. In Figure 5.16, you'll see that the OSD path and Icon path display the OSD and ICO files associated with the default application.

If you don't have the right icon path, the application should still launch, but the icon might not be what you expect.

However, these files need to be available via a share. So, your duty is to click Browse for the OSD path and the Icon path and make sure they are named with UNC paths, as seen in Figure 5.17.

At this point, don't click OK. We've got a little more tweaking to do.

FIGURE 5.16 You'll need to change the OSD and ICO paths before the Default App works.

FIGURE 5.17 The OSD and ICO paths should be UNC paths to a shared directory.

Shortcuts and Icons

For any published SoftGrid application, you can choose to have icons appear in various places. Clicking the Shortcuts tab enables you to choose where you want icons for the applications to appear.

By default, no shortcuts are created, which makes things a little confusing. I'm going to select the following, because I like to make sure I can always find my published applications. However, note that these selections are for this sample application and not other applications you publish.

To start, click Publish to Users' Desktop, but you can also select others, like I did in Figure 5.18.

File Associations

You can also associate file extensions with specific applications. Since this is a sample application, let's go ahead and associate the .SAM extension with this sample application. To do this, click the File Associations tab, and then click Add. In the New File Type Association dialog box, enter **SAM** as the Extension. Then, ensure that the "Create a new file type with this description" radio button is selected, as shown in Figure 5.19, and click OK.

Let's continue on with the Access Permissions tab.

FIGURE 5.18   You can tweak the location of an application's icons.

FIGURE 5.19   You can set up your own extensions for any application.

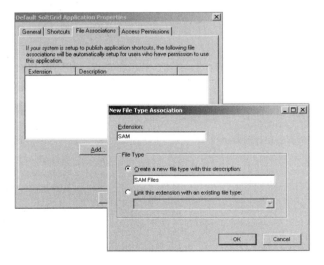

Access Permissions

The sample application is special, in that the sgUsers account (the users with any SoftGrid access at all) can start using the sample application right away. You can see this in Figure 5.20.

FIGURE 5.20   We're choosing to allow all SoftGrid users the ability to run this application.

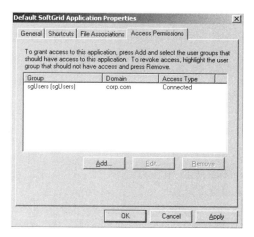

Later, when we set up our own applications, we'll have to specify which users and groups are valid for each application.

At this point, click OK to close the Default SoftGrid Application Properties screen.

Installing and Using the SoftGrid Client

Without the SoftGrid Client, you've got a server and nothing to use it. So, we'll get going with how to install and use the SoftGrid Client. We'll also log on as the first user and make sure the SoftGrid system is working as advertised.

The SoftGrid Client can be installed by hand or by using Group Policy Software Installation to get your clients installed, as you learned in the last chapter. I would suggest you use Group Policy Software Installation for all machines except the first one.

Installing the SoftGrid Client by Hand

The SoftGrid Client is located in the MDOP media. You saw the option to install this in Figure 5.4. The specific option is Install Microsoft SoftGrid Application Virtualization for Desktops. You can install the SoftGrid Client on XPPRO1 or Vista1 at this point.

Or, you could leap ahead and get the latest sanctioned version of the client, SoftGrid 4.2.1. This allows for a special superpower we'll explore later called Offline mode. I recommend using this latest version if possible. You can get it here http://support.microsoft.com/kb/941408.

WARNING   Be sure you download 4.2.1 and not 4.2.0, which is on the same page.

You can choose all the defaults until you get to the Cache Settings screen shown in Figure 5.21.

FIGURE 5.21   The SoftGrid Client cache settings.

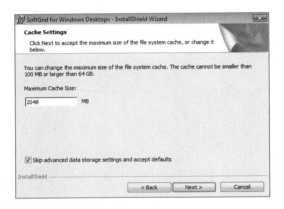

If you didn't think 2048MB (2GB) was enough to cache all the feature blocks of the applications your users might use, you can up the ante here.

NOTE   If you choose to uncheck "Skip advanced data storage settings and accept defaults," there are other client-side aspects to change, like the fake drive letter SoftGrid uses. In our case, let's leave them as they are.

At the Desktop Configuration Server screen, you'll need to enter a display name for Soft-Grid server (the one running the SVAS service), along with its proper hostname. It's suggested that you use the fully qualified domain name (FQDN) name like SoftGrid.corp.com, as seen in Figure 5.22.

After this, you'll be able to click through the rest of the installation. Finally, once the installation is complete, go ahead and reboot.

Testing the Default Application

At this point, log on to XPPRO1 or Vista1 as the Domain Administrator. I'm asking you to do this because earlier, I suggested you put the Administrator account into the sgUsers group, and the security upon the Default Application says that only members of the sgUsers group can use that application.

Launching via an Icon

When you log on as someone in the sgUsers group to the machine with the SoftGrid Client loaded, you should see the Default Application appear on the Desktop somewhere, as seen in Figure 5.23.

FIGURE 5.22 Telling a SoftGrid Client about its server.

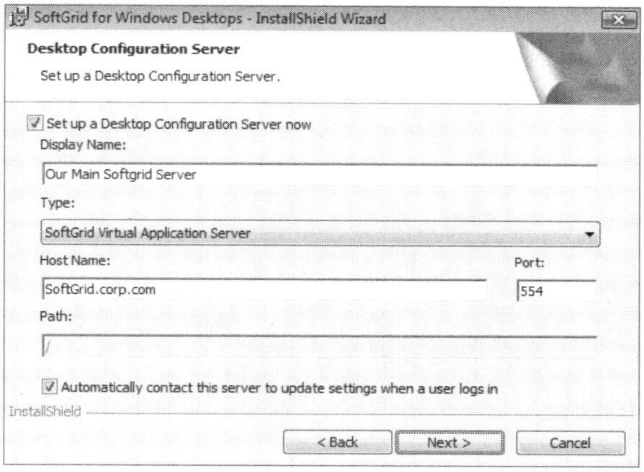

SoftGrid for Windows Desktops - InstallShield Wizard
Desktop Configuration Server
Set up a Desktop Configuration Server.
Set up a Desktop Configuration Server now
Display Name:
Our Main Softgrid Server
Type:
SoftGrid Virtual Application Server
Host Name:
Port:
SoftGrid.corp.com
554
Path:
/
Automatically contact this server to update settings when a user logs in
InstallShield
< Back
Next >
Cancel

FIGURE 5.23 SoftGrid applications' icons appear where you tell them to, in this case, the Desktop.

Recycle Bin
Default
SoftGrid
Application

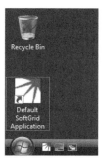

When you do, you'll see the sample application load from the server, go into the cache, and automatically launch as seen in Figure 5.24.

Launching via File Extension

Back in Figure 5.19, we told SoftGrid that whenever it sees a `.SAM` extension to auto-launch the sample application. If you'd like to test this, you can create a sample `.SAM` file on your desktop. The easiest way might be not through the GUI, but rather via the command line.

This is what I've done in Figure 5.25.

FIGURE 5.24   The SoftGrid sample application streaming down, then launching.

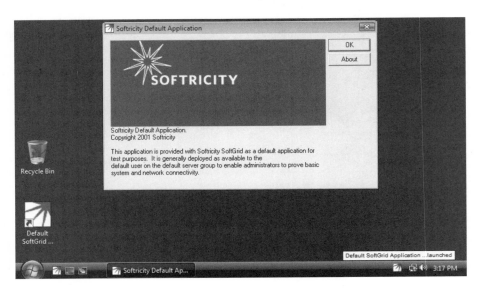

FIGURE 5.25   For our testing, create a new file with a .SAM extension.

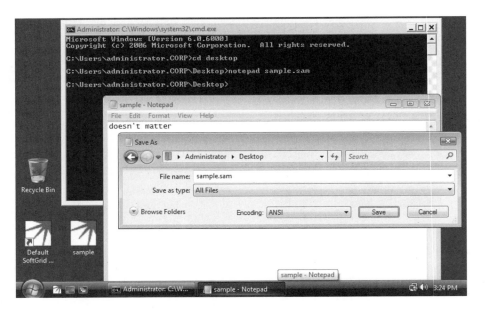

If you click the `Sample.sam` file (located above Internet Explorer in Figure 5.25) the sample file will automatically launch.

Ever-so-Brief Troubleshooting

If you're shouting, "I'm not seeing the Sample application!", make sure you've completed all of the following:

- You've got the SoftGrid server (the SVAS service) installed on a server and it's running.

- You've got a group who can use the SoftGrid system, like sgUsers, and you've got at least one user in that group. (In my example I just put the Domain Administrator in there for starters.)

- You've configured the sample application by using UNC paths for both the OSD file and ICO files.

- You've installed the SoftGrid Client on a Windows XP or Windows Vista machine (or, heck, even a Windows Server 2003 machine).

- You've logged into that Windows XP or Windows Vista (or Windows Server 2003) machine with a user who's in the sgUsers group.

 When I was first learning SoftGrid, the second and fourth bullets were my constant foes. I didn't point those files via UNC path, and I didn't log on as a user who was a member of the sgUsers group. So, I wasn't seeing the default application.

Hopefully, you're doing fine at this point.

If you can't get the sample application to load, I would recheck everything in this chapter up until this point. There's really no point in proceeding if you cannot get the sample application delivered to at least one client.

There is also a client log available at C:\Program Files\Softricity\SoftGrid for Windows Desktops named `sftlog.txt`. Open that log file and see if perhaps there's anything obviously "gunked up" in the works.

SoftGrid Sequencing

Sequencing is the act of taking an existing application and capturing its setup behavior into, basically, a single file. This single file will basically contain everything the application contains, and it's called a sequence. Once the application is sequenced, it can be deployed to any SoftGrid Client.

To sequence an application we need to have a SoftGrid "Sequencing Station." This will be our secret laboratory where we put the head of a chicken on a bat. Not really, but we will be pulling apart various applications here.

After that, we'll sequence our first application—nothing fancy—but we'll get the hang of the process.

Finally, we'll make sure we've got the application, I mean, sequence put on the server and streaming to our clients.

Let's get going!

Creating the Ideal SoftGrid Sequencing Station

You'll want to perform the sequencing on a clean SoftGrid Sequencing Station. A Sequencing Station doesn't have to be fancy. In fact, the less fancy, the better. The machine would ideally be (hold your breath here) a Windows 2000 machine with nothing but the operating system loaded.

Really, the only reason not to choose a Windows 2000 machine would be if the application you're sequencing doesn't support Windows 2000. So, if you don't choose a Windows 2000 machine, you will still want the "lowest common denominator" machine for all clients you're ever going to stream SoftGrid sequences to. Most people choose Windows XP, but again, the lowest common denominator is the rule to go by.

The machine should also have two partitions, and they need to be set up just so.

Partition 1   The C: drive. Load the OS here. Requires at least 4GB of free space, but 6GB is preferred.

Partition 2   The rest of the drive. At least 10GB of free space. Install nothing here. Format as NTFS and assign drive letter Q:. Yes, Q:.

Finally, load the SoftGrid Sequencing Station software. But don't load the SoftGrid Sequencing Software on a machine that already has the SoftGrid Client installed. That's a no-no.

You can see where to click to install the SoftGrid Sequencing Station back in Figure 5.4, where you can see the other parts of SoftGrid available for installation. However, that version is a little older than what's more recently available. You can get the latest SoftGrid Sequencing Software (version 4.2 as of this writing) at `http://support.microsoft.com/kb/941408` by clicking "Download the SoftGrid Sequencer 4.2.1.20 package now." It's a pretty unceremonious and uninteresting installation.

In my examples, I'll have an XP SoftGrid Sequence Station called XPSEQ, and I'll have configured it just as I've specified.

 Real World Scenario

Using a Virtual Machine for the Sequencer

Now, it's up to you, but I personally feel that this is just about the ideal situation in which to use either VMware Workstation or Virtual PC to help you with what lies ahead. You're about to load application after application on a machine, then wrap up each application as a sequence.

Except after you sequence an application, the ideal process would be to first wipe the machine clean. That way, the loading of the first application doesn't contaminate the second application. Between application installations, you have some choices. You could format the machine and reinstall the operating system each time, or capture an image using, say, Ghost. Or, better yet, take a virtual machine snapshot after you've got your clean machine all ready to go. Then, between sequences, snap back to the clean snapshot. The only trick is saving your Sequencer's SPRJ files somewhere that isn't within the virtual machine (because snapping back to a snapshot will obviously remove all files). Other than that, I heartily suggest using a virtual machine for the sequencer.

Sequencing Your First Application

A great first application to sequence is something small, such as Adobe Acrobat Reader or WinZip. Start out by downloading the installation and placing it on the Desktop of the Soft-Grid Sequencing Station.

You can see my copy of Acrobat Reader 7.0.9's setup program on the Desktop in Figure 5.26.

FIGURE 5.26   Put the application's installation somewhere handy.

 If you choose to sequence a different application, that's fine. But definitely stay away from big things like the Office suite or the full Acrobat (Writer) package. Those applications are a little harder to deal with; we'll tackle applications in that category in the next chapter.

To get started, fire up the SoftGrid sequencer by clicking Start ➤ Softricity ➤ SoftGrid Sequencer. (Note that someday, Microsoft will remove all Softricity references and replace them with Microsoft ones.)

When you do, the SoftGrid Sequencer will launch as seen in Figure 5.27. Get started by clicking File ➤ New Package.

The first question you're asked is, "Would you like some assistance in creating the package?" Let's click Yes, and then we'll walk through the wizard screens together. The wizard is roughly broken into three big sections.

First, get past the Introduction/Welcome screen by clicking Next.

Sequencing Wizard Part I

In this first section, we'll describe our package and specify what operating systems those packages will run with.

Package Information Screen

In Figure 5.28, you'll see the Package Information screen. In this screen, you can enter a Suite name (Acrobat Reader isn't really part of a suite like, say, Word 2000 is within Office 2000). So in my examples, I'll use the same name in the Suite Name and Title fields.

FIGURE 5.27 The SoftGrid Sequencer application.

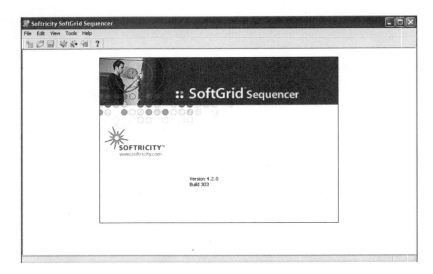

You can see that the Protocol box defaults to RTSP, or Real Time Streaming Protocol, which you can change to Secure RTSP, or RTSPS. We'll leave that default for now.

WARNING Don't even CLICK the little drop-down arrow under Protocol. Really! Don't. *I'm begging you.* If you do, you'll introduce a bug which you'll have to clean up later. Oops. Dang it, you clicked it already, didn't you? Well, if you did, and then later your package fails to work, be sure to read "Fixing the RTSP Bug in the OCD File" in the "SoftGrid Troubleshooting 101" section a little later.

FIGURE 5.28 Be careful not to click the Protocol drop-down (for now) as you could introduce a bug you'll have to clean up after later. Your job is to change the Hostname field to the actual name of your server (instead of the variable).

But here's the thing. Note that the hostname for the SoftGrid server is a variable named %SFT_SOFTGRIDSERVER%. The problem is that this variable needs to already exist on the target machine, and we haven't set that up yet. So for now, change this to the name of your SoftGrid server. In my case, it's SoftGrid.corp.com.

You can see this change in Figure 5.29.

FIGURE 5.29 Your hostname should be the exact name of your server.

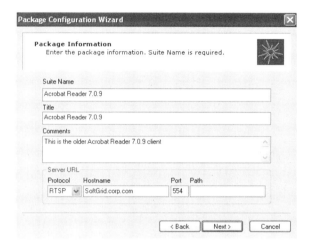

The Path field is an alternate path (relative to the content directory). So in plain English, let's say the sample app is stored at the root of the SoftGrid sgContent share. You could, if you like, store Acrobat Reader in a directory off the sgContent directory, called, say, \Acrobat7. So the full path would be *{server}*\sgContent\Acrobat7. In this case, you'd enter **Acrobat7** in the path.

You can leave this blank for now.

 To be frank, I think this wizard is a little odd, because you're being asked about the server and storage information at the same time you're doing the sequencing. I'm not saying these things aren't important, but I think it might be better if these questions were asked at a different time, like at the end of the sequence.

Operating Systems

In this screen, you select which operating systems this program is valid on. It's not a great idea to sequence an application on, say, Windows XP, then expect it to run on Windows 2000—but it might work (you'll have to test, test, test!).

However, this screen's main purpose is to filter which operating systems will even *see* the package (see Figure 5.30). In other words, if you want to be able to see this application on a particular operating system, be sure it's listed in the Selected Operating Systems box, then click Finish.

FIGURE 5.30   Select the operating systems this package can run on.

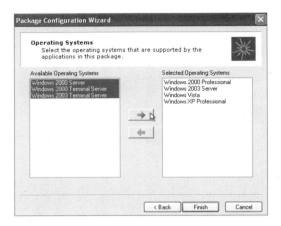

Sequencing Wizard Part II

You've made it past Part I. Now onto Part II. In this section, we'll address sequencing parameters, deal with the actual installation of the application, then add some key files to make sure our creation works.

Sequencing Parameters

In this screen, you can choose to compress the application using one of two protocols, or to keep it uncompressed. Compressed sequences are smaller, but uncompressed are faster. For this small application it doesn't matter.

Additionally, you can specify the Block Size list, as seen in Figure 5.31. The default size is 32KB, which means when more of the application is requested, it's delivered in 32KB chunks.

For now, keep it as 32KB and click Next.

FIGURE 5.31   You can set the block size to stream when applications need more—32KB is the default.

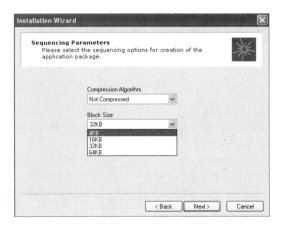

Monitor Installation

At this point, you can click Begin Monitoring. The idea here is that while you're doing the installation it's going to monitor the installation. Once it's done monitoring the installation, we can continue and make our particular tweaks if we want to. You can see the "Monitor installation" screen in Figure 5.32.

FIGURE 5.32 Monitor the application, then install it to the Q: drive.

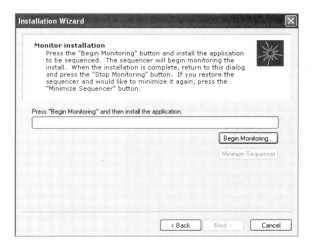

When you do, you're ready to install your chosen application.

The window will auto-minimize but stay running, ready to capture all that's about to go on.

Installing Your Application

You're just about ready to do your installation. But there are two important Don't Forgets before we run off and do it.

- Don't Forget #1: Remember that we set up our SoftGrid Sequencing station with two drives: the C: drive (like all our machines) and the Q: drive. Be sure to install your chosen application to the Q: drive.

- Don't Forget #2: When you install your application to the Q: drive, you can't go bananas and create a directory called My Creative Directory Name and install there. The installation directory needs to be old-school 8.3 folder names, such as Acro7.Rdr or Acrordr7.

See our FAQ section earlier regarding the Q: drive and the required old-school 8.3 names, if you're curious.

You can see me performing both of these Don't Forgets in one move, in Figure 5.33.

FIGURE 5.33   Install your application to the Q: drive.

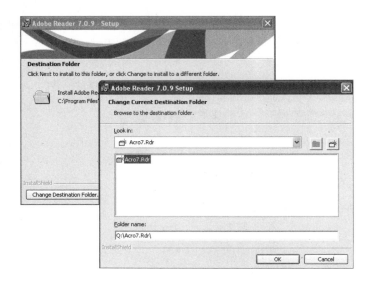

Now, go ahead and install Acrobat (or whatever other application you want).

Once Acrobat Reader is installed to the Q: drive, reopen the sequencer (remember, it's already running), then click Stop Monitoring in the sequencer.

Finishing Monitoring

When the application is done installing and you've clicked Stop Monitoring, you're then prompted for what directory you stored Acrobat Reader in by the Browse For Folder dialog as seen in Figure 5.34.

FIGURE 5.34   When you're finished monitoring, tell the sequencer where the application was installed.

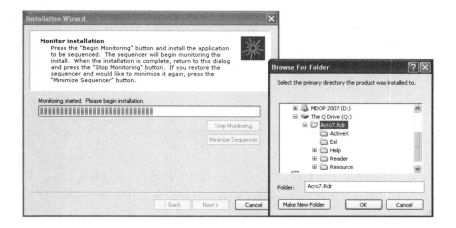

Select the Q:\Acro7.Rdr folder you used. You'll note that Start Monitoring is curiously available again. The idea is that, at this point, if you wanted to patch an application or make any settings changes (like never showing the EULA for Acrobat), you could do that at this time. You would click Begin Monitoring, make your changes, then click Stop Monitoring again. When you're finished, click Next.

Additional Files to Map to the VFS

What's interesting to note about SoftGrid is that it's really not all that smart. If you try to run a sequenced package, but the underlying guts which would normally be used to install that package aren't present within that package, the package installation fails. So the SoftGrid sequencer recommends a set of files used by the installer (msiexec.exe and supporting files) to actually run the sequenced application you just installed. You can see the default selections in Figure 5.35.

FIGURE 5.35 The sequencer needs some key .MSI components to work with your sequence.

Click Finish to continue.

Sequencing Wizard Part III

This is the final stage of the sequencer. In this section we're going to:

- Configure applications (their shortcuts, really), and
- Tell the sequencer how we want to launch our applications

   Then, finally, we'll have a fully sequenced package.

Configure Applications

In this screen, you can see all the steps that occurred regarding shortcuts when your application was installed. In Figure 5.36, we can see Acrobat Reader went a little overboard. It installed a piece that we don't really need—the Adobe Reader Speed Launch association, which put shortcuts in our Startup folder. Right-click over that entry, and click Remove as seen in Figure 5.36.

FIGURE 5.36 You can trim the fatty shortcuts from your applications.

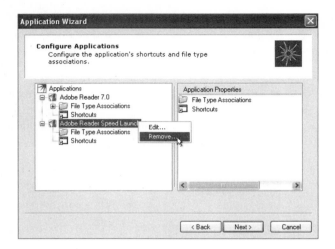

 Additionally, if you want to associate a file type that wasn't automatically detected during installation, just click the File Type Associations folder, then click Add.

When you're ready, click Next.

Launch Application

This is one of the more important screens during sequencing. It's at this screen where you get to do two things:

- You get to do a test flight for your application. You know, give it a spin around the block. Open up the key document types (like PDF for Acrobat Reader).

- You get to build Feature Block 1 (FB1) whenever you use more features within the application.

At this point, it's up to you how much poking around you want to do. The idea is that the more you poke around, the more you put into Feature Block 1. This has an upside and a downside.

The upside is that the FB1 chunk will contain more application components, meaning that once FB1 is loaded on the client, there's less for a user to need to download later.

The downside is that the FB1 chunk will be larger, which means it will initially take longer to stream; meaning the initial application startup (the very first time this application is launched) will take longer.

You'll build FB1 by clicking the application, and then clicking Launch (or just clicking Launch All), as seen in Figure 5.37.

Any other parts of application you don't run at this point will be part of FB2 and streamed to the client on demand.

FIGURE 5.37 You build FB1 by clicking Launch.

When you're finished, close Acrobat Reader to return to the Launch Applications screen. When you do, you should notice a little check mark next to the application which shows a successful launch. Finally, click Next.

 If there was a problem, you could click Back, and correct, say, a file association problem.

Sequence Package

At the Sequence Package screen, just wait for it to finish and click Finish. Pat yourself on the back. That was a long process and you survived.

Poking around in the Sequencer

All the work you've done up until this point was leading to here: the actual Sequence Editor. Across the top of the screen will be six tabs: Properties, Files, Virtual Registry, Virtual File System, Virtual Services, and OSD.

The idea is that you can poke around the sequencer (if you feel you know what you're doing) and change final parameters before saving out the project and the sequence. We'll be exploring these tabs a bit more in depth in the next chapter, but here's a quick overview:

 Be really careful in the Sequence Editor. This is where you can blow your foot off pretty easily.

Properties Most things here are read-only. You can change the Compression Algorithm if you'd like. The Launch Size indicates how large FB1 is in bytes, and how much space it will take up in your client's cache upon initial launch.

Files   This tab lets you take a look at every file that is contained in your sequence. Depending on the specific file, you can also set various options which let the SoftGrid Client know how to handle each specific file.

Virtual Registry   Remember when we said earlier that the Registry would be virtualized? Here is every Registry key that was created or modified as part of this installation.

Virtual File System   Looking back to Figure 5.33, we told our application that it was supposed to install to a specific location. Sometimes, application installations don't do what we ask them to do and end up putting files in other locations. Those other locations are mapped in the virtual file system, and you can see all of those other files and their locations here.

Virtual Services   Did you sequence an application that has a service or two? You can see what the services are on this tab.

OSD   The OSD tab lets you view or modify your OSD file. Want to know which operating systems you selected when you started your sequence? You can view them, or even change them, right here.

Saving the Sequence Files (and the Corresponding Project File) and Getting Them on the Server

The next steps are fairly straightforward. You're going to click File ➢ Save As and save your project somewhere. Be sure to name the project something meaningful (don't just go with the default `softapp.sprj`). In my example I chose the name `acroread7.sprj`. When you do, four files will be created: the ICO (icon) file, the OSD file (pre- and post-launch commands), the `.SFT` (sequenced application) file, and the SPRJ (Sequencer Project) file in case you need to reopen it for editing.

Next, your goal is to get them to the root of the sgContent directory on the server. You can use the network, a USB stick, or a carrier pigeon. We'll assume you got those files to your sgContent directory on your server as seen in Figure 5.38.

FIGURE 5.38   In our example, you can dump the files to the root of sgContent.

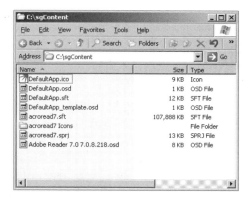

In real life you likely wouldn't just "dump" all your applications into the same directory. You'd create specific directories for each application. However, note that you'd have to change the path (seen in Figure 5.28) before you start the sequence, or, alternatively, you can change the OSD file, after the sequence is created, to point to a path inside the sgContent directory. Note that the path is also located in the SPRJ file as well; so, if you do decide to change it, be sure to change it in both locations to be consistent.

At this point, you're ready to deliver your new application to your users.

Delivering SoftGrid Applications

Sequencing the application for the SoftGrid server is only one part of the equation. The next big thing we need to do is to get it into our SoftGrid server and make it ready for deployment.

This is really the final frontier of a package: taking it from the sequenced blob that it is and making it available to our clients.

Then, our SoftGrid Clients can see the application and use it. It's a bunch of a little steps. So let's get started with the deliverin'.

Changing the Default Content Path

In our earlier example with the default application, we specified the path for both the OSD file and ICO file. You can see this in Figure 5.17.

However, it's also possible to just say that all packages will be coming from the same server and share. To do this, right-click over the server name and select System Options as seen in Figure 5.39.

When you do select the System Options item, you'll be able to put in a more permanent path to the sgContent share, such as \\softgrid\sgContent, like I did in Figure 5.40.

FIGURE 5.39 The System Options menu item is found when you right-click the main node for the server.

FIGURE 5.40   You can change the default content path so all applications can use it.

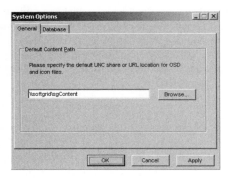

FIGURE 5.40   You can change the default content path so all applications can use it.

That way, all new applications we add to SoftGrid will automatically be found at \\softgrid\sgContent.

Adding a Sequenced Package to SoftGrid

Now that you have a sequenced package, it's not too hard to tell SoftGrid about it, as shown in the following steps:

1. In the SoftGrid console, drill down to SoftGrid Systems ➢ {*computer*} ➢ Applications, then right-click and select Import Applications, as seen in Figure 5.41.

2. When you do this, you can then select the Acrobat Reader's SPRJ file (which you already copied to \\{*server*}\sgContent). You'll then be automatically presented with the General Information screen shown in Figure 5.42.

3. You should see that the OSD Path and Icon path paths are automatically filled in with the path to the server (because you just changed the default content path). Leave the rest of the defaults as they are, and click Next.

FIGURE 5.41   Use Applications ➢ Import Applications to add your newly sequenced application.

FIGURE 5.42 Make sure your application's settings are set correctly (most importantly, the OSD Path and Icon Path entries).

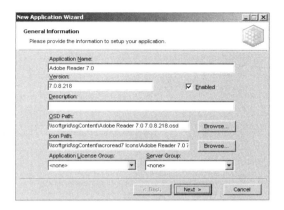

4. Next, you'll be able to choose where to display the application's icons. This is the same screen shown in Figure 5.18. Be sure to specify that the icon should be displayed on the desktop, and click Next.

5. Next, you'll have a chance to add file associations to or remove them from the application. For now, leave the defaults.

6. You'll then be at the Access Permissions screen. Remember earlier we created a group called sgAcroReaders and put one user, the Domain Administrator account, in there. Well, now's the time to select that sgAcroReaders group, as seen in Figure 5.43.

7. Click OK to close the Add/Edit User Group page, and click Next. Finally, you'll be presented with a Summary screen. Here, you can click Finish.

At this point, your application should be added to the Applications node as seen in Figure 5.44. You're pretty much ready to go. Let's move on to testing it all out.

FIGURE 5.43 Specify the group that contains the users that you want to allow to access your application.

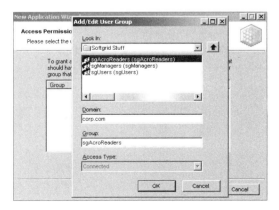

FIGURE 5.44 You should see your sequenced application added to the Applications node.

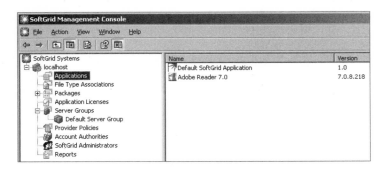

Testing out Your Application

All you need to do is log onto a client machine with the SoftGrid Client being someone who has access to SoftGrid and also to the specific package. In our example, the Administrator is a member of both sgUsers and sgAcroReaders.

Once you log on, you'll see the application's icons where you told them to be: in the Start Menu, on the Desktop, or both. When you double-click the application's icon, you'll see the application launching in the system tray shown in Figure 5.45.

What's really happening is that the first chunk (FB1) is coming down for the first time.

FIGURE 5.45 Your application will launch when it's streamed from the server.

At this point, you'll do a simple sanity check. That is, just for laughs, traverse to C:\Program Files and look for any trace of an Adobe directory. You won't find one. That's because, again, the application isn't ever installed within Windows. When you run it, you run it from the cache.

When you're done using it, it just goes away, as seen in Figure 5.46.

FIGURE 5.46 The SoftGrid Client alerts you when the application is shut down.

If the application fails to load, the first question you need to ask yourself is, "Did I get the sample application to work?" If the answer is no, then you're really going to need to go back and retest everything. I specifically put in that testing point to prevent deep heartache at this step when your newly sequenced application also fails to launch.

Now, if you're able to get the sample application to work but not your newly sequenced application, check out the next section "SoftGrid Troubleshooting 101" for some guidance on what the problem and the resolution might be.

 Real World Scenario

Using SoftGrid on the Road

Maybe while you've been experimenting with SoftGrid you've had the random thought, "Can I use this with laptops?" And the answer is, "Sure." The only issue would be what happens if you want the spell checker for the sequenced Microsoft Word at 30,000 feet, and you've never used that chunk of the application before.

That could be a problem. With this situation in mind, there are two solutions.

Solution #1, we'll explore here. That is, you can tell the client to load 100 percent of the application from the SoftGrid server. You can tell it to cache specific applications or all applications.

To tell the client to cache a specific application, you need to know the precise name of the OSD file. In Figure 5.37, you saw the result of the Adobe Acrobat Reader sequence and the corresponding OSD file it created. So, in this case, the command to cache 100 percent of my Adobe Reader sequence would be

```
sfttray.exe /load "Adobe Reader 7.0 7.0.8.218"
```

You can see the result of that action here.

Or, alternatively, I can cache all applications from the SoftGrid with the command:

```
sfttray.exe /loadall
```

However, note that that at no time can I exceed the client cache size. The default again is 2GB. It should be noted that once the cache fills up, the application that is currently streaming will simply stop streaming, and then display a Launch Failed message. Clicking the message will display an error code of xxxxxx-xxxxxx0A-0000E018.

Solution #2, we'll explore a little later. That is, the SoftGrid 4.2.1 Client can be set to work in Offline mode, which basically means that no SoftGrid server is required at all. How does that work? Well, mosey over to the section "Using an *.MSI* Package to Deliver SoftGrid Applications (via Group Policy and Other Methods)" to find out.

Ultimately, I think Solution #2 is the better solution, but be sure to spend some time checking it out and making sure it's right for you.

SoftGrid Troubleshooting 101

Even though it's a great tool, there are really a lot of ways SoftGrid can fail to work as advertised. The problems generally break down into three categories:

- No icons at all
- Application fails to launch
- Sequence didn't work as suspected

We'll tackle the first two in this chapter, but that last bullet gets a chapter all to itself. Check it out in Chapter 7, SoftGrid Sequencing Secrets.

So, we'll pull apart these three problems in the next little sections to get to the bottom of these potential issues.

No Icons at All

This is the most common symptom. Here's a quick hit list of things to check:

Are you sure the SoftGrid Client is loaded?   Check the Add/Remove applet in the Control Panel to really be sure the SoftGrid client is loaded. If it's not, definitely install it using Group Policy Software Installation, or by hand.

During your sequence, did you specify a path?   In our example, we didn't specify a path during sequencing (see Figure 5.28); but if you did, your files need to be inside the path you specified *within* the sgContent directory.

Did you pick all relevant operating systems when sequencing the application?   In our sequence example, I picked Windows 2000, Windows Server 2003, Windows XP, and Vista (as seen in Figure 5.30). If you are logged in on a different operating system than what's specified in the sequence, you won't see the icon.

You can correct this by editing the OSD file you saved in the sgContent directory. There should be a tag named <OS VALUE=*something*> where the *something* is an operating system list. For instance, my Acrobat Reader OSD file where I selected Windows 2000, Windows Server 2003, Windows XP, and Vista has lines that look like this:

```
<OS VALUE="Win2K"/>
<OS VALUE="Win2003Svr"/>
<OS VALUE="WinVista"/>
<OS VALUE="WinXP"/>
```

Be sure your OSD file lists the operating system you're currently on.

It's also possible to remove *every* OS VALUE tag in the OSD file and your application should still work. Without any OS VALUE tags, there is no check of the OS prior to launching. In other words, it attempts to launch on all operating systems. Whether the application actually works correctly or not is another story.

Check Group Membership

When we were testing out our Acrobat Reader deployment, we needed to be sure the test user was both a member of the sgUsers group (which permits the use of SoftGrid at all) and also a member of the application group (say, sgAcroReaders). Alternately, you can select the application inside the SoftGrid console, and then on the application's Access Permissions tab, you can add additional users and groups if necessary, as seen in Figure 5.47.

FIGURE 5.47 A common misconfiguration is forgetting to add a user to a group that is associated with an application.

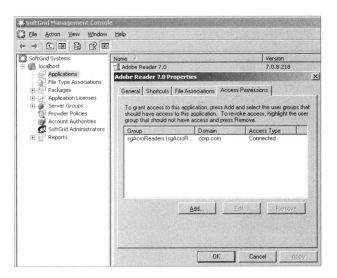

WARNING Remember that users must log off and back on to see any changed group membership. Without logging off and back on, you will not see the change take effect for the users.

Make Sure the Server Is Responding at All

At its heart, the SoftGrid server is really just a server which streams requested applications using IIS via a fancy protocol (RTSP) over a weird port (554). Knowing that, we can test to see if the server is responding to requests at all. Even if your SoftGrid server if working, you should give this a whirl, just to see what I'm talking about.

From a Windows XP or Windows Vista machine open up a command prompt and type this:

```
telnet {SoftGrid Servername or IP address} 554
```

When you do, the server should respond to you on port 554. Now, because neither you nor I know how to fool the server into thinking we're a client, we're not going to get very far. But if you hit Enter a couple of times, you should see the server respond with something like Bad Request, as seen in Figure 5.48.

Turns out Bad Request is a good thing! At least you can see that the server is *responding*. If your Telnet request is refused with an error (like "Error: Could not open the connection to {Servername} on port 554: Connect failed" or just hangs there, there could be a larger problem. Here are some things to check:

- Perhaps IIS stopped running.
- Perhaps the SoftGrid service stopped running (it's named SoftGrid Virtual Application Server).
- Perhaps there's a firewall between your client and your server. (Windows Server 2008 has a firewall turned on by default, so you'll need to specifically open up port 554 if you load SoftGrid server there.)
- There's another web service trying to use port 554.
- Your Windows XP or Windows Vista machine has a firewall preventing outbound traffic on port 554. (Not likely unless you're using third-party firewalls, but certainly possible.)

Once you can actually see that the server responds, even to a simple Telnet request on port 554, you can be pretty sure the issue is on the client.

FIGURE 5.48   You can use Telnet to see if your server is at least responding.

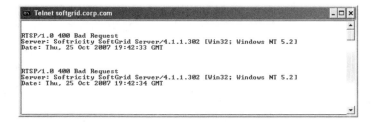

Application Fails to Launch

In this case, you see the application's icons, but you get a message that the application has "Failed to launch." There can be multiple reasons for this; let's explore some here.

Fixing the RTSP Bug in the OSD File

In Figure 5.28, you had the option to select the RTSP (not-secure) protocol or the RTSPS (secure) protocol. If you're curious like me, you might have clicked the drop-down to look at your selections before clicking Next. You might have even first clicked RTSPS, then changed your mind and gone back to RTSP.

In doing this, the OSD gets coded, by accident, with uppercase RTSP where it should say rtsp (lowercase). So, the result is that you get the icon files and can click them, but you get a "Failed to launch" message, because the specified protocol uppercase RTSP isn't valid. It has to be lowercase rtsp.

Grrrr.

A simple Find/Replace of the application's OSD using Notepad (as seen in Figure 5.49) to replace uppercase RTSP with lowercase rtsp does the trick.

Thanks to Joe Lurie for this tip.

Cracking the Failed to Launch Codes

When you get a "Failed to Launch" message, you can gather an error code for later use. Just click the message box that pops up in the lower right hand corner. When you do, you'll receive a box on the screen with a very cryptic error message.

FIGURE 5.49   Check to see if your OSD file has uppercase RTSP instead of lowercase rtsp.

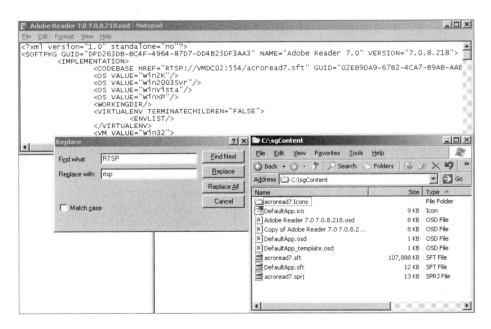

Take the last four digits of the error message, head on over to `http://support.microsoft.com`, and punch them in.

Even better, put them in Google (use `www.google.com/Microsoft` to use Google to search Microsoft's site). Hopefully, you'll find a document that tells you what the error message is and how to fix it.

Check out `http://tinyurl.com/23lot2` to read a posting on the SoftGrid Team blog with the top five error messages that are searched: of course, that top five is dated February 2007, but it's a helpful resource nonetheless.

Checking the SoftGrid Client Logs

As previously stated, the SoftGrid Client stores some log files in C:\Program Files\Softricity\SoftGrid for Windows Desktops. The key log file we want is named sftlog.txt.

It's chock full of useful information, so see if you can ferret out what's wrong.

As you're parsing the log file for clues about why your application isn't streaming, one possibility is that sometimes the pointer to the `.SFT` is wrong. Perhaps you specified a path, put the ICO file in the path, but forgot to place the `.SFT` file in the same path.

Deploying Your Applications to the Masses

There are many ways to deploy your application. We'll explore using group membership to deploy our applications (and we'll check in with that method again to make sure we get it). Then, we'll also explore the additional methods to get sequences delivered to target systems.

Using Group Membership to Deliver a SoftGrid Application

This is the most straightforward way to deliver the application. In fact, you've already done this one. Since you associated the Acrobat Reader application with the sgAcroReaders group, all you need to do is log on as someone who is a member of that group.

So, on XPPRO1, Vista1, or wherever you installed your SoftGrid Client, log on as Administrator. (If you're already logged on, log out and log on.)

You can also add new users to the sgAcroReaders group, and they'll magically get the application as well. The one thing to remember, of course, is that just because the user is a member of the group, that doesn't always mean he gets the application. That's because two other things positively need to be true:

- The user needs the SoftGrid Client installed on the target system. If the user roamed to a machine without the SoftGrid Client installed, no icons will appear.

- The user needs to be a part of the SoftGrid user group. In our examples we've used sgUsers. If the user isn't part of the sgUsers group, a whole lot of nothing happens.

Using the SoftGrid SMS Connector to Deliver a SoftGrid Application

SoftGrid ships with something called the SoftGrid SMS Connector. It's a neat piece of technology which enables an SMS administrator to deploy SoftGrid applications using the same SMS process they always did. You can learn more about this tool here: `www.microsoft.com/systemcenter/softgrid/solutions/sms.mspx`, shortened to: `http://tinyurl.com/yqaj5k`.

However, what's not generally known is that the SMS Connector has been deprecated (that means, put out to pasture). The problem with the SMS Connector isn't the technology itself; rather, the technology is too specific to a Microsoft solution. In other words, Microsoft wants a more generalized way to deploy SoftGrid applications to users, and that way should be through `.MSI`. Many technologies use `.MSI` to deploy applications including Microsoft SMS/ SCCM (the new version of SMS), Group Policy (yay!) and third-party application deployment methods like LanDesk or Altiris.

The official deprecation has occurred with the birth of the new MSI Converter tool is born (see the next section).

Using an *.MSI* Package to Deliver SoftGrid Applications (via Group Policy and Other Methods)

Very recently, a new way to deploy SoftGrid sequences has been made available. The tool is called the Microsoft SoftGrid Application Virtualization MSI Utility—SoftGrid MSI Utility for short, or just MSI Utility for even shorter.

It's a tool with a simple goal: wrap up the necessary SoftGrid application bits and put them into an `.MSI`. All the bits, that is, with the exception of the `.SFT` file, which might be too big to fit inside an `.MSI` file. Then, the idea is when you deploy the MSI application (using any tool you like), it simply directs the SoftGrid Client to use the ICO files locally and fetch the `.SFT` (the actual sequence) file and stick it all in the local SoftGrid cache.

So the end result is pretty cool: You no longer need to stream each application from the network. You can work offline, instead of always having to be connected to a server to request more of the application. And, if you know you have clients that aren't going to be connected for a while, you won't have to worry about setting them up in advance to cache the application before they go on the road. They'll already have it!

The best part is, you can deploy the `.MSI` using basically any tool you like that supports `.MSI` installation. Of course, my favorite, Group Policy, is totally supported!

No SoftGrid servers are involved in any part of the transaction. We'll call this Offline mode for short.

There are some caveats, however, in choosing to use Offline mode as opposed to streaming sequences directly off the server. Here are the main drawbacks:

- The `.MSI` isn't *running* from the SoftGrid server. The `.MSI` is deployed from any share you like (as long as the `.SFT` file is there and available too).

- The SoftGrid Client must be revision 4.2.1, which isn't in the box. It's an updated download.

- The SoftGrid Client can't switch on the fly between Offline mode and original streaming mode. So, you have to specifically dictate which SoftGrid Clients will work in Offline mode and which SoftGrid Clients will work in original streaming mode (Online mode).

- Any clients that use Offline mode are automatically exempt from SoftGrid's nifty auditing feature and software metering. This is because the whole sequence is running locally, not off the SoftGrid server. Therefore, there's no checking in with the SoftGrid server, and hence, no way to audit or meter for license overuse.

Right now, there is no hybrid mode where the client sometimes streams sequences online and sometimes uses sequences offline. So that means you'll need to do a little planning and decide which computers will work in which mode. I think this won't be too hard though. In short: you'll likely want to stay with the SoftGrid Client in the original streaming mode for desktops and you'll want to switch to the Offline mode for laptops. This is because desktops usually have pretty good connectivity and can generally get to the SoftGrid server. And that way, you can audit and perform licensing metering for (at least) the desktops. And you'll likely want to switch to Offline mode for laptops because you'll want to enable the fully offline capability that mode offers. You no longer have to actually rely on making sure you have contact with a SoftGrid server. Just deploy the .MSI, make sure the .SFT file is on the target machine (somehow), and go. (Don't worry. I'll show you my preferred method for getting the .SFT file on the target machine.)

Let's witness the process now.

Ensuring that the SoftGrid Client is Ready for Offline Mode

To make the magic happen with the MSI Tool for SoftGrid, you positively need one of the latest SoftGrid Clients installed. Earlier in the chapter, we installed the SoftGrid Client that came in the MDOP CD-ROM. But you'll need to upgrade (or freshly install) the SoftGrid 4.2.1 Client over your client population.

The SoftGrid 4.2.1 Client is available here: http://support.microsoft.com/kb/941408. I'm not sure why anyone wouldn't want to use the latest client, so stick with SoftGrid 4.2.1 Client if you're just getting started.

A quick note to save you heartache: be particularly careful that you're downloading the 4.2.1 client and not the 4.2.0 client. I spent four or five hours wondering why it wasn't working properly, and it was all because I downloaded the wrong client. Be really, really sure you have the right one.

Also note that the SoftGrid 4.5 beta client will not accept .MSI packages created using the MSI Utility. You must use 4.2.1 to perform the magic we're about to talk about.

 When you upgrade your SoftGrid Client, the applications cache is flushed and all packages need to be redownloaded.

Remember that the SoftGrid Client must be told "I want to use Offline mode," or it will naturally continue to use the original online mode. There are two ways to tell the SoftGrid 4.2.1 Client to use Offline mode: during the SoftGrid Client installation time, or after you've installed it.

Option two is easiest if you have lots of clients. You can deploy the client using Group Policy, then specify the necessary settings (also using Group Policy) to tell the client to use Offline mode. Let's explore both options.

Installing the SoftGrid Client Directly into .*MSI* Mode

This first option is easier if you have just one or two clients that you need to put into Offline mode. You'll just run the setup using the msiexec /i command with a MSIDEPLOYMENT=TRUE flag, as seen in Figure 5.50.

FIGURE 5.50 You next need to install the SoftGrid Client with the MSIDEPLOYMENT=TRUE switch using the msiexec command.

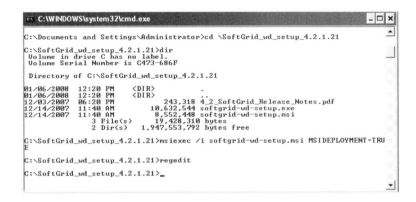

Next, set up the SoftGrid Client as normal (just like you did earlier in the "Installing the SoftGrid Client by Hand" section). However, when you get to the screen seen in Figure 5.51, enter in nothing and click Next. That's because the client doesn't require a connection to any server. Remember, it's working offline!

FIGURE 5.51 Installing the client in Offline mode requires no server.

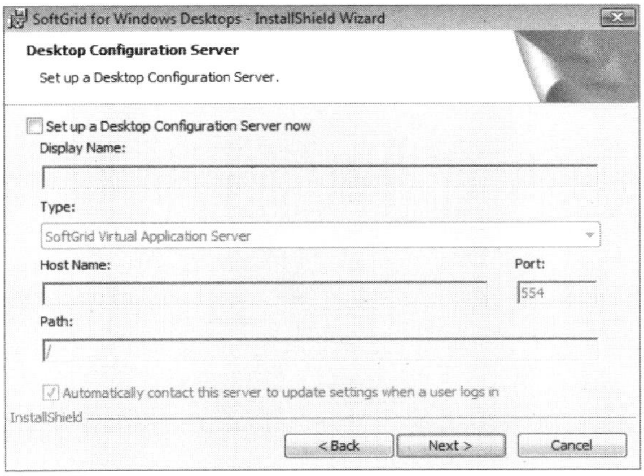

During this process, the client should have put in some Registry entries that tell it work in Offline mode. A quick test is to open up the client's Registry editor and dive down into HKEY_LOCAL_MACHINE\SOFTWARE\Softricity\SoftGrid Client\CurrentVersion\ Network and look for a key called Online. If Online is present and set to 0, your automatic installation succeeded.

However, it should be noted that one Registry option isn't automatically set correctly and really needs to be changed. That key is HKEY_LOCAL_MACHINE\SOFTWARE\Softricity\ SoftGrid Client\CurrentVersion\Network and the value is DOTimeoutMinutes. DOTimeoutMinutes should be a DWORD set to ffffff (that's six f's).

Read the next section to discover why.

Retrain the SoftGrid Client to Use .*MSI* Mode (After It's Been Installed)

In order to tell a SoftGrid 4.2.1 Client that it's supposed to use Offline mode, several Registry keys need to be present. The automatic installation mode we just explored will do the job. But if you're mass-upgrading SoftGrid Clients, using Group Policy Software Installation for instance, you won't be able to use the command line to make that automatic setup magic happen.

With that in mind, after you've installed the SoftGrid 4.2.1 Client, you can plunk in the needed Registry punches on each client by hand, or use the Group Policy Preference Registry Extension to get the job done on just the machines you need.

In Table 5.1, I have the values you'll need to convert a SoftGrid 4.2.1 Client from Online to Offline mode. To see a walkthrough of how to manually enter the values, see the MSI Utility Admin guide that comes with the MSI Utility. Make sure to read the warning following the table for a documentation bug.

To make the configuration changes, we're going to plunk values within folders inside HKEY_LOCAL_MACHINE\SOFTWARE\Softricity\SoftGrid Client\CurrentVersion. You can see that folder in Figure 5.52.

FIGURE 5.52   All required entries are within a folder inside the CurrentVersion folder.

TABLE 5.1   Registry Settings for a SoftGrid 4.2.1 Client from Online to Offline Mode

Folder	Value	Setting	Notes
Configuration	RequireAuthorizationIfCached	DWORD set to 0	Default value is 1. Need to change to 0.
Network	AllowDisconnectedOperation	DWORD set to 1	This is default value when client is installed with or without the MSIDEPLOYMENT=TRUE switch. But it needs to be verified that it wasn't somehow unset.
Network	Online	DWORD set to 0	Default value is 1. Need to change to 0.
Network	DOTimeoutMinutes	DWORD set to ffffff	(That's 6 f's) in HEX. Note that the MSI Utility documentation suggests 8 f's, but that's an invalid configuration and will be reset to the default hex value of 1fa40 (a value representing only 90 days) at reboot.
Network	LimitDisconnectedOperation	DWORD set to	Not automatically set when the MSIDEPLOYMENT=TRUE switch is used. If all the other entries are set correctly, this is okay, but ideally, you should set this value as specified.
Permissions	ToggleOfflineMode	DWORD set to 0	Default value is 1. Need to change to 0.

The MSI admin guide suggests you set DOTimeoutMinutes as eight f's. That value is actually invalid, and during a reboot will reset it to the original setting (1fa40) in hex, which is 90 days. However, six f's is a valid value and is equal to 31.9 years.

Now that you know all the Registry punches you'll need to convert a SoftGrid 4.2.1 Client from Online to Offline mode, you're ready to actually put those punches to work. You might want to create a GPO and link it to an OU, like **Traveling Sales Laptops** OU. Then, within the GPO, use the Group Policy Preference Registry Extension to dictate those specific settings listed earlier.

Also, don't forget: Even if you used the automatic setup routine (`msiexec /i` command with a `MSIDEPLOYMENT=TRUE` flag) there is still one Registry punch set incorrectly. Remember that the DOTimeoutMinutes value needs to be set to ffffff (that's 31.9 years) instead of the default, which is just under 90 days (1fa40).

In Figure 5.53, I'm specifically replacing the current value of `HKEY_LOCAL_MACHINE\ SOFTWARE\Softricity\SoftGrid Client\CurrentVersion\DOTimeoutMinutes` with ffffff (that's six f's).

FIGURE 5.53   You'll likely want to replace the defaults of DOTimeoutMinutes from 90 days to 31.9 years.

Again, here I'm simply showing one Registry change you'll likely always want to make. However, you can use this same trick to update the values on SoftGrid 4.2.1 Clients that are currently running in Online mode and convert them to Offline mode. Just replace the Registry values with what we described earlier. That will convert an Online client to an Offline client—just like that.

After punching the Registry, be sure to either restart the client's SoftGrid services (you'll find two of them) or restart the machine itself—that should save you from any trouble.

For a really good breakdown of the Registry values, be sure to read http:// desktopcontrol.blogspot.com/2007/12/msi-utility-explained.html (http://tinyurl.com/2nhbsz) and http://desktopcontrol.blogspot.com/ 2008/01/msi-utility-explained-pt2.html (http://tinyurl.com/2tynsg).

Converting a Sequence to an *.MSI*

Again, the whole point of working in Offline mode is to be able to run a sequence entirely in cache, without any maintained connection to a server. To do this, we'll use the SoftGrid MSI Utility to convert our existing packages and projects to an .MSI.

The MSI Utility can be found here http://tinyurl.com/2zlpyq. If it's not there, search for "MSI Utility for Microsoft Application Virtualization" and you should be able to find it. As of this writing, the tool's version was 1.0.0.16.

Installing it takes just a second. Then, the idea is to run it and have it find one of your existing package's project files. (Again, earlier, we stored this in the server's C:\sgContent directory.)

In Figure 5.54, you can see how I've pointed the MSI Utility toward the Acrobat Reader project file and how the output .MSI is created in the same directory.

FIGURE 5.54   The MSI Utility creates an .MSI from an existing SoftGrid project file.

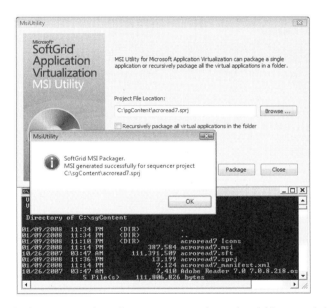

The whole process takes about two seconds. It should be noted that the large .SFT file isn't included in the new .MSI file. The .MSI file is simply a new way to launch the installation. The .SFT file still needs to stick around and be available at install time. Again, we're not actually installing an application (like Acrobat Reader), but we are installing the .MSI which pushes Acrobat Reader into the local SoftGrid cache.

Manually Running Applications in Offline Mode

Now that you've got your .MSI (and still have your .SFT file), you're ready for your first test. You're going to do three things:

- Create a directory on your client for your offline SoftGrid applications.
- Copy in the .MSI and .SFT files from the server to the client's directory.
- Install the .MSI file.

This is the easiest way to ensure that your client really is in Offline mode and ready to receive SoftGrid applications via Group Policy. In this example, I've copied the `acroread7.msi` and the (much larger) `acroread7.sft` file to my SoftGrid Client's `C:\sgMSIapps` directory, as seen in Figure 5.55.

The bad news is that to install virtualized applications using the MSI Utility, the user must have local administrative rights. If this test fails, try logging on as the local administrator and trying again. Don't worry, in the next section when we deploy the new .MSI file using Group Policy, that restriction is taken care of for us, and we'll be able to use it with normal users.

Then, simply run the `acroread7.msi` application for what appears to be an installation.

FIGURE 5.55 Even though you're installing the .MSI, you're not actually installing the Acrobat Reader application.

It will feel like you're actually *installing* the application, but you're really not. You're simply installing a little .MSI piece which puts the whole application into the SoftGrid cache for later use. Indeed, both feature blocks (FB1 and FB2) are put into the cache at this time.

Once the "installation" is complete, the application's icons will appear on the desktop and you can run it. There is nothing streaming down from the server, because 100 percent of the application is now local.

 Additionally, when it's run by hand in this way, the .SFT file must be in the same directory as the Virtual Application MSI file. If the .SFT file is not in the same directory as the .MSI file, the .SFT file location can be specified using `msiexec /I {misname.msi} /SFTPATH=<PathToSFTFile>`.

Automating Your SoftGrid Deployment to Offline Clients

Manual is great. If you only have a handful of machines you need to run around to. If you want to make the process more automatic, use the power of Group Policy to do the dirty work. The rules are pretty simple:

- Keep the .MSI and the .SFT file in the same share.
- Deploy these MSIs to computers, not users.

If you can keep those two things in mind, you're golden.

We'll see how to deploy to both Computers and Users, but deploying to Computers is usually better.

Let's check it out.

Using Group Policy to Assign SoftGrid *.MSI* Applications for Computers

In this section, we'll deploy to Computers and see how that works. In the next section, we'll deploy to Users and see what the scoop is there.

In Figure 5.56, you can see a GPO that I'm using to deploy Acrobat Reader to computers.

Note that the .MSI and .SFT files are in the same share, the sgContent share, also seen in Figure 5.56.

Remember that users need to be able read the .MSI file and the .SFT file through the share. So, be sure that the permissions are set to Read for Authenticated Users on both the share and within the underlying NTFS permissions. That way, both Users and Computers who are both considered (strangely enough) Authenticated Users can access the files. Without Read permissions to Authenticated Users your deployment will fail.

FIGURE 5.56   Use GPSI to deploy your .MSI to computers and ensure that the .MSI and .SFT files are in the same directory.

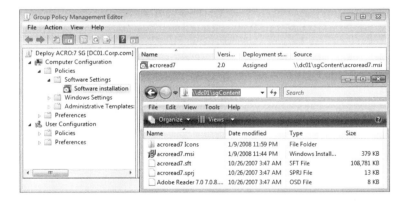

While creating the GPO that deploys the software, be sure to browse for the .MSI file over the network (e.g., \\DC01\sgContent\acroread7.msi), instead of browsing the local directories (e.g., C:\sgContent); that way clients will be able to find the package over the network too.

When a client that is set up for Offline mode reboots, they'll get a signal from Group Policy to deploy an application as seen in Figure 5.57. Windows XP is shown on the left, and Windows Vista is shown on the right. At this point the .MSI places 100 percent of the application into cache.

FIGURE 5.57   Upon reboot, SoftGrid 4.2.1 Offline clients will put the applications into cache.

While taking the Vista installation screenshot, I configured the client with the following Group Policy setting to enable verbose status messages: Computer Configuration ➢ Policies ➢ Administrative Templates ➢ System ➢ "Verbose vs normal status messages." Without this entry, Windows Vista users only see "Please wait" when software is installing.

Now, whenever any user logs onto the machine, they'll be pulling the application from the local cache and not from the server.

 If the package is targeted for regular, online clients, you might still see what's shown in Figure 5.57 each and every time they reboot. That's because the .MSI tries to process, but cannot successfully install, so it just times out. It's not a lot of time before it times out, but it does add to the computer startup time, each and every time for regular, online clients.

Using Group Policy to Assign SoftGrid .MSI Applications for Users (Basic)

Alternatively, instead of assigning the application to Computers as we just did, you can also assign the application to Users. However, in the end analysis, there's not much benefit. As you're doing your deployment, be sure to select the Basic option in the "Installation user interface options" section in the Deployment tab, as seen in Figure 5.58. If you don't, well, bad things happen (which, of course, you know I can't wait to show you in the next section!).

The application's .MSI appears to be installed in the Add/Remove Programs applet, but nothing is actually pushed into the SoftGrid cache. So, by default, no icons appear on the Start Menu, the Desktop, or anywhere else.

In order for a user to actually put the application into the cache in Windows XP, they need to be smart enough to traverse to Add/Remove Programs applet in Control Panel and select Add New Programs, as seen in Figure 5.59. For Windows Vista, navigate to Programs and Features ➢ Install a Program from the Network, or just search for Get Programs. You can see this in Figure 5.60.

FIGURE 5.58 The way to success is to deploy the .MSI using Basic interface options.

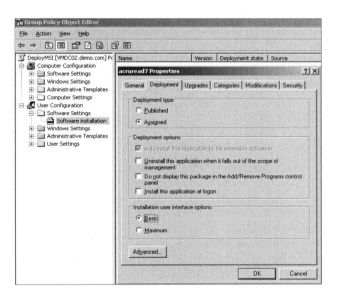

FIGURE 5.59 Users need to navigate to Add/Remove Programs Applet and select "Add New Programs" (for Windows XP clients).

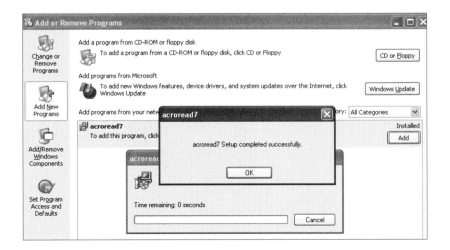

FIGURE 5.60 With Windows Vista, users need to navigate to Programs and Features ➤ Install a Program from the Network, or just Get Programs.

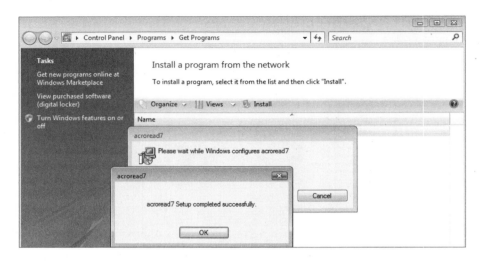

Now, here's the good news: A regular, nonadministrator user can run the .MSI and put the application into the SoftGrid cache. Then, the icons appear on the Start Menu, the Desktop, or wherever you specified in the SoftGrid package.

Here's the bad news: Once that first user puts the application into the cache, it's available for all users on that system.

Since all users get the package when the first user decides to execute it, I think you're better off simply assigning the application to the Computer, so all users can get the application right away anyway.

Using Group Policy to Assign SoftGrid *.MSI* Applications for Users (Maximum)

In Figure 5.58, I suggested that you should use the Basic setting. And that's because Basic works and Maximum doesn't. For more information about what these settings are supposed to do, be sure to read Chapter 4, where we talk about MSIs and their interface options.

But, in the spirit of completeness, let's show what happens should you choose to assign your users an application and select (oops!) the Maximum option in the "Installation user interface options" section in the Deployment tab.

When users go to install the application, it attempts to show the Maximum number of screens. And, in short, what you see in Figures 5.61, 5.62, and 5.63 are the quick road to Nowheresville for the poor user.

In short, the Maximum is incompatible with SoftGrid-wrapped MSIs, so be sure to use Basic instead.

FIGURE 5.61 What happens when users try to install software if the Maximum setting is selected by the administrator.

FIGURE 5.62 More trouble for users with the Maximum setting.

FIGURE 5.63 The final failure screen for users when Maximum has been selected.

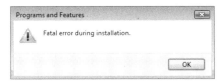

Final Thoughts on the SoftGrid MSI Utility and the SoftGrid 4.2.1 Client

The MSI Utility is super awesome, because now the link between SoftGrid and Group Policy is actually possible. Again, you must have the SoftGrid 4.2.1 Client installed and configured for Offline mode. You can read more about this tool in three web links:

- `http://tinyurl.com/2gzmat`
- `http://tinyurl.com/yrdd56`
- `http://tinyurl.com/2flgnk`
- `http://support.microsoft.com/?kbid=949050` (MSI Utility Troubleshooting tips)

However, you can actually get the converter here: `http://tinyurl.com/2zlpyq`. Be sure to read the included `.PDF` file that comes with the package; it does contain some helpful additional information.

Final Thoughts

Whew. For a chapter called "Application Virtualization and SoftGrid Essentials," we did an awful lot! SoftGrid is a big, big place and we needed a way to scratch the SoftGrid surface.

You've already come a long way. You've set up your SoftGrid server, you've installed your SoftGrid Client, you've tested SoftGrid's operation, and you've sequenced and deployed your first application.

You've also wrapped up your application as an `.MSI` and deployed the whole thing using Group Policy. To do this, you used the 4.2.1 client and made sure the client is configured to use Offline mode. Don't forget to change the `HKEY_LOCAL_MACHINE\SOFTWARE\Softricity\ SoftGrid Client\CurrentVersion\DOTimeoutMinutes` key and ensure that it has ffffff (that's six f's).

Remember, applications aren't really installed on the client. They're simply put in cache. That's the beauty of application virtualization.

Also note that you can get additional sequencing and other general SoftGrid help from various support forums:

- `www.appdeploy.com`
- `www.softgridguru.com`
- `www.GPanswers.com/community`
- `www.softgridanswers.com` (coming soon)

In the next chapters, we'll learn how to do some advanced SoftGrid magic and understand the SoftGrid management console a little more. Our goals are to understand exactly what power we've got under the SoftGrid hood on both the server and the client side.

Then we'll tear apart the dark arts of sequencing and learn the ins and outs of tricky applications. See you when you turn the page.

SoftGrid—Beyond the Basics

In the last chapter, we covered some of the basics for how to use SoftGrid—a SoftGrid 101 course, if you will. In that chapter, you learned how to set up a SoftGrid server, how to get a sample application sequenced, and how to make sure the whole thing is working properly.

In this chapter, we'll be expanding on what you previously learned and covering what's next: our SoftGrid 201 course. We'll be covering these three big things:

SoftGrid Management Console Every application starts out by being published in the Soft-Grid Management Console. Here's where we get to dictate exactly how a client receives that published application and perform other Advanced Administration tasks.

SoftGrid CMC Want to change the default behavior of your SoftGrid Clients? Find out how.

SoftGrid Client Applet Learn all the SoftGrid Client options available right from the system tray.

SoftGrid 4.5

All three of our SoftGrid chapters were written using the latest release of SoftGrid, which is version 4.2. Microsoft recently released a public beta of version 4.5 and has changed the name Soft-Grid to Microsoft Application Virtualization. As we journey through the various components of SoftGrid 4.2, we'll make note of some of the changes you can *probably* expect to see once 4.5 is officially released. Since it is a beta release, we still can't be totally sure what will or won't be included.

SoftGrid Management Console

In the last chapter, we installed the SoftGrid server and published the SoftGrid test application. We then sequenced Adobe Reader and published that application using the SoftGrid Management Console. As a quick reminder, we can launch the SoftGrid Management Console on the SoftGrid server by clicking Start ➤ Administrative Tools ➤ SoftGrid Management Console.

You can see the SoftGrid Management Console in Figure 6.1.

This Chapter written by Eric Johnson.

FIGURE 6.1 The SoftGrid Administrators node.

It's a pretty big world in there. But, don't worry. We'll steer you through it. Now let's learn all the *other* items in the SoftGrid Management Console:

SoftGrid Administrators   Need to change who can manage what within your SoftGrid system? Learn how in the first section, "SoftGrid Administrators Node."

Application Groups   In every company, there is a list of completely unrelated applications that every person uses. Learn how to take this unrelated set of applications and configure all of them at the same time to (almost) work together.

File Type Associations Node   Want to see just which applications have a particular file type association? Or, how about configuring a file type association for every user of a single application? This is the node for you.

Packages Node   Packages are used for one basic function: active upgrades. Learn how to actively upgrade your applications so users will always have the most current service pack, hotfix, or patch available for all of their applications.

Application Licenses Node   Concurrent licensing, named user licensing, and unlimited licensing—learn about all three types and why combining licenses can yield even more powerful licensing strategies.

Server Groups Node   A server group is a collection of SoftGrid servers. Learn why these collections of servers can benefit a multisite environment, and learn how you can make use of server groups even if you only have a single site.

Provider Policies Node   Everyone likes to make rules. No, wait. Everyone likes to *break* rules. Well, the provider policies are rules for the SoftGrid Clients (and they can't break the rules). Learn how to apply a set of rules (the policies) to the SoftGrid Clients that make connections to your SoftGrid servers (the providers) to launch applications.

Account Authorities Node   Remember the sgBrowser account we set up in the last chapter? That account helped us discover other accounts in Active Directory. This section helps us configure that account. You'll also learn more about what it is used for.

Reports Node   Have you ever wanted to find out just how often someone uses that really expensive application they just *had* to have? Or, if your company bought 1000 licenses of a specific software package, just how many are actually being used? Learn all about tracking application usage in the Reports node.

There are a lot of details to learn in the SoftGrid Management Console. Whenever you're ready, let's get started!

SoftGrid Administrators Node

In Chapter 5's "SoftGrid Accounts and Shares" section, we created a group called sgManagers. We then gave this group the ability to manage our SoftGrid system, as you can see if you turn back and review Figure 5.7.

The SoftGrid Administrators node allows us to grant the rights to administer the SoftGrid system to additional groups of users. It also allows us to remove rights of groups.

As you can see in Figure 6.1, we have highlighted the SoftGrid Administrators Node in the left hand pane of our SoftGrid Management Console. The middle pane then displays all of the Active Directory groups which have rights to administer the SoftGrid system. In our case, you can see the sgManagers group has been granted administrative rights to our SoftGrid system.

Deleting a Group from the SoftGrid Administrators

Deleting a group is as simple as right-clicking the name of the group in the middle pane of the management console and clicking Delete. Fortunately, if you attempt to delete the *only* group listed, you will receive the error message shown in Figure 6.2.

FIGURE 6.2   Don't delete the last group of SoftGrid Administrators.

There always has to be at least one group granting administrative rights.

Adding a Group to the SoftGrid Administrators

To add additional groups, right-click SoftGrid Administrators in the left-hand pane and click Add Administrator Group. Doing so will bring up the Add SoftGrid Administrators window seen in Figure 6.3.

You can find the group you want to add by browsing through your Active Directory and then highlighting it, or you can type the name in the Group field.

FIGURE 6.3 Add a group to the SoftGrid Administrators.

Adding a Group from Another Domain

At some point, your company might join forces with another company. You will go through the process of combining your IT departments and setting up the necessary permissions. When it comes to adding new groups to the SoftGrid Administrators groups, there are a few things that you need to know.

As you can see in Figure 6.4, we tried to add the Domain Admins group from `corp1.com`. The SoftGrid system displayed a yellow exclamation mark; if we pause our mouse cursor over it, a pop-up message appears stating, "Warning: this domain may not be trusted by the SoftGrid system."

FIGURE 6.4 Warning message when adding groups from another domain.

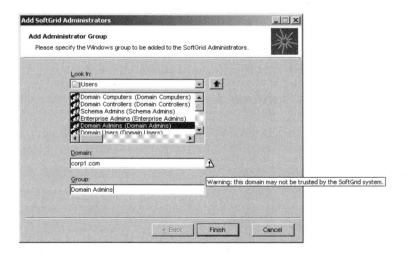

Even if the domain is a trusted domain, you still might get this error message. For example, every domain in a single forest can have a group as a member of the SoftGrid Administrators group. But even though, by default, all of those domains are trusted domains, SoftGrid still might warn you that the domain is not trusted. All of the users contained within the group will still be considered members of the SoftGrid Administrators group.

 Real World Scenario

Oh No! I Deleted the SoftGrid Administrators Group

Now, let's just say that by accident, someone *deleted* this group out of your Active Directory. Doh! Now, all of a sudden, the powerful sgManagers no longer exists in your Active Directory. (Don't really do this. We're just talking hypothetically.)

How do you manage your SoftGrid system now? You can't log into the SoftGrid Management Console and add users who have the right to manage SoftGrid, because the sgManagers group doesn't exist. Now what do we do? Panic? Yes, that is always an option. But what we really need to do is reset the SoftGrid Administrators group.

Referring back to Chapter 5, Figure 5.10, after you launch the SoftGrid Management Console, you will need to right-click SoftGrid Systems. Instead of clicking Connect to SoftGrid System, click Reset SoftGrid Administrators.

The first screen that comes up after clicking Reset SoftGrid Administrators is the Connect to the SoftGrid Data Store screen, shown here.

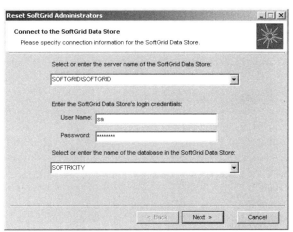

The first field we need to fill in is the server name of the SoftGrid Data Store. If we click the drop-down box, we are automatically presented with one option to select. In our case, the server name is SoftGrid, so go ahead and choose that.

Now, we need to enter the SoftGrid Data Store's login credentials. Because we are trying to log into the database, we will use the username "sa" and password "p@ssw0rd" that we entered back in Figure 5.5. (Remember, that's an at sign and a zero in the password.) Of course, if you don't know this username and password, you can always browse to the `C:\Program Files\Softricity\SoftGrid Server\conf` directory. Open up the `server.conf` file and the database username and password is stored there for you.

The name of the database by default is SOFTRICITY, so there isn't anything we need to change in the last field. You can click the drop-down to display other databases which are available on the SoftGrid server; however, there isn't any reason to do so. We want to access the SOFTRICITY database, so go ahead and click Next.

Reset SoftGrid Administrators

Now we are shown a list of the groups which currently have administrative rights in our Soft-Grid system, as shown next. Even if you have deleted the sgManagers group, it will still be listed here. Remember, we are looking in the database at this point for the members of the Soft-Grid Administrators group, not the groups in Active Directory.

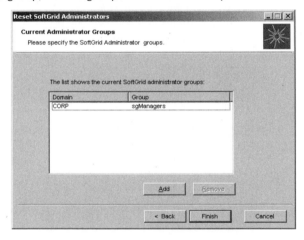

We can now remove the group that we no longer need. We can also add in the appropriate group or groups. Once we click Finish, the new groups will have administrative rights on our SoftGrid system.

Applications Node

Back in Chapter 5, you saw how to right-click the Applications node and use the Import Applications feature to add applications to the SoftGrid Management Console (see Figure 5.41). There are two other options in this menu; let's learn now what we can do with them.

First, we'll check out application groups. Then we'll check out how to add applications to SoftGrid through the New Application option.

New Application Group

An application group helps us manage as many applications as we want in the exact same way. So, let's say your marketing department has 17 applications, and every member of the Marketing users group needs those 17 applications. You can create an application group that lets you simultaneously manage all 17 applications. Want to put all the apps in a Marketing Applications folder off the Start Menu? Put all of the applications in an application group and configure the application group, rather than each application individually.

First, let's create an application group.

Clicking New Application Group brings up a window that lets us type in the name of an application group, as seen in Figure 6.5.

FIGURE 6.5   The New Application Group Wizard.

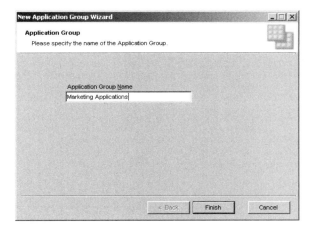

For this example, we'll call our application group Marketing Applications and then click Finish. If you look in the left-hand pane of the SoftGrid Management Console and click the plus sign by Applications, you can see our new application group, just like in Figure 6.6.

FIGURE 6.6   The Applications node lets us create an application group.

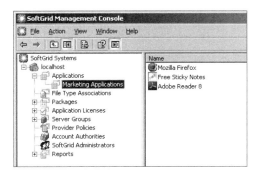

Now we can import applications directly into the Marketing Applications group and configure them all the same way. I've sequenced Firefox, Adobe Reader, and Free Sticky Notes and imported them into the Marketing Applications group. You can see in Figure 6.6 that those three applications are listed in the middle pane of the management console.

Application Group Properties

The Application Group Properties is where you can configure all of those applications you have added to the group as one application.

When I right-click the Marketing Applications group and click Properties, the window that is displayed looks similar to Figure 5.17, but as you can see in Figure 6.7, there is one tab that is missing: the File Associations tab, and with good reason.

FIGURE 6.7 The General tab of an Application Group.

Any change that I make in the properties of the Marketing Applications group affects *every* application within that group. If I had the ability to add a file type association, SoftGrid wouldn't know which application to use to launch the file type association. There are other differences on the tabs in an Application Group:

General Tab You can see a few differences on the General tab from a normal application properties window. With multiple applications, there will be multiple versions, OSD files, and icon paths, so those fields are grayed out.

I can enable and disable all of the applications in the group by checking or unchecking the Enabled box. I can also specify an application license group or a different server group for every application simultaneously. You'll learn more about license groups and server groups later in this chapter in the "Application Licenses Node" and "Server Groups Node" sections.

Shortcuts Tab Clicking the Shortcuts tab allows us to configure the location of the shortcuts for every application in the application group simultaneously, as seen in Figure 6.8.

If we wanted to have all of these applications show up on the user's Start Menu under the heading "Marketing Applications," we could do so here. Figure 6.9 shows what this will look like when we're done. You'll be a hero because all your users will know how to find *all* the applications they need to do specific types of tasks.

FIGURE 6.8 The Shortcut tab of an application group.

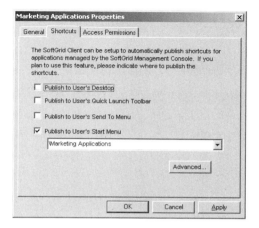

FIGURE 6.9 All of your marketing applications in the same location.

If you want to make sure none of these applications put a shortcut onto a user's desktop, uncheck the Publish to User's Desktop box.

Access Permissions   The last tab in the Marketing Applications Properties window is the Access Permissions tab, which you can see in Figure 6.10.

Here, we can configure the groups that have permissions to the applications contained within the application group. Rather than assigning access permissions for each application individually, we can hit all of them in one fell swoop. We can just as easily remove those groups, as well.

FIGURE 6.10 The Access Permissions tab of an application group.

New Application

You also have the ability to create a new application in the SoftGrid Management Console instead of importing an existing one. This option is available if you right-click the Applications node and select New Application.

FIGURE 6.11 The New Application Wizard.

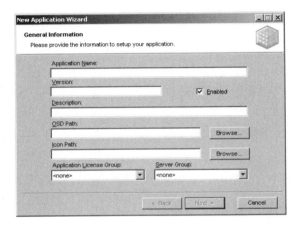

The screens in the New Application Wizard are identical to the screens displayed when you import an application. The major difference between choosing Import Application and choosing New Application? When you choose New Application, you have to manually fill out every little detail in every screen. While it is possible to use New Application, the likelihood of making a mistake in publishing your applications is much higher than if you use the Import feature. I'd recommend not using the New Application Wizard.

Deleting an Application

At some point in your career as a SoftGrid administrator, there will come a time when an application that is published on your SoftGrid system will no longer be used in your production environment. Because the application was never installed, you don't have to go through the process of uninstalling anything on your clients. Yay! What you will do, however, is delete the application off your SoftGrid system.

Instead of permanently deleting the folder containing the application that is no longer in use from your SoftGrid server, I recommend moving the folder from the content directory to an archive directory. You never really know when you might need to use an old application to open a file format that is no longer supported. If you still have the sequence, you can simply reimport it and stream it down to a client whenever you need.

Right-click the application and choose Delete. A message will appear telling you that your SoftGrid database will no longer have any information stored in it about the particular application. After that, you can never run a report to tell you how often it was used or who used it. All of the file types associated with this application will be removed as well.

 Deleting an application does not delete the associated package. You'll find out how to delete packages in the section "Packages Node" later on.

File Type Associations Node

Your company has finally made the decision to roll out Office 2007 across the entire enterprise. You spent the whole day sequencing and testing your package and have now made Office 2007 available to your organization. Of course, you don't want anyone using previous versions of Office, so you have removed all of your users' access to those applications, and every one of your users will be running Office 2007 when they walk in the next day. There is just one problem: out of the box, Office 2007 does not associate an XLS file with Excel 2007, nor a DOC file with Word 2007, nor a PPT file with PowerPoint 2007.

In fact, Office 2007 doesn't have *any* file type association for the previous Office document extensions.

But fear not, brave SoftGrid administrators. You have the File Type Associations node to quickly solve your problems. If you don't want your users to have to manually create this association, you can just walk through this wizard once on the server. Then, anyone who received the Office 2007 package will also receive the file type associations that you create for them for all of the previous Office document file types.

The File Type Associations node shows us every file type association that is configured in our SoftGrid system. By the time you have all of your applications sequenced, this list could contain well over 1000 file type associations. You can also create new file type associations right from this node.

Right-click File Type Associations and click New Association to launch the New File Type Association Wizard, which you can see in Figure 6.12. Type in the extension of the file type, and then we have a choice between two different buttons.

FIGURE 6.12 General page of the New File Type Association Wizard.

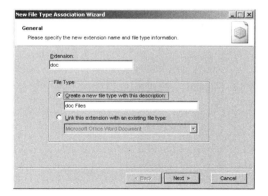

Create a new file type with this description   If we create a new file type, we can simply enter the description for the file type and then click Next to select the application.

Link this extension with an existing file type   The second button allows us to associate a new file type with an existing file type. In the case of associating a DOC file with Word 2007, we can very easily just select the Microsoft Office Word Document from the drop-down list. This selection automatically associates Word 2007 with DOC files, and changes the Next button to a Finish button—there is no additional screen.

Clicking Next brings up the screen you see displayed in Figure 6.13. Here we get to select the application and the icon our new file type association is going to use.

FIGURE 6.13   Application and icon selection.

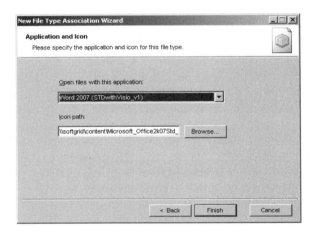

The Application and Icon selection screen are very simple and straightforward. Click the drop-down to choose which application to use to open the file type we just created from all of the currently published applications. Browsing through our content directory lets us pick which icon we would like to use for the file type we just created.

Once those two selections have been made, clicking Finish creates the file type association. Now, any user who performs an application refresh will receive the new file type association for that specific application.

Packages Node

Each application, or suite of applications, has a package associated with it. Office 2007 Standard edition has four major applications in it: Outlook, Excel, Word, and PowerPoint. If we sequenced Office 2007 Standard, we would have these four applications in our Applications node. But if we looked in our Packages node, there would be only one package. That is due to the one-to-one relationship between SFT (Softricity) files and packages.

Each package represents a single SFT file, which is one of the four major file types created in a sequenced application that we talked about in the "What Are the Four "Golden File Types" in SoftGrid?" section in Chapter 5.

In Figure 6.14, you can see the Packages node expanded to display all of the packages on our SoftGrid server.

FIGURE 6.14   The Packages node.

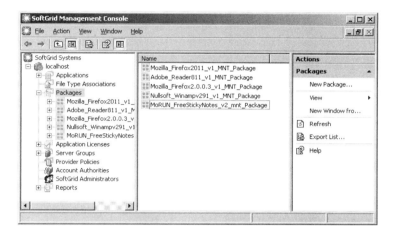

New Package

When you import an application, the associated package is created for you automatically. However, just as we have the ability to create a new application, we can also create a new package. Again, the difference between an application and a package is that packages are used to control the versions of the applications users are running. And that's an important reason why you'd want to create a new package.

Right-click the Packages node, and choose New Package. The New Package Wizard will start up, as shown in Figure 6.15.

We give our new package a name; in this case, we are calling it WinAmp. Now, we browse to the Softricity (SFT) file. On this first screen, we need to use a full path. This is because the SoftGrid Management Console actually opens up the SFT file to make sure it is a valid file.

Click Next to bring up the second screen of the New Package Wizard, as seen in Figure 6.16.

In Figure 6.15, we entered the full path for the Softricity file. If you click Back and copy all of the text to the right of \\SoftGrid\content\, you can paste that value into the Relative Path text box shown in Figure 6.16, as that is the correct relative path.

FIGURE 6.15 The New Package Wizard.

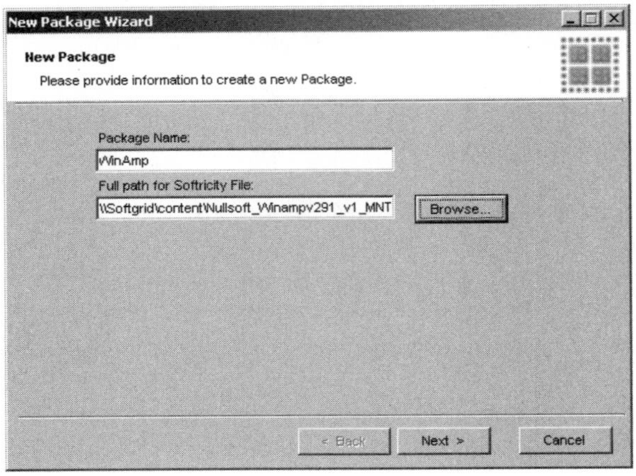

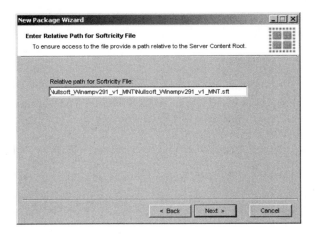

FIGURE 6.16 Enter the relative path.

Enter the relative path for the Softricity file. This information is stored in the database as the path *relative* to the SoftGrid System's specified content location.

We entered the SoftGrid System's content location in Chapter 5 in the "Changing the Default Content Path" section, and Figure 5.40 demonstrates this, as well.

Click Next to bring up the Summary screen shown in Figure 6.17.

FIGURE 6.17 The final screen of the New Package Wizard.

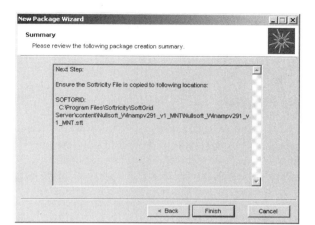

The location that is listed for the content directory in the Summary screen shown in Figure 6.17 was never entered like it is displayed. This is actually where the content directory was initially configured to be located during our installation of the SoftGrid Server. Refer back to Figure 5.9 to see where this value was initially entered.

Add Version

When we upgrade a package in our sequencer, we will need to add a version to the package in the SoftGrid system. Versioning a package allows us to add in hotfixes, patches, service packs, additional files, or any multitude of changes to our packages without causing any downtime. Our users can keep right on working, and the next time they launch the application whose associated package has been versioned, they will automatically receive the updated package. Not the *whole* package—just the difference between the package they were running and the new version. Versioning is all handled by the SoftGrid Client, which is on the workstation.

Right-clicking a specific package and clicking Add Version will allow us to do this, and the three-screen wizard is almost identical to adding a new package, which you just learned about.

You'll learn how to upgrade packages and add versions to packages in the next chapter, where we go into greater depth with the SoftGrid sequencer.

Deleting a Package

In the "Deleting an Application" section, you learned that when we delete an application, the corresponding package is not automatically deleted. We must then manually go into the Packages node and delete the appropriate package.

When we right-click a package and click Delete, we are prompted with the message telling us that when we delete a package, all of the versions of the package will be deleted as well.

Clicking Yes will then proceed to delete the package. However, if you attempt to delete a package that still has an associated application, you will get an error message stating that the package is still referenced by one or more applications. Remember to delete the application first, and then delete the package.

Application Licenses Node

SoftGrid has a licensing component built into it that allows you, the SoftGrid Administrator, to ensure licensing compliance across your organization. In fact, if you attempt to launch an application without a proper license, you will receive a launch failed message. When you click the launch failed message, you will be able to see that there is not an appropriate license for the application you are trying to run.

The Three Types of Application Licenses

There are three types of application licenses: unlimited license, concurrent license, and named license. Creating each type of license requires a two- or three-step wizard.

The first step of each licensing wizard is almost exactly the same; the only difference is in the title bar of the window. In Figure 6.18, you can see we are using an unlimited license, but again, for each license type, there isn't any difference in the data that's entered.

FIGURE 6.18   The first screen to create all license types.

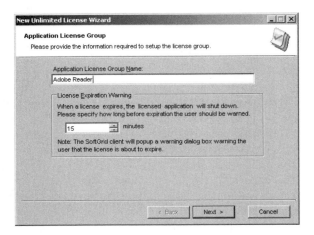

Application License Group Name   We'll learn what a license group is and what it is used for later in this section. For now, go ahead and name the license group. In Figure 6.18, you can see that I've named my license group Adobe Reader. I like to name my license group after the application I'm planning on licensing. It lets me easily see which applications have licenses and how the application is licensed.

License Expiration Warning   Every license can potentially expire, and you can set a pop-up message to display before it does. When the application license does expire, the application will shut down. It can't be launched again until a valid license is acquired.

You might have a piece of software that is not actually purchased but used on a subscription type of service. Perhaps you purchase use rights for a month, or even a year. You can set your license to expire on a specific date (you'll learn how shortly) and give your users a pop-up window telling them the application will shut down. This time can be anywhere from 0–100 minutes prior to the license expiring.

Now that you've learned about the initial screen in the licensing wizard, let's break each license out, learn what each type of license is, what it's used for and learn how to configure each license type.

Unlimited License

This type of license can be used when your entire company is licensed for an application. An unlimited license doesn't put any restrictions on the application using the license. In fact, if you look at the picture in the upper right-hand corner of the second dialog of the New Unlimited License Wizard displayed in Figure 6.19, you will see a blue infinity sign.

FIGURE 6.19   Configuring the unlimited license.

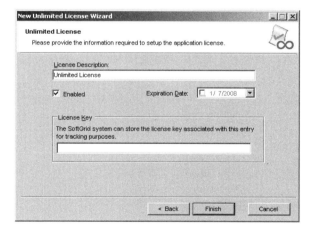

License Description   In this field, you describe the license; I like to use this field to say exactly what type of license we create. As you'll learn a bit later, when we have multiple license groups, naming them this way makes navigating through your licenses quicker.

Enabled   This check box signifies whether the license is enabled or not. Even if an application is attempting to make use of this license, if the license itself is not enabled, the application will run as if there were no license.

Expiration Date   Checking the box in the Expiration Date lets you set a specific date on which the license will expire. If you click the drop-down, you can now navigate to the proper date. Interestingly enough, you can set a date in the past and only generate a warning message. You can still create the license and apply it to a group. Of course, any application that uses this license will fail to launch.

License Key   This field provides you with an opportunity to store the license key for the application used by this license. It doesn't actually make use of the key, it's just a placeholder. Feel free to leave it blank.

> In previous versions of SoftGrid, there was a report called "License Compliance" that would provide you with license usage. In the case of an unlimited license, you would be able to see the number of distinct users that used applications assigned to that license. In SoftGrid 4.2, that report no longer exists. As a result, I recommend not using unlimited licenses.

Concurrent License

A concurrent license allows for a certain number of users to simultaneously access the application. Let's take a 24-hour type of environment like a call center, for example. There is a peak time where there are a maximum number of people in the call center. An application that is licensed concurrently can be set to have enough licenses for this peak time, even though there may be twice that number of employees who access the application on any given day. In Figure 6.20, you can see the second screen of the New Concurrent License Wizard.

Concurrent License Quantity

The only difference between Figure 6.20, which deals with a concurrent license, and Figure 6.19, which deals with an unlimited license, is the Concurrent License Quantity box. Change this number to the number of concurrent users you would like to allow for the application. You can make this any number from 1 all the way up to 32,767 concurrent users. That should be enough, right?

FIGURE 6.20   Configuring a concurrent license.

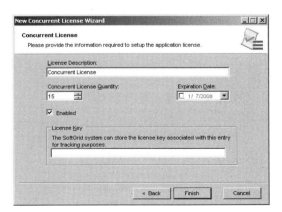

Named License

A named license allows only explicitly named users to have access to the applications associated with the license. If you want to explicitly track who can use a specific application, a named license is your ticket. If Pete in Accounting isn't explicitly named, he won't have access to the DogFoodMaker accounting software. It's that simple.

A named license is also the only license type that has three steps to creating a license group. You can see the second step in Figure 6.21, and you've already learned about the different components of this window.

FIGURE 6.21   The second step of the New Named License Wizard.

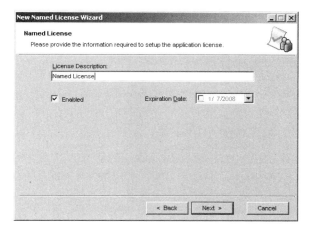

You'll notice there isn't a place to enter a license key. (You'll learn why in the "License Groups" section.) After naming the license, go ahead and click Next.

As shown in Figure 6.22, we now have the opportunity to add our named users to our license. Click the Add button to bring up the screen shown in Figure 6.23.

We can now navigate through our Active Directory to locate the user we want to add as a named user. Additionally, each named user can have their own license key and expiration date and have the license enabled or disabled for them.

License Groups

We briefly touched on the topic of license groups, but let's expand on it here. A license group is automatically created whenever you create a new license. Look closely at the icon to the left of the names listed under Application Licenses in Figure 6.24. You can see that it looks like there are multiple layers to the icon. This is because a *license group* can potentially contain *multiple licenses* within it. With multiple licenses, we can really create some powerful licensing options for our company.

Let's use an example. CAD software can be really expensive. So expensive, in fact, that we might want to do anything and everything we can to make sure we have only the licenses we need for it. In Figure 6.24, you can see we have a named user license already as part of our CAD software license group. We have our 25 CAD engineers listed in this named user license, but we also know that between vacation, sick leave, continuing education, trade shows, conferences, and so on that only 80 percent of our CAD engineers are ever using the software on any given day.

If we right-click our CAD software licensing group, we can select New Concurrent License. Up comes the License Wizard, without the first screen. We already have a licensing group, so we don't need to create another one of those. We just need to type in 80 percent of total number of engineers we have, or 20, and click Finish. Now, take a look at Figure 6.25. You can see we have both licenses in the license group.

FIGURE 6.22 Add a list of named users.

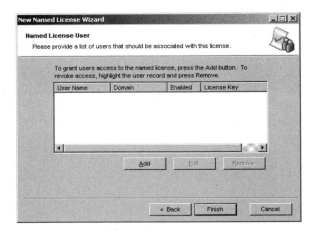

FIGURE 6.23 Adding a named user.

FIGURE 6.24   License groups.

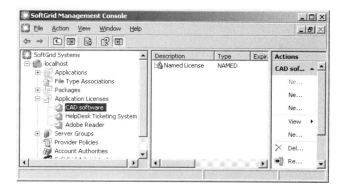

FIGURE 6.25   Two licenses in one license group.

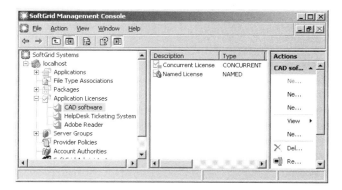

Once we configure our CAD software application to use this license group, our CAD engineers will be the only users who can run this software, and only 20 of them can run it at any one time.

We'll learn how to configure applications to use license groups when we talk about provider policies a bit later in the chapter.

Server Groups Node

The Server Groups node allows you to create groups of servers that have different characteristics. One group of servers can be configured one way, and another group of servers can be configured to log information differently.

Let's say we have multiple sites for our company: our main headquarters in Portland and a secondary site in Seattle. We have SoftGrid servers at both sites, and the two sites are connected by a T1. It is possible to have the Seattle SoftGrid servers log data to the main site in Portland, but would we want to send that data over our small pipe?

Instead, we can configure the Seattle servers to do all of their logging to a local database instead. We can save bandwidth by doing this and ensure the T1 is not clogged with SoftGrid logging data.

Creating a New Server Group

In the SoftGrid Management Console, right-click Server Groups and choose New Server Group. As you can see in Figure 6.26, the New Server Group Wizard appears.

FIGURE 6.26   The New Server Group Wizard.

Let's name our server group Seattle SoftGrid. We haven't created any additional provider policies at this point, so our only option is to choose Default Provider.

The Enabled check box is quite powerful: if you uncheck this box, either now or on a later day, all of the SoftGrid servers that are a member of this group will no longer accept any connections. They aren't enabled to do so. For our example, go ahead and leave this box checked and click Finish.

Now we have a second server group called Seattle SoftGrid, as seen in Figure 6.27.

FIGURE 6.27   Two server groups, not just one.

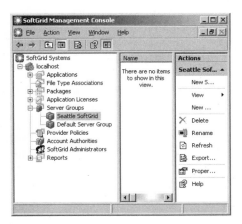

As you can see in Figure 6.27, however, there aren't any servers listed in our Seattle Soft-Grid Server Group. To remedy that situation, we just need to add them.

Adding a Server to the Server Group

Right-click the server group you want to add servers to, and choose New SoftGrid Virtual Application Server. The New Server Wizard will appear, as you can see in Figure 6.28.

FIGURE 6.28   Adding a new server to a Server Group.

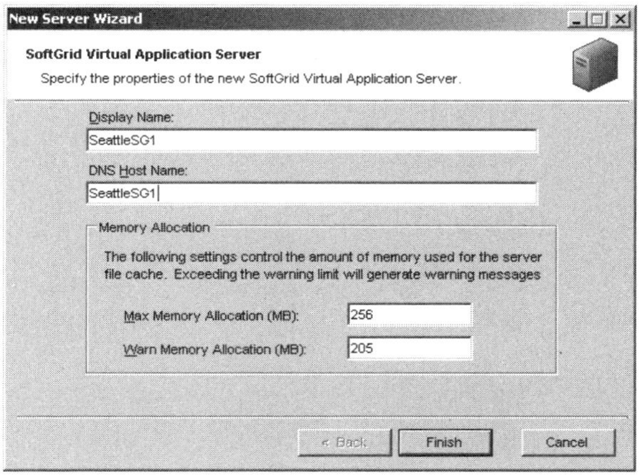

We don't actually have a second server to use, so for the purposes of this demonstration, we can go ahead and make one up. For the display name, you can enter anything you want. I've entered SeattleSG1, as you can see. I've entered that information into the DNS Host Name field as well. If we were actually setting this up, we would want to set the correct hostname for the real server.

The memory allocation section of the screen is used to support user sessions. You would think the more memory you have allocated, the more user sessions could be supported on a single server. It turns out the limiting factor is actually the processors, not the memory. You can read more about server sizing here: `http://tinyurl.com/3aphtt`.

For now, don't change either of these values. Go ahead and click Finish, and you will have a new server as a part of your server group, just like in Figure 6.29.

Since we now have a server to configure, go ahead and right-click the Seattle SoftGrid server group, and choose Properties. Let's configure our new Server group.

Server Group Properties

When we click Properties, as you can see in Figure 6.30, the General tab displays the provider policy we selected from Figure 6.26 and shows that the server group is enabled.

Let's click the Logging tab to configure logging for our Seattle SoftGrid server group. By default, logging is not enabled for any server group. You must manually configure your Soft-Grid system for logging. As you can see in Figure 6.31, we are logging to a SQL database.

FIGURE 6.29   Now we have a server in our server group.

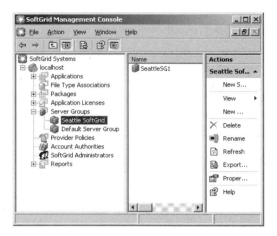

FIGURE 6.30   The General tab of the Seattle SoftGrid Server Group Properties window.

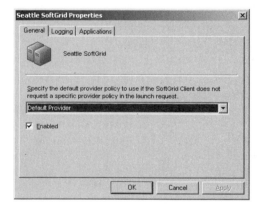

Click the Add button to display the Add/Edit Log Module window. If you click the Type drop-down, it is possible to log to a file. The biggest problem with doing that is you lose all reporting capabilities on the system-related problems. The report functionality, which you will learn about in the Reports Node section, can only query information in a SQL database, not a file. I'd set this to SQL Database.

If you click the Event Type drop-down, you'll see there are six options to choose from:

Transactions Only   For the purpose of logging, transactions deal only with licenses that have been set up and are being used on the system.

Fatal Errors   Fatal errors are errors the server had in handling more than one client session. They can also potentially prevent the server from taking *any* incoming requests.

FIGURE 6.31 Setting up logging for a server group.

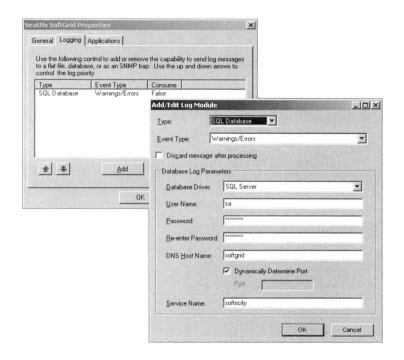

Errors Errors are problems the server had in handling one client session. It's not quite as catastrophic as a fatal error.

Warning/Errors Warnings are messages that give you a status update on something could be wrong with your system. They can also lead to trouble later on down the line if they are not dealt with. This level also logs errors.

Info/Warning/Errors This logging level includes messages related to general activity on the server and performance of the server as well as the Warning/Errors.

Verbose Everything and the kitchen sink. This logging level will tell you how the server handled every component of every request that it received. Be careful with this one.

There are a few other settings of note on the Add/Edit Log Module window shown in Figure 6.31. Let's learn about them now.

Discard Message after Processing

Enabling this will force the logging module to delete the logged messages rather than passing them onto the next system that will log messages. The default option is to pass all messages on.

Database Driver

For SQL database logging, you can choose a different driver to use to connect to the database. However, there are only two options, Oracle and SQL, and Oracle isn't supported.

The User Name and Password fields are self explanatory, so I won't go into detail here.

DNS Host Name

The DNS Host Name field contains the host name of the SQL server. In our case, we are using the same server for the SoftGrid server as for the SQL server, so we'll just enter SoftGrid.

We'll also leave the checkmark in the Dynamically Determine Port box, as well. This allows the SoftGrid server to communicate over a range of ports as opposed to a single defined port.

Service Name

In the Service Name field, just fill in the name of the database in the SQL server that is being used by the SoftGrid system.

Applications Tab

The last tab in the Server group Properties is the Applications tab, as you can see in Figure 6.32.

FIGURE 6.32 The Applications tab.

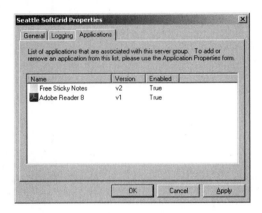

This tab is only informational, but it does have some value to it. You can tell which applications are being serviced by which server group and whether an application is enabled or not.

Provider Policies

The Provider Policies node is where we, as SoftGrid administrators, get to dictate how our clients and users interact with our SoftGrid system.

Out of the box, SoftGrid has the ability to enforce licensing. In fact, in the "Application Licenses Node" section, you learned how to set up those licenses. But it isn't until you properly set up a *provider policy* that those licenses will be enforced.

You also learned that in the File Type Associations node we can set file types for applications that apply to all users of that application. But, as you will learn in the "Client File Type Associations" section, we can also set file type associations in the SoftGrid Client. So, which association wins? The one set on the client, or the one set on the server? The answer: it depends on how your provider policy is set.

How do you set your provider policy? Let's dive in and learn the various settings.

There are three different screens to a provider policy, whether you are creating one from scratch or looking at the properties of a current provider policy. In our example, we'll start from scratch and create a brand new provider policy. Let's right-click Provider Policies node in the SoftGrid Management Console and click New Provider Policy to start the New Provider Policy Wizard, shown in Figure 6.33. As you can see, we'll need to give our new provider policy a name.

FIGURE 6.33 Naming the new provider policy.

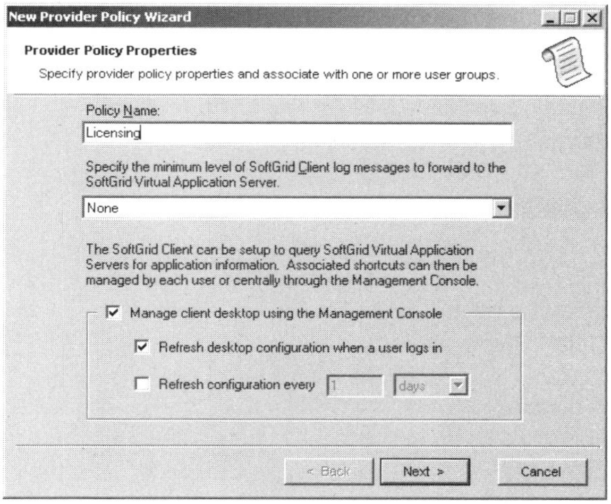

Since we will be using this new provider policy to start enforcing some of our licenses, I've gone ahead and named the policy just that: Licensing.

The first setting we can configure deals specifically with the client logging. If you click the drop-down, you'll see six different options to choose from. We'll cover five of those options in much more detail when we discuss logging in the "SoftGrid Client Management Console" section.

We can have every SoftGrid Client send their logging messages to the server to centralize client logging. While at first glance, this may sound like a good idea, it can make finding specific messages related to one individual client a bit troublesome. The default setting, which is also the sixth option, is None, which means no client messages are sent to the server. I've never seen a reason to change it from this setting.

Manage Client Desktop Using the Management Console

The box in the bottom half of Figure 6.33 deals with how the Desktop client queries the SoftGrid servers for applications. Earlier, we touched on the possibility that there might be file type associations set differently on both the client and the server and wondered which one would win. The answer depends on if the "Manage client desktop using the Management Console" box is checked. If the box is checked (and by default, it is checked). then the file type associations on the server override the client settings. If you uncheck it, then the client file type associations take precedence.

Refresh desktop configuration when a user logs in   By default, this check box is checked. This forces the Desktop client to contact the SoftGrid servers when a user logs in for updated configuration information. It's also one way to get new applications out to users. If this box is checked, the user can log out and log back in to get their new applications. You'll learn other ways to perform this function later in this chapter in the "SoftGrid Client Applet" section.

Refresh configuration every   This last check box, by default, is not checked. Therefore, there is no automatic refresh of the configuration information. However, if you check this box, you can force the Desktop client to refresh its configuration information as often as every 30 minutes, or as infrequently as every 999 days. For our licensing provider policy, we'll leave this unchecked.

Clicking Next brings us to the Group Assignment screen you see in Figure 6.34, which lets us add groups of users.

FIGURE 6.34   Adding groups to the provider policy.

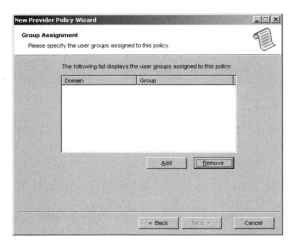

The default provider policy uses the Domain users group of the domain the SoftGrid server resides in. Since we are setting up a provider policy for a specific purpose (enabling licensing), we could choose a different group. Maybe we only want our Marketing users to comply with our SoftGrid licensing, so we can add only our Marketing users group here. For the purposes of this policy, however, click on the Add button. When the dialog box appears, browse to the Users folder and double-click on it. Then select the Domain users group and click Next.

 The dialog box that pops up to add groups will not let you browse every trusted domain to select a group. If you want to deliver applications from this SoftGrid system to users whose AD accounts reside in a different domain, for example, a company you just merged with, you will need to have a trust in place and then update the default provider policy with the appropriate groups to grant access.

We can now set the policies, as you can see in Figure 6.35.

FIGURE 6.35   Setting up authentication and licensing for the provider policy.

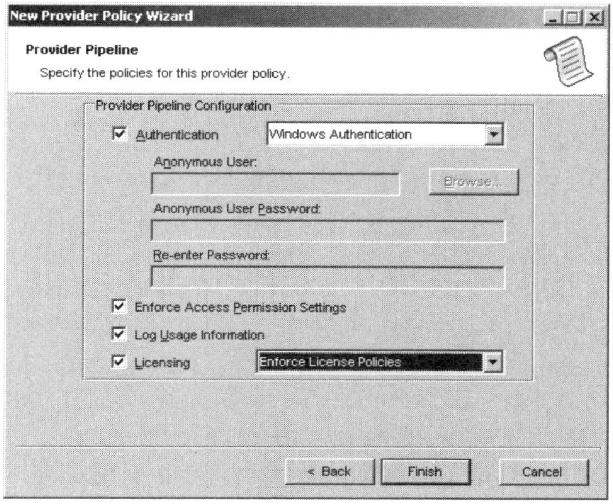

Authentication Methods

Let's talk about authentication. There are multiple ways to have users authenticate to the SoftGrid system. Here's a rundown of the three types of authentication supported by SoftGrid:

Windows Authentication   The default, type of authentication is Windows Authentication. When a user logs onto a workstation with the SoftGrid Client installed on it, the SoftGrid Client service starts with the credentials of the logged on user. Then, whenever an application refresh is initiated, the client passes those credentials to the SoftGrid server to receive updated configuration information.

Basic Authentication   If Basic Authentication is chosen, when a user launches an application, they will be prompted to enter their credentials. Of course, these credentials are not encrypted, so using this method is not as secure as using Windows authentication. If you do configure this, users will gain access to applications by providing a user ID and password that is authorized in the SoftGrid system to run the applications.

Anonymous Authentication   If you choose Anonymous Authentication, anyone who launches *any* application from the SoftGrid system will be able to use the account that is listed on this screen. You can grant this single-user right to all applications. If you do this, however, you will no longer be able to determine who is running which application. In essence, you are granting every user the right to run every application on your SoftGrid system. For obvious reasons, this isn't recommended.

Enforce Access Permissions Settings

The default is for this setting to be checked. This setting makes sure that a user is a member of the group before granting access to an application.

Log Usage Information

By default, this setting is checked, and that's a good thing. This setting ensures that all of the usage of an application is monitored and recorded for posterity and for reporting purposes, which we'll learn more about in our "Reports Node" section.

Licensing

Notice by default that licensing is not enabled. Since this provider policy is specifically for licensing, go ahead and enable it. We now have two drop-downs to choose from:

Audit License Usage only   Using this license will not ever prevent someone from using an application if there isn't a license available. In previous versions of SoftGrid, there was a report that would show license utilization, which made it easier to determine whether your software was licensed correctly. That report is no longer available, so I don't see a need for this type of license.

Enforce License Policies   This setting will enforce the licenses we created in the Application Licenses node. Every user who uses this provider policy will need to have a license for the application they are launching. If there is no available license, the application will not launch.

Select Enforce License Policies here, and then click Finish. You will now get a message telling you to restart the Virtual Application Server services; just click OK.

 Real World Scenario

Successfully Using SoftGrid Licensing

You now have all of the tools you need to successfully implement licensing in the SoftGrid system. We just need to put them all together. Creating a provider policy that enforces licensing is the first step, and we did that in the "Provider Policies" section.

We also have three license groups that we created in the "Application Licenses" section. For this example, let's use the Adobe Reader license group we created and put a named user license in the group. We'll only put one named user in the license.

Open up the properties of the Adobe Reader application by right-clicking the application in the Applications node and selecting Properties. You should be on the General tab of Adobe Reader, as seen next.

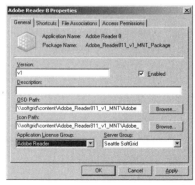

Click the Application License Group drop-down menu and select Adobe Reader. Now click OK.

This next part is the tricky part when it comes to licensing, so stick with me here. Browse to your content directory and find the folder containing the OSD file for Adobe Reader. Open up this file and find the following line:

```
HREF="rtsp://softgrid:554/Adobe_Reader811_v1_MNT/Adobe_Reader811_v1_MNT.sft"
```

This line needs to be modified to include the provider policy. Here's what the new line should look like:

```
HREF="rtsp://softgrid:554/Adobe_Reader811_v1_MNT/Adobe_Reader811_v1_
MNT.sft?Customer=Licensing"
```

Now, log in with your named user and see if Adobe works. Next, try it with a user who is *not* a named user. You can't use it. Pretty slick, eh?

To recap:

- Create the provider policy.

- Create the license group.

- Assign the license group to the application.

- Modify the HREF line in the OSD file by adding `?Customer=Name_of_Provider_Policy` at the end of the current HREF line, and before the quotes.

Account Authorities Node

The Account Authorities node will display the sgBrowser information we entered on initial setup of the SoftGrid system. If you refer back to Figure 5.6, you can see we entered the sgBrowser username and password.

But this account is never actually used to log into the network. In fact, if you check the last time this user logged in, you may find that they have never actually logged in. If your company is a security-conscious organization, it's possible someone might come along and disable this account because it might *appear* that it isn't being used, when in fact, it is used every day by the SoftGrid system.

So, if someone makes changes to this sgBrowser account in Active Directory, you might need to make changes to the account in the SoftGrid system. To do that, highlight the Account Authorities node in the left hand pane of the SoftGrid Management Console. In the middle pane, the domain name and domain type will be displayed, as in Figure 6.36.

If we right-click the information displayed in the middle pane and click Properties, we'll see the corp.com Properties box, shown in Figure 6.37.

You can see that our domain type in this case is Active Directory. If you click the drop-down, however, you will see Windows NT 4.0 domain is still listed as an option. I have run SoftGrid in an Active Directory domain and provisioned applications to user accounts in a trusted NT 4.0 domain. SoftGrid can be configured to work with NT 4.0; it just isn't a supported option.

FIGURE 6.36 Highlight the Account Authorities node.

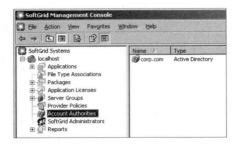

FIGURE 6.37 Properties of the Account Authority.

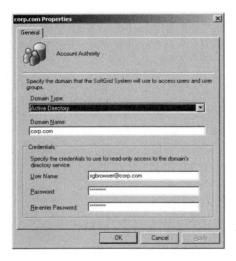

The domain is listed, as well as the sgBrowser account. Keep in mind that any changes made in Active Directory to the password of the sgBrowser account will also need to be changed here. If you haven't already, go back and configure the sgBrowser account with a nonexpiring password. Additionally, I recommend configuring the account so that should someone accidentally log in with this account, they cannot change the password.

Reports Node

You know what's frustrating for me? Not knowing what's going on. That's why reports were invented. Let me give you examples of three common problems that SoftGrid can help you solve with these three report types:

- Application Utilization report
- User/Group Activity report
- Software Audit report

Let's say that since you've been at your company, you have always heard that about 60 per-cent of the employees need a certain software. No one has ever questioned where that percent-age came from, it's just taken as fact. But now your company is undergoing some cost cutting measures, and you've been asked to ensure that your licensing situation is squared away. With an Application Utilization report, you can figure out *exactly* how many licenses of this soft-ware you need. You can even determine all of the people who haven't used the software in the last, say, three months. Talk about saving some money!

We all know users like Alice in Accounting. Alice needs 86 different applications on her com-puter. She also needs every application updated to the latest version or she "won't be able to do her job." But her boss is starting to get concerned about Alice and wants to know just how much she is using each piece of software. If you create a User/Group Activity report, you can track, down to the minute, just how long Alice has used each piece of software. Even better, you'll be able to see which pieces of software she hasn't ever used.

If you have thousands of users in your company, it's tough to know just how many people are actually using the various software packages you have available. Is anyone still using Adobe Reader 7, or did you upgrade everyone? How about Word 2000? You sequenced the Opera browser, but is it actually being used? Running a Software Audit report will tell you just how many people are using *every* published sequence on your Soft-Grid system.

Pretty sweet, eh?

The Reports node is the last node we'll learn about in the SoftGrid Management Console. If we right-click the Reports node, and click New Report, we'll see the screen displayed in Figure 6.38.

FIGURE 6.38   The first step in creating a new report.

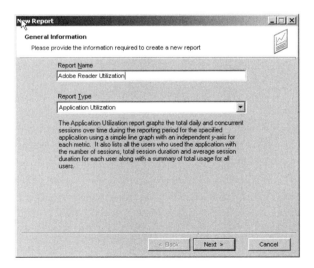

Types of Reports

First, we need to give our report a name. In this case, we'll call it Adobe Reader Utilization. Next, we need to choose the report type. There are five choices available on the Report Type drop-down menu. Here's what each type of report is and why it comes in handy:

System Utilization   This report type will tell us the number of daily and concurrent users over the period of time specified in the report. We can also choose to filter this based on the individual SoftGrid server or the server group or even look at every single SoftGrid server in our entire enterprise.

This report is useful in capacity planning situations. If you look at the Microsoft SoftGrid server sizing guide at `http://tinyurl.com/3aphtt`, you can see that each server can handle about 1,400 concurrent users. This report will tell you how close you are to hitting that mark.

Software Audit   This report type will give you application usage for *all* applications published in your SoftGrid system over the period of time specified in the report.

If you ever need to supply an overview of enterprise-wide application usage for a specific period of time, this report would be your best friend. It breaks down every application by user and how long they used it.

Application Utilization   This report type will tell you the number of daily and concurrent sessions over the time period specified for a specific application, broken down by username. It will tell you how many times they used it and how long they used it for.

Let's say we use a program called DogFoodMaker 2007 at `corp.com`. We have 16 folks who have licenses, but we are about to hire another person who should also most likely have rights to this application. The license for DogFoodMaker 2007 is a bit expensive, so we need to figure out if all 16 folks who have licenses are actually using the program. Application Utilization reporting to the rescue. You can run an Application Utilization report and determine exactly how much usage this application gets based on the user. You might even be able to reallocate a license if you figure out that someone hasn't actually used DogFoodMaker 2007 in the last six months.

User/Group Activity   This report type will tell you every application accessed by a specific user or group over the time period specified in the report. It will also tell you how many times each person used each application and for how long.

This report comes in handy when you need to determine just how often a specific department accesses a set of applications. How often does Sales use the DogFoodMaker suite of applications? They want an upgrade that is really expensive; do they use them often enough to justify the cost? This report will answer that question for you.

System Error   This report type will list the total number of fatal errors, errors, and warnings on a specific server, server group, or across the entire enterprise during the reporting period. It will also list each error individually, along with the time the error occurred.

This report is great for SoftGrid administrators to review on a periodic basis. Fatal errors affect more than one session and can potentially prevent the system from handling subsequent requests. They can be *fatal* to your SoftGrid system. Errors affect only one session and don't prevent the system from servicing any additional requests. Warnings are used to indicate unexpected events, but those events can automatically be recovered from. Of course, if the same warnings continue to happen, the warnings could eventually turn into errors, or even fatal errors.

Running a Report

Now that you understand all of the different report types, let's walk through creating each type of report.

System Utilization

Right-click the Reports node in the SoftGrid Management Console and click New Report. The screen shown in Figure 6.38 will pop up again, only this time, click the Report Type drop-down and choose System Utilization. Go ahead and name the report System Utilization, and click Next. You'll see the screen in Figure 6.39.

FIGURE 6.39   Select the time period for the report.

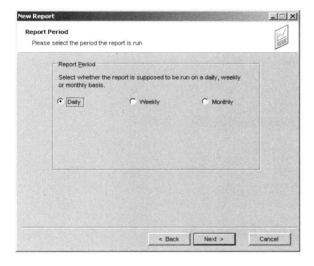

Go ahead and select the time period for the report, whether it's Daily, Weekly, or Monthly, and select Next. The Utilization Measurement screen will appear, as shown in Figure 6.40.

Go ahead and leave Sessions selected and choose Next. The Server screen will be displayed, which will allow you to select the server, server group, or enterprise you want to report on, as shown in Figure 6.41.

Click Finish and you have now created a System Utilization report; however, you can't run it just yet. Figure 6.42shows the entire SoftGrid Management Console.

Okay, you're going to have to stick with me here, because I'm about to show you something that's caused me lots of pain and confusion. In Figure 6.42, you can see the report we just created, System Utilization, is highlighted. Yet, in the right-hand pane, there's no option to run the report. Indeed, if you expand the Reports node and then right-click in the System Utilization report *without first selecting the Utilization report*, as I did in Figure 6.43, you still won't be able to run the report.

FIGURE 6.40 How do you want to measure system utilization?

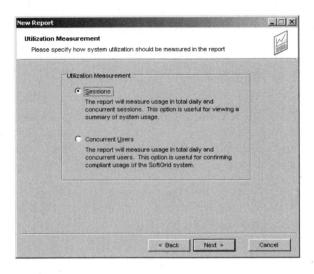

FIGURE 6.41 Select which server, server group, or enterprise to report on.

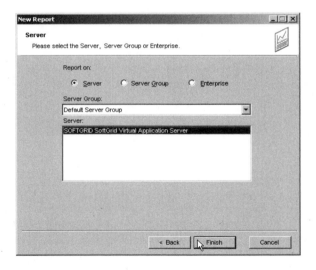

Now, go ahead and select the report, and look at what happens to the middle pane of the SoftGrid Management Console. See how it changed to a completely different type of window in Figure 6.44? Totally wacky!

FIGURE 6.42 Something is missing; there is no option to run the report.

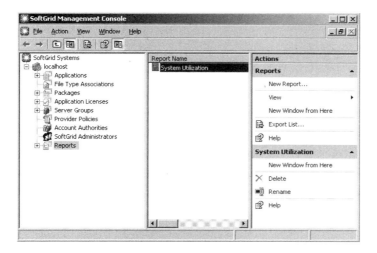

FIGURE 6.43 I still can't run my newly created report.

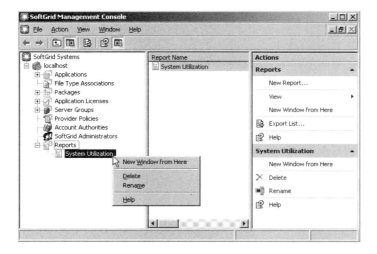

You can also see that the right-hand pane will let me run the report. If I right-click the report name under the Reports node, Run Report will be listed there, as well. This behavior exists for all newly created reports: you first must select the report and wait for the middle pane to change before you can run the report.

FIGURE 6.44   The middle pane looks different now. Note that you can now run the report using "Run Report" in the right page.

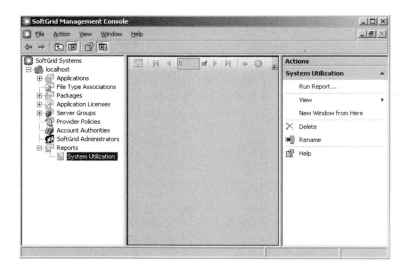

This behavior also occurs when you first launch the SoftGrid Management Console and try to run a saved report: you will still need to select the report and wait for the middle pane to change.

Okay, now that the middle pane has changed, we can actually run our report. Click Run Report. This is where things continue to get a bit weird *with reporting*. Even though we just configured the System Utilization report, choosing a daily report, sessions, and the SoftGrid server, we still have to choose the report period and which date we want for the reporting period, as shown in Figure 6.45.

In fact, we can even choose a completely different time period from the one we configured the report with. Go ahead and click Next here without changing anything.

FIGURE 6.45   Choosing the report period while running the report.

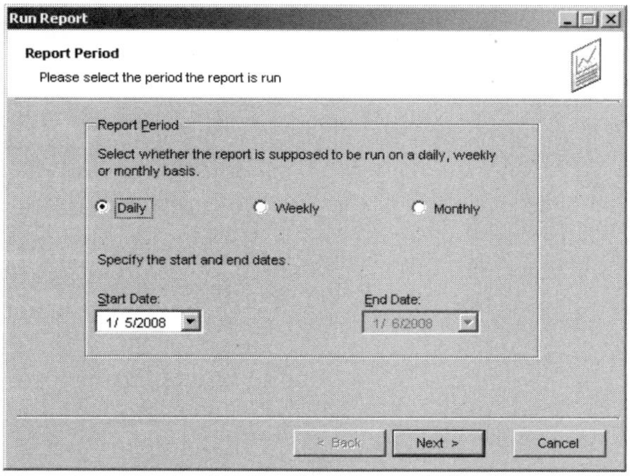

The Utilization Measurement screen comes up, except this time it's all grayed out, as in Figure 6.46.

FIGURE 6.46 Grayed out Utilization Measurement screen.

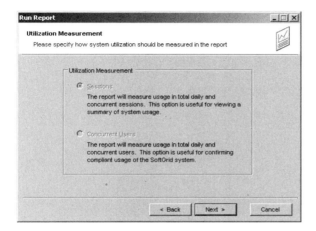

FIGURE 6.47 Select Server, Server Group, or Enterprise to run your report....again.

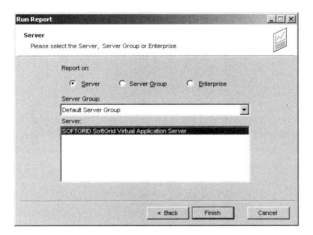

Click Next and you'll see the Server screen shown in Figure 6.41, only this time it's a Run Report window instead of a New Report window, as shown in Figure 6.47.

Click Finish, and the report will finally run. Hooray!

Go get yourself a soda and take a break. You earned it.

But don't take too long, we still have lots more SoftGrid fun to cover.

Sizing the SoftGrid Database

We have already seen the information that can be stored in our SoftGrid database. But now let's learn how to properly size our database to store all of that information. If you turn back to Figure 5.39, you can see the right-click menu options on the Server node. Choosing System Options brings up the System Options window displayed in Figure 5.40.

We set the default content path in the last chapter, so now click the Database tab as shown below.

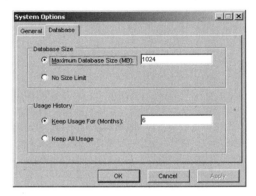

Database Size

The top section of the Database tab lets us specify a maximum database size or allow the database to grow to whatever size it needs. If you are limited by disk space, you might want to specify a maximum size.

TechNet has a guide for server sizing here: `http://tinyurl.com/3aphtt`.

If application logging is enabled, the database will grow based on application usage. The average transaction size for a user launching an application or shutting an application down is 1KB. So, for a company with 5000 employees with each employee launching, on average, five applications a day, the database will grow roughly 25MB per day.

Usage History

By default, usage information is logged for six months. You can also choose to either keep all usage history, or set a specific period of time to keep usage history, from 1 month to 120 months (yes, 10 years worth of application usage data!). Of course, this can also be completely disabled by making a change in the provider policy, which we covered earlier in the Provider Policies section.

Usage history comes into play when we start talking about creating reports. If there isn't any history, you can't create any useful reports now, can you?

SoftGrid Client Management Console

In the last chapter, you learned how to get the SoftGrid Client onto your target machines. Once the SoftGrid Client is installed on your own workstation, you can manage all of your client settings and do quite a bit of troubleshooting and problem resolution. This is where the magic happens, at least from the client perspective.

So, let's check things out.

On a machine that has the SoftGrid Client installed, click Start ➤ Control Panel ➤ Administrative Tools and launch the SoftGrid Client Management Console (CMC). You can see the result in Figure 6.48.

Now, we're ready to dive in and poke around.

FIGURE 6.48   The SoftGrid Client Management Console.

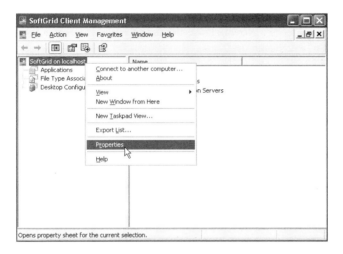

Figure 6.48 shows that we're working locally on this computer because the CMC displays "SoftGrid on localhost." But, of course, you can see this tool is meant to help us connect to *other* computers on the network, as well.

The CMC is kind of like the Windows Computer Management MMC snap-in. That is, the CMC snap-in works locally, but it also lets you remotely connect to another computer.

You'll learn how to use this tool to remotely manage machines a bit later. For now, let's check out what's available in Properties. Once you get the hang of it on your local system, you'll be able to manage remote systems in no time flat.

If you have a firewall enabled, including the Windows XP or Vista firewalls, there are two ports you'll need to open up to make this connection: TCP port 135 and TCP port 1041.

There are five big areas we're going to cover in this section:

General Properties   We'll cover all of the tabs within the General properties.

Applications Node   We'll see a list of sequenced applications on the computer and learn how to troubleshoot them.

File Type Associations Node   We'll go over all of the file type associations delivered through SoftGrid and all of the user-created associations.

Desktop Configuration Node   We'll see how this node lists the server(s) the SoftGrid Client talks to for application information and how often the client refreshes that configuration.

Remotely Managing Another Client   Now that we can manage all of the various settings on our own client, we'll learn what we can and can't do remotely on other clients.

General Properties of the SoftGrid Client Management Tool

When we installed the SoftGrid Client in the previous chapter, we set our Desktop configuration server and called it SoftGrid. Every other setting was a default configuration. The Properties tab is where we can find the rest of the settings we didn't configure and a few more on top of that.

We'll find those settings on the following tabs:

General   Includes log settings and data locations.

Interface   Configures SoftGrid components and messages visible to the end user.

File System   Configures system-wide settings related to the SoftGrid file system.

Network   Configures types of allowed connections, proxy servers, and remote administration settings.

Connectivity   Configures all settings related to using SoftGrid in Disconnected mode.

Permissions   Changes what a user can do with various components of the SoftGrid Client Management Tool.

General Tab

The General tab, shown in Figure 6.49, deals with the locations of a few key pieces of data: where client logs are stored and how detailed the reporting in them is; where the globally accessible SoftGrid data is stored; and where the user-specific SoftGrid data is stored.

FIGURE 6.49   The General tab.

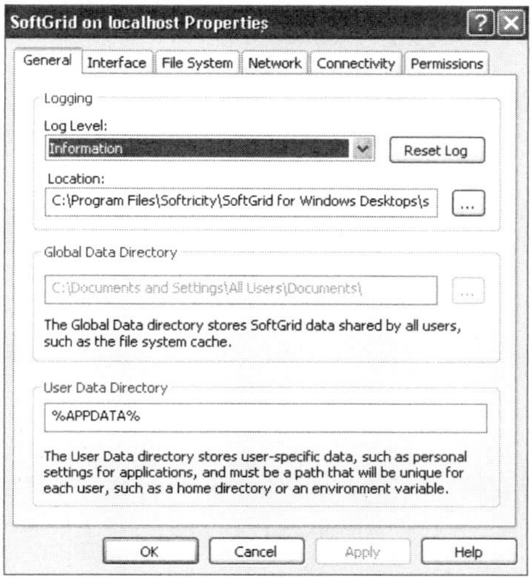

SoftGrid on localhost Properties

General | Interface | File System | Network | Connectivity | Permissions

Logging

Log Level:

Information | Reset Log

Location:

C:\Program Files\Softricity\SoftGrid for Windows Desktops\s | ...

Global Data Directory

C:\Documents and Settings\All Users\Documents\ | ...

The Global Data directory stores SoftGrid data shared by all users, such as the file system cache.

User Data Directory

%APPDATA%

The User Data directory stores user-specific data, such as personal settings for applications, and must be a path that will be unique for each user, such as a home directory or an environment variable.

OK | Cancel | Apply | Help

Logging

The top section in the General tab deals with the logging done by the client. By default, Log Level is set to Information; however, if you click the drop-down, you'll see there are five options to choose from: Critical, Error, Warning, Information, and Verbose. Each level builds on the next one. If you set the level to Critical, all you see are the critical messages. Setting the level to Warning means you will see Critical, Error, and Warning messages. Setting the level to Verbose lets you see all five different types of messages.

The 4.5 release of the SoftGrid Client (Microsoft Application Virtualization) will let us log events right to the Event Viewer if we so choose. Instead of scrolling through a text file, we can use the Application log in the Event Viewer and all of its filtering and searching options.

Changing the log level does require either a reboot or stopping and restarting the SoftGrid Client service. If you open the log file, shown in Figure 6.50, you can see that each message is classified by Log Level type.

Let's break down the log file shown in Figure 6.50:

- The first line in each log file entry contains the information needed to determine the type of log level message: INF means "information" and CRT means "critical."

- You can see one crucial entry toward the bottom of Figure 6.50 where the log shows, "The SoftGrid Client Core initialized correctly."

FIGURE 6.50 The SFTLOG.TXT file. The types of messages are circled here for clarity.

```
[01/28/2008 13:00:11.320 VSCM INF {tid=56C}
Starting Virtual Service Control Manager.

[01/28/2008 13:00:13.261 JGSW INF {tid=56C}
The SoftGrid file system was initialized successfully.

[01/28/2008 13:00:13.321 INTF CRT {tid=56C}
The SoftGrid Client Core initialized correctly.
Installed Product: SoftGrid for windows Desktops
Version: 4.2.0.302 (RTM)
Install Path: C:\Program Files\Softricity\SoftGrid for
windows Desktops
```

If you set Log Level to Critical, you will see just the Critical messages appear in your log after rebooting and not much else.

Here's a breakdown of other logging codes, what they mean, and what you can do about it.

ERR You might get an error message for the following reasons:

- When you receive a launch failed pop-up box and the application fails to launch, you can bet there will be an error message in this log file. The entry will include the long error code, as well, which can be used to help search in the Microsoft Knowledge Base.
- The SoftGrid Client is unable to stream down an application.

WRN You might see a warning message for the following reasons:

- The client system lost connectivity to the SoftGrid server and is now running in Disconnected mode.
- Your SoftGrid Client performed a background refresh of their Desktop configuration but was unable to update an OSD file that has changed on the server.
- The SoftGrid Client was unable to load a shortcut from the server.

Any of these issues could lead to trouble later on down the line.

INF You might see an information message for the following reasons:

- An application shut down.
- An OSD file was updated.
- The file system was successfully initialized.
- An application was deleted.
- An application was unloaded.
- An application took a certain amount of time to launch—down to the thousandth of a second.

VRB Anything goes with a verbose message. Rather than there being a specific reason a message might appear, you will see everything the SoftGrid Client is doing on your system, including the following:

- Checking each OS type.
- Checking suite names.

- Telling you the suite name is okay.
- Performing a `get` for the name of the SoftGrid server.

The list goes on and on. And on. I don't recommend using the Verbose setting unless you are looking for something very specific. It can make finding the informational and warning messages very difficult.

> **WARNING**   When Microsoft says "verbose," they really mean it. At one point, I changed my logging level to Verbose to troubleshoot a sequence that wasn't working properly, and I forgot to change the logging level back when I was done. The next day, I had a log file so large that it filled up the rest of my hard drive.

Troubleshooting a sequence can involve tackling the problem from different directions. It can be partly the sequence or the client's *reaction* to the sequence. With that in mind, we might have a need to perform the same task on the client repeatedly to see if the log files shows anything different. Rather than constantly appending information to the same log file, we can simply click the Reset Log button, which you can see in the Logging section of the General tab shown in Figure 6.49.

By resetting the log, the SoftGrid Client will automatically take the current log file, `sftlog .txt`, and move it to a backup copy called `sftlog0001.txt`. If the `sftlog0001.txt` file already exists, it will move the log file to a backup copy called `sftlog0002.txt`, and so on. This way, you can not only start with a fresh log file to parse, but also keep the previous log files for future reference.

Global Data Directory

In Chapter 5, we mentioned the all-encompassing `sftfs.fsd` file, the file that contains all of our virtual applications on the client. The Global Data Directory is where that file, along with local copies of OSD and icon files, resides. If you take a quick look back at Figure 6.49, you might be wondering why this section is grayed out. This is so you cannot change the values while the SoftGrid Client service is running.

You might think about shutting the SoftGrid Client service down so you can make a change here. If you do, the SoftGrid Client Management tool will automatically shut down, as a primitive fight or flight response. And then, when you start the tool back up, the service starts up!

So, you can't just go and change it, at least not without poking around in the Registry.

Stop the SoftGrid Client service. Now, open up `regedit`, and navigate to `HKLM\SOFTWARE\ Softricity\SoftGrid Client\CurrentVersion\Configuration` and look for the REG_SZ value called `GlobalDataDirectory`. You can change the value of that key and then restart your SoftGrid Client service.

The only time I can see someone wanting to move the Global Data Directory is if there's a space issue on a hard drive. If you only have a 20GB hard drive and want to allow for 25GB worth of applications, you could simply stick a second drive into your system and change the location of the Global Data Directory. Of course, if you change this location *after* you have already used applications, you'll have to stream all of your applications down to your system again.

User Data Directory

The User Data Directory houses all of the customizations we make to our SoftGrid delivered applications. If we add a toolbar to our default view, or change the color of something, those settings are stored here.

Think of this as an application data folder *just* for SoftGrid-delivered applications. By default, this folder is a part of our user account's application data folder. That's what the variable %APPDATA%, shown in Figure 6.49, means.

 Real World Scenario

It's a World of Variables with SoftGrid

You've learned about two different environment variables in the SoftGrid world, %SFT_SOFTGRIDSERVER% from the previous chapter, and %APPDATA%. The wonderful thing about using an environment variable is that we, the Enterprise Desktop Management gurus, get to decide what those variables really mean.

Open up a command prompt by clicking Start ➢ Run, typing **cmd**, and pressing Enter. Once the command prompt is open, type the word **set** and press Enter. All of the environment variables that are displayed here are ready for you to start using them.

If you scroll to the top of this list, you will see %APPDATA% listed there. It's already defined as the application data folder in your profile. This means we can do all kinds of things with the Soft-Grid user data, just by manipulating the application data folder, or %APPDATA%. How about redirecting the application data folder to the network using Group Policy as we learned about in Chapter 3. We could also roam this data as part of a roaming application data folder as well. It's even possible for us to change the %APPDATA% environment variable itself to point to a completely different location.

The other environment variable we have seen so far in SoftGrid, %SFT_SOFTGRIDSERVER%, is a client setting that can be used to define the SoftGrid server. In Figure 5.28 in the previous chapter, you can see that during sequencing, we changed this from %SFT_SOFTGRIDSERVER% to SoftGrid. In this case, we have a single server named SoftGrid, and we want to stream all of our applications from that one server.

But what if we have multiple SoftGrid servers in multiple sites? We can't call all of them "Soft-Grid," but we can make use of the %SFT_SOFTGRIDSERVER% environment variable. Let's say we have two sites, one in Seattle and one in Portland. There is a SoftGrid server in each site. The server in Seattle is called SGSEATTLE and the server in Portland is called SGPORTLAND. We want to be able to use the same set of sequenced applications in both sites. Moreover, we want people to be able to travel with their laptops between both sites and not stream applications from a city hundreds of miles away. In this case, we can use the new Group Policy Preferences to set an environment variable on the system, and then *filter* the policy based on the IP range of each site. Rather than a user needing to reboot their computers when they get to a new site to pick up the new environment variable, the policy will refresh in the background and change the environment variable without the user even realizing what is happening. One minute they are streaming from SGSEATTLE, the next minute from SGPORTLAND.

That is the flexibility of using environment variables.

Interface Tab

The next tab on our journey is the Interface tab, as seen in Figure 6.51. The Interface tab holds the configuration pieces for the tray icon in the "Run Settings" section and the status messages in the "Popup messages" section.

FIGURE 6.51   The Interface tab.

Run Settings

The default is to have the tray icon show up only after you've launched an application. I suggest that you set the icon to always be present. That way, you'll always have access to the right-click menu, as shown in Figure 6.52.

FIGURE 6.52   Right-click the SoftGrid Tray icon for menu options.

The right-click menu on the SoftGrid Client has a lot of power, which we'll cover in the section "SoftGrid Client Applet" a little later.

Popup Messages

When you launch an application delivered through SoftGrid, a little pop-up message appears just over the system tray. In some cases it will tell you what application is launching, whether the application launched successfully or even if the application launch failed. You'll see both information and error messages appear over the system tray.

Error messages *always* have to be displayed.

In fact, if we try and change the error message timeout to something less than 10 seconds, the application won't let us—that's how important errors are!

Informational messages, however, don't have this same restriction. In fact, you can even set the number of seconds to be 0 for the informational messages and they won't ever be displayed.

File System Tab

The File System tab, shown in Figure 6.53, deals with the size of the cache, the drive letter used by SoftGrid, and what happens when you import an application.

Cache Settings

With these settings, we can change the maximum size of the client's cache and see how much space is currently being used. If you do decide to change the size, you can never change the size to be any smaller then the value it was set at initially. That is, if you leave the default setting of 2048MB, then the smallest Cache Settings value you can ever have is 2048MB. You can always make it bigger, up to a maximum of 65536MB.

At some point, you will remove applications from your cache. Once the `sftfs.fsd` file has grown in size, however, it will never get smaller. Think of it as a dynamically expanding file that never contracts. If you stream down 1153MB worth of applications and then delete (flush, really) them all, the `sftfs.fsd` file will remain at 1153MB.

In the grand scheme of things, this really isn't a big deal. It's one file out of tens of thousands of files on your system. It's just going to take up space on your hard drive.

FIGURE 6.53 The File System tab.

 If you really want to start the sftfs.fsd file from scratch and reclaim the space on your hard drive, you can edit the REG_DWORD value called STATE in HKLM\SOFTWARE\Softricity\SoftGrid Client\CurrentVersion\AppFS and change the value to 0. Reboot, and your sftfs.fsd file will have no applications in it, nor will it be taking up any space on your hard drive. However, you will need to restream *everything* back down to your client at this point.

Drive Letter

We can change our drive letter here if we feel a burning desire to do so. It doesn't have to be Q:, but Q: seems to be rarely used for a mapped drive letter. Whether you change it or keep it as Q:, make sure the drive letter you install to on your sequencer and the drive letter on your client are the same. If the drive letter you pick using the sequencer isn't the same as the client machine, your apps may fail to run properly.

Import Search Path

We'll cover the Import function in more depth in the "Client Applications Node" section. Suffice to say, if you want to add specific locations to import a package from (such as a flash drive or an optical drive), this is where you specify those paths.

Network Tab

In Figure 6.54, you can see the next tab on our journey, the Network tab.

If you want to make changes to how the SoftGrid Client handles incoming or outgoing network traffic, this is the tab for you.

FIGURE 6.54   The Network tab.

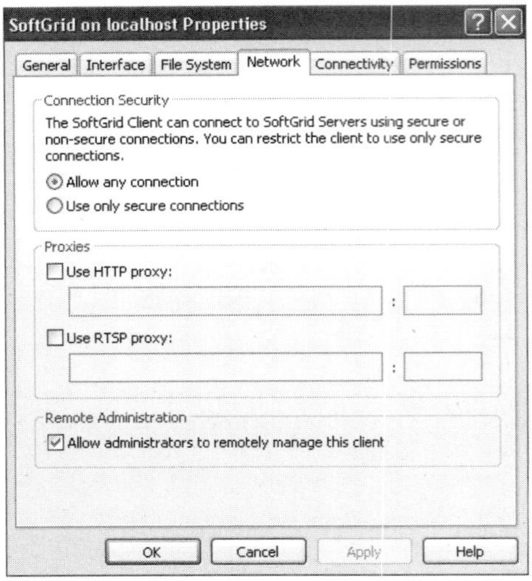

Connection Security

Out of the box, the SoftGrid Client is more than happy to send and receive unencrypted traffic across your network. It is possible to change the behavior to make the SoftGrid traffic encrypted. It really is just a question of if you should or not.

Encrypting and unencrypting network traffic will definitely slow down your application streaming and launch times. Of course, the benefit is that all SoftGrid related network traffic will be completely encrypted as it travels around your network.

I recommend leaving this setting at "Allow any connection." If someone were to stumble across SoftGrid packets flying around your network, capture them, and rebuild the packets into usable files, what could they do with them? Run Adobe Reader? Woo hoo…let's have a party!

If you decide encryption is for you, there are a few changes that you need to make. When you sequence your applications, you will need to make sure you choose the RTSPS protocol in the Package Configuration Wizard. Additionally, any applications that have already been sequenced will need to have a change made in their OSD file. At the top of the OSD file, look for the following line:

```
CODEBASE HREF="rtsp://SoftGrid:554/Path/application.sft"
```

You will need to change RTSP to RTSPS and perform a server refresh on your clients to download the new OSD files. Otherwise, your clients, who are only going to connect over a secured connection now, won't be able to run any of your applications.

I'm sure there are many tools that allow you to change RTSP to RTSPS on multiple files simultaneously, but my favorite is WildEdit, from the makers of TextPad, Helios Software Solutions. Take a look at it here: http://tinyurl .com/yg5hfq.

Proxies

Do your clients need to use a proxy server for HTTP or RTSP traffic on your LAN? If so, this section is where you would specify those values. You can specify the proxy setting using either a DNS name or an IP address.

Remote Administration

Remember earlier when I mentioned remotely connecting to a system using the SoftGrid CMC? The check box in this section needs to be checked in order to receive that connection, and it is by default.

What the Heck Is RTSP Anyway and Why Does SoftGrid Use It?

When a sequenced application is delivered to a client, the file transfer method that is used is RTSP, or Real Time Streaming Protocol. If you have ever listened to Internet radio, or watched a video on a website like YouTube, then you have used RTSP, perhaps without knowing about it. But why does SoftGrid use RTSP? Why not just do a straight file copy? The whole point is to get the application files to the client, right?

Yes, a normal file copy would get the appropriate files to the client, but one of the biggest advantages to using RTSP is the same one people notice the most when they are using it on the Internet. Let's say you are listening to an Internet-based radio station. Then, in the middle of your favorite song, the music suddenly stops for a moment. Then it resumes. You glance up at your application and see that it's busy "buffering" the file. In a few seconds, the music starts up again.

But what exactly happened? Any number of things really. There could have been some link congestion between you and the server. The server might not have had enough resources to serve up all the requests. It's also entirely possible the server you were connected to is now offline, and a different server is serving up your request.

From a streaming application perspective, that is a big deal, in a very good way. If I load balance my SoftGrid servers, and someone actively streams down Adobe Reader, I can take down the server currently serving up the stream—literally unplug the network cable if I want. Their stream will pause for a few seconds, reconnect to a *completely different server*, and restart right where it left off. My users are happy because all of their applications are available from any computer at any time. I'm happy because I can take a server down in the middle of the day and it won't generate a single help desk call. That's the power of using RTSP.

Connectivity Tab

The Connectivity tab, shown in Figure 6.55, has a bit of a strange name. It really deals with whether or not a client can run applications when a SoftGrid server is disconnected, and for how long.

FIGURE 6.55   The Connectivity tab.

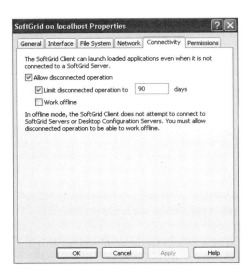

When a system running SoftGrid-delivered applications is connected to the network and can make contact to the virtual application servers, it is considered to be in a *connected* state.

But what happens if the client cannot talk to any virtual application servers? Will the applications still launch successfully and run? Of course they will....if we allow *disconnected operation*.

Figure 6.55 shows the default configuration for disconnected operation. That is, the check boxes are set up so we can run our applications even when we can't talk to a virtual application server.

However, the tricky part is that the default is set up to let us work offline for only 90 days. Indeed, it's possible to change that value to anything between 1 day and, get this, 999,999 days. This is handy should you need to run applications in disconnected mode for 2,739 years, or almost the next three millennia.

There are certainly cases in which we would want to restrict someone from running an application should they be unable to connect to a SoftGrid server. Let's say we bring a consultant into our organization, and they need to be able to run our very homegrown application, DogFoodMaker 7. Due to an application conflict, we can't have them install it locally, but we can have them install a SoftGrid Client. We then configure the SoftGrid Client so they can run in disconnected mode for only one day. They leave our company on Friday, and by next Monday, all they can do is uninstall the SoftGrid Client because DogFoodMaker 7 will not launch.

Be sure to read the section in Chapter 5 entitled: Using an .MSI Package to Deliver SoftGrid Applications for additional information on how to deploy applications so they can be used offline.

Permissions Tab

All the settings available on the Permissions tab are available to any local administrator, but a restricted user has only the permissions available that are checked. In addition to what is seen in Figure 6.56, I like to give everyone the ability to *delete* (flush, really) an application.

FIGURE 6.56 The Permissions tab.

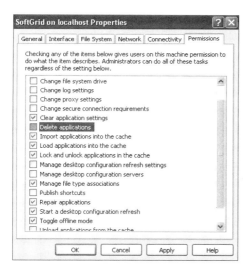

In my experience, over the course of time my users have discovered how to fix their own SoftGrid application issues (shocking, I know). Granting the rights to delete applications is just one more way to possibly prevent a call to the help desk.

All of the settings available on the Permissions tab can be controlled through a Group Policy setting. There is an ADM file available for this tab on GPanswers.com in the book resources section for this chapter.

Client Applications Node

The Applications node, shown in Figure 6.57, has a ton of information. Better refill that soda before we get started here.

Understanding the Column Headings within the Applications Node

Let's start with the columns across the top in the right-hand pane:

Application   This is the name of the application as it was created in your sequence.

FIGURE 6.57   The Applications node.

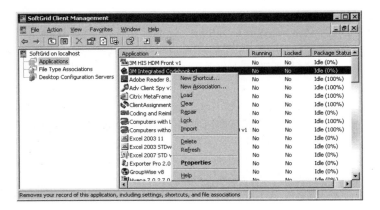

Running   The message in this column tells you whether or not the application is currently running. It is quite handy in cases where one of those nasty little terminate but stay resident (TSR) child processes is still running, but the application is not. If the TSR is still running, this column will say "Yes" even though the application itself is not running. And if an application is running, that means its package is in use.

Locked   When your cache hits its preset limit, unused chunks of applications are unceremoniously removed to make room for other application chunks. An application that is locked will not ever be removed from your cache (even if your cache fills up). You'll see how to lock an application to prevent it from ever being purged from your cache in just a bit.

Package Status   This column has two different values in it. The first is whether the *package*, not the application, is in use. For example, let's say we have Office 2007 Standard sequenced and we've published the three major applications, Word, Excel, and PowerPoint. If Word (the application) is currently running, all apps in the package (Word, Excel, and PowerPoint) will say "In Use." That's because they're all contained within the same SFT file, or package file, and it's in use. Packages that are in use can't be repaired, cleared, or deleted.

Those columns are just 4 of the 30 columns available for this view. To add more columns, click View ➢ Add/Remove Columns.

Due to space limitations, we can't go into detail on what each column will display. Come to GPanswers.com in the book resources section for this chapter for a table of the other columns.

Menu Items Regarding an Application

Right-clicking an individual application gives us a large menu of options:

New Association   Just one of the many ways we can create a new file type association for an application.

Load   Fully loads the application into cache. Loading any application that is part of a package will result in the entire package being fully loaded.

Clear   Deletes the PKG file, removes any shortcuts, and removes any file type associations. This does not remove the application from the system cache, however. (To do that, we would use a delete command, which I will cover in just a bit.) If you do clear an application, you will need to perform a server refresh before you can launch the application again.

You'll learn exactly what happens when we do a server refresh and why we have to perform one after using the Clear command on an application in the section "The Desktop Configuration Servers Node" later on.

Repair   Deletes the PKG file and nothing else. If an application that was working on a system previously is now failing to launch, using the Repair command on it can fix a large percentage of those pesky launch failed messages. This should be your first step in trying to get it working again. By deleting the PKG file, you are taking the application back to its original state. It'll be like the user has never even run the application. While not exactly the equivalent of uninstalling and reinstalling an application, it's a very quick way to reset an application back to its default state.

Lock   Locks a package into your cache. If a package is already locked, when you right-click it, you will be given the option to unlock it.

Import   We touched on this earlier when we talked about the File System tab. Let's dig a little deeper. A package that has not been fully loaded into cache can be *imported*. Import differs from simply performing a load because it allows you to specify from where you want to load the SFT file. Imagine Chuck, our CIO, is flying at 35,000 feet on his way across the country. He is happily editing his latest PowerPoint presentation, but before he left the office, he didn't fully load all of his packages into his client's cache. Now, he wants to use a feature that isn't loaded. So, he saves his PowerPoint file and shuts down the application. He then takes out his USB thumb drive (this could also be a folder on a local drive or a DVD) that has all of the SFT files he needs. He plugs it in, opens up the SoftGrid Client Management tool and goes to the Applications node. He then right-clicks PowerPoint, clicks Import, and navigates to the location that has the SFT file. The package containing PowerPoint will load to 100 percent, and he can then finish editing his presentation.

Delete   Removes all of the file type associations, user PKG files, and shortcuts *and* removes the package from the file system cache. After a deletion, two things have to happen prior to being able to run the application again. First, a server refresh needs to be performed. Then, on the first launch of an application, Feature Block 1 will need to stream down from the SoftGrid server.

Application Properties

Selecting an application's properties brings up a new window, shown in Figure 6.58, with two tabs: General and Package.

General   At some point, you will edit an OSD file. In fact, I'm so sure of it, there is an entire section of the next chapter dedicated to doing just that. But, once you edit an OSD file and launch it on a computer, the local OSD file gets updated with *whatever* changes you have made, whether they work or not. In order to remove any changes that were made, you have to know where the OSD file that was updated is stored.

To find that locally stored OSD file, you need to look at the properties of an application. See the Local OSD File line? You can scroll to the end of that field. If you do that, you'll find the specific OSD file that is used to launch Adobe Reader. Open it up and you can now remove any changes that were previously made.

Package   The Package tab, shown in Figure 6.59, shows some basic information regarding the actual package file.

FIGURE 6.58   The General properties of an application.

FIGURE 6.59   The Package tab.

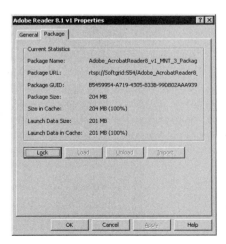

The name of the current SFT file is displayed under Package Name and where it was downloaded from is the Package URL. If you want to know how large the SFT file is, or how much space it is taking up in your client cache, you can find that information here, as well. The four buttons on this tab, Lock, Load, Unload, and Import, perform the same functions described on the Application's right-click menu.

Client File Type Associations Node

The File Type Associations node, shown in Figure 6.60, gives us a view of every file type association currently on the local system, a description of the extension, and what application the file type is associated with.

FIGURE 6.60 The File Type Associations node.

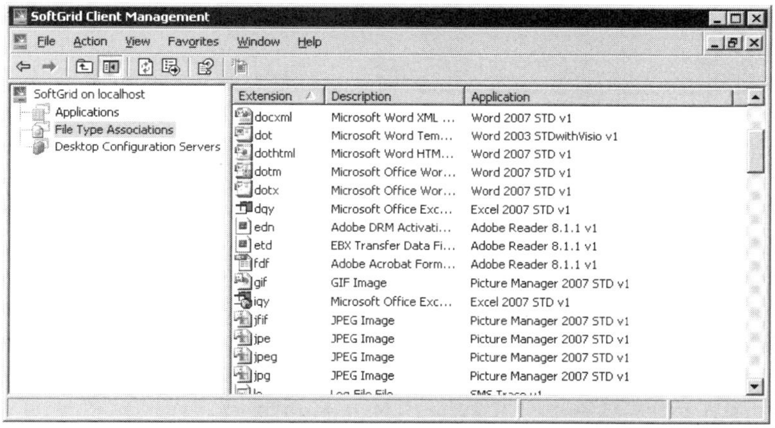

The File Type Associations node brings two distinct features to the table. First, we can create new file type associations here. Second, we can delete file type associations.

As an example of creating a new file type association, say we have a `DogFoodMaker7SalesOrder.doc` file, and we want to open it with Word 2007. Office 2007 does not natively support the previous Office document extensions, so we have to create that file type association to do so. Right-clicking File Type Associations and clicking New Association launches the two-step File Type Association Wizard. This wizard differs slightly from creating a file type association in the SoftGrid Management Console.

In Step 1, which you can see in Figure 6.61, we type in the extension of the file type and then have a choice between two different radio buttons.

Create a new file type with this description If we create a new file type, we also have the option of checking the "Apply this file type to all users" box. We'll talk more about the significance of this when we learn about how to remotely manage a SoftGrid Client in the "Remotely Managing Another Client" section. After we select this radio button, we click Next to select the application.

FIGURE 6.61   Step 1 of the File Type Association Wizard.

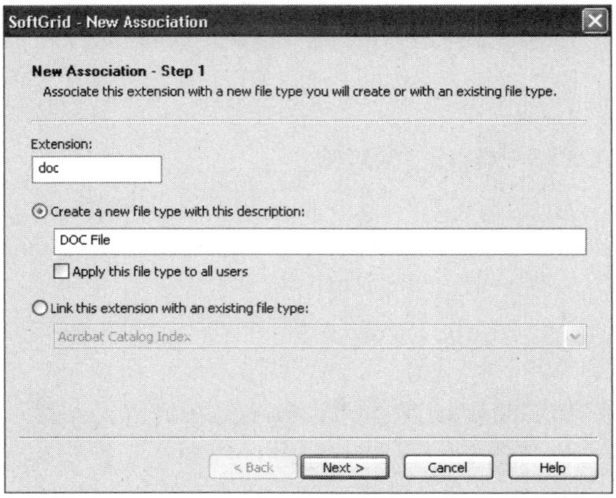

Link this extension with an existing file type   The second button allows us to associate a new file type with an existing file type. In the case of associating a DOC file with Word 2007, we can very easily select the Microsoft Office Word Document from the drop-down list. This automatically causes the user's computer to use Word 2007 to open a DOC file, the Next button changes to a Finish button, and there is no Step 2.

Clicking Next brings us to Step 2, shown in Figure 6.62. Here we get to select the icon and the application our new file type association is going to use.

FIGURE 6.62   Step 2 of the File Type Association Wizard.

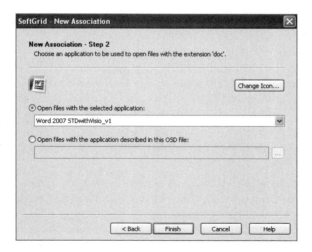

Clicking the Change Icon box allows us to select any icon we want to represent this file type association. If you want your DOC files to have some crazy icon, you can make that selection here.

We again have a choice between two radio buttons:

Open files with the selected application   Selecting this button and then choosing the drop-down will display a list of all the applications available to this user. Choose the application you want to use for this extension and then click Finish.

Open files with the application described in this OSD file   Selecting this button lets you browse to any OSD file you want. You can select any sequenced application. The user will need rights to launch the application once you choose it. I recommend sticking with applications that are already available to this user.

Of course, any new associations that we create will not follow us from machine to machine. They are only valid for the system we are currently using.

The other feature of the File Type Associations node is that we can delete file type associations, which comes in handy in a few different scenarios. We might get a help desk call from someone whose question goes something like, "How come when I try to open my spreadsheet, Microsoft Project opens up and then it says it can't open my file?" Well, it's entirely possible that a user has accidentally created a file type association for XLS so that any files saved with a XLS extension will open with Microsoft Project. It's certainly not a desired result, but I've seen it happen. In another case, we might want to delete any references to MDB. If we have numerous Access databases which were created using different versions of Access, we could very easily corrupt them by opening up and converting a database with the wrong version of Access. Now that would be a big mess, wouldn't it?

 Real World Scenario

Right-click, Open With

With applications being delivered virtually, one of the potential concerns is the lack of integration in the operating system. An example of this would be someone attempting to use Word as an HTML editor. For instance, if Word is locally installed, you can right-click an HTM file, choose Open With, and then select Word. The file will then be opened up with the locally installed version of Word.

With applications being delivered through SoftGrid, when you right-click an HTM file, the Open With menu has only a generic list of applications—Internet Explorer, WordPad, and Notepad—available to choose from as you can see in the graphic. However, if you select Choose Program and then choose the Softricity SoftGrid Client tray in the lower right-hand corner of your Desktop, a Choose Application box will pop up, just like the one shown. You can then select the virtual application to use to open this file.

Additionally, by default, a new file type association is created, unless you remove the check in the box that says "Always open 'htm' files with this application."

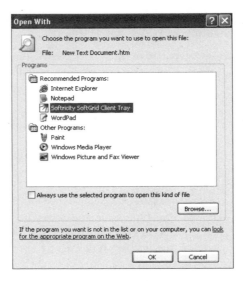

Desktop Configuration Servers Node

The Desktop Configuration Servers node, shown in Figure 6.63, shows the names of all of the SoftGrid servers we are currently talking to and when we will next perform a server refresh.

In the Desktop Configuration Servers node, we can add or delete a SoftGrid server by right-clicking the node name and clicking New Server. At some point, we will have an opportunity to upgrade our SoftGrid server to a new release. Adding in a test server will give us a chance to test our current client against an upgraded server. We'll be able to see which changes, if any, the client will see if they are connected to an upgraded server.

Similar to how we configured our initial SoftGrid server in Figure 5.22, the only two things we need to fill in here are the display name and hostname of the server.

The right-hand pane of the SoftGrid CMC displays the SoftGrid servers that your client is configured to use.

FIGURE 6.63   The Desktop Configuration Servers node.

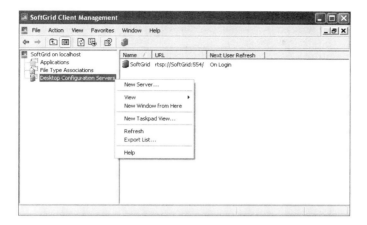

Understanding the Server Right-click Menu

As you can see in Figure 6.64, right-clicking the name of the server gives us five options:

FIGURE 6.64   Right-clicking the server in the Desktop Configuration Servers node.

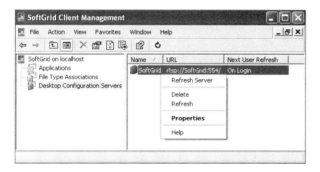

Refresh Server   Gets updated Desktop configuration information from the server. You may want to do this to receive the latest application set from the server.

Delete   Deletes the highlighted server. It is possible to delete all of the SoftGrid servers listed. If you do, the applications currently on your system will continue to function. However, no new applications will be able to be delivered.

Refresh   Refreshes the list of server information. Refresh is not the same as Refresh Server in the same menu.

Properties   Displays the Properties of the server. You'll learn everything about SoftGrid server properties in the next section.

Help   Opens a CHM file discussing the various aspects of the CMC.

Real World Scenario

A Behind-the-Scenes Look at a Server Refresh

When Chuck, our CIO, logs onto a system with a SoftGrid Client on it, the SoftGrid Client service starts up and captures Chuck's credentials. Now, whenever a server refresh is initiated, Chuck's credentials are passed to the SoftGrid server.

Let's say we wanted to give Chuck access to Adobe Reader. We just finished sequencing it in our last chapter, and now we want to deploy it. We add Chuck's active directory account to the sgAcroReaders group and have Chuck perform a server refresh. Chuck's credentials, which were captured by the SoftGrid Client service, are passed to the SoftGrid server.

The SoftGrid server uses the sgBrowser account we configured in Chapter 5 (see the section "SoftGrid Accounts and Shares") to look at the groups Chuck is a member of in Active Directory. Then it looks in the data store to see what applications Chuck can access based on his group membership. Because Chuck is a member of the sgAcroReaders group, the server knows Chuck has the ability to access Adobe Reader.

The SoftGrid server tells the SoftGrid Client where the ICO files and OSD files are for Adobe Reader. The client then pulls these files down to the local system, and an Adobe Reader shortcut appears on Chuck's desktop. Additionally, because we configured this Adobe Reader package to associate to PDF files, any PDF files will appear with the correct icon, too.

Now that you've learned about the five options when we right-click the server name, let's go ahead and click Properties.

Inside the Server Properties General Tab

The General tab, shown in Figure 6.65, lets us change the display name of the currently configured SoftGrid server and change the type of server, hostname, port, and path.

Type   Click the drop-down arrow in the Type field to see the four options to choose from:

SoftGrid Virtual Application Server   The default server type. Data is streamed to clients over port 554 using RTSP.

Secure SoftGrid Virtual Application Server   Utilizes encryption to stream data to clients over port 332 using RTSPS.

Standard HTTP Server   Using HTTP as the server type is a very limited use case scenario. The only time I can see why anyone would use HTTP (port 80, by default) is if there was something preventing RTSP from being used altogether.

Secure HTTP Server   Utilizes encryption to send data over port 443 using HTTPS.

Host Name   This field contains the DNS name of the SoftGrid server. This name can also reflect the virtual DNS name if more than one SoftGrid server is being load balanced.

FIGURE 6.65   The General tab of the Server Properties. This tab lets you change the display name of the SoftGrid server and change the hostname and port.

 Load balancing multiple SoftGrid servers is beyond the scope of this book. If you want to learn more about this topic, you can find more information on the Microsoft website at the following locations: `http://support.microsoft.com/kb/932017/` and `http://support.microsoft.com/kb/932018/`.

Port   This field will change as the type of server is changed. However, it can also be changed to any port number. If the port is configured so that it doesn't match the server port, then no connection to the server will be made.

Path   This field is only editable for either the HTTP server or the Secure HTTP server.

Inside the Server Properties Refresh Tab

The Refresh tab, shown in Figure 6.66, allows you to configure individual client refresh options specific to the computer you are working on.

By default, our client will perform a server refresh whenever we log in. It's also possible to set the client to perform an application refresh on a reoccurring basis over a period of minutes, hours, or even days. In fact, this time frame can be set to any duration between 30 minutes and 999 days. This feature can be used when you have a system that doesn't necessarily have a need to be logged out or rebooted. Like most IT folks, I leave my computer powered on all night in case I need to connect to it to perform some work-related function. I won't see new applications that are being pushed out unless I have a specific refresh cycle set up. I'm partial to setting this to refresh once a day, just to make sure that every system checks in at least once a day for new applications. That way, no matter what, I know that if I deploy a new app through SoftGrid, it will get to every system within one day at the most.

FIGURE 6.66 Server refresh properties.

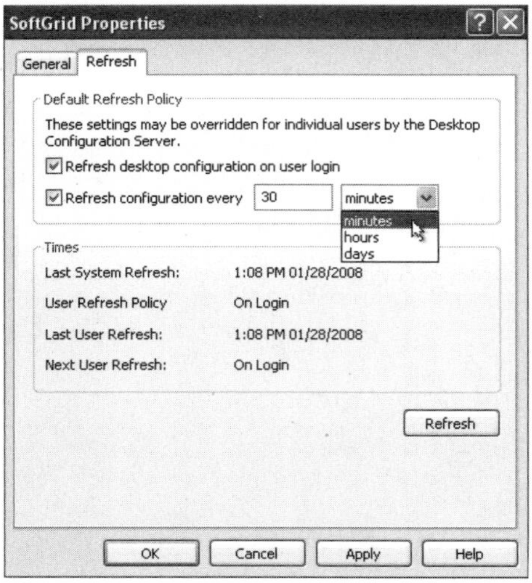

Remotely Managing Another Client

Earlier in this chapter, we briefly touched on the fact that you can remotely manage a SoftGrid Client from another workstation. Well now's the time to learn more about this.

Let's say we just opened up our SoftGrid CMC. Now, we right-click "SoftGrid on localhost" and pull up the menu as seen in Figure 6.48 earlier. This time, let's click "Connect to another computer," which brings up the window shown in Figure 6.67.

FIGURE 6.67 Connect to another computer.

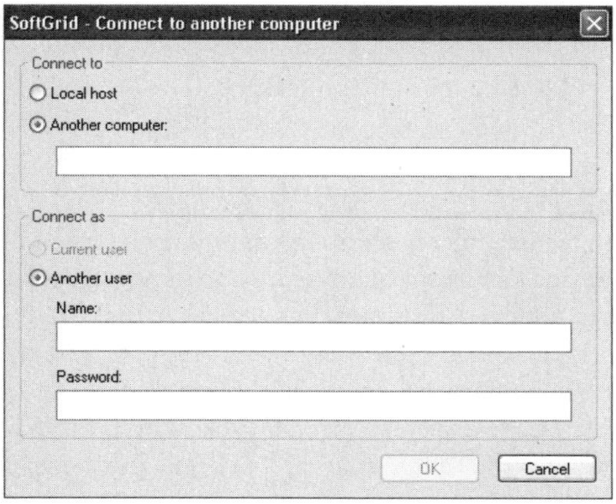

When you choose "Another computer" the first thing you'll notice is that in the "Connect as" section, "Another user" is selected by default. Even if you want to use your own user account, you still have to reenter your username and password. The username and password you use here determines what permissions you will have on the client system you want to make a connection to. If you have a second Windows XP system set up with the SoftGrid client, go ahead and put the name of that system in for the computer name, and enter a username and password with administrative rights as well. Then click OK.

Windows Vista will automatically record this connection in the Windows Logs\Security log as Event ID 4624. Windows XP will record this connection in its security log as Event ID 540, *provided the appropriate logging is enabled*. To enable the appropriate logging, create a Group Policy and change the **Audit logon events** setting, located at Computer Configuration ➤ Windows Settings ➤ Local Policies ➤ Audit Policy, to audit successful attempts, as shown in Figure 6.68.

FIGURE 6.68 Audit logon events Properties window

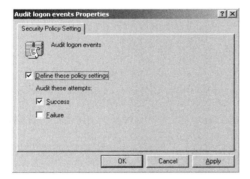

Changing this setting will allow the appropriate events to be displayed on your Windows XP systems. On both Desktop operating systems, the username you are using to make the connection and the computer name you are connecting from are displayed in the event log.

 As of the writing of this chapter, the ability to remotely manage other SoftGrid Clients has been removed in Microsoft Application Virtualization (SoftGrid 4.5).

What You *Can* Do When Remotely Managing a SoftGrid Client

When you remotely manage a SoftGrid Client, there are a few nuances you'll need to understand. Sometimes, the user needs to log off and log back on to see the changes, and sometimes a reboot is required. Let's learn about those situations.

General Properties of the SoftGrid Client   If you can make the change on your local client, you can make the change on the remote client. In that case, the behavior between the local client and the remote client is exactly the same. Any changes made that normally require the local system to reboot will also require the remote system to reboot in order to take effect. Any changes that are made on the Permissions tab will require the user to close the SoftGrid CMC and reopen it to take effect. All other settings (with one exception) take effect immediately after being changed on the remote system. The remote user will need to close the CMC and reopen it to see the changes that have been made.

The one exception is the Run settings on the Interface tab. As shown in Figure 6.51, the remote user will not see any changes to how the SoftGrid Client applet is displayed until they log off and log back on.

Applications   You can load and unload applications on a remote system. You can lock and unlock applications on a remote system. You can even delete, with one caveat, an application on a remote system. The caveat is that even if you delete an application on a remote system, you will not delete the PKG file for the user. If you are attempting to solve an issue where a user receives a launch failed message, you will still need to have the user perform the repair function.

File Type Associations   You have the ability to create new file type associations for any application that is currently on the remote system. Any file type association that is created on the remote system will apply to all users that log into that system, even if they do not have the ability to run the application.

Desktop Configuration Servers   Any changes to the Desktop Configuration Server can be accomplished remotely. Want to remotely add in a second SoftGrid server? Go for it. Want to change how often the user will refresh their configuration? It can all be accomplished remotely.

What You *Can't* Do When Remotely Managing a SoftGrid Client

While there are quite a few things you can do when you remotely manage another SoftGrid system, there are also a few things that can't be done remotely.

Applications   The Repair function is not supported when you're remotely managing a Soft-Grid Client. It is displayed, and you can click it, but you'll receive an error message when you do. Additionally, clearing an application is not listed as a remote option.

File Type Associations   While you can create file type associations for any file type you want and link to any application that is present on the remote system, you can't actually see any of the existing file type associations, *unless they are defined for all users*. In the section "Client File Type Associations Node," we talked about a scenario where a user might call the help desk because their spreadsheet is opening up with Project, not Excel. You won't be able to fix that particular problem remotely, because you can't see the file type associations on the remote system. As discussed in the "Client File Type Associations Node" section, we had the option of applying a new file type association to all users. If we manually created a file type association and applied it to all users, we will be able to see it when we remotely manage a SoftGrid Client. Otherwise, this section will be completely blank.

Desktop Configuration Servers   Refreshing the Desktop configuration information is not possible while you are remotely managing a SoftGrid Client. If you have a user who deletes an application, or you add a user to a group to gain access to a new application, the user themselves will have to perform the refresh.

Here's a quick parting tip: If you want to manage lots of SoftGrid clients at once, use Active Directory and Group Policy to help you. Go to www.LoginConsultants.com (specifically tinyurl.com/2yquhq) and download the SoftGrid 4.0 ADM template. This template lets you make changes en-mass to lots of clients at once. For more information on how to use ADM files, read *Group Policy Fundamentals, Security, and Troubleshooting in Chapter 7: ADM and ADMX Template Management.*

SoftGrid Client Applet

There's a lot of power a regular user can perform with the SoftGrid Client applet. That's right, Sally in Accounting can use the SoftGrid Client to get information about her SoftGrid applications and affect her own SoftGrid life. She likely won't; but it's good to know what type of trouble users *could* get into.

In Figure 6.52, you saw the menu items when you right-clicked over the SoftGrid Client icon in the system tray. Take a quick flip back to Figure 6.52 to recall what the system tray applet looks like. You'll see the following items:

- Refresh Applications
- Load Applications
- Message History
- Work Offline

(Exit is listed, as well, but that's no fun.) In this section, we'll explore the options the SoftGrid Client applet offers.

Refresh Applications

Clicking Refresh Applications is the exact same thing as the Server Refresh you learned about in the "Desktop Configuration Servers Node" section earlier. We are telling our SoftGrid Client to check in with our SoftGrid server to get any updated application configuration information. Having this option available right from the system tray comes in handy in a few ways.

Let's say we get a call from Jan in Marketing. Jan needs access to the DogFoodMaker Marketing 2007 application, but for some reason, she wasn't ever added to the group to grant her access. We can put her in the group, and she'll be able to refresh her applications right from the system tray and start using DogFoodMaker Marketing 2007 in a matter of moments.

Now, we get a call a few days later from Jan. DogFoodMaker Marketing 2007 isn't working, and as a troubleshooting step, we connect remotely to Jan's SoftGrid Client. We wind up deleting the application off of Jan's computer. As you just learned in our last section, "Remotely Managing Another Client," we can't trigger a server refresh to let Jan start running this application again. Jan will need to do this herself, and she can: right from the SoftGrid Client applet in the system tray shown in Figure 6.52.

Load Applications

Rather than right-clicking each application individually in the Applications node and then clicking Load, we can right-click the SoftGrid Client applet in the system tray and click Load Applications. This will load 100 percent of every application to the cache on the local system. There are a few reasons we should consider doing this.

Let's say that Jan in Marketing is going to get a new laptop. We can deliver her the new laptop, and when she logs in, she'll have the shortcuts to launch all of her applications. The first time she clicks each application, Feature Block 1 will stream down and the application will then launch. However, we can sidestep this initial launch by having Jan log in, right-click the SoftGrid Client applet, and click Load Applications. This will load all of her applications to 100 percent, and she won't need to worry about initially streaming down Feature Block 1 for any of her applications.

Now, Jan is going on a business trip for a week. We want to make sure that prior to leaving, she fully loads every application to 100 percent. That way, there won't be any potential issues with trying to use a part of an application that isn't on the local system. Just before Jan leaves, she can right-click her SoftGrid Client applet and click Load Applications. Every application will then fully load to her local system.

It's possible that Jan will start loading all of her applications and then change her mind and not want to load one of those applications—or maybe all of them. If you click the bar as the applications are loading, you'll be presented with a window similar to Figure 6.69 that will let you stop loading the current application or all of the applications.

FIGURE 6.69 Skip loading applications.

 It is possible to load all of the applications to a system from the Run line or a command prompt as well. Just type `sfttray /loadall`.

Message History

On every launch of an application, a message is displayed just above the system tray. If you refer back to Figure 5.45, you will see this message when Adobe Reader was launched. A message is also displayed when every application is shut down. And, anytime an application fails to launch, there will be an error message displayed in the same spot just above the system tray. All of these messages can be displayed using the Message History, shown in Figure 6.70.

While knowing when applications were launched and when they shut down is good information, the true value in using the Message History is when an application fails to launch correctly. Referring back to the Interface tab shown in Figure 6.51, you can see that, by default, error messages will only be displayed for 30 seconds. They also will only say Launch Failed, which doesn't give us much information.

FIGURE 6.70 Message History.

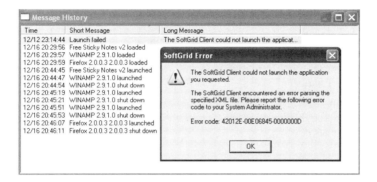

However, if you look in the Message History, you can see that a Launch Failed message contains more information. Double-clicking the Launch Failed message in the Message History will bring up an additional SoftGrid Error window, also shown in Figure 6.70. This window displays an error code that you can use to search within the Microsoft Knowledge Base to help you determine why an application failed to launch.

The Message History has been removed from the SoftGrid Client applet in version 4.5 (Microsoft Application Virtualization). Presumably, because we can configure the SoftGrid Client to use the Windows Event Log, the Message History can also be viewed there.

Work Offline

One of the most common questions I hear when I start talking about SoftGrid is, "How does this SoftGrid stuff work on a laptop when you aren't connected to the network?" And I have a real-life hard-knock experience to share!

When I was first learning to use SoftGrid, I configured (or so I thought) a laptop for my manager to use. He went on a road trip and was going to give a presentation from that very same laptop. Unfortunately, I didn't fully load PowerPoint. About an hour into his trip, he was editing his PowerPoint and it shut down. He couldn't get PowerPoint to relaunch, and he couldn't give his presentation.

But now, I can answer the question simply: To get SoftGrid to work on a laptop when you aren't connected to the network, you configure the SoftGrid Client to work in Offline Mode.

Preparing to Work Offline

The biggest concern when setting up your system to work offline is making sure 100 percent of each and every application is loaded on the client. In the previous chapter, Jeremy talked about creating Feature Block 1 and Feature Block 2 when creating your sequences. If we haven't fully loaded the entire application prior to going offline, including everything in the second feature block, and we try to use a feature that isn't loaded, the application will be forced to shut down.

So, the first thing we want to do prior to working offline is to load applications from the SoftGrid Client applet, just as you learned earlier.

The next thing is to go through and launch all of our applications one time. This does two things. First, it ensures that our applications will *most likely* work correctly when we are disconnected. (Although if an application requires a network connection to a piece of backend infrastructure like a database server, SoftGrid won't help in that situation.) Second, it ensures that all of our applications are properly authorized for use. Every application that is going to be used when disconnected from the network needs to have been run at least once to ensure the user is authorized to run it.

Working Offline

We've prepared to work offline. We've tested all of our applications and we've made sure 100 percent of our applications are on our mobile device. Now what? Unplug your system from the network and go. That's technically all there is to working offline. There are a few other nuggets of wisdom to learn, however.

Every time we launch a SoftGrid-delivered application, our system will attempt to talk to the SoftGrid server for a few different reasons. Are we authorized to run the application? Are we running the most recent version? Normally, this increases our launch time just a second or two. But, if there is no SoftGrid server to talk to, then it *really* increases the launch time. The SoftGrid Client waits a certain period of time, and then eventually launches the application. We can significantly decrease this launch time by right-clicking the SoftGrid Client applet and clicking Work Offline, as shown in Figure 6.71.

FIGURE 6.71   The SoftGrid Client applet with Work Offline checked.

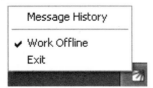

Two things now change with the SoftGrid Client applet. As you can see from Figure 6.71, we can no longer refresh or load applications. If you are offline, there is no SoftGrid server for your client to communicate with, so not having those options makes sense.

We also have a nice visible reminder that we are working offline. See that dotted line under our client tray icon? It's subtle, and you have to squint, but it's there. Even without right-clicking the tray icon, you can tell the SoftGrid Client is working offline.

 Be sure to read the section in Chapter 5 entitled: Using an .MSI Package to Deliver SoftGrid Applications for additional information on how to deploy applications so they can be used offline.

Final Thoughts

In this chapter, we've taken your understanding of the SoftGrid server and client pieces to the next level.

You learned how to use an application group to configure an entire group of applications instead of configuring each one individually. You also learned how to create file type associations right from the SoftGrid Management Console that all users of an application will receive. You even learned how to set up application licensing and how to use the built-in reporting pieces to monitor application usage.

On the SoftGrid Client, You learned how to manage every aspect of the client both locally and remotely. You also learned the ins and outs of working offline with the SoftGrid system.

In our next chapter, "SoftGrid Sequencing Secrets," you'll learn about the last of the three major components of SoftGrid, the sequencer.

You'll learn the ins and outs of the sequencer itself. You'll also learn how to troubleshoot problems with sequenced applications using a few common tools. We'll even cover some scripting within the SoftGrid system, both for troubleshooting purposes and for application configuration scenarios.

Whenever you're ready, we'll be waiting for you on the next page.

7

SoftGrid Sequencing Secrets

In the last chapter, we covered two of the major components that make up the SoftGrid system: the SoftGrid Management Console and the SoftGrid Client Management Console. You learned how to use the SoftGrid licensing component to restrict the number of users who can run a specific application. We created provider policies which allowed us to apply sets of rules to our SoftGrid Clients. We also used the built-in reporting features in the SoftGrid Management Console to learn about the utilization of our sequenced applications. In the SoftGrid Client Management Console, You learned how to administer the SoftGrid Client, which enabled us to more effectively troubleshoot client side issues and to remotely manage other clients as well as to assist our users from the comfort of our own desks.

In this chapter, we'll be covering the last major component of the SoftGrid system, the Sequencer, and how to troubleshoot application sequencing issues.

The following are the three big subjects we'll be covering in this chapter:

The SoftGrid Sequencer   Have you ever packaged an application and streamed it down to an end user, only to find that your username is in the package? Or tried to package an application that writes files to a temp directory but you weren't able to get those files to be added to your sequence? We'll take an in-depth look at what's inside the SoftGrid Sequencer application. We'll walk through all the tabs and wizards and explain exactly where everything might be used…or might *not* be used in some cases.

Advanced Sequencing   Can you package a shortcut to a website? How do you package an ActiveX plug-in? What do you do to perform an active upgrade? Why would you want to branch a package? If you have ever wanted to package something a bit out of the ordinary, this section will lead you in the right direction.

Troubleshooting Sequences   Sometimes when you package applications, things don't quite seem to work right the first time. Or the second time. Or the thirty-fifth time. I'll show you how to wiggle out of some sticky situations (and help you avoid those situations in the first place) by sharing some insights I've gleaned from sequencing hundreds of applications using SoftGrid.

This chapter was written by Eric Johnson.

Inside the SoftGrid Sequencer

In Chapter 5, you learned how to use the SoftGrid Sequencer to sequence Adobe Reader. We launched the sequence and walked through three wizards to sequence an application. We then saved the application and copied the saved sequence to our SoftGrid server to be published.

In this section, you'll learn about the other features available to us in the sequencer. Some of these will be used on a regular basis, and some will only be used occasionally, depending on the application we are sequencing.

Because of how the sequencer functions, this section will be broken down into two parts. In the first part, you'll learn all of the settings in the sequencer that we can make use of *before* we sequence an application. This will help you to better understand why you might want to change how the sequencer functions prior to starting a sequence.

In the second part, you'll learn all of the settings that are available *after* we've sequenced an application. Then you'll be able to see how we might modify our sequences after we are already done with the initial sequence.

Let's start up our sequencing virtual machine (we set this system up in Chapter 5), launch the sequencer, and dig in.

This next section might feel a little like a tour of your own house. You might think, "Hey, I know where the bathroom is." But stick with me. During this little tour of stuff you've already seen and played with, I'll be sprinkling in some hidden gems.

Before Sequencing an Application

As you can see in Figure 7.1, we have just launched our sequencer, but haven't started sequencing any applications yet.

FIGURE 7.1   The sequencer before we start to sequence

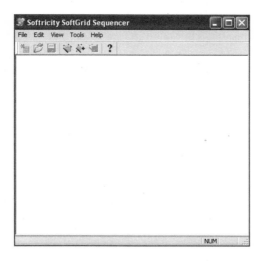

There is a whole lot of blank space up there on that screen, but there are a few menus that have some valuable information contained on them.

File Menu

Prior to completing a sequence, the File menu has three options: New Package, Open, and Open for Package Upgrade, as you can see in Figure 7.2.

FIGURE 7.2   What's on the File menu?

We'll talk more about Open and Open for Package Upgrade in the "Upgrading an Application Using an Active Upgrade" later in this chapter when we start to talk about upgrading applications after we've already deployed them.

New Package is the best place to start the sequencing process. . As Jeremy mentioned back in the "Sequencing Your First Application" section of Chapter 5,..when you click New Package, you are immediately asked if you want some assistance creating your new package. That's the first of the three sequencing wizards.

If, instead of clicking New Package, you use the shortcut keys, the wizard doesn't launch, and you have to manually start the sequencing process. Why doesn't the shortcut key do the exact same thing as the menu item? Who knows? It's just a little weird, that's all.

Edit Menu

The entire Edit menu is grayed out at this point. There isn't anything to edit, so there isn't anything for us to highlight. The Edit menu consists of four common functions: Undo, Cut, Copy, and Paste. There isn't any need to go into further detail as we have all used these functions at one time or another.

View Menu

The View menu has two sections separated by a line, as you can see in Figure 7.3. The top section can only be used once you have sequenced an application, so you'll learn about this later in the chapter.

The bottom section of the View menu has some items we can turn on or off.

FIGURE 7.3   The View menu

Toolbar

The toolbar is the set of seven icons under the menu names that is visible in Figure 7.4.

FIGURE 7.4   Here's a closer look at the toolbar

You can certainly uncheck Toolbar, and it will disappear. However, keeping the toolbar around will make your life a bit easier. Here's what the seven icons are and why you might want to keep the toolbar around:

The first three icons represent items on the File Menu:

- Rather than clicking File ➢ New Package, you can just click the first icon. It will start up the first of the three sequencing wizards.

- The second icon will let you open an existing package.

- The third icon will let you save the package you are currently working on.

The next three icons represent the three sequencing wizards:

- Package Configuration

- Installation

- Application

You can start up any of the three wizards right from the toolbar.

If you refer back to Figure 7.1 you will see the icon representing the Application Wizard is grayed out. You can't run the Application Wizard until you have run the Installation Wizard.

The last icon on the toolbar brings up the same information clicking Help ➢ About does.

Status Bar

The status bar is the bar along the bottom of the sequencer. Figure 7.5 shows the status bar displaying, "Show or hide the status bar" and tells you if Num Lock and Caps Lock are on as well.

FIGURE 7.5   The status bar

If you are ever curious about what a specific menu item does, the status bar can provide you with some guidance.

Tools Menu

The Tools menu has a host of options available, as shown in Figure 7.6.

Sequencing Wizards

This option lets you start up any of the three sequencing wizards. These are the same three wizards that are available on the toolbar and that you learned about in Chapter 5.

FIGURE 7.6   The Tools menu

Encoding Wizards

The Encoding Wizards deal with the directory that you have created on your Q: drive for your application. You can either encode the directory or decode *to* that directory.

Encode Directory   When you choose to encode a directory, you are actually able to take an entire directory and turn it into a package. You don't even have to run it through the sequencer. Of course, when you just encode a directory, you won't have any of the virtual Registry information. Additionally, you won't have any of the files or folders that were copied outside of the specific directory you just encoded, and you also will need to manually create an .OSD file.

Decode Directory   This option allows you to decode the current package, whether you have gone completely through the three sequencing wizards or have just used the Encode Directory option. Until that point, it is grayed out. Decoding a directory allows you to navigate through the files contained in the package and make changes to those files.

 The Encoding Wizards have been removed in the 4.5 release of SoftGrid (Microsoft Application Virtualization).

Diagnostics

The Diagnostics option lets us launch a command prompt within the sequenced application. The command prompt can be one of the most powerful tools in your arsenal when it comes to troubleshooting sequenced applications. We'll cover troubleshooting in the "Sequence Troubleshooting" section, so stay tuned for that.

Options

Clicking Options brings up the screen you see in Figure 7.7, which is the default configuration of the sequencer. Let's poke around here and learn all about the valuable options that are available.

FIGURE 7.7   The Options menu

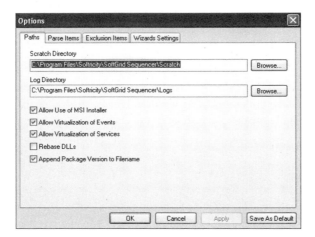

The Paths Tab   The Paths tab contains the following information:

Scratch Directory   The Scratch directory is used by the sequencer to store temporary files during the process of sequencing. Supposedly, if you want to potentially speed up your sequences, you can move the Scratch directory to a different physical drive. However, I have never seen much of a difference in how fast the sequencer operates after making this change. I still use the same system I started using to sequence applications two years ago and haven't seen a need to update it to state-of-the-art hardware. My system is a Pentium IV with two hard drives and 3GB of RAM, and it still does the job quite well at this point.

Log Directory   The Log directory houses all of the logs for the sequencer. We'll talk more about the sequencer logs in the "Sequence Troubleshooting" section. Depending on how you have set up your sequencer, it's possible this log will be overwritten on every sequence. The C: drive of your sequencer needs to be refreshed back to a state where no applications have been installed on it before every sequence. That includes this directory. If you want to keep your logs for all of your sequences, you should move this directory to a different location on your system, or even to the network.

Allow Use of MSI Installer   Keeping this box checked means that when an application is installed using the Windows Installer, the sequencer and the MSI Installer service in Windows can properly communicate during a sequence. If you are sequencing an application that doesn't make use of the Windows Installer Service, you could go into this menu and uncheck this box. However, leaving it checked during your sequence won't cause you any issues. It's checked by default because the assumption is that most packages you'll sequence will be MSI-based.

Allow Virtualization of Events   This check box does *not* refer to the Windows Event log, but to certain low-level operating system functions such as semaphores and mutexes. In the Chapter 5 section, "What, Exactly, Is Sequenced?", the last bullet item is semaphores and mutexes. By default, the sequencer will attempt to sequence these functions. You'll learn in the "Sequence Troubleshooting" section why you might want to turn *off* this feature.

If you want to know more about semaphores and mutexes, you can check it this Wikipedia entry: http://en.wikipedia.org/wiki/Semaphore_(programming). Be warned: it's a bit of a geeky entry with a large emphasis on programming.

Allow Virtualization of Services   SoftGrid has the ability to virtualize services. If the service doesn't need to start up when the system boots up, there is a good possibility you can virtualize the service. Once you have virtualized the service with SoftGrid, you can also configure how it will run in your virtual environment as well.

Rebase DLLs   Rebasing DLLs refers to the process of changing the base address of .DLL files in memory space. Checking this box can *potentially* save memory and improve application launch times on some systems. I've used this setting on a handful of sequences. I then tested launch times and memory usage. So far, I haven't come across any application that benefits by using this setting, so I don't use it. Also notice that, by default, it's not checked.

Append Package Version to Filename   This setting comes into play with active upgrades. An active upgrade is when you take an existing package, bring it back into the sequencer, and add additional components to it, like patches or hotfixes.

When you save a package after having performed an active upgrade on it, the .SFT file will save as the same name, with the version number appended to the end of it. As you see if you refer back to Chapter 5, Figure 5.38, the .SFT name for Adobe Reader is currently acroread7.sft. So, the first time you perform an active upgrade to your Adobe Reader package and save it, the .SFT file will be called acroread7_2.sft—as long as you leave this box checked.

When you go to perform the active upgrade, the wizard will prompt you for the name of the .SFT file. It's easy to see that the .SFT file with _2 at the end of it is the upgraded version. We'll walk through a complete active upgrade in the "Upgrading an Application Using an Active Upgrade" section, so you'll see this come into play very soon.

Parse Items Tab   Clicking the Parse Items tab brings up the information you see in Figure 7.8. Every location in the Windows Operating System has an identical location in the virtual world.

You can see that C:\Windows\system32 in the operating system correlates to %CSIDL_SYSTEM% in the virtual world. You can't make any changes to these settings, but when you are troubleshooting, the Parse Items tab can come in handy when you need to find out where a specific file might be located. If you know where the file normally shows up when you locally install an application, you can find the path it should reside in after you sequence it.

FIGURE 7.8 The Parse Items tab

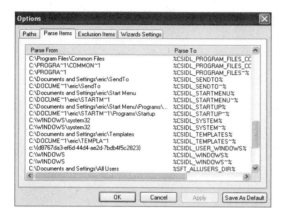

 CSIDL stands for constant special item ID list. CSIDL folders, like CSIDL_SYSTEM, are special folders that are used frequently by applications but may or may not be the same on different computers. On one computer, the system folder might be c:\windows, and on another, it might be c:\winnt. By using the CSIDL location of the folder, SoftGrid sequences will potentially function on more systems without a significant amount of rework by SoftGrid administrators.

Exclusion Items Tab   Clicking the Exclusion Items tab brings up a list of all of the locations that the sequencer will not monitor during sequencing. You can see this list in Figure 7.9.

As you can see, the sequencer won't monitor things like the scratch directory, or the Log directory of the sequencer, which makes sense. But there are times where you might need to change what is excluded during a sequence.

Let's look at a real world example of using these settings. Recently, I was working on a sequence for a medical application. This application stores files it needs to properly run in a temp directory. In Figure 7.9, you can see that the temporary directory in both the users profile and in Windows are not included in the sequence. In talking with the vendor, we decided the best thing to do would be to include the temporary directory in the sequence but to delete any of the files that are downloaded to the system during sequencing. This way, when any user launches the application, they will always download the latest set of files to the virtualized temp directory. If we left the files in the directory that were downloaded during sequencing, we might have some old files in our package that would constantly need to be updated.

FIGURE 7.9 The Exclusion Items tab

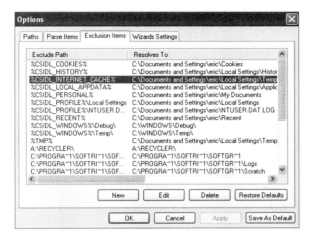

So how do we modify our exclusions for a sequence? Referring back to Figure 7.9, you can see there are four buttons under the list of exclusions:

New Clicking the New button brings up the screen you see in Figure 7.10. The Exclude Path can be an environment variable like %TMP%, or it can be a hard coded path such as C:\Program Files\Messenger.

FIGURE 7.10 Excluding the C:\Program Files\Messenger directory

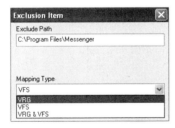

Under Mapping Type, there are three options available:

- VFS (Virtual File System) tells the sequencer the exclude path should not be included in the virtual file system.

- VRG (Virtual Registry) tells the sequencer the exclude path should not be part of the virtual Registry.

- VRG and VFS tell the sequencer the exclude path should not be a part of the virtual file system and the virtual Registry.

Edit The Edit button brings up the same window shown in Figure 7.10. However, the Exclude Path is already filled in and the correct mapping type is selected. You can then change both of these fields for predefined exclusions.

Delete   Highlighting an exclusion and clicking Delete will completely remove the exclusion that is highlighted. In the case of the medical application, we simply deleted the exclusion for the %TMP% directory.

Restore Defaults   If you have made a bunch of changes to your exclusions list and you want to bring everything back to the defaults so that your custom exclusions do not affect the next sequence that you do, click Restore Defaults, and you are ready to rock.

Wizard Settings Tab   Clicking the Wizard Settings tab displays the screen you see in Figure 7.11.

FIGURE 7.11   "Don't show me the wizard again" settings

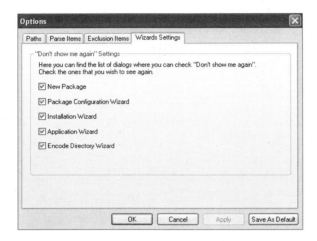

Every time you launch a wizard, you are asked if you want assistance using that wizard. If you have ever clicked the box that says "Don't ask me again in the future" you won't ever be asked if you want to use the wizard. But maybe you have had a change of heart and want to be asked if you want to use the wizard every time you start a sequence. If so, you'll need to come to the screen in Figure 7.11 and re-enable the dialog box. Check the box, click Apply, and you are right back to the default setting.

After Sequencing an Application

To learn how the sequencer is different *after* sequencing an application, we first need to sequence an application. Once our application is sequenced, you'll learn how the sequencer identifies the files to include in the sequence for the application. We'll also see what is contained within the virtual Registry as well.

I'll be using the latest version of Mozilla's Firefox, which I downloaded from www.mozilla.com.

We're not going to go over every step here, just the ones I want to explore in depth. For step-by-step instructions on how to sequence an application, see Chapter 5.

However, there are two specific things I want you to do in this sequence. First, when you begin to install Firefox, you'll have the option of selecting a Setup type; choose Custom, rather than Standard. Click Next twice, and you should come to the screen that allows you to choose the installation location. The second thing I want you to do is, instead of installing to the default location of C:\Program Files, put your Firefox installation files on the Q:\ drive. I chose to install Firefox to the Q:\frfx2011.v1 directory.

As we finish up this sequence, the installation location plays an important role in determining how efficiently our newly created sequence will run on our client systems. You'll learn why a bit later in a sidebar called "Should I Install to C: or Q: When Sequencing?".

Go ahead and finish the rest of the sequence without changing any other settings.

After you have finished the last of the three sequencing wizards, save the package to a folder called firefoxsequence on the Desktop. Your sequencer should look similar to what you see in Figure 7.12.

FIGURE 7.12   The Properties tab after saving a sequence

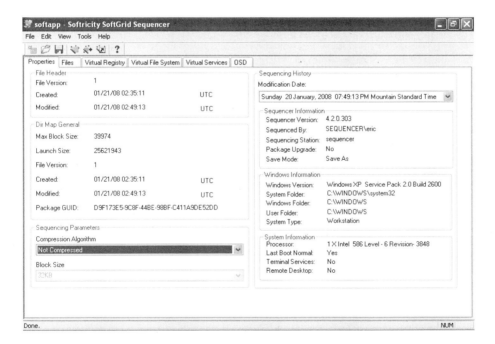

The Properties Tab

Your Properties tab won't look identical to mine, but if you sequenced the same application I did, it should look pretty close. There is a lot of information on this screen about the package you just created.

If you haven't saved the Firefox sequence you just created, the information in the Sequencing History box on the right-hand side of Figure 7.12 will not appear. The Sequencing History box only shows up after a save has been completed.

When it's time for someone to resequence Firefox, this information becomes very valuable. Resequencing Firefox might be necessary because a newer version might come out or you might be unable to patch your existing version.

Here is some other valuable information that appears on this screen:

Launch Size   The launch size is the actual size of Feature Block 1. In this case, you can see my Firefox package is roughly 25MB. Recall that FB1 is the bare minimum amount of code that will stream down to the client in order for Firefox to start up.

Sequencer Version   When it's time to troubleshoot a sequence, you can sometimes resolve your issues by resequencing the software with a new version of the sequencer. Indeed, the latest version of the sequencer is v4.2.1.20, and it can be downloaded here: http://support.microsoft.com/kb/941408. However, you have to know what version you used in the first place to know whether this is a worthwhile troubleshooting step. This label will tell you exactly what version you used.

Windows Information   A few years into your career as a SoftGrid Administrator, it's entirely possible you'll need to look at an old sequence. That's because for whatever reason, the sequence doesn't seem to perform quite right on your current operating system.

It may even be that your company is has begun to run Windows XP SP3 or Windows Vista, but the sequence might have been sequenced on an old operating system. It's good to know which version; this will tell you exactly that.

> Due to limitations on space in this book, we can't go into great lengths on every item on the Properties page. But, fortunately, we do have a great website where you *can* go into great detail on every little aspect of this page. Check out the additional download for this chapter in the "Book Resources" section on GPanswers.com.

The Files Tab

Click the Files tab now. You should see something similar to Figure 7.13. Now, if you didn't point the installation to the Q: drive, your screen might look a bit different. But, for now, let's assume you did.

If you double-click the folder name frfx2011.v1, you'll see the directory structure of the installation you just performed. Every file should be represented right here. As you can see in Figure 7.13, I've drilled down to the en-US.dic file in the dictionaries directory. This is the dictionary file for Firefox.

Softricity Attributes

In the lower right-hand corner of Figure 7.13, you'll see the Softricity Attributes section. Changing these attributes changes how certain files behave within the sequenced application.

FIGURE 7.13   This is the complete list of every file that was put on the Q: drive.

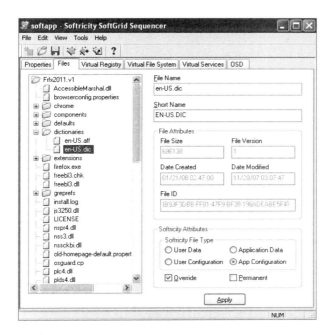

Softricity File Type   Currently, the dictionary file has the file type of App Configuration. The "App" portion of this means the dictionary file will be used by all users of this application on a system. The "Configuration" portion means that it is configurable, or it can be modified. So, if one person modifies this file, everyone who uses Firefox on this system can see the changes on this system.

Now, if we change this file to the Application Data file type, these become files that everyone uses but *can't* change. That is, everyone uses the same dictionary, but no one can change it. If you click through other files listed here, you will see that .DLL files have a Softricity file type of Application Data.

If we make this file type a User Configuration file type, every user will have their own copy of this file. Each user could make individual updates to this file, and no one else would see the changes that were made.

The User Data file type means that each user has their own specific copy of the file, but they can't update it.

Override   Let's say we've given a user the ability to create a custom dictionary in Firefox. But, now we have a hotfix to apply to our package, so we perform an active upgrade. The user streams down the *difference* between their existing version and the new version. If the Override check box is checked, the file will be overwritten by a newer version during an active upgrade.

Permanent   Let's say, again, we've given a user the ability to create a custom dictionary in Firefox and again we have a hotfix to apply to our package, so we perform an active upgrade. The user streams down the difference between their existing version and the new version. Of course, their current dictionary file will be different, but it will get overwritten anyway. Unless you check the Permanent check box: this makes it so the file doesn't ever get overwritten.

Now, stay with me here. Things are about to get a bit strange. I just said that if you check Override, a file *will* be overwritten by an active upgrade. I also said that if you check Permanent, a file *won't* be overwritten. So, what happens if you check both? Well, the sequencer will let you save your sequence without generating any errors. In that case, Permanent wins. It's supposed to be either/or, but it isn't.

The Virtual Registry Tab

Clicking the Virtual Registry tab displays all of the Registry keys that were tracked during the sequencing process. Additionally, you can drill down to an individual key, just like I did in Figure 7.14.

FIGURE 7.14   The Main Registry key in the Virtual Registry

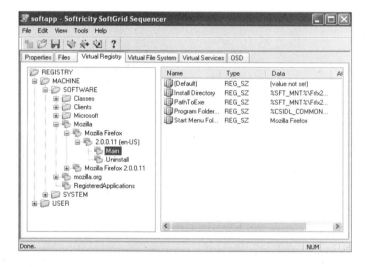

To drill down, double-click the Registry to display both the machine and the user sections of the Registry. Now expand the machine section until you get to the `Main` key under the `Mozilla Firefox` directory. Click `Main` once to display all of the values in the right-hand pane.

With a sequenced application, you aren't just packaging up an application. You are packaging a full runtime environment, including any changes to Registry keys you make when you initially configure the application as you sequenced it. If you type in your name and initials during the Word sequence, then everyone who uses the sequenced version of Word will create documents with your name and initials on them! Now is the time to delete any references to the username of the person who performed the sequence, as well as the computer name or any other specific information like that.

Now click the View menu, and click Show SoftGrid Variables. See how the right-hand pane changed to look like in Figure 7.15?

FIGURE 7.15   We're not displaying the SoftGrid variables anymore.

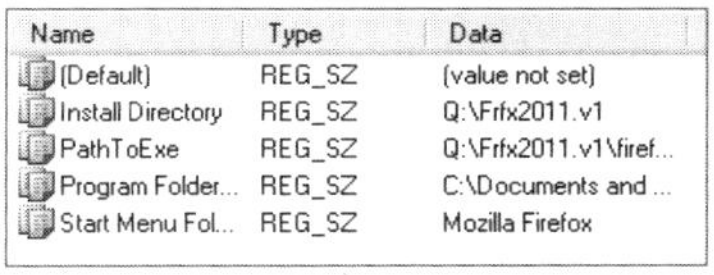

Name	Type	Data
(Default)	REG_SZ	(value not set)
Install Directory	REG_SZ	Q:\Frfx2011.v1
PathToExe	REG_SZ	Q:\Frfx2011.v1\firef...
Program Folder...	REG_SZ	C:\Documents and ...
Start Menu Fol...	REG_SZ	Mozilla Firefox

If you aren't sure what the path is behind the variable, you can always turn off the variables to display the full path.

The Virtual File System Tab

In our installation of Firefox, we made a point to install to a directory on the Q: drive. When we click the Virtual File System tab, as you can see in Figure 7.16, there are only a handful of files in the virtual file system.

The files listed here are shortcuts to launch Firefox, which were put in place by the Firefox installer. Additionally, remember that there are, by default, the five files the sequencer puts in place, so any applications requiring MSI installer functionality have the appropriate files available to them.

FIGURE 7.16   The Virtual File System

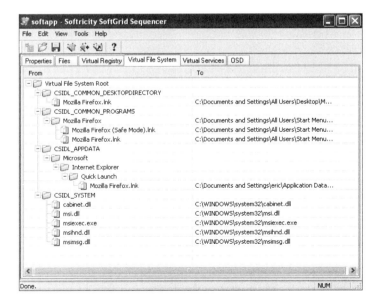

You can add any file you want to the virtual file system from this tab, as well. Sometimes the sequencer won't pick up all the files it needs for an application to run properly, and adding a file or two just might make the sequence function correctly. You'll learn how to do this in the "Sequence Troubleshooting" section later in this chapter.

The Virtual Services Tab

We don't have any virtual services in our Firefox package. We'll save our discussion of virtual services until we can work on some advanced sequences in the "Advanced Sequencing" section.

The OSD Tab

The last tab is the OSD tab, which lets us edit every field in every .OSD file in the package we are currently working on. In Chapter 5 you learned that the .OSD file is pushed down to the client and used to launch the sequenced application on the client. Figure 7.17 shows the Mozilla Firefox .OSD file.

FIGURE 7.17   The OSD file for the Mozilla Firefox shortcut

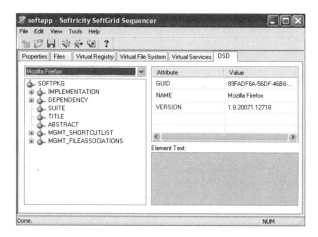

If you click the drop-down arrow at the top of the screen, you will see every other application in the package. You could select another application and then edit the .OSD file for that application.

We'll be editing .OSD files later in this chapter in the "Sequencing Troubleshooting" section.

Advanced Sequencing

In Chapter 5, you learned how to sequence an application from start to finish. We used an executable type of file to start the installation and then walked through the installation as if we were installing the application locally. Once the application was installed, we stopped the sequencer and finished packaging up the application.

A large percentage of applications you sequence will follow a process very similar to this. But it's not always so easy.

In this section, we'll talk about the types of applications that *don't* follow a simple process. You'll learn about the following kinds of applications:

Applications That Are ActiveX Plug-Ins   We've all seen websites that require additional components to be installed in order to successfully function. You'll connect to a website, download the required components, and everything on the website will then work. But how do you sequence a plug-in to a website? You're going to find out in the "Web-based Applications" section.

Applications That Are "Codependent"   You just got the new version of DogFoodMaker 2008, but the instructions state that Word 2003 must be already installed before DogFoodMaker will run correctly. Installing two or more applications in the same sequence is called an *application suite*. I'll show you how it's done in the "Creating an Application Suite" section.

A Group of Applications That Require Another Application to Be Installed   You've got a dozen applications that all need to have Word 2003 installed in order to function correctly, but it's a lot of work to sequence Word a dozen times, once for each application suite. You'll learn how to instead sequence Word 2003 once and save the sequence and how to take the sequence you just saved and create as many copies as you want. That is called *branching a package*, and I'll show you, step-by-step, how to accomplish this in the "Package Branching" section.

Applications That need a Hotfix or Service Pack Applied to Them   Almost every application at some point will eventually have a hotfix or a service pack released, and you'll need to update your sequences with the additional code. You could start from scratch and create a brand new sequence with the additional code in it. Or, you could perform an active upgrade and add the additional components to the existing package. It's quick, painless, and in some cases, your users won't ever know their applications are being updated. I'll show you how to make this happen in the "Upgrading an Application Using an Active Upgrade" section.

Let's get started!

Web-based Applications

For a Web-based application, there generally isn't an installation that you can launch. You usually wind up browsing to a website and then loading an ActiveX control when you are prompted to do so. And when you sequence an ActiveX control, the process is the same.

The somewhat tricky part of sequencing a web-based application comes during the last of the three sequencing wizards, the Application wizard. You'll learn what that tricky component is further down in the "Web-based Applications" section. For now, let's start up our sequencing system.

For our ActiveX plug-in, we'll be sequencing the Adobe Flash Player. (We will also use this sequence in the next section when you learn about active upgrades.) We'll need a directory on our Q: drive to give to the sequencer so it will know where we installed our application, so let's create one.

Normally, I would suggest naming the folder in such a way that you'll be able to identify the application that is installed. For something like Adobe Flash Player, I would use a folder such as Q:\flashply.v1. However, in this case, we are going to be putting more web-based components into the folder, so we should use something a bit more appropriate. We'll call our folder Q:\webstuff.v1 (you remember 8.3 naming conventions, right?).

In your sequencing career, you will run across many applications that can't be pointed to a specific location for installation. They might *only* install to the C: drive, or, like our ActiveX plug-in, they might download and install without any user interaction. However, in *every* sequence, you will need to have a folder on your Q: drive that you give to the sequencer to tell it where you installed the application, even if you really didn't install the application to the Q: drive.

Go ahead and start a new package on your sequencer. Walk through the Package Configuration Wizard just like we did in Chapter 5, and get to the point where you have just clicked Begin Monitoring. The sequencer should have minimized itself to the taskbar.

We are going to install Flash from the Adobe website, so launch Internet Explorer. Browse to Adobe's home page by typing **www.adobe.com** in the address bar and pressing Enter.

Click the Get Adobe Flash Player link in the lower right-hand corner of the website. That will bring you to the next screen, where you can uncheck the box next to the Google Toolbar. Then check the box to agree to the terms of service, and click the Install Now button.

After clicking the Install Now button, a gold bar will appear at the top of your browser window. Click it, and then click Install ActiveX Control.

When the installation box pops up, click Install. Once the installation is complete, you should see a message saying that Flash Player has been successfully installed.

Stop monitoring the sequence. When you are asked which directory the application was installed to, browse to your Q: drive, select the Q:\webstuff.v1 directory, and click OK.

Finish up the Installation Wizard, and launch the Application Wizard. What shortcut do you have? Internet Explorer, of course. Highlight Internet Explorer in the right-hand pane and click Edit. This will bring up the Edit application window, as shown in Figure 7.18. We are going to make some changes here.

FIGURE 7.18   This is the "before" shot of the Internet Explorer application.

In the Name field, change this name from Internet Explorer to Webstuff and change the Version field to v1. Next, change the OSD File Name field to `webstuff.osd` and click the Save button. Notice how the application name has changed, as in Figure 7.19.

FIGURE 7.19   Our newly configured Webstuff application

Those are the only changes I want you to make at this point to the application, so go ahead and click the Next button. Finish up your sequence and save it. Copy the sequence into the content directory of your SoftGrid server. Import the application and put a shortcut on your Desktop so it's easy to find, and stream the application down to a test client.

Launch both the local copy of Internet Explorer and the Webstuff shortcut. Now, let's hit a website that uses Flash to see if our package is working and to make sure the local browser doesn't still have Flash installed in it. One of my favorite websites is Desktop Tower Defense (which is fun and has lots of Flash content). Just point your browsers to this website: `http://tinyurl.com/2zjocv`.

You should see something similar to the screenshot in Figure 7.20. One browser should be prompting you to install Flash, and the other browser should be prompting you to select your language.

Recall that we changed the name and version of the application. We did this so that when you import an application into the SoftGrid server, the name and version are unique. If the name and version of an application *aren't* unique, you'll get an error message when you try to import an application into the SoftGrid Management Console, just as you see in Figure 7.21.

At this point, we're going to see how the changes we made back in Figure 7.19 are displayed on our Desktop client. To do this, right-click the Webstuff shortcut on the client and click Properties. You should see a screen just like the one in Figure 7.22.

Notice the shortcut target also uses the same name and version as the one displayed in the SoftGrid Management Console.

It's possible to launch SoftGrid sequenced applications from a batch file or script by executing the command contained in the target line of the shortcut.

FIGURE 7.20   Let the games begin!

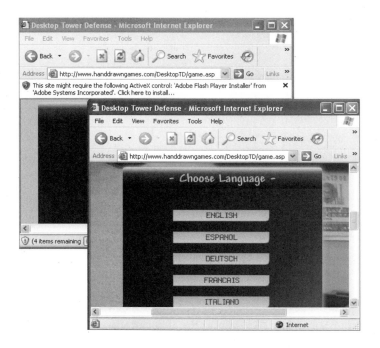

FIGURE 7.21   The name and version of an application must be unique.

Did you also notice the name of the shortcut on the client? It's Webstuff, which is what we renamed the application to when we edited the application. There are a lot of web-based applications out there these days. You might even have a few running in your company right now. You can package each one of them up individually with separate ActiveX plug-ins. By changing the name of the application, the users will be able to launch the correct shortcut to get to their web-based application. You can even create custom icons so that every web-based shortcut has a different icon, as opposed to using the standard Internet Explorer icon.

If you do choose to make custom icons, make sure they are a symmetrical shape: 16x16, 32x32, and so on. Asymmetrical icons, measuring 16x32, 32x48, and so on can cause some intermittent issues. Refer to Microsoft KB article 942687 for more information: http://support.microsoft.com/kb/942687.

FIGURE 7.22 Properties of the Webstuff shortcut

Let's take a look at our sequencer now. Your Files tab should look similar to mine, which is shown in Figure 7.23.

FIGURE 7.23 Notice how all of the files are stored in the VFS folder.

I've expanded the `webstuff.v1` folder so you can see where all of the files for the Flash installation are located. With the exception of the `osguard.cp` file, every other file wound up in the VFS (Virtual File system) folder.

> The osguard.cp file is a SoftGrid file that is created at the time that the sequence is saved. You can learn more about this file by reading a great post by Microsoft MVP Tim Mangan here: http://tinyurl.com/3yrpj8.

With this installation, we didn't have the choice of telling the files where to install. They wound up all over the system. Fortunately for us, our sequencer is able to find all of those files, ad package them up into our sequence. Otherwise, you would be turning to the last section of this chapter for tips on how to troubleshoot a sequence that isn't working correctly on a client.

🌐 Real World Scenario

Should I Install to *C:* or *Q:* When Sequencing?

One of the most common questions people ask me when they are first learning how to sequence is, "Why am I installing to the Q: drive when the sequence will work if I install the application to the C: drive anyway?" Yes, the sequence will *most likely* work if it is installed to the C: drive, but there is a very good reason to try to install to the Q: drive first.

In this chapter, there are two sequences where we can see the Files tab in the sequencer. In Figure 7.13 when we performed our Firefox install, we pointed the installation to a folder on the Q: drive called Q:\frfx2011.v1. In that figure, you can see that most of the files are in the root of that directory, or a folder or two underneath it.

Now compare the location of the Firefox files to the location of the Flash Player files in Figure 7.23. Almost every file for Flash Player is located in a VFS folder. When you expand that folder, you can see that every file is located in a folder that starts with CSIDL.

When it's time for the SoftGrid Client installed on the workstation to run these sequence applications, they will both function, but the Firefox package will run more efficiently. When the Firefox application is running and it needs to access another file within the application installation location, it can simply point to Q:\frfx2011.v1*somedirectory*. Almost all of the files it needs will be located in a named directory.

However, when the Flash Player application runs, the files will all be located in an area that is a bit more cumbersome to get to. Instead of being located right off the root of the Q:\webstuff.v1 directory, they are located in the Q:\webstuff.v1\vfs\CSIDL_*something* directory. In order for the SoftGrid Client to know what directory the files are in, the client must call another function to determine what the corresponding directory is. For every file. Every time.

It's a quick process to determine those locations. It's just not as efficient as installing the application to the Q: drive in the first place.

Upgrading an Application Using an Active Upgrade

We just finished getting an ActiveX plug-in sequenced and delivered it to our clients. Our users are so impressed with our handiwork, now they want to add Shockwave into the same package.

No problem! We'll perform an active upgrade on the package. If you haven't already, refresh your sequencing system back to its original state. Now, copy the files for the Webstuff sequence back down to the sequencing system.

Next, open the sequencer and click File ≻ Open for Package Upgrade, as shown in Figure 7.24.

FIGURE 7.24   Open up the Webstuff package for upgrade.

You'll be presented with the Open dialog box Navigate to the .SPRJ file of the package you want to upgrade, and double-click it.

You'll be presented with the Browse for Folder dialog box, just like the one you see in Figure 7.25.

FIGURE 7.25   Where do you want to put your application folder?

Always choose the Q: drive. Do not ever choose a folder within the Q: drive. *Always* choose the root of the Q: drive as the location where you want the Application Folder to be placed. If you choose something else, you might have some issues getting your package to work after you perform the upgrade.

Once we click OK, we are right back to where we were just after we saved the package initially, only now we are ready to install more components. In this case, we want to install Shockwave.

Rather than clicking the New Package icon, we will manually run the wizards that we want. Click Tools ➤ Sequencing Wizards ➤ Installation, as shown in Figure 7.26. This is the second of the three wizards and is the one that allows us to start monitoring changes to the sequence. While it's possible to make changes to the Package Configuration, we won't be doing that for this package.

FIGURE 7.26   Choose the Installation Wizard.

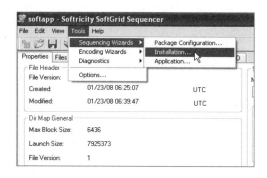

Once you select Installation, you are right back in a place in the sequencer you've seen many times before. Start monitoring the installation. Open up Internet Explorer and navigate to the Adobe website. You can see just below the Get Adobe Flash Player link that there is a link to click to get ShockWave. Click that link.

You'll come to a page that asks you to click the Install Now button to install Shockwave Player. Click that button and let the Shockwave installation begin.

Just as with Flash Player, you'll need to manually install the ActiveX plug-in. If prompted, choose not to install the Google toolbar.

Once the Shockwave installation is complete and you see a message stating this, close your browser and stop monitoring.

Now, when you did this, something interesting just happened in your sequencer. You weren't prompted for an installation location, right? When you initially told the sequencer where you wanted to put the application folder, the sequencer automatically knew where you wanted to save the application to as well. It's not going to ask you where you want to save the application when you are doing a package upgrade. Click Next and finish up the Installation Wizard.

In my testing, something odd happened during the third wizard. The Application Wizard didn't come up. You'll need to manually start this wizard by clicking Tools ➤ Sequencing Wizards ➤ Application.

Run through this wizard, but don't make any changes to the package at this point. Click File ➤ Save. You should be back to the screen you see in Figure 7.27.

FIGURE 7.27   The Properties tab after a Package Upgrade has been completed

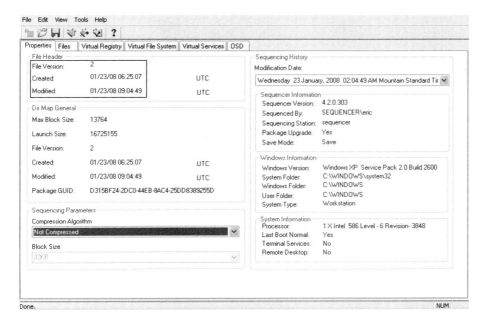

Notice in the File Header section that now we have a file version of 2 and that the created and modified dates are now different. On the right-hand side under Sequencer Information, you can also see that Package Upgrade now says Yes.

If you look at the files in the folder that we saved our package to and compare them to our original files that are still on the server, you'll see two differences, shown in Figure 7.28.

FIGURE 7.28   The files on the left are the original Webstuff sequence. The files on the right are the files after an active upgrade has been performed on our Webstuff sequence.

Name	Size	Type
softapp Icons		File Folder
softapp.sft	7,759 KB	SFT File
softapp.sprj	13 KB	SPRJ File
Webstuff.osd	2 KB	OSD File

Name	Size	Type
softapp Icons		File Folder
softapp.sprj	13 KB	SPRJ File
softapp_2.sft	16,374 KB	SFT File
Webstuff.osd	2 KB	OSD File

You'll notice first that the .SFT file on the right-hand side (which is called `softapp_2.sft`) is twice the size of the one on the left-hand side (which is called `softapp.sft`). Additionally, a "_2" has been added to the name. Turn back to Figure 7.7 and look at the last check box: Append Package Version to Filename. That's what has occurred with the .SFT file.

Now, take the .OSD file, the .SPRJ file, and the .SFT file that were just created by the package upgrade and copy them into the directory that the current package is running from. Both the .SPRJ file and the .SFT file will overwrite existing files, and the .SFT file will copy without overwriting anything.

Log onto the SoftGrid Management Console, and expand the Packages node. Right-click your package, and click Add Version, as shown in Figure 7.29.

FIGURE 7.29   Adding a version to a package

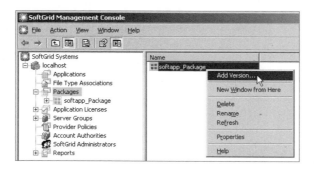

You will be asked to point to the new Softricity file. Browse to the location of the new .SFT file with the _2 in the name, as shown in Figure 7.30.

FIGURE 7.30   Browsing to the new Softricity file

Double-click the filename, and then click Next. You will be asked for the relative path of the filename, as shown in Figure 7.31. This path is relative to the Content directory. The easiest way to get this path is to click the Back button, and copy everything to the right of the content directory. Then click Next to get back to the Enter Relative Path screen.

FIGURE 7.31   Relative path for Softricity file

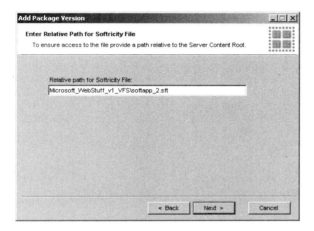

Clicking Next will bring up a summary screen; click Finish.

Jump back to your client and right-click the SoftGrid Client Applet tray icon. Click Refresh Applications. Wait for a few seconds for the client to refresh, and then launch Webstuff again. Webstuff will take a few seconds longer to launch while the SoftGrid Client downloads the updated code, and then Internet Explorer will launch.

Browse to the following website on both the local copy of Internet Explorer and the sequenced package:

`www.adobe.com/shockwave/welcome/`

You should see the same screen shown in Figure 7.32.

As you can see, our active upgrade worked like a charm. All your users need to do to receive an active upgrade is close the current application, refresh their applications using the SoftGrid Client applet, and then launch the application again. The SoftGrid Client will take care of the rest.

Creating an Application Suite

At some point you'll run across applications that are codependent on other applications to function. Let's use our fictitious DogFoodMaker 2008 as an example.

DogFoodMaker 2008 comes out, and it shows up on your desk. Your boss wants it to be available right away. That means you need to sequence it. You grab the box and read the requirements. Word 2003 must be installed in order for DogFoodMaker 2008 to run successfully.

FIGURE 7.32   Shockwave is installed in one browser but not in the other.

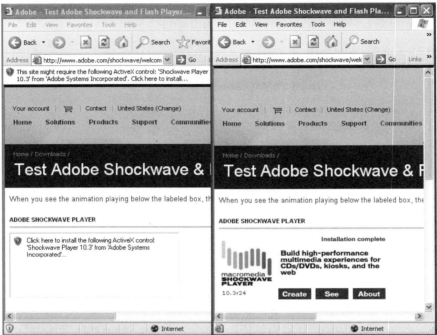

"That's a piece of cake," you think to yourself. You'll just create an *application suite* to handle the Word 2003 requirement. An application suite is where you run through multiple application installations within a single sequence.

Let's get started.

The first thing to do is create a folder on the Q: drive. We'll call it Q:\dfmaker.v1. Now, here is where things change just a bit because we are creating an application suite. We know we have to install Microsoft Word 2003 first, but we aren't going to install it to the Q:\dfmaker.v1 folder. Instead, we'll create a subfolder in the Q:\dfmaker.v1 folder to install Word. Let's call the folder Microsoft Word 2003. Our finished folder structure on the Q: drive should look just like the one in Figure 7.33.

 Subfolders under the root directory on your Q: drive do not have to follow the 8.3 naming convention for folder names. Any folder below the root folder on the Q: drive can have as many characters in the name as is allowed by the operating system.

Start up the sequencer, and go ahead and install Word. When the Type of Installation screen comes up, click the Browse button in the lower right-hand corner of the window to change the location of the installation to the Q: drive. Choose the Microsoft Word 2003 folder as the destination folder to install Word.

FIGURE 7.33 Folder structure for an application suite

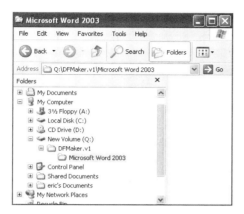

Continue sequencing Word, making sure to include any components required for DodFoodMaker. When the Word installation is finished, do not stop monitoring your sequence. Instead, start your installation of DogFoodMaker 2008. Install DogFoodMaker to the root of the `Q:\dfmaker.v1` folder.

Once DogFoodMaker is installed, stop monitoring. When the Browse for Folder window appears, select `Q:\dfmaker.v1` as the folder the application was installed to, as in Figure 7.34.

FIGURE 7.34 Choose the Q:\DFMaker.v1 folder as the primary directory the application was installed to.

Configure the rest of the sequence as you would any other sequence. Remove any unwanted application shortcuts, and publish your application. When your users launch DogFoodMaker, the application will have access to the components of Microsoft Word 2003 that it needs in order to successfully run.

Package Branching

You're starting to build up quite a library of packaged applications that are being delivered through SoftGrid. New application requests are coming in all the time, and you are able to deliver those applications to your end users.

It's possible that at some point, a request for a new package will come in, and that new package will be virtually identical to a package you already have created. Here are some scenarios that happen to me all the time:

- I need to make one small file change (like changing one line in an .INI file) in the new package.

- I need my Webstuff package to point to a completely different website.

- I need the exact same package, but I need to use a different parameter to tell the package to go to my test system instead of my production system.

- I want to use the exact same sequence I have already created for one application, but I need to modify it slightly to make a brand new application.

- I need to roll out a fix to my entire enterprise, but I want to have a few folks test the fix alongside the existing production application before going live across my enterprise.

You get the idea. I run across these scenarios all the time.

Wouldn't it be much easier to make a copy of an existing package and make a few minor modifications so that both the existing package and the new copy could run on the same system? Of course it would. And the method for doing so is called *branching* an application.

Let's say our education and training department is going to bring up a brand new application that is totally web-based. It has movies that play in Flash and training materials that require the newest versions of Java and Shockwave. They want a shortcut on everyone's Desktop, and they also want to use a special icon.

Doesn't it sound like we could just make use of our Webstuff sequence for this? We can just add the latest version of Java to the package and both packages will run simultaneously on our system once we finish branching the application. Let's get started!

Copy the Webstuff package to the sequencer system. Open up the SoftGrid Sequencer and click File ➤ Open for Package Upgrade, just as we did back in Figure 7.24. At this point, we can add in any additional changes to the package we want to by performing the exact same steps as in an active upgrade. We install the latest version of Java in our sequence and then, when we are ready to finish the package, instead of clicking File ➤ Save, we click File ➤ Save As.

A new dialog box pops up. In the bottom portion of this new dialog box, check the Save As New Package check box, as shown in Figure 7.35.

We need to make some changes in this dialog box in order to successfully branch our package.

Remember, the Package Root Directory is the directory at the root of our Q: drive that we saved our initial package into. We called it Q:\webstuff.v1 for our Webstuff package. The directory names need to be unique for each package, so we have to change that. Since we're branching our Webstuff package, let's change that to wsbranch.v1 (remember the 8.3 naming convention).

The suite name is the name we gave to the suite when we were initially creating the package. Fill in the Suite Name field to reflect the new package name by calling it Microsoft_WebStuffBranch_v1_VFS, as shown in Figure 7.36.

FIGURE 7.35 The Save As dialog box allows us to branch an application.

The filename is the name of the .SPRJ file that is used when we imported the package into the SoftGrid system. In this case, we can cut and paste the suite name into the File Name field.

If we clicked the Save button right now, we would save this package into the folder of the original package. Instead of saving the package there, click the Desktop icon on the left-hand side of the Save As dialog box and create a new folder on the Desktop using the Suite Name as the folder name. Now double-click the folder, and we are ready to save our package. Your screen should look like Figure 7.36 at this point.

FIGURE 7.36 We are ready to save our package branch.

Click Save, and a message pops up saying that we now have a brand new package that we can import into our SoftGrid system, but that the name and version of the applications contained *within* the package are the same as an existing package. Our Webstuff application is still configured identically to our existing package, which is why this message came up. Click Yes to this message, and the Reload Package window will pop up, shown in Figure 7.37.

FIGURE 7.37   Perform an active upgrade after you have saved the branched package.

We can now perform an active upgrade on our new package, and in fact, we *need* to do that. So click Yes here.

Follow the normal steps for doing an active upgrade. When it's time to choose the root of the Q: drive, you'll notice that there is already a Q:\WSBranch.v1 folder. This folder was created when you saved the branched package. Click the Q: drive and click OK. A message will pop up telling you the folder already exists, as shown in Figure 7.38.

FIGURE 7.38   Overwrite the contents of the folder?

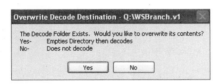

Click Yes to overwrite the contents of the folder. Once this is done, click Tools ➢ Sequencing Wizards ➢ Application to start up the Application Wizard.

Click Next to get past the introduction screen. You'll notice two things in the Configuration Applications screen, shown Figure 7.39, that need to be fixed.

First, there are two shortcuts. One is our original Webstuff shortcut, which we'll deal with in just a minute. The other one is an Internet Explorer shortcut. Go ahead and highlight the Internet Explorer shortcut in the right-hand pane and delete it. We already have one shortcut to Internet Explorer, and we don't need another one.

Now we just need to fix our Webstuff shortcut. Double-click the yellow exclamation mark and you'll see the message shown in Figure 7.40.

The path to the application is no longer valid. How did that happen? We didn't change where Internet Explorer was installed, did we? Click OK, and then highlight the Webstuff application. Now click Edit, and you'll see the Edit Application window displayed, as in Figure 7.41.

FIGURE 7.39   Let's make a few changes to our branched package.

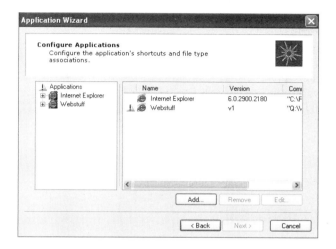

FIGURE 7.40   We've got a problem!

FIGURE 7.41   Look at the application path.

The only field we can edit is the Application Path field. Compare the path you see in Figure 7.41 to the path you saw in Figure 7.18. Instead of C:\Program Files, the path has been changed to Q:\WSBranch.v1. When you branch an application package, every application path is changed to reflect the new path.

Remember how we couldn't tell the installs of Flash or Shockwave to install to the Q: drive when we started creating our Webstuff package? Well, that just came back to bite us. When *any* sequence is created with the application installed directly to the C: drive and not the Q: drive, you will have to fix *all* of the applications within the package when the package is branched. This is one more reason to try and install applications to the Q: drive.

So let's edit the application path and change the name and .OSD filename. We'll name our application WSBranch and call our .OSD file WSBranch.osd. Your window should now look like Figure 7.42.

FIGURE 7.42   The WSBranch application can now be published.

By changing the Name field, we have also taken care of the warning message I described earlier in this chapter that warned the name and version of the applications contained within the package are the same as an existing package. We have given our application a unique name, so it can now be published and streamed to our clients alongside our preexisting Webstuff package. Click Save and finish up the Application Wizard.

To recap how to branch an application, here are the steps:

1. Copy the package to your sequencer.
2. Open the package for upgrade.
3. Click File ➢ Save As and save the package with the appropriate new names.
4. Open the package for an upgrade.
5. Start the Application Wizard.
6. Correct any incorrect application paths and rename the applications.
7. Save the package.

Sequence Troubleshooting

Properly sequencing applications is both an art and a science. Unfortunately, we don't have unlimited room in this chapter to handle too many "interesting" sequencing scenarios.

To give you an idea of the range of problems, the following link takes you to an MSKB article listing nine solutions to sequencing Office 2003:

`http://support.microsoft.com/kb/931914`.

This link takes you to a ten-page article showing you how to sequence Office 2007:

`http://support.microsoft.com/kb/939796`.

In short, it's not easy to get it all. It takes finesse and practice.

We're going to go over a few kinds of troubleshooting now, and then we have a special section for cracking open the `.OSD` file called "Troubleshooting Sequences by Modifying the .*OSD* File."

Let's explore a little more about sequence troubleshooting that will, I hope, help you get out of hot water.

Accessing the *Q:* Drive from Internet Explorer

Earlier in this chapter, you learned about active upgrades. With an active upgrade, we can bring our package back down to our sequencer, make a change, and then stream that change down to all of our SoftGrid Clients. That's great, but what if we want to test a few modifications to our sequenced applications—change a Registry key here, modify an `.INI` file there? Can we still use an active upgrade? Sure we can, but then *everyone* will stream down our changes. But we could branch our package, right? Of course we can—if we wanted to take the time to do that.

In some cases, the easiest thing to do is to take a client that already has the application streamed down to it and modify the sequenced application right on the client system. Yes, that's right. You can access the files and Registry for the sequenced application and make changes to them.

On one of your test systems that has a SoftGrid Client installed on it, log in with an account that has administrative rights and is also authorized to use the Webstuff package. You don't have to use the Webstuff package, but that is the package we'll be using for most of the examples in this section.

First, let's launch the Webstuff package. It will open up to whatever home page you have set. Now, in the address bar, change the address from a URL to `Q:`, just like the drive letter. Press Enter, and you should see something similar to what you see in Figure 7.43.

The six folders you see in Figure 7.43 are all the SoftGrid packages that have been streamed down to this system. This isn't dependent on which user is logged in. Every folder for every application that has been streamed down, regardless of who is logged in, is visible.

Click one of the folders that doesn't represent the Webstuff package. In Figure 7.44, you can see that I clicked the `WinAmp29.v1` folder.

FIGURE 7.43 You can see the contents of the Q: drive.

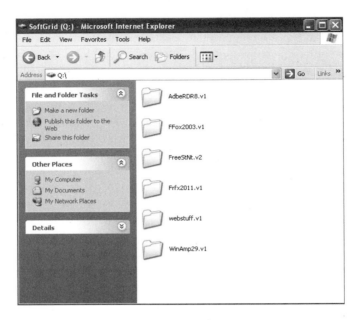

FIGURE 7.44 Just because I can see the folders, doesn't mean I have access to the folders.

The application that I launched is in the Q:\webstuff.v1 folder. If I click any of the other folders that are visible, I'm not able to access the contents of those folders.

Editing Files on the *Q:* Drive

Let's say you've got an application that has an .INI file for configuration purposes, and your users tell you something doesn't quite seem right. You contact the vendor, and they tell you to make a change in an .INI file to fix the problem. Rather than performing an active upgrade, open up your package and navigate to the .INI file in question, make the changes the vendor recommended, and try the application again.

If the change to the .INI file works, you can then perform an active upgrade to distribute the fix to all of your end users.

Editing the Registry on the *Q:* Drive

Let's say we have an application that we have sequenced, and our users tell us that a specific feature isn't quite working right. We contact the vendor, and he e-mails us a Registry key to try. That's all well and good, but how do we get into the virtual Registry to import it? We could pull the package back to the sequencer system and perform an active upgrade, but that's a bit cumbersome for a simple test. We can make changes to files, but there isn't a Registry file we can just open up and make changes to, which makes it more difficult.

Because we are SoftGrid Administrators, we already know how to have the Q: drive open and are happily browsing our Q:\webstuff.v1 folder. What is going to stop us from browsing out to, say, C:\windows and launching regedit.exe? Unless your Group Policy administrator has prevented you from running regedit.exe, it will launch correctly. In fact, let's go ahead and launch regedit.exe, and we can compare the local Registry (shown in Figure 7.45) against the Registry in the sequence (shown in Figure 7.46).

FIGURE 7.45   The local Registry

FIGURE 7.46   The Registry in the sequence

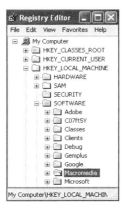

Figure 7.46 shows a Macromedia key. In Figure 7.45, this key doesn't exist. If we use regedit from within our sequence, we have full access to our sequenced Registry. Go ahead and import the Registry key from your vendor and try the application. If it fixes the problem your users have told you about, you can then perform an active upgrade on the package to distribute the key to all of your end users.

Using Process Monitor to Troubleshoot a Sequence

To figure out what's going on in a sequenced application, it's important to use every possible tool in your arsenal. Microsoft's Process Monitor tool was recently upgraded to allow you to see inside running sequences. You can learn more about this new ability in this SoftGrid blog entry: http://blogs.technet.com/SoftGrid/archive/2007/09/25/process-monitor-v1-23-released.aspx, shortened to: http://tinyurl.com/24f78t.

The two tricks (which they don't emphasize enough and so bear repeating) are as follows:

- The sequence and Process Monitor must be run on a Windows Vista or Windows Server 2003 machine. Any flavor of Windows XP whether it is right out of the box or has the latest and greatest service pack just isn't good enough for this purpose when you're using this version of the tool.

- The first time you run Process Monitor on Windows Vista, be sure to add the /hookregistry switch, which turns this special "see inside sequences" mode on. It doesn't work the second time, so you have to get it right the first time.

Of course, if you are running a SoftGrid Client on a Windows XP client system, you'll need to use a trick to launch Process Monitor so it has the ability to view all of the events happening inside the sequence Let's use our Adobe Reader package to learn how to do this.

Copy the .OSD file from our Adobe Reader package on the SoftGrid server down to our test system. Put it right on the Desktop. Open up the file using Notepad. Don't double-click it, or else you'll launch the Adobe Reader package.

Find the Dependency section and add the lines you see in Figure 7.47. (These lines are also available in the Book Resources section at GPanswers.com.)

FIGURE 7.47   Launching a command prompt before the application launches

```
</IMPLEMENTATION>
<DEPENDENCY/>
        <CLIENTVERSION VERSION="3.1.2.2"/>
                <SCRIPT EVENT="LAUNCH" TIMING="PRE" TIMEOUT="0" PROTECT="TRUE">
                        <SCRIPTBODY>
                        cmd.exe|
                        </SCRIPTBODY>
                </SCRIPT>
        </DEPENDENCY>
```

You'll learn more about what all of these changes mean later in the scripting section of this chapter, but for now, make the changes and save your .OSD file. Once the changes have been made, double-click the .OSD file to launch our Adobe Reader application.

You'll notice that a command prompt launches, and the application doesn't launch. At least not yet, anyway. We'll talk about why in the "Other Parameters" section. Navigate to the folder containing Process Monitor, and then launch procmon.exe, just as I did in Figure 7.48.

FIGURE 7.48   Launching Process Monitor on Windows XP from a command prompt

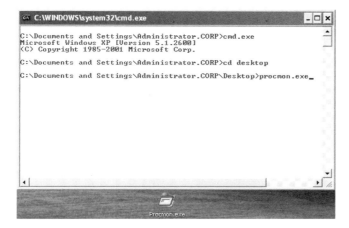

Once Process Monitor is up and running, exit the command prompt and you will capture all of the events occurring on your Q: drive during the launch of the application. If you don't start Process Monitor from within the sequenced application, Process Monitor won't be able to capture the critical events needed to help you troubleshoot your applications.

For my Windows XP test client systems, I'm using Windows XP SP2 without any other hotfixes applied. There isn't any software installed with the exception of the SoftGrid Client and the VM Tools from VMWare. When I attempted to run Process Monitor from within my sequence for the first time, I received an error message saying that Process Monitor was unable to load a device driver. In order to resolve that error, I installed the filter manager rollup package for Windows XP SP2, which can be found here: http://support.microsoft.com/kb/914882.

Process Monitor is really the key reason we don't want our application to launch before we close the command prompt. When an application fails to launch correctly, sometimes you have to capture every last little bit of data to find out why. If you can look at all of the files and Registry activity as the application is launching, you can sometimes figure out why the application won't launch correctly.

Now, all those hoops we just jumped through for our Windows XP systems disappear when we want to run Process Monitor on Windows Vista. We can get the exact same information on a sequenced application on Windows Vista without having to launch a command prompt. All we need to do is use the /hookregistry switch when we launch the application.

Learning how to use Process Monitor to troubleshoot applications is fairly straightforward. In fact, on the SoftGrid team blog, there is an entire post dedicated to just that. Take a look at it here: http://tinyurl.com/yvqwl4.

Troubleshooting Sequences by Modifying the *.OSD* File

Remember the .OSD file that is used to launch our applications? If you open it up, you'll see there are a bunch of XML commands that are used to tell the SoftGrid Client how to launch and run an application.

But we can also make changes to the .OSD file so that we can make our applications perform other actions. Want to map a drive? I'll teach you how. How about importing a Registry key? Yes, that can be done, as well. You'll learn how to do those things in the "Putting It All Together" section a bit later in our chapter, but let's start with learning how to modify the .OSD file for troubleshooting purposes.

We used a pretty simple application to start out our troubleshooting section. We launched our Webstuff application and then browsed to the install folder on the Q: drive by changing the address bar from a URL to a drive letter. It's fairly simple to gain access to the files and the Registry we want to work in when we have a way to see the Q: drive.

But what about an application like Adobe Reader? We can't open up Adobe Reader and get into our Q: drive, can we? No, not exactly. What we can do is make a change to our .OSD file to give ourselves the ability to launch a command prompt. And once we have the command prompt, we have quite a bit more flexibility with our sequenced application.

Launching a Command Prompt from the *.OSD* File

Use the edited Adobe Reader .OSD file we used in the earlier section, "Using Process Monitor to Troubleshoot a Sequence"; this will launch the command prompt.

With this command prompt, you can launch Internet Explorer or `regedit` for any application and gain access to the Q: drive for that application, as shown in Figure 7.49.

We started with an application that gave us easy access to the Q: drive. Now, it doesn't matter what sequenced application you want to modify. You can get to the Q: drive to modify your files till the cows come home.

FIGURE 7.49 Launch Internet Explorer or `regedit` for any application

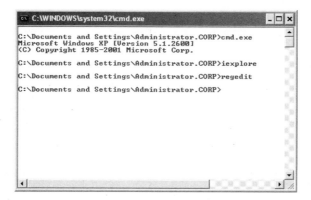

Terminating Children

If you find that you have an application that sometimes doesn't seem to shut down correctly, you're not alone. I've found this too, and here's a cool tip to help solve that.

In the .OSD file of every application, you will see the following line:

```
<VIRTUALENV TERMINATECHILDREN="FALSE">
```

This simple line makes all the difference. The children in this case refer to any child processes that are launched when the application is running. Terminating those child processes occurs when the main application is shut down. Rather than having child processes remain running, which therefore leaves the application running, you can change "False" to "True." When the main application shuts down, all of the child processes will shut down as well.

Policies

Policies are like rules for your sequenced application to follow. They tell your application to perform in a specific way for the entire time the application is running.

There are three policies that can be added to an .OSD file, and I'll cover those next.

Using LOCAL_INTERACTION_ALLOWED in the OSD

Here's a snippet you can put in your .OSD to allow your sequences to interact more with the local operating system.

```
<VIRTUALENV TERMINATECHILDREN="FALSE">
        <POLICIES>
            <LOCAL_INTERACTION_ALLOWED>
                    TRUE
            </LOCAL_INTERACTION_ALLOWED>
        </POLICIES>
        <ENVLIST/>
</VIRTUALENV>
```

The location interaction tag controls virtual eventing. Virtual eventing deals with things like semaphores and mutexes. If you turn back to Figure 7.7, you'll see we had the option to disable virtual eventing before starting the sequence. Turns out we can disable it after the fact as well.

This is generally used when you want your application to interact more with the local operating system. In fact, Microsoft recommends using this setting when sequencing Office 2007.

Using VIRTUAL_SERVICES_DISABLED in the OSD

Disabling the virtual services will stop the virtualized application from relying on the virtual services environment. Instead, the application will use the services that are present on the local system.

```
<VIRTUALENV TERMINATECHILDREN="FALSE">
        <POLICIES>
            <VIRTUAL_SERVICES_DISABLED>
```

```
                        TRUE
                </VIRTUAL_SERVICES_DISABLED>
            </POLICIES>
        <ENVLIST/>
</VIRTUALENV>
```

I've used this policy on one application in particular: Hyena from SystemTools. Hyena is an application that simplifies and centralizes day-to-day server and network administration tasks. One of the things it has the ability to do is view the services on remote systems. If I don't disable the virtual services using this policy, I can only see the services on the local system, no matter what remote computer I attempt to view.

Using SXS_32_ENABLED in the OSD

So far, there is only one application that is known to require this policy: Novell's Groupwise version 6.5.x e-mail client.

```
<VIRTUALENV TERMINATECHILDREN="FALSE">
        <POLICIES>
            <SXS_32_ENABLED>TRUE</SXS_32_ENABLED>
        </POLICIES>
        <ENVLIST/>
</VIRTUALENV>
```

I've been working with SoftGrid since v3.2, and the company I work for still uses Groupwise. When SoftGrid 4.0 first came out, we ran into an issue with our sequenced version of Groupwise. The first time we attempted to access the Address Book, we received an error message telling us the Address Book was not in the correct location. We had to click the Yes box three times, one for each type of address book. Once this was done, the error didn't come up again. At least until we closed Groupwise and reopened it. Then it happened all over again. This policy solved our issue.

Modifying Parameters Inside the OSD File

In our Webstuff package, we launched Internet Explorer and added Flash and Shockwave into our package. But let's say we want to force the application to launch to a specific web page every time, regardless of what the home page is. We can add a parameter to the .OSD to do this. Here's an example:

```
<CODEBASE HREF="rtsp://SoftGrid:554/Microsoft_WebStuff_v1_VFS/softapp_2.sft"
        GUID="D315BF24-2DC0-44EB-8AC4-25DD8389255D"
        PARAMETERS="http://www.gpanswers.com"
        FILENAME="%CSIDL_PROGRAM_FILES%\Internet Explorer\iexplore.exe"
        SYSGUARDFILE="webstuff.v1\osguard.cp"
        SIZE="16725155"/>
```

If we add the parameter `http://www.gpanswers.com`, our Webstuff package will open up to `www.gpanswers.com` every time, no matter what the home page is. We can also perform an active upgrade to set the home page to `www.gpanswers.com`.

Scripting

Earlier in this section when we were talking about sequence troubleshooting, we modified our Webstuff `.OSD` file to launch a command prompt. We did this using a script but didn't delve into too many details on scripting.

With an `.OSD` script, you can do anything you can do in a batch file. Even if there's something you can't do in a batch file, you can write a VBS script and call the VBS script from your `.OSD` file. Scripting is limited only by your imagination.

Let's learn the ins and outs of scripting.

When Can We Run a Script?

There are five different times we can run a script with a SoftGrid delivered application:

PRE STREAM   You can run a script before an application has started to stream down to the local client. For example, you might want to do this if a remote user needs to connect over a VPN before their application can successfully stream down to them. Script the VPN connection and then the application will be able to successfully stream down to them.

POST STREAM   You can run a script after the application has streamed down and the user is authorized to run the application, but before the virtual environment is setup. This is where I prefer to map any required drives for the application.

PRE LAUNCH   You can also run a script after the virtual environment is created, but before the application is launched. In the scripting example in our "Using Process Monitor to Troubleshoot a Sequence" section, this is when we launched a command prompt so that we could then launch Process Monitor.

POST LAUNCH   You would run this script after the application is launched if your script has a dependency on the application executable.

POST SHUTDOWN   You run this script after the application has shut down. This is a great time to delete any unneeded files, unmap drives, or remove any Registry keys that were required for the application.

Where Will Our Script Run?

There are only two options here that make sense. Either the script will run inside the virtual environment, which means we can make changes to our files and Registry inside the sequenced package, or the script will run outside of the virtual environment, which means any actions in the script will affect the locally installed operating system files and Registry.

PROTECT=TRUE   When we launched a command prompt earlier, we ran the script inside the virtual environment. Setting PROTECT=TRUE will allow our script to access the virtual environment. If you want to delete a Registry key in the virtual environment, you set PROTECT=TRUE.

PROTECT=FALSE In some cases, you will want your script to have the ability to interact with the nonvirtual environment. Maybe you want your script to edit the nonvirtual Registry. Or sometimes, no matter how hard you try, certain applications will still look for files or folders in the local operating system. You can build a script to check for the existence of those files, and if they aren't present, copy them down to the local system outside of the virtual environment.

Other Parameters

There are two other parameters that can be used for scripts, TIMEOUT and WAIT. Both parameters are timing parameters.

TIMEOUT={*some number of seconds*} With this parameter set, the client will wait a set period of time for the script to complete. If the script doesn't complete in the specified period of time, the client will return an error.

TIMEOUT=0 With the timeout value set to 0, the client will wait indefinitely for the script to complete. When you are launching Process Monitor from a command prompt, you should use TIMEOUT=0. This will allow you to get Process Monitor running so you can see every file and Registry key the application is using right when it first launches.

WAIT=TRUE Setting WAIT=TRUE is identical to setting TIMEOUT=0. The client will wait indefinitely for the script to complete.

WAIT=FALSE Setting WAIT=FALSE means the application launch will continue without waiting for the script to finish.

Putting It All Together

Let's take a look at a few different scripts, starting with the script we used for our troubleshooting purposes earlier:

```
<DEPENDENCY>
    <SCRIPT EVENT="LAUNCH" TIMING="PRE" TIMEOUT="0" PROTECT="TRUE">
        <SCRIPTBODY>
            cmd.exe
        </SCRIPTBODY>
    </SCRIPT>
</DEPENDENCY>
```

This is a prelaunch script, and we waited indefinitely for the script to finish before we continued on. Setting PROTECT=TRUE means we also want this script to launch within the virtual environment. This is the exact script you should use when you want to launch Process Monitor in your virtual environment.

Mapping a Network Drive

Here's a script for mapping a network drive during POST STREAM. I like to map drives for applications that aren't used very often in my `.OSD` files.

```
<DEPENDENCY>
    <SCRIPT EVENT="STREAM" TIMING="POST" TIMEOUT="0" PROTECT="TRUE">
        <SCRIPTBODY>
            NET USE T: \\\\SERVERNAME\\SHARENAME
        </SCRIPTBODY>
    </SCRIPT>
</DEPENDENCY>
```

Deleting a Network Drive Mapping

Here's a script for deleting a network drive mapping during POST SHUTDOWN. When your users no longer need to run that infrequently used application, why not get rid of that drive you mapped for them?

```
<DEPENDENCY>
    <SCRIPT EVENT="SHUTDOWN" TIMING="POST" TIMEOUT="0" PROTECT="TRUE">
        <SCRIPTBODY>
            NET USE T: /DELETE /Y
        </SCRIPTBODY>
    </SCRIPT>
</DEPENDENCY>
```

Importing Registry Keys

Let's say you have an application that requires a specific setting for its date and time. Maybe it's a 24-hour setting with a specific hour, minute, and second display. But you don't want the computer to always have those exact settings. Instead, you import a Registry key to set the date and time one way before the application runs, and when the application shuts down, you import another Registry key that sets the date and time back to the original settings.

```
<DEPENDENCY>
    <SCRIPT EVENT="LAUNCH" TIMING="PRE" TIMEOUT="0" PROTECT="FALSE">
     <HREF>regedit.exe -s \\servername\sharename\DATETIMEIN.REG
     </HREF>
    </SCRIPT>

    <SCRIPT EVENT="SHUTDOWN" TIMING="POST" TIMEOUT="0" PROTECT="FALSE">
     <HREF>regedit.exe -s \\servername\sharename\DATETIMEOUT.REG</HREF>
    </SCRIPT>
</DEPENDENCY>
```

Those are just a few examples to get you started. As I said at the beginning of this section, scripting is limited only by your imagination.

Final Thoughts

Application sequencing is really the heart and soul of SoftGrid. You can build up a fantastic server infrastructure and have all of your SoftGrid Clients installed and ready to go, but if you can't sequence the applications that need to be delivered, it's all for naught. If there is any one component of SoftGrid that you should spend most of your time learning, it is how to sequence applications and troubleshoot sequenced applications.

So before we bid a fond farewell to SoftGrid, let's review a few of the things we covered in this chapter:

- You learned the ins and outs of the sequencer application itself. Don't forget about the ability to change the file types within a sequence, especially in the case of files that will contain user-specific data.

- You learned some advanced sequences including creating application suites, branching applications, installing applications to the C: drive, and installing ActiveX plug-ins. Remember, you'll want to branch applications when you want to make a new package out of an existing package without having to go through the long process of starting a sequence from scratch.

- You learned how to troubleshoot sequenced applications by launching a command prompt to navigate the Q: drive and launching Process Monitor. The hard part about this is navigating through all of the entries in the Process Monitor log to find the one key piece of information you need. But if you remember how to use the filtering built into Process Monitor, you'll be fine.

- You learned how to make scripting changes within the .OSD file to perform specific tasks required by your applications. There are all sorts of reasons why this is awesome. In my example, I suggested importing and exporting Registry keys and mapping drives. But you could also install drivers, copy files down to the local system, or even run a VBScript to defragment your hard drive!

Finally, you should know that the information in Chapters 5 through 7 is based on the released version of SoftGrid. The next iteration, called Microsoft Application Virtualization, will likely have these new whiz-bang features:

- The ability to call one virtual application from within another virtual application. We talked about creating an application suite in our chapter, and we had to install all the applications we wanted to interact together into one sequence. With Dynamic Suite Composition, we'll be able to make changes to our .OSD files to allow us *not* to install all of our applications into one sequence, yet still have the ability to have those sequenced applications interact with each other.

- Lightweight streaming servers for branch offices. Similar to an SMS distribution point, the Application Virtualization Streaming Server will let us set up a SoftGrid server in every branch office without having to install the full SoftGrid Management Console, SQL server, or domain controller. We'll be able to control all of our branch office servers centrally from our servers that have a full management console installed on them.

- The ability to create MSI installer packages right from the sequencer instead of having to use a separate utility.

Won't that be great? And, yes, you can be sure we'll be there to cover the action when it all happens.

8

Client Security with WSUS 3.0 and MBSA

Over the years patch management for Microsoft products has grown from an occasional activity, principally completed during the irregular release of Service Packs, to a regular and seemingly constant task. Every Patch Tuesday, which is commonly the second Tuesday of every month, Microsoft releases its set of patches for that month. The sheer number of patches in each monthly release makes necessary the administrative function of not only installing them onto systems but managing which patches end up where. With hundreds of patches being released on a regular basis for virtually every application and OS written by Microsoft, as well as occasional third-party drivers, a system of managing those patches is critically necessary just in order to keep them straight.

Microsoft's big push in terms of patch management got its largest kickoff back in 2002 with the release of what is now known as the *Trustworthy Computing Memo*. This message, written by Bill Gates himself and distributed to employees throughout Microsoft, detailed Gates' realization that enhancing security in Microsoft's product stable was critically important to their positioning as a core resource for their customers. With the release of this memo, Gates and Microsoft announced to the world their intent to refocus code development activities on prioritizing security and the reduction or elimination of vulnerabilities. As Gates put it in the memo, "If we don't do this, people simply won't be willing—or able—to take advantage of all the other great work we do. Trustworthy Computing is the highest priority for all the work we are doing. We must lead the industry to a whole new level of Trustworthiness in computing" (Bill Gates, Trustworthy Computing memo, 1/15/2002).

Five months after the release of Gates' memo came the first iteration of Microsoft's product geared toward the patch management process: *Server Update Services*, also known as *SUS*. This initial release brought a single, centralized tool to the masses to distribute Microsoft patches to servers and Desktops. It was a great first attempt and served the IT community for nearly three years before eventually being replaced in June 2005 by the tool we use today: *Windows Server Update Services*, or *WSUS*.

SUS and WSUS were both very interesting additions to many IT environments for two very big reasons: first, both products worked fairly well. Other than a few early issues with deploying client components onto servers and Desktops, the use and management of SUS and WSUS installations was and is easy and the product relatively stable. The second reason was the price: free.

This chapter was written by Greg Shields.

In the early years of patch management's initial hypergrowth in popularity, many third-party companies rushed to release tools of their own to assist with the management and deployment of patches. Those tools invariably involved a cost to purchase and implement. As time passed and tools evolved, WSUS's stability and price both appeared to have a major effect on the economy of patch management tools, and today, few third-party patch-management tools remain that are solely targeted toward patching Microsoft products. That knowledge alone is a testament to the quality of Microsoft's WSUS platform and the embracement of it by IT organizations everywhere as the solution for patch management.

This chapter is dedicated to showing you the ins and outs of patch management with a specific focus not only on WSUS, but also its companion application, the *Microsoft Baseline Security Analyzer (MBSA)*. Whereas WSUS is dedicated to managing patches and the patching process, the MBSA augments these tasks by providing documentation of baseline security configurations that should be implemented on target systems. The MBSA, in addition to looking for security updates, also gives you an excellent set of reports associated with administrative vulnerabilities such as password complexity and firewall configuration, as well as security configurations associated with IIS and SQL. We'll start with a comprehensive discussion on WSUS and, later on in this chapter, show how MBSA can be used to illuminate even more information to keep your network safe.

We will be using prerelease software, specifically WSUS 3.0 SP1 RC and Windows Server 2008 RC1. There may be changes between the information shown here and what is realized in the final product.

Patch Management's Cast of Characters: WU, MU, MBSA, WSUS, SCE, and SCCM

Before we get into the down-and-dirty details of WSUS, we should first take a step back and look at the cast of characters that currently makes up Microsoft's patch-management products. You'll also find that depending on the size and complexity of your environment, options *other* than WSUS may be preferable. For extremely small environments, WSUS may not even be necessary component. That's because running a WSUS instance will require a server, which can be a premium in very small environments. For larger environments, other tools like System Center Essentials or System Center Configuration Manager may be needed to provide the level of configuration control you need. Let's take a look at each of these tools with an eye toward which one will work best for you:

WU and MU (Windows Update and Microsoft Update)   These two tools, which are often (though incorrectly) used interchangeably, actually describe two different tools used by Microsoft for the distribution of patches to client workstations. Traditionally, Windows Update is and was used for the distribution of patches specific to the Windows operating system. For Windows XP systems and earlier versions, Microsoft Update was an add-on functionality that added support for patching other Microsoft products like Office, SQL, Exchange, and others. With these operating systems, each individual client would go to `http://update.microsoft.com` to connect to the system and install needed patches.

With Windows Vista, the necessary components are available natively in the OS for connectivity to Microsoft Update. With Vista and Windows Server 2008, clients need only navigate to Start ➤All Programs ➤Windows Update to bring forward the Windows Update Control Panel where the same scanning and patch-deployment actions are now completed.

The major benefit of WU and MU is that any administrative user can connect to Microsoft and download patches as necessary to keep their system safe. But relying on individual users to "do the right thing" could be detrimental to your health (or at least the health of the business). MU and WU make available *some* patches that corporate IT may not want deployed to systems. More than anything, allowing individual systems to download patches independently and over the Internet negatively impacts bandwidth.

WSUS (Windows Server Update Services)   Because WU and MU are primarily meant for "individual" users rather than corporate ones, WSUS was implemented as a tool to centralize and localize the download, storage, and assignment of patches. WSUS solves two major problems not available in WU and MU. First, it provides a centralized management to the approval and distribution of patches. This means that you, the administrator, choose which patches to deploy and when. Second, it provides a single place on the local network from which patch code is stored and distributed. If every computer on your network attempted to contact Microsoft Update on a regular basis, the resulting network traffic could be a problem. With WSUS only one computer needs to download patches from locations off the local network. All other computers can then get their update installations from that server using high-speed LAN connections.

SCE and SCCM (System Center Essentials and System Center Configuration Manager)   WSUS alone, however, is only a tool for managing Microsoft patch installation. The only code available for installation via a WSUS instance is that which is provisioned through Microsoft. This means that third-party code and patches not distributed by Microsoft aren't available. For cases like these, other tools are necessary. System Center Essentials and System Center Configuration Manager are two very similar tools that allow for more rich management of individual systems within the IT environment. SCE is designed for smaller environments with less than 30 servers and 500 desktops, while SCCM is designed for larger environments. Though these tools both use the WSUS engine for deploying patches and other code, they also augment WSUS's capabilities with the ability to fully manage essentially all system configurations. This includes the ability to deploy third-party applications, drivers, and patches. I include them here as a counterpoint to WSUS's capabilities. If you expect that you'll need to deploy other types of applications, configuration changes, or non-Microsoft patches to your environment, consider implementing one of these two tools instead of WSUS. One important point is that unlike WSUS, neither of these tools is free.

MBSA (The Microsoft Baseline Security Analyzer)   WSUS alone is an excellent tool for managing the composition of installed and not-installed patches on servers and Desktops. But securing these machines involves more than simply ensuring its patches are up-to-date. Elements like password composition, administrative vulnerabilities, and IIS and SQL configurations are all critical to preventing outside entities from exploiting a machine. MBSA goes a step beyond WSUS in that it provides information about the security configuration on targeted machines. We'll talk more about these elements at the end of this chapter.

What is especially brilliant is the use of the Windows Update Agent by all these server-side tools. The Windows Update Agent is a small piece of client code installed to each managed computer, whether that computer is on, say, Windows XP or Windows Vista Desktop, an instance of Windows Server 2003, or Windows Server 2008. That code handles the interrogation of the machine to identify which patches are installed and which are yet needed. It also handles the installation of software as requested by any of these tools just listed.

There's a huge benefit to unifying the technology under a single client tool. As an example, consider how installations were done (and in some cases still are done) before the industry came to embrace Windows Installer: apps in many cases needed to build their own installation routines. The command line switches needed to install one piece of software were often very different than the ones used to install another. Unifying software installation under a single client tool now means that software installations are more predictable and easy to use. The same holds true for patch management. Whereas Windows Installer eased the software installation process, the Windows Update Agent eases the process of managing patches.

Better yet, you can start out with a free tool, like WSUS, and then later move up the pay-scale to SCE and SCCM with ease. That's because each of those products relies on the same underlying, already-installed client tools. As an example, if your environment has long used Microsoft Update as the tool for patching machines and you later want to implement WSUS, it's likely that you already have the necessary client pieces installed on your machines.

In this chapter we'll be exploring WSUS 3.0; a no-cost tool that's scalable from tens to tens of thousands of clients that can be set up in a number of different configurations depending on your requirements. WSUS is a capable solution for virtually any environment. Even though up to this point we've talked about some of the other tools that also enable patch management functions, the WSUS engine for deploying patches through any of them is the common denominator. Thus, if you know and understand how to use WSUS, you'll have the knowledge you need to later work with the other tools.

Now that we know why it's so great, let's start implementing!

Understanding the Components of WSUS

WSUS is a vast improvement over its predecessor SUS in that much of the internal workings of its client scanning process have been automated. With SUS, administrators were required to manually kickoff scans of machines on a regular basis to validate their configuration and see which patches needed installation. With WSUS, that process is changed such that clients scan themselves on a regular basis—every 22 hours by default—and automatically report their findings to the WSUS server behind the scenes.

Take a look at the multiple-site WSUS configuration in Figure 8.1. We'll talk in a minute about the specific kinds of architectures that can be set up for a WSUS infrastructure. For now, you can see here that WSUS has the ability to span across multiple, well-connected sites. These sites need not necessarily be Active Directory sites but are typically bounded by areas of high-speed network connectivity.

FIGURE 8.1   A graphical representation of a multisite WSUS architecture

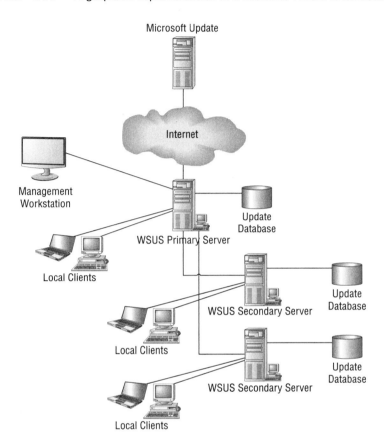

One of WSUS's primary responsibilities is to reduce the requirement for all machines to go directly to Microsoft Update to download patches. The WSUS server at the primary site communicates with Microsoft Update to download update metadata as well as the installation files. It then passes that data across the WAN to any configured secondary servers. Depending on how the WSUS architecture is set up, administrators in secondary sites can be either highly limited in what actions they can perform, or they can be given complete control over the configuration of their site.

Using Group Policy, clients in each location are pointed to a WSUS server in close network proximity to them. Their local WSUS server handles instructing clients which updates to download and install based on update approvals made by the administrator. The administrator uses a management workstation to run WSUS's MMC console to regularly make update approvals, manage the site's configuration, and add and remove clients from the WSUS database. WSUS includes its own set of internal groups, not related to Active Directory security groups, for setting permissions. By adding clients into these groups they can be given different patch schedules or assigned different patch approvals based on the software and/or OS installed on the client. There are many ways to populate WSUS client groups, which we'll talk about in a minute.

Scanning for presence or absence of needed patches is also done at the client, with the resulting report sent at regular intervals back to the server. Client scans are configured to involve relatively few resources while they are processing, which means that the scanning process should be relatively transparent to the user.

All of this is downloadable as a single package from Microsoft. Each of the server component pieces, as well as any necessary client pieces (with one exception for older OS versions that we'll discuss in a minute), can be downloaded from `http://tinyurl.com/2d15u5`.

Whether you have a single site with a few clients or dozens of sites with thousands of clients in each, WSUS's internal engine is built to scale to virtually any size. Throughout the rest of this chapter, we'll discuss the specifics of how you may want to configure your WSUS infrastructure. We'll talk about the different types of architectures that can support your needs, and you'll learn the best practices associated with WSUS, and patch management in general, that makes the process of managing this big, monthly task much easier.

What's New and Different between WSUS 2.0 and WSUS 3.0

Still running your patch management off WSUS 2.0? You should consider an upgrade to version 3.0, as the upgrade includes a number of new features, as well as better performance that makes the experience of using the tool much more user friendly. Let's look at a list of some of the important differences between WSUS 2.0 and 3.0:

- The user interface, which was a sometimes-very-slow web interface in 2.0, has been upgraded to a fully fledged MMC 3.0 interface.

- The new interface includes links to Microsoft Report Viewer, which does a much better job of providing nice reports for you, your managers, and those all-important auditors.

- E-mail notification is now an option, providing a way for your WSUS server to notify you when new status reports, updates, and categories are available.

- Clients can now be added into multiple groups when using Client-Side Targeting, which we'll discuss in a minute. This allows you to include your client computers into multiple WSUS groups within the console for testing purposes or for machines that support multiple roles.

- A new wizard is available in the WSUS interface that easily removes old and unnecessary data from the database. WSUS 2.0 mysteriously did not include any way to get rid of old machines and other data from the database, which eventually cluttered up the interface. With 3.0, the wizard can eliminate this clutter for you.

- High availability options are now available. If you want to make sure you always have servers available for patching, this is awesome. We'll discuss the specifics of how to set up high availability later in this chapter, but know that Windows Network Load Balancing clusters can now be used for front-end web servers, while the back-end SQL database can now also be clustered.

- Timing on synchronizations to upstream servers for patch data can now be configured to run multiple times per day. This is handy when you want to ensure that you have the most up-to-date data in your database.

- Network security options are also new to WSUS 3.0, adding the ability to use SSL to encrypt patch metadata as it is transferred between WSUS servers in your environment. Also, if you have concerns about rogue WSUS servers, you can require server-to-server authentication to prevent unauthorized WSUS servers from entering your infrastructure.

- The biggest priority for changes between WSUS 2.0 and 3.0 was the assurance that the upgrade process could be done in-place and as smoothly as possible. With few exceptions, the established method for upgrading an instance from WSUS 2.0 to 3.0 is to download the new WSUS 3.0 code from Microsoft and run it on your WSUS 2.0 server. The installation will identify that a WSUS instance is already present and automatically upgrade the necessary components and database. Once the upgrade is complete, you'll immediately get the benefits of the new features we've talked about here.

Installation Requirements and Prerequisites

Prior to installing WSUS, you'll need to ensure that you've got a few things set up in your environment. WSUS 3.0 SP1 will install onto Windows Server 2003 or Windows Server 2008 but is not supported on Windows 2000 Server. A WSUS instance for Windows Server 2003 works much like a client/server application. The server components install to the server and run there, while the client components can be run either on the server or on your management workstation. To simplify our environment, in most of our examples we'll run the client components from \\wsus, which is our example WSUS server.

As of this writing, WSUS is a separate download. It may also be possible to check for new roles once Server 2008 ships. There's some good info here on what may be coming: `http://tinyurl.com/23rgsv`. Before installing, be aware of the following additional installation prerequisites (which I cheerfully stole and listed here from the WSUS 3.0 SP1 Readme file):

- WSUS 3.0 SP1 is not supported on servers running Terminal Services. This does not include Remote Desktop, which can be enabled on the server.

- IIS must be installed and not running IIS 5.0 isolation mode (more on this in the "Installing the WSUS Server" section later).

- IIS on 64-bit servers must not be installed in compatibility mode.

- Other than the WSUS website, only one other website may be already be configured to listen on port 80. This is commonly done through the use of host headers running on port 80. Websites beyond the single additional one must be removed prior to starting the installation.

- Disable antivirus applications prior to beginning the WSUS 3.0 SP1 installation.

- If using SQL Server as the database for WSUS 3.0 SP1, the nested triggers option must be enabled. (But SQL isn't required; you can use the Windows Database, as we do in our upcoming examples.)

- SQL databases on servers other than the WSUS server can be used for the WSUS 3.0 SP1 database, with the following assumptions:

  - The remote SQL server cannot be a Domain Controller and Terminal Services cannot be running.

  - The remote SQL server must be at least Microsoft SQL Server 2005 SP1 for Windows Server 2003 or Microsoft SQL Server 2005 SP2 for Windows Server 2008.

- For desktop installations, client components can be installed to Windows XP SP2 or later or Windows Vista clients. For server installations, client components can be installed to Windows 2000 SP4 or later, or any version of Windows Server 2003 or 2008.

- The following required components must be installed to the WSUS 3.0 SP1 server:

  - IIS. For Windows Server 2008, ensure that the following components are enabled: Windows Authentication, Static Content, ASP.NET, IIS 6 Management Compatibility, and IIS 6 Metabase Compatibility.

  - Microsoft .NET Framework Version 2.0 Redistributable Package.

  - Microsoft Management Console 3.0.

  - Microsoft Report Viewer.

  - SQL Server 2005 or Windows Internal Database.

- WSUS 3.0 SP1 cannot be installed onto compressed drives.

- The server installation requires a minimum of 1GB on the server's system partition and 2GB for database files. 20GB is required for storage of content. Note that although the amount of data for the system partition and database is not likely to increase beyond the requirements, the level of storage required for content can be vastly different based on the number and type of updates and classifications you intend to store locally as well as the number of languages you need to support.

Be aware that additional requirements may be added by the time the RTM version of WSUS 3.0 SP1 is released. Check the Readme file to verify any additional requirements at the time of release.

WSUS Architectures

Though not immediately obvious during the installation of the software, there are seven possible configurations for WSUS. Each of these configurations may be used depending on the size of the network, as well as the managing IT group's requirements. The level of trust between IT groups is also an important determinant in selecting an architecture. When the IT team at the primary site does not trust those at secondary sites to perform certain patch management tasks, you'll see that it is possible to limit what kinds of activities can be done by those downlevel teams. For environments that have laptops or special network requirements, other architectures that support those needs are available. In the next sections, we'll discuss each of the seven architectures at a high level. Later in this chapter, I'll show you the actual configurations necessary to enable each of these seven architectures.

Simple

The *Simple* architecture is, as the name says, the easiest way to deploy a WSUS infrastructure to an environment. Here, a single WSUS server services a single well-connected site of computers. Typically, the Simple architecture is used when there are only a few clients in the environment—so few, in fact, that no client groupings are necessary to separate clients or enable different patch distribution schedules.

Simple with Groups

As we discussed earlier in the section on WSUS's architecture, WSUS has its own internal groups that allow for the separation of clients. Those groups, which can be either manually populated or can be populated through Group Policy and OU membership, are typically used to categorize client types (such as servers versus desktops versus laptops, etc.) or to allow for different patching schedules.

The *Simple with Groups* architecture is effectively the same single-server architecture as the Simple architecture. What is different here is the use of WSUS groups. With WSUS groups, the determination of how machines are separated is done by the managing administrator.

For smaller environments with only a single site, this architecture is the most-often deployed configuration. This is usually due to the need of many organizations to minimally configure some groups for testing prior to patch distribution.

Centralized

Whereas the first two architectures work well in smaller environments with only a single well-connected site, there are times when multiple sites wish to share the same WSUS infrastructure. We refer to those WSUS servers as "chained" together. Chaining can occur in one of two different ways.

In the first, called the *Centralized* architecture, downstream WSUS servers are connected to the primary WSUS server as slaves or "replicas." Administrators in downstream sites have little control over WSUS configuration. WSUS groups are defined at the primary server. Those group names and characteristics then flow down automatically to any configured downstream server. Downstream administrators have the rights to add computers to these predefined groups but do not have the ability to approve or schedule updates.

The Centralized architecture is useful in situations where administrators at the primary site want to retain control of the types of patches applied and when they are distributed but do not want the responsibility of ensuring that machines are kept in the proper groups. As an example, imagine the situation where no skilled IT administrators are located in a downstream site. Patching at that remote site still needs to be done, but the decisions about what to patch should likely be made by the skilled IT people at the primary site. Using the Centralized architecture, local unskilled people at the downstream site can be easily trained to put computers in the right groups. The approving of patches, which is a more skilled activity, can then be done solely from the primary site. The Centralized architecture is also handy when the IT team at the primary site wants to retain complete control over the patch baseline from a single location.

Distributed

The *Distributed* architecture is similar in form to the Centralized architecture, where multiple WSUS servers are chained together to form a single infrastructure. However, in this architecture, downstream administrators have more configuration control over their local site. Groups flow down from the primary server, but group memberships do not. Update approvals and schedules similarly do not flow down.

Whereas the Centralized architecture is used primarily for control of updates, the Distributed architecture is used for site-to-site distribution of patch code. In this configuration, only the primary WSUS server contacts Microsoft for update code. Once downloaded from Microsoft, updates are transferred from WSUS server to WSUS server through the WAN infrastructure. The Distributed architecture is an excellent configuration when IT organizations wish to use a centralized infrastructure for reporting and patch distribution yet retain local control.

An example of where this architecture may be useful is in a company where skilled IT administrators are present both at the primary and downstream sites. Downstream IT teams may have a better knowledge of what updates need to be approved for their site. Thus, they will want to control which patches they approve. This can be done using the Distributed architecture. All updates are still downloaded from Microsoft through a single WSUS server and transferred to other servers through the WAN, but each site controls every aspect about patch approval and distribution.

Combinations of the Centralized and Distributed architectures can be used. Some sites can be connected to upstream servers using one model while others use another. As we'll discuss in a minute, any WSUS server's configuration can be manipulated to suit the needs of local IT teams.

Disconnected

Some networks are completely isolated from the Internet and other internal networks. These networks are often test and development environments or have governmental restrictions on network connectivity. In these cases, it is possible to migrate metadata, as well as the updates themselves, from one WSUS server to another. This manual process, which we'll discuss later, creates a type of *Disconnected* architecture between the network-connected WSUS infrastructure and the isolated one.

Classified (as in governmental) environments are a perfect example of where the Disconnected architecture works very well. These highly secured environments usually do not allow connectivity to the regular Internet, so a direct connection from the WSUS server to Microsoft

Update is prohibited. In the case here, a separate WSUS server that is allowed access to the Internet can be used to download metadata and update files and can then be synchronized to the disconnected WSUS server through a manual process.

Roaming

Some environments involve machines that are off the network for long periods of time. Or, they may have high local Internet connectivity but low intersite connectivity. In these cases, it is possible to configure WSUS to distribute only update metadata (such as schedules and approvals) through the WAN. Clients are then configured to receive the actual update distribution directly from Microsoft.

This is of particular use for laptops which may be away from the network for extended periods of time. When laptops connect to the WAN they receive their approvals from the WSUS server. When they are later attached to the Internet, they download and install updates as instructed by the WSUS infrastructure. This configuration requires that off-network computers connect to the WAN at irregular intervals to receive update instructions.

High Availability

Some environments require high availability to prevent single points of failure. In environments where high availability is critical, it is possible to configure multiple, redundant WSUS instances for each site. We'll discuss how to set this up later on in this chapter, but the WSUS front end can be made highly available through the use of Microsoft Network Load Balancing. The back-end database can be further made highly available by configuring the database as a failover cluster. Combining these two eliminates single points of failure within the WSUS infrastructure.

 As with the combinations of the Centralized and Distributed architectures, combinations of Disconnected, Roaming, and High Availability architectures are also possible. In fact, when more than one WSUS server is present in the environment, any combination of architectures can be used as needed by IT.

Installing the WSUS Server

Now that we have an understanding of the history and potential architectures associated with our WSUS infrastructure, let's go through the installation step by step to illustrate the necessary procedure. In this section, we'll discuss the steps necessary to install a single instance of WSUS to Windows Server 2008. Our Windows Server 2008 computer has already been installed and added to the corp.com domain.

Installing WSUS Prerequisites

Before we can ever begin installing our WSUS server, it requires the installation of some needed prerequisites. These prerequisites enable its components to run properly. If you miss a prerequisite before starting the installation, the install will let you know what you've missed.

Installing the Web Server (IIS) Role and Needed Role Services

Even though WSUS 2.0 no longer uses a web interface as its tool for managing the instance, WSUS 3.0 still leans heavily on IIS for functionality. To install it, launch Server Manager and right-click the Roles node. Choose Add Roles and add the Web Server (IIS) Role, as well as any required features. When prompted, also ensure that the following Role Services are enabled in addition to the defaults: Windows Authentication, Static Content, ASP.NET, IIS 6 Management Compatibility, and IIS 6 Metabase Compatibility.

Installing the Microsoft Report Viewer

From the Microsoft Download Center, download and install the Microsoft Report Viewer to the server. This component is used by WSUS to manage and build reports within its interface. This can be found at `http://tinyurl.com/ytjo3v`.

Installing Microsoft SQL Server 2005 SP2 (Optional)

WSUS can run atop either a local installation of the Windows Internal Database or Microsoft SQL Server 2005 SP2. Typically the Windows Internal Database is used when the size of the WSUS environment is small, while SQL Server is used when the size is large or when you want the additional resiliency, performance, and restoration capabilities of SQL Server. If desired, install SQL Server either locally to the WSUS server or to a separate server using the SQL Server documentation. Typically, WSUS does not make heavy use of its database, so except for the largest of environments, it is usually not necessary to install a separate instance of SQL Server for WSUS alone. Using a shared SQL Server on another computer often provides the performance and scalability needed for a nominally sized WSUS infrastructure.

WARNING   While installation of the WSUS database using the Windows Internal Database is free, using SQL Server can involve the added cost of a SQL Server license.

Installing WSUS 3.0 SP1

Once you've completed the preceding steps, you'll need to download the WSUS installation files from the Microsoft website at this address: `http://tinyurl.com/22anrz`. Then, run the installation.

During the installation, you will be asked lots of questions. We'll run down the questions you'll be asked and some suggested ways to answer them.

Installation Mode Selection   To begin, we'll need to install the "Full server installation including Administration Console" to the server we've chosen to be our WSUS server. Another option exists on this screen called "Administration Console only." Later on, when we're ready to install the console to our local Desktop for management, we can use this same installation to install the console there. But, for now on the server, let's choose to start the full installation.

License Agreement   Accept the license agreement to continue.

Select Update Source   In the Roaming architecture, as we've discussed, if clients are to receive their updates directly from Microsoft instead of through the WSUS infrastructure, deselect the check box, as seen in Figure 8.2. Otherwise, if clients are to receive their updates directly from the WSUS server itself, ensure that the check box is selected. Also, provide a location where a minimum of 6GB and a recommended 20GB of disk space is available.

FIGURE 8.2   During installation, the WSUS server can be configured to store updates locally, or clients can get them directly from Microsoft.

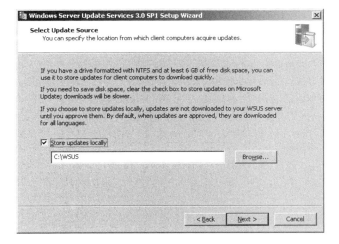

For this chapter and our examples, we're going to check the box marked "Store updates locally" and use the default location for storing our updates.

Database Options   On the next screen, the WSUS instance can be configured to install and use an instance of the Windows Internal Database, an existing SQL database on the same computer, or a remote SQL instance. For this chapter and our examples, we're going to select the option "Install the Windows Internal Database on this computer" and use the default location for the database, which is C:\WSUS.

Website Selection   In this screen, you can choose to use the existing IIS Default website or use another website that defaults to port 8530, rather than the traditional port 80. The wizard recommends that you use the default website as this simplifies the naming of the site. However, if you are already using this server as a web server for another reason, or you want to incorporate the added security that changing the website port provides, you can select the option "Create a Windows Server Update Services 3.0 SP1 Website." For this chapter and our examples, we're going to select the option "Use the existing IIS Default Website."

Windows Server Update Services Configuration Wizard

Once the installation is complete, the Windows Server Update Services Configuration Wizard will appear. This wizard will take you through most of the initial configurations necessary to get your WSUS infrastructure online and fully operational. Let's take a look at each of the steps you may see as part of this wizard.

Join the Microsoft Update Improvement Program   Similar to the Windows Customer Experience Improvement Program seen within Vista's Error Reporting configuration, WSUS has the ability to send information to Microsoft about the health and configuration of your WSUS infrastructure. If you wish to participate and send this information to Microsoft, you can do so by checking the box here. The decision to send this information to Microsoft is completely your own. While the information is kept in confidence, it is used to help Microsoft identify and understand the use and experience of Microsoft products, as well as to build a database of errors and why they occur.

Choose Upstream Server   An important decision needs to be made at the Choose Upstream Server screen, which is seen in Figure 8.3. You need to decide which type of architecture this WSUS will use:

- To configure the server as either a Simple or Simple with Groups architecture with only a single WSUS instance, choose Synchronize from Microsoft Update.

- To configure the server to use a Centralized architecture, choose "Synchronize from another Windows Server Update Services server" and select the option "This is a replica of the upstream server."

- To configure the server to use a Distributed architecture, choose "Synchronize from another Windows Server Update Services server" and deselect the option "This is a replica of the upstream server."

- If you want to use SSL to encrypt traffic between the servers, select that box, as well. All servers in an infrastructure must be similarly configured as to the use of SSL.

Specify Proxy Server   Enter any proxy server information that is required by your corporate security infrastructure for servers to connect to the Internet.

Connect to Upstream Server   The update catalog for WSUS is constantly changing as Microsoft adds and removes updates, products, and languages. Thus, in order to make an initial selection of the categories and types of updates you want to synchronize locally, you must first download the update catalog. The next screen starts that connection. The result of the download in this step will determine the options that can be enabled in the following screens.

Choose Languages   The languages in which your environment has been localized are chosen in the next screen. Choose only the languages for which you currently support localization in your environment.

 Don't select the "Download updates in all languages, including new languages" button unless you really mean it! Selecting all languages will significantly increase the amount of data the WSUS server will attempt to download.

FIGURE 8.3   The initial WSUS Configuration Wizard allows you to define where this server will receive its updates. This selection defines the architecture used to distribute patches.

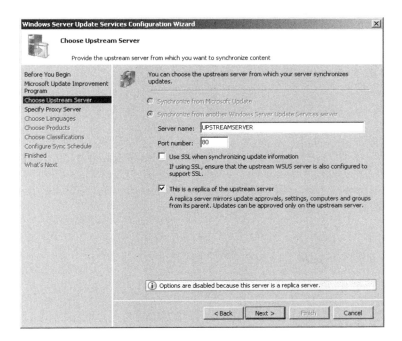

Choose Classifications   The next two screens allow for the selective downloading of only those products and classifications needed for your environment. The same rules hold true here as for the preceding screen where you choose languages. Because Microsoft releases thousands of updates for many different products, it will make update administration easier if you select only the classifications for products you have in your environment. For example, if you do not have Windows 2000 machines in your environment, you needn't download patches for them. Be aware that it is possible to change these settings later on if necessary.

More update classifications also increase the amount of storage space required to store their updates. By default, WSUS will only download update installation code once that update has been set to Approved in the interface.

Configure Sync Schedule   Synchronization is the process of updating the local WSUS server with information from upstream. If the upstream server is another WSUS server, the local server will sync its information with that server. Otherwise, it will sync its information from Microsoft. Though you can sync manually, it is recommended that you set a schedule, since this can take some time to complete and can use network bandwidth.

Once the initial configuration is complete, you will likely want to select the option in the second-to-last page of the wizard to begin an initial synchronization, as well as to bring up the WSUS console. All other activities within WSUS will take place within the console.

Distributing the Windows Update Agent

In most cases, the Windows Update Agent already installed onto each client in your environment will be at a level where WSUS can interact with it. All instances of the Windows Update Agent (WUA) on Windows XP Service Pack 2, Windows Vista, and Windows Server 2008 are already at this level. Windows XP RTM, Windows 2003, and earlier systems, however, require a manual installation of the correct agent version to function with the WSUS infrastructure.

To obtain the client, download the Windows Update Agent from the Microsoft website at http://tinyurl.com/2v3aqb, or search for "How to Install the Windows Update Agent on Client Computers" at Microsoft.com. Use this downloaded package to install the client to any machines that are at Windows XP RTM or earlier. Clients will not appear in the WSUS interface until the process has been completed for older operating systems.

Once the agent is installed to all machines and WSUS can communicate with the agent, WSUS itself will automatically update the client as necessary and as Microsoft releases new versions of the client itself. This self-update process happens automatically and requires no additional configuration.

WSUS and Group Policy

All parts of the WSUS client are managed through Group Policy. This includes the behavior of the client itself, when it contacts the WSUS server, its rebooting policy, and more. WSUS policy settings are born from the file WindowsUpdate.admx, which either lives in the C:\Windows\ PolicyDefinitions folder or your domain's Group Policy Central Store. You can learn more about creating the Group Policy Central Store in Chapter 7 of the companion book.

Fifteen different WUA client computer-based settings are available within WindowsUpdate .admx. These are located within the Group Policy Management Editor at Computer Configuration ➢ Policies ➢ Administrative Templates ➢ Windows Update.

Three more user-based settings are found in the same path under User Configuration. Let's take a look at each of these 18 different settings and how they will impact your use of WSUS within your environment.

It is possible to manage WSUS configurations manually through the Registry. But really, with Group Policy at your side, why would you want to? Refer to the WSUS manual for excellent documentation on the specific Registry settings needed to do this in a non-Active Directory or non-Group Policy environment.

WSUS configurations deployed through Group Policy can utilize any of the usual Group Policy mechanisms for targeting machines. This includes OU membership, AD group memberships, and WMI filters. Though we focus on OU membership in much of this text, your ability to target groups is limited only by your ability to target any Group Policy.

Computer Configuration Settings

Now we're getting into the real meat of WSUS. Once it's installed and operational, its use is relatively straightforward—if you set it up in the best way possible. Though every environment is different, in this section I'll suggest what I think are the best ways to set up Group Policy to make your life as easy as it can possibly be. In a later the section, "Best Practices in Patch Management," I'll continue with what I think are the best ways to ensure that you get patches installed the fastest with the least interruption to your users.

Specifically, in this section we'll discuss the Group Policy settings that you can implement to configure each client's Windows Update Agent. In the upcoming sections I'll show you how settings are commonly configured and where you may want to be careful. Some settings have unintended consequences associated with their use that may impact network bandwidth usage or the speed of client updates.

Configure Automatic Updates   This is the master toggle switch for Automatic Updates (AU). Enabling this configuration turns on AU for all clients that receive the GPO. Here, it is also possible to configure the time and day of the week for the scheduled install, as well as how updates are downloaded and installed, either automatically or manually. Here is a list of possible options within the policy setting:

> **Notify for download and notify for install.**   WUA will notify you when updates are ready for download and again when they're ready for installation.

> **Auto download and notify for install.**   WUA will automatically download updates but notify you when they're ready for installation.

> **Auto download and schedule the install.**   WUA will automatically download and install updates using the defined schedule. This configuration provides the most centralized control for administrators using WSUS. It also eliminates any notifications for download or install that can irritate or confuse users.

> **Allow local admin to choose setting.**   The local administrator will be allowed to choose which of the preceding three settings are used to handle update download and installation. This setting is useful for clients that are in a WSUS testing group. Then you, the administrator, can make the decision about how you want updates downloaded.

Specify Intranet Microsoft Update Service Location   Locations for the intranet update service and the intranet statistics server are specified here. Configure the location of the local WSUS server in the format http://servername for both entries. By not configuring or disabling this setting, the client will refer to Microsoft Update rather than a local WSUS server.

Automatic Updates Detection Frequency   By default, all clients check for new updates every 22 hours (plus or minus 20 percent). Setting a different time here can extend or shorten the amount of time between client update checks. Narrowing the amount of time can decrease the amount of time needed to recognize new updates but can have a negative impact on network bandwidth. It's generally not a good idea to increase the frequency past the 22-hour default.

Allow Nonadministrators To Receive Update Notifications   By default, only administrators will receive balloon notifications that updates require processing. By enabling this setting, nonadministrators will also receive notifications. As we'll discuss later in our best practices section, unless you want your users to be aware that they're being patched, I recommend disabling this setting. The balloons that appear for nonadministrators tend to confuse rather than help nontechnical users.

Allow Automatic Updates Immediate Installation   Some updates do not require a reboot or a service restart for a complete installation. In the case of these updates, it is possible to instruct the client to automatically install the update immediately and without waiting for the scheduled update period to occur. Since the patch can be installed immediately, it is usually a good idea to configure this setting to speed the distribution of these types of updates.

Turn On Recommended Updates via Automatic Updates   Recommended updates are updates that are not critical to the safety and security of the operating system or its immediate stability. Thus, they are not necessarily required. Some recommended updates introduce new features to the operating system or driver sets. This setting configures clients to download any recommended updates when available. If you don't want these "extra" installations to occur automatically, it may be a good idea to leave this disabled until you see a specific recommended update that you want installed.

No Auto-Restart for Scheduled Automatic Updates Installations   Some updates require you to restart the operating system for a complete installation. When these updates are installed, the client will automatically restart within five minutes of the installation. Often, this restart can interrupt users if the update occurs in the middle of their workday. Enabling this setting ensures that the patch will be installed only when the user or some other process reboots the client. As you'll see later on, I really like enabling this setting and using a script or some other tool to reboot my clients. Doing reboots this way helps you avoid irritating your users!

Delay Restart for Scheduled Installations   When users receive a reboot notification, they are given a predefined number of minutes to either complete and save work in preparation for the reboot or postpone the reboot. When this policy is set to Not Configured or Disabled, that default interval is 5 minutes. Enabling this setting will change the default number of minutes before an automatic reboot occurs. If you do want WUA to manage the post-installation reboots, it's probably a good idea to increase this to a larger number, such as the maximum value of 30 minutes, and give users as much time as possible to determine how they want to handle the reboot. Although, the maximum value of 30 minutes is long enough for many users, think about users who leave documents open during their hour-long lunch. Later on in the section on best practices we'll talk about another way to get around this limitation, primarily through the complete elimination of the WUA-initiated reboot.

Reprompt for Restart with Scheduled Installations   When a reboot notification is given to the user, the user is allowed to postpone the reboot for a certain number of minutes. When this policy is set to Not Configured or Disabled, the default interval is 10 minutes. Enabling this setting allows the default postponement interval to be changed to a different number up to a maximum of 1440 minutes, or 24 hours. The situation here is the same as in the setting just discussed. If you choose to let WUA do reboots for you, it might be a good idea to increase this number. That way when users are working on a high-priority project, they can postpone the reboot until a more convenient time.

Reschedule Automatic Updates Scheduled Installations   Sometimes clients are powered off when updates are scheduled to be installed. When those clients are powered back on, the updates will begin to install. This setting allows for a predetermined number of minutes to elapse prior to beginning the installation. This is most important when updates require reboots, since depending on other configurations, the update installation can enforce a post-installation reboot. If this setting is disabled, the missed update is rescheduled to occur with the next set of updates. If not configured, the update will be installed in 1 minute. When this setting is enabled, you can wait to update installation up to a maximum of 60 minutes.

Be careful with this setting. By enabling or not configuring this setting, any updates that aren't installed because a machine was powered off will get installed a few minutes after the power on. The effect for the user is that they start their machine and can work for only a short time before they're rebooted again, which is really irritating!

Enable Client-side Targeting   There are two ways that clients can be put into groups within WSUS: Client-Side Targeting and Server-Side Targeting. Setting this to Disabled or Not Configured instructs WSUS to use Server-Side Targeting. Enabling this setting and entering in a group name instructs WSUS to use Client-Side Targeting. In the next section we'll discuss the differences between Client-Side and Server-Side Targeting.

We've talked before about the new WSUS 3.0 feature of multiple targeting. You can force machines into multiple groups by putting multiple group names into this box, separated by a semicolon. An example of where this might be useful is when you have a SQL Server that is also a Windows Media Server.

Allow Signed Updates from an Intranet Microsoft Update Service Location   WSUS has the ability to deploy some third-party updates, such as drivers, through its infrastructure. Enabling this setting instructs the client to accept these updates if they are signed by a certificate that is trusted by the client.

Do Not Display the 'Install Updates and Shut Down' Option in Shut Down Windows Dialog Box   When patches are available for installation, users can install updates and then shut down. Enabling this setting removes that ability from the Shut Down menu. If you are attempting to remove visual notifications from the view of your users, you may consider enabling this setting.

Do Not Adjust Default Option to 'Install Updates and Shut Down' in Shut Down Windows Dialog Box   By default, if patches are available for installation (but not yet installed) users will be prompted to Install Updates and Shut Down as the default option when shutting down. By enabling this setting, the last known setting (such as Hibernate, Shut Down, and so on) is used.

Enabling Windows Update Power Management to Automatically Wake up the System to Install Scheduled Updates   For Windows computers that are configured with power management features (such as Windows Vista and Windows Server 2008), when a system is in hibernation mode and updates are scheduled to be installed or a deadline is reached, enabling this setting will instruct the Windows Update Agent on the client to wake up the machine and install the update. If the machine is running on batteries, this is detected during startup and the machine is shut down automatically after two minutes without installing any updates. Enabling this setting helps with improving update compliance in environments where hibernation is routinely used.

User Configuration Settings

In addition to the settings that configure the Windows Update Agent for the computer, there are three settings that can be targeted toward users. Two of these settings are redundant with those in Computer settings, but are available in case you want to adjust the policy definition by individual rather than by computer. The third of these is effectively the master toggle switch for WSUS. Providing that capability here allows for WSUS to be disabled completely for certain users.

Do Not Display the 'Install Updates and Shut Down' Option in Shut Down Windows Dialog Box   This setting is effectively the same as the one in Computer Configuration, but targeted toward specific users. This is handy when you have certain users, such as administrators, that may want more control over when updates are installed.

Do Not Adjust Default Option to 'Install Updates and Shut Down' in Shut Down Windows Dialog Box   As with the preceding setting, this setting is effectively the same as the one in Computer Configuration but targeted toward specific users.

Remove Access to Use all Windows Update Features   This setting effectively shuts down Windows Update entirely, preventing the use of its native control panels and blocking access to the Windows Update website. For environments that do not want WSUS or WU/MU updates to function whatsoever, that restriction can be enabled by setting this configuration.

Client Targeting (aka Group Assignment)

As we talked about earlier in this chapter, WSUS has its own internal groups that can be used to separate clients. But you should be aware that WSUS groups are not Windows-style Active Directory groups.

They are used only within WSUS to separate clients. This is most often done to provide for multiple patch schedules or to separate out approvals. Since some groups will likely require some patches and others will not, dividing clients into multiple groups can be helpful in approving only the necessary updates for each type of client.

There are two different ways in which clients can be added into groups in WSUS. Depending on the processes and procedures of the IT department, the structure of Organizational Units in the domain, and the desire of administrators, either type of targeting can be used.

   Only one kind of targeting can be used per WSUS server.

Client targeting is configured in two places, in the WSUS console and also within Group Policy. The configuration must match between the two locations for targeting to work properly. First, from within the WSUS console, click Options ➢ Computers. You'll see a screen similar to Figure 8.4.

FIGURE 8.4 This screen determines how clients are assigned into groups within WSUS.

There, you can select the option "Use the Update Services console" or "Use Group Policy or registry settings on computers." Using the console to assign clients into groups is called *Server-Side Targeting*, while using Group Policy to assign clients is called *Client-Side Targeting*.

Server-Side Targeting Server-Side Targeting is really a fancy way to say, "Let me just drop my machines into the groups myself within the WSUS management console." When doing this, ensure that the Enable Client Side Targeting setting is disabled and the radio button is set to "Use the Update Services console." New computers will be automatically positioned in the Unassigned Computers group within the WSUS console and must manually be moved to the correct group by an administrator.

When using Server-Side Targeting, the onus of responsibility for ensuring that clients are in the correct groups is on the administrator. So, returning back to the WSUS console regularly to look for new machines within the Unassigned Computers group is critical when you choose this option.

Client-Side Targeting In the "Computer Configuration Settings" section, we discussed the Enable Client Side Targeting setting. Enabling that setting also allows you to enter the name of a group for the machines that are assigned the Group Policy Object. When this setting is enabled, the setting in WSUS should be set to "Use Group Policy or registry settings on computers."

When the OU structure for the domain mimics the group structure you wish your WUA clients to follow, Client-Side Targeting is an effective tool to automatically drop clients into the proper groups based on their OU membership. However, when the OU structure is much different than the desired WSUS structure, Server-Side Targeting should be used.

Multiple Targeting   When using Client-Side Targeting in WSUS 3.0, it is possible to assign machines into multiple groups by separating group names with a semicolon when configuring the Group Policy Object. Once the GPOs have been embraced by the client and clients have contacted the WSUS server, they will appear in multiple locations within the WSUS console as targeted within Group Policy. This is handy for clients that may play multiple roles or that operate as both production as well as patch-testing machines.

You have the option of choosing either Client-Side or Server-Side Targeting for each of your WSUS servers. Making that decision is critical to how your clients will get dropped into their correct groups. Client-Side Targeting is an easier and less manual mechanism for getting clients into their correct groups, but using Client-Side Targeting means that your Active Directory Organizational Unit structure must match what you want your WSUS groups to be. This is because Client-Side Targeting leans on Group Policy for its application. Multiple targeting can also be used in this scenario and is typically used when an OU full of clients needs to belong to more than one WSUS group.

If your OU structure doesn't match what you want your WSUS group structure to be, you'll be forced to use the more manual (but more flexible) Server-Side Targeting method.

Setting Up Our Example Environment

In the next section, we'll be taking a look at the WSUS Console and each of the components within it. In order to let us see the same things when doing this, let's make sure that we've configured our example environment to prepare for console administration.

To do this, first make sure you've installed WSUS and its necessary prerequisites onto a computer in your test environment. In my example, I've named my test computer \\wsus. When installing that WSUS server, make sure you've selected the options discussed earlier in this chapter.

Once the server is installed, bring up the WSUS console by first creating an empty Microsoft Management Console. Do this by typing **mmc** into the command prompt window. From the resulting console, choose File ➢ Add/Remove Snap-in and then add in the snap-in for Update Services. If you are not doing this directly on the WSUS server, you'll the need to right-click the Update Services node and select Connect to Server. Enter the WSUS server name to initiate the connection. Another way to access the WSUS console is to go to Start ➢ Administrative Tools ➢ Microsoft Windows Server Update Services 3.0 SP1, which has the server connected by default.

We must do two things to create our example environment. First, we must ensure that our server is configured correctly for the upcoming examples. Then, we'll need to create a Group Policy that applies the correct configuration to our clients.

To check our server settings, select the Options node in the tree, choose WSUS Server Configuration Wizard, and then configure the following options:

1.   In the Microsoft Update Improvement Program window, check the box "Yes, I would like to join the Microsoft Update Improvement Program." Click Next.

2. In the Choose Upstream Server window, select Synchronize from Microsoft Update. Click Next.

3. In the Specify Proxy Server window, enter any proxy server information that relates to your environment in this screen. Click Next.

4. Next is the Connect to Upstream Server window; click the Start Connecting button. The server will take a minute to download the updated products and classifications list. When it has finished, click Next.

5. In the Choose Languages window, select "Download updates only in these languages" and check the box for your primary language. Click Next.

6. Next comes the Choose Products window. Check the boxes for Office and Windows only. Later on we can add other products as necessary. Click Next.

7. On the Choose Classifications screen, select the default options, which are Critical Updates, Definition Updates, and Security Updates. Click Next.

8. In the Configure Sync Schedule window, select "Synchronize automatically" and set the first synchronization to 3:00:00 am, and 1 Synchronization per day. Click Next.

9. In the last window, check the box for "Begin initial synchronization" to start the first update synchronization. Click Finish to return to the WSUS console.

We now need to set up the Group Policy that will configure our clients to connect to this WSUS server and behave in the way we wish for our example environment. This will be a minimal policy that does little more than tell our clients to start reporting to WSUS. You can later change the Group Policy to add additional configurations that make sense for your environment.

To do this, first add the `WindowsUpdate.admx` file to your Group Policy Central Store so we can see the selections of interest to us. Then create a new Group Policy in the GPMC and link it to an OU that includes a set of computers you want to use for testing. Within that OU, configure the following settings in Computer Configuration ➢ Policies ➢ Administrative Templates ➢ Windows Update:

Configure Automatic Updates   Set to Enabled. Set Configure automatic updating to "4 – Auto download and schedule the install." Set the Scheduled install day to "0 – Every day" and the Scheduled install time to 04:00.

Specify intranet Microsoft update service location   Set to Enabled. The name of the server we're using in this example is `\\wsus`, so in both the "Set the intranet update service for detecting updates" box and the "Set the intranet statistics server" box, enter **http://wsus**. Note the http:// at the beginning of the server name here—formatting is very important with this setting.

Automatic Updates detection frequency   Set to Enabled. In the "Check for updates at the following interval (hours)" box, enter **1**. Normally, we would not reduce the update check interval to this low a number in a production environment, but here we want to speed up the process during our testing. When using this in a production scenario, it is a good idea to use the default of 22 hours.

Once you've completed these three tasks, you'll need to wait for the clients to download the Group Policy and then begin a detection cycle. This can take some time. It is possible to speed up this process by using these three commands in this order:

```
gpupdate /force
```

then two WSUS client agent command lines:

```
wuauclt /resetauthorization /detectnow
wuauclt /reportnow
```

This should significantly reduce the amount of time needed to see clients within the WSUS interface.

The WSUS Console

Now that we've installed our WSUS server and configured our Group Policy, the remainder of the work and virtually all of the daily operational activities are done through the WSUS console. As stated earlier, the WSUS console arrives as a snap-in to the Microsoft Management Console. The WSUS console can be run either from a management workstation or from the WSUS server itself. Upon installing the server, the WSUS console will be available on the system as a snap-in to the MMC. However, in order to use the console from a remote computer, you'll need to run the WSUS installation on that remote computer. When prompted, choose to install "Administration console only." This will make the WSUS console MMC snap-in available on the remote computer.

WSUS's console is relatively sparse in comparison with some Microsoft products, containing only six nodes at the top level. In this section, we'll take a look at each of those nodes and see where they come in handy.

First, before clicking through any of the individual nodes in the WSUS screen, check out the top-level node described with the server name. Clicking here will give you a series of charts and graphs showing the overall health of the WSUS infrastructure. Also shown here is the WSUS To Do List, which shows items you should check in order to bring your WSUS infrastructure to maximum health. The To Do List is a handy feature, as it rolls up together all the important tasks such as approving updates and looking at new products and classifications.

Computers

Let's start out by looking at the Computers node in the WSUS console. This is where computers and the groups they belong to are managed. If Server-Side Targeting is enabled for this instance, you will be required to look through this node from time to time to find new machines within the environment and drop them into the correct groups. As you can see in Figure 8.5, we have chosen to use Server-Side Targeting. Because of this, when machines first arrive into WSUS, they arrive in the Unassigned Computers group.

FIGURE 8.5   The management console for WSUS shows update status by machine and group.

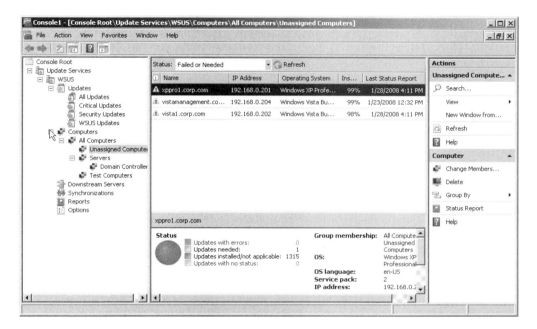

The machines that make up our environment are listed here. Each has provided a status report showing the patches currently installed as well as those missing. One of the major benefits of a WSUS instance is the Needed Patches categorization, which helps the administrator discover which patches each client within their environment needs in order to be fully compliant.

Changing the filtering for computers is done via the Status element in the upper-center of the screen. As shown in Figure 8.5, the status for this view is currently set to Needed or Failed. It is possible to limit the view by those systems with a status of Any, Failed, Needed, Installed/ Not Applicable, or No Status.

You can also see a status report in the middle-bottom of the screen that shows some handy information about the status and composition of updates for the highlighted machine. In Figure 8.5, the system \\xppro1 has 1315 updates that are either installed or do not relate to the machine. One update is currently needed but not installed. Additional details such as make and model of the computer, processor, and BIOS version are also available.

Another new element for WSUS 3.0 is the ability to create nested groups. You can see in Figure 8.5 that the Domain Controllers group is nested within the Servers group. This allows for greater extensibility in terms of assigning update configurations to groups, as well as creating reports.

Right-clicking any computer within the Computers node brings up a context menu that, among other elements, allows you to change the group membership of that machine or produce a status report. Producing a status report brings forward the Microsoft Report Viewer with detailed information about the status of the target machine, including its installed and needed patches. These reports are handy for identifying the compliance status of machines in the infrastructure. A sample report for \\xpprol is shown in Figure 8.6. Notice at the top of the screen that the report can be filtered down to produce just the information of interest, including update classification, product, and status.

FIGURE 8.6   WSUS can provide filterable status reports on specific machines.

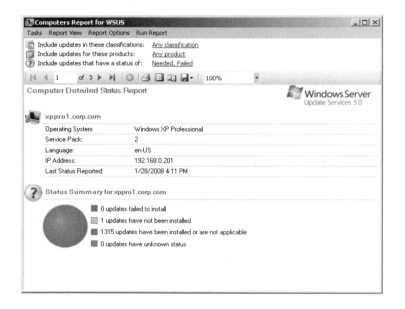

Updates

You do a lot of your work with WSUS in the Updates node. Here, updates are approved or disapproved for installation to clients. As shown in Figure 8.7, four default views are available for Updates: All Updates, Critical Updates, Security Updates, and WSUS Updates. Each of these views provides a look at the potentially thousands of updates under management by WSUS.

Approving an update for a computer group is simple within this interface. You just right-click the update you want and select Approve. The resulting screen will show a list of the computer groups that you can approve for the update. Click the down arrow to the left of the appropriate groups and/or subgroups and click Approved for Install. Conversely, if the patch should not be installed (or even removed), click the appropriate setting within the interface.

Once an update is set to Approved for Install, WSUS clients will begin downloading and installing the patch using the schedule identified within Group Policy. By default, clients are configured to check in with the WSUS server every 22 hours. This lengthy default ensures that clients aren't saturating network bandwidth with repeated checks. Once the client check-in has completed, the client will then install the patch based on how the **Configure Automatic Updates** policy setting has been set.

FIGURE 8.7   WSUS's Updates node, showing the Critical Updates currently available for the environment

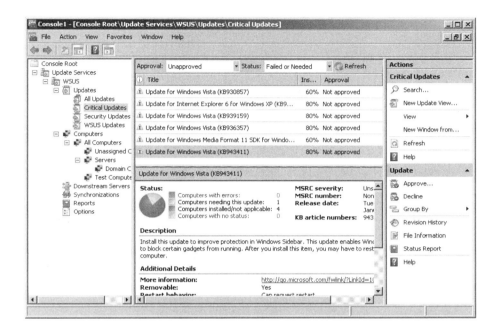

Depending on how you configure the detection frequency and the install time, it is possible for clients to take an extended period of time to install patches, so plan your Group Policy settings accordingly.

On this screen you can also set a deadline for the installation of the update. Deadlines allow for the overriding of the Group Policy–configured patch installation time. By setting a deadline, you are telling the client to install the patch at a specified time rather than their configured time. This mechanism can be used to speed up the time for patch installation should your configured time be too far in the future. Note that deadlines will automatically reboot machines if patches require a reboot no matter how WUA configuration is set within Group Policy.

This screen gives you the ability to pull additional information about updates, similar to the Computers node. Right-clicking the context menu associated with any particular update pulls up a status report associated with that update, information about the files that make up the update, and a revision history that shows if the update has experienced any changes or updates over its lifecycle. This information is useful in helping determine whether or not to deploy the update to clients around your network. You may find that certain updates do not relate to clients within your environment and as such do not need to be approved for installation.

Approving only those updates that relate to your environment reduces the total number of updates you must manage over time.

If the four default views do not provide the granularity you need in order to best find and deploy updates, it is possible to create custom views with WSUS 3.0. These views can be tailored to show just the updates of interest and remain persistent when you close and reopen the WSUS console. To create a custom view, right-click the node in Updates that you want the view to be created under, and select New Update View.

In the resulting screen, shown in Figure 8.8, the view can be tailored to show updates by classification, product, assigned group, and date, as well as to focus only on WSUS updates. Once a property is set in the upper window, the specifics associated with that property are configured in the bottom window.

FIGURE 8.8 A custom view within WSUS that will show only critical Exchange 2007 patches approved for a particular group that have been synchronized within the past two months

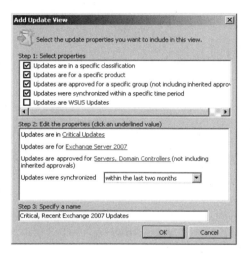

Downstream Servers

The third node provides information about downstream servers within a multiserver WSUS infrastructure. When multiple WSUS servers are chained together, information about downstream servers can be obtained here, such as status and last synchronization.

This node is intended as a location for checking the status of downstream servers. Configuration of downstream servers is done through each server's Options node.

Synchronizations

The Synchronizations node provides information about the last synchronizations between the highlighted server and its upstream server (including Microsoft Update). As with the Downstream Servers node, this is mainly a reporting location to show the status of syncs. Right-clicking any synchronization in the middle pane will bring forward a report with more detail about the status and success of the synchronization.

Reports

WSUS has a limited capability for generating reports associated with the status of updates, computers, and synchronizations that have occurred. By clicking the Reports node, you will find the seven standard reports available natively within the WSUS interface. These are the only reports that can be pulled natively within the WSUS interface. Custom reports over and above these must be pulled programmatically through a direct connection to the WSUS database. Later on in this chapter we'll talk more about the process for doing this.

Clicking any of the seven reports brings up the Microsoft Report Viewer. It is possible to limit any of the reports by various elements like classification, product, computer group, and status. An example of the Update Detailed Status Report is shown in Figure 8.9.

FIGURE 8.9   An example report showing summary status for needed updates

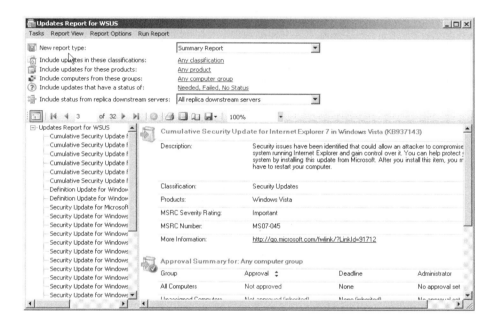

As an example, one very useful report to pull is a listing of all patches that are listed with a status of Needed by clients. This gives you a single-glimpse listing of every update that clients anywhere within your infrastructure believe they are missing. In order to do this, click to open the Update Status Summary report. In the resulting screen, leave all options as default with the exception of "Include updates that have a status of," which should be set to Needed. The resulting report provides you with a list of any patches that are needed by clients in the infrastructure.

The links at the very bottom of the screen under "Approval Summary for Any computer group" are clickable and bring forward the approval screen for that update, making this report even more useful.

Options

Within the WSUS interface is the Options node, which contains the server-side configurations for WSUS. Most of these configurations were set during the WSUS installation within the WSUS Server Configuration Wizard. That same wizard is available for later use within the Options node if portions of the initial setup need reconfiguration. There are, however, a few settings that were not configured as part of that initial configuration. Let's take a look now at each of these new settings and where they may be useful.

Update Files and Languages   Many of the settings here were already set after the installation using the WSUS Server Configuration Wizard. However, one we haven't talked about is the setting "Download express installation files." By instructing WSUS to download express installation files, the file size transferred from WSUS server to the client during update installation is smaller than normal. However, the file size for synchronizations between WSUS servers and Microsoft or between WSUS servers is increased. Depending on the configuration of your network, using express installation files may improve or in some cases, as we'll see later, reduce performance.

Automatic Approvals   If the process of individually approving updates through the WSUS interface is too time-consuming, it is possible to instruct WSUS to automatically approve updates that meet certain criteria. By setting those criteria in this configuration, those updates will be automatically approved once they are synchronized to the local WSUS server. You can also automatically approve any WSUS-specific updates or revisions of already-approved updates.

Server Cleanup Wizard   Earlier versions of WSUS lacked a way to remove clients and other objects from the WSUS interface once they were added. WSUS 3.0 includes the server cleanup wizard to do this. Running the wizard will search for updates, computers, and files that are no longer used within the WSUS infrastructure. It is a good idea to run this wizard from time to time to remove extraneous data from the WSUS server.

Reporting Rollup   Reports within the reporting node can be focused on the local WSUS server only, or they can include all data from every chained server below the local WSUS instance. This selection changes how reports are shown between those two options.

E-mail Notifications   If you tire of logging into the interface on a regular basis just to see if updates or computers are available, you can configure a regular notification to be e-mailed to you. The notification can include information on new updates and status reports.

Personalization   The personalization element allows for rollup information from downstream WSUS servers, such as computers and status, to be included within reports pulled from the local WSUS server. Also, you can also select the elements in the WSUS To Do List here. Narrowing down the items that appear in the To Do List helps reduce notification clutter.

As you can see, other than the installation and Group Policy configuration, actually using WSUS and its console is relatively easy. The console does a great job of illustrating the updates you need to stay aware of, as well as assisting you to find the computers that aren't at your proper patch baseline.

That being said, there are times when patches simply won't install, or when clients refuse to show up in the console. In our next section we'll talk about some of these problems and some common solutions that will get you back up and running quickly.

Troubleshooting WSUS

When WSUS begins having problems, there are only a few places to look for error messages that illuminate those problems' source. As the WUA client is little more than a mechanism for scanning client systems and installing software code, it is a relatively simple set of code. This makes it easy to troubleshoot. Luckily, much can be gleaned by digging into the error messages you see when problems occur.

Event Logs and Log Files

There are five locations to look when problems occur either on a client or on the WSUS server itself: the Windows Event log, two log files on the WSUS server itself, one log file on each client, and the Windows Update Control Panel. These five locations provide much of the debugging support for tracking down problems with update identification and installation.

Windows Event Log

WSUS automatically performs two types of health checks against itself on a regular basis. Its "detect cycle" polls WSUS components every ten minutes to look for and report on changes in status. Its "refresh cycle" occurs every six hours and logs errors and warnings. This polling looks for issues with WSUS core components, the database, web services, and clients. Any events generated by either of these two cycles are posted to the Application Event log with a source of Windows Server Update Services. Thus, monitoring the Application Event log is useful when problems are occurring with the WSUS server itself.

WindowsUpdate.log

On each WUA client is a file, located in `%windir%\WindowsUpdate.log`, which includes a fairly high level of logging activity associated with the client. Here, virtually every activity performed by the client in scanning itself, requesting the appropriate updates, installing those updates, and validating successful installation is provided in a time-ordered format. An example from this log associated with the update download process is listed here:

```
2008-01-09  01:40:12:558  744  14a0  DnldMgr  **************
2008-01-09  01:40:12:558  744  14a0  DnldMgr  ** START **  DnldMgr: Downloading
updates [CallerId = AutomaticUpdates]
2008-01-09  01:40:12:558  744  14a0  DnldMgr  *********
2008-01-09  01:40:12:558  744  14a0  DnldMgr  * Call ID = {7B124073-3C96-48C1-
9B16-0DD583912705}
2008-01-09  01:40:12:558  744  14a0  DnldMgr  * Priority = 2, Interactive = 0,
Owner is system = 1, Explicit proxy = 0, Proxy session id = -1, ServiceId =
{7971F918-A847-4430-9279-4A52D1EFE18D}
2008-01-09  01:40:12:558  744  14a0  DnldMgr  * Updates to download = 1
2008-01-09  01:40:12:558  744  14a0  Agent    * Title = Update for Windows
Vista for x64-based Systems (KB943302)
```

```
2008-01-09  01:40:12:558  744  14a0  Agent     * UpdateId = {62E062EB-F82A-414E-
A319-3D5D836D0126}.102
2008-01-09  01:40:12:558  744  14a0  Agent     * Bundles 1 updates:
2008-01-09  01:40:12:558  744  14a0  Agent     * {3EB48727-4957-4781-B45F-
8B40302A1099}.102
2008-01-09  01:40:12:559  744  14a0  DnldMgr  *********** DnldMgr: Regulation
Refresh [Svc: {7971F918-A847-4430-9279-4A52D1EFE18D}]  ***********
2008-01-09  01:40:12:559  744  14a0  DnldMgr  * Regulation call complete.
0x00000000
```

Two elements to notice are the sections marked UpdateID and BundleID. The *UpdateID* identifies the general update, whereas the *BundleID* identifies the package to be downloaded that is associated with the update. These two pieces of information can be used to assist in identifying updates that are causing problems. Searching for key words such as FATAL or WARNING can further help in finding failed updates. For more information about how to read the `WindowsUpdate.log` file, see MSKB article 902093 at `http://support` `.microsoft.com/kb/902093`.

Should the information provided within the `WindowsUpdate.log` file not have the level of detail necessary to locate the problem, it is possible to increase that file's log level by adding two values to the Registry. First, in `HKEY_LOCAL_MACHINE\SOFTWARE\Microsoft\Windows\` `CurrentVersion\WindowsUpdate\Trace`, set the `REG_DWORD` value for Flags to 7. Then, in the same Registry key, set the `REG_DWORD` value for Level to 4.

Change.log

This file on the WSUS server itself provides a list of all recent approvals and the individual who made those approvals. Found in `%Program Files%\Update Services\LogFiles\change.log`, this log is useful in discovering what changed in the WSUS infrastructure and who made the change.

```
2008-01-21 20:07:59.828 UTC   Synchronization manually started
2008-01-21 20:12:09.156 UTC   Successfully deployed deployment(Install) of
Update for Background Intelligent Transfer Service (BITS) 2.0 and WinHTTP 5.1
(KB842773) by WUS Server UpdateID:3E1EE9BF-A5F6-4CD8-BF9F-310F4CFDBAD1 Revision
Number:101 TargetGroup:All Computers
```

In this sample, the log shows the start of a synchronization activity followed by a change to the update KB842773. The text "by WUS Server" means that changes made by this user were done automatically by WSUS as part of an automatic approval.

SoftwareDistribution.log

This log file gives information about software updates as they are synchronized from an upstream source (including Microsoft itself) and the local WSUS server. Unfortunately, of the three logs available, this one is the most difficult to decipher. The following text shows the download of a portion of update metadata to the local database.

```
2008-01-21 20:46:09.847 UTC  Info  w3wp.13
SusEventDispatcher.TriggerEvent  TriggerEvent called for NotificationEventName:
DeploymentChange, EventInfo: DeploymentChange
```

2008-01-21 20:46:13.379 UTC   Info   w3wp.8
SusEventDispatcher.TriggerEvent TriggerEvent called for NotificationEventName:
DeploymentChange, EventInfo: DeploymentChange

2008-01-21 20:46:13.441 UTC   Info   w3wp.24
SusEventDispatcher.DispatchManagerWorkerThreadProc DispatchManager Worker
Thread Processing NotificationEvent: DeploymentChange

2008-01-21 20:46:13.441 UTC   Info   w3wp.24
DeploymentChangeNotification.InternalEventHandler deployment change event
received

2008-01-21 20:46:13.582 UTC   Info   w3wp.24
RevisionIdCacheChangeNotificationDispatcher.InternalEventHandler
Get event DeploymentChange from dispatchmanager

2008-01-21 20:46:14.457 UTC   Info   WsusService.7
SusEventDispatcher.TriggerEvent TriggerEvent called for NotificationEventName:
DeploymentChange, EventInfo: DeploymentChange

2008-01-21 20:46:14.847 UTC   Info   w3wp.13
SusEventDispatcher.TriggerEvent TriggerEvent called for NotificationEventName:
DeploymentChange, EventInfo: DeploymentChange

2008-01-21 20:46:16.879 UTC   Info   WsusService.28
CatalogSyncAgentCore.ImportMultipleUpdates Imported 100/100 updates in 1
iterations; 0 will be retried

2008-01-21 20:46:16.879 UTC   Info   WsusService.28
CatalogSyncAgentCore.GetUpdateDataInChunksAndImport357 updates to go

Windows Update Control Panel

One of the easiest places to look for problems with update installation is within the Windows Update Control Panel. When updates incur problems during their installation they will show a status of Failed. Right-clicking any update with a Failed status and selecting View Details will present a window similar to Figure 8.10, where the Installation Status is Failed and an error code is provided in the Error details field. Details about the reasons for that code can be researched either by clicking the "Get help" link or by searching the Internet.

FIGURE 8.10   The Windows Update Control Panel shows error codes associated with failed update installations.

A list of all the WSUS error codes and associated descriptions is available on the Internet at http://tinyurl.com/78pvo.

Patch Distribution and Network Usage Issues

In multisite environments, it is possible to set up a WSUS infrastructure with multiple hops between the primary servers and the farthest downstream server. It is further possible to set up chaining between servers with very slow bandwidth connecting them. In either of these cases, it is possible to set up a situation where bandwidth is being saturated through the update synchronization process between disparate WSUS servers. There are a number of ways to reduce the overall network usage associated with patch distribution.

Eliminate Unnecessary Patches   Many WSUS administrators initially bring all possible updates and update categories under local management in case they may be needed. This is most often done though the creation of Automatic Approval rules. But not all updates relate to every environment. WSUS will only download update code when updates are set to Approved for Install. Thus, approving only the minimum possible set of updates will reduce the total number of updates that must be transferred through the WSUS infrastructure. Beware of setting automatic approval rules too loosely, as they can trigger large numbers of update downloads.

Stagger Update Distribution   When setting the synchronization schedules among chained servers in a WSUS infrastructure, it can be useful to stagger the synchronization time. Ensure that the primary server completes its synchronization schedule before secondary servers attempt to synchronize or they may not get the most recent set of updates. Also, if tertiary servers are present, stagger their synchronization as well with secondary servers. Above all, be careful not to set synchronizations to occur all at the same time, as this can cause excessive consumption of bandwidth when all of the WSUS servers attempt to synchronize at once.

Express Installation Files   Express installation files involve the download of larger amounts of code from the upstream server. By downloading a larger file size to the WSUS server, the size of that update's distribution to clients is reduced. But express installation files reduce file sizes for WSUS-to-client connections only. WSUS-to-WSUS synchronizations can actually involve larger amounts of data in order to synchronize the express installation files between servers. So be careful about using express installation files in chained WSUS infrastructures with low bandwidth.

Throttle BITS   It is possible to reduce the overall bandwidth used by BITS for all transfers. BITS is the protocol used for all WSUS file transfers. Using Group Policy, it is possible to set a limit on the bandwidth used by BITS, which will increase the overall time needed to complete a transfer but can help with network saturation problems. Do this in Group Policy by navigating to Computer Configuration ➢ Administrative Templates ➢ Network ➢ Background Intelligent Transfer Service. There, set the configurations for the setting "Maximum network bandwidth for BITS background transfers." You'll be able to configure the transfer rate and the time of day to limit transfers.

WARNING By default, BITS is configured to use all available and unused bandwidth. So, it is normal to see an unconfigured BITS instance consume all unused bandwidth on a network link.

WSUS from the Command Line

In addition to its graphical user interface, WSUS can also be managed from the command line in several ways. You can use shell commands, VBScript, and PowerShell scripting exposure for some client and server elements, as well as a few precompiled API samples. Each of these is available to extend the usefulness of WSUS and its database.

Shell Commands

There are three commands commonly used to administer your WSUS instance from the command line. Two are used at the client side to assist with client administration, and the third is used on the WSUS server itself to trigger some common tasks.

wuauclt

The wuauclt command is used to speed up the process of client communication with the server. This tool is especially handy when adding new clients into a WSUS infrastructure as it instructs the client to begin communicating with the WSUS server immediately. Three switches are commonly used with wuauclt:

/detectnow   This switch instructs the client to immediately attempt to contact its configured server for a detection cycle.

/resetauthorization   This switch initiates a background search for applicable updates. When adding new clients into the WSUS infrastructure, this switch is often used with the /detectnow switch to begin detection and update searching all at once.

/reportnow   This switch sends any queued reports to the WSUS server immediately and helps with speeding the transfer of information to the server about the status of the client.

gpupdate

For new clients or clients that have recently been added to an OU with applicable Group Policy, it is useful to run the gpupdate /force command to speed up the processing of Group Policy. As WSUS configuration most often comes through Group Policy, running this command before wuauclt on new clients will speed up Group Policy application and ensure that the client is properly configured prior to attempting a detection.

wsusutil

The wsusutil command is used to initiate actions on the server. This command is located in the %ProgramFiles%\Update Services\Tools folder on the WSUS server itself and can only be run on the server. It may not automatically be available within your path. Wsusutil includes twelve switches, each performing a different action on the server:

configuressl　This switch updates host headers via the Registry after the IIS configuration has changed. Additionally, the ServerCertificateName switch can be used in combination with this switch to set the correct certificate for SSL use.

healthmonitoring　This switch is used in conjunction with numerous parameters for setting or checking various WSUS health parameters and conditions. For a list of the switches that can be used with healthmonitoring, enter the command **wsusutil healthmonitoring**.

export　This switch is used to export update data from the WSUS server. It is commonly used in disconnected architectures to transfer update information from a connected WSUS server to a disconnected WSUS server.

import　This switch does the opposite of the export switch, importing update data to a WSUS server.

movecontent　Should WSUS content need to be moved from one location to another, usually due to a disk drive failure or having filled up, this switch will move the data and update the WSUS database with the new location.

listfrontendservers　This switch, as you might expect, lists the front-end servers in a Microsoft Network Load Balancing configuration.

deletefrontendserver　This switch deletes identified front-end servers in a Microsoft Network Load Balancing configuration. Using this command removes only the server from the database. WSUS must also be separately uninstalled from the front-end server.

checkhealth　Using this switch triggers an immediate health check of the WSUS server. As with all health checks, results are written to the Application Event log.

reset　This switch is used to verify metadata within the WSUS database and whether that data corresponds with update files stored on the server. This command is useful if database corruption is suspected or immediately after a data restoration activity.

listinactiveapprovals　This switch is used to identify the approvals that are configured as permanently inactive. This is done when language options are changed on an upstream server.

removeinactiveapprovals　When language options are changed and the number of permanently inactive approvals is different between chained servers, this switch will remove those approvals that are inactive due to the change.

usecustomwebsite　Using this switch resets the WSUS website from port 80 to port 8530.

WSUS Scripts

WSUS and the Windows Update Agent both include VBScript and PowerShell exposure for the creation of scripts and other custom tools for managing a WSUS infrastructure. Scripts for the

WUA client allow for client-side listing of updates, search and service properties, and modifying the update schedule, among others. For the WSUS server, scripts are available to provide server status, start synchronizations, show server status, and more.

Sample scripts in both VBScript and PowerShell languages are available from the TechNet ScriptCenter at `www.microsoft.com/technet/scriptcenter`. Look in the Windows Update section for details about available scripts.

 Real World Scenario

WSUS API Samples

Along with scripting exposure is a fully realized API that can be used for performing custom tasks and creating custom reports associated with WSUS data. The WSUS API Samples are available from Microsoft's WSUS website at `http://technet.microsoft.com/en-us/wsus` and arrive as a set of precompiled tools along with each tool's associated source code.

Although their use is unsupported by Microsoft, the tools can come in handy for certain activities as they enable functionality that in some cases is not natively available in the WSUS interface. The ability to see the source associated with each sample also assists developers in understanding the WSUS API. The available API Samples that can be obtained for WSUS 3.0 include:

ADImporter   This tool prepopulates WSUS groups with computers from Active Directory and helps with the initial population of WSUS after installation. The ADImporter tool looks like the image seen here:

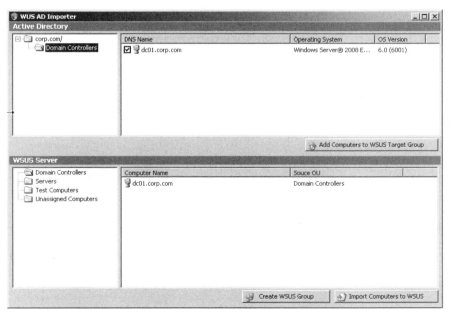

ApprovedUpdatesToXML   This tool creates an XML file that includes a list of updates and their associated approval information.

ApproveForOptionalInstall   Running this tool against a specified update adds the update to the Add/Remove Programs Control Panel, allowing users to optionally install the update.

CleanStaleComputers   This tool removes computers from the WSUS database that have not contacted the WSUS server within a configurable amount of time.

ComputerStatusToXML   Running this tool creates a list of computers currently listed within the WSUS server and also updates status information for each computer.

ComputersNeedingReboot   This tool creates an HTML report that lists computers that have installed updates but require a reboot to complete the installation.

ListApprovedUpdates   Running this tool displays a list of updates that were approved after a configurable date.

UpdateStatusToCSV   This tool creates a CSV file that includes updates and their approval information.

UpdateStatusToXML   This tool provides the same information as UpdateStatusToCSV but with the resulting file in an XML format.

UpdatesToXML   This tool creates an XML file that includes all updates and related information.

WsusMigrate   This tool helps in the migration of update approvals and target groups from one WSUS server to another.

Tips and Tricks for a Smooth WSUS Experience

So far, we've talked about many of the standard uses of WSUS within a computing environment. But some environments have special requirements like high availability or privilege granularity. In this section we'll discuss some of those "extra added features" provided by WSUS 3.0 for special needs.

Implementing WSUS Reporters

Upon installing WSUS, two local groups are created on the WSUS server. The first group, WSUS Administrators, identifies the users who have full rights to the WSUS instance on the server. This group is in addition to the Administrators group that natively has full rights to perform any action within WSUS.

The second group is called WSUS Reporters. This group is granted the permission to run reports within WSUS but not change any configurations, modify update approvals, or add computers. Using the WSUS Reporters group is useful when nonadministrative users need to use the WSUS Console to create and view reports associated with update status and environment compliance.

WSUS Reporters will be able to view all nodes of the WSUS tree, including update and computer information, but any options for making changes will be grayed out with the exception of running and manipulating reports.

Implementing Network Load Balancing

In order to eliminate the single point of failure that occurs when installing only a single WSUS server within an environment, it may be desired to configure a Network Load Balancing (NLB) cluster among all front-end WSUS web servers. The process to set up an NLB cluster is not trivial and involves a number of careful steps. The specifics associated with creating an NLB cluster are documented in the WSUS 3.0 Deployment Guide, but the general steps for creating a cluster are discussed next.

Configure a Remote SQL Server As multiple WSUS servers will be participating in the NLB cluster, a single SQL store for update metadata is required. Installing the back-end WSUS database to this SQL server allows all front-end web servers to point to a single location for their update metadata.

> It is also possible to configure a failover SQL cluster to eliminate the single point of failure of the SQL database. Doing this is beyond the scope of this chapter, but the process to set up a SQL cluster for WSUS is similar to the process for setting up any SQL cluster.

Install and Configure WSUS on Front-end Web Servers Once the SQL store is created, run the WSUS installation on each of the front-end web servers. Ensure that the front-end servers are configured to use the back-end SQL server rather than creating their own internal database. Once the installation is complete, ensure that all front-end WSUS web servers are using a central proxy server and authenticate via the same username and password.

Configure a DFS Share for Content As with the central SQL store for update metadata, a single DFS share should be used for content storage. All front-end WSUS web servers will use this single DFS share for distributing updates.

Enable IIS Remote Access IIS must be specifically configured to use remote data for the content directory. This is done in IIS by modifying the virtual directory for the content node to use a share located on another computer.

Relocate Content The first WSUS server created will have local content that can be moved to the DFS share. Do this using the `wsusutil movecontent` command.

Configure the NLB Cluster The next step is to set up the NLB cluster between the network cards of the participating servers. During this step, cluster and host parameters, as well as port rules, will be configured as desired for the environment.

Point Clients to the NLB Cluster Once the cluster creation is complete, use Group Policy to reconfigure clients to point to the NLB cluster's shared address.

There are some critical steps to properly implementing an NLB cluster for the WSUS front-end web server. Reference the WSUS Deployment Guide for further instructions.

Implementing Intranetwork Roaming

In the beginning of this chapter I explained the Roaming architecture that can be used within a WSUS instance. Setting up a WSUS server for roaming clients off the network involves ensuring that clients who VPN into the network can resolve internal addresses to receive WSUS metadata. Once they have received their approval metadata and have attached to the Internet again, those clients can then download update files directly from Microsoft.

Another manifestation of roaming is when clients remain on the WAN but roam internally from site to site. In this case, for bandwidth reasons, it is often best for these clients to download updates from a WSUS server that is in close proximity. Doing this involves configuring a server for each subnet likely to be used by roaming clients, which means it can be a potentially expensive architecture. To set up intranetwork roaming, you must do the following:

Identify WSUS Servers One server must be identified on each subnet to be used as a roaming WSUS server. Install WSUS onto these servers.

Configure Hostnames Set up a DNS hostname (that is, an A record) for each WSUS server. In every case, the DNS hostname should be the same for each WSUS server.

Configure DNS Round Robin and Netmask Ordering DNS netmask ordering is a protocol that ensures that when multiple DNS records are available and configured for round robin, the address in the same subnet as the client is provided first. Within the DNS console, right-click the DNS server node and choose Properties and then the Advanced tab. In the Server options box, ensure that "Enable round robin" and "Enable netmask ordering" is checked.

Configure WSUS Servers and Clients Ensure that the WSUS servers are configured with the proper networking as entered into DNS. Then, reconfigure clients to point to the single hostname that is used in DNS for all WSUS servers.

By configuring WSUS servers in this way, the same DNS A record is used to contact all WSUS servers within the infrastructure. DNS netmask ordering will ensure that when a client attempts to resolve the IP address for the WSUS server, the server will be on the same subnet as the client. This ensures that clients are always talking to the closest WSUS server.

Obviously, doing this involves the installation of many WSUS servers. You'll need one WSUS server per subnet. If a WSUS server is not present on the same subnet as the client, netmask ordering will resolve the next IP address as identified by the round robin. That server could be located anywhere on the network.

Hacking WSUS's Database

If you're using SQL 2005 to run your WSUS database, it is possible to use the SQL 2005 administration tools to review the structure and data within the database. Leveraging that structure and using the proper joins between tables, it is also possible to create your own queries of the database to generate custom reports based on WSUS data. Since WSUS's own reports are limited in what they will provide, doing this is sometimes necessary to get the specific kinds of reports you may need.

When using the Windows Internal Database instead of SQL, extra tools are required in order to see the database tables and create custom queries. One graphical tool that makes this process easy is the SQL Server 2005 Management Studio Express Edition, which can be downloaded from the Microsoft website at http://tinyurl.com/j7wjl. Similar to the full SQL 2005 Management Studio, this tool can be used to review the database structure, look at the contents of various tables, and even create your own custom queries.

Be aware that, by default, the Windows Internal Database does not allow remote connections. To enable remote connections, install SQL Server Express 2005 and run the Surface Area Configuration Utility and the SQL Server Configuration Utility. In both tools enable the TCP/IP protocol on the database to enable remote access. This is required if scripts will be used against the WSUS database.

Alternatively, if only the SQL Server 2005 Management Studio Express is used on the same server as the WSUS database, it is possible to connect without enabling remote access. Do this by connecting using Windows Authentication to the address \\.\pipe\MSSQL$MICROSOFT##SSEE\ sql\query.

The tables used by WSUS are highly normalized, which means that you'll need to join multiple tables in order to get useful information. Microsoft does not publish the database structure for WSUS, so discovering the proper table joins can be a challenging activity.

To get you started, the following code shows one query that can be run against a WSUS instance to match security bulletin naming to Knowledge Base article naming (also known as "the MS number" to "the Q number"). This code can be input into the SQL Server 2005 Management Studio Express Edition tool. The results from this query will resemble Figure 8.11.

```
SELECT dbo.tbSecurityBulletinForRevision.SecurityBulletinID,
    dbo.tbLocalizedProperty.Title FROM
    dbo.tbLocalizedPropertyForRevision INNER JOIN dbo.tbLocalizedProperty ON
    dbo.tbLocalizedPropertyForRevision.LocalizedPropertyID =
    dbo.tbLocalizedProperty.LocalizedPropertyID INNER JOIN
    dbo.tbSecurityBulletinForRevision ON
    dbo.tbLocalizedPropertyForRevision.RevisionID =
    dbo.tbSecurityBulletinForRevision.RevisionID WHERE
    (dbo.tbLocalizedPropertyForRevision.LanguageID = 1033) ORDER BY
    dbo.tbSecurityBulletinForRevision.SecurityBulletinID
```

This code is available as a download from this chapter's resources at www.gpanswers.com.

FIGURE 8.11 SQL Server Management Studio Express showing query results

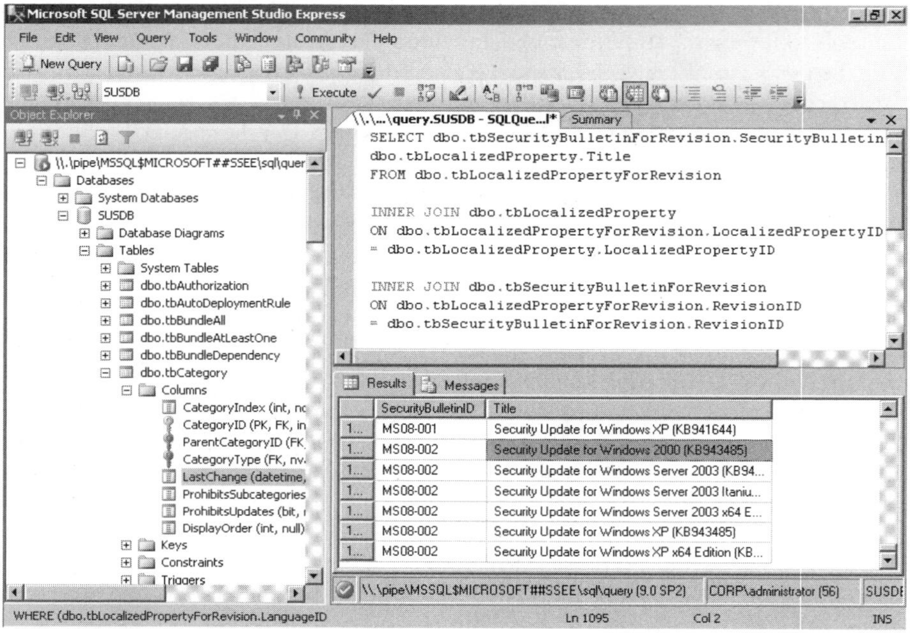

Best Practices in Patch Management

Managing patches and updates in your environment is more than just clicking Approved for Install when they appear every Patch Tuesday. There is a need for a holistic patch management strategy within your organization if you're to test each patch thoroughly and get them installed as quickly as possible while annoying your users as little as possible. In this section, we'll talk quickly about a few best practices for doing just that. Getting updates installed is one matter, but doing so in a way that makes the process easy and relatively trivial every month is yet another.

Considerations for Desktops

In most IT environments, desktops are vast in number, and keeping them all straight can be the biggest challenge associated with their patch management. WSUS includes numerous tools that assist with getting updates installed onto servers, though the procedures in which you deploy WSUS's Group Policy configurations can mean the difference between an annoyed user base and one that never knows or needs to worry that they're being patched.

From the perspective of the user, there are three activities that occur regularly with every month's patch cycle: the regular machine scan, the update installation, and the post-update reboot. WSUS scans each client system every day, a process that is relatively transparent to the user. The WUA client process that scans the system consumes a level of resources but does so over a short period of time, so the scan's impact to the user can be considered relatively small.

The patch download and installation process can be quite different. Depending on how WUA is configured, the user can be highly involved with the patch process. They can be notified when patches are being downloaded and installed. They can be alerted that reboots are about to occur, and they may need to make adjustments to their workflow to prepare for unexpected reboots.

Alternatively, the user can be kept out of the patching process entirely. If you configure Group Policy to prevent all notifications to users, they will never be notified when updates are coming down and applied. From personal experience, this tends to work the best for users (whether they agree or not). Users should be responsible for completing their work tasks. IT should be responsible for patching systems. Thus, making the conscious decision to keep users out of the patching process allows them to be blissfully ignorant of what is occurring behind the scenes.

One element of restricting the user's involvement with the patch process is involved with the post-update reboot. When reboots are scheduled to occur after patch installation, the likelihood is increased that interruptive reboots will occur during the workday. When users' machines are powered off during the install time, updates can be set to automatically install immediately after reboot. This reboot-after-power-on can further annoy users.

> One of the highest considerations for patching desktops, in my experience, is to prioritize the prevention of user workflow interruptions caused by patching and subsequent reboots.

You can most easily prevent user interruptions by enabling the Group Policy setting "No auto-restart for scheduled Automatic Updates installations." Doing this, however, means that you'll need to figure out some other way to reboot workstations as necessary to complete patch installation, such as a script that is run regularly through a Scheduled Task or using the Group Policy Preference Extensions' Scheduled Tasks feature to create a reoccurring task. You get the idea.

As another note of personal experience, it is usually safe to use the patch-and-delay process with Microsoft updates. This process involves the installation of an update but a delay of the post-update process until a future time. Enabling the preceding Group Policy effectively implements the patch-and-delay process to WSUS. WSUS will install any approved patches but will not reboot the client after installation.

Obviously, a reboot is still required to complete the installation of the patch. Another consideration is to use an out-of-band process such as a script to reboot machines on a regular basis. This incorporates the concept of *outage windows* to the desktop patching process. Using Scheduled Tasks on a server to schedule the triggering of a reboot script, an administrator can reboot all desktops in the environment, for example, twice per week on Thursday and Sunday mornings starting at 1:00 am. As Microsoft patches typically arrive on Tuesday afternoons with testing and deployment on Wednesdays, this schedule ensures a post-installation reboot. Doing this through an out-of-band procedure also eliminates the user workflow interruptions sometimes incurred when WSUS handles reboots.

Considerations for Servers

Servers can also benefit from the patch-and-delay approach, though obviously with greater levels of testing involved prior to deploying patches. Incorporating patch-and-delay into server operations reduces the overall outage window associated with installing patches and invoking the post-patch reboot. This happens because patches can be pushed without reboots during the workday, relegating only the reboot to the end of the day. Utilizing virtualization in server environments also adds the ability to snapshot servers prior to update installation, granting the administrator the ability to roll back if the update installs poorly.

In environments where hot-swappable RAID 1 is in place, another server option is often called "The RAID 1 Undo." To create an effective snapshot of a server that uses RAID 1 drives, pull one of the drives immediately prior to installing the update. This breaks the mirror but keeps a "good" copy of the server on the pulled drive. That drive can then be used to boot the system back into its previous state if the update installs badly. If the update installs correctly with the post-installation reboot, the secondary drive is simply snapped back into place once the server is back to a steady state. This allows the mirror to reestablish itself and the server to continue operating as normal.

Typically, the OU structure for servers mimics the servers' roles. Because of this, the OU structure can be a good way to populate WSUS groups when you're using Client Side Targeting. By populating groups in this manner, you can more easily discover and approve the correct updates that are appropriate for each class of server. Since updates typically align by Microsoft products, and server OU membership typically relates to their installed products, this can go far in helping you keep the classifications of approved updates straight for each server's OU, and therefore for the WSUS group.

With operating systems such as Windows Server 2008, the idea of componentization has been added into the development of the OS code. Componentization means that capabilities that are not specifically installed onto the server are not present on the drive whatsoever. This reduces the patching requirements for that server since patches that do not relate to the composition of Roles, Role Services, and Features of the server do not need to be applied.

The Microsoft Baseline Security Analyzer

Patching is a critically important component of securing a Windows network, but as we've said before in this chapter, there's more to security than just getting patches onto clients. Another major component of security is in ensuring that clients are configured in the best way possible to ensure exploits can't make use of unsecured components. WSUS alone handles only the patch management component of security. In order to view more information about individual security configurations, other tools are required.

One tool that can check for certain security configurations is the Microsoft Baseline Security Analyzer, as shown in Figure 8.12, which is downloadable from the Microsoft website at `http://tinyurl.com/2e5fe`. This tool, in addition to looking for security updates, also reviews administrative vulnerabilities such as password complexity and firewall configuration. In addition, it scans the configuration of add-on services like SQL and IIS to validate that these other tools are configured in ways considered secure. As of this writing, the current version of the MBSA is version 2.1, which includes support for Windows Vista.

FIGURE 8.12   The results of an MBSA scan showing administrative vulnerabilities for the targeted server

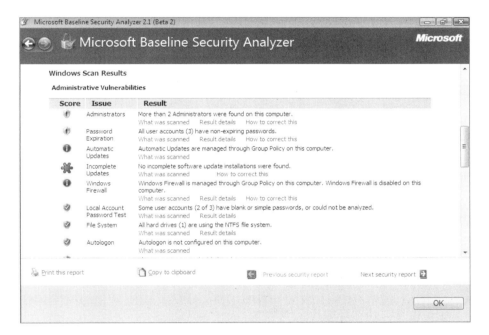

Performing Scans

MBSA is an exceptionally simple tool, with only a very few options available for the user. Scans can be performed against the local computer or remote computers, a single computer or a group of them. You can run a multiple-machine scan against an entire domain of computers or an IP address range. The IP address range is good for very large domains as the scanning process can take an extended period of time.

As you can see in Figure 8.13, a number of additional options are available that allow you to define which scans are done against the targeted computer. Although most of the option check boxes are relatively self-explanatory, two should be explained in greater detail:

Configure computers for Microsoft Update and scanning prerequisites   For clients that do not have the proper Windows Update Agent components in place, checking this box will automatically install or update the agent to the proper level so that a scan can successfully complete.

FIGURE 8.13 The MBSA tool provides limited options for scanning machines.

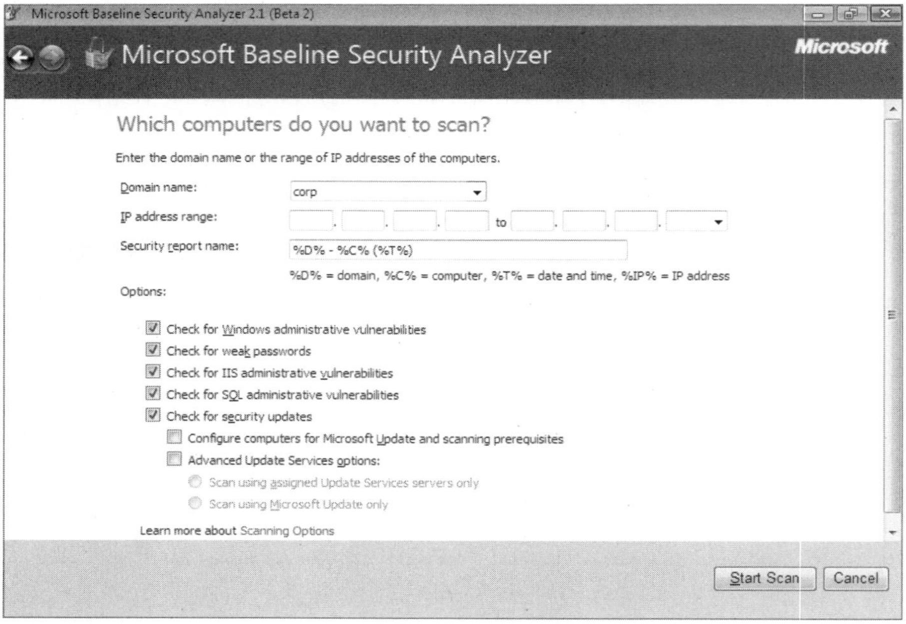

Advanced Update Services options When scanning a system for installed patches, this selection allows you to choose the baseline by which the client's composition is compared. It is possible to compare the client against Microsoft Update or in relation to the approved patches from its connected WSUS (Update Services) baseline.

MBSA at the Command Line

In many cases, it can be more valuable to use MBSA from the command line. Using MBSA in this way provides a textual result associated with the scans you've created. The command line tool `mbsacli.exe` is installed along with the MBSA and can be used to perform many of the same functions as are available in the GUI. The only feature of the GUI not available in the command line version is the ability to view previously run reports. So, if you only intend to run a few reports, the command line can provide you with everything you need.

There are quite a few switches for `mbsacli.exe`, used for identifying scan ranges, the types of scans to perform, and how to display the data. Rather than showing you a list of the switches, let's look at a few combinations that you'll likely use most often. For a complete list of all the available switches, use the command `mbsacli.exe /?`.

mbsacli /r 10.0.0.1-10.0.0.200 This combination sets off a scan of the computers in the IP range of 10.0.0.1 through 10.0.0.200.

mbsacli /listfile {computers.txt} /n SQL+IIS   This combination sets off a scan of each computer contained within the file {`computers.txt`}. The /n switch also instructs the process to skip the SQL and IIS scan components.

mbsacli /d {domain} /wa   This combination sets of a scan of each computer in the domain. The /wa switch instructs the process to compare the results of each computer's scan with the list of approved patches currently configured in WSUS.

Interpreting Scan Results

Once a scan is completed, a report associated with each scanned client is stored within the interface. As you saw previously in Figure 8.12, links are provided for each scanned area that show what was scanned, the results of that scan, and the correct actions that are required in order to correct any problems.

The process of securing systems can typically have multiple involved steps. These steps are necessary to validate that completed changes as suggested by previous scans are correctly applied. The typical life cycle for using MBSA against systems resembles the following:

1. Scan. All target systems are scanned and reports are given on their current security status.

2. Report. Reports are then analyzed and items to be changed are noted.

3. Patch/Reconfigure. Those items that need to be updated, reconfigured, or patched are then completed.

4. Scan. Another scan against the target system is completed.

5. Report. The result of the second scan is analyzed to verify and validate that the necessary changes are correct.

This five-step process is repeated as necessary until all targeted systems are considered compliant. What is important to recognize with this process is that these five steps should be rerun from time to time—often at the same time as the monthly patch cycle—to continuously verify the compliance of all targeted systems.

Back during the days of SUS, the predecessor to WSUS, the MBSA was more heavily used as part of the patch management lifecycle. Regularly scanning machines was part of the routine security activities required of a systems administrator. However, with the release of WSUS and its client-focused approach to reporting and status updates, you'll find yourself using the MBSA less and less. With WSUS managing the patch composition on each of your managed machines, the utility of the MBSA has changed to assisting with security configurations and one-off machines that are not a part of your WSUS infrastructure. Your mileage will vary.

For the most part, I suspect you'll use MBSA relatively rarely. When? Likely immediately after completing the build on a new server and prior to putting it into service. You may also use it as a regular checkup activity on a quarterly or annual basis, to ensure that any administrative configurations, IIS, or SQL settings haven't been changed to something less secure.

Troubleshooting MBSA

If proper network resolution and connectivity is available between the computer running the scans and the computers targeted by the scans, then relatively few problems should be expected from MBSA. It is worthwhile to note, however, that there are some requirements on the part of the systems being scanned in order for the scan to properly complete:

OS   For Windows Server systems, the computer must be running Windows 2000 Service Pack 3 or later. For Windows Desktop systems, the computer must be running Windows XP or later.

Internet Explorer   Internet Explorer 5.01 or later is required.

XML parser   An XML parser must be installed on all target systems. It is recommended that the latest version of the Microsoft XML Parser is installed to all target systems. (It likely is, but double-check if you have issues.) You can find it at `http://support.microsoft.com/kb/269238`.

Services   The Workstation and Client for Microsoft Networks services must be enabled for scans to complete successfully.

Correct network connectivity between systems is required. When firewalls are enabled between systems participating in the scans, those firewalls can impede the success of the scan. Incorrect network name resolution between systems can also prevent clients from being reached. Verifying resolution and connectivity between the computer running the scan and the computers being scanned will help to ensure the success of the scan process.

Final Thoughts

Throughout this chapter, we've talked about some of the tools provided by Microsoft that can assist with the securing of a network. Patching and patch management is a critical component of keeping networks safe. WSUS is one useful tool that arrives with a very compelling price (free) that can assist with that process. Being scalable from tens to thousands of systems, WSUS is an effective tool in managing the patching process for all types of IT environments.

Also available from Microsoft is the MBSA. This no-cost tool augments the capabilities of WSUS by providing further information about client security configuration and necessary changes to that configuration to secure the client against external attack.

If you'd like to learn more about WSUS, the MBSA, and all things having to do with Windows Server, feel free to join me at my Realtime Windows Server Community, where I post regular thoughts and occasional podcasts on topics, trends, and technology associated with managing Windows systems. Check us out at `www.realtime-windowsserver.com`. We also have a community forum on GPanswers.com that answers WSUS questions.

9

Network Access Protection with Group Policy

Group Policy has a lot of responsibility on your network. Sure, it's got its touchy-feely side, like setting the desktop background and delivering applications' settings. But it's also got a kicking-butt side, too. And that's the side we want to show you here.

In this chapter, I'll cover just one topic but a very hot one: how to ensure that only healthy, validated machines make it onto your production network.

Without knowing the "health status" of your machines, you're just letting any machine join your network, regardless of what's running on them; and that's clearly unhealthy.

By using a new Windows Server 2008 technology, called Network Access Protection, in conjunction with Group Policy to configure it all, we'll have a network that automatically decides who lives and dies, er, gets on our network or not.

So, strap in. It's prime time butt kicking, Group Policy style.

Network Policy Services and Network Access Protection

If you've ever had to put a child in public school (or a dog in doggy day care), you know that you need to get your kid (or "fur kid") vaccinated first. Then, you need a certification of health that proves they've actually had the necessary vaccinations. Let's say that when you introduce your kid to this one particular school on the first day, the principal at the front door of the school looks at the vaccination report, validates that the kid is really vaccinated (and is likely healthy enough not to infect others), and then permits your kid to come inside the building.

If your kid hasn't been vaccinated, this school will cheerfully give you two options: walk down a specific hallway that has no kids that your child could possibly infect, and meet with the school nurse at the nurse's office to get vaccinated immediately. Or stay outside.

Your choice.

Why is introducing new creatures into the environment so harsh? Because we want to maintain a healthy environment. Now, it is perfectly true that just because every kid in the school *has* been vaccinated doesn't *actually* guarantee there won't be an outbreak. It just means that certain criteria have been met which meet the baseline of healthy.

Got the idea?

Well, welcome to Network Access Protection, or NAP, for Windows Server 2008 (with client components for Windows Vista and Windows XP/SP3). NAP's goal for your client machines is similar to the preceding example with the unvaccinated kids. Here's how it works:

- A computer already has a specific configuration (Windows Vista or Windows XP/SP3 and above). Note that Windows Server 2008 as a client is also supported but cannot be used with the health agent built into Vista and XP SP3 that monitors Windows Security Center.

- A Health Agent on the computer presents the "truth" as it knows it about that configuration. (This is the vaccination record in the previous analogy.)

- A Health Validator on the server interprets the client computer's Health Agent's report. (This is the administrator in the previous analogy.)

- If the client computer is healthy enough, as you define it, the computer can join the rest of the computers on the regular network.

- If the client computer isn't healthy enough, the computer can only go to the doctor's office, er, can only communicate with Remediation Servers for assistance (while it's kept in a quarantine environment until the issue is addressed).

There are lots of ways NAP can come in handy on your network:

- It can ensure that your loaner laptops are healthy before they reconnect to the company network.

- It can ensure that traveling salesdudes' laptops weren't infected while away on company business.

- It can ensure that people using VPNs (i.e., home computers used for business but that also have teenagers using them) connect to your company from computers in a healthy state.

- It can ensure that consultants' and outsiders' laptops are healthy enough to be put on your internal network when they visit.

Now, before you start jumping up and down all excited about the possibilities, there is one catch. You need to think of NAP as a "framework for stuff that's potentially awesome" instead of "something itself that's immediately awesome." That's because Windows ships with exactly *one* Health Agent (that's the client piece that checks how healthy you are) and one Health Validator (that's the server piece that interprets the client's Health Agent report).

The client piece is called the *System Health Agent*, or *SHA*. Windows Vista and Windows XP/SP3 ship with one SHA called *Windows Security Health Agent*, or *WSHA*. Note, strangely, Windows Server 2008 is capable of hosting SHAs, but doesn't ship with any.

The server piece is the *System Health Validator*, or *SHV*. Windows Server 2008 ships with one SHV called *Windows Security Health Validator*, known as *WSHV*.

Catchy, names right?

The WSHA client piece is already built into Windows Vista and will be built into XP/SP3 (it won't be available for XP/SP2 or older). Windows Security Health Validator is included in Windows Server 2008 when we load Network Access Protection. The WSHA (client) and WSHV (server) combination can poke around and make sure that the following things are true:

- The client computer has antivirus software installed and running.
- The client computer has current antivirus updates installed.
- Microsoft Update Services is enabled on the client computer.
- The client computer has firewall software installed and enabled.
- The client computer has antispyware software installed and running. (Available on Windows Vista only.)
- The client computer has current antispyware updates installed. (Available on Windows Vista only.)

 The Antivirus and Antispyware software must be recognized by Windows Security Center, which runs on Windows XP and Windows Vista. Check out http://support.microsoft.com/kb/883792, and also check with your vendor to make sure your software actually *is* recognized by Windows Security Center (or you'll be pulling your hair out wondering why it's not working).

That's it. There isn't a whole lot of stuff WSHA and WSHV can really check for.

If you wanted to do something fancier, like ensure that a specific DLL was installed for an application, or a data file was present, or the latest corporate application was installed—you can't really do that out of the box. However, many partners are working on solutions which will snap into NAP as Health Agents and Health Validators.

 There's a huge list of NAP partners at www.microsoft.com/windowsserver2008/nap-partners.mspx.

For instance, one company, UNET, makes a product called Anyclick for NAP which does a pretty neat job of checking stuff on a client computer. For instance, you can check the Registry and file systems for the presence or absence of specific entries, check the hash value of certain files, check the operating system version, and more. So, if you want to go above and beyond the (very, very basic) checking abilities that ship in the box, check out the third-party NAP list. UNET's Anyclick for NAP can be found at http://unetsystem.co.kr/nap/.

What's interesting about SHAs is that they have the ability to be told to auto-remediate if possible, depending on the noncompliant situation. In the case of the WSHA that ships with Windows Vista and Windows XP/SP3, turning on auto-remediation means that it will try to turn on the Windows Firewall, update the latest antispyware, and/or update the antivirus definitions if the computer is deemed noncompliant.

That's a pretty neat trick.

NAP is part of a bigger picture called *NPS*, or *Network Policy Server*. Network Policy Server is really a fancy way of saying Microsoft's RADIUS. NPS is the replacement for the Internet Authentication Service (IAS) in Windows Server 2003, which also basically performed the RADIUS function.

RADIUS is an open protocol that enables multiple sources to authenticate to one point, and then have the RADIUS server, er, I mean, the Network Policy Server take those requests and pass them around the network to various authentication points. So, the two basically must be used together: you can't really do NAP without NPS.

There was something like NAP available for Windows Server 2003, but it was a real pain in the neck to use. It was called *Network Access Quarantine Control*, or *NAQC*. If you positively cannot use Windows Server 2008 with NPS and NAP, you can learn more about NAQC at http://tinyurl.com/2u5rfu, http://tinyurl.com/27q8bn, and http://tinyurl.com/yukn7s.

You can learn more about the RADIUS protocol here: http://en.wikipedia.org/wiki/RADIUS. You can also read a neat Windows/Linux interoperability example (but not a NAP example) in my book, *Windows & Linux Integration*, which can be found at www.WinLinAnswers.com/book.

So what we're going to do next is really take a full, no-kidding-around NAP test drive. Once this is set up, I swear this is going to be so cool, you'll want to show the boss how sexy it really is. So, do these steps in a test lab, make sure they really work, then call the boss over and show them how smart you are. There are lots of ways you can "do" NAP, and we're only going to go over one big way. But you'll learn a lot.

How You Can Use NAP

We're going to go through a quick (well, not so quick) example to get the hang of NAP. Let me jump to the end of the story and tell you that this example is the easiest possible one to set up. And that's saying a lot, considering the number of steps we're about to embark upon.

There are really four main ways to NAP your network. We're going to use DHCP as our enforcement point. That is, when a new client requests a DHCP address, we'll ensure that they're compliant with our wishes. Not compliant? Go to the doctor's office for a shot in the arm.

But there are other ways you can handle enforcement. The following are the other main methods:

- Via IPsec; that is, when your clients use IPsec to communicate you can ensure that they're healthy.

- Via 801.1X; that is, when your clients use the 802.1X capabilities of your network switch, you can ensure that they're healthy.

- Via VPN; that is, when your clients make contact over a VPN to connect to the network, you can ensure that they're healthy.

I'll provide some resources a little later if you want to check out these methods on your own. Our goal is to just check out the simple case: via DHCP enforcement.

Now, before we get going here, let's have a quick word about why using DHCP enforcement for NAP *isn't* such a great idea. The downside of using DHCP as our only point of enforcement is that, well, a savvy user (with rights) can just statically add a valid IP address to his client computer, avoid the DHCP server entirely, and then never get checked for health! Doh!

So, if we know that, why am I going to show you DHCP enforcement over some of the other methods? Because at least you'll get the idea of how NAP is supposed to work. Then, once you've successfully completed this run-through and learned how to troubleshoot it, I'll point you toward some other guides which have stronger enforcement methods.

Figure 9.1 has a diagram of how requests come in from NAP-capable computers (bottom left), are validated by NAP Enforcement Servers (middle), and are finally allowed on the network via NPS servers (bottom right). And, if your system's a bad boy, it can only talk with Remediation Servers or System Health Servers.

FIGURE 9.1   A diagram of how NAP clients interface with NAP servers, NPS servers, and supporting servers

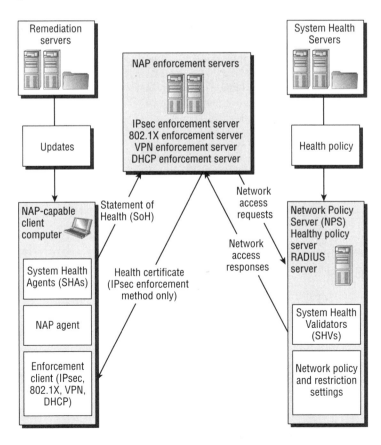

Setting up a Quick NAP Test Lab with Specific Goals in Mind

Let's come up with a testing scenario we can all hang our hats on.

Let's assume you're the security administrator. Your job is to keep computers that aren't up to health standards off of your network, until such time as they're healthy. But you have a new intern working in the desktop support department. He didn't get the memo that all Windows Vista and Windows XP/SP3+ machines need to come from the team with the Windows Firewall enabled. Sometimes he double-checks and ensures that the Windows Firewall is enabled (which is the default, actually), and sometimes he forgets (and then unknowingly turns it off).

Silly example, but just go with me on this one, okay?

With that in mind, you want to ensure that certain "health points" are valid before your computers get full access to the live network. In this case your health point is, "Is the Windows Firewall installed and enabled on our client?"

If the answer is yes, we'll say they're healthy enough. And, here's the kicker, if the firewall isn't enabled, you want to auto-enable it if at all possible.

Well, the built-in WSHA (client) and WSHV (server) combination can't do a whole heck of a lot. But one of the things it *can* actually do is ensure that the client computer has the Windows Firewall enabled.

 If, during these tests, you wanted to substitute in one of other things that WSHA and WSHV can check for, like ensuring that the client computer has antivirus software installed and running, that's totally fine too, but you'll have to get that software on your test client yourself and ensure that the Windows Security Center can see that software.

To give this a shot, you need some computers to test this out on. Here's what we'll need:

DC01   This is our Domain Controller. If you didn't already set this up as a DHCP server, we'll do that now. Additionally, we'll make it our NPS and our NAP server, which will validate whether or not the client is healthy enough. This must be a Windows Server 2008 machine.

REM1   This is our Remediation Server. This is a server that we'll permit unhealthy clients to talk with. That way, if they need updates they can at least talk with this server, which will have them. This isn't expressly needed in the scenario I'm setting up here (because we won't be downloading any updates to become compliant). But we'll make use of it anyway to see the NAP moving parts work. If you don't want to bring up a whole new server for the test, that's fine. We'll play pretend and assume a server named REM1 exists at IP address 192.168.2.16 (feel free to substitute any open IP address on your test network here). You can actually see the NAP moving parts work without bringing up this new server. You could also put DNS on this machine and have your noncompliant machines use REM1 for DNS and not the Domain Controller. We won't be doing that in our examples, but it's likely a good idea.

NAPCLIENT1   This is a new Vista machine or Windows XP/SP3+ machine that we've never joined to the network before. We'll pretend we're the intern, and just for our tests, we'll make sure the Windows Firewall is (gasp!) off. But don't join the domain, we'll do that together a little later.

Setting up DC01 for New Roles: DHCP, NPS, and NAP Server

Again, DC01 is about to take on three new roles: DHCP, NPS, and NAP. Our goal is that clients will report their state of health (in our case, if the Windows Firewall is on or not) while they ask for a DHCP address. So, we'll add the DHCP, NPS, and NAP server roles now, then configure each one, in that order:

1. Start out by logging into DC01 as the domain Administrator, and then running Windows Server 2008's Computer Management by clicking Start ➢ All Programs ➢ Administrative Tools ➢ Server Manager.

2. Click Roles, then click Add Roles. The Server Manager will try to get as much data from you to get started, including a nearly full setup of DHCP on the fly. These are the steps as they were presented to me; your situation may vary somewhat.

3. Next, you'll get the Before You Begin page. Click Next. You can see I'm adding the DHCP and Network Policy and Access Services roles in Figure 9.2. Click Next.

FIGURE 9.2   You need the DHCP, Network Policy, and Access Services roles installed for our tests.

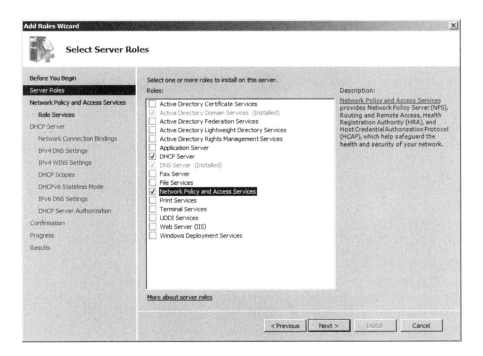

4. You'll be prompted with some more information to read at the Network Policy and Access Services introduction page. Click Next.

5. You'll be at the Select Role Services page as seen in Figure 9.3. For our purposes, we need only the Network Policy Server entry. The others are for more advanced options, like using a VPN or using your Cisco switch as an authentication point. Again, I'll point you toward documentation later that uses these features if you want to give them a try on your own. For now, select only Network Policy Server, as seen in Figure 9.3, and click Next.

FIGURE 9.3 Once the Network Policy Server role is installed, you automatically get NAP services.

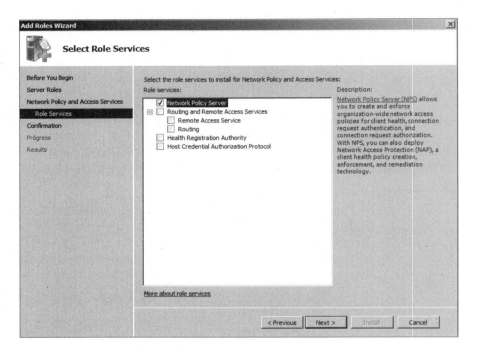

6. At the DHCP Server introduction page, click Next.

7. At the Select Network Connections Bindings page, ensure that you have a hardwired connection that has a fixed IP address, and click Next.

8. At the Specify IPv4 DNS Server Settings page (page 1) make sure your domain name (corp.com) is listed in the Parent Domain entry and the IP address of the server is listed in the Preferred DNS Server IPv4 Address entry. Click Next.

9. At the Specify IPv4 WINS Server Settings page (page 2), you can specify that "WINS is not required for applications on this network," and click Next.

10. At the "Add or Edit DHCP Scopes" page, you can click Add and add in a valid scope for your tests. In my tests, I'm adding a range of 192.168.2.20–192.168.2.50 with a subnet mask of 255.255.255.0. Your test network may vary. The most important field here, however, is Scope Name. I'm going to call mine ALLOWED, as shown in Figure 9.4. The

idea is that if the client machine is healthy it can get an IP address from the ALLOWED scope. Once you've filled in the scope name, click OK, then click Next.

FIGURE 9.4   The Add Roles Wizard can help you set up your DHCP scope for the first time.

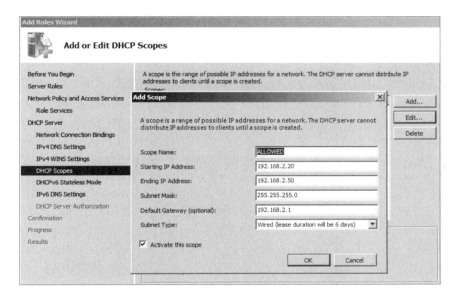

11. At the Configure DHCPv6 Stateless Mode page, select "Disable DHCPv6 stateless mode for this server," and click Next.

12. At the Authorize DHCP Server page, select "Use current credentials" (because you're logged in as the domain Administrator), and click Next.

13. At the Confirm Installation Selections page, select Install.

14. You should see your components install, then finally, at the Installation Results page, click Close.

Testing DHCP

Just as a quick test, bring up a new client and ensure that client is getting DHCP from your new DHCP server. If not, make sure the DHCP service is started on Windows Server 2008, it's authorized, and the scope is active and has the correct addresses.

A quick side note: if you're using Windows Vista, I don't know about you, but I find using the ol' tried and true `ipconfig /release` and `ipconfix /renew` to be less than helpful. If you're in fits getting Windows Vista to try to fetch an IP address via DHCP, right-click over the network icon in the tray, and select Diagnose and Repair. Then reset the network adapter. When you do, you'll see what's in Figure 9.5.

Confirm that you got an IP address from the DHCP server by pulling up a command prompt, typing `ipconfig`, and checking, as seen in Figure 9.6.

FIGURE 9.5 Use the network icon's Diagnose and Repair if ipconfig doesn't seem to want to work. This is the result when Windows Vista is attempting to repair a network connection.

Windows Network Diagnostics
Repairing...
Cancel
System Pr...
Comman...
Windows ...
3:25 PM

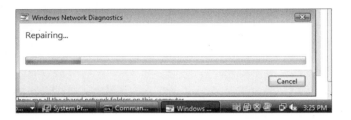

FIGURE 9.6 Ensure that you have a valid IP address from the DHCP server.

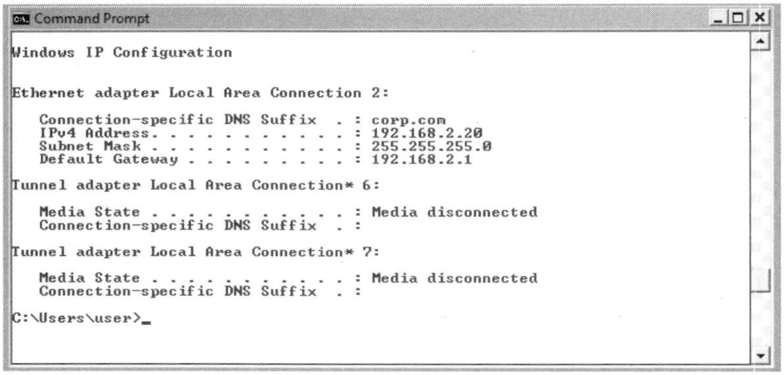

Command Prompt
Windows IP Configuration
Ethernet adapter Local Area Connection 2:
Connection-specific DNS Suffix . : corp.com
IPv4 Address. . . . . : 192.168.2.20
Subnet Mask . . . . : 255.255.255.0
Default Gateway . . . . : 192.168.2.1
Tunnel adapter Local Area Connection* 6:
Media State . . . . : Media disconnected
Connection-specific DNS Suffix . :
Tunnel adapter Local Area Connection* 7:
Media State . . . . : Media disconnected
Connection-specific DNS Suffix . :
C:\Users\user>_

Configuring NAP via the NAP Wizard

Now we're ready to configure NAP. We do this within the Network Policy Server snap-in, which is located within Start ➢ All Programs ➢ Administrative Tools. When you select that snap-in, the Network Policy Server (NPS) console loads and focuses on the NPS (Local) topmost node.

Here we'll use the NAP Wizard (though it's not really called a wizard here) to configure NAP. At the topmost node of NPS, you'll be presented with a Getting Started page, as seen in Figure 9.7.

Ensure that Network Access Protection (NAP) is seen in the drop-down, and click Configure NAP to get started.

At the "Select Network Connection Method for Use with NAP" window, select Dynamic Host Configuration Protocol (DHCP) in the drop-down, as seen in Figure 9.8. When you do, a NAP policy name of NAP DHCP is automatically assigned for you, but it's not shown in Figure 9.8. Click Next.

FIGURE 9.7 The topmost node of the Network Policy Server has a wizard to help you configure NAP.

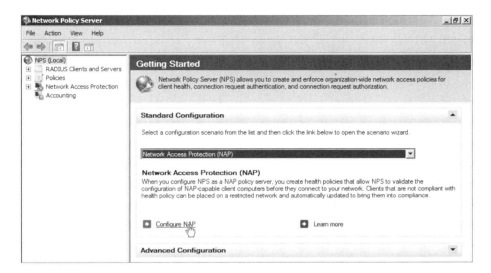

FIGURE 9.8 You can select a NAP connection method (in our case, we're using DHCP).

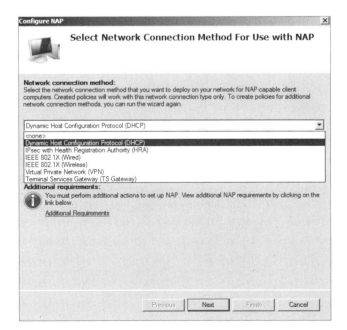

The next screen is Specify NAP Enforcement Servers Running DHCP Server. For our tests, you won't enter anything here and just click Next. This screen is asking for "RADIUS clients," which really means "RADIUS proxy servers" (because in RADIUS terminology, a RADIUS proxy server acts as a client). So, in our tests, we're running everything (DHCP, NPS, NAP) on one box; we don't need to enter anything extra here.

The next screen is Specify DHCP Scopes. In our examples, we have just one DHCP scope. If you had multiple scopes being served from DHCP, you would use this to marry a collection of settings to a particular scope. For our examples you can safely skip this screen.

The next screen is "Configure User Groups and Machine Groups." On that screen, you could identify specific machines and/or users that have to adhere to the policy. In this initial configuration, we'll assume *everyone* has to comply. If you want to change this later so only some users or some machines must comply, that's fine. But leave this empty for now and click Next.

The next screen is called "Specify a NAP Remediation Server Group and URL," as seen in Figure 9.9. Here, you'll decide exactly which computers are considered Remediation Servers. Note that this isn't an Active Directory group (which is confusing), it's just a collection of machines that that noncompliant computers can still talk to if they're unhealthy.

In our first tests, we're not going to use this setting, but we will in our second tests. So let's set it up now, for later. Start out by clicking New Group as seen in Figure 9.9 and give a name to your server group, then add in your remediation server or servers. In short, these are the only possible servers that noncompliant machines will be able to communicate with. In our tests, we'll limit the testing to REM1. We'll talk more about this later. While we're here, we'll also set up a Troubleshooting URL that will be part of a pop-up and help people get to some information you can provide to ensure that they can get help if they need it. You can also see this in Figure 9.9.

The next screen is called Define NAP Health Policy, as seen in Figure 9.10.

Here you'll decide three things:

- Which WSHA (Windows System Health Agent) to use (remember, Windows only ships with one, and you can add others with third-party snap-ins).

- Whether or not to turn on the auto-remediation feature. Again, this feature will automatically turn on the firewall or update the latest antivirus or do whatever the health agent is capable of doing. In our case, we'll leave it on, because we want to demonstrate how the firewall can be automatically turned on, even if our intern turned it off.

- What to do if a client is simply non-NAP-capable (also called NAP-ineligible). Think Windows 2000 machines or even Windows XP/SP2 (because the NAP agent only comes with Windows XP/SP3+!). If one of these machines comes onto the network, you have two choices (presented here) and a third choice (not presented here, but you can learn about it in the Real-World Scenario, "Denying All Network Access"):

  - Choice 1 is to restrict them to "Allow access to a restricted network only" (this is the default). This makes sense. If you're going to be serious about using NAP, put all non-compliant machines (and non-NAP-capable machines) in miniquarantine so you can address them.

  - Choice 2 is to grant them "full network access." This seems a little silly because why go through the motion of restricting NAP-capable machines but then let the non-NAP-capable machines on the network?

For our purposes, let's keep all the defaults and click Next.

 **Real World Scenario**

Denying All Network Access

Choice 3 isn't listed in the Define NAP Health Policy window, but you can enable it manually later if you like. That is, you can actually Deny all network access. In the case of the DHCP agent, it will just plumb refuse to give a DHCP address, thus preventing users from getting on the network. This is kind of a misleading, because in the case of the DHCP agent, it simply won't serve up a DHCP address. A very savvy user could just pop in his own IP address (if he had rights) and voilà, be on the network.

It's true that the DHCP agent we're using is the least powerful, but it's the easiest to demonstrate. For better (much better) security, you can use 802.1x agents, but that requires smarter switch or access point hardware (and for our example, I didn't want to assume you had it). In our case, let's leave the default as Deny as seen in Figure 9.10. That way, if anyone isn't 100 percent compliant, they won't get on our network.

FIGURE 9.9 Enter the list of servers that unhealthy clients can still communicate with.

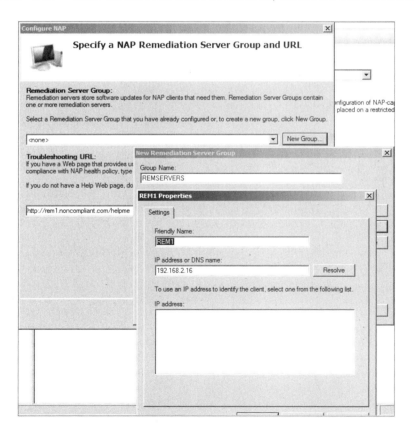

FIGURE 9.10   You can decide how to handle unhealthy clients.

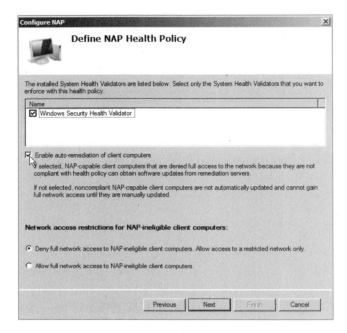

The final screen is the "Completing NAP Enforcement Policy and RADIUS Client Configuration" page and isn't shown here. This is a summary page for reference. Click Finish when you're ready.

Next, we'll soon make sure the wizard "did the right thing" for us and then spend a little time making sure only the "healthy kids" can get on our network.

Inspecting Our Wizard Work

Now that we're finished with the NAP Wizard, let's see what we've done so far. If you click on NPS ➤ Policies ➤ Network Policies, you'll see a list of Policy Names, as seen in Figure 9.11.

You can see that there are three NAP policies created:

NAP DHCP Compliant   The client is NAP-enabled, and all is right in the world. That is, all the Health Validators have passed. If so, this policy applies.

NAP DHCP Noncompliant   The client is NAP-enabled, but one of the Health Validators fails. If so, this policy applies.

NAP DHCP Non NAP-Capable   The client isn't NAP-enabled (the NAP agent service isn't running, or it's not a Windows Vista or Windows XP/SP3+ machine). In this case, this policy applies.

Now you're ready to continue setting up the rest of the system.

FIGURE 9.11   The Network Policies show you the possible ways a client can match. Then the NAP server can take action.

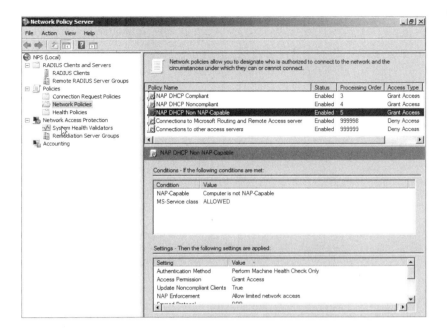

Setting Up the Windows System Health Validators

Now, we need to tell NAP what our definition of *noncompliant* is. Remember, the goal is to keep out machines which we feel aren't healthy enough to be on our network.

In our scenario, we're going to say that, "A computer is noncompliant if the Windows Firewall is disabled."

Yep, that's it; we're keeping it simple for now. To express this, we need to configure the System Health Validators. And, again, Windows only ships with one, called the Windows Security Health Validator.

In our tests, the only thing we care about is if the Windows Firewall is enabled or not. So, drill down to NPS ➢ Network Access Protection ➢ System Health Validators. You'll see only one, because Windows only ships with one. And, heck, it's already configured!

Except it's configured too strongly for our little tests. So double-click the Windows Security Health Validator entry to get to its properties. Click the Configure box on the Windows Security Health Validator Properties page to get to the Windows Security Health Validator entries. All the windows in those steps can be seen in Figure 9.12.

You'll see two tabs in the Windows Security Health Validator window: Windows Vista and Windows XP. It really should say Windows Vista and Windows XP/SP3+, but maybe I'm splitting hairs. Anyway, for our tests, we're not going to leave anything checked except for the validation that the firewall is enabled. Remember our intern who creates our PC images? Again, the idea is that sometimes he turns it off and other times he leaves it on. Our goal is to check to make sure he actually has it turned on. So, for our tests, only add the check mark seen in Figure 9.13.

FIGURE 9.12   The default options for the Windows Vista WSHV

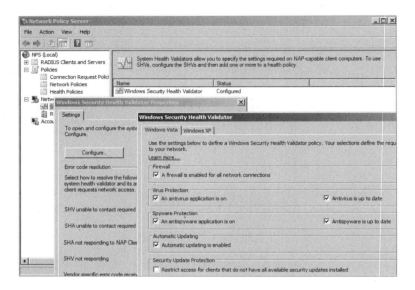

FIGURE 9.13   If you're using Windows Vista for our tests, just deselect everything except "A firewall is enabled for all network connections."

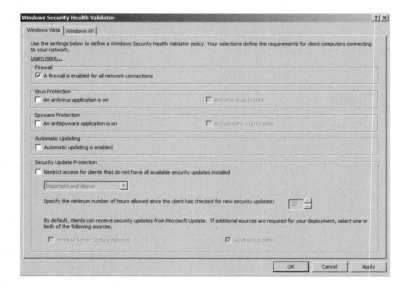

When you click OK, you'll be back at the Windows Security Health Validator Properties window, as seen in Figure 9.14.

FIGURE 9.14   You can specify what happens if the NAP client or server components have some sort of failure. The default behavior in that case is that clients are considered noncompliant.

Here, you'll be able to specify what happens should the communication fail between the NAP client and the NAP server. In short, the most secure configuration is "If I can't make contact to the NAP server, let's assume the client computer is noncompliant."

That's a pretty good bet, because if something tampers with the operating system, you'll want to make sure you can get that machine healthy again before admitting it back into your population. So, for our examples, I'm going to leave everything here as-is and click OK.

Configuring DHCP to Use NAP

Until we complete this step, NAP won't do anything. That's because we need to tell DHCP about NAP.

To do this, fire up the DHCP management tool (Start ➤ All Programs ➤ Administrative Tools ➤ DHCP), then right-click over the scope and select Properties. Select the Network Access Protection tab, and then select "Enable for this scope" and ensure that "Use default Network Access Protection profile" is enabled.

You can see this in Figure 9.15.

But we're not done. We have to specify what our clients *should* be given when they're noncompliant. To do this, right-click over Scope Options and select Configure Options. In the

Advanced tab, pull the User Class drop-down so it shows Default Network Access Protection Class. Then select the 006 DNS Servers option, and specify which DNS servers noncompliant and non-NAP-capable computers should use.

FIGURE 9.15 Select "Use default Network Access Protection profile" to turn NAP on for this scope.

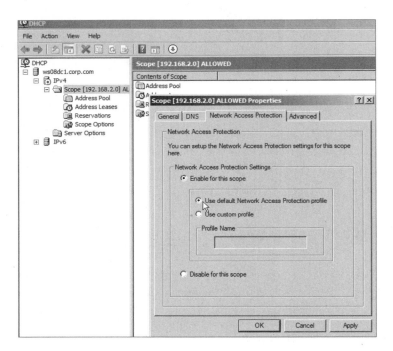

In our case, we only have one server that has DNS, which is our Domain Controller, DC01 (192.168.2.111). But in real life, you'd likely specify a server that's less sensitive than a Domain Controller as your DNS server. If you have DNS set up on REM1, you could put that IP address as the DNS server. I'm not doing that in these examples, but you can if you like. So, as seen in Figure 9.16, enter the IP address of the DNS server you'd like for noncompliant machines to use.

Also set the 015 DNS Domain Name option to something that demonstrates that the machines are noncompliant. In Figure 9.17, I've specified noncompliant.corp.com.

Once you click OK to close the Scope Options properties page, you'll see the scope options for the DHCP server for both compliant and noncompliant conditions, as seen in Figure 9.18.

FIGURE 9.16   Specify the DNS servers that unhealthy computers should use.

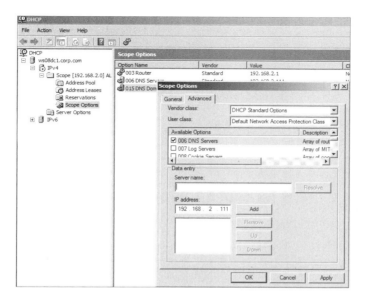

FIGURE 9.17   Specify a special DNS domain name for noncompliant computers.

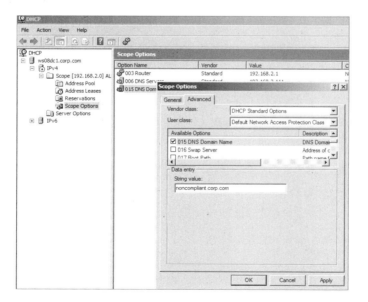

FIGURE 9.18   The scope will have entries for the Default Network Access Protection class and entries for no class.

Testing NAP with Non-NAP-Enabled Clients

Now, any client that isn't NAP-capable won't get on our network. So, let's first review what NAP-capable means:

- The machine must be Windows Vista or Windows XP/SP3+, and
- The NAP agent service must be enabled and running (we'll do this in a minute), and
- The NAP Enforcement Client must be enabled (we'll also do this in a minute).

That's right: every Windows Vista machine and every Windows XP/SP3+ machine is technically non-NAP-capable out of the box, because those last two steps aren't done (yet). So, if we just try to release and renew the IP address (or try to reset the adapter), we should be considered non-NAP-capable, even though we're using a Windows Vista or Windows XP/SP3+ machine. That's because we haven't turned on the NAP agent service or turned on the NAP Enforcement Client (again, that's next).

So, let's try to fetch an IP address on our Windows Vista machine via DHCP again. Because this machine isn't considered NAP-capable (yet), when you do, you'll see what's in Figure 9.19.

FIGURE 9.19   You should get an IP address back, but the DNS suffix should show your noncompliant settings.

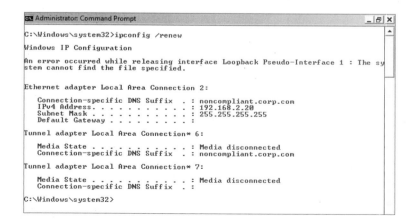

The default behavior in this situation is pretty clear: get an IP address, change the DNS suffix to show that it's noncompliant, and only be able to get to machines which are listed as remediation servers (and *also* the machine which gave out the DHCP address).

 In our case, this is a liiiitle more access than we would normally want versus how you would deploy in the real world. That's because you'd ensure that the DHCP server in the real world wasn't a file server, print server, Domain Controller, and other-stuff-server, like we're using here in this book.

In Figure 9.20, we can see that the DNS suffix shows that the machine is considered noncompliant (well, non-NAP-capable, really). And look at the crazy subnet mask. It's all 255s, or fully masked! That means that the machine can only use static routes to get from place to place.

And that's what NAP will do: use static route maps to ensure that the client can only get to the remediation servers. You can validate that the technology is working the way it should while if you're on your non-NAP-capable client—type `route print` and see the output as seen in Figure 9.20.

FIGURE 9.20   Noncompliant (unhealthy) or non-NAP-capable machines are static route mapped to remediation servers (in this case, REM1 at 192.168.2.16).

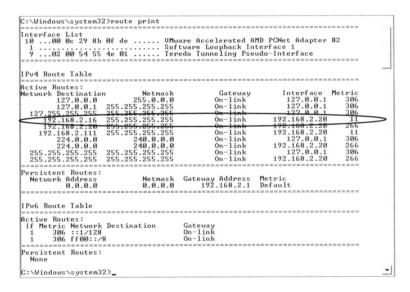

So, if a machine becomes noncompliant (that is, a policy matches which restricts access), NAP does the following:

- Removes the default gateway (which under normal conditions would show up in route print as Network Destination 0.0.0.0 with the netmask of 0.0.0.0)

- Changes the subnet mask to fully masked (255.255.255.255)

- Produces a classless static route to all servers in the remediation server group

Basically, we've just achieved our first big goal. We've just ensured that clients we can't really be too sure of aren't just walking on our networks and sniffing around. They can only walk down specific hallways and talk to specific servers. (See, I told you this was sexy!)

Preparing for Domain-Joined NAP-Capable Machines

Now that we can predict what happens to non-NAP-capable machines, let's deal with our normal clients. That is, Windows Vista and Windows XP/SP3+ machines that are joined to the domain. We'll use our secret Group Policy weapons to ensure a smooth ride for clients who are first-class citizens.

In my examples, I'm going to have one GPO that does three things:

- Always ensures that the Windows Security Center is enabled

- Always ensures that the NAP agent is enabled (NAP client service, really)

- Utilizes at least one NAP Client Enforcement Agent (in our case, the DHCP Enforcement Agent)

Once complete, I'll link the GPO to the domain. By making sure this GPO affects all computers in the domain, I can be sure everyone is getting a uniform policy. However, depending on your situation, you may want to set up GPOs and link them to OUs if you're using different NAP Enforcement Agents (like 802.1X instead of the DHCP agent we're using here).

Ensuring that Client Computers Have the Security Center Enabled While in the Domain

This step isn't strictly required, but it can help in troubleshooting. That's because the NAP client (the SHA) relies on the Security Center service to see that the Windows Firewall is enabled or that there's antivirus or antispyware loaded, and so on. The Security Center Service is always running (by default on Windows Vista and Windows XP), but the Security Center's UI is disabled when the computers are joined to the domain. That's a little frustrating, because even under the hood, the Security Center is actually still running, you just can't see what it thinks is happening.

To make sure the Security Center is enabled (and therefore ensure that WSHA can see your antibadware software), be sure you have a Group Policy linked to the domain (or just an OU containing the client computers) that turns it back on.

That policy setting is Computer Configuration ➢ Policies ➢ Administrative Templates ➢ Windows Components ➢ Security Center ➢ **Turn on Security Center (Domain PCs only)**, and set to Enabled, as seen in Figure 9.21.

Using Group Policy to Ensure that the NAP Service Is Turned On for Clients

Because you've already got the Group Policy Preference Extensions bits on your Windows Vista and Windows XP/SP3+ machines, you can leverage the Services Extension to ensure that the NAP agent is automatically started.

Drill down to Computer Configuration ➢ Preferences ➢ Control Panel Settings ➢ Services and configure the NAP agent service such that the Service action is set to "Start service," as shown in Figure 9.22.

FIGURE 9.21 While not strictly required, turning on the view to Windows XP and Windows Vista Security Center can help in troubleshooting.

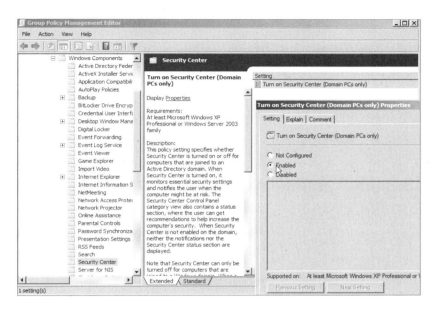

FIGURE 9.22 Use the Group Policy Preference Extensions to always ensure that the client's NAP agent service is started.

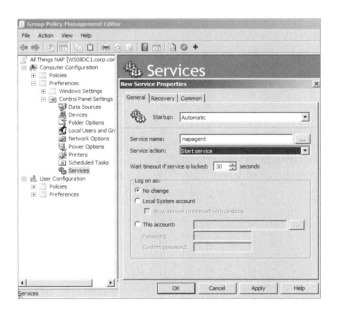

Ensuring Client Computers Have NAP Enforcement Clients Enabled

Finally, we'll need to tell the NAP service which Enforcement Clients we want to work with. (Again, we're working with the DHCP Enforcement Client, but you can see the others in Figure 9.23.)

We do this by drilling down into Computer Configuration ➤ Policies ➤ Windows Settings ➤ Security Settings ➤ Network Access Protection ➤ NAP Client Configuration ➤ Enforcement Clients. Then, right-click over DHCP Quarantine Enforcement Client and select Enable. Your Enforcement Clients should look like Figure 9.23, because we're only using the DHCP Quarantine Enforcement Client.

FIGURE 9.23 At least one NAP Client Enforcement Agent must be selected. In our case, we're using the DHCP Enforcement Client.

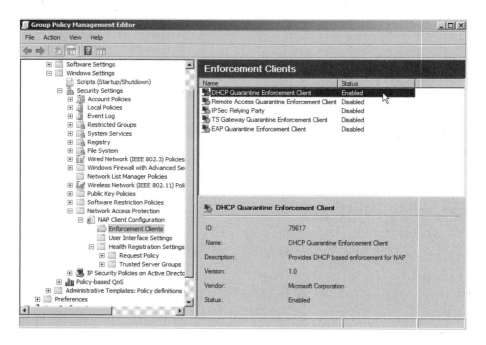

Now here's the trick: even when you close the GPO editor, your changes aren't saved. That's right. There's a bug in this interface which says that you've enabled the Enforcement Client. But you haven't. You need to update the GPO. How do you do that? Well, it's not quite a bug, but it is really, really confusing. I like to call this little problem the "pop-down" problem. Because we all know what a pop-up is, of course. That's when a dialog box pops up and asks you a question.

Except when you close the GPO, you don't see the pop-up, er, pop-down. Because it's popped down somewhere and not popped up. In short, you need to close all windows and hunt around for an open window, which has what you see in Figure 9.24.

FIGURE 9.24   You positively need to find this window and say Yes in order to save your Group Policy changes.

Finally, when you click Yes in Figure 9.24, you've saved the contents of the GPO and saved the day, er, saved the GPO.

I don't know why this was coded this way; just a bug I suppose. But it's maddening if you don't know the trick. Without saving the settings inside the GPO, it will seem like the contents of the GPO aren't applying—because they're not.

Special Case for 802.11 Enforcement on Windows XP/SP3

Note that there is one lone Administrative Templates policy for Windows XP/SP3 that can enable the enforcement of 802.1x. It's found at Computer Configuration ➢ Policies ➢ Administrative Templates ➢ Windows Components ➢ Network Access Protection and is called **Allow the Network Access Protection client to support the 802.1x Enforcement Client component.** You can see it in Figure 9.25. It's not needed for our scenario, but I thought you might want to know about it. Also note, the Requirements listed in the window are wrong for this policy setting. The NAP agent service is only available for Windows XP/SP3 (and above) even though the policy says it's for at least Windows XP/SP2.

FIGURE 9.25   To use 802.1x enforcement with Windows XP clients, this policy must be selected. (It's not used in our examples.)

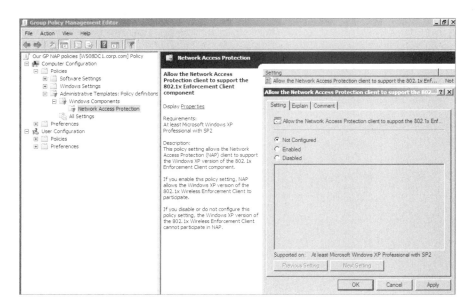

NAP Clients in a Domain-Joined Environment

Once your client is domain-joined, they'll pick up the three policy settings we configured earlier. However, let's make super-sure the things we need are really set before we go gangbusters and test out NAP. So, log onto your NAPCLIENT1 machine as domain Administrator (just for now) and we'll run some pretests before we really test out NAP. Indeed, you can almost think of this little section as "Pretroubleshooting NAP," and it's all good stuff to try if clients start to fail and NAP isn't letting people on the network.

Ensuring that the NAP Service is Running on the Client

The first big thing you really need to make sure of is that the NAP agent (service) is running, or your clients will continue to act like non-NAP-capable machines. The Network Access Protection agent's status should be listed as Started, as seen in Figure 9.26.

FIGURE 9.26   Ensure that the NAP client service is running on your Windows XP/SP3+ or Windows Vista client.

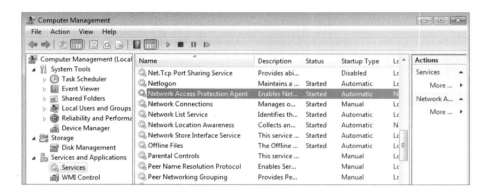

Quick NAP Agent Status Check (*ipconfig /all*)

Then, since the NAP agent is running, you can now take advantage of two tips to help you determine what your NAP status is. At a command prompt, type `ipconfig /all` as seen in Figure 9.27.

FIGURE 9.27   You can see your System Quarantine State with `ipconfig /all`.

```
Administrator: C:\Windows\system32\cmd.exe
C:\Users\administrator>ipconfig /all

Windows IP Configuration

    Host Name . . . . . . . . . . . . : NAPCLIENT1
    Primary Dns Suffix  . . . . . . . : Corp.com
    Node Type . . . . . . . . . . . . : Hybrid
    IP Routing Enabled. . . . . . . . : No
    WINS Proxy Enabled. . . . . . . . : No
    DNS Suffix Search List. . . . . . : Corp.com
    System Quarantine State . . . . . : Not Restricted
```

Here, you'll see the System Quarantine State is set to Not Restricted, which means that we've passed all the health validation tests. Again, note that System Quarantine State information only shows up in `ipconfig /all` as long as the Network Access Protection Agent Service is started.

Quick NAP Group Policy Check

To make sure your client really got the settings from Group Policy, there's a special command you can run. Yes, this command needs to be run on the target machine. The command is

`Netsh nap client show grouppolicy`

With this command you'll see which settings are brought down from Group Policy, as shown in Figure 9.28. If you don't see your DHCP Enforcement Agent set to Enabled, definitely go back and re-edit the GPO and make positively sure the settings were set inside the GPO. Again, if you don't click Yes to the "pop-down" as seen back in Figure 9.24, you never really saved the GPO.

FIGURE 9.28   The netsh command can show the NAP settings from Group Policy.

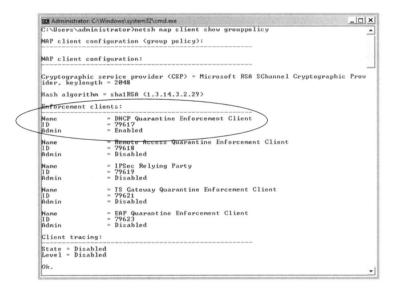

Quick NAP Enforcement Client Check

Just having the NAP agent running isn't enough. Again, we need to ensure that the DHCP Quarantine Enforcement Client is active. You can check the client's event viewer, but the only way I know to do that is by typing in:

`netsh nap client show state`

as seen in Figure 9.29.

You're looking to see if the DHCP agent was initialized. Remember, you set a GPO that set this property. This is just verifying to make sure the client got the message.

FIGURE 9.29 You can see the DHCP Enforcement Client is Initialized, but the others are not.

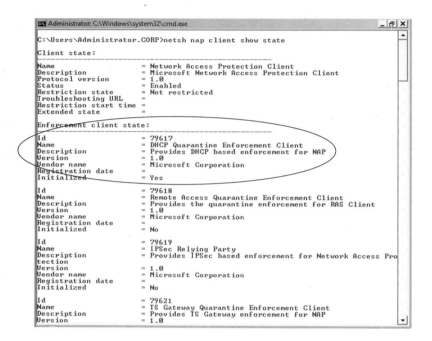

If you don't see that your client has Initialized = Yes within the DHCP Quarantine Enforcement Client block, try running gpupdate /force to repull down the GPO and/or try restarting the NAP agent service.

There's a local editor to the NAP Enforcement Clients called NAPCLCFG.MSC. However, if the Enforcement Client policies are set via Group Policy, the editor does not show it. Only the netsh command shown in Figure 9.28 will genuinely show you if the Enforcement Agent has been successfully embraced. If you chose not to use Group Policy to set the Enforcement Agent, you can run netsh nap client show config to see the same information, but only if the policy is set locally using NAPCLCFG.MSC.

Quick NAP Agent Check with *napstat.exe*

There is another check you can do, but it's not as useful as the previous one. That is, you can run napstat.exe. When you do, a little pop-up balloon shows up on the system tray and tells you the overall health status, as shown in Figure 9.30.

FIGURE 9.30   napstat.exe will show you the overall health of the computer.

Clicking the balloon provides more information, but it's not super useful, as seen in Figure 9.31.

FIGURE 9.31   Clicking the pop-up balloon will show more information.

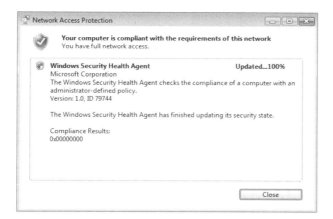

Specifically, there's no information about which health policy was met, and that's kind of frustrating. And if, for instance, you had no client Enforcement Agents active, but you did have just the NAP agent started, the overall health status is considered A-OK, because you're not telling it to enforce anything. That's more than a little annoying, which is why I recommend you use the `netsh` command shown earlier to specifically demonstrate that a Quarantine Enforcement Client is set (in our case, the DHCP Quarantine Enforcement Client).

Testing out Auto-Remediation of a NAP Client

At this point, we're ready to see if the NAP client can auto-remediate an unhealthy condition. Again, the only unhealthy condition we're specifically checking for is if the Windows Firewall is turned off.

Now, because you're logged into NAPCLIENT1 as the domain Administrator, you can specifically turn off the Windows Firewall if it's on. In Figure 9.32, I'm turning off NAPCLIENT1's firewall and selecting OK.

When I click OK, the firewall status changes to Off as seen in Figure 9.33. This state is automatically changed in about two seconds back to the "healthy" state, as seen in Figure 9.34.

FIGURE 9.32 Just try to turn the firewall off. I dare you!

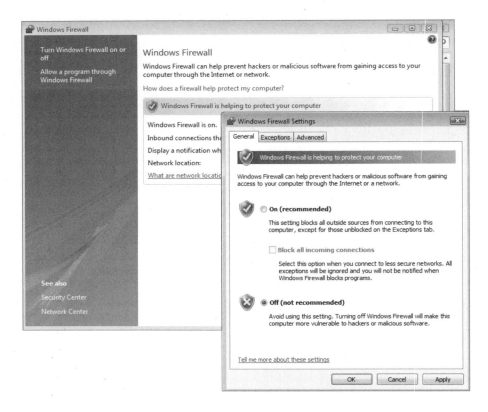

FIGURE 9.33 The firewall will stay off for about a second or two.

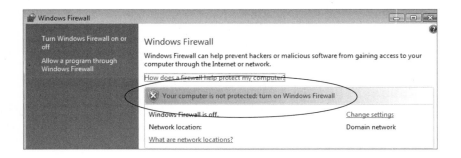

FIGURE 9.34   The auto-remediation feature of NAP will pop the Windows Firewall back on.

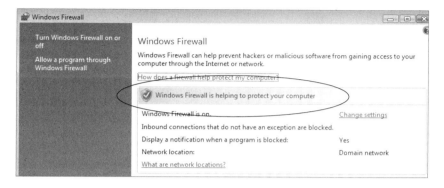

This auto-remediation stuff is fascinating. I often get the question of precisely when auto-remediation will happen. It happens whenever a "statement of health" is generated. And a statement of health is generated when the following happens:

- The IP profile changes
- Group Policy updates
- The health state of something that's being monitored changes
- The NAP agent starts
- And, depending on the agent involved, when the VPN connection succeeds and/or the certificate for IPsec is updated or expires

Auto-remediation is the place you want to be. Think about it: clients that aren't healthy enough just *fix themselves*. No interaction required. Not all SHAs support auto-remediation, but the one that ships in Windows does (WSHA). Even so, be sure to fully test out auto-remediation to make sure it's working the way you expect before rolling into production.

Turning Off Auto-Remediation and Forcing the Users to Get Help (Just for Fun)

We've met our goal. If our intern screws up our machines and leaves the firewall off, NAP will turn it back on before allowing the machine to come on the production network.

But I wanted to show you one more thing you can do with NAP if you wanted to. Again, the point of NAP is that it's a framework. And, you might have a situation in the future where you wanted to inform the user they were noncompliant and give them more information on how to get compliant manually.

In Figure 9.11, we saw that we have three Network Policies, one being the "NAP DHCP Noncompliant" policy. When this policy hits (in other words, it's a NAP-enabled client, but something fails in the health check) we've told it to auto-remediate. But let's turn that off.

First, find that health policy at NPS ➢ Policies ➢ Network Policies ➢ NAP DHCP Noncompliant policy, then in the Settings tab, click NAP Enforcement, and uncheck "Enable auto-remediation of client computers," as seen in Figure 9.35.

FIGURE 9.35   You can turn off auto-remediation for noncompliant machines if you like.

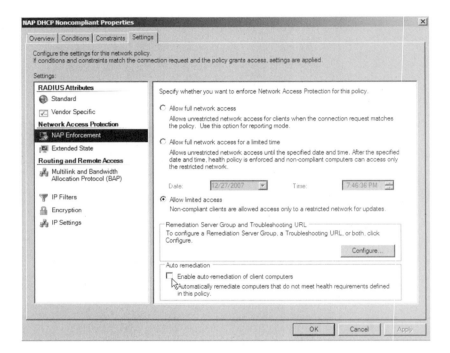

After you uncheck this setting, go get a cup of coffee. I'm not sure why exactly, but this setting takes a while to be reflected on the client. Sometimes restarting the NAP agent at the client helps speed this along (and other times it doesn't).

Now, when you turn off the Windows Firewall, you'll get a pop-up (because auto-remediation is turned off), as seen in Figure 9.36.

FIGURE 9.36   Users receive a pop-up balloon when they become noncompliant.

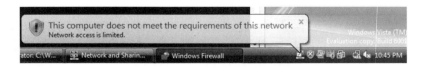

If you click the balloon, you'll get more information as seen in Figure 9.37.

Here the user can see what it would take to achieve the remediation (in our case, re-enabling the Windows Firewall would do it). And, if the user clicks the More Information button they are brought to the web address that you set up way back in Figure 9.9 as the URL where noncompliant computers could get more information. My link doesn't show anything because I didn't actually set up the server, but you get the idea.

FIGURE 9.37   The More Information button sends them to the URL you chose in Figure 9.9.

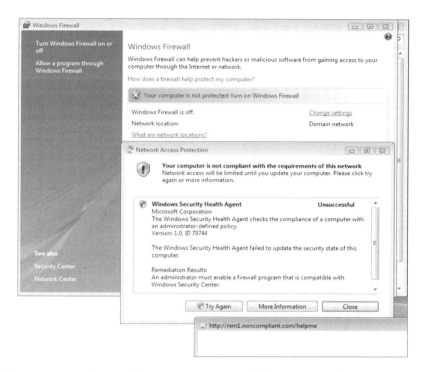

However, note that regular users cannot just click Try Again. That prompt requires administrator credentials—I'm not really sure why.

Again, this idea of presenting the remediation results and more information is really only a good idea if the user genuinely can do something about it, or at the very least they can be brought to a web page where they can call the help desk. And I'm sure the help desk would be happy to call you on your cell phone for help.

Troubleshooting NAP

NAP troubleshooting isn't a no-brainer. By its very definition, NAP is meant to keep people out of your network. And discovering why they're out of your network can be difficult. There are several areas you can check to get to the bottom of NAP woes:

- Group Policy RSoP
- Client logs

- Server logs
- Tracing logs
- The NPS server configuration

However, before you even jump into logging again, I heartily recommend that you check out the obvious stuff that I already described in the "NAP Clients in a Domain-Joined Environment" section (the same goes for a nondomain joined client):

- Ensure that the NAP Service is running on the client.
- Do a Quick NAP Agent Status Check (`ipconfig /all`).
- Do a Quick NAP Enforcement client check.
- Do a Quick NAP Agent Check with `napstat.exe`.

Beyond that, we'll inspect some additional issues I'm sure you'll run into. For instance, if NAP keeps clients off your network, how can they join the domain? That's the first topic up at bat. Then, if you suspect client connection issues, where can you go for more troubleshooting? That's second, third, fourth, and fifth at bat.

Domain-Joining Issues When NAP Is Engaged

When joining a freshly installed computer (Windows XP SP3+ or Windows Vista) to a NAP-protected domain, there's a chance you might not be able to make contact with the Domain Controller and get joined up.

That's because, without the NAP agent service running (from the GPPE setting), and without the NAP Quarantine Enforcement settings (from the domain GPO), the client will not be able to contact a Domain Controller on the network.

Remember: the clients are going to be put into a Restricted mode, and the client cannot contact anything except the DHCP/NPS server that gave them the address as well as any servers in the remediation group. In other words, without the NAP agent and instructions from the domain, the client won't be able to contact our regular DNS and Domain Controllers, which of course makes it impossible to join the domain. So why are we able to join the domain in our sample environment?

It's only possible in our simplified scenario because the NAP server is *also* the DHCP server *and* DNS server *and* Domain Controller (DC). Behind the scenes, a route has been added with the intention of making communication between the DHCP client and the DHCP server possible. However, that same route can be used by the client to contact the DNS server for name resolution and the Domain Controller when you're ready to join it up.

So, in a real-world scenario this might not be possible, because not everyone will make their Domain Controller a NAP server with DHCP like I did in this simple example.

If your Domain Controllers are separate from your NAP servers and your DHCP servers in the real world, what can you do? A junky workaround would be that you assign a static IP address and DNS info for every machine you're about to join to the domain. Then, after it's joined, remove the static maps. But, alas, that is cumbersome, complicated, and insecure.

Is there a better solution? Well, to answer that, we need to break down the two problems we have:

- Problem 1: You don't already have the NAP agent started because you haven't joined the domain. And because you haven't joined the domain, you can't receive the GPO that starts the NAP agent and sets the NAP agent to Automatic.

- Problem 2: You don't have the DHCP Enforcement Agent started because you haven't joined the domain, and the GPO that sets the DHCP Enforcement Agent hasn't been applied yet.

Okay, so you need to join the domain and be NAP compliant. What's the trick?

Well, to solve Problem 1, you can go to the Services console and start the NAP Agent manually and set it to automatic. You can do this in your build or by hand when you're ready to join the machine to the domain.

To solve Problem 2, you need to turn on the DHCP Enforcement Agent. There are two ways to do this. One way is to use the local editor to the NAP Enforcement Clients. This is called NAPCLCFG.MSC, and you can run it right from the command line. You can see NAPCLCFG.MSC, which only runs against the local computer, in Figure 9.38. In this example, I'm locally turning on the Enforcement Client.

FIGURE 9.38   You can turn on the NAP DHCP Quarantine agent without Group Policy if you're not yet domain joined.

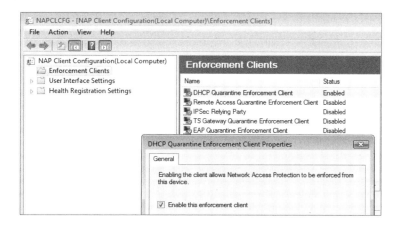

The second option is to use a NETSH command to help you turn on NAP's DHCP Quarantine Enforcement Client. The following command can do the same thing the local NAPCLCFG.MSC can do. So, a command like:

```
NETSH NAP CLIENT SET ENFORCEMENT ID = 79617 ADMIN = "ENABLE"
```

will turn on the DHCP Quarantine Enforcement Client. If you want to turn on the others, you just need to know their codes. And here they are. Just substitute the right code after ID = in the preceding line of code, and you've got the Enforcement Agent working for you.

- 79617 = Enforcement ID of DHCP Quarantine Enforcement, other IDs
- 79618 = Remote Access Quarantine Enforcement Client
- 79619 = IPSec Relying Party
- 79621 = TS Gateway Quarantine Enforcement Client
- 79623 = EAP Quarantine Enforcement Client

You may want to consider having these settings defined within your client image if you plan to get serious about NAP.

Group Policy RSoP

Remember the "pop-down" bug that happens when you set the Enforcement Agent within the GPO, as seen earlier in Figure 9.24? Because of this, you might not actually be getting the GPO's settings!

You'll want to make sure the setting was really set within the GPO, as seen here in Figure 9.39. That is, the GPO has Enforcement Client Settings with your Enforcement Agent set to Enabled.

Then, you can also run Group Policy Results Reports to ensure that the User and Computer combination you're checking really gets the GPO.

FIGURE 9.39 First make sure the Enforcement Client is enabled within the GPO by checking the GPO's Settings tab.

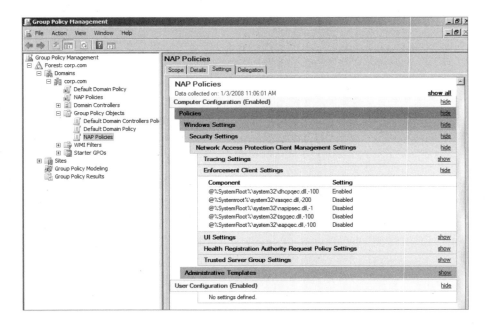

Client Logs

If you've got Windows Vista NAP clients, you'll want to check out the NAP-specific logs. Those are found in Event Viewer ➤ Applications and Services Logs ➤ Microsoft ➤ Windows ➤ Network Access Protection ➤ Operational. You can see an event in Figure 9.40.

FIGURE 9.40   Windows Vista events are in the Network Access Protection Operational log.

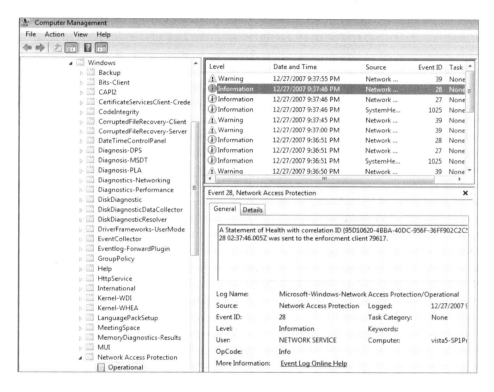

This isn't the easiest place to get feedback from about what the client thinks is going on. However, you can at least determine if the NAP agent is running and what it thinks is going on.

Note that you might see an excessive amount of Warnings with Event ID 39. Those represent a bug when using the DHCP Enforcement Client and can be safely ignored.

Windows XP/SP3+ NAP clients will find events in their SYSTEM logs.

Server Logs

The NAP server also has logs about what happens when clients connect. You'll want to look in the Security log of the NAP server. Here you'll usually find events with the Task Category listed as Network Policy Server, as seen in Figure 9.41.

In Figure 9.41, you can see that the server has denied the client access because there wasn't a health policy that it matched with.

FIGURE 9.41 Without a match to any network policy, the client is denied access.

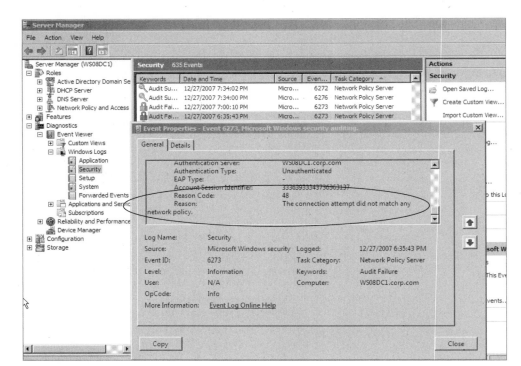

Tracing

After event logs on the client and server come tracing logs. And, in short, that would be another 30 pages or so to walk through. So, instead, I'm going to take the lazy way out and point you toward a couple really great references. Check out these two websites for NAP tracing:

- http://blogs.technet.com/wincat/archive/2007/10/29/the-definitive-guide-to-nap-logging.aspx (shortened to http://tinyurl.com/yudj5p)

- http://forums.microsoft.com/TechNet/ShowPost.aspx?PostID=1050230&SiteID=17 (shortened to http://tinyurl.com/26y28a)

NPS Configuration

Remember that the basis for NAP is NPS (the RADIUS) server. You can glean all sorts of information about the NPS server by running this command:

```
Netsh nps show config
```

Final Thoughts

NAP is great. It keeps the unhealthy kids off your network until they can be proven fit. Again, it doesn't guarantee that there won't be an outbreak of some kind. But it does represent that a minimum baseline of health is achieved before computers run through the halls of your network.

In this chapter, we used the built-in SHA and SHV that ship with Windows. And, again, together they can do some neat tricks, like figure out if your clients have the firewall turned on or not or if they've got Antivirus software running. But it doesn't do things like check to see if the latest DLL is present, a Registry punch has been made, or a certain file is present. That's because NAP is more of a framework for neat technology. Introducing more agents that check for more neat stuff is the job of third-party health agents.

Here's a gaggle of NAP resources to help you take it to the next level:

- All things NAP at Microsoft: www.microsoft.com/nap

- NAP FAQ: www.microsoft.com/technet/network/nap/napfaq.mspx

- NAP blog: http://blogs.technet.com/nap/

- Quick 30-minute overview of NAP: http://support.microsoft.com/kb/921070

- Network Access Protection Platform Architecture whitepaper http://tinyurl.com/25trgu

- NAP architecture: http://tinyurl.com/2ot3ud

- Step-by-Step Guide: Demonstrate 802.1X NAP Enforcement in a Test Lab: http://tinyurl.com/yks6dg

- Step-by-Step Guide: Demonstrate DHCP NAP Enforcement in a Test Lab http://tinyurl.com/yrqjqa

- Step-by-Step Guide: Demonstrate IPsec NAP Enforcement in a Test Lab http://tinyurl.com/2anqks

- Step-by-Step Guide: Demonstrate VPN NAP Enforcement in a Test Lab http://tinyurl.com/ysmpmb

- Using NAP with a new Windows Server 2008 Terminal Services Gateway: http://tinyurl.com/2kx5c6

- NAP Clients for Linux: Linux client: www.avendasys.com/products/nap.shtml

- Implementing NAP and NAC Security Technologies: The Complete Guide to Network Access Control: www.wiley.com/WileyCDA/WileyTitle/productCd-0470238380.html (shortened to http://tinyurl.com/279ofk)

- Microsoft Press book on NAP: www.microsoft.com/MSPress/books/11160.aspx

- NAP + SMS, er, SCCM 2007: http://technet.microsoft.com/en-us/library/bb693725.aspx

10

Finishing Touches with Group Policy: Controlling Hardware, Deploying Printers, and Implementing Shadow Copies

We've come a long way so far in this book. We've got our new machines deployed using WDS and Microsoft Deployment. We've set up Roaming Profiles, Redirected Folders, and Offline Files. We've deployed software using Group Policy Software Installation and SoftGrid. And, we've made sure unhealthy machines can't get on our network, with NAP.

We've made a pretty big cake. But no frosting.

Now it's time for what I like to call "the finishing touches."

In this chapter we'll cover three big topics which can round out your desktop experience:

Restricting Access to Hardware   Want a way to ensure that only the hardware you sanction gets on to your network? Well, giddy-up!

Setting up Printers   Nobody really *loves* printer management, but together we can make it easier for everyone.

Implementing Shadow Copies   How long does it take you to recover a user's file if he deletes it? If the answer is "over 30 seconds" you're going to want to learn how to implement Shadow Copies.

In the first two sections we'll be leveraging the new Group Policy Preference Extensions to provide some extra horsepower to your desktop machines.

We'll check out one of the Group Policy Preference Extensions right away when we talk about restricting access to hardware. Then, we'll continue to use it to help deploy our printers with style.

So, let's get started with the finishing … touches, that is!

Restricting Access to Hardware via Group Policy

You know it's true: Those USB thumb-disk keys and removable media doo-dads make your personal life easier, but your professional life harder. You want a way to control which hardware devices can be installed by users and which can't.

Thank you, Group Policy, for coming to the rescue.

Imagine this scenario: You allow users to have USB mice, but disallow USB Disk on Keys. You could allow CD-ROM readers, but not DVD writers. You could allow Bluetooth, but disallow PCMCIA.

You're in control, letting Group Policy do the work for you.

There are two ways to make this magic happen. One way disables the device, which is nice. But the other way actually restricts the driver itself from even loading. The first way uses the new Group Policy Preference Extensions' (GPEE) Devices extension.

The GPPEs are valid for Windows XP, Windows Vista, and Windows Server 2003 (when loaded), and they're installed in Windows Server 2008 by default.

The second way is via Group Policy's Administrative Templates. This method is valid for Windows Vista or Windows Server 2008 clients.

Table 10.1 will be the basis of our discussions. Here we'll be able to see how the two Group Policy technologies compare and contrast. And when you're done reading this big section, come back to this table to make your final decision about which one to use (or, heck, maybe you'll decide to use 'em both!).

TABLE 10.1 GPPE Devices versus Group Policy Device Installation Restriction

Feature Evaluation	GPPE Devices Extension	Device Installation Restriction
Valid for	XP and onward	Windows Vista and Windows Server 2008
Mechanism	Disables the device	Prevents the driver from loading
Better for	Any device	Devices that are unplugged, then plugged back in
Requirements	Group Policy Preference Extensions CSE loaded on client machine	Windows Vista or Windows Server 2008
User can avoid?	Possible: With admin rights, can re-enable	Possible: With admin rights, can avoid the Group Policy altogether, but more difficult

TABLE 10.1   GPPE Devices versus Group Policy Device Installation Restriction *(continued)*

Feature Evaluation	GPPE Devices Extension	Device Installation Restriction
Notification of restriction	None	Pop-up balloon that doesn't always appear (not sure why)
Granularity	Works only to restrict Device Class and Device Type	Works to restrict from very specific hardware ID or generic Device IDs up to restricting the entire hardware class

Devices Extension

In Chapter 10 of the companion book, *Group Policy Fundamentals, Security, and Troubleshooting* (Sybex, 2008), you learned about the Group Policy Preference Extensions. One of those extensions is the Devices extension.

The Devices extension works for Windows XP and higher, provided the GPPE CSE is already loaded.

> For more information about how to install the CSE, see Chapter 10 of the companion book.

The Devices GPPE disables the actual device or port but *doesn't* prevent the driver from loading. The new Devices extension node is found by navigating to Computer Configuration ➢ Preferences ➢ Control Panel Settings ➢ Devices or User Configuration ➢ Preferences ➢ Control Panel Settings ➢ Devices. You can see the Devices Extension in Figure 10.1.

Why is it on both sides?

You'll use the Computer side when you want all users on the same machine to be affected by your edict. Use the User side when you want a specific person to be affected by your edict.

Most organizations will choose the Computer side. That way, everyone on the machine can be restricted from using, say, USB flash disks or floppy disk drives.

Deciding to Disable the Device Class or Device Type

In Figure 10.2, we can see the Select a Device Class or a Device dialog. Here you can select a root class (like **Ports (COM & LPT)**) or a specific device, like **Communication Port (COM1)**.

If you choose just the device class, only the "Device class" block gets filled in. If you choose the actual device, then both the "Device class" *and* "Device type" get filled in, as seen in Figure 10.2.

What Happens When a Device Is Restricted?

When a specific device is restricted, it is simply disabled, shown as the little down-arrow icon in Figure 10.3.

However, if you went the extra mile and disabled the class, then usually *all* devices within that class are restricted, as seen in Figure 10.4.

FIGURE 10.1   The Group Policy Preference Extensions have the ability to restrict devices and device classes. Here, I'm selecting a whole class to disable.

FIGURE 10.2   Restricting a specific device.

FIGURE 10.3   The Devices extension simply disables devices.

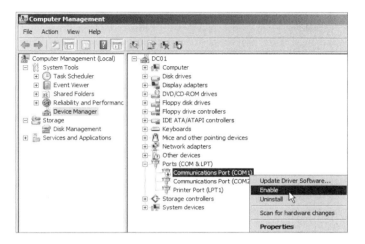

FIGURE 10.4   Disabling the whole class will disable all devices within that class.

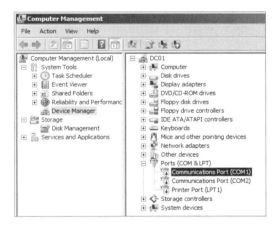

The issue is that with proper rights, any user could right-click and re-enable the device (also seen in Figure 10.4). Now, by default, regular users (on Windows XP and Windows Vista) cannot re-enable devices that are disabled like this. But because many organizations run their users as local admins, this is very easy for any admin-user to do. However, because Group Policy Preference Extensions are Group Policy, they take effect during the background refresh (about every 90 minutes or so). At that time, the device will once again be restricted.

 You cannot disable some devices. For example, on my Windows Vista machines, I was unable to disable Processors. I'm pretty sure this is a "Good Thing."

Dealing with Devices That Aren't Listed

This is kind of a problem with the Devices extension: You cannot specify a piece of hardware that you don't already have on your management station.

So, while it's a snap to disable USB ports altogether, it's a lot harder to eliminate just USB Disk on Keys, or something specific like a 30GB color video iPod. In short, the easiest way to disable a device is to track one down and get it hooked into your management station. Then, you'll be able to just point to it and you're done.

Now, if you can't get a hold of the device, but you know someone who has one, you might still be in luck. That's right! Just the very act of knowing someone with the device might be able to help you get out of a jam. Instead of having to schlep that device over to your management station (or make the machine with the device a temporary management station) you can simply ask your pal to tell you what the device properties are and jam them into the XML code of the preference you created. (We go into how to edit the underlying XML code of a preference in Chapter 10 of the companion book, *Group Policy Fundamentals, Security, and Troubleshooting*.)

Table 10.2 shows what you need from the device property details and how to set them within the XML attribute.

TABLE 10.2 Device Property Details and Their Appropriate XML Attributes

XML Attribute	Device Property from Details Tab of Device Properties
deviceClass	Class long name
deviceType	Device description
deviceClassGUID	Device class GUID
deviceTypeID	Device Instance Path

The CSE has to have the deviceClassGUID and the deviceTypeID exactly as they are displayed in the device properties to correctly enable/disable the device.

Why Is There an Option to Disable and Enable?

A keen eye will spot that the Devices extension has both Disable *and* Enable.

The idea is simple: You can use GPO filtering or Group Policy Preference Extensions Item Level Targeting to decide, perhaps, who should get which hardware enabled or disabled. For instance, everyone who gets the GPO will have their USB ports disabled. Except for Lab Technicians, who need USB ports *enabled*.

To do something like this, you might set the GPO at a high level (maybe a high-level OU or at the domain level) and then set it to Disabled. Then lower down, say at the **Lab Technicians** OU, set the USB ports as Enabled.

In my testing, Devices GPPE worked perfectly when I used Computer Configuration ➢ Preferences ➢ Control Panel Settings ➢ Devices. I restricted the hardware and ran the gpupdate.exe command, and my hardware was disabled. However, when I did the same thing using User Configuration ➢ Preferences ➢ Control Panel Settings ➢ Devices and restricted the same hardware, it didn't always take effect right away.

Restricting Driver Access with Policy Settings for Windows Vista (and Windows Server 2008)

In the last section, we talked about the Group Policy Preference Extensions and how in using that technology, you can disable devices. That's great. But you can take it to the next level with two areas of Group Policy. There are two sections of Group Policy that we're going to talk about now to help you secure your hardware even further:

- Computer Configuration ➢ Policies ➢ Administrative Templates ➢ System ➢ Removable Storage Access (seen in Figure 10.5)

- Computer Configuration ➢ Policies ➢Administrative Templates ➢ System ➢ Device Installation ➢ Device Installation Restriction (seen in Figure 10.6)

The first set (Removable Storage Access) is fairly self-explanatory: If you enable a policy setting for that kind of removable storage (CD/DVD, floppy, and so on), you can make it so that the whole device type cannot be read or written to. But it doesn't have the "superpower" the second set (Device Installation Restrictions) has.

FIGURE 10.5   There are some predefined hardware restrictions you can leverage in Group Policy.

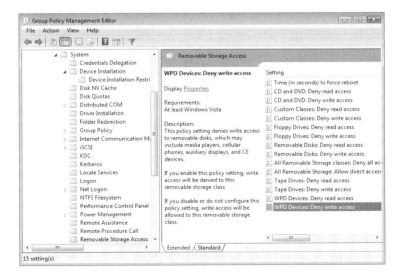

FIGURE 10.6 You can customize the kinds of hardware you want to restrict.

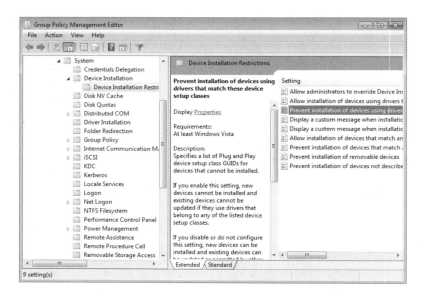

In the first set there is a policy setting group named **Custom Classes: Deny read access** and **Custom Classes: Deny write access.** It sounds like it has a similar ability to what we're about to explore. However, there is one difference. The Removable Storage Access policy set doesn't actually prevent the drivers from being installed. So, the driver for the class will be installed when the hardware is detected, but this policy prevents it from being read or written to. In the next section, when we explore the Device Installation Restrictions policy settings, we'll put the real smackdown on the driver itself.

Getting a Handle on Classes and IDs

First things first: you need to know what you want to restrict.

Think big.

Or small.

That's because, like the Devices extension, you can restrict a specific "class" of devices or get super-specific and restrict a single hardware type. Or, you can do the converse, as well, and allow only specific device classes, like USB mice.

Here's the trick though: similar to the Devices extension, to really be effective you're going to need to track down the hardware you'll want to restrict.

So, if you want to say, "No joystick drivers can be installed on my Windows Vista machines," and "Only USB mice can be installed on my Windows Vista machines," you'll likely need to get a hold of a joystick and a USB mouse. Now, this isn't always true. You can try to use the Internet to track down one of the following pieces of information:

- Hardware ID
- Compatible ID
- Device Class

But, again, it's much easier if you just have one of these devices in front of you. That way, you can introduce it to a Windows Vista machine and see for yourself what the Hardware ID, Compatible ID, or Device Class is. Once you know that, you'll know how to squash it (or leave it available).

In this example, we'll squash a specific sound card family: a Creative AutoPCI ES1371/ ES1373. If you want to squash something else, (like specific USB devices, or even USB ports, and so on), just follow along and substitute the device you want.

To do this, fire up Device Manager on a machine that already has the hardware items installed. Then, when you find the device, right-click it and select Properties and select the Details tab. By default you'll see a "Device description." While interesting, it's not that useful. Select the Property drop-down and select "Hardware Ids" as seen in Figure 10.7.

The "Hardware Ids" page shows you, from top to bottom, the most specific to least specific Device ID. If you look closely at the topmost item in the "Hardware Ids" value list, you'll see this sound card is specifically a Rev 2 of the ES1371 soundboard. That's pretty darned specific. As you go down the list, the description becomes less specific to encompass the whole family.

FIGURE 10.7   The Details tab of the device helps you determine how to squash it.

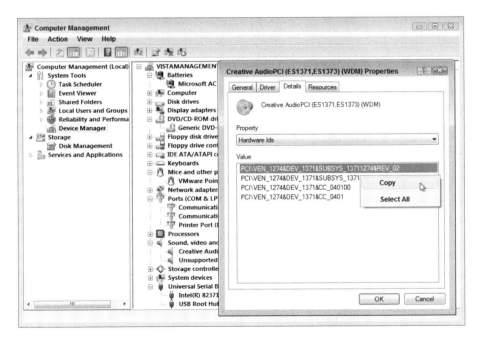

Additionally, you can also change the Property to "Compatible Ids." These also describe the hardware and are considered less specific than what you'll find in "Hardware Ids." You might choose to use the information found in "Compatible Ids" to try to corral more hardware that's similar into the "don't use" list—because it's less specific and might actually net you more results. Of course, the tradeoff is always that you might restrict something you didn't want to as you get less specific.

And, finally, the least specific category can be found by selecting Device Class from the Property drop-down. In my case, the sound card shows up as simply Media. But lots of things could be considered Media, so, again, caution should be used the less specific you go.

Once you've decided which value you want to leverage, right-click it, select Copy, and paste it into Notepad for safekeeping. Copying it directly as it's presented is important because, in the next steps, the value must be entered exactly. If there are upper- and lowercase characters in the value, they must be transferred precisely.

If you wanted to be a command-line commando instead of using the Device Manager to capture the Hardware IDs or Device Classes, check out the devcon command-line utility at `http://support.microsoft.com/kb/311272`.

Microsoft has a bunch of identifiers for common classes here which may be helpful if you don't have any physical access to the device: `http://go.microsoft.com/fwlink/?LinkId=52665`.

Restricting or Allowing Your Hardware via Group Policy

While we'll explore all the policy settings located in Computer Configuration ➢ Administrative Templates ➢ System ➢ Device Installation ➢ Device Installation Restriction (seen in Figure 10.8), there is really only one we'll need to complete this initial example.

FIGURE 10.8   Paste the Device ID to ensure you've captured the device description exactly.

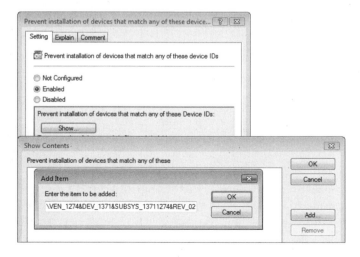

Create a GPO and link it to an OU (or domain, and so on) that contains the Windows Vista machines you want to control. Then edit the GPO and drive down into Computer Configuration ➤ Administrative Templates ➤ System ➤ Device Installation ➤ Device Installation Restriction ➤ **Prevent installation of devices that match any of these device IDs.** Select Enabled in the policy setting, click Show (also in the policy setting), and select Add in the Show Contents dialog. Then in the Add Item dialog box, paste in the information from the device you got before. All this can be seen in Figure 10.8.

Now, before we go on, here's the trick: if a machine already has the device installed, it doesn't magically uninstall and restrict access to the device. So, if you're going to restrict hardware, I suggest you do this early in your Windows Vista deployment. Or, check out the Real-World Scenario "Using Group Policy Preference Extensions' Scheduled Tasks Extension and Devcon to Force the Removal of Hardware."

When you turn on a machine which has never seen the hardware device before, you'll see the machine try to install the hardware device and provide pop-up balloon status information as to its progress. When completed, the goal is that the hardware is restricted, as seen in Figure 10.9.

FIGURE 10.9   When implemented properly, the device driver will be prevented from installing.

That will remove all COM ports, as seen here.

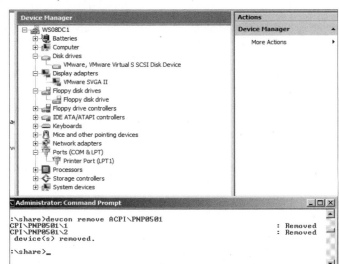

The question is, how do you reach out and disconnect existing hardware?

With the Group Policy Preference Extensions, of course!

The Scheduled Tasks Extension can throw tasks to Windows XP, Windows Server 2003, Windows Vista, and Windows Server 2008 machines. (Note that only the Scheduled Tasks and not the Immediate Tasks will work for Windows Vista or Windows Server 2008 machines.)

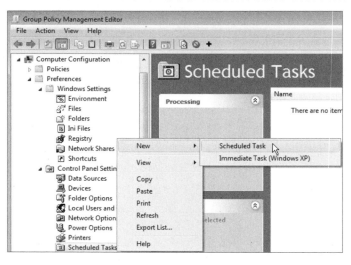

Once we set up a new Scheduled Task, we instruct devcon to run (in my example, directly from a shared folder) where the Arguments field simply says remove {hardware ID}, as seen here.

You don't need to check "Run as" because this task will run as SYSTEM, which is fine. Finally, in the Schedule tab, specify when you want the task to run. We can set this to run just once, as seen here.

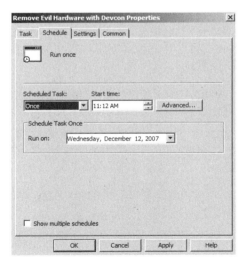

When we do, the hardware will be removed. And, since we've already got the **Prevent installation of devices that match any of these device IDs** Group Policy setting working for us, the pesky hardware we want banished can never return!

Understanding the Remaining Policy Settings for Hardware Restrictions

In the example we just went though, we squashed the use of just one device. You could, if you wanted, go the opposite route, which is restrict *all* hardware by default and allow only *some*. This can be done using the policy settings described next. Again, you can see a list of these policy settings in Figure 10.6, which shows the Computer Configuration ➢ Administrative Templates ➢ Device Installation ➢ Device Installation Restrictions branch of Group Policy.

Allow Administrators to Override Device Installation Restrictions

By default, local administrators on the Windows Vista machine must honor the restrictions that are put in place. If you enable this setting, local administrators can install whatever hardware they want.

Allow Installation of Devices Using Drivers that Match These Setup Classes

By entering in device descriptions in this policy setting, you're expressly allowing these hardware devices as "allowed" into the system. Note this policy setting honors only setup classes and not Device IDs (like those we used in the working example).

Prevent Installation of Devices Using Drivers that Match These Device Setup Classes

In the working example we used the Device ID to describe our hardware and used another policy setting, entitled **Prevent Installation of devices that match any of these device IDs.** It should be noted that the setting we used does not honor Class ID descriptions. To use Class ID descriptions you need to use this policy setting.

Display a Custom Message When Installation Is Prevented by Policy (Balloon Text) and (Balloon Title)

These are two policy settings to help you customize the message like what is seen in Figure 10.9. However, I've noticed that sometimes the custom text just fails to show up, and only the default text is shown.

Allow Installation of Devices that Match Any of These Device IDs

In the working example we used the Device ID to describe our hardware. However, I also stated that the least specific way to describe our hardware is based on hardware class. It should be noted that this policy setting does not honor Class ID descriptions. To use Class ID descriptions, use the policy settings **Allow installation of devices using drivers that match these device setup classes** or **Prevent installation of devices using drivers that match these device setup classes.**

This setting is best used with another setting entitled **Prevent installation of devices not described by other policy settings**. By preventing everything (by default), then using this setting, you can specify precisely which devices you want to allow to be installed.

Prevent Installation of Devices that Match Any of These Device IDs

In the working example, this is the policy setting we used to restrict a specific type of hardware based on Device IDs. If we wanted to restrict using Device Classes, we would have to leverage other specific policy settings such as **Allow installation of devices using drivers that match these device setup classes** or **Prevent installation of devices using drivers that match these device setup classes.**

Prevent Installation of Removable Devices

This setting is a generic and quick way to restrict any hardware device which describes itself as "removable," including USB devices. I wouldn't count on this particular policy setting that often. Use the techniques described earlier to get moderately restrictive Device IDs and lock them down specifically. This setting is vague enough and there's no telling what the hardware is telling Windows about itself to really be sure it's locking down what you think it is.

Prevent Installation of Devices not Described by Other Policy Settings

This is the catch-all policy setting to basically restrict all hardware, unless you've specifically dictated that something can install. This policy in conjunction with the various "Allow" policies (such as **Allow installation of devices that match any of these device IDs**) can make a really powerful combination to allow only the hardware you want in your environment.

Assigning Printers via Group Policy

Let me guess what another of your biggest headaches is.

Printers.

So, wouldn't it be great if we could just zap printers down to our Windows 2000, Windows XP, and Windows Vista client machines? Or, whenever Sally roams from Desktop to Desktop, she had access to the same printers?

Those are two different goals, and we're about to approach both of them here.

Before we get too far along, let me explain that the goal is the same: deploying printers to our Windows 2000, Windows XP, and Windows Vista clients (or servers, too, I suppose). However, there are three potential ways to get there:

- Using the Group Policy Preference Extensions
- Using the Printers snap-in
- Using `pushprinterconnections.exe` in conjunction with the Printers snap-in

We're going to explore these in this order, but in short, here's why you choose one method over another.

You would use the Group Policy Preference Extensions when…

- The target machines are Windows XP, Windows Vista, Windows Server 2003, and Windows Server 2008.
- The Group Policy Preference Extensions client is already loaded.

You would use the Printers snap-in when…

- You were unable to get the Group Policy Preference Extensions loaded in your environment (technical or political reasons).
- Your target machines are Windows Vista machines.

You would use `pushprinterconnections.exe` in conjunction with the Printers snap-in when…

- You were unable to get the Group Policy Preference Extensions loaded in your environment (technical or political reasons).
- Your target machines are Windows 2000 or Windows XP.

Don't worry. We'll walk though all the scenarios and you can decide as you go along which one is best.

(Hint, hint: The first option's the best!)

Using the Printers Group Policy Preference Extensions

Ideally, you'll use the Group Policy Preference Extensions to zap printers to your users and computers. But, of course, the catch is that the Group Policy Preference Extensions client component needs to be already on your Windows XP and Windows Vista machines.

If you cannot do this for whatever reason (usually, political issues where people cannot change clients without a ludicrous amount of testing), you can skip this section and go on to the next one, "Using the Printers Snap-in and *pushprinterconnections.exe*." That's because those components are all in-the-box and you don't need to get the Group Policy Preference Extensions client on the target machine.

But, if you have been able to get the Group Policy Preference Extensions on your target machines, let's explore how to zap printers down to your users.

Zapping Down Printers to Users and Computers

The Printers Extension exists on both the Computer and User sides. Except on the Computer side, you can't map shared printers, only TCP/IP and Local Printers, as seen in Figure 10.10. On the User side, you can map all three kinds of printers, as seen in Figure 10.11.

Setting up a shared printer on the User side is easy, as seen in Figure 10.12. Just set the share path to the printer share, and voilà. Instant printer for the user. The bonus here is that the user doesn't need to be an administrator to install the drivers that will come down from the server when this connection happens. The Group Policy engine does it on the user's behalf, so it's just done, lickety-split.

FIGURE 10.10   The Printers extension on the Computer side allows only for mapping TCP/IP and Local Printers.

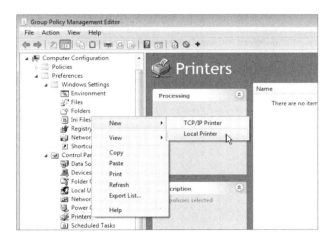

FIGURE 10.11   The Printers extension on the User side can deploy all three types of printers.

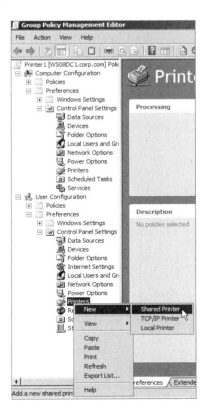

FIGURE 10.12   Shared printers are usually what most people set up.

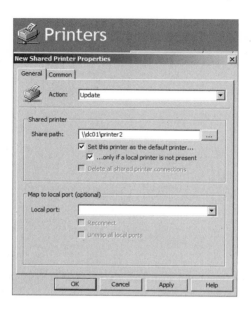

Trickier: Zapping Down Specific Printers to Users on Specific Machines

Oh sure, you can use the Printers extension to map a specific printer to a specific user. But that means that no matter which computer a user travels to, they get exactly the same printers.

Maybe that's not what you want.

I talk with lots and lots of people who have the same problem: how to map printers based on the computer the user is on at that moment.

Take Figure 10.13 for example. Here you can see four zones:

- Zone 1 with Printer 1: IT computers
- Zone 2 with Printer 2: Human Resources
- Zone 3 with Printer 3: Sales
- Zone 4 with Printer 4: Marketing

And, just for fun, I'm adding an additional challenge; a special circumstance where I have a shared computer in each zone that should not only print to the normal printer in that zone, but should also map to an additional shared printer specific to the shared computers.

In Figure 10.13, our shared computer and shared printer are shaded. In these examples, the shared computers have the word "shared" in their names. This will be helpful later as we craft our printing experience.

So the dream is that whenever anyone logs onto any computer in the zone, they get mapped to the printer for that zone.

FIGURE 10.13 In our sample company, we have four zones and one special shared printer requirement.

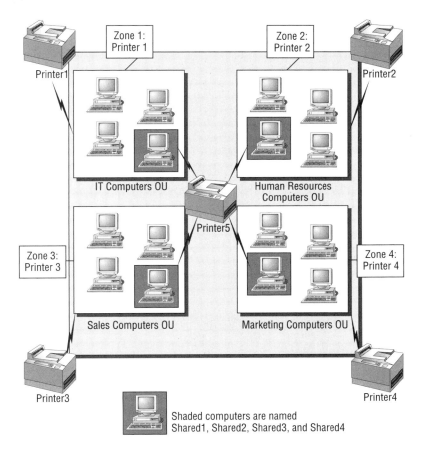

To achieve the goal, we'll break this out into two steps:

1. Deploy the specific zone printer to all computers in the same zone.

2. Deploy the shared printer to only the shared computers in all zones.

Deploying the Same Printer to All Computers in the Zone

To accomplish our first goal, we want to make sure all computers in Human Resources get the same printer, Printer 2. You'll repeat this same procedure for other areas of your universe, but we'll just show Human Resources as an example.

We've already seen how you can't deploy Shared Printers to computers. That's a bummer, because our goal is that whenever anyone logs onto a Human Resources computer, they get Printer 2.

And, natively, you can't do that. (You could do it with Group Policy Loopback in Merge mode, but you may end up getting unintended Group Policy Objects this way.)

But with a little one-two Group Policy Preference Extensions punch, we can do it without any Loopback hassle.

Punch #1: Put an Environment Variable on All Computers in the Zone   What we need is a way to tag the specific computers with a little marker, so that once we can see this marker, we can take action on it. We can use environment variables to make this little tag on specific computers, which will indicate that specific computers should use specific printers. We'll use the Group Policy Preference Environment Extension to do this for us.

Punch #2: Map Shared Printers Only to Users Whose Computers Have the Environment Variable   Once we have the little tag on each computer, we'll use the GPPE Printers extension. We'll map shared printers to users, but only if the tag is present on the machine that specifies a printer.

Before we get started, make sure your **Human Resources** OU looks like mine does in Figure 10.14. You can see I've got **Human Resources Computers** and **Human Resources Users** within the **Human Resources** OU.

FIGURE 10.14   Make sure your Human Resources structure looks like mine.

Next, we'll create a GPO and link it over to the **Human Resources Computers** OU. We'll use the GPPE Environment extension to put a System variable on the computer called PRINTER2, and give it a value of 1, meaning true.

So the idea is that if a computer in Zone 2 sees a variable with Printer2, that computer should get that printer.

You can see this in Figure 10.15.

Then, create a GPO and link it to the domain level (or any higher level such that all the zones you want are covered). I'm calling my GPO "Universal Printer Map for Users." This GPO will affect all user accounts. It will use the GPPE Printers extension on the User side to map a shared printer, as seen in Figure 10.16.

Now, if we stopped right here, we'd have a problem. That's because right now we're saying "Everyone should get \\dc01\printer2," and that's not right. What we want to say is "Everyone should get \\dc01\printer2...if they're using a computer that's tagged with the environment variable PRINTER2=1."

FIGURE 10.15   Use a System variable to tag specific computers to use specific printers.

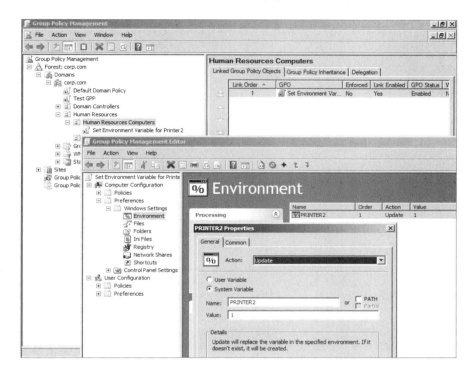

FIGURE 10.16   Use the GPPE Printers extension to map a printer to everyone.

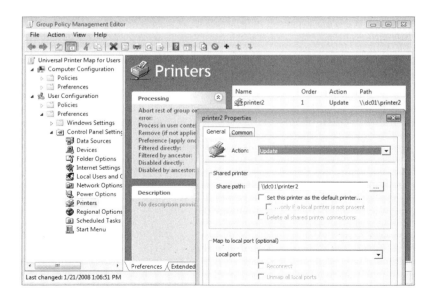

So now, click the Common tab in the Printer extension properties. Then click "Item-level targeting," as seen in Figure 10.17, and select the Targeting button to open the Targeting Editor.

Add a New Item, select the environment variable, and specify that the PRINTER2 environment variable must be set to 1, as seen in Figure 10.17.

FIGURE 10.17 Use Item Level Targeting to specify that the PRINTER2 environment variable must be set to 1.

If all goes well, two things happen on the client system: they get the message that they should get the environment variable and, because of that environment variable, anyone who logs onto that computer with the variable gets the printer.

Magic!

You can see this magic in Figure 10.18. The command prompt shows the environment variable PRINTER2=1, and the Printers dialog shows the newly mapped printer based on the environment variable.

Because this "Universal Printer Map for Users" GPO is linked to the domain, it already affects every user account. And inside this GPO, you'll want to create a new preference item *for every printer*. The goal, again, is to make it such that the mapping of the printer only happens when computers have the environment variable present.

Deploying a Shared Printer to Only the Shared Computers in All Zones

In the previous example, we got everyone to use the specific printer for the computers in their zone.

FIGURE 10.18   Based on the environment variable, anyone who uses this computer gets the printer.

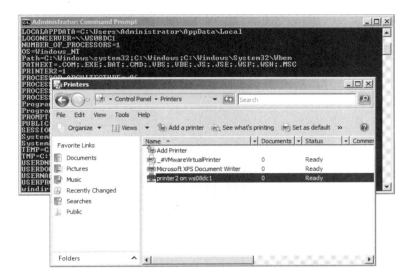

However, remember that we have one special requirement. That is, we want all the shared computers (in our examples they're named SHARED1, SHARED2, SHARED3, and SHARED4) to use the same printer: Printer 5.

However, this time, we'll use a trick in the Item Level Targeting feature to specify that all computers with "shared" in the name will map to the same printer.

To do this, we'll create a GPO at the domain level called "Special Map for Public Computers" and use the Printers extension on the Users side to map \\dc01\printer5, but only when the computer name is SHARED-something.

To do this, we use the * indicator, as in SHARED*. You can see this in Figure 10.19.

The star will evaluate to true for any computer named SHARED1, SHARED2, and so on.

Now, you've done it! You've got a universal way to ensure that people get a specific printer based on the specific computer they're logging onto. Indeed, if you were to log onto SHARED2, which is in the **Human Resources Computers** OU, you would now get two printers: You'd get Printer2 because you were in Zone 2 (from the first exercise), and Printer5 because you were on a shared computer, as seen in Figure 10.20.

Using the Printers Snap-in and *pushprinterconnections.exe*

I actually hope you won't need to use the material in this section. This section is only necessary for people who positively cannot get the Group Policy Preference Extensions installed on their Windows XP and Windows Vista machines. I know who you are, and I feel your pain.

Anyway, this section is for you.

FIGURE 10.19 You can map printers to users based on the computer name.

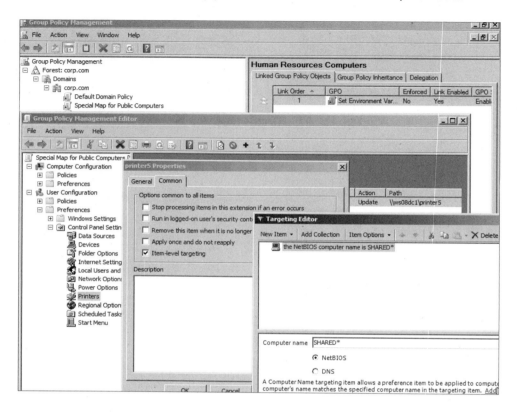

FIGURE 10.20 Because you logged into SHARED2, you got two printers.

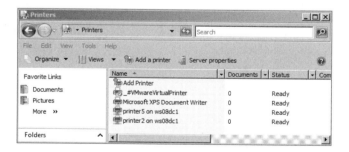

The fact is, there's an alternative way to deploy printers, which existed before the Group Policy Preference Extensions. The idea is that there's a way to "add" the ability to zap printers down to users and computers.

Now, again, I'm not "anti" the method I'm about to show you. It's just that the GPPE Printer extensions are a more elegant way to achieve a similar goal. And, it's a lot (really, a lot) more reliable for Windows XP machines than what I'm about to show you. However, it should be noted that it's really the only way to push printers down to Windows 2000 machines, because the Group Policy Preference Extensions aren't supported on Windows 2000 machines.

With that in mind, we need to embrace that three things must be true:

- The Active Directory schema version must be at least level 31 (I'll explain what that means in a second).

- The correct snap-in needs to be present on your management station.

- We need a special EXE to be run on our Windows XP and Windows 2000 machines to actually make the printer mapping work.

We'll check out how to make sure what level our Active Directory schema is at, and upgrade it if necessary. Then, we'll get the correct snap-ins on our management stations and start deploying some printers.

Discovering Our Schema Level

You can figure out what schema version your Active Directory is using pretty quickly. Just mosey over to a Domain Controller and check a specific Registry subkey. You can find this subkey in the following location:

HKEY_LOCAL_MACHINE\System\CurrentControlSet\Services\NTDS\Parameters

and look for the schema Version values. Here's what you might find, and what it means:

- Level 13 = Microsoft Windows 2000

- Level 30 = Original release version of Microsoft Windows Server 2003 and Microsoft Windows Server 2003 Service Pack 1 (SP1)

- Level 31 = Microsoft Windows Server 2003 R2

- Level 44 = Windows Server 2008

You can find more about schema version values at http://support.microsoft .com/kb/917385.

For our purposes, and to deploy printers using the Printers snap-in, we need to have at least level 31.

Updating Our Schema (to at Least Level 31)

To zap printers down to our Windows XP and Windows Vista machines, we need to first update the Active Directory schema.

In Chapter 9 of the companion book, *Group Policy Fundamentals, Security, and Troubleshooting*, we also had to update our Active Directory schema, but that was to support the new Windows Vista wireless policy.

Updating the schema is likely the hardest part of the job, because you'll need approval from your Active Directory bigwigs that this is okay. Once you have approval, this operation is best performed directly upon the Schema Master Domain Controller in your domain.

The reason for the schema upgrade is that our printer connection objects get a new "fast query" lookup via LDAP in Active Directory. This way, tools like Windows Server 2003/R2's and Windows Server 2008's Print Management Console (which we really won't be going into here) don't have to inspect every GPO in the domain to figure out where printers are currently deployed.

You need to decide which schema level to upgrade to. You have two choices:

- Windows Server 2003/R2 schema, Level 31
- Windows Server 2008 schema, Level 44

> **WARNING**   Windows Vista schema is also level 31—more like pre-Level 31. Apparently the schema on the shipping Windows Vista DVD is a *beta* schema (wow...that's nice). Learn more about this issue here: http://support.microsoft.com/kb/933585/en-us.

So, if you want Level 31, the Windows Server 2003/R2 version, you need to run the command `adprep /forestprep`, which is located in the `\cmpnents\r2\adprep` directory.

If you want Level 44, the Windows Server 2008 version, you need to run the command `adprep /forestprep`, which is located in the `\sources\adprep` directory on the Windows Server 2008 DVD.

You can see the running of the command in Figure 10.21.

FIGURE 10.21   In order to get the ability to zap printers down to your users, you need to extend the schema with the Windows Server 2003/R2 schema.

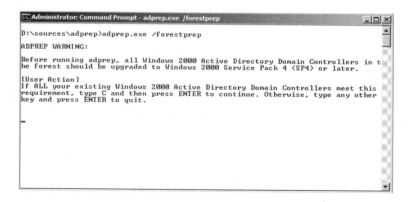

The Printers Group Policy Snap-in

Your management station is where you edit GPOs from. And in this book, we're assuming it's a Windows Vista or Windows Server 2008 machine. However, for this procedure, the management station can be Windows XP, Windows Vista, or Windows Server 2008 (although Windows Vista and Windows Server 2008 are preferred).

Here's a list of which machines can host the Printers snap-in and how to get them.

Printers Snap-in for Windows XP or Windows Server 2003/R2   Once again, leveraging a Windows Vista management station will save you time. You can do all the magic we're about to explore from, say, a Windows Server 2003 server or a Windows XP management station. But that requires extra components that I don't really want to explore here. (For a full rundown of these components, check out an article I wrote about these new print management features available at Microsoft Technet Magazine at `http://tinyurl.com/ymawtq`.)

Printers Snap-in for Windows Vista   The printers snap-in is already built into Windows Vista management station. There's nothing you need to do if you're already using a Windows Vista management station.

Printers Snap-in on Windows Server 2008   If you're using a Windows Server 2008 management station, there are some steps you'll need to get the printers snap-in. In Figure 10.22, you can see there is no printers snap-in listed within the Group Policy Editor.

To install the printers snap-in, use Server Manager, add the feature named Remote Server Administration Tools, and add the Print Services Tools, as seen in Figure 10.23.

FIGURE 10.22   On a Windows Server 2008 machine the Printers snap-in is missing until you install it.

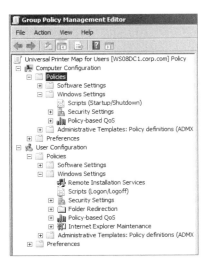

FIGURE 10.23   Add the Print Services Tools to get the GPO snap-in.

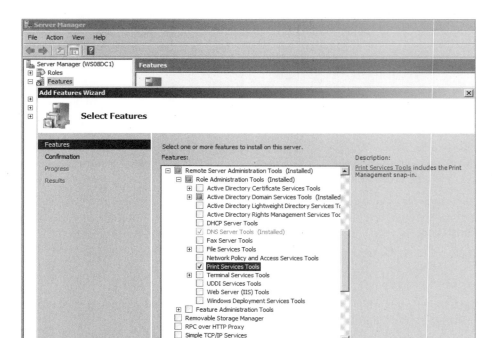

Once installation is complete, you'll see the Deployed Printers snap-in, which can be seen in Figure 10.24 a little later.

Zap Printers Down from Your Vista or Windows Server 2008 Management Station

From here, we'll assume you want to test drive this on your Windows Vista or Windows Server 2008 management station. We'll also assume you have a test printer connected on a server somewhere. If not, you can follow along by running through the Add Printer Wizard on your server and sharing out a (fake) printer if you like.

To zap a printer down to your users or computers, you start out by creating a GPO and linking it to an OU containing either users or computers; say, the Human Resources OU.

You can see where to zap printers down in the two "Deployed Printers" nodes in the Group Policy Object Editor (or, on newer machines, the Group Policy Management editor). One is under Computer Configuration ➢ Policies ➢ Windows Settings ➢ Deployed Printers and the other is under User Configuration ➢ Policies ➢ Windows Settings ➢ Deployed Printers.

Once you select User Configuration ➢ Policies ➢ Deployed Printers ➢ Deploy Printers (as seen in Figure 10.24) or Computer Configuration ➢ Policies ➢ Deployed Printers ➢ Deploy Printers, you'll be ready to blast new printer assignments down. Just type **\\server\printer** into the "Enter printer name" dialog, click Add, and you're done. (Note that my screenshots in Figures 10.24 and Figures 10.25 are somewhat older, because I dug up an old Windows Vista machine to play with, so the Policies node isn't present.)

Now, if you didn't actually upgrade the schema, you'll see what's seen in Figure 10.24. That is the Connection Status field will say "Addition failed."

But, if the schema was successfully upgraded, you'll see what's shown in Figure 10.25.

FIGURE 10.24   If you didn't upgrade the schema and try to zap a printer down, you'll get an "Addition failed" message.

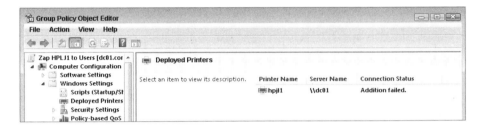

FIGURE 10.25   If the schema was upgraded properly, there is no Connection Status information.

Verifying Printer Assignment on a Windows Vista Target

If you have all Windows Vista client machines, you're done. If you wait until Group Policy refreshes, you'll see the printer just pop into place, as in Figure 10.26. Just log off and back on (for users) or reboot (for computers) and, like magic, you'll have printers assigned.

However, if you try this on a Windows XP machine, you won't see this work. That's because Windows Vista has a CSE (Client-Side Extension) that does the work. Neither Windows XP nor Windows 2000 have this CSE, and, hence, won't map the printer automatically.

To do this, we need a little "helper" application.

FIGURE 10.26 Group Policy will naturally just pop this printer into place.

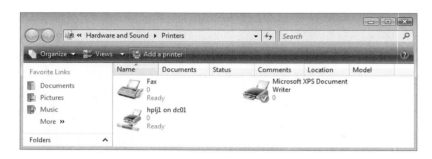

Adding PushPrinterConnections to the GPO to "Help" Windows XP and Windows 2000

To make Windows XP (and Windows 2000 for that matter) "wake up and smell the printers" you need to have it run a little program. This trick is done through an executable program that you have to kick off via a Login script (for printers assigned to users) or Startup script (for printers assigned to computers).

The "moving part" to make the printer assignment work on Windows XP and Windows 2000 is a little EXE called `pushprinterconnections.exe`. Here's the bad news (so brace yourself). This little EXE is only available if you own a copy of Windows Server 2003/R2 or Windows Server 2008.

If you own one copy of either server type, you can use it in your domain. If you don't own Windows Server 2003/R2 or Windows Server 2008, you cannot download this little executable anywhere else.

You'll find the `pushprinterconnections.exe` on your Windows Server 2003/R2 in the `\windows\PMCSnap` directory, along with some other bits associated with the Print Management Console.

On Windows Server 2008, `pushprinterconnections.exe` is in your `\windows\system32` directory.

Once you've located `pushprinterconnections.exe`, here's what you do:

- If you're deploying printers to users, the EXE needs to be run in the user's Login Script.

- If you're deploying printers to computers, it needs to be run in the computer's Startup Script.

Here are the rough steps to do this (as seen in Figure 10.27):

1. While editing the GPO, drill down to the script type (User Login or Computer Startup).

2. Click the Show Files button.

3. Copy the `pushprinterconnections.exe` into the window that opens up.

4. Back at the properties of the script, click Add and locate and select the `pushprinterconnections.exe` file.

5. Optionally, you can enter **-log** in the Script Parameters field to start a log file on the Windows XP or Windows 2000 client.

6. Click OK.

FIGURE 10.27 Add in pushprinterconnections.exe as part of the Logon script for this user (or Startup script for this computer).

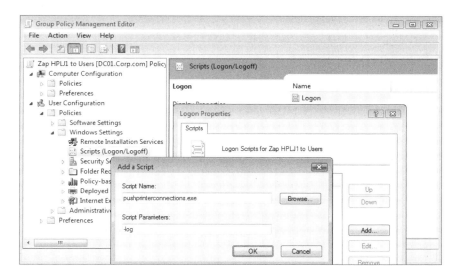

The key point is that the location where it starts out isn't the location where you need to run it from. Your job is to take the file and plunk it directly into the GPO itself.

> Optionally, you can put the pushprinterconnections.exe program in a shared place that everyone can get to.

A troubleshooting log file is generated with a -log typed in the Script Parameters box. A per-user debug log file will be written to %temp%. A per-machine debug log will be written to %windir%\temp. (Note that these are totally different directories.)

It's worth noting that you shouldn't use the -log parameter in a production environment—you wouldn't want the utility filling up your client machine hard disks with megabytes of log files.

So what happens if a Windows Vista machine runs pushprinterconnections.exe? Absolutely nothing. The first thing that pushprinterconnections.exe does when you run it is to check if it is running on Windows Vista. If it is running on a Vista machine, the utility exits without doing anything—so network administrators don't have to worry if they accidentally push out the pushprinterconnections.exe utility down to Windows Vista clients.

In other words, you can use the same GPO to assign printers to Windows Vista and Windows XP or Windows 2000 machines.

Verifying Printer Assignment (Again) for Windows XP Machines

If you log in as Frank Rizzo on your Windows XP machine, you should see a printer in the Printers and Faxes section of Control Panel.

Note that Windows XP printers won't "change" during background refresh after you're already logged in. That's because the `pushprinterconnections.exe` only runs at login or startup.

Final Thoughts on Zapping Printers Using the Printers Snap-in

Some more thoughts about all this printer stuff before we move on:

- Windows 2000 machines only support per-user printer connections via the Printers snap-in.

- Windows Vista, Windows XP, and Windows 2003 support per-user or per-computer printer connections.

But, in practice, I've seen `pushprinterconnections.exe` simply fail to map the printers to both users and computers.

The Group Policy Preference Extensions are really the best way to deploy printers.

Use that method when you can.

One extra thing we didn't mention is that the Print Management Console gives a one-stop-shop view of printers deployed via GPOs. Again, space prevents us from walking through the Print Management Console. However, you can read my full article here: `http://tinyurl.com/ymawtq` or read Microsoft's guide to the Printer Management Console at `http://tinyurl.com/n2pvh`.

Windows Server 2008 has the Print Management Console built in, and you can run it by typing **printmanagement.msc** in the Start box.

Shadow Copies (aka Previous Versions)

The idea behind Shadow Copies is awesome: preserve some number of copies of the user's precious files on the server. When the user performs a CLM (Career-Limiting Move) by deleting a file or overwriting a file with data that cannot be undone, they can simply get that file back from a point in time. Microsoft's code name for this feature was Time Warp, and I think that pretty much says it all.

Technically, the system doesn't precisely store "copies" of a file, it preserves a "point-in-time" copy of a file—not a copy of all the bytes that compose the entire file. Sometimes, this magic is referred to as Snapshots, though, technically again, it's not a direct bitwise snapshot of the file.

There are two versions of this feature:

- One works when the data is stored on a Windows Server 2003 machine. The clients can be Windows 2000, Windows XP, or Windows Vista.

- The other version is built in locally to Windows Vista. So, if a user whacks a file on the local computer (and it wasn't ever saved on the network), you've still got them covered.

Setting up and Using Shadow Copies for Local Windows Vista Machines

By default, Windows Vista's System Protection is enabled. This system allows you to restore to a point-in-time backup if the operating system should have problems. This system existed in Windows XP as well but didn't capture the changes to data files. In Windows Vista, that's changed.

Again, System Protection is enabled, so Windows Vista is automatically "doing its thing" and protecting the files. There isn't really anything to "set up." System Protection *restore points* are created once every day and before a new driver is installed. You can also create a manual snapshot from the System Protection section of the System applet in Control Panel. Or, disable System Protection altogether (not recommended though). Again, do this at Control Panel ➢ System ➢ System Protection.

When you're ready to restore a previous version of a file, you'll use the same interface we're about to explore. As you'll see a bit later, it's as simple as right-clicking the file and selecting Previous Versions to get a file back.

Because we only have so much space, we're just going to show the version when files are stored on the server.

Setting up Shadow Copies on the Server

You must take care of two tasks before the user can use Shadow Copies:

- Set up Windows Server 2003/2008 to start creating these snapshots.

- Deliver the Shadow Copies client piece to the desktops. You need to do this for Windows 2000 and Windows XP (pre-SP2). The Shadow Copies client piece is already integrated into Windows XP/Service Pack 2+ and Windows Vista.

So, let's do that now.

Shadow Copies work because you're making a *point-in-time* copy of the users' data files, which preserves them in case of a future calamity. The best place to do this is on the volume to which you've redirected Documents/My Documents. However, first you need to ask yourself several questions:

- How much junk, I mean, data, are my users taking up on each drive on the server?

- How much more space on this drive am I willing to cordon off to preserve previous versions of files?

- How often do I want to take a snapshot to preserve user data?

Once you answer these questions, follow these steps:

1. Right-click a drive letter on a server and choose Properties from the shortcut menu to open the Properties dialog box, as shown in Figure 10.28.

2. Click the Shadow Copies tab, select a drive letter, and click the Settings button to open the Settings dialog box, as shown in Figure 10.29.

FIGURE 10.28   You set the Shadow Copies characteristics on a per-volume basis.

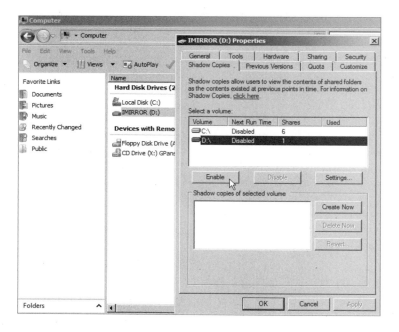

FIGURE 10.29   You can specify how much space to dedicate when files change, set a schedule to make Shadow Copies, and specify where to locate the storage area.

Here you can specify how much space you want to set aside for this particular volume. My recommendation is to set aside about 20–30 percent. The point of Shadow Copies isn't to keep backup copies of *all* user files forever; rather, similar to the Offline Caching mechanism, user files that get old will be flushed out of this space to make room for new files. Although Shadow Copies are a great preventive measure, they're not a substitute or replacement for general backups should the file turn out not to be available for restore.

1. In the Use Limit spin box, specify the size, and then click the Schedule button to open up the Schedule tab for the volume.

2. The Schedule tab is pretty self-explanatory. You might just wish to leave the defaults for now. When ready, click OK to confirm a changed schedule, or click Cancel to return to the Settings dialog. Click OK or Cancel again to return to the Properties tab.

The default schedule for any enabled volume is at 7:00 a.m. and 12:00 p.m. workdays (Monday through Friday). The idea is that you'll snag points in time of the data before the workday begins and again at the halfway point in the workday. If a user screws up and deletes a file, you've got at least two potentially restorable files from just today! If you have even more space available, you can store days or weeks of restorable data! Set the schedule however you want, but note two things:

-   Shadow Copies keep a maximum of 64 previous versions of a file. Every time you take a snapshot, you're *potentially* dumping older files. The default schedule is usually pretty good for most organizations; it's estimated that it should provide about a month's worth of previous versions.

-   The server will be hammered for a bit while the Shadow Copy snapshot is being made. Consequently, taking multiple snapshots during the day might not be such a hot idea. Therefore, you might want to perform fewer snapshots, say, once a day.

Delivering Shadow Copies to the Client

Once you set up the server, you're ready to deploy the client piece. If your clients are already using Windows Vista or Windows XP/Service Pack 2+, they have got the client piece built in, and you can skip this section.

The good news is that the Shadow Copy client is valid for Windows XP (pre-SP2) and even Windows 2000. Although a version of the Shadow Copies client is on the Windows 2003 Server CD, it's better to download the update, which you'll find at `www.microsoft.com/windowsserver2003/downloads/shadowcopyclient.mspx`.

To do the deployment, simply take what you learned in the previous chapter and use it to your advantage:

-   Share the file out on a shared folder or DFS (see the section "Using DFS to Provide Access to Volumes that Contain Shadow Copies" here: `http://tinyurl.com/32tuxj` if you want to use DFS with Shadow Copy).

-   Round up the computers you want to get the Shadow Copy client into an OU.

-   Create a GPO, link it to the OU, and then use GPSI to deploy the MSI file.

Figure 10.30 demonstrates how to assign the application to your Windows 2000 and Windows XP computers.

FIGURE 10.30   You can simply use GPSI to deploy the Shadow Copy client to your Windows 2000 and Windows XP (pre-SP2) machines.

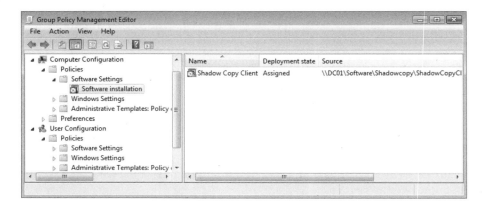

Restoring Files with the Shadow Copies Client

Before you can restore a file, the data must be Shadow Copied at least once, changed, and then Shadow Copied again. This process maintains a point in time of the volume—in its changed state and ready to be reverted to a previous version or restored if it was deleted altogether.

Reverting to a Previous Version of a File

Oftentimes, users inadvertently overwrite their documents with data. As a result, you have now given them the ability to revert to a previous version of the file. To do so, users follow these steps:

1. Open the Documents folder, right-click any file, and choose Properties from the shortcut menu to open the Properties dialog box, as shown in Figure 10.31. And, in Windows Vista, right-clicking a file in most cases will also have a "Restore previous versions" option which goes to the same place.

2. Click the Previous Versions tab.

3. Select the version you want, and then click Open, Copy, or Restore:

    Open (was View pre-Vista)   Clicking Open or View launches the program associated with the file type, and you can view the file. You might be able to make temporary changes in the document, but you cannot save them back to the same place on the server as the original document. You can do a Save As and save the file somewhere else.

    Copy   You can copy the file to an alternate location. A popular location is the Desktop, but any locations that users have access to are equally valid.

Restore   The title of this button is sort of a misnomer. When I think of the word *Restore*, I think of restoring a deleted file, but the file needn't be fully deleted in order to use this option. Clicking this button will cause the selected file to revert to the previous version. Note, however, that it will overwrite the current version. So, use this Restore button with caution, because any changes in the document since a Shadow Copy was performed are deleted.

FIGURE 10.31   After at least one change is preserved, users can revert to a point-in-time file.

Restoring a Previous Version of a File

If a user actually deletes a copy of a preserved file, you or they can restore it. Since we're using Shadow Copies on the volume that houses our redirected My Documents/Documents, we can leverage this magic.

Off the Start Menu, locate My Documents or Documents. Then right-click the user's My Documents folder, choose Properties from the shortcut menu to open the Properties dialog box, and click the Previous Versions tab, as shown in Figure 10.31.

This doesn't seem to work if you're already in Windows Vista's *Documents* and then right-click Favorite Links in the left pane and select Use Previous Versions. Seems like a bug. Seemingly, in Windows Vista this only works when right-clicking directly off the Start Menu.

You'll have the same three options as before: Open, Copy, or Restore. My suggestion is to select View and then drag the file you need to the intended location, as shown in Figure 10.32.

Restore is quite dangerous, actually. It will restore the *entire contents of the folder* upon the live copy. This is not a good idea. In Windows XP, it just lets you do this. In Windows Vista, it gets a little smarter and UAC pops up and asks for administrative credentials before restoring the whole shootin' match, as shown in Figure 10.33.

FIGURE 10.32 You can restore the entire contents of the folder, or just use View to drag and drop the file to be restored to an alternate location.

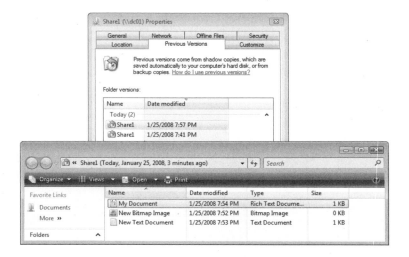

FIGURE 10.33 In Windows Vista, users are prevented from overwriting their entire Documents folder until admin credentials are provided.

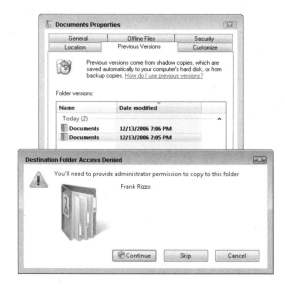

Clicking Copy copies the entirety of the folder to a specific location; this is not all that useful either, as the user might not want to restore the entirety of the point in time of the folder.

Shadow Copies complete the circle of user data protection. Without it, the only data protection (other than normal, regularly scheduled backups) is Offline Files. Offline Files is a good piece of technology, but ultimately not enough if the data on the server is deleted or inadvertently overwritten.

Final Thoughts

The cake might be yummy, but we appreciate the frosting first.

In this chapter, we added some frosting to our already hearty secure and managed desktop cake. We used Hardware Control to keep the bad devices off our network, ensured that users had Printers exactly when they needed them, and made sure we could recover user's junk, I mean, files, using Shadow Copies.

And we did a lot of it using the new Group Policy Preference Extensions. If you haven't gotten your head around all the ins and outs of those, be sure to check out Chapter 10 of the companion book, *Group Policy Fundamentals, Security, and Troubleshooting*, where we give them the full treatment.

In if at this point, you still aren't feeling secure enough, prepare to strap in for a rocket ride to Secureville. See you in the next chapter.

11

Full Lockdown with Windows SteadyState

All the deliverables we've put together thus far using Group Policy, the managed Desktop, and SoftGrid are awesome. Once they've been implemented your IT life won't ever be the same. You'll have more free time to "think the big thoughts" that made IT worth getting into in the first place.

But even with all that massaging using the technology we've put in place, there is still one missing piece. "How do I use Group Policy to put the full lockdown on a machine?" is a question I get a lot.

You learned how to do bits and pieces of this already:

- You can use mandatory profiles to prevent users from preserving their Desktop view.

- You can use Group Policy settings to control the way Windows Explorer behaves.

- You can use custom Group Policy settings to prevent users from seeing specific drive letters. (You can check out www.gpanswers.com/faq/?id=19 for the how-to on this one.)

But is that really enough? It feels like there's a missing piece here. In all cases, we're relying on the operating system to do the honorable thing. For instance, we've got to assume that Windows Explorer is really preventing users from getting to those drive letters. But maybe some other application lets them skate through. And if a user does manage to bust through these protections, what's to stop them from going even further?

NTFS permissions, for one. But depending on the environment, users can still surf to malicious websites, install dubious applications, and perform other insecure actions that affect Windows at its core.

What you need is a way to guarantee that a Desktop can't be messed with. Group Policy can take you only so far. Group Policy's job is to deliver instructions to each operating system component—and we have to hope that component is doing its job.

But imagine if you really could prevent changes to the hard drive. Really prevent them. Then you'd have something. You'd have full lockdown the way you want it—forever.

That's what Windows SteadyState, or just SteadyState for short, or WSS, is all about.

The *Windows SteadyState Handbook* is full of useful information to get you started on your journey. My goal isn't to replicate that manual. This chapter isn't a series of step-by-steps, but rather a collection of guidance, insights, and techniques where the Windows SteadyState manual leaves off. Hopefully, these insights will be useful for you if your machine is joined to the domain or not joined to the domain. To be successful with SteadyState, I suggest using this chapter in conjunction with the *Windows SteadyState Handbook*, FAQ, and other resources:

- SteadyState technical FAQ: `http://tinyurl.com/2hncut`
- *Windows SteadyState Handbook*: `http://tinyurl.com/yvy5sf`
- Microsoft Community support forum for SteadyState: `http://tinyurl.com/3c5jel`
- `www.GPanswers.com/community`

If you've never used SteadyState before, I heartily suggest you initially use the program on a computer that isn't joined to the domain (that's where we'll go first on our tour). Then, try to apply the concepts to your domain-joined computers. That's the second big section. But again, I suggest you work though the first big section first.

So, read through my guidance here; then read through the *Windows SteadyState Handbook* and FAQ second. Together, you'll have all the pieces you need to really achieve a fully locked down system.

Windows SteadyState Concepts and Installation

How would you ensure that you kept a clean machine, and ensure that users can use a "fresh copy" every time they walked up and wanted to use the system? Well, that's what SteadyState does. The idea is simple when you decide to use SteadyState:

- Create the perfect machine with all the software you want. We'll call this the computer *baseline*.
- Cache all hard drive writes (to the volume containing Windows).
- Then, when the computer is rebooted, all those hard drive writes are dumped.

That way, your computer returns to its baseline state—regardless of what was written to the hard drive. But before we install it everywhere, let's make sure we're using the right tool (SteadyState) for the right job. It's not meant to be installed everywhere; just on the "right" machines.

SteadyState Concepts

SteadyState is primarily meant to be loaded upon what are known as *shared computers*—the first version of SteadyState was actually called Shared Computer Toolkit for just that reason. A shared computer means, well, just that: situations where multiple people use the same machine. And the underlying question is: can you trust each and every user on that machine to be on their best behavior?

Let's take a look at some ways that SteadyState can be potentially handy in your environment, figure out why the problem is difficult to solve, and understand how SteadyState can help.

General Machine Shared Computer Use

These are the kinds of computers where many people might "walk up" and use them. These might be found in:

- Airport kiosks and conference centers for Internet access
- Hotels where people use them for airline boarding passes, word processing, printing, and other general use
- Universities/colleges for student machines so they can check their grades, e-mail, and use instant messaging
- Internet cafes for all sorts of good and nefarious uses

And the worst part is, you have no idea as to the quality of the users' "hygiene." They could be downloading the worst virus, rootkit, or spyware known to man. Or, worse, they could just play solitaire all day and tie up the system!

In these cases, you really don't care about the identity of the person using the system. You just want to make sure the system keeps working when they're done using it. These systems might be good candidates for nondomain-joined use. That is, these computers need not be joined to the domain to perform these general-purpose computing tasks.

Internal Corporate Shared Computer Use

There are certainly other times when multiple people could be using the same machine. For instance, the idea of "loaner laptops" is quite popular in many corporations. Just take a machine before you go on that business trip, and it's preloaded with the company software. (We'll talk more about that case later.)

Other areas where you might have multiple people using the same machine in a corporate environment might be the following:

- Cafeteria machines for quick e-mail, eBay, and Amazon.com use during lunch
- Library machines for general access
- Shop floor machines and lab machines to run test equipment
- CD/DVD-ROM burning stations

In these cases, you might want to ensure that the person using the system is authenticated. You'll need to make sure the machine is joined to the domain to ensure that the person using the system is authenticated to Active Directory before allowing them to use the system. But even then, you'll want to make sure that one person's actions don't bring down this shared system.

Why Shared Computing Is Hard

The difficulty in creating a truly stable multiperson environment is easy to understand. Windows really wasn't designed from the ground up to "firewall" one person's actions from another person's actions. Think about all of the things one person could do that could affect all other users on the same machine:

- Something as simple as changing the clock or time zone
- John gets a virus, and so does Mary

- One rootkit affects the whole machine
- Items in the "All Users" profile affect everyone

Moreover, there are certainly some instances where one user might able to view another's information, like his Internet History and Temp files, or other bits and pieces that maybe should be kept secret from other users.

 In XP, users need Admin rights to change the time zone and clock. Windows Vista has adjusted for this. Some tips for allowing an XP user to change the time zone can be found here: http://tinyurl.com/cn4us.

The SteadyState Mission

Really, the goal isn't to totally throw out *any* changes made to the volume holding Windows. Rather, the goal is to throw out unwanted changes. With that in mind, what kinds of changes are wanted?

Well, for one, the applications you, the administrator, install.

And patches; both the kind that you need for your applications and the ones for the operating system itself. And let's not forget Antivirus, antispyware, and other patches too. Just because your system is going to be protected, doesn't mean it can't practice "safe hex" and protect others.

There are four big parts to SteadyState:

Windows Disk Protection (WDP)   This is the actual driver and service that prevents writes from going straight to the system volume. Disk write changes are cached by this service.

Windows Restrictions   This is a quick way to guarantee a baseline of settings, like ensuring that users cannot get to the Control Panel. It's a lot of your favorite Group Policy settings wrapped up into one place.

User Profiles   Similar to the user profiles we've already explored, this gives users their own home on these machines. This allows for interesting scenarios, like a teacher who has more access on one computer than a student does.

System Updates   Even though your system is nigh invulnerable once Windows Disk Protection is enabled, it's still a good idea to get the latest Windows security updates and antivirus updates. WSS has a built-in facility to update these kinds of patches, as well as those you might need for your own applications.

Preparing for Windows SteadyState

We'll start out our SteadyState journey in a nondomain-joined environment. That way we can get a feel for how it works, then take our knowledge and use it in a domain-joined environment if we need to. The following are the various steps to get started:

- Preparing a clean machine and activating Windows
- Using Windows Genuine Advantage (WGA) to "WGA-ify" a machine
- Loading SteadyState

Preparing a New Clean Machine

You'll want to start with as clean a machine as possible. And, that machine must be Windows XP, and not Windows Vista (for now, anyway). Just load the operating system, Service Pack 2 (for Windows XP), last-minute patches from Windows update, and any hotfixes you know you need.

 As of this writing WSS doesn't support Vista, but hopefully by the time you read this book, WSS 2.5 will be out with Windows Vista support. WSS 2.5 will also support SP3 for Windows XP.

After you prepare a clean machine, depending on the version of Windows XP you're licensed for, you may need to Activate it to prove you've got a legitimate copy. This is only necessary for those without a Volume License Key (VLK). You can activate your copy here:

http://www.microsoft.com/windowsxp/evaluation/features/activation.mspx

At this point you're not loading any applications; you're just loading the operating system and updates.

You should, however, install any antivirus or antispyware applications you have and get those updates and signature files as well. Indeed, SteadyState has specific support for three antivirus programs. That means it can automatically detect the presence of and, at a set interval, automatically update the antivirus definitions. Those specific programs are

- TrendMicro OfficeScan 6.5, 7.0, 7.3, 8.0
- CA eTrust 7.0
- McAfee VirusScan

 For TrendMicro support, you will need to install the clnupdnow.exe tool from their website. Also, note that WSS does not support the TrendMicro Internet Security version of their product.

You'll need to be mindful about the amount of free space remaining once everything is fully installed. The Windows Disk Protection service will gobble up about half the remaining free space. You'll need at least 4GB of free space remaining *after everything you want to install is installed*, because WDP requires a minimum of 2GB of space for the cache.

A good baseline is to have about 6–10GB free, so half that space can be used for the cache.

Installing Windows SteadyState

At this point, you've prepared your machine, you've WGA-ified your machine and, right now, it's not joined to any domain. Machines that are not joined to the domain should only have one account (a user who is a member of the Administrator's group and has no password). And because the machine isn't joined to the domain, there is no ability to log onto the domain, as seen in Figure 11.1.

FIGURE 11.1 For our examples, this machine has one user, named SteadyState, for us to use.

For an extra step (which might help with overall speed), you might want to defragment your hard drive before you install SteadyState. We're going to download it first, so if the goal is to put this machine in a shop floor or other area without full Internet connectivity, you could do the defrag once you have the SteadyState on some media (like a USB stick) that you can use for installation.

At this point, let's get the SteadyState application on your machine. The home page for SteadyState is at `www.microsoft.com/windows/products/winfamily/sharedaccess/default.mspx` (`http://tinyurl.com/ytknan`), and the specific download page for SteadyState is at `http://tinyurl.com/376exg`.

I was lucky to get a beta version of SteadyState to use for this book. By the time you get this, SteadyState version 2.5 will be out, so be sure to get that version when exploring this chapter.

The installation is pretty uneventful. The longest part of the installation occurs while SteadyState checks to see if the machine is WGA-ified, as seen in Figure 11.2. It doesn't need to be on the Internet to do this; this all happens locally. When installed, you should see a message similar to Figure 11.3.

FIGURE 11.2   Sometimes pressing the Validation button could keep you waiting for a moment or two.

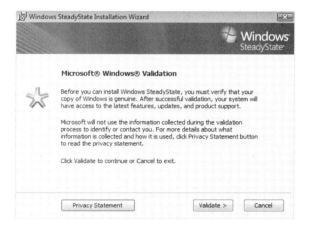

FIGURE 11.3   A successful SteadyState installation

In the Installation Successful dialog, click Next and you should get the choice to install Windows Live Toolbar. The default is to install it, but for our examples, I'm going to leave it out. You can see it, though, in Figure 11.4.

At the final dialog window, click Finish to complete the installation.

FIGURE 11.4 For our examples, we won't be installing the Windows Live Toolbar.

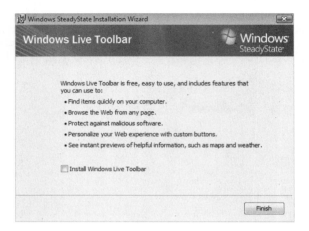

Configuring Windows SteadyState (for Nondomain-Joined Computers)

Again, I'd really like for you to get started with your SteadyState tour on a machine that's not domain-joined. Go ahead and log on with the local Windows XP Administrator account. Then start out by selecting Start ➢ All Programs ➢ Windows SteadyState.

When you do, you'll be able to get started using the SteadyState console. As you can see in Figure 11.5, there are various things to do here. Let's explore what it takes to get a minimal configuration going for your quick testing.

You'll want to first deal with the User Settings, then Set Computer Restrictions, Schedule Software Updates, and finally Protect the Hard Disk. The SteadyState Getting Started manual is also there for reference if you need it.

User Settings

In nondomain-joined environments, you need to add a user. This is done in several steps.

Creating a Public User

You may want to call this user Public or Walkup. You won't want to use Guest because it's a special system name. In my examples, I'll use Public with a password of public, as you can see in Figure 11.6.

FIGURE 11.5   SteadyState is running and has a great built-in help.

FIGURE 11.6   We're going to create a new user called Public.

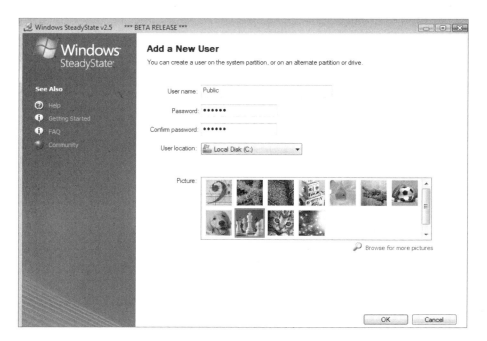

We'll talk about the User Location a little later when we talk about Multi-Tier access environments, like in a Teacher/Student scenarios.

When you're ready, click OK to set up precisely how this user should react on this system.

Setting the User Settings

Windows SteadyState Handbook and the FAQ do a pretty good job explaining these areas, so I won't bore you.

However, one further recommendation I'd like to share is to use Low Restrictions while installing software, then slowly increase the restriction level while testing each application. Keep in mind that some restrictions may have unexpected consequences that impact the usability or functionality of an application. In that case, you might have to back off a little bit until you get it just right. When you finally have the maximum restrictions that still enable you to do the work you've set up for this machine, stop. You've got it. We'll briefly discuss application installation strategy around the corner.

Let's look at each of the main tabs within the SteadyState User settings and see what they can do for us.

General You can see this tab in Figure 11.7. Here you can set things like a session timer to forcefully log users out before they hog up the machine all day, or to log out when idle.

FIGURE 11.7 The User Settings has multiple tabs to configure. Don't select "Lock profile to prevent the user from making permanent changes" right away.

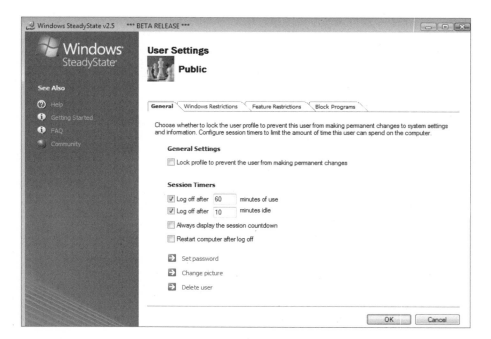

Also, remember that the computer only flushes its WDP cache during a reboot—not a logoff. But you can check the "Restart computer after log off" check box to force the machine to flush the cache. There's also a "Lock profile to prevent the user from making permanent changes" check box, which we'll discuss later.

For now, I heartily recommend not changing these settings until you've read the "Application Installation Strategy (for Nondomain-Joined Windows SteadyState Machines)" section.

Windows Restrictions   You can see this tab in Figure 11.8. Here you can change a lot of look-and-feel settings including which Windows Explorer bits and pieces are available for use. You can also hide drive letters. However, these drive letters are only hidden if the application honors the standard shell interfaces. You might have an application which uses its own interfaces; in that case, you're not protected from seeing the drives.

FIGURE 11.8   Select the restrictions and the drives you want to hide. You might not want to select "High restrictions" right away.

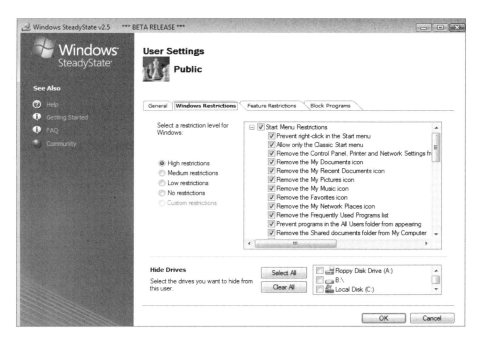

There are High, Medium, and Low presets, plus a "Custom restrictions" button where you can make your own restrictions as you see fit. The idea here is that you may want to start low and go higher depending on your needs. For now, set this to "No restrictions."

Feature Restrictions   Here you'll find restrictions that apply to Internet Explorer and Microsoft Office, like preventing printing from Internet Explorer, restricting web access to specific web pages, and other interesting options. This can be seen in Figure 11.9. For now, set this to "No restrictions."

FIGURE 11.9 Select the Feature Restrictions you want to enable. You may not want to select "High restrictions" right away.

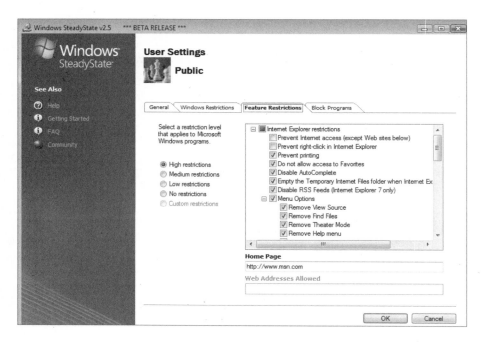

Block Programs This uses a local Software Restriction Policy to secure any applications you like. Sure, you'll be locking down the Start Menu, so they shouldn't be able to find applications. But in Figure 11.10, you can see the Block Programs tab, which provides an extra safety gate should they stumble across an application that looks tempting. SteadyState populates the Block Programs list with programs (and shortcuts to programs) found in the common programs folder (typically `C:\Documents and Settings\All Users\Start Menu\Programs`) and the common Desktop folder (typically `C:\Documents and Settings\All Users\Desktop`).

You can Browse for additional applications that SteadyState did not automatically populate. For now, do not name any additional programs or specifically perform any blocking.

Once you're done, click OK. You should be back at the Windows SteadyState main screen.

A nice touch is that when you're ultimately finished with your user account or accounts, you can export them. That way, if you create The perfect Public account, you can export it here, then import it on other SteadyState systems without having to duplicate your efforts on multiple machines.

FIGURE 11.10   WSS uses Software Restriction Policies to block specific applications.

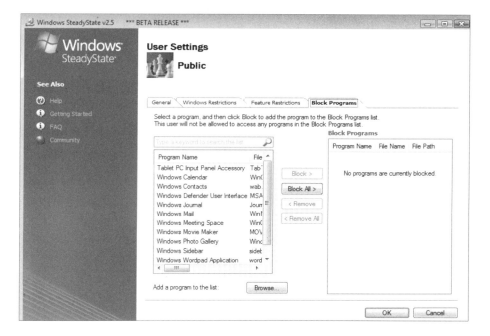

Global Computer Settings

There are three big things you can do within Global Computer Settings. And the name does say it all. That is, the settings here affect all users of the machine. So far, we've talked about the Public account (some standard random user) using the machine. But there are certainly other scenarios, as well. Indeed, later we'll be talking about the Student and Teacher scenario where one user should have more power than another on the box.

But Global Computer Settings affect all users equally.

The three big actions here are named "Set Computer Restrictions," "Schedule Software Updates," and "Protect the Hard Disk."

Set Computer Restrictions

As stated, these settings affect everyone. Some settings are turned on automatically by default, as seen in Figure 11.11.

The most interesting setting here is "Remove the Administrator user name from the Welcome screen." Indeed, right underneath this setting, it's clearly stated, "Press CTRL+ALT+DEL twice to log on to accounts not listed," like the local Administrator account. Be sure to remember this in two weeks after you've set up SteadyState then need to make a settings change.

Schedule Software Updates

Here is where you set up your daily updates. You can see this screen in Figure 11.12.

FIGURE 11.11 Computer restrictions affect all users on the machine. Be careful when selecting "Prevent users from creating folders and files on drive C:\".

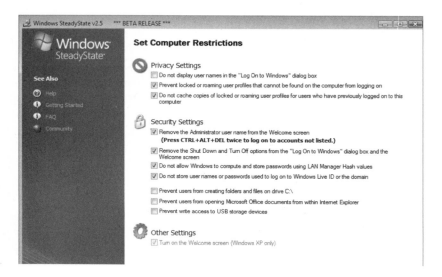

FIGURE 11.12 You can set when to perform updates for Windows, Windows Defender, and any detected security programs and/or to do custom updates.

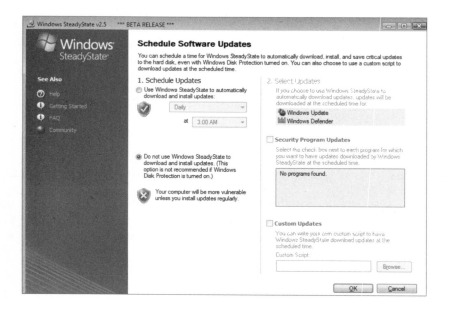

Let's examine this page further, and I'll also share some neat tips and show you what's going on under the hood here.

The Schedule Software Updates Options

There are four sections on this page:

Schedule Updates   Here you can schedule your frequency of Windows Updates.

Select Updates   Windows Update (the little world with the Windows logo) is available and also Microsoft Defender if that's installed, too. Those are the only Microsoft-specific updates available here.

Security Program Updates   As previously stated, SteadyState specifically supports three anti-virus vendors for automatic definitions updates. If any supported program is found, you can choose to update those at the appointed time, as well.

Custom Updates   Here is where you can enter in a script of your choice to do any custom updating. Perhaps you have a shop floor machine that needs the latest daily statistics to do its job, or some other custom update to another program. You can specify a batch file here (that doesn't ask for input) to be run. This runs in the SYSTEM account context, so you should be able to do just about anything you want here.

While it's possible to enter a local path for a script (like `c:\myscript.bat`), I suggest you enter in a `\\server\share\myscript.bat` combination. That way, if you ever want to change what the script is doing, you can just change it on the server and not worry about trotting out to the machine, turning off Windows Disk Protection, updating the script, then turning back on Windows Disk Protection. Oy, what a pain.

If you use a script on a server, it's a no-brainer to update.

> WSS checks to ensure that a custom script has ACLs placed on it so that members of the Users group cannot write it, well, rewrite it, really. That way, they cannot introduce a security problem by inadvertently specifying a custom script that any user could modify.

The Scheduled Updates Process

We'll assume you have Windows Disk Protection enabled and now the appointed time for Scheduled Updates occurs. So what exactly happens at the scheduled time?

At the appointed time, the following occurs:

1. Any users currently logged on are logged off. A pop-up message like the one seen in Figure 11.13 comes up when the time approaches.

2. Windows reboots to clear out any of the day's changes.

3. Windows prevents users from logging on. A message appears after reboot like the one seen in Figure 11.14.

4. SteadyState automatically changes the state of Windows Disk Protection mode to "Retain all changes permanently" (but just temporarily). (See the additional notes at the end of this section for other situations.)

5. The following security scripts/actions are run:

- Windows installs the latest Windows Updates (via Windows Update or WSUS connection).

- Your Custom Update script runs, if present.

- Windows then installs any antivirus updates (only those automatically supported from the aforementioned three vendors).

6. Windows Disk Protection mode returns to "Remove all Changes at Restart."

7. Windows reboots.

8. Users are able to log on again.

FIGURE 11.13 Users are forced off the system at Scheduled Update time.

FIGURE 11.14 Users are informed that they cannot log on until SteadyState is finished with its updates.

Each security action and script is allowed to run for 30 minutes by default. If the script takes longer than that, WSS will stop waiting for it and move on to the next action or script. If this happens, an event is written to the event log. The timeout value is configurable in the Registry: [HKLM\System\CurrentControlSet\Services\Windows SteadyState\Parameters] "UpdateScriptTimeLimitMinutes"=dword:30.

Daily updates occur whether or not Windows Disk Protection is currently enabled. If WDP is not in use, or if WDP is in "Retain changes temporarily" mode, the WDP mode is not changed. In the case of "Retain changes temporarily" the downloaded updates simply remain in the cache. When that mode expires, the updates are discarded and the next update cycle will download them again.

What if WSUS Is Used?

You can use Group Policy to set WSUS settings for this machine. And, if you do, the WSUS settings will take precedence. But note that WSUS will *not* turn off Windows Disk Protection or change the mode.

So, in order to use WSUS, you have to time it perfectly to coincide with the window of time when Windows Disk Protection is off. If you miss the window (that is, you write WSUS updates during at a time that WDP is set to discard changes), the WSUS changes will be lost.

Therefore, I recommend that you don't use WSUS with WSS machines, and just stick with each WSS machine phoning home to the mother ship to get the individual updates it needs at your specified time.

The power-conscious admin can have the system set to go into Suspend mode (suspend-to-RAM; not hibernate/suspend-to-disk). At the prescribed time, SteadyState will automatically wake the machine to download and apply updates. WSS won't automatically suspend the machine again when this is done, but will instead rely on the system's power management settings (e.g., sleep after 60 minutes of inactivity) to put the machine in Suspend mode again.

Protect the Hard Disk

By default, Windows Disk Protection is not working for you. That is, it's off. And you (and your users) can write anything to the hard drive (provided they have permissions). This is good and bad.

It's good because you can still install software (and write those changes to the disk). It's bad because during this time if you were to turn over this machine to a user, they could do some damage.

We'll be reviewing Application Installation Strategy next, so let's get familiar with the options on this page:

Off   If Windows Disk Protection is turned on, turning it Off will delete the cache and force a reboot of the computer. At that point, your system is unprotected. Note that the other restrictions, like User and other Global Computer Settings are still in effect. It's just that Windows Disk Protection isn't working for you.

On: Remove all changes at restart   This is the default when you click "On." Again, the magic only happens at restart time. That is, the cache is only cleaned during a reboot, not at a logoff. This is the normal operating mode for Windows Disk Protection. See the Real World Scenario "Fun with Windows Disk Protection (and How to Further Protect Yourself)" for a quick guide to what not to do to a regular machine, and to see what's possible with a machine with Windows Disk Protection turned on.

On: Retain changes temporarily   In this mode, your users will feel like it's a regular machine (except for the User restrictions and Global Computer settings). That's because with the proper permissions, it'll feel like they're able to install software, save documents to the hard drive, and reboot the machine with no problems at all. That is, until the expiration date and time. Then, the next reboot after the expiration date will simply flush those changes down the drain. This is great if you're setting up a room of machines, say, for a three-day conference and want to flush all the data on the fourth day.

On: Retain all changes permanently   In this mode, changes made to the disk exist in the cache file until the next reboot. At that time, the changes are written out to disk and the system reboots to finalize those changes. This mode is almost like you've turned off WDP, except that you haven't spend the extra time to delete the cache file. You might use this mode to install a lot of software, then, return to "On: Retain all changes at restart" when you're done installing all of your software and want to put the full smackdown on again.

 Real World Scenario

Fun with Windows Disk Protection (and How to Further Protect Yourself)

If you haven't turned on Windows Disk Protection on a machine yet, you really should try it out. It's amazing. Indeed, you can do some ludicrously damaging actions to your Windows XP machine and still survive the damage.

That's because Windows Disk Protection is silently caching all disk writes. So, you can do things you'd never want to do, like:

- Stop and disable every service.

- Blow away all the key boot files in the root, like the boot.ini and NTLDR.

- Delete the entire contents of the Windows directory.

And more. And as long as you can find the Reset button on the machine, it'll survive.

However, what's really important to note about these scenarios is that Windows is still running when the damage occurs. In other words, Windows is active, the Windows Disk Protection service is cookin' along and saving your bacon.

But there can be scenarios where you're *not* protected. Specifically, if you boot an alternate copy of Windows on the same machine (say, a dual boot machine), or boot from Windows PE or Bart PE or a Linux Rescue Boot CD. In all these cases, you'll be able to access the file system outside of Windows Disk Protection's normal control.

With that in mind, be sure to also physically secure your machines so your little attackers (students, children, your boss, etc.) cannot boot from a CD-ROM or USB key. Do this by physically locking up the box and/or via BIOS control with a password.

Only then, when you know Windows is booting, can you be sure you're protected.

Oh, and they can't bypass Windows Disk Protection by booting into Safe Mode either. They would need to know the local Administrator password because SteadyState disables all other accounts in Safe Mode.

And only *you* have that account information, right?

Application Installation Strategy (for Nondomain-Joined Windows SteadyState Machines)

Now that you've got a feel for all the settings here, let's talk about how to best deal with installing packages.

Installing Packages before Turning on Windows Disk Protection

Earlier, I suggested that you not turn on any (or many) user restrictions for the Public account, and that you should also be careful with the Global Computer Restrictions that affect everyone. And what I mean is that, sure, you'll want to turn them all on to get the ultimate lockdown. But before you do that, you have a hard job to do: installing applications on this machine.

And if you crank down the thumbscrews too early in the application installation process, you're simply not going to be able to effectively install anything. Some applications might have to be installed as the user (indeed, in some instances you may need temporarily to give them elevated rights during the install). But, if you look closely at Figure 11.11, there's an option called "Prevent users from creating folders and files on drive C:\" Sounds like a great idea… and it is. But only when you're ready to turn it on!

So, don't crank down the settings until you've tested your applications as the Public user. Then, ease into some restrictions. Test some more. Crank down some more. Test some more.

Additionally, don't forget that some applications you'll install as the administrator, but you want the user to be able to run them. That's fine (if the application supports that). But don't forget the Public user might not have the icon to launch the application in his profile. You might need to do a little finessing here. Just right-click Start and select "Explore all users" to start moving icons around to the Public user's profile.

For more information about the ins and outs of profiles, be sure to read Chapter 2.

Finally, when you're sure you've got all the applications you want to install locally ready to go, turn on Windows Disk Protection.

Installing and Upgrading Packages after Turning on Windows Disk Protection

So now that Windows Disk Protection is in full force, things get a little bit harder. When you log on as the Administrative user, you do, thankfully, get a little reminder about Windows Disk Protection, as seen in Figure 11.15.

FIGURE 11.15 SteadyState demonstrates that Windows Disk Protection is enabled at logon time for administrators.

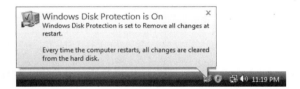

This warning is a big one. The idea is that if you were to, say, install DogFoodMaker 5.0 (an upgrade from DogFoodMaker 4.0) and then you reboot, you'd lose all your changes and be back to square 1, er, DogFoodMaker 4.0.

So, here's the plan. Install or upgrade your application. Hopefully you can do this as the local Administrator. If you need to do the installation or upgrade as the Public user, this gets a little more complicated because you might have to back out some of your restrictions first.

Finally, once you're done there, test as the Public user. But don't reboot!

Indeed, whenever you try to even log off as the Administrator, you get the pop-up shown in Figure 11.16 (for Windows XP) and Figure 11.17 for Windows Vista.

The correct option while you're still installing, tweaking, or configuring is "Continue without saving changes." This will log you off as the Administrator and you can test out the Public user's ability to use the application.

Finally, when you're done with your duty, log back in as the Administrator. Be sure to turn back on any user restrictions (or Global Computer restrictions) you backed off from during the installation or upgrade. See the Real World Scenario called "Making WSS Application Installation Even Easier" for a tip from the WSS team.

Finally, click "Save changes and restart the computer." When you do, the computer will reboot and during the reboot, you'll see your changes being embraced by the system (as seen in Figure 11.18). The system will reboot one more time before users are able to log on again.

FIGURE 11.16   The Windows Disk Protection shutdown dialog for Windows XP

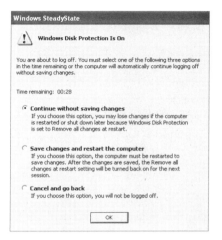

FIGURE 11.17   The Windows Disk Protection shutdown dialog for Windows Vista

FIGURE 11.18   You can see when SteadyState is committing changes during reboot.

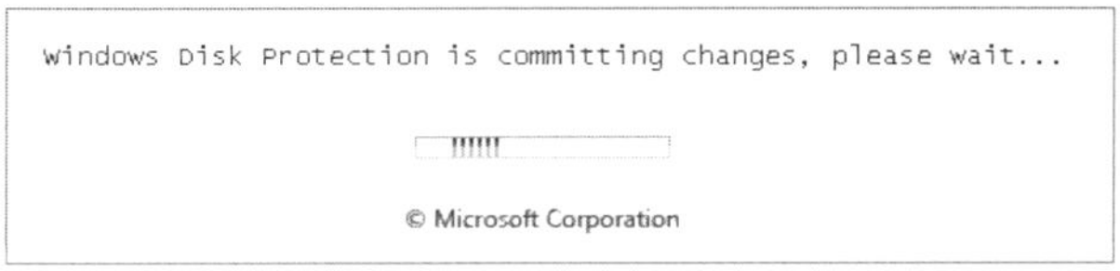

Windows Disk Protection is committing changes, please wait...

© Microsoft Corporation

You can combine this methodology with the command-line /import and /export functions to ease making changes to multiple users.

Real World Scenario

Making WSS Application Installation Even Easier

Here's a suggestion for easing the pain of re-restricting a user after installing software.

First, create a new user named Unrestricted and select No Restrictions for both Windows and Program restrictions. Export this profile as unrestricted.ssu. Now delete the Unrestricted user. Next, export the user you want to unrestrict (e.g., to public.ssu).

At this point you have two important SSU files, one with no restrictions and one with the restrictions you want to enforce.

Before you install your software, use the Import function to import unrestricted.ssu on top of the user Public.

Now Public is unrestricted and you can install software or adjust the user's environment at will. Once you have your machine set up just so, it's time to log back in as Administrator and import public.ssu on top of user Public.

This restores the original restrictions in place on Public!

You can learn more about exporting and importing from the WSS guide.

It's not super easy to just install applications anymore—not when User and Computer restrictions are putting the hurt on. And it gets even harder when Windows Disk Protection is enabled, because you have to specifically remember to log back in as the admin and embrace the changes.

Multi-Tier Access Environments

Now that we've set up our Public user, you may want to proceed with some advanced configurations. There are lots of possible ideas here. Think Parents vs. Kids: Who should be able to get to what websites and access what files. Shop Foreman vs. Worker Bee: Who should be able to access what program.

Or, something simple like Teacher vs. Student where the teacher has access to GradeMaker 3.0 and the students have KidPro 6.0. You get the idea.

This whole idea is called Multi-Tier Access because the student gets one level of privilege and the teacher gets another.

Setting User Profiles for Multi-Tier Access Environments

As you're thinking of these scenarios, you may want to add additional users to the SteadyState system. You saw how to do this earlier in Figure 11.6. But, in Figure 11.19, you can see how to add, say, a user called Teacher. Note that I'm saving the Teacher profile's User Location to a drive that isn't the C: drive. That's because Windows Disk Protection will completely wipe out any changes to the C: drive on reboot (as its default behavior).

The idea is simple: If the teacher stores something as simple as say, an Internet Explorer bookmark, it's not being written to the C: drive. So, if you put the profiles of the users who need this kind of capability on what's known as a Persistent disk (in my case, the E: drive) you'll be able to maintain the profile changes even with Windows Disk Protection in full force.

FIGURE 11.19 You can have other users who do save state if you store their profiles on alternate drives.

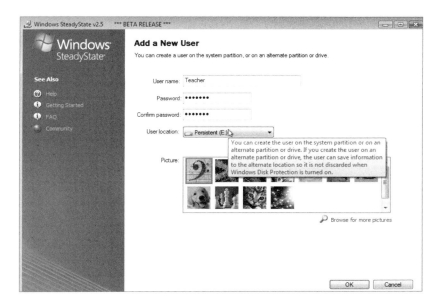

Persistent Storage Space for Your Users

To continue our example a little bit, let's say the teacher uses GradeMaker 3.0 and needs to save data directly to the hard drive. Again, saving data on the C: drive is a bad idea, because upon reboot, those grade changes will be gone.

In this situation, we want to use a persistent drive. Then, it's an easy matter to carve out some space for the user for them to save data and such.

So, assuming you have a second partition available to save persistent data to, say, the E: drive, just create a new directory. In this example, I'm creating a writeable area for the Teacher account. Then, right-click, select Properties, and select the Security tab.

If you don't see the Security tab, it's likely that you have Simple File Sharing enabled. To disable it, in Windows Explorer click Tools ➢ Folder Options then select View and uncheck "Use simple file sharing (Recommended)."

Depending on how your drive is configured, the usual default is Everyone:Full Control. Your goal is to set up the permissions such that only the teacher (and maybe the Administrators group) has access to this directory.

You may have to uninherit permissions from the parent, clear out any entries, then specifically add the teacher. The end result will appear similar to what you see in Figure 11.20.

FIGURE 11.20 Set rights on a directory on the E: drive where only teachers (and maybe Administrators) have access.

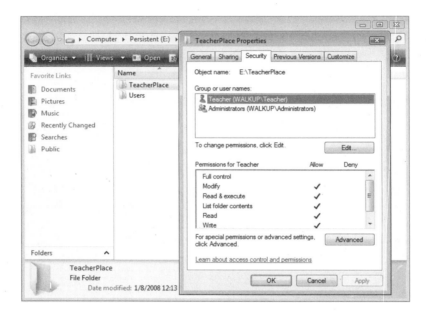

So with the Teacher profile writable on the E: drive and the Teacher's data also writeable to the E: drive, you've got an ideal platform to maintain multiple users with different purposes on this machine.

Configuring Windows SteadyState (for Domain-Joined Computers)

Before we continue, you may be asking yourself: why would I even need SteadyState in a domain-joined environment? Sure, it makes sense to have a way to restrict computers like we just did in a nondomain-joined environment.

But with the power of Group Policy, don't we have everything we need for a real lockdown? In fact, the answer is no. Group Policy doesn't make any consideration for the actual security or sanctity of the hard drive contents. Group Policy's goal is to *deliver* settings.

SteadyState's Windows Disk Protection is the real key here to preventing changes from any evil software from making their way (permanently) onto your hard drive. With that in mind, here are the basic steps we'll perform for my WSS domain-joined recipe:

1. Join the computer to the domain and move the computer to an appropriate OU.

2. Create a GPO that will affect all users who use the computer. You'll then control Windows Disk Protection.

   - In WSS 2.0, you'll need to turn on the Windows Disk Protection manually, but then you can remotely change the state.

   - In WSS 2.5, you'll be able to remotely turn on Windows Disk Protection and also, naturally, remotely change the state.

3. Tweak the machines so a logoff equals a reboot (optional).

   Then, later, we'll remotely:

1. Deploy and update software applications.

2. Tweak software update settings.

Windows SteadyState Handbook actually has a whole section dedicated to domain-joined computers. And while they do a good job describing some of the issues, some issues require a little Group Policy finesse, which we will address here.

In my consulting practice I find that most clients want the following to happen:

- Have the user walk up and log on with their own username and password.

- Use the machine they need with their own assigned software plus whatever software is special on the machine.

- Log off and be done.

In the nondomain-joined scenarios, we used a public user for our machines. That's great— except that's not how I usually see people wanting to use SteadyState. Like I said, most people seem to want to leverage their own credentials to log onto a machine, not some generic public account. The SteadyState Handbook suggests that you might want to create an Active Directory user account named something like Public then leave a little sticky note next to the computer saying "Use the Public account with password of Public to log onto this machine."

If you really want this setup, use Active Directory Users and Computers to prevent the Public account from only logging onto domain-joined SteadyState computers, as seen in Figure 11.21.

But in many environments, that's still considered insecure computing (for good reasons). You might want to enable auditing to see who actually logged on and used that machine for the day. And if you use a generic account named Public, you won't know what Fred was doing on the system.

While *Windows SteadyState Handbook* is a really excellent document, I don't necessarily agree with all their recommendations. Meanwhile, there are also some important missing pieces when dealing with domain-joined computers—which we'll go into, as well.

With that in mind, let's walk through my suggested way to set up SteadyState in a domain environment. I would still encourage you to read *Windows SteadyState Handbook* (starting on page 64 of the SteadyState 2.5 Handbook) for their domain-joined recipe, in case there's some extra insights you discover using their method with or without my method.

FIGURE 11.21   Use Active Directory Users and Computers to ensure that specific accounts can only log onto specific domain-joined machines.

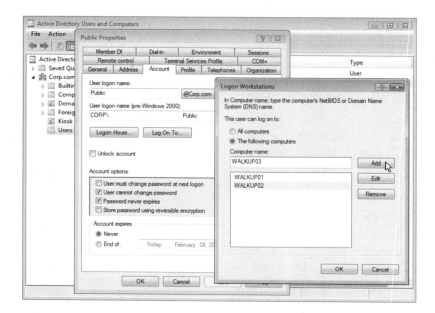

Joining the Computer to the Domain and Moving It into Its OU

While we'll be working with one domain-joined computer, we'll assume you'd do the same thing for one computer that you would for multiple computers. For instance, if you had 30 CD/DVD-ROM burning stations you would join them to the domain. Then, you'd move them to an OU named for that purpose.

In my example, I'll call my OU Kiosk. In Figure 11.22, you can see WALKUP moved to a newly created OU named Kiosk.

FIGURE 11.22   Put your SteadyState computers into a specific OU.

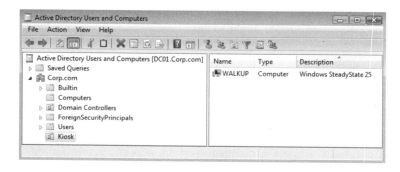

Create GPOs That Will Affect All Users Who Use the Computer

SteadyState ships with an ADM template that performs just about all the Windows Restrictions and General Restrictions you saw earlier in Figures 11.7 and 11.8. It's called SCTSettings.adm, and the name is rather confusing. You can find it within C:\Program Files\Windows SteadyState\ADM.

To be successful with the SCTSettings.adm, we need to perform three big steps:

- Creating the GPO and linking it to the right place.
- Setting restrictions using the ADM template.
- Guaranteeing settings for all users on the computers in the Kiosk OU.

So, let's get started.

 SCT is the Shared Computer Toolkit, the old name for Windows SteadyState.

Creating and Linking the GPO and Setting up Restrictions for SteadyState

Our goal is to use the ADM template to control our users on our machines. Therefore, use the GPMC, and create a new GPO linked to the Kiosk OU, as seen in Figure 11.23.

Then, edit the GPO. When you do, you'll want to add in the SCTsettings.adm template. Do this by going to User Configuration ➢ Policies, right-clicking the words Administrative Templates, and selecting Add/Remove Templates, as seen in Figure 11.24.

FIGURE 11.23   Start out by linking a GPO to an OU containing domain-joined SteadyState computers (like Kiosk).

FIGURE 11.24   Add the SCTsettings.adm file.

Click Add, and locate the SCTsettings.adm file, which is part of the SteadyState installation. Once it's added (as seen in Figure 11.25), click Close.

FIGURE 11.25   Adding the SCTsettings ADM template to a GPO

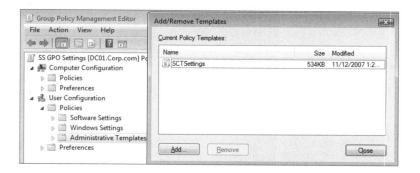

Checking out the *SCTsettings.adm* Restrictions

Now, you'll see a new node under User Configuration ➤ Policies ➤ Administrative Templates ➤ Classic Administrative Templates (ADM) called All Windows SteadyState Restrictions, as seen in Figure 11.26.

At this point, you're welcome to explore all the settings available here. Note that many are "copies" of settings found elsewhere within the Group Policy Management Editor. That is, the settings are originally found in other ADM templates. However, they're rounded up here in a nice little "greatest hits" package for your use.

FIGURE 11.26 SCTsettings.adm contains basically the same restrictions that SteadyState does.

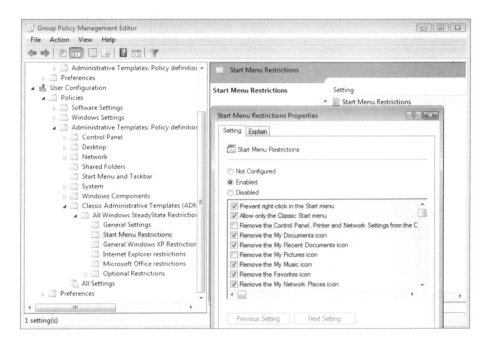

You don't actually have to have SteadyState loaded on the target computer to make use of most of the settings. You could use the "greatest hits" template on machines anywhere in Active Directory—not just SteadyState machines. They're simply packaged up nicely for your use in any way you see fit.

Note how in some cases, like in Figure 11.26, there is a single policy setting named "Start Menu Restrictions." It doesn't just control one little item, it controls a gaggle of items. Once Enabled, you can check or uncheck the various little settings it controls.

You can get yourself into trouble quickly here with all these restrictions. I would start small, and gradually increase your protections until you feel you've restricted enough.

Now, you may have noticed that the settings are contained on the User configuration side of things. And, if you've read the companion book, *Group Policy Fundamentals, Security, and Troubleshooting* (Sybex, 2008), specifically Chapter 2, "Managing Group Policy with the GPMC," you'll recall that User-side settings cannot affect computers. And that's the situation we have here. We put the computer account into the Kiosk OU and now we're linking a GPO that contains only User-side settings on this OU (which only contains computers).

With only this setup (and nothing more) we will never see the results we desire. That's because computers cannot pick up User-side settings. By default, that is. But we can adjust that with Group Policy Loopback Processing, as seen in the next section.

 We'll assume you have a handle on Group Policy Loopback Processing and what it does. So, we're just going to blast through the required steps here to make our wishes come true. For more information, come to www.GPanswers.com/book to get your own copy of *Group Policy Fundamentals, Security, and Troubleshooting* to catch up. You'll find Loopback Processing detailed in Chapter 4, "Group Policy Processing Behavior," in the section entitled "Group Policy Loopback Processing."

One other quick note here about the template. It doesn't specifically help create the default Software Restriction Policies (SRP) you saw earlier when we were running SteadyState in a nondomain-joined environment. If you want to re-create the same level of SRP, you'll need to do that manually. *Windows SteadyState Handbook* (page 71 in the current SteadyState 2.5 beta handbook) has a section named "Duplicating Software Restrictions by Using Software Restrictions Policies in Windows XP." Use the knowledge there to re-create them.

 We'll assume that you have a handle on Software Restriction Policy and what it does. If you need more information on SRP, check out Chapter 7 of *Group Policy Fundamentals, Security, and Troubleshooting* in the "Software Restriction Policy" section.

Creating a Loopback Group Policy Object

Our goal is to make all users who use the WALKUP computer contained within the Kiosk OU get the same settings. To do this, we'll use Group Policy Loopback in Replace mode.

I suggest you create a new GPO to perform the Loopback function; though it's certainly possible and acceptable to use the same GPO you created earlier when you put in your SteadyState restrictions.

In Figure 11.27, I've created a GPO named Loopback Enable and linked it to the Kiosk OU.

Then edit the GPO you created. You want to traverse to Computer Configuration ➤ Policies ➤ Administrative Templates ➤ System ➤ Group Policy and select **User Group Policy loopback processing mode**. Then Enable the policy setting and set the mode to Replace, as shown in Figure 11.28.

This will dictate that everyone who uses a computer in the Kiosk OU will get the exact same user-side settings.

FIGURE 11.27   Set a GPO which enables Loopback:Replace mode upon your SteadyState Kiosk computers.

FIGURE 11.28   Ensure that you have a GPO set to Loopback:Replace.

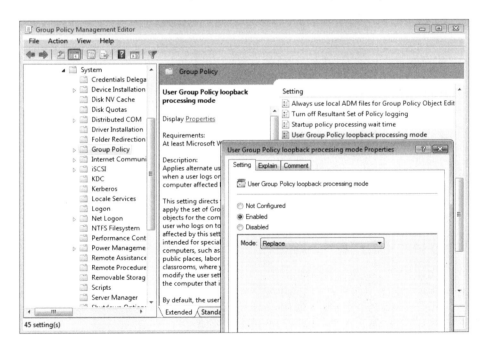

Testing Your Group Policy

At this point, log on as, well, anyone in your domain, including the domain administrator, to your WALKUP machine. The restrictions you put in place should be evident, regardless of who walks up to the WALKUP machine. You can see the results in Figure 11.29.

FIGURE 11.29   A SteadyState machine with some various restrictions enabled

If you don't want the administrator to be restricted by the SteadyState Group Policy you created, you can use Group Policy filtering to have this GPO pass over the administrator so he's unaffected.

> To learn more about Group Policy filtering, check out the companion book's Chapter 2 in the "Filtering the Scope of Group Policy Objects" section. You can pick up a copy at www.GPanswers.com/book.

Turning on Windows Disk Protection

Getting the machine just right is definitely going to take some time. But, let's jump ahead a little bit and assume you're perfectly happy with the way the machine reacts when any user logs on. At this point, you're ready to turn on WDP and enable the full lockdown. There are two ways you can do this: manually or remotely.

Manually Turning on WDP

You'll do this the same way you did earlier. Just log on as the local Administrator (or domain Administrator) and run the SteadyState administration console. Then, select "Protect the Hard Disk" and select On ➢ Remove all changes at restart.

Remotely Turning on WDP

The whole point of having a domain-joined machine is that you don't have to run out and touch it often, if ever. If you've deployed this domain-joined machine to China, it might be hard to reach out and touch the machine to turn on the hard disk protection.

There are two ways to reach out and touch the machine if you need to: via the command line and via script.

Turn Windows Disk Protection On or Off via the Command Line

The ability to turn WDP on and off is only available with Windows SteadyState 2.5. To turn it on, use the command

```
sctui.exe /EnableWDP
```

then reboot to have it take effect.

To turn it off, use the command

```
sctui.exe /DisableWDP
```

then reboot to have it take effect.

Use a tool like psExec from Microsoft (`http://tinyurl.com/24x3cu`) to run the command remotely (provided you have administrative privileges).

Turn Windows Disk Protection On or Off via Script

You can also use a WMI script to remotely affect WDP. That is, from your machine you can send a signal to the WALKUP computer (or any computer with SteadyState installed) to turn on, turn off, or flush the contents of the cache. The one trick, however, is that the target machine needs to be configured such that administrators can send signals to it through the network. And, because Windows XP (and Vista and Windows Server 2008) all have the firewall turned on by default, you'll either need to turn that target machine's firewall off, or at least poke the required holes for remote administration.

For more information about tweaking Windows XP (and Vista's) firewall settings (including how to open up specific ports for remote administration), be sure to read Chapters 6 and 7 of the companion book, *Group Policy Fundamentals, Security, and Troubleshooting*, which deal with security and network functions. Come to www.GPanswers.com/book for more information.

Assuming that the firewall is correctly configured on the target machine, you can use the sample script listed here (based on the one at `http://support.microsoft.com/kb/938335`) to remotely turn on WDP—without ever having to actually touch the machine.

```
' WDP_Control.CurrentStatus will return one of these values:
const WDP_ACTIVE  = 0
const WDP_PASSIVE = 1

' WDP_Control.CurrentMode will return or can be set to:
const WDP_MODE_DISCARD = 0
const WDP_MODE_PERSIST = 1
const WDP_MODE_COMMIT  = 2


' Identify the computer to manage.  "." means the local computer.
strComputer= "."

set objWbemServices = GetObject ("winmgmts:\\" & strComputer & "\root\wmi")
set setWdpObjects   = objWbemServices.ExecQuery ("SELECT * FROM WDP_Control")

for each objWdp in setWdpObjects
   objWdp.CurrentMode  = WDP_MODE_COMMIT
   objWdp.Put_
next
```

We'll also have this script available for download at GPanswers.com in the Book Resources section for this chapter.

Deciding When to Clean Up

Because WDP only flushes the cache (and cleans up) during a reboot, you might want to think about when you want the clean up to occur. Perhaps you may want to clean up once a day at 3:00 a.m. or something. The only issue with that is that during the whole day junk is being loaded on the machine. So, the machine isn't ever clean for anyone except that very first person of the day. That might be okay, but you might also want to reboot during every logoff to ensure squeaky cleanliness for everyone's experience. Of course, that means it's going to take a bit longer to get started.

I'm going to suggest three potential solutions on how you might want to clean up the computer when it's joined to a domain.

In a nondomain-joined environment, you can use "Restart computer after log off" in the General tab of the Public profile. The only challenge is that this will reboot the computer every single time. You might be able to use these alternate techniques if you'd like to help mitigate that issue.

Option 1: Set a Scheduled Task to Restart the Machine

In both cases, you're going to use a helper program that comes with SteadyState called ForceLogoff.exe (which reboots the computer as well).

A quick walkthrough of how to leverage scheduled tasks in XP can be found here: http://support.microsoft.com/kb/308569. A similar guide for Windows Vista can be found here: http://tinyurl.com/3ynyjp.

Just be sure to use the ForceLogoff.exe command found in C:\Program Files\Windows SteadyState and additionally be sure to leverage the /Restart flag, as seen in Figure 11.30.

F I G U R E   1 1 . 3 0   You can force a logoff and a restart at a specific appointed time.

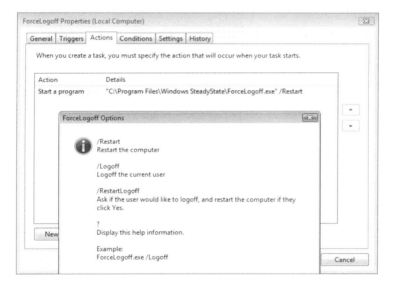

This option isn't great because all of a sudden—boom! Users are working along and suddenly the machine is rebooted. This option isn't bad, however, if you specify a reboot after hours when you know no one is logged on.

Option 2: Use a Logoff Script to Force a Reboot

You can also leverage a logoff script for a similar purpose. So, whenever a user logs off, they also force a reboot using the ForceLogoff.exe /Restart command. Figure 11.31 shows how to do this using Group Policy.

Preferably, you'd use the same GPO that contains the SteadyState restrictions as seen in the figure.

For more information about logon, log off, shut down, and startup scripts, be sure to read Chapter 6 of the companion book, which deals with these topics. Come to www.GPanswers.com/book for more information.

FIGURE 11.31   You can specify a reboot to clear changes when anyone logging onto SteadyState machine logs off.

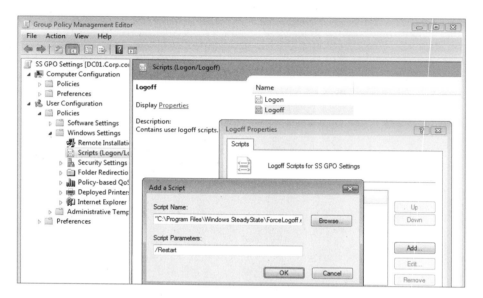

Option 3: The Best of All Worlds—Rebooting and Cleaning up When No One Is Around

So rebooting at a scheduled time is nice, but that only cleans out the machine once a day (or whatever the schedule is set to). And rebooting every time the user logs off is a real pain in the neck because of the wait time involved for the next user to use the machine.

Wouldn't it be great if there was a way for the system to detect if there wasn't anyone who wanted to use the machine right now? And, if so, just reboot the machine to clean it up?

Here's my vision:

- Let a user use the machine.

- Let the user make a mess.

- Let the user log off.

- If no one is jumping on the machine right away (say, no one has logged in within five minutes), then automatically reboot the machine.

The upshot is as follows:

- A reboot will clear out the nasties introduced to the system (if no one is around).

- But if someone really wants to use the machine, they can do so right away, without waiting for a reboot. Sure, there might be some nasties on the box, but I'm willing to take that risk, because I want the user to be able to log on right away.

Sounds great, right? How do we do this? I asked my friend Jakob Heidelberg, the Technical Editor of this book to solve the problem, and here's what he came up with. In Figure 11.32, we can see the basic flow. After the computer starts up, nothing happens until the first user logs on. Then, after the first user logs off, the countdown starts. After five minutes of no one logging on (configurable if you like), the computer automatically reboots. But, if someone does log on within that five minutes—the process is halted. No reboots. It just waits until no one is logged in again and then starts the countdown to the five-minute mark before rebooting.

Magic!

FIGURE 11.32 The flowchart of ActivityMonitor.vbs

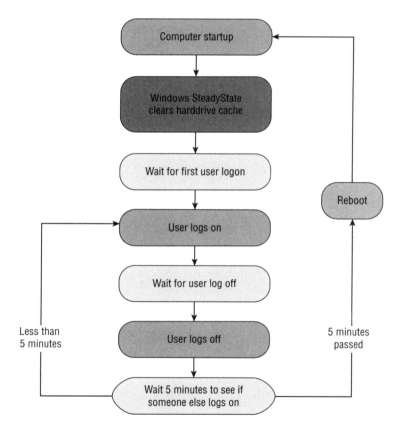

To do this, Jakob produced two scripts, `ActivityMonitor.vbs` and `CallActivityMonitor.vbs`. They're kind of long and involved, so we're not going to list them here. But in short, if you put both scripts on the computer locally in, say, the `C:\scripts` directory, all you need to do is create a GPO (or set a local Group Policy) so it runs `CallActivityMontior.vbs` as a Startup script, as shown in Figure 11.33. Then reboot the computer to engage the Startup script.

So, when the computer starts up, it begins watching for activity and really starts paying attention after the first person logs on. You can tweak the script if you want to: it's fully documented and configurable. For instance, if you want to restart after 1 minute or 20 minutes of inactivity (with no one logged on), you can do that.

Also, there's a neat activity log the script generates to C:\ActivityLog.txt if you want some feedback about its operation.

Check out www.GPanswers.com in the Book Resources section of this chapter for these scripts.

FIGURE 11.33   Use a Startup Script to run the local C:\scripts\CallActivityMonitor.vbs.

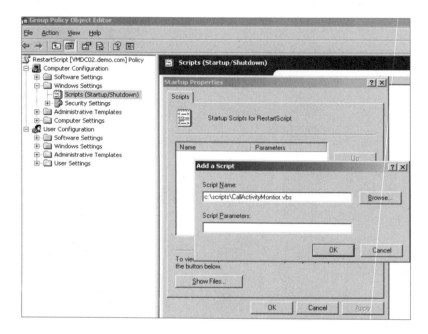

Deploying Software When Using Windows SteadyState

There's certainly nothing preventing you from preinstalling software before you leave that machine out there to fend for itself. That's perfectly acceptable. But there might be times when you want to remotely deploy software. My two preferred techniques for deploying software are via Group Policy Software Installation and SoftGrid.

Deploying Software Using GPSI

You can normally use Group Policy Software Installation to deploy software to either the user or the computer. But, since, in our examples, we're using Group Policy Loopback (Replace Mode) to toss out the user's normal settings (and replace them with our restrictions), that's not such a hot choice.

You can, however, deploy software to the computer—but on the user side!

You can see what I mean in Figure 11.34 where I'm using Group Policy Software Installation to deploy to the user side.

FIGURE 11.34   Deploy any software you like using Group Policy Software Installation to SteadyState computers (but on the user side).

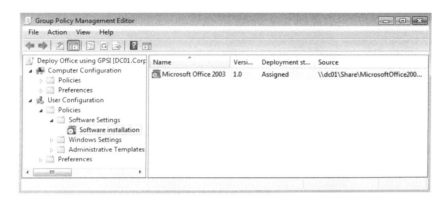

This is a little odd, of course. But again, the idea is that you want everyone who logs onto the machine to get exactly the same settings. And that's precisely what happens when you deploy a GPO linked to the Kiosk OU when Loopback Replace is engaged.

When the user logs on, they'll see the software on the Start Menu, as seen in Figure 11.35.

FIGURE 11.35   Group Policy can deploy software to SteadyState machines when users log on.

Deploying Software Using SoftGrid

In previous chapters, you learned all about how stream applications to your users based on group membership. The same rule applies here. Just be sure the SteadyState machine has the SoftGrid client loaded *before* you turn on Windows Disk Protection.

Then, whenever any users log on with their normal accounts, they'll be restricted because of the GPOs we utilized (and a little help with Loopback policy). Then, once they log on, the SoftGrid client will check their group membership and present them with the applications they've got access to.

In Figure 11.36, a sample user logs onto a machine with SteadyState and sees the application's icon for the SoftGrid package. Double-clicking it streams down the application for use.

FIGURE 11.36 SteadyState plus SoftGrid is a magic combination.

That application will remain in cache until the computer is rebooted. Then, it's a simple double-click of the icon to get it in cache next time it's needed.

It's simplicity at its best.

Remotely Updating the Custom Updates Script

So far, we've been able to perform 100 percent of our installation tasks remotely. There is, however, one critical part of SteadyState that doesn't have any inherent remote ability—that is, remotely changing the Custom Updates script, as seen in Figure 11.37.

FIGURE 11.37 You can use the Custom Updates section to specify a custom script.

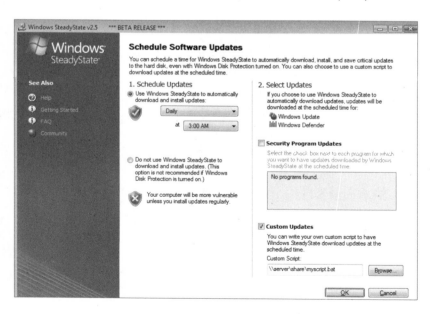

By knowing the little technique I'm about to show you, you can do some neat tricks. For instance, you can have the Custom Updates script start out by pointing to \\server\share\myscript.bat then another day pointing to \\newserver\newshare\newscript.bat.

Turns out, that value is controlled by HKLM\SYSTEM\CurrentControlSet\Services\Windows SteadyState\Parameters with the OtherUpdateScript value. You can see this Registry item in Figure 11.38.

The question is, how do you modify that value remotely?

The answer is: via the new Group Policy Preference Extensions. You just use the Registry extension to deploy a new setting, as seen in Figure 11.39.

For more information about the Group Policy Preference Extensions, like the Registry extension, be sure to read Chapter 10 of the companion book, *Group Policy Fundamentals, Security, and Troubleshooting*, which deals with these topics. Come to www.GPanswers.com/book for more information.

FIGURE 11.38   The OtherUpdateScript value controls the GUI entry for Custom Updates.

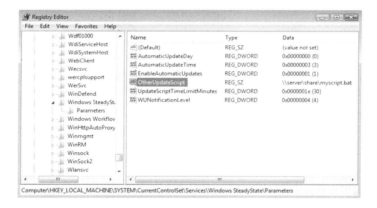

FIGURE 11.39   Use the Group Policy Preference Registry Extension to specify the value remotely.

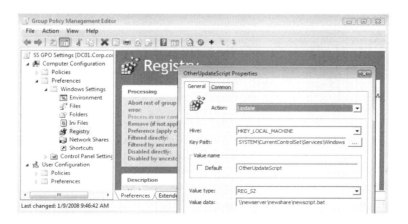

⊕ **Real World Scenario**

Mass Deployment of Windows SteadyState

If you're going to use SoftGrid in a domain environment, it's likely you'll want to deploy SteadyState to a gaggle of machines and sprinkle them around your universe. That's great, but you'll need to figure out a way to perform a mass rollout of your systems.

The most optimal way is by using a Ghost-style tool to deploy Windows SteadyState.

Just install the operating system, activate Windows, WGA-ify the machine, load SteadyState, then load the applications you want (unless you're going to use Group Policy or SoftGrid to deploy them).

Basically, you're going to craft the machine exactly the way you want and prepare to clone it. But don't turn on Windows Disk Protection yet. We'll do that last.

But before we actually clone our machine, we need to remember the supported method. That way is to use Microsoft Sysprep to shut the machine down, generate a new SID, and create a unique identity for this machine. Then, use a tool like Ghost and turn on the resulting Ghosted machines.

However, if you're using that method, you will positively need to reactivate and then also re-WGA-ify the machines once they're turned on. Ouch. That's a lot of work.

If only there was a way to not have to reactivate and re-WGA-ify the machines. With that in mind, I did a quick test with the old Sysinternals tool called NewSID (now owned by Microsoft). Officially, this tool is not supported when cloning machines, but it did seem to work in my tests. You can find NewSID at `www.microsoft.com/technet/sysinternals/Utilities/NewSid.mspx` (`http://tinyurl.com/yabqqe`).

Other tools like Ghostwalker, which act similarly, may or may not work. I tested an older version of Ghostwalker, and it didn't succeed in my tests. Be sure to test for yourself.

Again, in no case is anything other than Sysprep the officially supported method.

Final Thoughts for This Chapter and for the Book

Group Policy can only take you so far. That's because while Group Policy appears to be a security mechanism, it's not. It's a delivery mechanism. Sure, it can deliver security settings, and that's awesome. But to achieve true security and manageability on the Desktop we need more than just Group Policy alone.

In Chapter 1, we deployed our Desktop in an automated fashion.

In Chapters 2 and 3, we set up roaming profiles and redirected folders and offline files to help us manage our user's computer-hopping experiences.

In Chapters 4, 5, 6, and 7, we worked on getting software to our users and computers via GPSI and SoftGrid.

In Chapter 8, we started making sure our computers were more secure with WSUS and MBSA.

In Chapter 9, we ensured that only healthy computers were allowed on the network.

In Chapter 10, we put on some finishing touches to ensure that users enjoyed their Desktop experience and were more productive.

And here in Chapter 11, we got even more secure with SteadyState, where we performed a true lockdown using Windows Disk Protection, which traps all disk writes.

I hope you enjoyed this book. It was fun to share with you some of my favorite secrets to Desktop nirvana. I hope you'll join me at www.GPanswers.com and explore the rest of the resources we have:

- A killer newsletter

- Constantly updated newletter and weekly tips.

- A video series

- A community room to help get your most pressing questions answered

- And, of course, my hands-on training to take your game to the next level.

Thanks for making it to the end of the book. See you at GPanswers.com—where *smart* Group Policy admins come to get *smarter*!

Jeremy

Moskowitz

Index

Note to the Reader: Throughout this index **boldfaced** page numbers indicate primary discussions of a topic. *Italicized* page numbers indicate illustrations.

M

T

Your Group Policy Companion.

For Windows Server® 2008 and Windows Vista®

When you're doing something tough or learning something new, it's always nice to have help—a companion or two to make things easier for you. And if you're enhancing your skills in Active Directory Group Policy, you'll want to have Group Policy MVP Jeremy Moskowitz and his two fully-updated companion books on Group Policy at your side.

Stay Informed

Get additional resources, downloa eChapters, and get follow-up tips and tricks at Jeremy's website www.GPanswers.com/books.

About the Books

Group Policy Fundamentals, Security and Troubleshooting builds on previous editions to cover the lates in Group Policy essentials. Get updates and new coverage for Windows Vista, Windows Server 2008, the Advanced Group Policy Management tool, Group Policy with PowerShell, and the all-new Group Policy Preference Extensions.

Creating the Secure Managed Desktop: Using Group Policy, SoftGrid®, Microsoft® Deployment Toolkit, and Other Management Tools picks up where the first book leaves off. Here, you'll learn the secrets of crafting the smoothest possible desktop experience. Save money and implement faster using the tools Microsoft already provides, and ensure the best experience possible for your users.

Jeremy Moskowitz, Group Policy MVP, is the Chief Propeller-Head for Moskowitz, inc., and GPanswers.com. He is a nation ally recognized authority on Windows Server, Active Directory, Group Policy, and other Windows management topics. He is one of less than a dozen Microsoft MVPs in Group Policy. He runs GPanswers.com, ranked by *Computerworld* as a "Top 20 Resourc for Microsoft IT Professionals." Jeremy frequently contributes to *Microsoft TechNet Magazine, Windows IT Pro* magazine and *Redmond* magazine. Jeremy is a sought-after speaker at many industry conferences and, in his training workshops, helps thousa of administrators every year do more with Group Policy. Contact Jeremy by visiting GPanswers.com.

Go to www.sybex.com/go/moskowitz for more information

An Imprint of Ⓦ W
Now you know